PUBLISHED
EXPRESSLY FOR
THE PERSONAL LIBRARY
OF

The Easton Press

of
MICE
and
MEN

JOHN STEINBECK (1902–1968)

JOHN STEINBECK

of MICE
and MEN

With Illustrations by FLETCHER MARTIN

and an Introduction by JOHN T. WINTERICH

COLLECTOR'S EDITION
BOUND IN GENUINE LEATHER

the Easton Press

NORWALK, CONNECTICUT

PUBLISHER'S PREFACE

ACCORDING to the terms of Alfred Nobel's bequest, the Nobel Prize for Literature is awarded each year "to the person who shall have produced . . . the most distinguished body of work of an idealistic tendency." Relatively few American authors have won the Nobel Prize since the awards were instituted at the beginning of this century. John Steinbeck, who received the honor in 1962, was the sixth, his predecessors having been Sinclair Lewis, Eugene O'Neill, Pearl Buck, William Faulkner, and Ernest Hemingway.

The Pulitzer Prizes have been distributed annually since 1917. Steinbeck won his in 1940 for *The Grapes of Wrath*. Three years earlier a dramatic version of his novella, *Of Mice and Men*, had received the Drama Critics Circle award. Few books have achieved the stature of a classic in so short a period as *Of Mice and Men*. The simple-minded giant, Lennie Small, his compassionate friend George Milton, and their tragic

3

tale—of best-laid plans that went *agley*—are among the most unforgettable creations in American literature.

The life and work of John Steinbeck are sympathetically traced in our Introduction by the American man of letters, John T. Winterich. The book has been illustrated by the distinguished American painter, Fletcher Martin.

Like Steinbeck, Fletcher Martin is a rugged westerner, hailing from Palisades, Colorado, where he was born the same year as Steinbeck, 1902. Like Steinbeck, too, he was a wanderer. Before joining the Navy in 1922 he had been a lumberjack and—also like Steinbeck—a migrant harvester. He played, he fought, he taught himself to paint, he read exhaustively, and he made friends with practitioners of every form of art. But his first trade was printing, which he learned at his father's shop.

Martin was in his thirties before giving up printing to devote full time to painting, but soon began winning prestigious prizes from such institutions as the Pennsylvania Academy of Fine Arts and the National Academy of Design. There followed a succession of one-man shows in New York's Madison Avenue galleries, and retrospective exhibitions in various parts of the United States. Two books have been devoted to the art of Fletcher Martin, one as early as 1954, the second—published by Harry N. Abrams, Inc.—as recently as 1977.

His extensive teaching career commenced in 1940, when he succeeded Grant Wood as artist-in-residence at the State University of Iowa. To the many books he has illustrated, Fletcher Martin brings dynamic realism, intuitive understanding of character, and vigorous portrayal of action. *Of Mice and Men* inspired him to paint five double-spread water colors and eighteen two-color drawings. For this Collector's Edition he has in addition painted the frontispiece portrait of John Steinbeck.

Being one of the extremely rare artists who have been practical printers, Fletcher Martin was also commissioned to plan the book's format and typography—a task he performed with tremendous flair. For the text of the novella he selected a special cutting of the large eighteen-point Janson type, which is based on one that was cut around 1670 by the Dutch letter-founder Anton Janson. For the titles and the chapter initials, Martin drew a series of ruggedly decorative capital letters that echo the forcefulness of the story and fit comfortably into the book's quarto-size pages.

4

Apart from its unusually large dimensions, the volume gains impressiveness from the numerous costly elements that have gone into its production. It is these marks of quality that give distinction to the Collector's Editions of *The 100 Greatest Books Ever Written*.

THE EASTON PRESS

INTRODUCTION

JOHN ERNST STEINBECK, novelist, short-story writer, syndicated columnist, dramatist, motion-picture script writer, essayist, reporter, whilom poet, and general surveyor of the human scene, was born in Salinas, California, on February 27, 1902. The valley of the Salinas River is one of this nation's great fruit baskets, vegetable bins, and grain repositories. But the general area is by no means lacking in literary associations. The first unit of Frank Norris' three-volume epic of the wheat, called *The Octopus*, was published the year before John Steinbeck was born; the setting was the Salinas valley. Later Robinson Jeffers, though not a native son (neither was Frank Norris), made California's Big Sur country his own. Edwin Markham, a native of rural Oregon, grew up in central California, turned poet, and was widely read by thousands who had not previously gone in for poetry. He will always be remembered for *The Man with the Hoe* (1899), which many people considered pretty radi-

7

cal, but men who wielded hoes for a living did not regard it as radical enough. Judge for yourself:

> *Bowed by the weight of centuries he leans*
> *Upon his hoe and gazes on the ground,*
> *The emptiness of ages in his face,*
> *And on his back the burden of the world.*

Sixty-odd years before Markham achieved his pinnacle of fame, a temporary dropout from Harvard College had stepped ashore at the port of Monterey, California, where John Steinbeck's father would one day serve as county treasurer. The young man was Richard Henry Dana, Jr., who had embarked at Boston on a two-year voyage designed to cure his ailing eyesight, which had been damaged by an attack of measles. At Monterey, young Dana had been a member of a work detail charged with stowing aboard cattle-hides, which, he whimsically philosophized, would be taken to Massachusetts and there made into shoes for a fresh crop of foremast hands to wear out in Monterey, and so on ad infinitum.

There appears to be no record of John Steinbeck's ever having piled hides, but he did perform many backbreaking agricultural chores alongside the floating population of field hands. And he read widely and to good purpose. His mother was a schoolteacher, and she apparently held to the principle that pedagogy should begin at home. John's early reading, some of it inspired by his mother, included such titles as Dostoevski's *Crime and Punishment*, Hardy's *The Return of the Native*, and Milton's *Paradise Lost*. The choice of *Paradise Lost* is particularly interesting. The title of Steinbeck's first major novel, *In Dubious Battle*, was taken from *Paradise Lost*. And let it not be forgotten that one of the protagonists of *Of Mice and Men* is George Milton.

In 1920 Steinbeck enrolled at Leland Stanford Jr. University at Palo Alto, but he did not register for a degree. This is by no means the worst possible way to get a college education. Four years later he took off for New York.

No annotator of the career of John Steinbeck has ever failed to mention the fact that on his arrival in the metropolis, he went into construction work, and that his high point in this activity was helping to rear the edifice of Madison Square Garden. There have been, of course, *three* Madison Square Gardens in Manhattan. Garden II—erected in the 1920s

8

at Forty-ninth Street and Eighth Avenue—was where John Steinbeck laid his bricks true, or carried a hod, or both, and this location should not be omitted from any future itineraries of John Steinbeck's New York.

Steinbeck got down to serious writing in the late 1920s. As a youth he had contributed bits and pieces—most of them funny, or so intended—to newspapers in the Salinas area and to the Stanford University literary magazine. It was not until 1929 that he published his first book, *Cup of Gold*, a romanticized account of the freebooter Henry Morgan. Then came October of that year, and the Great Depression was on. During that period of doom and gloom, books took on a popularity they had never known before. Bread lines were long and library reading rooms were packed (a perfect instance of cause and effect). Steinbeck kept at his writing, and in 1932 came out with a book of short stories, *The Pastures of Heaven*, in the scenes of which he returned to California farm people. *To a God Unknown* followed in 1933; but not until he produced *Tortilla Flat*, in 1935, did Steinbeck become if not a great author at least a known author.

John Steinbeck's abounding sense of pity for his toiling fellow man, particularly for the hewer of wood and the drawer of water, rings loud and clear through much of his work, and it rings loudest and clearest in three successive novels: *In Dubious Battle* (1936), *Of Mice and Men* (1937), and *The Grapes of Wrath* (1939). All are superb examples of proletarian literature.

I have always liked William Rose Benét's definition of proletarian literature: "It has for its aim a sympathetic portrayal of the lives and sufferings of the proletariat and an exposure of injustices and economic inequalities seen by its writers in the society in which they lived, with a view to inducing amelioration."

Accepting this definition (as I hope he does), the reader of John Steinbeck's proletarian novels must admit that *Of Mice and Men* is the least proletarian of all his proletarian novels. George Milton and Lennie Small do not complain about their lot, or turn up their noses at their quarters, or beef about the beef; the only amelioration they are interested in is a piece of land that they can call home. The double tragedy that tears them apart has no slightest concern with time-and-a-half for overtime, or Social Security, or fringe benefits.

The Grapes of Wrath was a shoo-in for the Pulitzer prize in fiction in 1940. Sometimes, it seems to me, the Pulitzer judges have picked the right

9

authors but the wrong books. It was not thus in 1940. The conjunction of title and author was perfect. In 1962 Steinbeck was awarded the Nobel prize for literature. The two prizes do not by any means parallel each other. The most radical divergence, of course, is the size of the awards; the Nobel is many, many times more profitable than the Pulitzer. The Pulitzer is credited to a specific book, the Nobel to the complete canon of a single author's work.

Steinbeck was the sixth American to win the Nobel prize for literature since its establishment in 1901. In the order of the calendar, the American winners preceding him were as follows: 1930, Sinclair Lewis; 1936, Eugene O'Neill; 1937, Pearl S. Buck; 1949, William Faulkner; 1953, Ernest Hemingway. (Thomas Stearns Eliot, a native St. Louisan who spent most of his life in England and became a British subject—as Henry James had done before him—was awarded the Nobel in 1948, but his denaturalization disqualifies him from the roster.)

Steinbeck went on writing industriously. His next novels were *The Moon Is Down* (1942) and *Cannery Row* (1945). Notable among their successors were *The Wayward Bus* (1947) and *East of Eden* (1952).

He became a permanent resident of New York in 1961. In a survey of the author's career in *The New York Times*, Alden Whitman called this "a complete change of milieu that, in the opinion of many critics, adversely affected the quality of his fiction." Whitman cites specifically an adverse judgment of the Nobel award by Arthur Mizener, who wrote in the *Times:* "It is difficult to find a flattering explanation for awarding this most distinguished of literary prizes to a writer whose real but limited talent is, in his own best books, watered down by twentieth-rate philosophizing and, in his worst books, is overwhelmed by it."

Steinbeck's last book publication was *America and Americans*, for which he wrote a long essay to accompany a series of photographs; issued in 1966, it was highly acclaimed for the author's deep social insight.

But we are here concerned with the pre-Nobel Steinbeck, with a novel that is a very short novel. There is, of course, no law specifying how many or how few words a novelist is entitled to. Does a novelist ever say to himself, as he pulls his pad of ruled yellow paper toward him (that was what John Steinbeck used, anyway), "I've set the meter for this one at three hundred and twenty-five pages"? That would be ridiculous, of course. But such a fine pro as Charles Dickens operated on a system something like that. Most of the great Dickens novels (many of which, by the way, were simon-pure proletarian literature) originally appeared in monthly parts of thirty-two pages each, so that when Dickens set to work on a part, he knew where he was going to come out almost to the letter. Each of these massive parts-productions totaled something like a third of a million words. *Of Mice and Men* is just about the length of one Dickens part. So is it, strictly, a novel? I think so, though part of my argument is based on my dislike of the term novelette.

You can play this length game another way: by chapters. Most novels, as we all well know, are divided into chapters, although the anomaly of a chapterless novel is not unknown. On the other hand, we recall with pleasure two great nineteenth-century English novels which are composed of one hundred chapters each: George Borrow's *Lavengro* and Charles Reade's *The Cloister and the Hearth*. *Of Mice and Men* has a mere six chapters, which may be a record (the issue will not be pressed here).

Of Mice and Men was published in September, 1937, and ended the year as number eight on the best-seller list. If every novel did that well, everybody would rush into the publishing business.

For some time John Steinbeck had toyed with the idea of making his six-chapter novel into a play. Sensibly regarding himself as a rank amateur in this area, he looked around for a Grade A collaborator. He picked a good one: George S. Kaufman, who may well go down in American theatrical history as the great collaborator. He wrote several plays on his own and more than a dozen in association, chiefly with Marc Connelly. The dramatic version of *Of Mice and Men* won the New York Drama Critics Circle award for 1937. The night the play opened on Broadway, Steinbeck was in a California migrant camp in company with a group of displaced Oklahomans.

John Steinbeck died at his New York City home, a brownstone residence on East Seventy-second Street, December 20, 1968. *The New York Times* for the following day carried a comprehensive obituary that began on page one and broke over inside to total five full columns of text and halftones. At the funeral service, held two days before Christmas at St. James's Episcopal Church, Henry Fonda, who had starred in the motion-picture version of *The Grapes of Wrath*, read verses by John Millington Synge, Alfred Lord Tennyson, and Robert Louis Stevenson which had given Steinbeck pleasure. The ashes were flown to Salinas for burial. John Steinbeck had come full circle.

Ever since before the Second World War, Steinbeck's work has been receiving competent critical attention and evaluation. The most impressive and detailed study to appear so far is *The Wide World of John Steinbeck* by Peter Lisca, published in 1958 and frequently reprinted—a noteworthy record for a work of scholarship. A few weeks before Steinbeck's death there was announced the establishment, at Ball State University in Muncie, Indiana, of the John Steinbeck Bibliographical Society. He appears to be firmly fixed in the pantheon of American authors.

JOHN T. WINTERICH

of
MICE
and
MEN

A FEW miles south of Soledad, the Salinas River drops in close to the hillside bank and runs deep and green. The water is warm too, for it has slipped twinkling over the yellow sands in the sunlight before reaching the narrow pool. On one side of the river the golden foothill slopes curve up to the strong and rocky Gabilan mountains, but on the valley side the water is lined with trees—willows fresh and green with every spring, carrying in their lower leaf junctures the debris of the winter's flooding; and sycamores with mottled, white, recumbent limbs and branches that arch over the pool. On the sandy bank under the trees the leaves lie deep and so crisp that a lizard makes a great skittering if he runs among them. Rabbits come out of the brush to sit on the sand in the evening, and the damp flats are covered with the night tracks of 'coons, and with the spread pads of dogs from the ranches, and with the split-wedge tracks of deer that come to drink in the dark.

There is a path through the willows and among the sycamores, a path beaten hard by boys coming down from the ranches to swim in the deep pool, and beaten hard by tramps who come wearily down from the highway in the evening to jungle-up near water. In front of the low horizontal limb of a giant sycamore there is an ash pile made by many fires; the limb is worn smooth by men who have sat on it.

Evening of a hot day started the little wind to moving among the leaves. The shade climbed up the hills toward the top. On the sand banks the rabbits sat as quietly as little gray, sculptured stones. And then from the direction of the state highway came the sound of footsteps on crisp sycamore leaves. The rabbits hurried noiselessly for cover. A stilted heron labored up into the air and pounded down river. For a moment the place was lifeless, and then two men emerged from the path and came into the opening by the green pool.

They had walked in single file down the path, and even in the open one stayed behind the other. Both were dressed in denim trousers and in denim coats with brass buttons. Both wore black, shapeless hats and both carried tight blanket rolls slung over their shoulders. The first man was small and quick, dark of face, with restless eyes and sharp, strong features. Every part of him was defined: small, strong hands, slender arms, a thin and bony nose. Behind him walked his opposite, a huge man, shapeless of face, with large, pale eyes, with wide, sloping shoulders; and he walked heavily, dragging his feet a little, the way a bear drags his paws. His arms did not swing at his sides, but hung loosely.

The first man stopped short in the clearing, and the follower nearly ran over him. He took off his hat and wiped the sweat-band with his forefinger and snapped the moisture off. His huge companion dropped his blankets and flung himself down and drank from the surface of the green pool; drank with long gulps, snorting into the water like a horse. The small man stepped nervously beside him.

"Lennie!" he said sharply. "Lennie, for God' sakes don't drink so much." Lennie continued to snort into the pool. The small man leaned over and shook him by the shoulder. "Lennie. You gonna be sick like you was last night."

Lennie dipped his whole head under, hat and all, and then he sat up on the bank and his hat dripped down on his blue coat and ran down his back. "Tha's good," he said. "You drink some, George. You take a good big drink." He smiled happily.

George unslung his bindle and dropped it gently on the bank. "I ain't sure it's good water," he said. "Looks kinda scummy."

Lennie dabbled his big paw in the water and wiggled his fingers so the water arose in little splashes; rings widened across the pool to the other side and came back again. Lennie watched them go. "Look, George. Look what I done."

George knelt beside the pool and drank from his hand with quick scoops. "Tastes all right," he admitted. "Don't really seem to be running, though. You never oughta drink water when it ain't running, Lennie," he said hopelessly. "You'd drink out of a gutter if you was thirsty." He threw a scoop of water into his face and rubbed it about with his hand, under his chin and around the back of his neck. Then he replaced his hat, pushed himself back from the river, drew up his knees and embraced them. Lennie, who had been watching, imitated George exactly. He pushed himself back, drew up his knees, embraced them, looked over to George to see whether he had it just right. He pulled his hat down a little more over his eyes, the way George's hat was.

George stared morosely at the water. The rims of his eyes were red with sun glare. He said angrily, "We could just as well of rode clear to the ranch if that bastard bus driver knew what he was talkin' about. 'Jes' a little stretch down the highway,' he says. 'Jes' a little stretch.' God damn near four miles, that's what it was! Didn't wanta stop at the ranch gate, that's what. Too God damn lazy to pull up. Wonder he isn't too damn good to stop in Soledad at all. Kicks us out and says, 'Jes' a little stretch down the road.' I bet it was *more* than four miles. Damn hot day."

Lennie looked timidly over to him. "George?"

"Yeah, what ya want?"

"Where we goin', George?"

The little man jerked down the brim of his hat and scowled over at Lennie. "So you forgot that awready, did you? I gotta tell you again, do I? Jesus Christ, you're a crazy bastard!"

"I forgot," Lennie said softly. "I tried not to forget. Honest to God I did, George."

"O.K.—O.K. I'll tell ya again. I ain't got nothing to do. Might jus' as well spen' all my time tellin' you things and then you forget 'em, and I tell you again."

"Tried and tried," said Lennie, "but it didn't do no good. I remember about the rabbits, George."

"The hell with the rabbits. That's all you ever can remember is them rabbits. O.K.! Now you listen and this time you got to remember so we don't get in no trouble. You remember settin' in that gutter on Howard street and watchin' that blackboard?"

Lennie's face broke into a delighted smile. "Why sure, George, I remember that . . . but . . . what'd we do then? I remember some girls come by and you says . . . you say . . ."

"The hell with what I says. You remember about us goin' into Murray and Ready's, and they give us work cards and bus tickets?"

"Oh, sure, George. I remember that now." His hands went quickly into his side coat pockets. He said gently, "George . . . I ain't got mine. I musta lost it." He looked down at the ground in despair.

"You never had none, you crazy bastard. I got both of 'em here. Think I'd let you carry your own work card?"

Lennie grinned with relief. "I . . . I thought I put it in my side pocket." His hand went into the pocket again.

George looked sharply at him. "What'd you take outa that pocket?"

"Ain't a thing in my pocket," Lennie said cleverly.

"I know there ain't. You got it in your hand. What you got in your hand—hidin' it?"

"I ain't got nothin', George. Honest."

"Come on, give it here."

Lennie held his closed hand away from George's direction. "It's on'y a mouse, George."

"A mouse? A live mouse?"

"Uh-uh. Jus' a dead mouse, George. I didn't kill it. Honest! I found it. I found it dead."

"Give it here!" said George.

"Aw, leave me have it, George."

"Give it here!"

Lennie's closed hand slowly obeyed. George took the mouse and threw it across the pool to the other side, among the brush. "What you want of a dead mouse, anyways?"

"I could pet it with my thumb while we walked along," said Lennie.

"Well, you ain't petting no mice while you walk with me. You remember where we're goin' now?"

Lennie looked startled and then in embarrassment hid his face against his knees. "I forgot again."

20

"Jesus Christ," George said resignedly. "Well — look, we're gonna work on a ranch like the one we come from up north."

"Up north?"

"In Weed."

"Oh, sure. I remember. In Weed."

"That ranch we're goin' to is right down there about a quarter mile. We're gonna go in an' see the boss. Now, look—I'll give him the work tickets, but you ain't gonna say a word. You jus' stand there and don't say nothing. If he finds out what a crazy bastard you are, we won't get no job, but if he sees ya work before he hears ya talk, we're set. Ya got that?"

"Sure, George. Sure I got it."

"O.K. Now when we go in to see the boss, what you gonna do?"

"I . . . I," Lennie thought. His face grew tight with thought. "I . . . ain't gonna say nothin'. Jus' gonna stan' there."

"Good boy. That's swell. You say that over two, three times so you sure won't forget it."

Lennie droned to himself softly, "I ain't gonna say nothin' . . . I ain't gonna say nothin' . . . I ain't gonna say nothin'."

"O.K.," said George. "An' you ain't gonna do no bad things like you done in Weed, neither."

Lennie looked puzzled. "Like I done in Weed?"

"Oh, so ya forgot that too, did ya? Well, I ain't gonna remind ya, fear ya do it again."

22

A light of understanding broke on Lennie's face. "They run us outa Weed," he exploded triumphantly.

"Run us out, hell," said George disgustedly. "We run. They was lookin' for us, but they didn't catch us."

Lennie giggled happily. "I didn't forget that, you bet."

George lay back on the sand and crossed his hands under his head, and Lennie imitated him, raising his head to see whether he were doing it right. "God, you're a lot of trouble," said George. "I could get along so easy and so nice if I didn't have you on my tail. I could live so easy and maybe have a girl."

For a moment Lennie lay quiet, and then he said hopefully, "We gonna work on a ranch, George."

"Awright. You got that. But we're gonna sleep here because I got a reason."

The day was going fast now. Only the tops of the Gabilan mountains flamed with the light of the sun that had gone from the valley. A water snake slipped along on the pool, its head held up like a little periscope. The reeds jerked slightly in the current. Far off toward the highway a man shouted something, and another man shouted back. The sycamore limbs rustled under a little wind that died immediately.

"George—why ain't we goin' on to the ranch and get some supper? They got supper at the ranch."

George rolled on his side. "No reason at all for you. I like it here. Tomorra we're gonna go to work. I seen thrashin' machines on the way down. That means we'll be bucking grain bags, bustin' a gut. Tonight I'm gonna lay right here and look up. I like it."

Lennie got up on his knees and looked down at George. "Ain't we gonna have no supper?"

"Sure we are, if you gather up some dead willow sticks. I got three can of beans in my bindle. You get a fire ready. I'll give you a match when you get the sticks together. Then we'll heat the beans and have supper."

Lennie said, "I like beans with ketchup."

"Well, we ain't got no ketchup. You go get wood. An' don't you fool around. It'll be dark before long."

Lennie lumbered to his feet and disappeared in the brush. George lay where he was and whistled softly to himself. There were sounds of splashings down the river in the direction Lennie had taken. George stopped whistling and listened. "Poor bastard," he said softly, and then went on whistling again.

In a moment Lennie came crashing back through the brush. He carried one small willow stick in his hand. George sat up. "Awright," he said brusquely. "Gi'me that mouse!"

But Lennie made an elaborate pantomime of innocence. "What mouse, George? I ain't got no mouse."

George held out his hand. "Come on. Give it to me. You ain't puttin' nothing over."

Lennie hesitated, backed away, looked wildly at the brush line as though he contemplated running for his freedom. George said coldly, "You gonna give me that mouse or do I have to sock you?"

24

"Give you what, George?"

"You know God damn well what. I want that mouse."

Lennie reluctantly reached into his pocket. His voice broke a little. "I don't know why I can't keep it. It ain't nobody's mouse. I didn't steal it. I found it lyin' right beside the road."

George's hand remained outstretched imperiously. Slowly, like a terrier who doesn't want to bring a ball to its master, Lennie approached, drew back, approached again. George snapped his fingers sharply, and at the sound Lennie laid the mouse in his hand.

"I wasn't doin' nothing bad with it, George. Jus' strokin' it."

George stood up and threw the mouse as far as he could into the darkening brush, and then he stepped to the pool and washed his hands. "You crazy fool. Don't you think I could see your feet was wet where you went acrost the river to get it?" He heard Lennie's whimpering cry and wheeled about. "Blubberin' like a baby! Jesus Christ! A big guy like you." Lennie's lip quivered and tears started in his eyes. "Aw, Lennie!" George put his hand on Lennie's shoulder. "I ain't takin' it away jus' for meanness. That mouse ain't fresh, Lennie; and besides, you've broke it pettin' it. You get another mouse that's fresh and I'll let you keep it a little while."

Lennie sat down on the ground and hung his head dejectedly. "I don't know where there is no other mouse. I remember a lady used to give 'em to me — ever' one she got. But that lady ain't here."

George scoffed. "Lady, huh? Don't even remember who that lady was. That was your own Aunt Clara. An' she stopped givin' 'em to ya. You always killed 'em."

Lennie looked sadly up at him. "They was so little," he said, apologetically. "I'd pet 'em, and pretty soon they bit my fingers and I pinched their heads a little and then they was dead—because they was so little.

"I wish't we'd get the rabbits pretty soon, George. They ain't so little."

"The hell with the rabbits. An' you ain't to be trusted with no live mice. Your Aunt Clara give you a rubber mouse and you wouldn't have nothing to do with it."

"It wasn't no good to pet," said Lennie.

The flame of the sunset lifted from the mountain-tops and dusk came into the valley, and a half darkness came in among the willows and the sycamores. A big carp rose to the surface of the pool, gulped air and then sank mysteriously into the dark water again, leaving widening rings on the water. Overhead the leaves whisked again and little puffs of willow cotton blew down and landed on the pool's surface.

"You gonna get that wood?" George demanded. "There's plenty right up against the back of that sycamore. Floodwater wood. Now you get it."

Lennie went behind the tree and brought out a litter of dried leaves and twigs. He threw them in a heap on the old ash pile and went back for more and more. It was almost night now. A dove's wings whistled over the water. George walked to the fire pile and lighted the dry leaves. The flame cracked up among the twigs and fell to work. George undid his bindle and brought out three cans of beans. He stood them about the fire, close in against the blaze, but not quite touching the flame.

"There's enough beans for four men," George said.

Lennie watched him from over the fire. He said patiently, "I like 'em with ketchup."

"Well, we ain't got any," George exploded. "Whatever we ain't got, that's what you want. God a'mighty, if I was alone I could live so easy. I could go get a job an' work, an' no trouble. No mess at all, and when the end of the month come I could take my fifty bucks and go into town and get whatever I want. Why, I could stay in a cat house all night. I could eat any place I want, hotel or any place, and order any damn thing I could think of. An' I could do all that every damn month. Get a gallon of whisky, or set in a pool room and play cards or shoot pool." Lennie knelt and looked over the fire at the angry George. And Lennie's face was drawn with terror. "An' whatta I got," George went on furiously. "I got you! You can't keep a job and you lose me ever' job I get. Jus' keep me shovin' all over the country all the time. An' that ain't the worst. You get in trouble. You do bad things and I got to get you out." His voice rose nearly to a shout. "You crazy son-of-a-bitch. You keep me in hot water all the time." He took on the elaborate manner of little girls when they are mimicking one another. "Jus' wanted to feel that girl's dress — jus' wanted to pet it like it was a mouse—— Well, how the hell did she know you jus' wanted to feel her dress? She jerks back and you hold on like it was a mouse. She yells and we got to hide in a irrigation ditch all day with guys lookin' for us, and we got to sneak out in the dark and get outta the country. All the time somethin' like that—all the time. I wisht I could put you in a cage with about a million mice an' let you have fun." His anger left him suddenly. He looked across the fire at Lennie's anguished face, and then he looked ashamedly at the flames.

It was quite dark now, but the fire lighted the trunks of the trees and the curving branches overhead. Lennie crawled slowly and cautiously around the fire until he was close to George. He sat back on his heels. George turned the bean cans so that another side faced the fire. He pretended to be unaware of Lennie so close beside him.

"George," very softly. No answer. "George!"

"Whatta you want?"

"I was only foolin', George. I don't want no ketchup. I wouldn't eat no ketchup if it was right here beside me."

"If it was here, you could have some."

"But I wouldn't eat none, George. I'd leave it all for you. You could cover your beans with it and I wouldn't touch none of it."

George still stared morosely at the fire. "When I

think of the swell time I could have without you, I go nuts. I never get no peace."

Lennie still knelt. He looked off into the darkness across the river. "George, you want I should go away and leave you alone?"

"Where the hell could you go?"

"Well, I could. I could go off in the hills there. Some place I'd find a cave."

"Yeah? How'd you eat. You ain't got sense enough to find nothing to eat."

"I'd find things, George. I don't need no nice food with ketchup. I'd lay out in the sun and nobody'd hurt me. An' if I foun' a mouse, I could keep it. Nobody'd take it away from me."

George looked quickly and searchingly at him. "I been mean, ain't I?"

"If you don' want me I can go off in the hills an' find a cave. I can go away any time."

"No—look! I was jus' foolin', Lennie. 'Cause I want you to stay with me. Trouble with mice is you always kill 'em." He paused. "Tell you what I'll do, Lennie. First chance I get I'll give you a pup. Maybe you wouldn't kill *it*. That'd be better than mice. And you could pet it harder."

Lennie avoided the bait. He had sensed his advantage. "If you don't want me, you only jus' got to say so, and I'll go off in those hills right there—right up in those hills and live by myself. An' I won't get no mice stole from me."

George said, "I want you to stay with me, Lennie. Jesus Christ, somebody'd shoot you for a coyote if you was by yourself. No, you stay with me. Your Aunt Clara wouldn't like you running off by yourself, even if she is dead."

Lennie spoke craftily, "Tell me—like you done before."

"Tell you what?"

"About the rabbits."

George snapped, "You ain't gonna put nothing over on me."

Lennie pleaded, "Come on, George. Tell me. Please, George. Like you done before."

"You get a kick outta that, don't you? Awright, I'll tell you, and then we'll eat our supper. . . ."

George's voice became deeper. He repeated his words rhythmically as though he had said them many times before. "Guys like us, that work on ranches, are the loneliest guys in the world. They got no family. They don't belong no place. They come to a ranch an' work up a stake and then they go inta town and blow their stake, and the first thing you know they're poundin' their tail on some other ranch. They ain't got nothing to look ahead to."

Lennie was delighted. "That's it—that's it. Now tell how it is with us."

George went on. "With us it ain't like that. We got a future. We got somebody to talk to that gives a damn about us. We don't have to sit in no bar room blowin'

in our jack jus' because we got no place else to go. If them other guys gets in jail they can rot for all anybody gives a damn. But not us."

Lennie broke in. "*But not us! An' why? Because . . . because I got you to look after me, and you got me to look after you, and that's why*." He laughed delightedly. "Go on now, George!"

"You got it by heart. You can do it yourself."

"No, you. I forget some a' the things. Tell about how it's gonna be."

"O.K. Someday—we're gonna get the jack together and we're gonna have a little house and a couple of acres an' a cow and some pigs and ——"

"*An' live off the fatta the lan'*," Lennie shouted. "An' have *rabbits*. Go on, George! Tell about what we're gonna have in the garden and about the rabbits in the cages and about the rain in the winter and the stove, and how thick the cream is on the milk like you can hardly cut it. Tell about that, George."

"Why'n't you do it yourself? You know all of it."

"No . . . you tell it. It ain't the same if I tell it. Go on . . . George. How I get to tend the rabbits."

"Well," said George, "we'll have a big vegetable patch and a rabbit hutch and chickens. And when it rains in the winter, we'll just say the hell with goin' to work, and we'll build up a fire in the stove and set around it an' listen to the rain comin' down on the roof—Nuts!" He took out his pocket knife. "I ain't got time for no more." He drove his knife through the top of one of the bean cans, sawed out the top and passed the can to Lennie. Then he opened a second can. From his side pocket he brought out two spoons and passed one of them to Lennie.

They sat by the fire and filled their mouths with beans and chewed mightily. A few beans slipped out of the side of Lennie's mouth. George gestured with his spoon. "What you gonna say tomorrow when the boss asks you questions?"

Lennie stopped chewing and swallowed. His face was concentrated. "I . . . I ain't gonna . . . say a word."

"Good boy! That's fine, Lennie! Maybe you're gettin' better. When we get the coupla acres I can let you tend the rabbits all right. 'Specially if you remember as good as that."

Lennie choked with pride. "I can remember," he said.

George motioned with his spoon again. "Look, Lennie. I want you to look around here. You can remember this place, can't you? The ranch is about a quarter mile up that way. Just follow the river?"

"Sure," said Lennie. "I can remember this. Di'n't I remember about not gonna say a word?"

" 'Course you did. Well, look. Lennie—if you jus' happen to get in trouble like you always done before, I want you to come right here an' hide in the brush."

"Hide in the brush," said Lennie slowly.

"Hide in the brush till I come for you. Can you remember that?"

"Sure I can, George. Hide in the brush till you come."

"But you ain't gonna get in no trouble, because if you do, I won't let you tend the rabbits." He threw his empty bean can off into the brush.

"I won't get in no trouble, George. I ain't gonna say a word."

"O.K. Bring your bindle over here by the fire. It's gonna be nice sleepin' here. Lookin' up, and the leaves. Don't build up no more fire. We'll let her die down."

They made their beds on the sand, and as the blaze dropped from the fire the sphere of light grew smaller; the curling branches disappeared and only a faint glimmer showed where the tree trunks were. From the darkness Lennie called, "George—you asleep?"

"No. Whatta you want?"

"Let's have different color rabbits, George."

"Sure we will," George said sleepily. "Red and blue and green rabbits, Lennie. Millions of 'em."

"Furry ones, George, like I seen in the fair in Sacramento."

"Sure, furry ones."

" 'Cause I can jus' as well go away, George, an' live in a cave."

"You can jus' as well go to hell," said George. "Shut up now."

The red light dimmed on the coals. Up the hill from the river a coyote yammered, and a dog answered from the other side of the stream. The sycamore leaves whispered in a little night breeze.

THE bunk house was a long, rectangular building. Inside, the walls were whitewashed and the floor unpainted. In three walls there were small, square windows, and in the fourth, a solid door with a wooden latch. Against the walls were eight bunks, five of them made up with blankets and the other three showing their burlap ticking. Over each bunk there was nailed an apple box with the opening forward so that it made two shelves for the personal belongings of the occupant of the bunk. And these shelves were loaded with little articles, soap and talcum powder, razors and those Western magazines ranch men love to read and scoff at and secretly believe. And there were medicines on the shelves, and little vials, combs; and from nails on the box sides, a few neckties. Near one wall there was a black cast-iron stove, its stovepipe going straight up through the ceiling. In the middle of the room stood a big square table littered with playing cards, and around it were grouped boxes for the players to sit on.

At about ten o'clock in the morning the sun threw a bright dust-laden bar through one of the side windows, and in and out of the beam flies shot like rushing stars.

The wooden latch raised. The door opened and a tall, stoop-shouldered old man came in. He was dressed in blue jeans and he carried a big push-broom in his left hand. Behind him came George, and behind George, Lennie.

"The boss was expectin' you last night," the old man said. "He was sore as hell when you wasn't here to go out this morning." He pointed with his right arm, and out of the sleeve came a round stick-like wrist, but no hand. "You can have them two beds there," he said, indicating two bunks near the stove.

George stepped over and threw his blankets down on the burlap sack of straw that was a mattress. He looked into his box shelf and then picked a small yellow can from it. "Say. What the hell's this?"

"I don't know," said the old man.

"Says 'positively kills lice, roaches and other scourges.' What the hell kind of bed you giving us, anyways? We don't want no pants rabbits."

The old swamper shifted his broom and held it between his elbow and his side while he held out his hand for the can. He studied the label carefully. "Tell you what—" he said finally, "last guy that had this bed was a blacksmith—hell of a nice fella and as clean a guy as you want to meet. Used to wash his hands even *after* he ate."

"Then how come he got graybacks?" George was working up a slow anger. Lennie put his bindle on the neighboring bunk and sat down. He watched George with open mouth.

"Tell you what," said the old swamper. "This here blacksmith—name of Whitey—was the kind of guy that would put that stuff around even if there wasn't no bugs—just to make sure, see? Tell you what he used to do—At meals he'd peel his boil' potatoes, an' he'd take out ever' little spot, no matter what kind, before he'd eat it. And if there was a red splotch on an egg, he'd scrape it off. Finally quit about the food. That's the kinda guy he was—clean. Used ta dress up Sundays even when he wasn't going no place, put on a necktie even, and then set in the bunk house."

"I ain't so sure," said George skeptically. "What did you say he quit for?"

The old man put the yellow can in his pocket, and he rubbed his bristly white whiskers with his knuckles. "Why . . . he . . . just quit, the way a guy will. Says it was the food. Just wanted to move. Didn't give no other reason but the food. Just says 'gimme my time' one night, the way any guy would."

George lifted his tick and looked underneath it. He leaned over and inspected the sacking closely. Immediately Lennie got up and did the same with his bed. Finally George seemed satisfied. He unrolled his bindle and put things on the shelf, his razor and bar of soap, his comb and bottle of pills, his liniment and leather wristband. Then he made his bed up neatly with blankets. The old man said, "I guess the boss'll be out here in a minute. He was sure burned when you wasn't here this morning. Come right in when we was eatin' breakfast and says, 'Where the hell's them new men?' An' he give the stable buck hell, too."

George patted a wrinkle out of his bed, and sat down. "Give the stable buck hell?" he asked.

"Sure. Ya see the stable buck's a nigger."

"Nigger, huh?"

"Yeah. Nice fella too. Got a crooked back where a horse kicked him. The boss gives him hell when he's mad. But the stable buck don't give a damn about that. He reads a lot. Got books in his room."

"What kind of a guy is the boss?" George asked.

"Well, he's a pretty nice fella. Gets pretty mad sometimes, but he's pretty nice. Tell ya what—know what he done Christmas? Brang a gallon of whisky right in here and says, 'Drink hearty boys. Christmas comes but once a year.' "

"The hell he did! Whole gallon?"

"Yes sir. Jesus, we had fun. They let the nigger come in that night. Little skinner name of Smitty took

after the nigger. Done pretty good, too. The guys wouldn't let him use his feet, so the nigger got him. If he coulda used his feet, Smitty says he woulda killed the nigger. The guys said on account of the nigger's got a crooked back, Smitty can't use his feet." He paused in relish of the memory. "After that the guys went into Soledad and raised hell. I didn't go in there. I ain't got the poop no more."

Lennie was just finishing making his bed. The wooden latch raised again and the door opened. A little stocky man stood in the open doorway. He wore blue jean trousers, a flannel shirt, a black, unbuttoned vest and a black coat. His thumbs were stuck in his belt, on each side of a square steel buckle. On his head was a soiled brown Stetson hat, and he wore high-heeled boots and spurs to prove he was not a laboring man.

The old swamper looked quickly at him, and then shuffled to the door rubbing his whiskers with his knuckles as he went. "Them guys just come," he said, and shuffled past the boss and out the door.

The boss stepped into the room with the short, quick steps of a fat-legged man. "I wrote Murray and Ready I wanted two men this morning. You got your work slips?" George reached into his pocket and produced the slips and handed them to the boss. "It wasn't Murray and Ready's fault. Says right here on the slip that you was to be here for work this morning."

George looked down at his feet. "Bus driver give us a bum steer," he said. "We hadda walk ten miles. Says we was here when we wasn't. We couldn't get no rides in the morning."

The boss squinted his eyes. "Well, I had to send out the grain teams short two buckers. Won't do any good to go out now till after dinner." He pulled his time book out of his pocket and opened it where a pencil was stuck between the leaves. George scowled meaningfully at Lennie, and Lennie nodded to show that he understood. The boss licked his pencil. "What's your name?"

"George Milton."

"And what's yours?"

George said, "His name's Lennie Small."

The names were entered in the book. "Le's see, this is the twentieth, noon the twentieth." He closed the book. "Where you boys been working?"

"Up around Weed," said George.

"You, too?" to Lennie.

"Yeah, him too," said George.

The boss pointed a playful finger at Lennie. "He ain't much of a talker, is he?"

"No, he ain't, but he's sure a hell of a good worker. Strong as a bull."

Lennie smiled to himself. "Strong as a bull," he repeated.

George scowled at him, and Lennie dropped his head in shame at having forgotten.

The boss said suddenly, "Listen, Small!" Lennie raised his head. "What can you do?"

In a panic, Lennie looked at George for help. "He

can do anything you tell him," said George. "He's a good skinner. He can rassel grain bags, drive a cultivator. He can do anything. Just give him a try."

The boss turned on George. "Then why don't you let him answer? What you trying to put over?"

George broke in loudly, "Oh! I ain't saying he's bright. He ain't. But I say he's a God damn good worker. He can put up a four hundred pound bale."

The boss deliberately put the little book in his pocket. He hooked his thumbs in his belt and squinted one eye nearly closed. "Say—what you sellin'?"

"Huh?"

"I said what stake you got in this guy? You takin' his pay away from him?"

"No, 'course I ain't. Why ya think I'm sellin' him out?"

"Well, I never seen one guy take so much trouble for another guy. I just like to know what your interest is."

George said, "He's my . . . cousin. I told his old lady I'd take care of him. He got kicked in the head by a horse when he was a kid. He's awright. Just ain't bright. But he can do anything you tell him."

The boss turned half away. "Well, God knows he don't need any brains to buck barley bags. But don't you try to put nothing over, Milton. I got my eye on you. Why'd you quit in Weed?"

"Job was done," said George promptly.

"What kinda job?"

"We . . . we was diggin' a cesspool."

42

"All right. But don't try to put nothing over, 'cause you can't get away with nothing. I seen wise guys before. Go on out with the grain teams after dinner. They're pickin' up barley at the threshing machine. Go out with Slim's team."

"Slim?"

"Yeah. Big tall skinner. You'll see him at dinner." He turned abruptly and went to the door, but before he went out he turned and looked for a long moment at the two men.

When the sound of his footsteps had died away, George turned on Lennie. "So you wasn't gonna say a word. You was gonna leave your big flapper shut and leave me do the talkin'. Damn near lost us the job."

Lennie stared hopelessly at his hands. "I forgot, George."

"Yeah, you forgot. You always forget, an' I got to talk you out of it." He sat down heavily on the bunk. "Now he's got his eye on us. Now we got to be careful and not make no slips. You keep your big flapper shut after this." He fell morosely silent.

"George."

"What you want now?"

"I wasn't kicked in the head with no horse, was I, George?"

"Be a damn good thing if you was," George said viciously. "Save ever'body a hell of a lot of trouble."

"You said I was your cousin, George."

"Well, that was a lie. An' I'm damn glad it was. If I

44

was a relative of yours I'd shoot myself." He stopped suddenly, stepped to the open front door and peered out. "Say, what the hell you doin' listenin'?"

The old man came slowly into the room. He had his broom in his hand. And at his heels there walked a drag-footed sheep dog, gray of muzzle, and with pale, blind old eyes. The dog struggled lamely to the side of the room and lay down, grunting softly to himself and licking his grizzled, moth-eaten coat. The swamper watched him until he was settled. "I wasn't listenin'. I was jus' standin' in the shade a minute scratchin' my dog. I jus' now finished swampin' out the wash house."

"You was pokin' your big ears into our business," George said. "I don't like nobody to get nosey."

The old man looked uneasily from George to Lennie, and then back. "I jus' come there," he said. "I didn't hear nothing you guys was sayin'. I ain't interested in nothing you was sayin'. A guy on a ranch don't never listen nor he don't ast no questions."

"Damn right he don't," said George, slightly mollified, "not if he wants to stay workin' long." But he was reassured by the swamper's defense. "Come on in and set down a minute," he said. "That's a hell of an old dog."

"Yeah. I had 'im ever since he was a pup. God, he was a good sheep dog when he was younger." He stood his broom against the wall and he rubbed his white bristled cheek with his knuckles. "How'd you like the boss?" he asked.

"Pretty good. Seemed awright."

"He's a nice fella," the swamper agreed. "You got to take him right."

At that moment a young man came into the bunk house; a thin young man with a brown face, with brown eyes and a head of tightly curled hair. He wore a work glove on his left hand, and, like the boss, he wore high-heeled boots. "Seen my old man?" he asked.

The swamper said, "He was here jus' a minute ago, Curley. Went over to the cook house, I think."

"I'll try to catch him," said Curley. His eyes passed over the new men and he stopped. He glanced coldly at George and then at Lennie. His arms gradually bent at the elbows and his hands closed into fists. He stiffened and went into a slight crouch. His glance was at once calculating and pugnacious. Lennie squirmed under the look and shifted his feet nervously. Curley stepped gingerly close to him. "You the new guys the old man was waitin' for?"

"We just come in," said George.

"Let the big guy talk."

Lennie twisted with embarrassment.

George said, "S'pose he don't want to talk?"

Curley lashed his body around. "By Christ, he's gotta talk when he's spoke to. What the hell are you gettin' into it for?"

"We travel together," said George coldly.

"Oh, so it's that way."

46

George was tense, and motionless. "Yeah, it's that way."

Lennie was looking helplessly to George for instruction.

"An' you won't let the big guy talk, is that it?"

"He can talk if he wants to tell you anything." He nodded slightly to Lennie.

"We jus' come in," said Lennie softly.

Curley stared levelly at him. "Well, nex' time you answer when you're spoke to." He turned toward the door and walked out, and his elbows were still bent out a little.

George watched him out, and then he turned back to the swamper. "Say, what the hell's he got on his shoulder? Lennie didn't do nothing to him."

The old man looked cautiously at the door to make sure no one was listening. "That's the boss's son," he said quietly. "Curley's pretty handy. He done quite a bit in the ring. He's a lightweight, and he's handy."

"Well, let him be handy," said George. "He don't have to take after Lennie. Lennie didn't do nothing to him. What's he got against Lennie?"

The swamper considered. . . . "Well . . . tell you what. Curley's like a lot of little guys. He hates big guys. He's alla time picking scraps with big guys. Kind of like he's mad at 'em because he ain't a big guy. You seen little guys like that, ain't you? Always scrappy?"

"Sure," said George. "I seen plenty tough little guys.

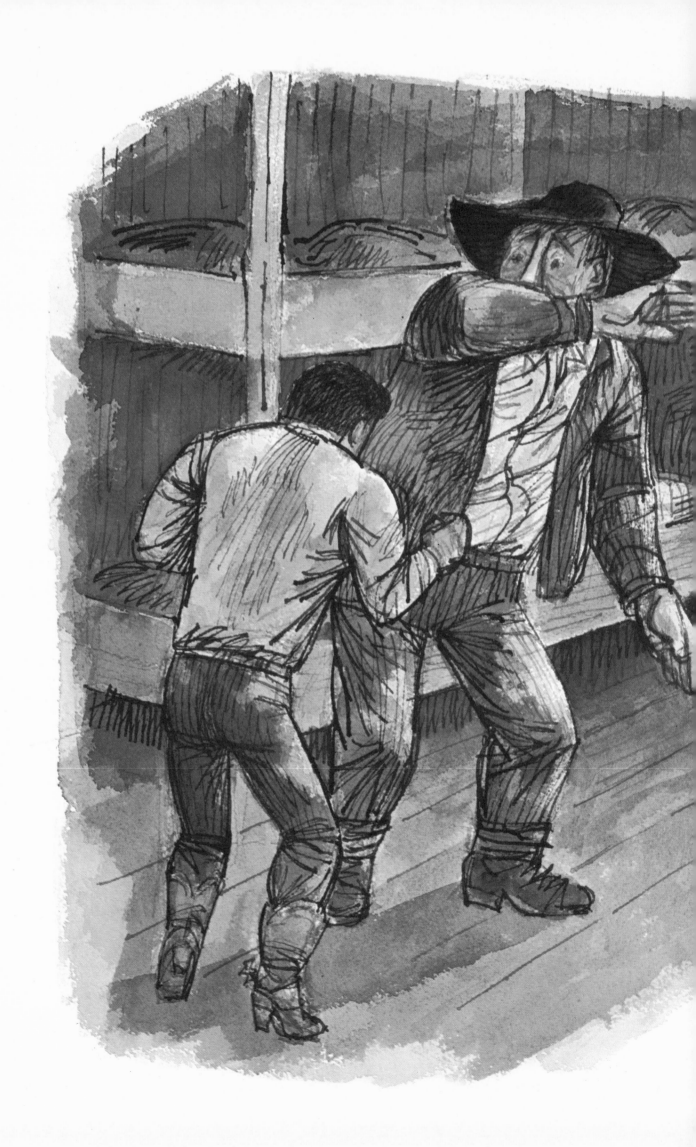

But this Curley better not make no mistakes about Lennie. Lennie ain't handy, but this Curley punk is gonna get hurt if he messes around with Lennie."

"Well, Curley's pretty handy," the swamper said skeptically. "Never did seem right to me. S'pose Curley jumps a big guy an' licks him. Ever'body says what a game guy Curley is. And s'pose he does the same thing and gets licked. Then ever'body says the big guy oughtta pick somebody his own size, and maybe they gang up on the big guy. Never did seem right to me. Seems like Curley ain't givin' nobody a chance."

George was watching the door. He said ominously, "Well, he better watch out for Lennie, Lennie ain't no fighter, but Lennie's strong and quick and Lennie don't know no rules." He walked to the square table and sat down on one of the boxes. He gathered some of the cards together and shuffled them.

The old man sat down on another box. "Don't tell Curley I said none of this. He'd slough me. He just don't give a damn. Won't ever get canned 'cause his old man's the boss."

George cut the cards and began turning them over, looking at each one and throwing it down on a pile. He said, "This guy Curley sounds like a son-of-a-bitch to me. I don't like mean little guys."

"Seems to me like he's worse lately," said the swamper. "He got married a couple of weeks ago. Wife lives over in the boss's house. Seems like Curley is cockier'n ever since he got married."

George grunted, "Maybe he's showin' off for his wife."

The swamper warmed to his gossip. "You seen that glove on his left hand?"

"Yeah. I seen it."

"Well, that glove's fulla vaseline."

"Vaseline? What the hell for?"

"Well, I tell ya what—Curley says he's keepin' that hand soft for his wife."

George studied the cards absorbedly. "That's a dirty thing to tell around," he said.

The old man was reassured. He had drawn a derogatory statement from George. He felt safe now, and he spoke more confidently. "Wait'll you see Curley's wife."

George cut the cards again and put out a solitaire lay, slowly and deliberately. "Purty?" he asked casually.

"Yeah. Purty . . . but ——"

George studied his cards. "But what?"

"Well—she got the eye."

"Yeah? Married two weeks and got the eye? Maybe that's why Curley's pants is full of ants."

"I seen her give Slim the eye. Slim's a jerkline skinner. Hell of a nice fella. Slim don't need to wear no high-heeled boots on a grain team. I seen her give Slim the eye. Curley never seen it. An' I seen her give Carlson the eye."

George pretended a lack of interest. "Looks like we was gonna have fun."

The swamper stood up from his box. "Know what I

think?" George did not answer. "Well, I think Curley's married . . . a tart."

"He ain't the first," said George. "There's plenty done that."

The old man moved toward the door, and his ancient dog lifted his head and peered about, and then got painfully to his feet to follow. "I gotta be settin' out the wash basins for the guys. The teams'll be in before long. You guys gonna buck barley?"

"Yeah."

"You won't tell Curley nothing I said?"

"Hell no."

"Well, you look her over, mister. You see if she ain't a tart." He stepped out the door into the brilliant sunshine.

George laid down his cards thoughtfully, turned his piles of three. He built four clubs on his ace pile. The sun square was on the floor now, and the flies whipped through it like sparks. A sound of jingling harness and the croak of heavy-laden axles sounded from outside. From the distance came a clear call. "Stable Buck — ooh, sta-able Buck!" And then, "Where the hell is that God damn nigger?"

George stared at his solitaire lay, and then he flounced the cards together and turned around to Lennie. Lennie was lying down on the bunk watching him.

"Look, Lennie! This here ain't no set up. I'm scared. You gonna have trouble with that Curley guy. I seen that kind before. He was kinda feelin' you out. He figures he's got you scared and he's gonna take a sock at you the first chance he gets."

Lennie's eyes were frightened. "I don't want no trouble," he said plaintively. "Don't let him sock me, George."

George got up and went over to Lennie's bunk and sat down on it. "I hate that kinda bastard," he said. "I seen plenty of 'em. Like the old guy says, Curley don't take no chances. He always wins." He thought for a moment. "If he tangles with you, Lennie, we're gonna get the can. Don't make no mistake about that. He's the boss's son. Look, Lennie. You try to keep away from him, will you? Don't never speak to him. If he comes in here you move clear to the other side of the room. Will you do that, Lennie?"

"I don't want no trouble," Lennie mourned. "I never done nothing to him."

"Well, that won't do you no good if Curley wants to plug himself up for a fighter. Just don't have nothing to do with him. Will you remember?"

"Sure, George. I ain't gonna say a word."

The sound of the approaching grain teams was louder, thud of big hooves on hard ground, drag of brakes and the jingle of trace chains. Men were calling back and forth from the teams. George, sitting on the bunk beside Lennie, frowned as he thought. Lennie asked timidly, "You ain't mad, George?"

"I ain't mad at you. I'm mad at this here Curley bastard. I hoped we was gonna get a little stake together —

maybe a hundred dollars." His tone grew decisive. "You keep away from Curley, Lennie."

"Sure I will, George. I won't say a word."

"Don't let him pull you in—but—if the son-of-a-bitch socks you—let 'im have it."

"Let 'im have what, George?"

"Never mind, never mind. I'll tell you when. I hate that kind of a guy. Look, Lennie, if you get in any kind of trouble, you remember what I told you to do?"

Lennie raised up on his elbow. His face contorted with thought. Then his eyes moved sadly to George's face. "If I get in any trouble, you ain't gonna let me tend the rabbits."

"That's not what I meant. You remember where we slep' last night? Down by the river?"

"Yeah. I remember. Oh, sure I remember! I go there an' hide in the brush."

"Hide till I come for you. Don't let nobody see you. Hide in the brush by the river. Say that over."

"Hide in the brush by the river, down in the brush by the river."

"If you get in trouble."

"If I get in trouble."

A brake screeched outside. A call came, "Stable — Buck. Oh! Sta-able Buck."

George said, "Say it over to yourself, Lennie, so you won't forget it."

Both men glanced up, for the rectangle of sunshine in the doorway was cut off. A girl was standing there looking in. She had full, rouged lips and wide-spaced eyes, heavily made up. Her fingernails were red. Her hair hung in little rolled clusters, like sausages. She wore a cotton house dress and red mules, on the insteps of which were little bouquets of red ostrich feathers. "I'm lookin' for Curley," she said. Her voice had a nasal, brittle quality.

George looked away from her and then back. "He was in here a minute ago, but he went."

"Oh!" She put her hands behind her back and leaned against the door frame so that her body was thrown forward. "You're the new fellas that just come, ain't ya?"

"Yeah."

Lennie's eyes moved down over her body, and though she did not seem to be looking at Lennie she bridled a little. She looked at her fingernails. "Sometimes Curley's in here," she explained.

George said brusquely, "Well he ain't now."

"If he ain't, I guess I better look some place else," she said playfully.

Lennie watched her, fascinated. George said, "If I see him, I'll pass the word you was looking for him."

She smiled archly and twitched her body. "Nobody can't blame a person for lookin'." she said. There were footsteps behind her, going by. She turned her head. "Hi, Slim," she said.

Slim's voice came through the door. "Hi, Good-lookin'."

"I'm tryin' to find Curley, Slim."

"Well, you ain't tryin' very hard. I seen him goin' in your house."

She was suddenly apprehensive. " 'Bye, boys," she called into the bunk house, and she hurried away.

George looked around at Lennie. "Jesus, what a tramp," he said. "So that's what Curley picks for a wife."

"She's purty," said Lennie defensively.

"Yeah, and she's sure hidin' it. Curley got his work ahead of him. Bet she'd clear out for twenty bucks."

Lennie still stared at the doorway where she had been. "Gosh, she was purty." He smiled admiringly. George looked quickly down at him and then he took him by an ear and shook him.

"Listen to me, you crazy bastard," he said fiercely. "Don't you even take a look at that bitch. I don't care what she says and what she does. I seen 'em poison before, but I never seen no piece of jail bait worse than her. You leave her be."

Lennie tried to disengage his ear. "I never done nothing, George."

"No, you never. But when she was standin' in the doorway showin' her legs, you wasn't lookin' the other way, neither."

"I never meant no harm, George. Honest I never."

"Well, you keep away from her, 'cause she's a rat-trap if I ever seen one. You let Curley take the rap. He

let himself in for it. Glove fulla vaseline," George said disgustedly. "An' I bet he's eatin' raw eggs and writin' to the patent medicine houses."

Lennie cried out suddenly—"I don' like this place, George. This ain't no good place. I wanna get outa here."

"We gotta keep it till we get a stake. We can't help it, Lennie. We'll get out jus' as soon as we can. I don't like it no better than you do." He went back to the table and set out a new solitaire hand. "No, I don't like it," he said. "For two bits I'd shove out of here. If we can get jus' a few dollars in the poke we'll shove off and go up the American River and pan gold. We can make maybe a couple of dollars a day there, and we might hit a pocket."

Lennie leaned eagerly toward him. "Le's go, George. Le's get outta here. It's mean here."

"We gotta stay," George said shortly. "Shut up now. The guys'll be comin' in."

From the washroom nearby came the sound of running water and rattling basins. George studied the cards. "Maybe we oughtta wash up," he said. "But we ain't done nothing to get dirty."

A tall man stood in the doorway. He held a crushed Stetson hat under his arm while he combed his long, black, damp hair straight back. Like the others he wore blue jeans and a short denim jacket. When he had finished combing his hair he moved into the room, and he moved with a majesty only achieved by royalty and master craftsmen. He was a jerkline skinner, the prince of the ranch, capable of driving ten, sixteen, even twenty mules with a single line to the leaders. He was capable of killing a fly on the wheeler's butt with a bull whip without touching the mule. There was a gravity in his manner and a quiet so profound that all talk stopped when he spoke. His authority was so great that his word was taken on any subject, be it politics or love. This was Slim, the jerkline skinner. His hatchet face was ageless. He might have been thirty-five or fifty. His ear heard more than was said to him, and his slow speech had overtones not of thought, but of under-standing beyond thought. His hands, large and lean, were as delicate in their action as those of a temple dancer.

He smoothed out his crushed hat, creased it in the middle and put it on. He looked kindly at the two in the bunk house. "It's brighter'n a bitch outside," he said gently. "Can't hardly see nothing in here. You the new guys?"

"Just come," said George.

"Gonna buck barley?"

"That's what the boss says."

Slim sat down on a box across the table from George. He studied the solitaire hand that was upside down to him. "Hope you get on my team," he said. His voice was very gentle. "I gotta pair of punks on my team that don't know a barley bag from a blue ball. You guys ever bucked any barley?"

"Hell, yes," said George. "I ain't nothing to scream

60

about, but that big bastard there can put up more grain alone than most pairs can."

Lennie, who had been following the conversation back and forth with his eyes, smiled complacently at the compliment. Slim looked approvingly at George for having given the compliment. He leaned over the table and snapped the corner of a loose card. "You guys travel around together?" His tone was friendly. It invited confidence without demanding it.

"Sure," said George. "We kinda look after each other." He indicated Lennie with his thumb. "He ain't bright. Hell of a good worker, though. Hell of a nice fella, but he ain't bright. I've knew him for a long time."

Slim looked through George and beyond him. "Ain't many guys travel around together," he mused. "I don't know why. Maybe ever'body in the whole damn world is scared of each other."

"It's a lot nicer to go around with a guy you know," said George.

A powerful, big-stomached man came into the bunk house. His head still dripped water from the scrubbing and dousing. "Hi, Slim," he said, and then stopped and stared at George and Lennie.

"These guys jus' come," said Slim by way of introduction.

"Glad ta meet ya," the big man said. "My name's Carlson."

"I'm George Milton. This here's Lennie Small."

"Glad ta meet ya," Carlson said again. "He ain't very

small." He chuckled softly at his joke. "Ain't small at all," he repeated. "Meant to ask you, Slim—how's your bitch? I seen she wasn't under your wagon this morning."

"She slang her pups last night," said Slim. "Nine of 'em. I drowned four of 'em right off. She couldn't feed that many."

"Got five left, huh?"

"Yeah, five. I kept the biggest."

"What kinda dogs you think they're gonna be?"

"I dunno," said Slim. "Some kinda shepherds, I guess. That's the most kind I seen around here when she was in heat."

Carlson went on, "Got five pups, huh. Gonna keep all of 'em?"

"I dunno. Have to keep 'em a while so they can drink Lulu's milk."

Carlson said thoughtfully, "Well, looka here, Slim. I been thinkin'. That dog of Candy's is so God damn old he can't hardly walk. Stinks like hell, too. Ever' time he comes into the bunk house I can smell him for two, three days. Why'n't you get Candy to shoot his old dog and give him one of the pups to raise up? I can smell that dog a mile away. Got no teeth, damn near blind, can't eat. Candy feeds him milk. He can't chew nothing else."

George had been staring intently at Slim. Suddenly a triangle began to ring outside, slowly at first, and then faster and faster until the beat of it disappeared into one ringing sound. It stopped as suddenly as it had started.

"There she goes," said Carlson.

Outside, there was a burst of voices as a group of men went by.

Slim stood up slowly and with dignity. "You guys better come on while they's still something to eat. Won't be nothing left in a couple of minutes."

Carlson stepped back to let Slim precede him, and then the two of them went out the door.

Lennie was watching George excitedly. George rumpled his cards into a messy pile. "Yeah!" George said, "I heard him, Lennie. I'll ask him."

"A brown and white one," Lennie cried excitedly.

"Come on. Le's get dinner. I don't know whether he got a brown and white one."

Lennie didn't move from his bunk. "You ask him right away, George, so he won't kill no more of 'em."

"Sure. Come on now, get up on your feet."

Lennie rolled off his bunk and stood up, and the two of them started for the door. Just as they reached it, Curley bounced in.

"You seen a girl around here?" he demanded angrily.

George said coldly. "'Bout half an hour ago maybe."

"Well what the hell was she doin'?"

George stood still, watching the angry little man. He said insultingly, "She said—she was lookin' for you."

Curley seemed really to see George for the first time. His eyes flashed over George, took in his height, measured his reach, looked at his trim middle. "Well, which way'd she go?" he demanded at last.

"I dunno," said George. "I didn't watch her go."

Curley scowled at him, and turning, hurried out the door.

George said, "Ya know, Lennie, I'm scared I'm gonna tangle with that bastard myself. I hate his guts. Jesus Christ! Come on. They won't be a damn thing left to eat."

They went out the door. The sunshine lay in a thin line under the window. From a distance there could be heard a rattle of dishes.

After a moment the ancient dog walked lamely in through the open door. He gazed about with mild, half-blind eyes. He sniffed, and then lay down and put his head between his paws. Curley popped into the doorway again and stood looking into the room. The dog raised his head, but when Curley jerked out, the grizzled head sank to the floor again.

ALTHOUGH there was evening brightness showing through the windows of the bunk house, inside it was dusk. Through the open door came the thuds and occasional clangs of a horseshoe game, and now and then the sounds of voices raised in approval or derision.

Slim and George came into the darkening bunk house together. Slim reached up over the card table and turned on the tin-shaded electric light. Instantly the table was brilliant with light, and the cone of the shade threw its brightness straight downward, leaving the corners of the bunk house still in dusk. Slim sat down on a box and George took his place opposite.

"It wasn't nothing," said Slim. "I would of had to drowned most of 'em anyways. No need to thank me about that."

George said, "It wasn't much to you, maybe, but it was a hell of a lot to him. Jesus Christ, I don't know how we're gonna get him to sleep in here. He'll want to sleep right out in the barn with 'em. We'll have trouble keepin' him from getting right in the box with them pups."

"It wasn't nothing," Slim repeated. "Say, you sure was right about him. Maybe he ain't bright, but I never seen such a worker. He damn near killed his partner buckin' barley. There ain't nobody can keep up with him. God awmighty I never seen such a strong guy."

George spoke proudly. "Jus' tell Lennie what to do an' he'll do it if it don't take no figuring. He can't think of nothing to do himself, but he sure can take orders."

There was a clang of horseshoe on iron stake outside and a little cheer of voices.

Slim moved back slightly so the light was not on his face. "Funny how you an' him string along together." It was Slim's calm invitation to confidence.

"What's funny about it?" George demanded defensively.

"Oh, I dunno. Hardly none of the guys ever travel together. I hardly never seen two guys travel together. You know how the hands are, they just come in and get their bunk and work a month, and then they quit and go out alone. Never seem to give a damn about nobody. It jus' seems kinda funny a cuckoo like him and a smart little guy like you travelin' together."

"He ain't no cuckoo," said George. "He's dumb as

66

hell, but he ain't crazy. An' I ain't so bright neither, or I wouldn't be buckin' barley for my fifty and found. If I was bright, if I was even a little bit smart, I'd have my own little place, an' I'd be bringin' in my own crops, 'stead of doin' all the work and not getting what comes up outa the ground." George fell silent. He wanted to talk. Slim neither encouraged nor discouraged him. He just sat back quiet and receptive.

"It ain't so funny, him an' me goin' aroun' together," George said at last. "Him and me was both born in Auburn. I knowed his Aunt Clara. She took him when he was a baby and raised him up. When his Aunt Clara died, Lennie just come along with me out workin'. Got kinda used to each other after a little while."

"Umm," said Slim.

George looked over at Slim and saw the calm, God-like eyes fastened on him. "Funny," said George. "I used to have a hell of a lot of fun with 'im. Used to play jokes on 'im 'cause he was too dumb to take care of 'imself. But he was too dumb even to know he had a joke played on him. I had fun. Made me seem God damn smart alongside of him. Why he'd do any damn thing I tol' him. If I tol' him to walk over a cliff, over he'd go. That wasn't so damn much fun after a while. He never got mad about it, neither. I've beat the hell outa him, and he coulda bust every bone in my body jus' with his han's, but he never lifted a finger against me." George's voice was taking on the tone of confession. "Tell you what made me stop that. One day a bunch of guys was standin' around up on the Sacramento River. I was feelin' pretty smart. I turns to Lennie and says, 'Jump in.' An' he jumps. Couldn't swim a stroke. He damn near drowned before we could get him. An' he was so damn nice to me for pullin' him out. Clean forgot I told him to jump in. Well, I ain't done nothing like that no more."

"He's a nice fella," said Slim. "Guy don't need no sense to be a nice fella. Seems to me sometimes it jus' works the other way around. Take a real smart guy and he ain't hardly ever a nice fella."

George stacked the scattered cards and began to lay out his solitaire hand. The shoes thudded on the ground outside. At the windows the light of the evening still made the window squares bright.

"I ain't got no people," George said. "I seen the guys that go around on the ranches alone. That ain't no good. They don't have no fun. After a long time they get mean. They get wantin' to fight all the time."

"Yeah, they get mean," Slim agreed. "They get so they don't want to talk to nobody."

" 'Course Lennie's a God damn nuisance most of the time," said George. "But you get used to goin' around with a guy an' you can't get rid of him."

"He ain't mean," said Slim. "I can see Lennie ain't a bit mean."

" 'Course he ain't mean. But he gets in trouble alla time because he's so God damn dumb. Like what happened in Weed——" He stopped, stopped in the mid-

68

dle of turning over a card. He looked alarmed and peered over at Slim. "You wouldn't tell nobody?"

"What'd he do in Weed?" Slim asked calmly.

"You wouldn' tell? . . . No, 'course you wouldn'."

"What'd he do in Weed?" Slim asked again.

"Well, he seen this girl in a red dress. Dumb bastard like he is, he wants to touch ever'thing he likes. Just wants to feel it. So he reaches out to feel this red dress an' the girl lets out a squawk, and that gets Lennie all mixed up, and he holds on 'cause that's the only thing he can think to do. Well, this girl squawks and squawks. I was jus' a little bit off, and I heard all the yellin', so I comes running, an' by that time Lennie's so scared all he can think to do is jus' hold on. I socked him over the head with a fence picket to make him let go. He was so scairt he couldn't let go of that dress. And he's so God damn strong, you know."

Slim's eyes were level and unwinking. He nodded very slowly. "So what happens?"

George carefully built his line of solitaire cards. "Well, that girl rabbits in an' tells the law she been raped. The guys in Weed start a party out to lynch Lennie. So we sit in a irrigation ditch under water all the rest of that day. Got on'y our heads sticking out from the side of the ditch. An' that night we scrammed outa there."

Slim sat in silence for a moment. "Didn't hurt the girl none, huh?" he asked finally.

"Hell, no. He just scared her. I'd be scared too if he

grabbed me. But he never hurt her. He jus' wanted to touch that red dress, like he wants to pet them pups all the time."

"He ain't mean," said Slim. "I can tell a mean guy a mile off."

"'Course he ain't, and he'll do any damn thing I——"

Lennie came in through the door. He wore his blue denim coat over his shoulders like a cape, and he walked hunched way over.

"Hi, Lennie," said George. "How do you like the pup now?"

Lennie said breathlessly, "He's brown an' white jus'
like I wanted." He went directly to his bunk and lay
down and turned his face to the wall and drew up his
knees.

George put down his cards very deliberately. "Lennie," he said sharply.

Lennie twisted his neck and looked over his shoulder. "Huh? What you want, George?"

"I tol' you you couldn't bring that pup in here."

"What pup, George? I ain't got no pup."

George went quickly to him, grabbed him by the

shoulder and rolled him over. He reached down and picked the tiny puppy from where Lennie had been concealing it against his stomach.

Lennie sat up quickly. "Give 'um to me, George."

George said, "You get right up an' take this pup back to the nest. He's gotta sleep with his mother. You want to kill him? Just born last night an' you take him out of the nest. You take him back or I'll tell Slim not to let you have him."

Lennie held out his hands pleadingly. "Give 'um to me, George. I'll take 'um back. I didn't mean no harm, George. Honest I didn't. I jus' wanted to pet 'um a little."

George handed the pup to him. "Awright. You get him back there quick, and don' you take him out no more. You'll kill him, the first thing you know." Lennie fairly scuttled out of the room.

Slim had not moved. His calm eyes followed Lennie out the door. "Jesus," he said. "He's jes' like a kid, ain't he?"

"Sure he's jes' like a kid. There ain't no more harm in him than a kid neither, except he's so strong. I bet he won't come in here to sleep tonight. He'd sleep right alongside that box in the barn. Well—let 'im. He ain't doin' no harm out there."

It was almost dark outside now. Old Candy, the swamper, came in and went to his bunk, and behind him struggled his old dog. "Hello, Slim. Hello, George. Didn't neither of you play horseshoes?"

"I don't like to play ever' night," said Slim.

Candy went on. "Either you guys got a slug of whisky? I gotta gut ache."

"I ain't," said Slim. "I'd drink it myself if I had, an' I ain't got a gut ache neither."

"Gotta bad gut ache," said Candy. "Them God damn turnips give it to me. I knowed they was going to before I ever eat 'em."

The thick-bodied Carlson came in out of the darkening yard. He walked to the other end of the bunk house and turned on the second shaded light. "Darker'n hell in here," he said. "Jesus, how that nigger can pitch shoes."

"He's plenty good," said Slim.

"Damn right he is," said Carlson. "He don't give nobody else a chance to win——" He stopped and sniffed the air, and still sniffing, looked down at the old dog. "God awmighty, that dog stinks. Get him outa here, Candy! I don't know nothing that stinks as bad as an old dog. You gotta get him out."

Candy rolled to the edge of his bunk. He reached over and patted the ancient dog, and he apologized, "I been around him so much I never notice how he stinks."

"Well, I can't stand him in here," said Carlson. "That stink hangs around even after he's gone." He walked over with his heavy-legged stride and looked down at the dog. "Got no teeth," he said. "He's all stiff with rheumatism. He ain't no good to you, Candy.

An' he ain't no good to himself. Why'n't you shoot him, Candy?"

The old man squirmed uncomfortably. "Well — hell! I had him so long. Had him since he was a pup. I herded sheep with him." He said proudly, "You wouldn't think it to look at him now, but he was the best damn sheep dog I ever seen."

George said, "I seen a guy in Weed that had an Airedale could herd sheep. Learned it from the other dogs."

Carlson was not to be put off. "Look, Candy. This ol' dog jus' suffers hisself all the time. If you was to take him out and shoot him right in the back of the head —" he leaned over and pointed, "— right there, why he'd never know what hit him."

Candy looked about unhappily. "No," he said softly. "No, I couldn' do that. I had 'im too long."

"He don't have no fun," Carlson insisted. "And he stinks to beat hell. Tell you what. I'll shoot him for you. Then it won't be you that does it."

Candy threw his legs off his bunk. He scratched the white stubble whiskers on his cheek nervously. "I'm so used to him," he said softly. "I had him from a pup."

"Well, you ain't bein' kind to him keepin' him alive," said Carlson. "Look, Slim's bitch got a litter right now. I bet Slim would give you one of them pups to raise up, wouldn't you, Slim?"

The skinner had been studying the old dog with his calm eyes. "Yeah," he said. "You can have a pup if you want to." He seemed to shake himself free for speech.

74

"Carl's right, Candy. That dog ain't no good to himself. I wisht somebody'd shoot me if I got old an' a cripple."

Candy looked helplessly at him, for Slim's opinions were law. "Maybe it'd hurt him," he suggested. "I don't mind takin' care of him."

Carlson said, "The way I'd shoot him, he wouldn't feel nothing. I'd put the gun right there." He pointed with his toe. "Right back of the head. He wouldn't even quiver."

Candy looked for help from face to face. It was quite dark outside by now. A young laboring man came in. His sloping shoulders were bent forward and he walked heavily on his heels, as though he carried the invisible grain bag. He went to his bunk and put his hat on his shelf. Then he picked a pulp magazine from his shelf and brought it to the light over the table. "Did I show you this, Slim?" he asked.

"Show me what?"

The young man turned to the back of the magazine, put it down on the table and pointed with his finger. "Right there, read that." Slim bent over it. "Go on," said the young man. "Read it out loud."

" 'Dear Editor:' " Slim read slowly. " 'I read your mag for six years and I think it is the best on the market. I like stories by Peter Rand. I think he is a whing-ding. Give us more like the Dark Rider. I don't write many letters. Just thought I would tell you I think your mag is the best dime's worth I ever spent.' "

Slim looked up questioningly. "What do you want me to read that for?"

Whit said, "Go on. Read the name at the bottom."

Slim read, " 'Yours for success, William Tenner.' " He glanced up at Whit again. "What you want me to read that for?"

Whit closed the magazine impressively. "Don't you remember Bill Tenner? Worked here about three months ago?"

Slim thought. . . . "Little guy?" he asked. "Drove a cultivator?"

"That's him," Whit cried. "That's the guy!"

"You think he's the guy wrote this letter?"

"I know it. Bill and me was in here one day. Bill had one of them books that just come. He was lookin' in it and he says, 'I wrote a letter. Wonder if they put it in the book!' But it wasn't there. Bill says, 'Maybe they're savin' it for later.' An' that's just what they done. There it is."

"Guess you're right," said Slim. "Got it right in the book."

George held out his hand for the magazine. "Let's look at it?"

Whit found the place again, but he did not surrender his hold on it. He pointed out the letter with his forefinger. And then he went to his box shelf and laid the magazine carefully in. "I wonder if Bill seen it," he said. "Bill and me worked in that patch of field peas.

76

Run cultivators, both of us. Bill was a hell of a nice fella."

During the conversation Carlson had refused to be drawn in. He continued to look down at the old dog. Candy watched him uneasily. At last Carlson said, "If you want me to, I'll put the old devil out of his misery right now and get it over with. Ain't nothing left for him. Can't eat, can't see, can't even walk without hurtin'."

Candy said hopefully, "You ain't got no gun."

"The hell I ain't. Got a Luger. It won't hurt him none at all."

Candy said, "Maybe tomorra. Le's wait till tomorra."

"I don't see no reason for it," said Carlson. He went to his bunk, pulled his bag from underneath it and took out a Luger pistol. "Let's get it over with," he said. "We can't sleep with him stinkin' around in here." He put the pistol in his hip pocket.

Candy looked a long time at Slim to try to find some reversal. And Slim gave him none. At last Candy said softly and hopelessly, "Awright — take 'im." He did not look down at the dog at all. He lay back on his bunk and crossed his arms behind his head and stared at the ceiling.

From his pocket Carlson took a little leather thong. He stooped over and tied it around the old dog's neck. All the men except Candy watched him. "Come boy. Come on, boy," he said gently. And he said apologetically to Candy, "He won't even feel it." Candy did not move nor answer him. He twitched the thong. "Come on, boy." The old dog got slowly and stiffly to his feet and followed the gently pulling leash.

Slim said, "Carlson."

"Yeah?"

"You know what to do."

"What ya mean, Slim?"

"Take a shovel," said Slim shortly.

"Oh, sure! I get you." He led the dog out into the darkness.

George followed to the door and shut the door and set the latch gently in its place. Candy lay rigidly on his bed staring at the ceiling.

Slim said loudly, "One of my lead mules got a bad hoof. Got to get some tar on it." His voice trailed off. It was silent outside. Carlson's footsteps died away. The silence came into the room. And the silence lasted.

George chuckled, "I bet Lennie's right out there in the barn with his pup. He won't want to come in here no more now he's got a pup."

Slim said, "Candy, you can have any one of them pups you want."

Candy did not answer. The silence fell on the room again. It came out of the night and invaded the room. George said, "Anybody like to play a little euchre?"

"I'll play out a few with you," said Whit.

They took places opposite each other at the table under the light, but George did not shuffle the cards. He rippled the edge of the deck nervously, and the little snapping noise drew the eyes of all the men in the room, so that he stopped doing it. The silence fell on the room again. A minute passed, and another minute. Candy lay still, staring at the ceiling. Slim gazed at him for a moment and then looked down at his hands; he subdued one hand with the other, and held it down. There came a little gnawing sound from under the floor and all the men looked down toward it gratefully. Only Candy continued to stare at the ceiling.

"Sounds like there was a rat under there," said George. "We ought to get a trap down there."

Whit broke out, "What the hell's takin' him so long? Lay out some cards, why don't you? We ain't going to get no euchre played this way."

George brought the cards together tightly and studied the backs of them. The silence was in the room again.

A shot sounded in the distance. The men looked quickly at the old man. Every head turned toward him.

For a moment he continued to stare at the ceiling. Then he rolled slowly over and faced the wall and lay silent.

George shuffled the cards noisily and dealt them. Whit drew a scoring board to him and set the pegs to start. Whit said, "I guess you guys really come here to work."

"How do ya mean?" George asked.

Whit laughed. "Well, ya come on a Friday. You got two days to work till Sunday."

80

"I don't see how you figure," said George.

Whit laughed again. "You do if you been around these big ranches much. Guy that wants to look over a ranch comes in Sat' day afternoon. He gets Sat' day night supper an' three meals on Sunday, and he can quit Monday mornin' after breakfast without turning his hand. But you come to work Friday noon. You got to put in a day an' a half no matter how you figure."

George looked at him levelly. "We're gonna stick aroun' a while," he said. "Me an' Lennie's gonna roll up a stake."

The door opened quietly and the stable buck put in his head; a lean Negro head, lined with pain, the eyes patient. "Mr. Slim."

Slim took his eyes from old Candy. "Huh? Oh! Hello, Crooks. What's' a matter?"

"You told me to warm up tar for that mule's foot. I got it warm."

"Oh! Sure, Crooks. I'll come right out an' put it on."

"I can do it if you want, Mr. Slim."

"No. I'll come do it myself." He stood up.

Crooks said, "Mr. Slim."

"Yeah."

"That big new guy's messin' around your pups out in the barn."

"Well, he ain't doin' no harm. I give him one of them pups."

"Just thought I'd tell ya," said Crooks. "He's takin'

'em outa the nest and handlin' them. That won't do them no good."

"He won't hurt 'em," said Slim. "I'll come along with you now."

George looked up. "If that crazy bastard's foolin' around too much, jus' kick him out, Slim."

Slim followed the stable buck out of the room.

George dealt and Whit picked up his cards and examined them. "Seen the new kid yet?" he asked.

"What kid?" George asked.

"Why, Curley's new wife."

"Yeah, I seen her."

"Well, ain't she a looloo?"

"I ain't seen that much of her," said George.

Whit laid down his cards impressively. "Well, stick around an' keep your eyes open. You'll see plenty. She ain't concealin' nothing. I never seen nobody like her. She got the eye goin' all the time on everybody. I bet she even gives the stable buck the eye. I don't know what the hell she wants."

George asked casually, "Been any trouble since she got here?"

It was obvious that Whit was not interested in his cards. He laid his hand down and George scooped it in. George laid out his deliberate solitaire hand — seven cards, and six on top, and five on top of those.

Whit said, "I see what you mean. No, they ain't been nothing yet. Curley's got yella-jackets in his drawers, but that's all so far. Ever' time the guys is around she shows up. She's lookin' for Curley, or she thought she lef' somethin' layin' around and she's lookin' for it. Seems like she can't keep away from guys. An' Curley's pants is just crawlin' with ants, but they ain't nothing come of it yet."

George said, "She's gonna make a mess. They's gonna be a bad mess about her. She's a jail bait all set on the trigger. That Curley got his work cut out for him. Ranch with a bunch of guys on it ain't no place for a girl, specially like her."

Whit said, "If you got idears, you ought ta come in town with us guys tomorra night."

"Why? What's doin'?"

"Jus' the usual thing. We go in to old Susy's place. Hell of a nice place. Old Susy's a laugh — always crackin' jokes. Like she says when we come up on the front porch las' Sat'day night. Susy opens the door and then she yells over her shoulder, 'Get yor coats on, girls, here comes the sheriff.' She never talks dirty, neither. Got five girls there."

"What's it set you back?" George asked.

"Two an' a half. You can get a shot for two bits. Susy got nice chairs to set in, too. If a guy don't want a flop, why he can just set in the chairs and have a couple or three shots and pass the time of day and Susy don't give a damn. She ain't rushin' guys through and kickin' 'em out if they don't want a flop."

"Might go in and look the joint over," said George.

"Sure. Come along. It's a hell of a lot of fun — her

crackin' jokes all the time. Like she says one time, she says, 'I've knew people that if they got a rag rug on the floor an' a kewpie doll lamp on the phonograph they think they're running a parlor house.' That's Clara's house she's talkin' about. An' Susy says, 'I know what you boys want,' she says. 'My girls is clean,' she says, 'an' there ain't no water in my whisky,' she says. 'If any you guys wanta look at a kewpie doll lamp an' take your own chance gettin' burned, why you know where to go.' An' she says, 'There's guys around here walkin' bow-legged 'cause they like to look at a kewpie doll lamp.''

George asked, "Clara runs the other house, huh?"

"Yeah," said Whit. "We don't never go there. Clara gets three bucks a crack and thirty-five cents a shot, and she don't crack no jokes. But Susy's place is clean and she got nice chairs. Don't let no goo-goos in, neither."

"Me an' Lennie's rollin' up a stake," said George. "I might go in an' set and have a shot, but I ain't puttin' out no two and a half."

"Well, a guy got to have some fun sometime," said Whit.

The door opened and Lennie and Carlson came in together. Lennie crept to his bunk and sat down, trying not to attract attention. Carlson reached under his bunk and brought out his bag. He didn't look at old Candy, who still faced the wall. Carlson found a little cleaning rod in the bag and a can of oil. He laid them on his bed and then brought out the pistol, took out the magazine and snapped the loaded shell from the chamber. Then he fell to cleaning the barrel with the little rod. When the ejector snapped, Candy turned over and looked for a moment at the gun before he turned back to the wall again.

Carlson said casually, "Curley been in yet?"

"No," said Whit. "What's eatin' on Curley?"

Carlson squinted down the barrel of his gun. "Lookin' for his old lady. I seen him going round and round outside."

Whit said sarcastically, "He spends half his time lookin' for her, and the rest of the time she's lookin' for him."

Curley burst into the room excitedly. "Any you guys seen my wife?" he demanded.

"She ain't been here," said Whit.

Curley looked threateningly about the room. "Where the hell's Slim?"

"Went out in the barn," said George. "He was gonna put some tar on a split hoof."

Curley's shoulders dropped and squared. "How long ago'd he go?"

"Five — ten minutes."

Curley jumped out the door and banged it after him.

Whit stood up. "I guess maybe I'd like to see this," he said. "Curley's just spoilin' or he wouldn't start for Slim. An' Curley's handy, God damn handy. Got in the finals for the Golden Gloves. He got newspaper

86

clippings about it." He considered. "But jus' the same, he better leave Slim alone. Nobody don't know what Slim can do."

"Thinks Slim's with his wife, don't he?" said George.

"Looks like it," Whit said, "'Course Slim ain't. Least I don't think Slim is. But I like to see the fuss if it comes off. Come on, le's go."

George said, "I'm stayin' right here. I don't want to get mixed up in nothing. Lennie and me got to make a stake."

Carlson finished the cleaning of the gun and put it in the bag and pushed the bag under his bunk. "I guess I'll go out and look her over," he said. Old Candy lay still, and Lennie, from his bunk, watched George cautiously.

When Whit and Carlson were gone and the door closed after them, George turned to Lennie. "What you got on your mind?"

"I ain't done nothing, George. Slim says I better not pet them pups so much for a while. Slim says it ain't good for them; so I come right in. I been good, George."

"I coulda told you that," said George.

"Well, I wasn't hurtin' 'em none. I jus' had mine in my lap pettin' it."

George asked, "Did you see Slim out in the barn?"

"Sure I did. He tol' me I better not pet that pup no more."

"Did you see that girl?"

"You mean Curley's girl?"

"Yeah. Did she come in the barn?"

"No. Anyways I never seen her."

"You never seen Slim talkin' to her?"

"Uh-uh. She ain't been in the barn."

"O.K.," said George. "I guess them guys ain't gonna see no fight. If there's any fightin', Lennie, you keep out of it."

"I don't want no fights," said Lennie. He got up from his bunk and sat down at the table, across from George. Almost automatically George shuffled the cards and laid out his solitaire hand. He used a deliberate, thoughtful, slowness.

Lennie reached for a face card and studied it, then turned it upside down and studied it. "Both ends the same," he said. "George, why is it both ends the same?"

"I don't know," said George. "That's jus' the way they make 'em. What was Slim doin' in the barn when you seen him?"

"Slim?"

"Sure. You seen him in the barn, an' he tol' you not to pet the pups so much."

"Oh, yeah. He had a can a' tar an' a paint brush. I don't know what for."

"You sure that girl didn't come in like she come in here today?"

"No. She never come."

George sighed. "You give me a good whore house every time," he said. "A guy can go in an' get drunk and get ever'thing outa his system all at once, an' no messes. And he knows how much it's gonna set him back. These here jail baits is just set on the trigger of the hoosegow."

Lennie followed his words admiringly, and moved his lips a little to keep up. George continued, "You remember Andy Cushman, Lennie? Went to grammar school?"

"The one that his old lady used to make hot cakes for the kids?" Lennie asked.

"Yeah. That's the one. You can remember anything if there's anything to eat in it." George looked carefully at the solitaire hand. He put an ace up on his scoring rack and piled a two, three and four of diamonds on it. "Andy's in San Quentin right now on account of a tart," said George.

Lennie drummed on the table with his fingers. "George?"

"Huh?"

"George, how long's it gonna be till we get that little place an' live on the fatta the lan' — an' rabbits?"

"I don' know," said George. "We gotta get a big stake together. I know a little place we can get cheap, but they ain't givin' it away."

Old Candy turned slowly over. His eyes were wide open. He watched George carefully.

Lennie said, "Tell about that place, George."

"I jus' tol' you, jus' las' night."

"Go on — tell again, George."

"Well, it's ten acres," said George. "Got a little win'mill. Got a little shack on it, an' a chicken run. Got a kitchen, orchard, cherries, apples, peaches, 'cots, nuts, got a few berries. They's a place for alfalfa and plenty water to flood it. They's a pig pen ——"

"An' rabbits, George."

"No place for rabbits now, but I could easy build a few hutches and you could feed alfalfa to the rabbits."

"Damn right, I could," said Lennie. "You God damn right I could."

George's hands stopped working with the cards. His voice was growing warmer. "An' we could have a few pigs. I could build a smoke house like the one gran'pa had, an' when we kill a pig we can smoke the bacon and the hams, and make sausage an' all like that. An' when the salmon run up river we could catch a hundred of 'em an' salt 'em down or smoke 'em. We could have them for breakfast. They ain't nothing so nice as smoked salmon. When the fruit come in we could can it — and tomatoes, they're easy to can. Ever' Sunday we'd kill a chicken or a rabbit. Maybe we'd have a cow or a goat, and the cream is so God damn thick you got to cut it with a knife and take it out with a spoon."

Lennie watched him with wide eyes, and old Candy watched him too. Lennie said softly, "We could live offa the fatta the lan'."

"Sure," said George. "All kin's a vegetables in the garden, and if we want a little whisky we can sell a few eggs or something, or some milk. We'd jus' live there. We'd belong there. There wouldn't be no more runnin' round the country and gettin' fed by a Jap cook. No,

90

sir, we'd have our own place where we belonged and not sleep in no bunk house."

"Tell about the house, George," Lennie begged.

"Sure, we'd have a little house an' a room to ourself. Little fat iron stove, an' in the winter we'd keep a fire goin' in it. It ain't enough land so we'd have to work too hard. Maybe six, seven hours a day. We wouldn't have to buck no barley eleven hours a day. An' when we put in a crop, why, we'd be there to take the crop up. We'd know what come of our planting."

"An' rabbits," Lennie said eagerly. "An' I'd take care of 'em. Tell how I'd do that, George."

"Sure, you'd go out in the alfalfa patch an' you'd have a sack. You'd fill up the sack and bring it in an' put it in the rabbit cages."

"They'd nibble an' they'd nibble," said Lennie, "the way they do. I seen 'em."

"Ever' six weeks or so," George continued, "them does would throw a litter so we'd have plenty rabbits to eat an' to sell. An' we'd keep a few pigeons to go flyin' around the win'mill like they done when I was a kid." He looked raptly at the wall over Lennie's head. "An' it'd be our own, an' nobody could can us. If we don't like a guy we can say, 'Get the hell out,' and by God he's got to do it. An' if a fren' come along, why we'd have an extra bunk, an' we'd say, 'Why don't you spen' the night?' an' by God he would. We'd have a setter dog and a couple stripe cats, but you gotta watch out them cats don't get the little rabbits."

Lennie breathed hard. "You jus' let 'em try to get the rabbits. I'll break their God damn necks. I'll . . . I'll smash 'em with a stick." He subsided, grumbling to himself, threatening the future cats which might dare to disturb the future rabbits.

George sat entranced with his own picture.

When Candy spoke they both jumped as though they had been caught doing something reprehensible. Candy said, "You know where's a place like that?"

George was on guard immediately. "S'pose I do," he said. "What's that to you?"

"You don't need to tell me where it's at. Might be any place."

"Sure," said George. "That's right. You couldn't find it in a hundred years."

Candy went on excitedly, "How much they want for a place like that?"

George watched him suspiciously. "Well—I could get it for six hundred bucks. The ol' people that owns it is flat bust an' the ol' lady needs an operation. Say — what's it to you? You got nothing to do with us."

Candy said, "I ain't much good with on'y one hand. I lost my hand right here on this ranch. That's why they give me a job swampin'. An' they give me two hunderd an' fifty dollars 'cause I los' my hand. An' I got fifty more saved up right in the bank, right now. Tha's three hunderd, and I got fifty more comin' the end a the month. Tell you what ——" He leaned forward eagerly. "S'pose I went in with you guys. Tha's three

94

hunderd an' fifty bucks I'd put in. I ain't much good, but I could cook and tend the chickens and hoe the garden some. How'd that be?"

George half-closed his eyes. "I gotta think about that. We was always gonna do it by ourselves."

Candy interrupted him, "I'd make a will an' leave my share to you guys in case I kick off, 'cause I ain't got no relatives nor nothing. You guys got any money? Maybe we could do her right now?"

George spat on the floor disgustedly. "We got ten bucks between us." Then he said thoughtfully, "Look, if me an' Lennie work a month an' don't spen' nothing, we'll have a hunderd bucks. That'd be four fifty. I bet we could swing her for that. Then you an' Lennie could go get her started an' I'd get a job an' make up the res', an' you could sell eggs an' stuff like that."

They fell into a silence. They looked at one another, amazed. This thing they had never really believed in was coming true. George said reverently, "Jesus Christ! I bet we could swing her." His eyes were full of wonder. "I bet we could swing her," he repeated softly.

Candy sat on the edge of his bunk. He scratched the stump of his wrist nervously. "I got hurt four years ago," he said. "They'll can me purty soon. Jus' as soon as I can't swamp out no bunk houses they'll put me on the county. Maybe if I give you guys my money, you'll let me hoe in the garden even after I ain't no good at it. An' I'll wash dishes an' little chicken stuff like that. But I'll be on our own place, an' I'll be let to work on our own place." He said miserably, "You seen what they done to my dog tonight? They says he wasn't no good to himself nor nobody else. When they can me here I wisht somebody'd shoot me. But they won't do nothing like that. I won't have no place to go, an' I can't get no more jobs. I'll have thirty dollars more comin', time you guys is ready to quit."

George stood up. "We'll do her," he said. "We'll fix up that little old place an' we'll go live there." He sat down again. They all sat still, all bemused by the beauty of the thing, each mind was popped into the future when this lovely thing should come about.

George said wonderingly, "S'pose they was a carnival or a circus come to town, or a ball game, or any damn thing." Old Candy nodded in appreciation of the idea. "We'd just go to her," George said. "We wouldn't ask nobody if we could. Jus' say, 'We'll go to her,' an' we would. Jus' milk the cow and sling some grain to the chickens an' go to her."

"An' put some grass to the rabbits," Lennie broke in. "I wouldn't never forget to feed them. When we gon'ta do it, George?"

"In one month. Right squack in one month. Know what I'm gon'ta do? I'm gon'ta write to them old people that owns the place that we'll take it. An' Candy'll send a hunderd dollars to bind her."

"Sure will," said Candy. "They got a good stove there?"

"Sure, got a nice stove, burns coal or wood."

"I'm gonna take my pup," said Lennie. "I bet by Christ he likes it there, by Jesus."

Voices were approaching from outside. George said quickly, "Don't tell nobody about it. Jus' us three an' nobody else. They li'ble to can us so we can't make no stake. Jus' go on like we was gonna buck barley the rest of our lives, then all of a sudden some day we'll go get our pay an' scram outa here."

Lennie and Candy nodded, and they were grinning with delight. "Don't tell nobody," Lennie said to himself.

Candy said, "George."

"Huh?"

"I ought to of shot that dog myself, George. I shouldn't ought to of let no stranger shoot my dog."

The door opened. Slim came in, followed by Curley and Carlson and Whit. Slim's hands were black with tar and he was scowling. Curley hung close to his elbow.

Curley said, "Well, I didn't mean nothing, Slim. I just ast you."

Slim said, "Well, you been askin' me too often. I'm gettin' God damn sick of it. If you can't look after your own God damn wife, what you expect me to do about it? You lay offa me."

"I'm jus' tryin' to tell you I didn't mean nothing," said Curley. "I jus' thought you might of saw her."

"Why'n't you tell her to stay the hell home where

she belongs?" said Carlson. "You let her hang around bunk houses and pretty soon you're gonna have som'pin on your hands and you won't be able to do nothing about it."

Curley whirled on Carlson. "You keep outta this les' you wanta step outside."

Carlson laughed. "You God damn punk," he said. "You tried to throw a scare into Slim, an' you couldn't make it stick. Slim throwed a scare inta you. You're yella as a frog belly. I don't care if you're the best welter in the country. You come for me, an' I'll kick your God damn head off."

Candy joined the attack with joy. "Glove fulla vaseline," he said disgustedly. Curley glared at him. His eyes slipped on past and lighted on Lennie; and Lennie was still smiling with delight at the memory of the ranch.

Curley stepped over to Lennie like a terrier. "What the hell you laughin' at?"

Lennie looked blankly at him. "Huh?"

Then Curley's rage exploded. "Come on, ya big bastard. Get up on your feet. No big son-of-a-bitch is gonna laugh at me. I'll show ya who's yella."

Lennie looked helplessly at George, and then he got up and tried to retreat. Curley was balanced and poised. He slashed at Lennie with his left, and then smashed down his nose with a right. Lennie gave a cry of terror. Blood welled from his nose. "George," he cried.

99

"Make 'um let me alone, George." He backed until he was against the wall, and Curley followed, slugging him in the face. Lennie's hands remained at his sides; he was too frightened to defend himself.

George was on his feet yelling, "Get him, Lennie. Don't let him do it."

Lennie covered his face with his huge paws and bleated with terror. He cried, "Make 'um stop, George." Then Curley attacked his stomach and cut off his wind.

Slim jumped up. "The dirty little rat," he cried. "I'll get 'um myself."

George put out his hand and grabbed Slim. "Wait a minute," he shouted. He cupped his hands around his mouth and yelled, "Get 'im, Lennie!"

Lennie took his hands away from his face and looked about for George, and Curley slashed at his eyes. The big face was covered with blood. George yelled again, "I said get him."

Curley's fist was swinging when Lennie reached for it. The next minute Curley was flopping like a fish on a line, and his closed fist was lost in Lennie's big hand. George ran down the room. "Leggo of him, Lennie. Let go."

But Lennie watched in terror the flopping little man whom he held. Blood ran down Lennie's face, one of his eyes was cut and closed. George slapped him in the face again and again, and still Lennie held on to the closed fist. Curley was white and shrunken by now, and his struggling had become weak. He stood crying, his fist lost in Lennie's paw.

George shouted over and over, "Leggo his hand, Lennie. Leggo. Slim, come help me while the guy got any hand left."

Suddenly Lennie let go his hold. He crouched cowering against the wall. "You tol' me to, George," he said miserably.

Curley sat down on the floor, looking in wonder at his crushed hand. Slim and Carlson bent over him. Then Slim straightened up and regarded Lennie with horror. "We got to get him in to a doctor," he said. "Looks to me like ever' bone in his han' is bust."

"I didn't wanta," Lennie cried. "I didn't wanta hurt him."

Slim said, "Carlson, you get the candy wagon hitched up. We'll take 'um into Soledad an' get 'um fixed up." Carlson hurried out. Slim turned to the whimpering Lennie. "It ain't your fault," he said. "This punk sure had it comin' to him. But — Jesus! He ain't hardly got no han' left." Slim hurried out, and in a moment returned with a tin cup of water. He held it to Curley's lips.

George said, "Slim, will we get canned now? We need the stake. Will Curley's old man can us now?"

Slim smiled wryly. He knelt down beside Curley. "You got your senses in hand enough to listen?" he asked. Curley nodded. "Well, then listen," Slim went

on. "I think you got your han' caught in a machine. If you don't tell nobody what happened, we ain't going to. But you jus' tell an' try to get this guy canned and we'll tell ever'body, an' then will you get the laugh."

"I won't tell," said Curley. He avoided looking at Lennie.

Buggy wheels sounded outside. Slim helped Curley up. "Come on now. Carlson's gonna take you to a doctor." He helped Curley out the door. The sound of wheels drew away. In a moment Slim came back into the bunk house. He looked at Lennie, still crouched fearfully against the wall. "Le's see your hands," he asked.

Lennie stuck out his hands.

"Christ awmighty, I hate to have you mad at me," Slim said.

George broke in, "Lennie was jus' scairt," he explained. "He didn't know what to do. I told you nobody ought never to fight him. No, I guess it was Candy I told."

Candy nodded solemnly. "That's jus' what you done," he said. "Right this morning when Curley first lit intil your fren', you says, 'He better not fool with Lennie if he knows what's good for 'um.' That's jus' what you says to me."

George turned to Lennie. "It ain't your fault," he said. "You don't need to be scairt no more. You done jus' what I tol' you to. Maybe you better go in the wash room an' clean up your face. You look like hell."

Lennie smiled with his bruised mouth. "I didn't want no trouble," he said. He walked toward the door, but just before he came to it, he turned back. "George?"

"What you want?"

"I can still tend the rabbits, George?"

"Sure. You ain't done nothing wrong."

"I di'n't mean no harm, George."

"Well, get the hell out and wash your face."

CROOKS, the Negro stable buck, had his bunk in the harness room; a little shed that leaned off the wall of the barn. On one side of the little room there was a square four-paned window, and on the other, a narrow plank door leading into the barn. Crooks' bunk was a long box filled with straw, on which his blankets were flung. On the wall by the window there were pegs on which hung broken harness in process of being mended; strips of new leather; and under the window itself a little bench for leather-working tools, curved knives and needles and balls of linen thread, and a small hand riveter. On pegs were also pieces of harness, a split collar with the horsehair stuffing sticking out, a broken hame, and a trace chain with its leather covering split.

106

Crooks had his apple box over his bunk, and in it a range of medicine bottles, both for himself and for the horses. There were cans of saddle soap and a drippy can of tar with its paint brush sticking over the edge. And scattered about the floor were a number of personal possessions; for, being alone, Crooks could leave his things about, and being a stable buck and a cripple, he was more permanent than the other men, and he had accumulated more possessions than he could carry on his back.

Crooks possessed several pairs of shoes, a pair of rubber boots, a big alarm clock and a single-barreled shotgun. And he had books, too; a tattered dictionary and a mauled copy of the California civil code for 1905. There were battered magazines and a few dirty books on a special shelf over his bunk. A pair of large gold-rimmed spectacles hung from a nail on the wall above his bed.

This room was swept and fairly neat, for Crooks was a proud, aloof man. He kept his distance and demanded that other people keep theirs. His body was bent over to the left by his crooked spine, and his eyes lay deep in his head, and because of their depth seemed to glitter with intensity. His lean face was lined with deep black wrinkles, and he had thin, pain-tightened lips which were lighter than his face.

It was Saturday night. Through the open door that led into the barn came the sound of moving horses, of feet stirring, of teeth champing on hay, of the rattle of halter chains. In the stable buck's room a small electric globe threw a meager yellow light.

Crooks sat on his bunk. His shirt was out of his jeans in back. In one hand he held a bottle of liniment, and with the other he rubbed his spine. Now and then he poured a few drops of the liniment into his pink-palmed hand and reached up under his shirt to rub again. He flexed his muscles against his back and shivered.

Noiselessly Lennie appeared in the open doorway and stood there looking in, his big shoulders nearly filling the opening. For a moment Crooks did not see him, but on raising his eyes he stiffened and a scowl came on his face. His hand came out from under his shirt.

Lennie smiled helplessly in an attempt to make friends.

Crooks said sharply, "You got no right to come in my room. This here's my room. Nobody got any right in here but me."

Lennie gulped and his smile grew more fawning. "I ain't doing nothing," he said. "Just come to look at my puppy. And I seen your light," he explained.

"Well, I got a right to have a light. You go on get outta my room. I ain't wanted in the bunk house, and you ain't wanted in my room."

"Why ain't you wanted?" Lennie asked.

"'Cause I'm black. They play cards in there, but I can't play because I'm black. They say I stink. Well, I tell you, you all of you stink to me."

Lennie flapped his big hands helplessly. "Ever'body

108

went into town," he said. "Slim an' George an' ever'-body. George says I gotta stay here an' not get in no trouble. I seen your light."

"Well, what do you want?"

"Nothing — I seen your light. I thought I could jus' come in an' set."

Crooks stared at Lennie, and he reached behind him and took down the spectacles and adjusted them over his pink ears and stared again. "I don't know what you're doin' in the barn anyway," he complained. "You ain't no skinner. They's no call for a bucker to come into the barn at all. You ain't no skinner. You ain't got nothing to do with the horses."

"The pup," Lennie repeated. "I come to see my pup."

"Well, go see your pup, then. Don't come in a place where you're not wanted."

Lennie lost his smile. He advanced a step into the room, then remembered and backed to the door again. "I looked at 'em a little. Slim says I ain't to pet 'em very much."

Crooks said, "Well, you been takin' 'em out of the nest all the time. I wonder the old lady don't move 'em someplace else."

"Oh, she don't care. She lets me." Lennie had moved into the room again.

Crooks scowled, but Lennie's disarming smile defeated him. "Come on in and set a while," Crooks said. "'Long as you won't get out and leave me alone, you

might as well set down." His tone was a little more friendly. "All the boys gone into town, huh?"

"All but old Candy. He just sets in the bunk house sharpening his pencil and sharpening and figuring."

Crooks adjusted his glasses. "Figuring? What's Candy figuring about?"

Lennie almost shouted, "'Bout the rabbits."

"You're nuts," said Crooks. "You're crazy as a wedge. What rabbits you talkin' about?"

"The rabbits we're gonna get, and I get to tend 'em, cut grass an' give 'em water, an' like that."

"Jus' nuts," said Crooks. "I don't blame the guy you travel with for keepin' you outa sight."

Lennie said quietly, "It ain't no lie. We're gonna do it. Gonna get a little place an' live on the fatta the lan'."

Crooks settled himself more comfortably on his bunk. "Set down," he invited. "Set down on the nail keg."

Lennie hunched down on the little barrel. "You think it's a lie," Lennie said. "But it ain't no lie. Ever' word's the truth, an' you can ast George."

Crooks put his dark chin into his pink palm. "You travel aroun' with George, don't ya?"

"Sure. Me an' him goes ever' place together."

Crooks continued. "Sometimes he talks, and you don't know what the hell he's talkin' about. Ain't that so?" He leaned forward, boring Lennie with his deep eyes. "Ain't that so?"

"Yeah . . . sometimes."

"Jus' talks on, an' you don't know what the hell it's all about?"

"Yeah . . . sometimes. But . . . not always."

Crooks leaned forward over the edge of the bunk. "I ain't a southern Negro," he said. "I was born right here in California. My old man had a chicken ranch, 'bout ten acres. The white kids come to play at our place, an' sometimes I went to play with them, and some of them was pretty nice. My ol' man didn't like that. I never knew till long later why he didn't like that. But I know now." He hesitated, and when he spoke again his voice was softer. "There wasn't another colored family for miles around. And now there ain't a colored man on this ranch an' there's jus' one family in Soledad." He laughed. "If I say something, why it's just a nigger sayin' it."

Lennie asked, "How long you think it'll be before them pups will be old enough to pet?"

Crooks laughed again. "A guy can talk to you an' be sure you won't go blabbin'. Couple of weeks an' them pups'll be all right. George knows what he's about. Jus' talks, an' you don't understand nothing." He leaned forward excitedly. "This is just a nigger talkin', an' a busted-back nigger. So it don't mean nothing, see? You couldn't remember it anyways. I seen it over an' over — a guy talkin' to another guy and it don't make no differ- ence if he don't hear or understand. The thing is, they're talkin', or they're settin' still not talkin'. It

112

don't make no difference, no difference." His excitement had increased until he pounded his knee with his hand. "George can tell you screwy things, and it don't matter. It's just the talking. It's just bein' with another guy. That's all." He paused.

His voice grew soft and persuasive. "S'pose George don't come back no more. S'pose he took a powder and just ain't coming back. What'll you do then?"

Lennie's attention came gradually to what had been said. "What?" he demanded.

"I said s'pose George went into town tonight and you never heard of him no more." Crooks pressed forward some kind of private victory. "Just s'pose that," he repeated.

"He won't do it," Lennie cried. "George wouldn't do nothing like that. I been with George a long time. He'll come back tonight ——" But the doubt was too much for him. "Don't you think he will?"

Crooks' face lighted with pleasure in his torture. "Nobody can't tell what a guy'll do," he observed calmly. "Le's say he wants to come back and can't. S'pose he gets killed or hurt so he can't come back."

Lennie struggled to understand. "George won't do nothing like that," he repeated. "George is careful. He won't get hurt. He ain't never been hurt, 'cause he's careful."

"Well, s'pose, jus' s'pose he don't come back. What'll you do then?"

Lennie's face wrinkled with apprehension. "I don'

know. Say, what you doin' anyways?" he cried. "This ain't true. George ain't got hurt."

Crooks bored in on him. "Want me ta tell ya what'll happen? They'll take ya to the booby hatch. They'll tie ya up with a collar, like a dog."

Suddenly Lennie's eyes centered and grew quiet, and mad. He stood up and walked dangerously toward Crooks. "Who hurt George?" he demanded.

Crooks saw the danger as it approached him. He edged back on his bunk to get out of the way. "I was just supposin'," he said. "George ain't hurt. He's all right. He'll be back all right."

Lennie stood over him. "What you supposin' for? Ain't nobody goin' to suppose no hurt to George."

Crooks removed his glasses and wiped his eyes with his fingers. "Jus' set down," he said. "George ain't hurt."

Lennie growled back to his seat on the nail keg. "Ain't nobody goin' to talk no hurt to George," he grumbled.

Crooks said gently, "Maybe you can see now. You got George. You *know* he's goin' to come back. S'pose you didn't have nobody. S'pose you couldn't go into the bunk house and play rummy 'cause you was black. How'd you like that? S'pose you had to sit out here an' read books. Sure you could play horseshoes till it got dark, but then you got to read books. Books ain't no good. A guy needs somebody — to be near him." He whined, "A guy goes nuts if he ain't got nobody. Don't

make no difference who the guy is, long's he's with you. I tell ya," he cried, "I tell ya a guy gets too lonely an' he gets sick."

"George gonna come back," Lennie reassured himself in a frightened voice. "Maybe George come back already. Maybe I better go see."

Crooks said, "I didn't mean to scare you. He'll come back. I was talkin' about myself. A guy sets alone out here at night, maybe readin' books or thinkin' or stuff like that. Sometimes he gets thinkin', an' he got nothing to tell him what's so an' what ain't so. Maybe if he sees somethin', he don't know whether it's right or not. He can't turn to some other guy and ast him if he sees it too. He can't tell. He got nothing to measure by. I seen things out here. I wasn't drunk. I don't know if I was asleep. If some guy was with me, he could tell me I was asleep, an' then it would be all right. But I jus' don't know." Crooks was looking across the room now, looking toward the window.

Lennie said miserably, "George wun't go away and leave me. I know George wun't do that."

The stable buck went on dreamily, "I remember when I was a little kid on my old man's chicken ranch. Had two brothers. They was always near me, always there. Used to sleep right in the same room, right in the same bed — all three. Had a strawberry patch. Had an alfalfa patch. Used to turn the chickens out in the alfalfa on a sunny morning. My brothers'd set on a fence rail an' watch 'em — white chickens they was."

Gradually Lennie's interest came around to what was being said. "George says we're gonna have alfalfa for the rabbits."

"What rabbits?"

"We're gonna have rabbits an' a berry patch."

"You're nuts."

"We are too. You ast George."

"You're nuts." Crooks was scornful. "I seen hunderds of men come by on the road an' on the ranches, with their bindles on their back an' that same damn thing in their heads. Hunderds of them. They come, an' they quit an' go on; an' every damn one of 'em's got a little piece of land in his head. An' never a God damn one of 'em ever gets it. Just like heaven. Ever'-body wants a little piece of lan'. I read plenty of books out here. Nobody never gets to heaven, and nobody gets no land. It's just in their head. They're all the time talkin' about it, but it's jus' in their head." He paused and looked toward the open door, for the horses were moving restlessly and the halter chains clinked. A horse whinnied. "I guess somebody's out there," Crooks said. "Maybe Slim. Slim comes in sometimes two, three times a night. Slim's a real skinner. He looks out for his team." He pulled himself painfully upright and moved toward the door. "That you, Slim?" he called.

Candy's voice answered. "Slim went in town. Say, you seen Lennie?"

"Ya mean the big guy?"

"Yeah. Seen him around any place?"

"He's in here," Crooks said shortly. He went back to his bunk and lay down.

Candy stood in the doorway scratching his bald wrist and looking blindly into the lighted room. He made no attempt to enter. "Tell ya what, Lennie. I been figuring out about them rabbits."

Crooks said irritably, "You can come in if you want."

Candy seemed embarrassed. "I do' know. 'Course, if ya want me to."

"Come on in. If ever'body's comin' in, you might

just as well." It was difficult for Crooks to conceal his pleasure with anger.

Candy came in, but he was still embarrassed. "You got a nice cozy little place in here," he said to Crooks. "Must be nice to have a room all to yourself this way."

"Sure," said Crooks. "And a manure pile under the window. Sure, it's swell."

Lennie broke in, "You said about them rabbits."

Candy leaned against the wall beside the broken collar while he scratched the wrist stump. "I been here a long time," he said. "An' Crooks been here a long time. This's the first time I ever been in his room."

Crooks said darkly, "Guys don't come into a colored man's room very much. Nobody been here but Slim. Slim an' the boss."

Candy quickly changed the subject. "Slim's as good a skinner as I ever seen."

Lennie leaned toward the old swamper. "About them rabbits," he insisted.

Candy smiled. "I got it figured out. We can make some money on them rabbits if we go about it right."

"But I get to tend 'em," Lennie broke in. "George says I get to tend 'em. He promised."

Crooks interrupted brutally. "You guys is just kiddin' yourself. You'll talk about it a hell of a lot, but you won't get no land. You'll be a swamper here till they take you out in a box. Hell, I seen too many guys. Lennie here'll quit an' be on the road in two, three weeks. Seems like ever' guy got land in his head."

Candy rubbed his cheek angrily. "You God damn right we're gonna do it. George says we are. We got the money right now."

"Yeah?" said Crooks. "An' where's George now? In town in a whore house. That's where your money's goin'. Jesus, I seen it happen too many times. I seen too many guys with land in their head. They never get none under their hand."

Candy cried, "Sure they all want it. Everybody wants a little bit of land, not much. Jus' som'thin' that was his. Somethin' he could live on and there couldn't nobody throw him off of it. I never had none. I planted crops for damn near ever'body in this state, but they wasn't my crops, and when I harvested 'em, it wasn't none of my harvest. But we gonna do it now, and don't make no mistake about that. George ain't got the money in town. That money's in the bank. Me an' Lennie an' George. We gonna have a room to ourself. We're gonna have a dog an' rabbits an' chickens. We're gonna have green corn an' maybe a cow or a goat." He stopped, overwhelmed with his picture.

Crooks asked, "You say you got the money?"

"Damn right. We got most of it. Just a little bit more to get. Have it all in one month. George got the land all picked out, too."

Crooks reached around and explored his spine with his hand. "I never seen a guy really do it," he said. "I seen guys nearly crazy with loneliness for land, but ever' time a whore house or a blackjack game took what it takes." He hesitated. ". . . If you . . . guys would want a hand to work for nothing — just his keep, why I'd come an' lend a hand. I ain't so crippled I can't work like a son-of-a-bitch if I want to."

"Any you boys seen Curley?"

They swung their heads toward the door. Looking in was Curley's wife. Her face was heavily made up. Her lips were slightly parted. She breathed strongly, as though she had been running.

"Curley ain't been here," Candy said sourly.

She stood still in the doorway, smiling a little at them, rubbing the nails of one hand with the thumb and forefinger of the other. And her eyes traveled from one face to another. "They left all the weak ones here," she said finally. "Think I don't know where they all went? Even Curley. I know where they all went."

Lennie watched her, fascinated; but Candy and Crooks were scowling down away from her eyes. Candy said, "Then if you know, why you want to ast us where Curley is at?"

She regarded them amusedly. "Funny thing," she said. "If I catch any one man, and he's alone, I get along fine with him. But just let two of the guys get together an' you won't talk. Jus' nothing but mad." She dropped her fingers and put her hands on her hips. "You're all scared of each other, that's what. Ever' one of you's scared the rest is goin' to get something on you."

After a pause Crooks said, "Maybe you better go along to your own house now. We don't want no trouble."

"Well, I ain't giving you no trouble. Think I don't like to talk to somebody ever' once in a while? Think I like to stick in that house alla time?"

Candy laid the stump of his wrist on his knee and rubbed it gently with his hand. He said accusingly, "You gotta husban'. You got no call foolin' aroun' with other guys, causin' trouble."

The girl flared up. "Sure I gotta husban'. You all seen him. Swell guy, ain't he? Spends all his time sayin' what he's gonna do to guys he don't like, and he don't like nobody. Think I'm gonna stay in that two-by-four house and listen how Curley's gonna lead with his left twict, and then bring in the ol' right cross? 'One-two' he says. 'Jus the ol' one-two an' he'll go down.' " She paused and her face lost its sullenness and grew interested. "Say — what happened to Curley's han'?"

There was an embarrassed silence. Candy stole a look at Lennie. Then he coughed. "Why . . . Curley . . . he got his han' caught in a machine, ma'am. Bust his han'."

She watched for a moment, and then she laughed. "Baloney! What you think you're sellin' me? Curley started som'pin' he didn' finish. Caught in a machine — baloney! Why, he ain't give nobody the good ol' one-two since he got his han' bust. Who bust him?"

Candy repeated sullenly, "Got it caught in a machine."

122

"Awright," she said contemptuously. "Awright, cover 'im up if ya wanta. Whatta I care? You bindle bums think you're so damn good. Whatta ya think I am, a kid? I tell ya I could of went with shows. Not jus' one, neither. An' a guy tol' me he could put me in pitchers. . . ." She was breathless with indignation. " — Satiday night. Ever'body out doin' som'pin'. Ever'body! An' what am I doin'? Standin' here talkin' to a bunch of bindle stiffs — a nigger an' a dum-dum and a lousy ol' sheep — an' likin' it because they ain't nobody else."

Lennie watched her, his mouth half open. Crooks had retired into the terrible protective dignity of the Negro. But a change came over old Candy. He stood up suddenly and knocked his nail keg over backward. "I had enough," he said angrily. "You ain't wanted here. We told you you ain't. An' I tell ya, you got floozy idears about what us guys amounts to. You ain't got sense enough in that chicken head to even see that we ain't stiffs. S'pose you get us canned. S'pose you do. You think we'll hit the highway an' look for another lousy two-bit job like this. You don't know that we got our own ranch to go to, an' our own house. We ain't got to stay here. We gotta house and chickens an' fruit trees an' a place a hunderd time prettier than this. An' we got fren's, that's what we got. Maybe there was a time when we was scared of gettin' canned, but we ain't no more. We got our own lan', and it's ours, an' we c'n go to it."

Curley's wife laughed at him. "Baloney," she said.

"I seen too many you guys. If you had two bits in the worl', why you'd be in gettin' two shots of corn with it and suckin' the bottom of the glass. I know you guys."

Candy's face had grown redder and redder, but before she was done speaking, he had control of himself. He was the master of the situation. "I might of knew," he said gently. "Maybe you just better go along an' roll your hoop. We ain't got nothing to say to you at all. We know what we got, and we don't care whether you know it or not. So maybe you better jus' scatter along now, 'cause Curley maybe ain't gonna like his wife out in the barn with us 'bindle stiffs.'"

She looked from one face to another, and they were all closed against her. And she looked longest at Lennie, until he dropped his eyes in embarrassment. Suddenly she said, "Where'd you get them bruises on your face?"

Lennie looked up guiltily. "Who — me?"

"Yeah, you."

Lennie looked to Candy for help, and then he looked at his lap again. "He got his han' caught in a machine," he said.

Curley's wife laughed. "O.K., Machine. I'll talk to you later. I like machines."

Candy broke in. "You let this guy alone. Don't you do no messing aroun' with him. I'm gonna tell George what you says. George won't have you messin' with Lennie."

"Who's George?" she asked. "The little guy you come with?"

Lennie smiled happily. "That's him," he said, "That's the guy, an' he's gonna let me tend the rabbits."

"Well, if that's all you want, I might get a couple rabbits myself."

Crooks stood up from his bunk and faced her. "I had enough," he said coldly. "You got no rights comin' in a colored man's room. You got no rights messing around in here at all. Now you jus' get out, an' get out quick. If you don't, I'm gonna ast the boss not to ever let you come in the barn no more."

She turned on him in scorn. "Listen, Nigger," she said. "You know what I can do to you if you open your trap?"

Crooks stared hopelessly at her, and then he sat down on his bunk and drew into himself.

She closed on him. "You know what I could do?"

Crooks seemed to grow smaller, and he pressed himself against the wall. "Yes, ma'am."

"Well, you keep your place then, Nigger. I could get you strung up on a tree so easy it ain't even funny."

Crooks had reduced himself to nothing. There was no personality, no ego — nothing to arouse either like or dislike. He said, "Yes, ma'am," and his voice was toneless.

For a moment she stood over him as though waiting for him to move so that she could whip at him again; but Crooks sat perfectly still, his eyes averted, everything that might be hurt drawn in. She turned at last to the other two.

126

Old Candy was watching her, fascinated. "If you was to do that, we'd tell," he said quietly. "We'd tell about you framin' Crooks."

"Tell an' be damned," she cried. "Nobody'd listen to you, an' you know it. Nobody'd listen to you."

Candy subsided. "No . . ." he agreed. "Nobody'd listen to us."

Lennie whined, "I wisht George was here. I wisht George was here."

Candy stepped over to him. "Don't you worry none," he said. "I jus' heard the guys comin' in. George'll be in the bunk house right now, I bet." He turned to Curley's wife. "You better go home now," he said quietly. "If you go right now, we won't tell Curley you was here."

She appraised him coolly. "I ain't sure you heard nothing."

"Better not take no chances," he said. "If you ain't sure, you better take the safe way."

She turned to Lennie. "I'm glad you bust up Curley a little bit. He got it comin' to him. Sometimes I'd like to bust him myself." She slipped out the door and disappeared into the dark barn. And while she went through the barn, the halter chains rattled, and some horses snorted and some stamped their feet.

Crooks seemed to come slowly out of the layers of protection he had put on. "Was that the truth what you said about the guys come back?" he asked.

"Sure. I heard 'em."

"Well, I didn't hear nothing."

"The gate banged," Candy said, and he went on, "Jesus Christ, Curley's wife can move quiet. I guess she had a lot of practice, though."

Crooks avoided the whole subject now. "Maybe you guys better go," he said. "I ain't sure I want you in here no more. A colored man got to have some rights even if he don't like 'em."

Candy said, "That bitch didn't ought to of said that to you."

"It wasn't nothing," Crooks said dully. "You guys comin' in an' settin' made me forget. What she says is true."

The horses snorted out in the barn and the chains rang and a voice called, "Lennie. Oh, Lennie. You in the barn?"

"It's George," Lennie cried. And he answered, "Here, George. I'm right in here."

In a second George stood framed in the door, and he looked disapprovingly about. "What you doin' in Crooks' room. You hadn't ought to be in here."

Crooks nodded. "I tol' 'em, but they come in anyways."

"Well, why'n't you kick 'em out?"

"I di'n't care much," said Crooks. "Lennie's a nice fella."

Now Candy aroused himself. "Oh, George! I been figurin' and figurin'. I got it doped out how we can even make some money on them rabbits."

George scowled. "I though I tol' you not to tell nobody about that."

Candy was crestfallen. "Didn't tell nobody but Crooks."

George said, "Well you guys get outta here. Jesus, seems like I can't go away for a minute."

Candy and Lennie stood up and went toward the door. Crooks called, "Candy!"

"Huh?"

"'Member what I said about hoein' and doin' odd jobs?"

"Yeah," said Candy. "I remember."

"Well, jus' forget it," said Crooks. "I didn' mean it. Jus' foolin'. I wouldn' want to go no place like that."

"Well, O.K., if you feel like that. Goodnight."

The three men went out of the door. As they went through the barn the horses snorted and the halter chains rattled.

Crooks sat on his bunk and looked at the door for a moment, and then he reached for the liniment bottle. He pulled out his shirt in back, poured a little liniment in his pink palm and, reaching around, he fell slowly to rubbing his back.

ONE end of the great barn was piled high with new hay and over the pile hung the four-taloned Jackson fork suspended from its pulley. The hay came down like a mountain slope at the other end of the barn, and there was a level place as yet unfilled with the new crop. At the sides the feeding racks were visible, and between the slats the heads of horses could be seen.

It was Sunday afternoon. The resting horses nibbled the remaining wisps of hay, and they stamped their feet and they bit the wood of the mangers and rattled the halter chains. The afternoon sun sliced in through the cracks of the barn walls and lay in bright lines on the hay. There was the buzz of flies in the air, the lazy afternoon humming.

130

From outside came the clang of horseshoes on the playing peg and the shouts of men, playing, encouraging, jeering. But in the barn it was quiet and humming and lazy and warm.

Only Lennie was in the barn, and Lennie sat in the hay beside a packing case under a manger in the end of the barn that had not been filled with hay. Lennie sat in the hay and looked at a little dead puppy that lay in front of him. Lennie looked at it for a long time, and then he put out his huge hand and stroked it, stroked it clear from one end to the other.

And Lennie said softly to the puppy, "Why do you got to get killed? You ain't so little as mice. I didn't bounce you hard." He bent the pup's head up and looked in its face, and he said to it, "Now maybe George ain't gonna let me tend no rabbits, if he fin's out you got killed."

He scooped a little hollow and laid the puppy in it and covered it over with hay, out of sight; but he continued to stare at the mound he had made. He said, "This ain't no bad thing like I got to go hide in the brush. Oh! no. This ain't. I'll tell George I foun' it dead."

He unburied the puppy and inspected it, and he stroked it from ears to tail. He went on sorrowfully, "But he'll know. George always knows. He'll say, 'You done it. Don't try to put nothing over on me.' An' he'll say, 'Now jus' for that you don't get to tend no rabbits!'"

Suddenly his anger rose. "God damn you," he cried. "Why do you got to get killed? You ain't so little as mice." He picked up the pup and hurled it from him. He turned his back on it. He sat bent over his knees and he whispered, "Now I won't get to tend the rabbits. Now he won't let me." He rocked himself back and forth in his sorrow.

From outside came the clang of horseshoes on the iron stake, and then a little chorus of cries. Lennie got up and brought the puppy back and laid it on the hay and sat down. He stroked the pup again. "You wasn't big enough," he said. "They tol' me and tol' me you wasn't. I di'n't know you'd get killed so easy." He worked his fingers on the pup's limp ear. "Maybe George won't care," he said. "This here God damn little son-of-a-bitch wasn't nothing to George."

Curley's wife came around the end of the last stall. She came very quietly, so that Lennie didn't see her. She wore her bright cotton dress and the mules with the red ostrich feathers. Her face was made up and the little sausage curls were all in place. She was quite near to him before Lennie looked up and saw her.

In a panic he shoveled hay over the puppy with his fingers. He looked sullenly up at her.

She said, "What you got there, sonny boy?"

Lennie glared at her. "George says I ain't to have nothing to do with you — talk to you or nothing."

She laughed. "George giving you orders about everything?"

Lennie looked down at the hay. "Says I can't tend no rabbits if I talk to you or anything."

She said quietly, "He's scared Curley'll get mad. Well, Curley got his arm in a sling — an' if Curley gets tough, you can break his other han'. You didn't put nothing over on me about gettin' it caught in no machine."

But Lennie was not to be drawn. "No, sir. I ain't gonna talk to you or nothing."

She knelt in the hay beside him. "Listen," she said. "All the guys got a horseshoe tenement goin' on. It's on'y about four o'clock. None of them guys is goin' to leave that tenement. Why can't I talk to you? I never get to talk to nobody. I get awful lonely."

Lennie said, "Well, I ain't supposed to talk to you or nothing."

"I get lonely," she said. "You can talk to people, but I can't talk to nobody but Curley. Else he gets mad. How'd you like not to talk to anybody?"

Lennie said, "Well, I ain't supposed to. George's scared I'll get in trouble."

She changed the subject. "What you got covered up there?"

Then all of Lennie's woe came back on him. "Jus' my pup," he said sadly. "Jus' my little pup." And he swept the hay from on top of it.

"Why, he's dead," she cried.

"He was so little," said Lennie. "I was jus' playin' with him . . . an' he made like he's gonna bite me . . . an'

I made like I was gonna smack him . . . an' . . . an' I done it. An' then he was dead."

She consoled him. "Don't you worry none. He was jus' a mutt. You can get another one easy. The whole country is fulla mutts."

"It ain't that so much," Lennie explained miserably. "George ain't gonna let me tend no rabbits now."

"Why don't he?"

"Well, he said if I done any more bad things he ain't gonna let me tend the rabbits."

She moved closer to him and she spoke soothingly. "Don't you worry about talkin' to me. Listen to the guys yell out there. They got four dollars bet in that tenement. None of them ain't gonna leave till it's over."

"If George sees me talkin' to you he'll give me hell," Lennie said cautiously. "He tol' me so."

Her face grew angry. "Wha's the matter with me?" she cried. "Ain't I got a right to talk to nobody? Whatta they think I am, anyways? You're a nice guy. I don't know why I can't talk to you. I ain't doin' no harm to you."

"Well, George says you'll get us in a mess."

"Aw, nuts!" she said. "What kinda harm am I doin' to you? Seems like they ain't none of them cares how I gotta live. I tell you I ain't used to livin' like this. I coulda made somethin' of myself." She said darkly, "Maybe I will yet." And then her words tumbled out in a passion of communication, as though she hurried before her listener could be taken away. "I lived right in Salinas," she said. "Come there when I was a kid. Well, a show come through, an' I met one of the actors. He says I could go with that show. But my ol' lady wouldn' let me. She says because I was on'y fifteen. But the guy says I coulda. If I'd went, I wouldn't be livin' like this, you bet."

Lennie stroked the pup back and forth. "We gonna have a little place — an' rabbits," he explained.

She went on with her story quickly, before she should be interrupted. " 'Nother time I met a guy, an' he was in pitchers. Went out to the Riverside Dance Palace with him. He says he was gonna put me in the movies. Says I was a natural. Soon's he got back to Hollywood he was gonna write to me about it." She looked closely at Lennie to see whether she was impressing him. "I never got that letter," she said. "I always thought my ol' lady stole it. Well, I wasn't gonna stay no place where I couldn't get nowhere or make something of myself, an' where they stole your letters. I ast her if she stole it, too, an' she says no. So I married Curley. Met him out to the Riverside Dance Palace that same night." She demanded, "You listenin'?"

"Me? Sure."

"Well, I ain't told this to nobody before. Maybe I ought'n to. I don' *like* Curley. He ain't a nice fella." And because she had confided in him, she moved closer to Lennie and sat beside him. "Coulda been in the movies, an' had nice clothes — all them nice clothes like they wear. An' I coulda sat in them big hotels, an' had pitchers took of me. When they had them previews I coulda went to them, an' spoke in the radio, an' it wouldn'ta cost me a cent because I was in the pitcher. An' all them nice clothes like they wear. Because this guy says I was a natural." She looked up at Lennie, and she made a small grand gesture with her arm and hand to show that she could act. The fingers trailed after her leading wrist, and her little finger stuck out grandly from the rest.

Lennie sighed deeply. From outside came the clang of a horseshoe on metal, and then a chorus of cheers. "Somebody made a ringer," said Curley's wife.

Now the light was lifting as the sun went down, and the sun streaks climbed up the wall and fell over the feeding racks and over the heads of the horses.

Lennie said, "Maybe if I took this pup out and threw him away George wouldn't never know. An' then I could tend the rabbits without no trouble."

Curley's wife said angrily, "Don't you think of nothing but rabbits?"

"We gonna have a little place," Lennie explained patiently. "We gonna have a house an' a garden and a place for alfalfa, an' that alfalfa is for the rabbits, an' I take a sack and get it all fulla alfalfa and then I take it to the rabbits."

She asked, "What makes you so nuts about rabbits?"

Lennie had to think carefully before he could come to a conclusion. He moved cautiously close to her, until he was right against her. "I like to pet nice things.

136

Once at a fair I seen some of them long-hair rabbits. An' they was nice, you bet. Sometimes I've even pet mice, but not when I could get nothing better."

Curley's wife moved away from him a little. "I think you're nuts," she said.

"No I ain't," Lennie explained earnestly. "George says I ain't. I like to pet nice things with my fingers, sof' things."

She was a little bit reassured. "Well, who don't?" she said. "Ever'body likes that. I like to feel silk an' velvet. Do you like to feel velvet?"

Lennie chuckled with pleasure. "You bet, by God," he cried happily. "An' I had some, too. A lady give me some, an' that lady was — my own Aunt Clara. She give it right to me — 'bout this big a piece. I wisht I had that velvet right now." A frown came over his face. "I lost it," he said. "I ain't seen it for a long time."

Curley's wife laughed at him. "You're nuts," she said. "But you're a kinda nice fella. Jus' like a big baby. But a person can see kinda what you mean. When I'm doin' my hair sometimes I jus' set an' stroke it 'cause it's so soft." To show how she did it, she ran her fingers over the top of her head. "Some people got kinda coarse hair," she said complacently. "Take Curley. His hair is jus' like wire. But mine is soft and fine. 'Course I brush it a lot. That makes it fine. Here — feel right here." She took Lennie's hand and put it on her head. "Feel right aroun' there an' see how soft it is."

Lennie's big fingers fell to stroking her hair.

"Don't you muss it up," she said.

Lennie said, "Oh! That's nice," and he stroked harder. "Oh, that's nice."

"Look out, now, you'll muss it." And then she cried angrily, "You stop it now, you'll mess it all up." She jerked her head sideways, and Lennie's fingers closed on her hair and hung on. "Let go," she cried. "You let go!"

Lennie was in a panic. His face was contorted. She screamed then, and Lennie's other hand closed over her mouth and nose. "Please don't," he begged. "Oh! Please don't do that. George'll be mad."

She struggled violently under his hands. Her feet battered on the hay and she writhed to be free; and from under Lennie's hand came a muffled screaming. Lennie began to cry with fright. "Oh! Please don't do none of that," he begged. "George gonna say I done a bad thing. He ain't gonna let me tend no rabbits." He moved his hand a little and her hoarse cry came out. Then Lennie grew angry. "Now don't," he said. "I don't want you to yell. You gonna get me in trouble jus' like George says you will. Now don't you do that." And she continued to struggle, and her eyes were wild with terror. He shook her then, and he was angry with her. "Don't you go yellin'," he said, and he shook her; and her body flopped like a fish. And then she was still, for Lennie had broken her neck.

He looked down at her, and carefully he removed his hand from over her mouth, and she lay still. "I don't want ta hurt you," he said, "but George'll be mad if you yell." When she didn't answer nor move he bent closely over her. He lifted her arm and let it drop. For a moment he seemed bewildered. And then he whispered in fright, "I done a bad thing. I done another bad thing."

He pawed up the hay until it partly covered her.

From outside the barn came a cry of men and the double clang of shoes on metal. For the first time Lennie became conscious of the outside. He crouched down in the hay and listened. "I done a real bad thing," he said. "I shouldn't of did that. George'll be mad. An' . . . he said . . . an' hide in the brush till he come. He's gonna be mad. In the brush till he come. Tha's what he said." Lennie went back and looked at the dead girl. The puppy lay close to her. Lennie picked it up. "I'll throw him away," he said. "It's bad enough like it is." He put the pup under his coat, and he crept to the barn wall and peered out between the cracks, toward the horseshoe game. And then he crept around the end of the last manger and disappeared.

The sun streaks were high on the wall by now, and the light was growing soft in the barn. Curley's wife lay on her back, and she was half covered with hay.

It was very quiet in the barn, and the quiet of the afternoon was on the ranch. Even the clang of the pitched shoes, even the voices of the men in the game seemed to grow more quiet. The air in the barn was dusky in advance of the outside day. A pigeon flew in

140

through the open hay door and circled and flew out again. Around the last stall came a shepherd bitch, lean and long, with heavy, hanging dugs. Halfway to the packing box where the puppies were she caught the dead scent of Curley's wife, and the hair rose along her spine. She whimpered and cringed to the packing box, and jumped in among the puppies.

Curley's wife lay with a half-covering of yellow hay. And the meanness and the plannings and the discontent and the ache for attention were all gone from her face. She was very pretty and simple, and her face was sweet and young. Now her rouged cheeks and her reddened lips made her seem alive and sleeping very lightly. The curls, tiny little sausages, were spread on the hay behind her head, and her lips were parted.

As happens sometimes, a moment settled and hovered and remained for much more than a moment. And sound stopped and movement stopped for much, much more than a moment.

Then gradually time awakened again and moved sluggishly on. The horses stamped on the other side of the feeding racks and the halter chains clinked. Outside, the men's voices became louder and clearer.

From around the end of the last stall old Candy's voice came. "Lennie," he called. "Oh, Lennie! You in here? I been figuring some more. Tell you what we can do, Lennie." Old Candy appeared around the end of the last stall. "Oh, Lennie!" he called again; and then he stopped, and his body stiffened. He rubbed his smooth wrist on his white stubble whiskers. "I di'n't know you was here," he said to Curley's wife.

When she didn't answer, he stepped nearer. "You oughten to sleep out here," he said disapprovingly; and then he was beside her and — "Oh, Jesus Christ!" He looked about helplessly, and he rubbed his beard. And then he jumped up and went quickly out of the barn.

But the barn was alive now. The horses stamped and snorted, and they chewed the straw of their bedding and they clashed the chains of their halters. In a moment Candy came back, and George was with him.

George said, "What was it you wanted to see me about?"

Candy pointed at Curley's wife. George stared. "What's the matter with her?" he asked. He stepped closer, and then he echoed Candy's words. "Oh, Jesus Christ!" He was down on his knees beside her. He put his hand over her heart. And finally, when he stood up, slowly and stiffly, his face was as hard and tight as wood, and his eyes were hard.

Candy said, "What done it?"

George looked coldly at him. "Ain't you got any idear?" he asked. And Candy was silent. "I should of knew," George said hopelessly. "I guess maybe way back in my head I did."

Candy asked, "What we gonna do now, George? What we gonna do now?"

George was a long time in answering. "Guess . . . we

gotta tell the . . . guys. I guess we gotta get 'im an' lock 'im up. We can't let 'im get away. Why, the poor bastard'd starve.'' And he tried to reassure himself. "Maybe they'll lock 'im up an' be nice to 'im.''

But Candy said excitedly, "We oughtta let 'im get away. You don't know that Curley. Curley gon'ta wanta get 'im lynched. Curley'll get 'im killed.''

George watched Candy's lips. "Yeah,'' he said at last, "that's right, Curley will. An' the other guys will.'' And he looked back at Curley's wife.

Now Candy spoke his greatest fear. "You an' me can get that little place, can't we, George? You an' me can go there an' live nice, can't we, George? Can't we?''

Before George answered, Candy dropped his head and looked down at the hay. He knew.

George said softly, "—I think I knowed from the very first. I think I knowed we'd never do her. He usta like to hear about it so much I got to thinking maybe we would.''

"Then — it's all off?'' Candy asked sulkily.

George didn't answer his question. George said, "I'll work my month an' I'll take my fifty bucks an' I'll stay all night in some lousy cat house. Or I'll set in some poolroom till ever'body goes home. An' then I'll come back an' work another month an' I'll have fifty bucks more.''

Candy said, "He's such a nice fella. I didn' think he'd do nothing like this.''

George still stared at Curley's wife. "Lennie never

done it in meanness," he said. "All the time he done bad things, but he never done one of 'em mean." He straightened up and looked back at Candy. "Now listen. We gotta tell the guys. They got to bring him in, I guess. They ain't no way out. Maybe they won't hurt 'im." He said sharply, "I ain't gonna let 'em hurt Lennie. Now you listen. The guys might think I was in on it. I'm gonna go in the bunk house. Then in a minute you come out and tell the guys about her, and I'll come along and make like I never seen her. Will you do that? So the guys won't think I was in on it?"

Candy said, "Sure, George. Sure I'll do that."

"O.K. Give me a couple minutes then, and you come runnin' out an' tell like you jus' found her. I'm going now." George turned and went quickly out of the barn.

Old Candy watched him go. He looked helplessly back at Curley's wife, and gradually his sorrow and his anger grew into words. "You God damn tramp," he said viciously. "You done it, di'n't you? I s'pose you're glad. Ever'body knowed you'd mess things up. You wasn't no good. You ain't no good now, you lousy tart." He sniveled, and his voice shook. "I could of hoed in the garden and washed dishes for them guys." He paused, and then went on in a singsong. And he repeated the old words: "If they was a circus or a baseball game . . . we would of went to her . . . jus' said 'ta hell with work,' an' went to her. Never ast nobody's say so. An' they'd of been a pig and chickens . . . an'

144

in the winter . . . the little fat stove . . . an' the rain comin' . . . an' us jus' settin' there." His eyes blinded with tears and he turned and went weakly out of the barn, and he rubbed his bristly whiskers with his wrist stump.

Outside the noise of the game stopped. There was a rise of voices in question, a drum of running feet and the men burst into the barn. Slim and Carlson and young Whit and Curley, and Crooks keeping back out of attention range. Candy came after them, and last of all came George. George had put on his blue denim coat and buttoned it, and his black hat was pulled down low over his eyes. The men raced around the last stall. Their eyes found Curley's wife in the gloom, they stopped and stood still and looked.

Then Slim went quietly over to her, and he felt her wrist. One lean finger touched her cheek, and then his hand went under her slightly twisted neck and his fingers explored her neck. When he stood up the men crowded near and the spell was broken.

Curley came suddenly to life. "I know who done it," he cried. "That big son-of-a-bitch done it. I know he done it. Why — ever'body else was out there playin' horseshoes." He worked himself into a fury. "I'm gonna get him. I'm going for my shotgun. I'll kill the big son-of-a-bitch myself. I'll shoot 'im in the guts. Come on, you guys." He ran furiously out of the barn. Carlson said, "I'll get my Luger," and he ran out too.

Slim turned quietly to George. "I guess Lennie done

145

it, all right," he said. "Her neck's bust. Lennie coulda did that."

George didn't answer, but he nodded slowly. His hat was so far down on his forehead that his eyes were covered.

Slim went on, "Maybe like that time in Weed you was tellin' about."

Again George nodded.

Slim sighed. "Well, I guess we got to get him. Where you think he might of went?"

It seemed to take George some time to free his words. "He — would of went south," he said. "We come from north so he would of went south."

"I guess we gotta get 'im," Slim repeated.

George stepped close. "Couldn' we maybe bring him in an' they'll lock him up? He's nuts, Slim. He never done this to be mean."

Slim nodded. "We might," he said. "If we could keep Curley in, we might. But Curley's gonna want to shoot 'im. Curley's still mad about his hand. An' s'pose they lock him up an' strap him down and put him in a cage. That ain't no good, George."

"I know," said George. "I know."

Carlson came running in. "The bastard's stole my Luger," he shouted. "It ain't in my bag." Curley followed him, and Curley carried a shotgun in his hand. Curley was cold now.

"All right, you guys," he said. "The nigger's got a

147

shotgun. You take it, Carlson. When you see 'um, don't give 'im no chance. Shoot for his guts. That'll double 'im over."

Whit said excitedly, "I ain't got a gun."

Curley said, "You go in Soledad an' get a cop. Get Al Wilts, he's deputy sheriff. Le's go now." He turned suspiciously on George. "You're comin' with us, fella."

"Yeah," said George. "I'll come. But listen, Curley. The poor bastard's nuts. Don't shoot 'im. He di'n't know what he was doin'."

"Don't shoot 'im?" Curley cried. "He got Carlson's Luger. 'Course we'll shoot 'im."

George said weakly, "Maybe Carlson lost his gun."

"I seen it this morning," said Carlson. "No, it's been took."

Slim stood looking down at Curley's wife. He said, "Curley — maybe you better stay here with your wife."

Curley's face reddened. "I'm goin'," he said. "I'm gonna shoot the guts outa that big bastard myself, even if I only got one hand. I'm gonna get 'im."

Slim turned to Candy. "You stay here with her then, Candy. The rest of us better get goin'."

They moved away. George stopped a moment beside Candy and they both looked down at the dead girl until Curley called, "You George! You stick with us so we don't think you had nothin' to do with this."

George moved slowly after them, and his feet dragged heavily.

148

And when they were gone, Candy squatted down in the hay and watched the face of Curley's wife. "Poor bastard," he said softly.

The sound of the men grew fainter. The barn was darkening gradually and, in their stalls, the horses shifted their feet and rattled the halter chains. Old Candy lay down in the hay and covered his eyes with his arm.

THE deep green pool of the Salinas River was still in the late afternoon. Already the sun had left the valley to go climbing up the slopes of the Gabilan mountains, and the hilltops were rosy in the sun. But by the pool among the mottled sycamores, a pleasant shade had fallen.

A water snake glided smoothly up the pool, twisting its periscope head from side to side; and it swam the length of the pool and came to the legs of a motionless heron that stood in the shallows. A silent head and beak lanced down and plucked it out by the head, and the beak swallowed the little snake while its tail waved frantically.

A far rush of wind sounded and a gust drove through

the tops of the trees like a wave. The sycamore leaves turned up their silver sides, the brown, dry leaves on the ground scudded a few feet. And row on row of tiny wind waves flowed up the pool's green surface.

As quickly as it had come, the wind died, and the clearing was quiet again. The heron stood in the shallows, motionless and waiting. Another little water snake swam up the pool, turning its periscope head from side to side.

Suddenly Lennie appeared out of the brush, and he came as silently as a creeping bear moves. The heron pounded the air with its wings, jacked itself clear of the water and flew off down river. The little snake slid in among the reeds at the pool's side.

Lennie came quietly to the pool's edge. He knelt down and drank, barely touching his lips to the water. When a little bird skittered over the dry leaves behind him, his head jerked up and he strained toward the sound with eyes and ears until he saw the bird, and then he dropped his head and drank again.

When he was finished, he sat down on the bank, with his side to the pool, so that he could watch the trail's entrance. He embraced his knees and laid his chin down on his knees.

The light climbed on out of the valley, and as it went, the tops of the mountains seemed to blaze with increasing brightness.

Lennie said softly, "I di'n't forget, you bet, God damn. Hide in the brush an' wait for George." He pulled his hat down low over his eyes. "George gonna give me hell," he said. "George gonna wish he was alone an' not have me botherin' him." He turned his head and looked at the bright mountain tops. "I can go right off there an' find a cave," he said. And he continued sadly, "— an' never have no ketchup — but I won't care. If George don't want me . . . I'll go away. I'll go away."

And then from out of Lennie's head there came a little fat old woman. She wore thick bull's-eye glasses and she wore a huge gingham apron with pockets, and she was starched and clean. She stood in front of Lennie and put her hands on her hips, and she frowned disapprovingly at him.

And when she spoke, it was in Lennie's voice. "I tol' you an' tol' you," she said. "I tol' you, 'Min' George because he's such a nice fella an' good to you.' But you don't never take no care. You do bad things."

And Lennie answered her, "I tried, Aunt Clara, ma'am. I tried and tried. I couldn' help it."

"You never give a thought to George," she went on in Lennie's voice. "He been doin' nice things for you alla time. When he got a piece a pie you always got half or more'n half. An' if they was any ketchup, why he'd give it all to you."

"I know," said Lennie miserably. "I tried, Aunt Clara, ma'am. I tried and tried."

She interrupted him. "All the time he coulda had such a good time if it wasn't for you. He woulda took

154

his pay an' raised hell in a whore house, and he coulda set in a pool room an' played snooker. But he got to take care of you."

Lennie moaned with grief. "I know, Aunt Clara, ma'am. I'll go right off in the hills an' I'll fin' a cave an' I'll live there so I won't be no more trouble to George."

"You jus' say that," she said sharply. "You're always sayin' that, an' you know sonofabitching well you ain't never gonna do it. You'll jus' stick around an' stew the b'Jesus outa George all the time."

Lennie said, "I might jus' as well go away. George ain't gonna let me tend no rabbits now."

Aunt Clara was gone, and from out of Lennie's head there came a gigantic rabbit. It sat on its haunches in front of him, and it waggled its ears and crinkled its nose at him. And it spoke in Lennie's voice too.

"Tend rabbits," it said scornfully. "You crazy bastard. You ain't fit to lick the boots of no rabbit. You'd forget 'em and let 'em go hungry. That's what you'd do. An' then what would George think?"

"I would *not* forget," Lennie said loudly.

"The hell you wouldn'," said the rabbit. "You ain't worth a greased jack-pin to ram you into hell. Christ knows George done ever'thing he could to jack you outa the sewer, but it don't do no good. If you think George gonna let you tend rabbits, you're even crazier'n usual. He ain't. He's gonna beat hell outa you with a stick, that's what he's gonna do."

Now Lennie retorted belligerently, "He ain't neither. George won't do nothing like that. I've knew George since — I forget when — and he ain't never raised his han' to me with a stick. He's nice to me. He ain't gonna be mean."

"Well he's sick of you," said the rabbit. "He's gonna beat hell outa you an' then go away an' leave you."

"He won't," Lennie cried frantically. "He won't do nothing like that. I know George. Me an' him travels together."

But the rabbit repeated softly over and over, "He gonna leave you, ya crazy bastard. He gonna leave ya all alone. He gonna leave ya, crazy bastard."

Lennie put his hands over his ears. "He ain't, I tell ya he ain't." And he cried, "Oh! George — George — George!"

George came quietly out of the brush and the rabbit scuttled back into Lennie's brain.

George said quietly, "What the hell you yellin' about?"

Lennie got up on his knees. "You ain't gonna leave me, are ya, George? I know you ain't."

George came stiffly near and sat down beside him. "No."

"I knowed it," Lennie cried. "You ain't that kind."
George was silent.
Lennie said, "George."
"Yeah?"
"I done another bad thing."

"It don't make no difference," George said, and he fell silent again.

Only the topmost ridges were in the sun now. The shadow in the valley was blue and soft. From the distance came the sound of men shouting to one another. George turned his head and listened to the shouts.

Lennie said, "George."

"Yeah?"

"Ain't you gonna give me hell?"

"Give ya hell?"

"Sure, like you always done before. Like, 'If I di'n't have you I'd take my fifty bucks ——' "

"Jesus Christ, Lennie! You can't remember nothing that happens, but you remember ever' word I say."

"Well, ain't you gonna say it?"

George shook himself. He said woodenly, "If I was alone I could live so easy." His voice was monotonous, had no emphasis. "I could get a job an' not have no mess." He stopped.

"Go on," said Lennie. "An' when the enda the month come ——"

"An' when the end of the month come I could take my fifty bucks an' go to a . . . cat house . . ." He stopped again.

Lennie looked eagerly at him. "Go on, George. Ain't you gonna give me no more hell?"

"No," said George.

"Well, I can go away," said Lennie. "I'll go right off in the hills an' find a cave if you don' want me."

158

George shook himself again. "No," he said. "I want you to stay with me here."

Lennie said craftily—"Tell me like you done before."

"Tell you what?"

"'Bout the other guys an' about us."

George said, "Guys like us got no fambly. They make a little stake an' then they blow it in. They ain't got nobody in the worl' that gives a hoot in hell about 'em —"

"*But not us*," Lennie cried happily. "Tell about us now."

George was quiet for a moment. "But not us," he said.

"Because —"

"Because I got you an' —"

"An' I got you. We got each other, that's what, that gives a hoot in hell about us," Lennie cried in triumph.

The little evening breeze blew over the clearing and the leaves rustled and the wind waves flowed up the green pool. And the shouts of men sounded again, this time much closer than before.

George took off his hat. He said shakily, "Take off your hat, Lennie. The air feels fine."

Lennie removed his hat dutifully and laid it on the ground in front of him. The shadow in the valley was bluer, and the evening came fast. On the wind the sound of crashing in the brush came to them.

Lennie said, "Tell how it's gonna be."

George had been listening to the distant sounds. For

a moment he was business-like. "Look acrost the river, Lennie, an' I'll tell you so you can almost see it."

Lennie turned his head and looked off across the pool and up the darkening slopes of the Gabilans. "We gonna get a little place," George began. He reached in his side pocket and brought out Carlson's Luger; he snapped off the safety, and the hand and gun lay on the ground behind Lennie's back. He looked at the back of Lennie's head, at the place where the spine and skull were joined.

A man's voice called from up the river, and another man answered.

"Go on," said Lennie.

George raised the gun and his hand shook, and he dropped his hand to the ground again.

"Go on," said Lennie. "How's it gonna be? We gonna get a little place."

"We'll have a cow," said George. "An' we'll have maybe a pig an' chickens . . . an' down the flat we'll have a . . . little piece alfalfa ——"

"For the rabbits," Lennie shouted.

"For the rabbits," George repeated.

"And I get to tend the rabbits."

"An' you get to tend the rabbits."

Lennie giggled with happiness. "An' live on the fatta the lan'."

"Yes."

Lennie turned his head.

160

"No, Lennie. Look down there acrost the river, like you can almost see the place."

Lennie obeyed him. George looked down at the gun.

There were crashing footsteps in the brush now. George turned and looked toward them.

"Go on, George. When we gonna do it?"

"Gonna do it soon."

"Me an' you."

"You . . . an' me. Ever'body gonna be nice to you. Ain't gonna be no more trouble. Nobody gonna hurt nobody nor steal from 'em."

Lennie said, "I thought you was mad at me, George."

"No," said George. "No, Lennie. I ain't mad. I never been mad, an' I ain't now. That's a thing I want ya to know."

The voices came close now. George raised the gun and listened to the voices.

Lennie begged, "Le's do it now. Le's get that place now."

"Sure, right now. I gotta. We gotta."

And George raised the gun and steadied it, and he brought the muzzle of it close to the back of Lennie's head. The hand shook violently, but his face set and his hand steadied. He pulled the trigger. The crash of the shot rolled up the hills and rolled down again. Lennie jarred, and then settled slowly forward to the sand, and he lay without quivering.

George shivered and looked at the gun, and then he

threw it from him, back up on the bank, near the pile of old ashes.

The brush seemed filled with cries and with the sound of running feet. Slim's voice shouted, "George. Where you at, George?"

But George sat stiffly on the bank and looked at his right hand that had thrown the gun away. The group burst into the clearing, and Curley was ahead. He saw Lennie lying on the sand. "Got him, by God." He went over and looked down at Lennie, and then he looked back at George. "Right in the back of the head," he said softly.

Slim came directly to George and sat down beside him, sat very close to him. "Never you mind," said Slim. "A guy got to sometimes."

But Carlson was standing over George. "How'd you do it?" he asked.

"I just done it," George said tiredly.

"Did he have my gun?"

"Yeah. He had your gun."

"An' you got it away from him and you took it an' you killed him?"

"Yeah. Tha's how." George's voice was almost a whisper. He looked steadily at his right hand that had held the gun.

Slim twitched George's elbow. "Come on, George. Me an' you'll go in an' get a drink."

George let himself be helped to his feet. "Yeah, a drink."

164

Slim said, "You hadda, George. I swear you hadda. Come on with me." He led George into the entrance of the trail and up toward the highway.

Curley and Carlson looked after them. And Carlson said, "Now what the hell ya suppose is eatin' them two guys?"

WORLD *of* SOCIOLOGY

WORLD *of* SOCIOLOGY

Joseph M. Palmisano, *Editor*

Volume 2
N-Z

GALE GROUP

Detroit
New York
San Francisco
London
Boston
Woodbridge, CT

GALE GROUP STAFF

Library of Congress Cataloging-in-Publication Data

World of sociology/Joseph M. Palmisano, editor
    p.cm.
  Includes bibliographical references and indexes.
  ISBN 0-7876-4965-1 (set) - ISBN 0-7876-5070-6 (vol. 1) - ISBN 0-7876-5071-4 (vol. 2)
  1. Sociology-Encyclopedias. I. Palmisano, Joseph M.

HM585.W67 2000
301'.03-dc21   00-048399

Printed in the United States of America
10 9 8 7 6 5 4 3 2 1

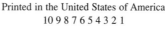

CONTENTS

Introduction

Welcome to the *World of Sociology*. The 1,000 individual entries in this two–volume ready–reference source explain in concise, detailed, and jargon–free language some of the most important topics, theories, discoveries, concepts, and organizations in sociology. Brief biographical profiles of the people who have made a significant and lasting impact on the field of sociology and society in general are also included. More than 230 photographs, statistical charts, and graphs aid the reader in understanding the topics and people covered in the reference work.

World of Sociology has been designed and written with students and non–experts in mind. In so doing, we have compiled a vast array of straightforward, alphabetically arranged entries that will be useful to students who need accessible and concise information for school–related work, as well as to others who want reliable and informative introductions to the numerous aspects of the discipline of sociology.

It becomes increasingly important for all people to have a practical, theoretical, and historical understanding of sociology because it reflects real world issues—from aging, bioethics, and crime to terrorism, voting behavior, and women's studies. We hope that the entries contained in the *World of Sociology* will help you understand some of these and other important issues and how they affect you and the world in which you live.

How to Use This Book

This first edition of the *World of Sociology* has been designed with ready reference in mind.

- **Entries are arranged alphabetically**, rather than chronologically or by subdiscipline.
- **Boldfaced terms** direct readers to related entries.
- **Cross–references** at the end of entries alert readers to related entries that may not have been specifically mentioned in the body of the text.
- A **Sources Consulted** section lists many worthwhile print and electronic materials encountered in the compilation of this volume. It is offered to readers who want additional information on the topics, theories, discoveries, concepts, organizations, and people covered in this reference source.
- The **Historical Chronology** includes over two hundred significant events in the social sciences and related fields spanning from 1640 through 2000.
- A **Nationality Index** assists those readers seeking biographical profiles by national heritage.
- A **General Index** guides readers to all topics, theories, discoveries, concepts, organizations, and people mentioned in the book. Page numbers appearing in boldface indicate major treatment of entries. Italicized page numbers refer to photos, statistical charts, or graphs found throughout the *World of Sociology*.

Acknowledgments

Advisory Board

In compiling this edition, we have been fortunate in being able to call upon the following people, our panel of advisors who contributed to the accuracy of the information in this premiere edition of the *World of Sociology*. To them we would like to express sincere appreciation:

Eric D. Albright
Head of Public Services
Duke Medical Center Library, Duke University
Durham, North Carolina

Bette J. Dickerson
President
Association of Black Sociologists
Professor of Sociology
American University
Washington, D.C.

Tom Horne
Selection Librarian
Seattle Public Library
Seattle, Washington

Carla B. Howery
Deputy Executive Officer
American Sociological Association, Committee on the
    Status of Women in Sociology
Washington, D.C.

Muqtedar Khan
Primary Contact
Association of Muslim Social Scientists
Professor of Political Science
Washington College
Herndon, Virginia

Harry D. Perlstadt
Primary Contact
Commission of Applied Clinical Sociology
Professor of Sociology
Michigan State University
Lansing, Michigan

Joseph H. Strauss
Executive Director
Western Social Science Association
Professor of American Indian Studies
University of Arizona
Tucson, Arizona

Contributors

Maureen Aitken, Matthew Archibald, Geraldine Azzata, Gianpaolo Baiocchi, Virginia Battista, Kari Bethel, Rose Blue, Stephanie A. Bohon, David Boyns, Rebecca Brooks, Lilian Brown, Kimberly Burton, M. Jean Campo, Neal Caren, C Lyn Carr, Bob Carrothers, Ruth Chananie, James Ciment, Corey Colyer, Amy Cooper, Heith Copes, Danielle Currier, Akosua Darkwah, Gretchen Dehart, Jeffery Dennis, Catherine Dybiec Holm, T. D. Eddins, Carla D. Edwards, Chris Fairclouth, Tina Fetner, Lydia Fink-Cox, Lara Foley, Joah Francoeur, Ellis Godard, Richard Goe, Chad Goldberg, Teresa Gowan, Jill Griffin, Terrence Hill, Laura Holland, Shirley Hollis, Kathleen Hunt, Arthur Jipson, Jodi T. Johnson, Andrew Jolivette, Steven Jones, Kent Kerley, Nikki Khanna, Paul Lachelier, Steph Lambert, Lawrence Lanahan, Jason LaTouche, Leslie Lockart, Martha Loustaunau, Maureen McClarnon, Matthew McKeever, Melodie Monahan, Gillian Murphy, Sally Myers, Corinne Naden, Pat Nation, Stephanie Nawyn, Mya Nelson, Carolette Norwood, Patricia Onorato, Erica Owens, Jean-Pierre Reed, Monica Robbers, Pamela Rohland, Melanie Sberna, Lisa L. Sharp, Elizabeth Shostak, Catherine Siebel, Karrie Snyder, Donald Stewart, Tammy Reedy Strother, Andrea Trombley, Judy Van Wyk, Dane Walker, Susan Marnell Weaver, Laura West, Esther I. Wilder, Jonathan R. Wivagg, Aaron Young, Nicole Youngman.

N

NATIONAL AMERICAN WOMAN SUFFRAGE ASSOCIATION (NAWSA)

The women's suffrage movement was closely intertwined with the abolitionist and **peace** movements of the nineteenth and early twentieth centuries. Former anti-slavery activists founded both the National Woman Suffrage Association (NWSA) and the American Woman Suffrage Association (AWSA) in 1869. The two groups had deep philosophical and tactical differences, however. The NWSA, led by **Elizabeth Cady Stanton** and **Susan B. Anthony**, refused to support the Fifteenth Amendment if it excluded women. But the AWSA, led by Lucy Stone and Henry Blackwell, did not want to jeopardize winning suffrage for black men by insisting that women be included right away. The National American Woman Suffrage Association (NAWSA) was formed when these two groups merged in 1890.

Following many other women's movements of the Progressive era, NAWSA framed their issue as a form of "municipal housekeeping." Enfranchised women, they argued, would be better able to raise their children and protect their families by demonstrating the duties of citizenship, fighting corruption and violence, and working for safer food and working conditions. NAWSA worked with labor unions, veterans of the British suffrage movement, and to some extent, African-American organizations. Many black women were active in the suffrage movement, including Ida B. Wells, best known for her anti-lynching campaign, and Mary Church Terrell, who founded the National Association of Colored Women.

However, divisions within the movement persisted. NAWSA denied funds to the southern-based Woman Suffrage Conference, which supported a "states' rights" approach to suffrage that sought to enfranchise white women at the expense of blacks, though NAWSA's own relationship with black organizations was shaky. And in 1913, Alice Paul left NAWSA to form the Congressional Union, which became the National Women's Party in 1916. In 1917, the NWP began protesting constantly in front of the White House, going on hunger strikes when members were arrested. Though they were frequently brutalized, NWP activists also generated much support for their cause and made NAWSA look calm and reasonable by comparison.

Meanwhile, NAWSA president Carrie Chapman Catt had revitalized the organization and begun a "winning plan" which coordinated state and local suffrage groups across the country. But the onset of World War I made criticizing the government seem anti-American, and despite the objections of the Women's Peace Party (whose membership overlapped NAWSA's), Catt instructed her **organization** to work for the war effort. This tactic solidified President Wilson's support, and the Nineteenth Amendment was finally ratified in 1920.

NATIONAL ORGANIZATION FOR WOMEN (NOW)

The National Organization for Women was formed in 1966 by activists who wanted "an NAACP for women" that would fight against sexism and sexual discrimination in U.S. society. Many founding members were veterans of the Civil Rights Movement; others, such as Betty Friedan, Kate Millett, and Gloria Steinem, were well-known writers whose work challenged assumptions about gender roles. The organization's charter stated, "The purpose of NOW is to take action to bring women into full participation in the mainstream of society now, exercising all the privileges and responsibilities thereof in truly equal partnership with men." NOW's first activities included urging the Equal Employment Opportunity Commission to force an end to the practice of sex-segregated "help wanted" ads, which were common at the time, and to support flight attendants in their legal struggles against airlines, which portrayed them as sex objects in their advertisements and forced them to quit if they got married or reached their thirties.

NOW's positions on various issues over the past few decades have caused controversies both inside and outside of

Under the leadership of Eleanor Smeal, NOW organized boycotts against states that had not ratified the Equal Rights Amendment *(Corbis Corporation [Bellevue]).*

the organization. Barbara Ryan wrote: "Organizational disputes are important movement events because they force participants to confront meaningful issues. Rather than maintaining unity by denying the existence of controversial subjects, participants are led to consider the issues and the organizations are forced to articulate a position." In the late 1960s and early 1970s, NOW struggled to define both itself and its spectrum of acceptable feminist issues. Founding president Friedan insisted that NOW should work for the legalization of abortion, which caused some members to decide the organization was too radical and leave. Likewise, some labor union activists left over NOW's decision to fight against "protective" labor laws for women workers, which the NOW leadership insisted trapped women in lower-paying jobs. NOW has also faced disputes regarding its hierarchical organizational structure, and its image as a white, middle-class organization.

Probably the most difficult and divisive issue for NOW shortly after its founding was lesbian rights. In an era when accusations of lesbianism (sometimes referred to as "dyke-baiting") were enough to ensure that women would not be taken seriously, Friedan warned of a "lavender menace" and refused to acknowledge the contributions of lesbians in the movement. But when Millett's bisexual orientation was widely publicized by the media, the majority of NOW members stood behind her. Kate Millet stated: "Women's liberation and homosexual liberation are both struggling towards a common goal: a society free from defining and categorizing people by virtue of their gender and/or sexual preference. 'Lesbian' is a label used as a psychic weapon to keep women locked into their male-defined 'feminine role.'"

NOW grew rapidly in the late 1970s and early 1980s as the organization focused on passing the Equal Rights Amendment, which stated "Equality of rights under the law shall not be denied or abridged by the United States or by any state on account of sex." Under the leadership of Eleanor Smeal, NOW organized boycotts and other forms of political pressure against states which had not yet ratified the amendment. By that time a considerable anti-feminist backlash had also developed. Ryan wrote: "The noticeable increase in feminist activism paralleled the growth of the New Right as the ERA became the focal political activity for both feminist and anti-feminist forces." The amendment's eventual defeat in 1982 was a severe blow for NOW and for the feminist movement overall, which had lost its central organizing issue.

However, the 1980s and 1990s presented a wide variety of issues for NOW to organize around. NOW's priorities shifted to fighting for reproductive freedom and lesbian rights, promoting diversity, ending violence against women, and protecting the rights of women on welfare. At the close of the century, the organization claimed approximately 500,000 members in 550 chapters around the country. NOW has continued to use a variety of tactics to further its causes, from traditional lobbying and legal efforts to marches and non-violent civil disobedience. And it has continued to be criticized by some as too radical and by others as too mainstream. In a 1999 interview, President Patricia Ireland stated: "I do think that there has been some expanded understanding of equality that all of us have gained...In one sense we've always been willing to step out and say things that make other people uncomfortable, and push to make what is seen initially as a very radical idea become mainstream...I think we have to have an inside and an outside strategy."

NATIONAL WOMAN'S PARTY (NWP)

The National Woman's Party (NWP), originally founded in 1913 as the Congressional Union for Woman Suffrage (CU), was a militant offshoot of the National American Woman Suffrage Association's (NAWSA). The non-partisan organization changed to its present name in 1916. The CU was originally founded by Alice Paul and Lucy Burns, who were acting as chair and vice-chair of the NAWSA Congressional Committee. They influenced a contingent of NAWSA members to work to bring about a federal suffrage amendment, rather than following the state by state approach taken by Carrie Chapman Catt and the NAWSA. Though it has suffered a membership

decline, today the NWP advocates a broad range of issues including the ratification of an equal rights amendment, the elimination of violence against women, the retaining of reproductive choice, the minimizing of **poverty** among women, support for **child care**, and heightening awareness of women's health concerns. It also supports an international platform which promotes equality of the sexes and the ratification of the Convention on the Elimination of All Forms of **Discrimination** Against Women.

The NWP was known for its militant suffragist tactics and demonstrations. In 1917, in one of the most famous protests, members of the NWP were imprisoned for picketing the White House. As a result of the demonstration, they claimed status as political prisoners. Alice Paul, Lucy Burns and 96 other suffragists were sentenced for up to six months in prison, where many of the women went on hunger strikes. They were heralded as national heroes by some, but their actions were denounced by other more conservative suffragists and members of the public. Their arrests were declared invalid by the District of Columbia Court of Appeals in 1918. The public furor over the arrests and the agenda of the NAWSA led President Woodrow Wilson to support suffrage, but it was voted down in 1918. The NWP held the Democratic Party accountable for this loss and opposed Wilson's re-election, as well as the Democratic candidates for Congress but had little real impact on the elections. The NWP lacked political clout despite its large membership. From 1919 to 1920, the NWP had between 35,000 and 60,000 members.

After the passage of the Nineteenth Amendment in 1920, membership in the NWP declined. The party had only 152 members in 1921. The NWP sought to broaden its concerns in 1920, and in 1923, the leadership of the NWP proposed the Equal Rights Amendment (ERA). The ERA was introduced into every session of Congress until 1972, and has been again since 1982, when it failed to gain state ratification. The newsletter *Equal Rights* was founded in 1923 and still exists. In addition to advocating women's rights, the NWP maintains the NWP Equal Rights and Suffrage Art Gallery and Museum in Washington D.C.

NATIONALISM

Nationalism is an **ideology** based on a constructed group's ethno-history which espouses political self-determination for that **group**. The idea of nationalism developed in the late eighteenth century with the French Revolution as the first major nationalist movement. It makes sense that the concept of nationalism developed concurrently with the concept of the modern state, for the two are closely linked. The legitimate modern state is the representation of a particular nation. The state is constructed to embody only the will of the people. In order to defend this cultural construction, the ''people'' must be also constructed so that conceivable that such a single will is possible. Nationalism is the commonality that defines the people of the state. Likewise, part of the ideology of nationalism is the desire for self-determination. If the group is unified and dis-

Reform nationalism seeks to redefine an existing state in order to benefit a subgroup that is recreated as the "true" nation, such as the Nazi movement of the twentieth century *(AP/Wide World Photos, Inc.)*.

tinct from other groups, then it must govern itself, for it can be part of no other nation. Therefore, nationalist movements generally seek to be state-forming.

Historian Louis Snyder described several characteristics common to most nationalist groups. Nations are typically characterized by a sense of group consciousness and common social **identity**. Often this identity is based on the belief in a shared history. Nations, especially those already incorporated into nation-states, may also be defined by a shared **territory**, language, religion, and/or **ethnicity**.

John Breuilly has outlined four types of nationalism, based on their relationship to both existing and forming states. Separatist nationalism emphasizes the distinction between the nationalist group and any currently existing state. Thus, separatist nationalist movements tend to seek the formation of a new state. During the early 1990s, several post-Soviet republics, like Belarus, for instance, formed separate states, claiming national self-determination. Unification nationalism seeks to bring several political communities together into a unified state. The reunification of Germany was orchestrated under discourse emphasizing a common ethnic and historical background of the people of East and West Germany. Reform na-

tionalism seeks to redefine the nation of an existing state in order to benefit a subgroup that is recreated as the "true" nation. As in the central European fascism of the early twentieth century, this type of nationalism tends to characterize extremist movements. Anti-colonial nationalism seeks politically to consolidate indigenous interests in order to wrest power from a colonizer, for example, the Indian independence movement led by Mahatma Gandhi.

Social scientific research on nationalism has focused on how nationalism in general and particular nationalisms are developed and spread and how they spur **collective action**. In his influential work *Imagined Communities*, Benedict Anderson described how the technology of the printing press, which made possible the mass reproduction of written texts, was instrumental in the creation of national consciousness. Print language created a unified field of **communication** that did not require face-to-face communication, allowing ideas to be easily shared by individuals who remain unknown to one another. Further, the printed word allowed for a new "fixity" of language; a written document is consistent across space and time. And finally, the state use of written language allowed for the possibility of a single official state language, the legitimate language of the nation. Following another line of inquiry, sociologists Hank Johnston and David A. Snow have investigated how subcultures may spawn nationalist social movements. Their interviews with Estonian activists revealed a **subculture** that shifted its strategies as the political climate shifted, growing more oppositional as opportunities arose. As Soviet repression lessened, gradually a full-fledged separatist nationalist movement developed and eventually an independent Estonian state.

Within the nationalism research literature, there are several prominent debates. One debate centers on the historical identity claims of nationalists and the extent to which these claims are based in fact and the extent to which they are recently constructed. Jürgen Habermas has pointed out that, even though the modern nation is closely tied to the modern state, the idea of nationalism is premodern and prepolitical. In contrast, Anthony Smith purports that nationalism is part of modernity and is closely linked with industrialization, bureaucratization, and **capitalism**. A second debate centers on whether nationalist movements are inherently violent. The link between the nation and the state and the power of the state to render one nation "official" and delegitimatize others may mean that conflict is part of the idea of nationalism, particularly in states with diverse populations. On the other hand, nationalism can be consensus-building and may be necessary for **democracy**.

Nation-State

A nation-state is a political unit with clear geographical boundaries and populated by a predominantly homogenous people. Modern states, then, form a contrast to earlier forms because such states did not have the adminstrative capabilities to develop cultural cohesion within their borders. Nation-state refers

to a centrally organized political unity that operates independently from other governmental powers. In general, the people within the geographical borders share a common language, religion, and history. Due to migration and immigration, most nation-states are not, however, ethnically homogenous. Instead, many nation-states have become mulitcultural in that a number of diverse cultures thrive within the boundaries of a single state. The nation-state, regardless of the cultures of individuals, retains central power and the ability to interact with other nation-states on behalf of its people.

Anthony Giddens claimed that nation-states are "bordered power containers" and have a much greater adminstrative ability than traditional states. Modern nation-states are generally components of a nation-state system, or an international circuit of political entities. In this network, individual nation-states, according to Giddens, are characterized by their preparation for and participation in **war** with other nation-states in the system. The modern nation-states became models for the development of states in Africa and Asia. Moreover, the modern nation-state is characterized by its predominance over other social institutions and even its growing power over the economic system.

Native American Identity

Native American **Identity** within the discipline of **sociology** continues to become more significant in understanding and explicating the ways in which race and **ethnicity** in the United States is a complex process, that according to Michael Omi and Howard Winant, involves the construction of racial projects which situate various groups within a core or peripheral cultural location. The Native American has gone through a historic process in which two types of representations have been evoked at different historical moments to serve a similar purpose. The Native American in early anthropological studies was portrayed as a "noble savage" unable to think for himself allowing the United States government to become involved in a racial project to assimilate and acculturate Native Americans into mainstream, i.e. white, society.

Since the 1980 **census**, the second representation of the Native "Other" as exotic, romanticized, or old and wise has created enormous economic and socio-cultural exploitation of Indian culture(s). However, the second representation like the first serves as a way for the United States to continue to hold onto and control the images and narratives of Native American identity. Paternalistic U.S. policy toward Indian tribes has affected the ability of Indians to move from dependency to self-reliance. The non-native control over definitions of "Indianness" creates problems for sociologists studying the Native American population or examining Native American identity. The issues of identity cannot be reduced to an image from a certain point in history when *all* Native Americans were supposedly the *same*.

Issues of gender and sexual identity, as well as disparate levels of economic mobility within the **community**, are a few basic distinctions which make over simplification of Native

American identity useless. Urban Indians are different from their rural counterparts who live in tribal- specific communities. Urban natives tend to maintain pan-Indian or inter-tribal enclaves.

Sociologists who study Native American identity contend with previous models that have been used to understand this population; however, a growing segment of the discipline is attempting to create innovative frameworks for conducting both qualitative and quantitative forms of social inquiry. The trend in Native American identity studies has been based on essentialist categories which limit who can be a ''real'' Indian based defined parameters of blood quantum (the percentage of ancestry an individual must have in order to be an enrolled member of a tribe according to the United States government), tribal enrollment, and federal recognition.

By allowing the United States to decide which tribes can be federally recognized and which cannot, tribes lose their authority to determine for themselves who are members of their specific communities/nations. Sociologists are faced with the fact that no other ethnic individuals in the United States are asked to prove their membership in the **group**.

This identity ''policing'' phenomenon emerges as an important issue in sociological studies of Native American identity, especially given the rate of Native American interracial marriages. Sociological examination of the complexity of Native American identity will provide a basis for studying other racially mixed American ethnic groups to understand the ways in which power, class, and, **race** remain intersections that illustrate why and how categories of identity are constructed, reconstructed, and constantly used as a hegemonic tool that reduces the importance of difference.

NATIVE AMERICAN STUDIES

Sociological examination of **race** and **ethnicity** has complicated assumptions about biological and cultural frameworks used to understand **group** identity, particularly among groups of color in the United States. In the case of American Indians, this study has been further complicated by racial narratives which represent Natives as primitive, stoic, and, unchanging symbols of an American past. In Native American Studies much academic work has focused on diverse topics, such as American Indian **identity**, power and politics, the global economy, and commodification of American Indian art and **culture**. In the past, much research on Native Americans was done in anthropology; today works in Native American Studies come from diverse disciplinary and interdisciplinary fields, such as **sociology**, history, American studies, ethnic studies, women's studies, philosophy, theology, literature, and film studies. Native American Studies has both theoretical and practical implications for sociology in the twenty-first century.

To understand Native American Studies as a sub-field within Sociology, one must first consider the concept of modernism and how it affects academic studies of the ''native'' and the ''non-native.'' Modernism refers to the period after capitalist and industrial expansion in the United States and fol-

lows the Traditional Period (1900-1950). The Modernist Phase, as articulated by Norman Denzin and Yvonna Lincoln, extends from about 1950 through the 1970s (and is present in some later works) and builds on the work of the Traditional Period. Modernism focuses on social **realism**, naturalism, and slice-of-life ethnographies. According to Steven Seidman, an original ''moral vision'' provided the impetus behind much modern sociological research. The 1960s Civil Rights Movement, a response to the modernist value of a moral vision, directed attention to under- represented groups, such as Native Americans.

Though modernism has sought social equality, it has often struggled, at least theoretically, with questions of difference and representation. Modernist thinking informed many studies of race and ethnicity, such as Nathan Glazer's Melting Pot Theory which argued for the assimilation of minority groups into mainstream U.S. culture. The modernist approach continues to be toward universalism, a theoretical framework which does not take cultural differences into consideration. While the ''Red Power'' Movement of American Indians in the 1960s directed attention to the issue of difference, a dynamic demographic shift slowly emerged as U.S. citizens identified themselves as Native American.

Responding to the modernist project of universalism, the Civil Rights Movement and Red Power Movement provided impetus for a transformation in the American Indian **community** and the creation of American Indian and Native American Studies programs throughout the United States. The Third World Student Strikes of 1968 were key in the development of the first Ethnic Studies and Native American Studies Programs at San Francisco State University and the University of California/Berkeley.

Matthew Snipp and Joane Nagel, examining demographic developments in the Native American population, found Native American population increased significantly after 1960 and connected the resurgence of American Indian identity to **student movements** calling for equality and representation. According to Nagel, the number of Native Americans increased eightfold from 1900 to 1990, with much of the growth occurring in the decades after 1960, from the low point in 1900 to 523,591 in 1960 to 1.88 million in 1990.

Demographic shifts within the American Indian community have been linked to several factors: increased American Indian activism and visibility; greater opportunities to identify oneself as Native American without fear of severe oppression; and economic opportunities available to Native Americans from scholarship funds, grants, benefits, rare art, and gaming enterprises. The shift in Native American Studies from sociological **demography** to class analysis has also caused investigation into racial and ethnic identity, with a particular focus on blood quantum, federal recognition, and, enrollment status as cultural markers of legitimacy that only Native Americans must face.

Given the increased benefits in identifying as American Indian, many scholars have examined the **political economy** of ''being Native.'' The federal government's role in implementing policies that determine if a tribe is federally recognized has

become an essential aspect of most projects that involve Native American Studies and class analysis. Historian Vine Deloria Jr. has asserted that with the Congressional policy changing from termination to support for self-sufficiency, Indian tribes may be able to become economically independent in the next generation. Many tribes have become more independent and in some cases contribute significant funds to surrounding cities and governments while maintaining their own self-government. However, other segments of the Indian population remain socioeconomically disenfranchised. Some tribes, according to Deloria, may take up to ten million dollars a year in government programs and private grants; however, the struggle for modernism now prominent in Native American Studies is the concept of the universal.

Sociological theory since the 1970s turned toward difference and representation as fluid and dynamic concepts which resist reduction. Native American Studies investigates the postmodern, and sociologists use a postmodern framework to attempt to understand partial truths rather than total truths as representative of entire ethnic communities. The postmodern in Native American Studies allows sociology to challenge traditionally-held models of race and ethnicity.

Diversity and difference characterize Native American Studies and the Native American population of the United States. While demographic trends continue to demonstrate that more citizens are choosing to identify as Indian, sociologists must focus on postmodernist lessons which indicate the value of seeing beyond universalist or essentialist categories for defining a community as complex and changing as the Native American.

NATURE VERSUS NURTURE

The nature versus nurture debate, a controversial topic within the field of **sociology**, asks whether human behavior is biologically inherited or socially learned. Although most sociologists see humans as social by nature, the extent to which biology influences social behavior sparks much disagreement. Many sociologists assert that **socialization** processes are solely responsible for human social behavior. Others contend that humans possess inherited biological tendencies that cannot be explained through socialization alone. Sociologists who investigate these biological tendencies specialize in the subfield referred to as **sociobiology**.

Socialization is the process through which individuals learn the ways of their **culture**. Such learning takes place within a social environment. Assuming that human beings are blank slates at birth, strict socialization theorists assert that the social environment is exclusively responsible for molding human behaviors. It is therefore argued that biology plays no **role** in shaping how individuals behave. "Nurture," not "nature," shapes human social interaction.

While sociobiologists do not deny that socialization processes shape human behavior, they argue that "nature" also plays a significant role. Advocates of sociobiology assert that humans possess certain genetic templates that predispose them

to behave in specific ways under varying circumstances. Although they do not attempt to explain all behavior in biological terms, sociobiologists contend that specific forms of social interaction are largely influenced by biological and genetic tendencies. For instance, it is argued that aggression, male dominance, and **incest** avoidance are patterns of social interaction that have been programmed by human "nature." Socialization theorists, on the other hand, assert that these behaviors can only be understood in a social context.

The examination of **sexual behavior** is a central and highly controversial topic in the ongoing nature versus nurture debate. In an effort to explain behavioral differences between the sexes, sociobiologists assert that males and females have been programmed differently with regard to sexual behavior. It is argued that these behavioral differences function to ensure that an individual's genes continue into the next generation. According to sociobiologists, the survival of one's genetic material is the most important goal in the practice of sexual behavior.

Sociobiologists assert that men have historically been more sexually promiscuous than women because it is in a male's genetic interests to inseminate as many females as possible. Promiscuous sexual behavior helps a male maximize the transmission of his genetic material to the next generation. A female, however, fares better by seeking out one reliable partner who will assist her in providing for the few offspring that she is able to bear. This more conservative sexual behavior among females serves two functions. First, it assures the desired male that he is indeed the father of a female's offspring, thus making him more willing to contribute to their survival. Second, it allows a female to maximize the time and effort spent on ensuring the survival of her offspring. Working toward the survival of her offspring is the primary way a female can ensure the transmission of her genes into the next generation.

Socialization theorists counter this sociobiological explanation of sexual behavior by asserting that behavioral differences between the sexes do not automatically indicate differential biological programming. Rather, it is more likely that such differences provide evidence of gender inequality in various societies. These sociologists argue that relations of gender inequality offer a more accurate explanation for male/female differences in sexual behavior. They also point out that men and women do not always conform to strict gender specific sexual behaviors described by sociobiologists.

While socialization theorists assert that sociobiological explanations of human sexual behavior are inaccurate and biased, most contemporary sociobiologists would contend that sexual behavior involves more than just the expression of biology and genes. Sexual behavior occurs in a social context. Furthermore, while sociobiologists argue that socialization theorists fail to recognize the biological bases of sexuality, most socialization theorists acknowledge that sexual behavior does involve the transmission of genetic material and thus bears some biological significance.

Although the nature versus nurture debate shows little sign of dissipating soon, most sociologists would agree that

both biology and environment play important roles in social interaction. The main focus in this debate, however, explores which exerts greater influence over human behavior, biology or environment, nature or nurture.

NEED

A need is anything that is deemed essential for the proper functioning or maintenance of any person, system, animal, etc. For example, humans need food in order to survive. In the social sciences, which frequently studies needs, they are often contrasted by ''wants.'' Wants, by definition, are not essential but desired. Whereas a person would die without water, one would not die without a new car. The notion of a need further suggests that these requirements are necessary conditions that must be satisfied to sustain life. There is a great deal of debate regarding the differences between needs and wants. There is, moreover, often disagreement regarding the extent of these needs.

For functionalists, a need is often analogous to what sociologist Talcott Parsons described as the functional prerequisites of a social system. That is to say, according to Parsons, these prerequisites or needs are absolutely crucial to the survival of the **society**; without them, it would parish. Similarly, researchers operating under the Marxist **paradigm** tend toward speaking to the needs of capitalist society. They are primarily the needs for production, reproduction, and legitimation. Some critics have indicated that the identification of needs with any type of accuracy may lead to circular or tautological reasoning.

NEGATIVE ASSOCIATION

Negative association refers to one possible direction in which two variables can be correlated. It is the opposite of a positive relationship. When two variables are correlated, researchers can estimate the extent to which scores on one variable move up or down, in conjunction with a rise or fall in scores on a second variable. A negative association occurs when scores on one variable fall and scores on the other variable rise.

To illustrate a **correlation** between two variables, picture a graph in which one variable's scores are listed along the horizontal axis from low to high scores and the other variable's scores appear along the vertical axis in ranked order from lowest scores to highest. Each case is then plotted with a dot that corresponds to each respondent's scores on each of the two variables. Then, a line is fitted to the dots that represents the least squared distance from each dot to the line itself. This is called a **regression** line. The **regression line** describes the strength of the relationship among the variables and the direction of the relationship. If the regression line slopes downward from low scores to high scores along the horizontal (or X) axis (something like this: ¤), then there is a negative relationship between the two variables. When scores along the horizontal axis rise, scores along the vertical axis (or Y axis) fall.

Now let's use an example. Picture the graph again. Scores along the horizontal (X) axis represent age and range from 18 to 65. Scores along the vertical (Y) axis represent physical energy levels and range from low to high scores. If we plot respondent's age with each respondent's energy level, then fit a regression line that represents the least squared distance from each dot to the line itself, we would probably find that the line slopes downward from left to right. Thus, the older people are, the less energy they have. This represents a negative relationship between age and level of physical energy.

NEOCOLONIALISM

The prefix ''neo-'' refers to a previous event or time period which has again become significant for sociological and political study. In this case neocolonialism is the study of events and social phenomena which have occurred after the colonial period (1492–1865). This concept is used to analyze the events transpiring after initial European contact in the Americas (1492) as well as after the United States slavery period (post–1865). Neocolonialism enjoyed its greatest use in sociological studies during the Woodrow Wilson (early 1900s and after) an era when the United States created an imperialist policy that sought to expand control of other islands, countries, and provinces (i.e., Cuba, Panama, Puerto Rico, Mexico, and the Philippines). Many of these expansionist goals took place in an international context and also had tremendous and lasting effects on domestic affairs.

A few examples are the Dawes Act of 1887, Cherokee Indian Removal, and the Trail of Tears which opened up the western United States and American Indian land to European immigrant settlers living in the eastern and central regions. These examples represent the ways in which the United States government used neocolonialism as a methodological approach in removing Indians and extracting their lands (by legal and illegal means). Neocolonialism effectively provides a framework for understanding the ways in which U.S. federal policy after 1865 focused on expanding the previous work of **colonialism** in new but similar ways, such as creating laws and policies that in a national and international context would allow government and corporate companies to expand physically, militarily, and economically without limitations and at whatever cost to mostly indigenous populations.

The colonial period itself began a process of **domination** and economic exploitation in not only the Americas and the Caribbean but countries on the continent of Africa, in India, Australia, and the Pacific Islands. Following the colonial period, the greatest form of political contestation evolved out of a struggle for world power and dominance. The results of this struggle were World Wars I and II, the Korean War, the Vietnam War, as well as the Persian Gulf War. These wars, along with anti-immigrant policies such as the Chinese Exclusion Act of 1882 and the Gentlemen's Agreement Act of 1908, allowed the United States to emerge ''victorious'' as a ''first world nation'' that had surpassed the British level of dominance during the colonial era.

However, it is the Cold War 1945–1990 (a battle between communist Russia and the capitalist United States)

which was the most significant war (although it involved non-traditional conflict more political than military in nature) in the neocolonial period. This war sealed the U.S. fate as the most economically dominant nation in the world; however, since the 1990s and the end of the Cold War, the U.S. government has continued to use whatever means possible to maintain its control over emerging nations such as Japan and countries in the Middle East. Today scholars continue to struggle with the effects of neo-colonialism which has in many ways devastated the political and economic structures of many countries throughout the world. Neocolonialism, many could argue, has created a dichotomy between the "core and periphery" the countries that dominate in terms of economic, political, and, military control and those marginal countries which are under-developed, also termed "third world" nations. Neocolonialism will continue to be an area of significance for post-colonial studies and **sociology**, particularly as underdeveloped nations begin to develop and gain greater economic and political **autonomy** in the twenty-first century.

NEOCONSERVATISM

The neoconservative movement in the U.S. was begun in the 1950s and 1960s by a group of intellectuals, led by Irving Kristol, who became disillusioned with **liberalism** and the Old Left. While not embracing conservative doctrine entirely, neoconservatives have been extremely critical of what they perceive as the excessive **individualism** and laissez-faire moral attitude of modern society. **Anthony Giddens** wrote that "The neoconservatives accept the pervasive influence that **capitalism**, and liberal **democracy**, have come to have over our lives today; but they see the bourgeois order as destroying traditional symbols and practice on which a meaningful social existence depends." Neoconservatives trace their **philosophy** back to classical times, focusing on the "republican virtue tradition" that insists that political liberty must rest upon a strong moral foundation of shared **community values**. They are particularly interested in maintaining the traditional institutional structures of religion and family life.

Mark Gerson wrote that there is "not one political position that can be considered distinctly neoconservative"; rather, it is "a philosophical movement with political relevance." Even so, neoconservatives have been interested in circulating ideas that will influence public policy and have been suspicious of large government programs such as public housing and welfare, though they generally do not seek to do away with them altogether. Because they believe that social life is too complex to be fully understood by anyone, they feel our ability to change it is limited. Thus, government attempts to do so are likely to fail, particularly given the difficulties of overcoming immorality in **society**. For instance, the Moynihan Report, a study published by the Department of Labor in 1965 that was predominantly written by Senator Daniel Patrick Moynihan, was heavily criticized by liberals for focusing on a "tangle of pathology" in black families, which were often female-headed and had high rates of **poverty** and welfare dependency. Moyni-

han was accused of being racist and blaming the victim for his insistence that African Americans could best be assisted through government efforts to help strengthen their disintegrating families. Neoconservatives, however, defended Moynihan's approach, with what the Senator called "a much higher level of intellectual honesty."

Gerson wrote that "Neoconservatism is now coming to an end, as it becomes clear that only one generation of thinkers identifies itself as such." What were once considered "neoconservative" ideas have been adopted by those who consider themselves "conservative," so that making distinctions becomes increasingly difficult.

NEOFUNCTIONALISM

Neofunctionalism is a modification of structural functional **theory** and is used by international relations scholars. Neofunctionalists claim that states cooperate (as a means) to increase their gains (to an end). The economic integration among states results in a political dynamic that increases integration even more, resulting in an ever-increasing cycle of integration. This is because increased economic cooperation and integration requires political coordination in order for the individual states and the group to function properly. Although there are different incarnations of neofunctionalist theory, most neofunctionalists tend to downplay the functionalist aspect of the theory. It is one of the most complex integration theories because it is both a political strategy and a set of theories within a theoretical development that has many phases. This theory has been instrumental in the development and explanation of political/economic systems such as the European Economic **Community** (EEC).

Neofunctionalists recognize the same complex interdependency of states posited by neoliberalism, but differ in that they say that states cooperate for political rather than economic reasons. They say that states recognize the process and advantages of **collective action** both within individual states and within collectives of states (federations). States begin to cooperate for practical and functional reasons, but continue the cooperation because of the potential gains in political power. States with greater power and influence are able to affect groups' decisions that positively effect their own domestic agendas. Thus, certain states will initially reap more benefits from the integration, but eventually, all states will reap the gains of cooperation, and there will be increased support for collective action. As there is successful cooperation in one area, the populace, particularly the elites and politically powerful, recognize the benefits of cooperation and become increasingly supportive of the idea. Political elites will begin to reject the concepts of nationalism and **individualism**, transcending their individual agendas and focusing on the integrated unit. Thus, the political elites will generate popular support for the integrated whole in their individual states. Cooperation can become self-perpetuating and create a "spill over" effect whereby cooperation extends into other than political and economic arenas. Through this process, states extend the areas in which

they cooperate, which leads to greater political power both individually and collectively. This spill over is part of the ultimate strategy of neofunctionalism, which is to create a federation, a supranational regional integration. This political strategy includes a gradual step-by-step transfer of **authority** from several regions or states to a new center.

The biggest critique of neofunctionalism is for its complexity and its focus on the idea of states using cooperation as a means to an end. This interpretation limits an understanding of the state by implying that it acts as an autonomous unit solely to acquire gains and ignores the other complex functions of the state as an entity. It is also criticized for the difficulty of accurately explaining spill over. This concept does not adequately account for the effects of external conditions on the potential integration process; it focuses too much on the internal process within individual states.

Some critics also claim that neofunctionalists assume an automatic tendency to spill over, although this assumption was rejected early in the development of the theories by neofunctionalists themselves. Another criticism is that it is undemocratic and elitist and focuses too much on the institutional level of analysis. In addition, some criticize the assumption that elites will transfer their loyalties away from their own states to the integrated unit, saying that even if they did, it would not necessarily lead to the solid formation of a new and inclusive political community. The final criticism has been that neofunctionalist theory did not accurately explain or predict the developments and crises that have faced the EEC over the decades, thus failing to support itself in the real world.

NETWORK THEORY

Network **theory** explores the structure of relations among social entities and suggests that the pattern of social ties affects allocation of resources and, therefore, has implications for **social change** beyond the scope of individual agency. Relations among organizations, individuals, or groups may be studied from this perspective. Network theory has enabled the quantitative analysis of the structure of relationships and interactions.

Rooted in the work of **Georg Simmel**, network theory conceptualizes social relations as sets of roles and positions and describes the links between them. Individuals are seen as occupying positions and roles rather than existing as compilations of specific attributes. Network theory derives its power not from classifying individuals by their attributes but by aggregating regularities in the patterns of relations among actors. These patterns of ties affect the behaviors available to individual actors.

In the extreme view, some sociologists contend that all social phenomena can be explained by social structure. This exclusively structuralist standpoint rejects the individual agency championed by rational choice theorists and others. Network theory has been used in empirical studies of diverse topics such as explorations of the structure of effective relationships, flows of goods or information between organiza-

tions, shared membership of boards of directors, and patterns of sexually-transmitted disease transmission. What these studies have in common is an ability to link micro-level and macro-level processes.

NEW STRUCTURALISM

New **structuralism** is a response to the individualistic assumptions implicit in **status** attainment and **human capital** theories of wage inequality. A new structuralist approach focuses on institutional **culture** and organizational behaviors that create inequalities in the labor market. Focusing on structural features of inequality and the individual criteria necessary for social mobility within the hierarchical organization, new structuralism presents inequality arguments that center on aspects of the labor market that affect individuals within those positions. Thus, issues of power tend to influence explanations of inequality for new structuralists.

New structuralists see evidence through research that earning differentials are affected by the nature of the business, whether public or private, and the wage earner's ability to bargain for their earnings. From this new paradigm come explanations of inequality that describe the process between individual and structural factors.

New structuralism attempts to describe, predict, and explain the affects that structural positions have upon labor markets. Thus, firms with more capital, larger and more extensive networks, and unionization are more likely than firms without these characteristics to pay higher wages and produce distinctive features of inequality. This hypothesis was supported in new structuralist research on labor market issues. Further research and applications of new structuralism demonstrate the causal mechanisms behind interorganizational and interindustry pay differentials. New structuralism refocuses inequality discussions surrounding pay differences in order to envision the aspects that cause it within a particular organization or firm. For example, one new line of research attributes some wage inequality to particular positions that are available within a given **structure**.

According to James Baron new structuralism is focused on processes that differentiate mobility and attainment among individuals rather than the contexts under which these occur. New structuralist Michael Piore argues that there are two markets, which offer different kinds of jobs to employees, the primary and secondary markets. In the primary market jobs are high paying, secure, and stable, while the secondary market is much less attractive in terms of these qualities. According to Piore these markets both attract and prevent some persons from working in them, therefore creating wage inequalities. Furthermore, Mark Granovetter argued that earnings are determined by a complex relationship between personal qualities, characteristics of the job, and the process by which these two sets of characteristics are matched.

In sum, the new structuralism outlines the effects that positions have on the individuals who hold them rather than focusing on the **role** that the individual plays in maintaining

Friedrich Nietzsche *(Archive Photos, Inc.)*

a position and the prestige of that position. The new structuralism redirects the social scientist's attention to the structural side of wage inequalities and away from the variables that are attributable to human beings.

NIETZSCHE, FRIEDRICH WILHELM (1844-1900)

German philosopher and poet

The German philosopher Friedrich Nietzsche foresaw a European collapse into nihilism. In works of powerful and beautiful prose and poetry he struggled to head off the catastrophe. Friedrich Nietzsche was born on October 15, 1844, in Röcken, a village in Saxony where his father served as a Lutheran pastor. The father's death, when the child was four years old, was a shattering blow to which Nietzsche often referred in his later writings. This death left Nietzsche in a household of women: his mother, grandmother, several aunts, and a sister, Elizabeth.

After attending local schools in Naumburg, in 1858 Nietzsche won a scholarship to Pforta, one of the best boarding schools in Germany. Here he received a thorough training in the classics and acquired several lifetime friends. At the end of this period of schooling, Nietzsche, who had earlier fully shared the genuine piety of his family, found that he had ceased to accept Christianity—a view that soon hardened into outright atheism.

In 1864, Nietzsche enrolled in the University of Bonn where he pursued classical studies with Friedrich Ritschl, and when the latter, within the year, moved to Leipzig, Nietzsche followed him. Nietzsche attempted to enter into the social life of the students, but he soon discovered that his sense of his own particular mission in life had isolated him from his fellow students. At this time, too, Nietzsche contracted syphilis in a Leipzig brothel. The incurable disease gradually undermined his strong constitution. In middle life he suffered almost constantly from migraine and gastric upsets. Loneliness and physical pain were thus the constant background of his life—though Nietzsche later came to interpret them as the necessary conditions for his work.

Nietzsche's early publications in classical philology so impressed his teacher that when a chair of philology opened up at Basel, Ritschl was able to secure it for Nietzsche, then only 24 years old and still without his degree. This the University of Leipzig gave him on the strength of his writings without requiring an examination, and Nietzsche entered upon a teaching career. Important for Nietzsche's intellectual development was his discovery in these Leipzig years of the philosophy of **Arthur Schopenhauer** and Friedrich Lange and the music dramas of Richard Wagner.

When Nietzsche took up residence in Basel, Wagner was nearby at Tribschen, and Nietzsche was soon drawn into his circle. Friendship with the charismatic but egocentric Wagner was, however, incompatible with independence of thought, the quality Nietzsche most valued. Before long he began to reassert his own ideas and plans. This led finally to a break.

Prior to the break, Wagner had greatly influenced Nietzsche's first book *The Birth of Tragedy* (1872), which gave an imaginative account of the forces that led to the rise of Athenian tragedy and to its subsequent decline. Nietzsche's book ends with a rousing advocacy of Wagner's music drama as a revival of Hellenic tragedy. But no sooner had it been published than Nietzsche began to perceive the difference between Wagner's musical genius and the shabby pseudophilosophy of the Wagnerian cult. From then on, though he still felt affection for Wagner's person, Nietzsche attacked ever more vigorously the ''decadence'' of Wagner's political and philosophical ideas.

Nietzsche's teaching at Basel was interrupted frequently by prolonged bouts of sickness and by several months of service as a medical orderly during the Franco-Prussian War, which further aggravated his illness. In April 1879 his health had deteriorated so much that he was driven to resign. He was given a small pension, and he now began a ten year period of wandering in search of a tolerable climate. Though racked by increasing pain from the relentless progress of his disease, Nietzsche managed to produce ten substantial books before his final collapse. They belong to the first rank of German literature and contain a provocative set of philosophical ideas.

Nietzsche believed that European man was standing at a critical turning point. The advance of scientific enlightenment, in particular the Darwinian theory, had destroyed the old religious and metaphysical underpinnings for the idea of human dignity. "God is dead," declares Nietzsche's spokesman Zarathustra, and man, no longer "the image of God," is a chance product of a nature indifferent to purpose or value. The great danger is that man will find his existence meaningless. Unless a new grounding for **values** is provided, Nietzsche predicted a rapid decline into nihilism and barbarity.

Nietzsche aimed in all his work to provide a new meaning for human existence in a meaningless world. In the absence of any transcendent sanction, men must create their own values. Nietzsche's writings are either analyses and criticisms of the old system of values or attempts to formulate a new system. For European man, the Judeo-Christian tradition was the source of the old values. Nietzsche attacked it head on in such works as *A Genealogy of Morals* (1887) and *The Antichrist* (1888).

In his constructive works Nietzsche sought to find in life itself a force that would serve to set human existence apart. He found it in the hypothesis of the will to power—the urge to dominate and master. All creatures desire this, but only man has achieved sufficient power to turn the force back upon himself. Self-mastery, self-overcoming: these are the qualities that give a unique value to human life. The ideal man, the "superman," will achieve a fierce joy in mastering his own existence, ordering his passions, and giving style to his character. The sublimation of passion and of life's circumstances that the ideal man achieves in his self-overcoming will release in him a flood of creative energy. The lives of such men will be the justification of reality; their preferences will constitute the standard of value.

All **morality** is thus the result of self-overcoming, but Nietzsche discerned a criterion by which to distinguish the morality of the superman from the "decadent" morality of **Christianity**. The latter undercuts earthly life in favor of an illusory afterlife, condemns self-assertion as pride, and perverts bodily functions with guilt and fear. Its tendency is toward nihilism and the denial of life. The new morality, on the other hand, will affirm life, encourage self-assertion, and eliminate guilt consciousness. In *Thus Spake Zarathustra* (1883) Nietzsche formulated the ultimate test of the superman's affirmations. Confronted with the hypothesis of eternal recurrence, the notion that the world process is cyclical and eternal, the superman still affirms life. Let it be—again and again—with all its joys and sorrows.

On January 3, 1889, Nietzsche collapsed on a street in Turin, Italy. When he regained consciousness, his sanity was gone. He began to send off wild letters to friends and strangers signed "Dionysus—the Crucified." He was taken to his mother's home and lived on in a twilight condition, sinking ever further from the real world until his death on August 25, 1900.

NOMADS

Nomads are cultural groups characterized by their tendency to move from place to place with no permanent residence. This

Nomads are cultural groups characterized by their tendency to move from place to place with no permanent residence (*Corbis Corporation [Bellevue]*).

manner of existence can be traced back to the earliest humans. Gradually, over thousands of years, permanent residence, whether urban or rural, replaced nomadism as the more common way of living.

Nomads are generally either hunter-gatherers or herders and move based on the supply of game or grazing land for their animals. Sometimes this movement is seasonal, based on climatic conditions, but it may also be more random: a process of following the migrational patterns of the animals on which the nomads depend.

The Bedouin of northern Africa and the Middle East and the Mongols of the Gobi Desert have historically relied on nomadic herding. Their lifestyle has been greatly altered, but many still follow the ancient practices mixed liberally with modern conveniences. Small-scale subsistence farming is also engaged in by some nomadic peoples. Often they live in areas where soil is thin or of poor quality. It may quickly become depleted, in which case they move on to fresh soil and start again. This method is practiced by many small groups in the Amazon rain forest.

As agriculture has evolved to favor cash crops at the expense of subsistence food production, nomadism has diminished. The territories of these peoples have been encroached upon by modern civilizations and artificial barriers, such as new national borders, have restricted their traditional movements.

Ironically, modern **communication** and improved modes of transportation have created a new form of nomadism in which individuals or families move from place to place following the job supply. Concurrently, national borders and local cultures have become blurred by the global economy, and people are less connected to a particular country or region than in the past.

NON-LITERATE SOCIETY

Non-literate societies are defined as peoples or cultures that exist without a written **language**. In addition to the lack of a written language, people in non-literate societies are usually relatively isolated, have small populations and relatively simple social institutions, and show a slow rate of socio-cultural change. Anthropologists make a distinction between "non-literate" and "illiterate" societies, where illiterate designates a person or group of people within a literate **society** who have not learned to read or write. They stress that even in literate societies, not every member participates in literacy and that there are varying degrees of literacy; for example, some members may only write their names but not be able to read or write more than that. Non-literate societies have often been designated as "primitive," "preliterate," "preurban," or "savage." In the tradition of the colonial mind, many have interpreted this level of **culture** to be inferior, hence the application of such highly charged terms. Cultural anthropologists prefer to avoid these terms, however, because they represent a simplistic view of the complexity and the worth of other cultures.

Non-literate societies often participate in an oral tradition, by which social knowledge can be communicated through stories passed on from generation to generation. It may be true that non-literate societies abound; while thousands of languages have been spoken, relatively few have been written. Orality has been debated as a form of literacy because most cultures that rely solely on oral tradition do not express the "consequences" of literacy such as modernization, political and economic development, and innovation. Yet these consequences reflect a Western bias towards literacy that manifests certain assumptions about language, education, and power. Anthropologists generally prefer to stress the diverse uses of oral communication and its benefits in tracing a people's history and culture.

NONPARAMETRIC STATISTICS

Nonparametric statistics are used when some assumptions about the population cannot be made. This situation usually arises when nominal and/or ordinal data are used, and population parameters, such as means and standard deviations, cannot be calculated. If **data** were interval level, means and standard deviations could be compared to the **normal distribution**, and inferences about the population could be made. Further, if the data violate some other assumption for a parametric test, for example, the data may be skewed or the sample size small, a nonparametric test is more appropriate. Where data are skewed, it is inappropriate to use statistics that use the **mean** since the mean is influenced by outlying cases. Such data should be analyzed with nonparametric, median-based tests.

The most widely used nonparametric alternative to the **t-test** is *chi-square*. Chi-square is used when data is categorical or nominal. This test can be used as a one-sample **median** test or a test of differences among samples. Both tests are based on whether observed frequencies differ from expected frequencies. Chi-square can thus be thought of as a discrepancy statistic—one that measures the discrepancy between observed and expected frequencies. For example, a researcher is trying to ascertain whether an electronic monitoring program is more effective than regular probation by comparing recidivism rates. The sample size is small and contains skewed data. The null hypothesis would state that there is no difference between recidivism rates of offenders in regular probation and offenders in electronic monitoring programs. The alternative would state that there is a difference in recidivism rates. The chi-square statistic is then calculated. The larger the chi-square statistic is, the more likely the researcher is to find a statistically significant difference. If the data are nominal, it is also possible to analyze more than two categories of several variables using log-linear models.

A second commonly used nonparametric statistic is the *Mann Whitney U* test for rank ordered or ordinal data. This test is the nonparametric alternative to the independent groups t-test. Mann Whitney U tests whether two samples have the same distribution or come from the same population. For example, a researcher evaluates whether an intensive six week statistics course is associated with higher grades than a regular 15-week statistics course. Two groups of students are randomly selected and placed in the two programs. Six students complete the intensive course and 16 students complete the regular course. The intensive group is designated as group one since it has a smaller sample size. The scores are ranked and the U statistic calculated. The **research hypothesis** would state that the students are from different populations, while the null would state that the students are from the same population. An extension of this test is the Kruskal-Wallis test.

The Wilcoxon matched-pairs signed-ranks test is a third nonparametric test. Its parametric equivalent is the matched-pairs t-test. Suppose a researcher wished to research whether observing a convicted murderer being put to death by lethal injection changes attitudes toward the death penalty. Prior to the observation, the researcher would survey a group to determine attitudes toward the death penalty. The group would then observe the state-imposed sentence and would be surveyed again. The researcher is thus comparing the scores of the same group prior to and after the observation. The null hypothesis would state that there is no difference between the pairs of scores and the research hypothesis would state that there is a difference. The scores are paired up and ranked, and the Wilcoxon T-statistic is calculated. It is sometimes necessary to employ nonparametric **regression** techniques, particularly when there are outlying cases affecting regression estimates. Using smooth curves, such as band regression, is one example of nonparametric regression.

Nonparametric tests are useful when the assumptions for parametric tests cannot be met. The researcher must be mindful, however, that nonparametric tests are not as powerful as parametric tests. Power refers to the probability that a statistical test will find a difference when there is one. Thus, nonparametric tests are not as sensitive to finding differences or providing proof for research hypotheses as parametric tests.

Because of this shortcoming, many researchers will transform data so that they meet the requirements for parametric tests. There are a number of transformation techniques that range from simply re-coding variables into scales that can be thought of as interval to complex statistical transformations. The danger with transformations is that the researcher runs the risk of finding results that he or she can no longer explain clearly, make no practical sense or which are artificial and have little meaning. In such situations, it is more beneficial to run non-parametric tests.

NONRESPONSE

Several survey errors with which researchers must contend include coverage error, **sampling error**, **measurement** error, and nonresponse error. When a research study is being designed, a sample is selected and then contacted. Some contacted individuals do not respond. For example, asurvey may be sent to 10,000 college graduates. Of the 10,000 individuals contacted, 7,500 people may ultimately agree to participate and return the **surveys**. This yields a response rate of 75 percent. Response rates vary, especially depending on the way respondents are contacted. For example, the pressure of being contacted by someone directly (either in person or over the telephone) may produce a higher response rate than just sending a survey through the mail. Sending a pre-notice before the survey and a reminder message afterward may improve mail response rates further.

Overall response rates are taken to be indicators of representativeness. Nonresponse error is when those who fail to respond differ in some systematic way from those who do respond. If those who do not respond differ in some fundamental way, then the respondents cannot be considered representative of the entire population from which the sample was chosen. Differences have to be in some way critical to the purpose of the research project. For example, if a study is being conducted concerning the environment, a survey might be sent out to a random sample of individuals. If those who respond to the survey are more active in environmental organizations than those who do not, the set of respondents cannot be considered representative. Their responses may be biased toward high levels of concern for the environment. Differences in social class, gender, and age between respondents and nonrespondents may also be fundamental to representativeness in a study of the environment. There is, of course, no way to be sure when those who respond and those who do not are different in ways that impair the representativeness of the sample and the generalizability of the results. For this reason, response rates are used as a proxy for representativeness. Typically, a **response rate** of fifty percent is considered adequate, sixty percent is considered good, and seventy percent is considered very good.

NORMAL DISTRIBUTION

A normal distribution, also called a normal **probability** distribution, is a bell-shaped probability distribution used for statistical inference. A special property of many sample and population distributions is that they approximate the normal distribution. The normal distribution is characterized by its **mean**, *(the Greek letter mu)* and its standard deviation, *(the Greek letter theta)*. The curve of the normal distribution is symmetric about its mean, and its shape is determined by the **values** of the mean and standard deviation. The height and the width of the curve are greater for larger values of the mean and standard deviation, respectively. A normal distribution with a large mean and small standard deviation will be tall and narrow, while the shape of the curve for a sample that has a small mean but large standard deviation will be short and wide. For every possible combination of mean and standard deviation there is only one normal distribution that has those values.

Probabilities are determined by the area underneath the curve. The probability falling within z standard deviations of the mean is the area under the curve bounded by ($-z($ and ($+ z($. The area under the curve that extends one standard deviation ($z=1$) in each direction from the mean includes 68 percent of the total area. It follows that there is 68 percent probability under the curve. Ninety-five percent of the area falls within two standard deviations ($z=2$), and 99.7 percent falls within three standard deviations ($z=3$). Ninety-five percent of cases fall within two standard deviations of the mean, and 99.7 percent fall within three standard deviations of the mean. The exact probability for other values of z can be determined by examining tables of standard normal probability distributions or from statistical software packages.

NORMATIVE THEORY

Normative **theory** is any theory that aims to establish the values or **norms** that best fit the overall needs or requirements of **society**, either societies in general or particular societies, and that would be morally justified. For those who see the purpose of modern social science as descriptive and explanatory and not prescriptive, such a goal is not acceptable. Therefore, in these circumstances ''normative theory'' can have a negative connotation. For others, however, the purpose of assessing and establishing values is an important goal, perhaps the most significant goal, of the social sciences.

NORMS

Much daily social life involves conforming to certain social guidelines; obeisance to these social **rules** is often reflexive. A norm is an ideal standard that regulates behavior in a particular social setting and determines what is socially desirable or appropriate. Although norms lack the formal status of rules, persons' adherence to such standards largely determines the extent to which they are considered deviant. The concept of normative behavior is largely based upon the idea that social life is an ordered and enduring process which cannot continue without common expectations and obligations to which the majority of its participants adhere. This adherence is enforced

through positive or negative sanctions prescribing such behavior, which is known as social control. Norms can be either proscriptive, forbidding a certain action, or prescriptive, which encourages a particular deed.

Two types of norms are **folkways** and **mores**. The former describes everyday conventions of social life, the violation of which is rarely (if ever) serious. Poor table manners are an example of a folkway violation. Mores, however, are significantly more serious, and a violation of these often contradicts what we consider to be morally correct behavior and elicits strong social reactions. An example of such a violation would be the desecration of a religious symbol.

Norms and normative behavior became a central focus of the work of Talcott Parsons (1902-1979) and other structural functionalists in the 1950s and 1960s. This perspective argues that norms become part of one's social makeup and, thus, are adhered to out of an internalized desire to conform to the rights and obligations of their various roles. This view has declined in popularity, largely because it suggests that social **interaction** is static, rather than fluid, in nature. The idea of norms was further developed through the social identity **theory**, which views norms as actions that are carried out because they are expected to validate one's sense of **identity** through the approval of others. In other words, people behave in ways that will gain approval and thus build a sense of identity.

See also Folkways; Mores

NORTH AMERICAN FREE TRADE AGREEMENT

The North American Free Trade Agreement (NAFTA) went into effect on January 1, 1994, creating the world's largest and wealthiest trading bloc of over 360 million people with an annual economic output exceeding $6.5 trillion. Proponents claimed that by lowering trade barriers over a 15-year period, NAFTA would increase trade, moderate prices, and create jobs in all three participating countries—the United States, Canada, and Mexico. Opponents in the United States and Canada feared widespread job loss to Mexico's cheap labor market. They also voiced deep concerns over Mexico's lax enforcement of safety and environmental standards.

In 1990 the United States and Mexico first announced plans to initiate negotiations for a comprehensive free trade agreement. Canada, through its commitment to the U.S.-Canada Free Trade Agreement of 1988, became a third party to NAFTA in 1991. In early 1991 President Bush formally entered into treaty discussions and petitioned Congress for fast-track authority, which was granted in May. In June, Congress extended fast-track procedures for two years. Fast-track authority allows the president to present a negotiated treaty to Congress for approval without amendments. Congress then has ninety days to approve or reject the treaty as a whole.

The trilateral discussions ended in agreement on August 12, 1992. The two-thousand-page treaty addressed six areas: market access, regulations, services, investment, intellectual property, and dispute settlement. According to the U.S. Department of State, the objective of the agreement was to provide the means that would "eliminate barriers to trade in... goods and services between the territories of the parties." In short, NAFTA's creators proposed that the agreement would improve living conditions in all three countries by supporting the free trade of goods, capital, and services. On November 17, 1993, after an eleven-hour debate involving 240 speeches and one interruption by protestors in the balcony who showered the House with fake fifty-dollar bills that read "Stop NAFTA Now," Congress ratified the treaty by a 234 to 200 margin. It went into effect on January 1, 1994.

NAFTA's success was hampered by recession in Mexico that began in December 1994 and resulted in the peso losing fifty percent of its value. Many U.S. businesses that had intended to expand into Mexico curtailed their plans, including Wal-Mart, Ford, and Mercedes-Benz. For Mexican workers, the recession was crushing. Factory wages dropped by 29 percent between 1994 and 1998 to an average of $55.77 a week, forcing sixty percent of the Mexican labor force to live below the **poverty** line. In NAFTA's first five years, 28,000 Mexican small businesses failed.

NAFTA and the Mexican recession combined to make manufacturing along the border very appealing. NAFTA supporters had argued that by eliminating tariffs and other trade barriers, industry would spring up in Mexico's interior, where land and costs are cheaper. However, few businesses materialized in the interior, but fueled by cheap labor and close access to the U.S. markets, the number of border industries, or *maquiladoras*, rose dramatically. This pattern led to renewed concerned by environmentalists who correlate the growing number of maquiladoras with increased birth defects, occurrence of hepatitis A, and concerns over air pollution and the proper disposal of toxic waste. By 1998, half of all U.S. produce was being imported from Mexico; however, between 1994 and 1998, the amount of imported food that was inspected fell from eight percent to less than two percent.

Along with food inspection issues, safety concerns have focused on the number and condition of Mexican trucks coming into the United States. With the increase in imports from Mexico has come an increase in truck traffic, with over 3.3 million trucks crossing the border every year. Whereas U.S. highways are built to withstand 80,000 pounds, Mexican trucks weigh up to 120,000 pounds. Only one percent are inspected and of those, over half are turned back due to improper licenses, faulty tires or brakes, unsecured loads, underage drivers, or presence of hazardous cargo. Also, Mexican drivers are not drug-tested, nor are the number of driving hours regulated.

NAFTA's success is a matter of ongoing debate. In terms of jobs and wages, the reviews are mixed. Opponents point to numerous areas where they claim NAFTA has failed, including jobs and wages, environmental concerns, public health, and safety. However, the statistics regarding jobs and wages are complicated by numerous interpretations of the **data**. Opponents note that the United States' traditional trade surplus with Mexico turned into a trade deficit of $13.2 billion by 1998 and claim that over 200,000 U.S. workers lost their

jobs due to NAFTA. Proponents, on the other hand, quote U.S. Commerce Department figures showing that U.S. trade with Canada increased 56 percent from $211.7 billion to $329.9 billion and trade with Mexico jumped 113 percent from $81.5 billion to $173.4 billion. Consensus among moderates is that, less than a decade after NAFTA's inception, it appears that the gains have not been as extreme as its advocates promised nor have the losses been as dramatic as its opponents predicted.

NULL HYPOTHESIS

In order to test research **data**, researchers make statements about the relationship she or he believe exists between variables in the analysis. Researchers can then conduct statistical tests on the statements and determine whether the hypotheses are supported. Hypotheses generally fall into two categories, null hypotheses and research hypotheses.

The null hypothesis is the hypothesis of a statistical test which states that no relationship exists between the variables and is symbolized by H_0. This is not the conclusion researchers expect to find, but it is what they test. For example, if researchers want to test whether a relationship exists between the variables of female literacy rate for a country and its infant mortality rate, a null hypothesis might be stated as "no relationship exists between the female literacy rate of a country and its infant mortality rate." The research hypothesis might state that the variables are related. By design, the null hypothesis contradicts the **research hypothesis**. While the research hypothesis claims the appearance of a relationship between variables is due to an actual relationship existing between the variables, the null hypothesis says that any relationship which may seem to exist (meaning if there is any difference at all in values) is merely the result of sampling error and not because of a true relationship. If the null hypothesis is supported by the data, researchers say they fail to reject the null hypothesis instead of claiming to accept the null hypothesis because there is a possibility that if they had chosen to test the data at a different alpha level (how willing they are to be wrong), the results may have supported a different conclusion.

Since researchers expect the data to support the statements made by the research hypothesis, statistical analyses actually test the null hypothesis, with hopes of being able to demonstrate that it is a false statement. Researchers may be able to find evidence to support the research hypothesis, yet for the variables to have no real relationship with one another. Therefore, researchers must attempt to support or disprove the lack of a relationship in order to make a statement about the relationship. If the probability is small that the evidence supporting the existence of the relationship may simply be the result of the randomness of the sample, the researchers can reject the null hypothesis.

NURSING HOMES

Nursing homes are institutions where mostly older individuals live when they are no longer able to care for themselves inde-

Nursing homes, sometimes referred to as long-term care facilities, are the only alternative for some older individuals in the United States (*Corbis Corporation [Bellevue]*).

pendently. Nursing homes employ doctors, nurses, and other staff members who take care of the daily needs of their patients. Round the clock nursing care is also provided, including bathing, distributing medications, physical therapy, speech therapy and provision of social events. People who move into nursing homes usually do so when their caretaker (spouse, children) can no longer care for them. Nursing homes, sometimes referred to as **long-term care** facilities, are the only alternative for some older individuals in the United States.

Most nursing homes are private businesses whose aim is to make a profit. Many facilities charge high fees and provide first-rate service. Other facilities charge reasonable rates but are overcrowded, understaffed, and in some cases unsanitary and dangerous. In the last few years some nursing homes have received negative media attention regarding unlawful occurrences. Staff members were found neglecting the elderly and, in some cases, physically, mentally, and sexually abusing residents. In such cases, action has been taken and guilty parties have been punished, but it is still leaves a mark on the rep-

utation of nursing homes. On the whole, however, nursing homes are safe and effective places for people who require care.

A common misconception about nursing homes and long time care facilities is that a large proportion of the elderly population reside in them. In actuality, less than five percent of the elderly reside in such facilities. Most older adults either live independently in their homes or are cared for by family members. When looking at the makeup of nursing home populations in the United States, minority groups are found to be underrepresented in the nursing home population. White Americans make up ninety percent of the nursing home population while African Americans make up seven percent, Hispanics two-and-a-half percent, and Native Americans and Asian Americans less than one percent.

The fastest growing portion of the United States population is the 65 and older age group. Nursing home populations are expected to grow as the baby boom generation (people born in the 1950s and 1960s) begins to age. With newer and better medical technology people are able to live longer. In 1900 only four percent of the population was over age sixty-

five. In 2000, that age group represents thirteen percent of the population and researchers predict that by the year 2030 twenty percent of the population will be over age sixty-five. The need for nursing homes and long term care facilities will increase with this trend.

Many Americans fear being placed in a nursing home. Many who enter nursing homes suffer psychological problems such as depression. To many, entering a nursing home is a ultimate sign that they have lost their independence and death is imminent. While nursing homes are many times the only option for the elderly, some wish to seek other alternatives. Some alternatives to nursing homes are home care, assisted living, or adult day care centers. These provide care without the elderly person feeling institutionalized. However, home care nurses are expensive, assisted living is sometimes not enough care, and adult day care covers only for a few hours during the day. As the elderly population grows, new alternatives to nursing homes will be established to meet the needs of the **aging** baby boom generation.

See also Long-Term Care

O

OBJECTIVISM

Objectivism is the philosophical view that all objects of knowledge have a reality of their own. According to Émile Durkheim, an early objectivist, the subject matter of **sociology** is overt, readily observable social phenomena, or the things that can be measured, counted, and correlated. Objectivism views "wholes" or "collectives" as real in the sense that they are external to individuals and have a reality that is independent to our knowledge of it. These wholes have properties of their own that are different from the sum of individual action. That is, the whole is more than the sum of its constituent parts.

This view suggests that social behavior is determined by antecedent, external causes. The object of study for sociology, human behavior, is thought to be a product of social forces. Durkheim stated that social facts constrain our behavior, a point that can be shown in how we raise our children. Education is used to impose on children ways of seeing, thinking, and acting which they would not have arrived at spontaneously. The child is eventually shaped into the image of **society**. This observation implies that most of our ideas and tendencies are not developed by ourselves but come from the outside.

Those who adhere to objectivism, such as August Comte and Émile Durkheim, are staunch positivists. They apply the scientific approach to studying social phenomena. One of the primary rules set forth by Durkheim is that social facts are things and must be viewed externally. Sociologists must be neutral and observe from the outside. Durkheim presents three corollaries for studying social facts. First, researchers must discard all preconceptions about what they are studying. Second, they must define beforehand the subject matter by using certain external characteristics. The definition must express the phenomena as a function of its inherent properties and not the researchers' notions of it. This process allows the facts to be grounded in reality. Finally, sociologists should strive to consider social facts from a viewpoint where they present themselves in isolation from their individual manifestations. Objectivists place a strong emphasis on quantitative tech-

niques. They use surveys, experiments, secondary **data** analysis and the like. Objectivism has contributed to sociology being considered a science and has provided a better understanding of the social world.

OCCUPATIONAL AND CAREER MOBILITY

Occupational mobility is a popular concept in the sociological investigation of stratification and **social inequality**. Occupational and **career** mobility refers to the movement of individuals between different levels of the occupational hierarchy. Often this mobility is assessed in terms of a gradational scale of occupational status or prestige. Mobility can be either upward, involving an increase in status or prestige, or downward, resulting in a loss or decrease of prestige. A high degree of mobility implies that there is openness and fluidity in a society. Mobility can be studied in several different ways. Research is extensive on both intergenerational and intragenerational mobility. Intergenerational mobility refers to the similarities or differences in occupational attainment that occurs between an individual and his or her parents. Intragenerational mobility focuses on the changes in the occupational level of the same individuals over the courses of their lives. Another distinction in mobility research is between absolute and relative rates of mobility. Absolute mobility refers to the proportion of individuals who are mobile or immobile starting at some base category. Relative mobility refers to the relative chances of individuals of different class backgrounds to reach particular occupational levels. Relative mobility rates allow researchers to compare different nations in terms of their fluidity.

Two types of mobility patterns have been established in research. Sponsored mobility involves an early identification of children for certain occupational levels and stratifies children along this decision, thus yielding little occupational mobility. R.H. Turner's research in the 1960s used this term to

describe the system of occupational mobility in Britain. Contest mobility, used to describe the United States, involves delaying selection as long as possible. Such a system is assumed to be a more egalitarian system because occupational mobility is supposedly possible for all individuals, as is characteristic of a **meritocracy**. Contemporary research has shown little difference between the United States and Britain, and the extent to which the United States is an example of contest mobility is itself debated. Education is recognized as an **institution** that is intimately connected to expectations, opportunities, and barriers related to occupational mobility. It is assumed in a meritocracy that education is equally available to all individuals and that the amount of work an individual puts in will determine his or her rewards. Some see the institution of education to be such a system in the United States, one that encourages mobility and fluidity. Others argue that the institution of education reproduces the advantages and disadvantages present in society, known as a process of social reproduction.

Research on occupational and career mobility addresses issues from several directions. Some research focuses on patterns in mobility, such as who is recruited to various occupational levels. Other research concentrates on the factors that influence mobility and how certain individuals reach various occupational levels. In terms of the factors affecting occupational mobility, researchers have focused on both ascribed and achieved characteristics. Ascribed characteristics include such aspects as **race**, **ethnicity**, and gender. Achieved characteristics include education and training. Other research explores mobility as an **independent variable** and looks at the effects of mobility or lack of mobility on individuals and their families. Mobility both within and between generations can impact relationship dynamics. Occupational and career mobility should not be confused with **social mobility**. While the two processes are related, social mobility involves movement between different positions in society more generally. While work is an important aspect of general status and position within a social **structure**, mobility in one's occupation and career involves a more specific transition and may have more acute effects.

OCCUPATIONAL PRESTIGE

The study of occupational prestige is part of the larger body of research on **social stratification**, the area of **sociology** that focuses on who achieves higher social standing. Stratification researchers focus on the unequal distribution of social **status** as measured by jobs, income, health, and housing or other possessions. While it is relatively easy to rank houses and incomes, the ranking of jobs is not so obvious. Thus in order to describe who is getting the best jobs researchers must first agree on some measure of what constitutes a better job. Scales of occupational prestige are one means of classifying occupations as higher or lower in the social system, so that researchers can then analyze what types of people are able to get ahead in the labor market.

Occupational prestige is differentiated from other ways of evaluating occupations in the focus on the relative place-

ment of jobs by all members of a **society**. A ranking of occupational prestige seeks to explain which jobs people think have a higher social standing. Occupations are thus ranked according to the social honor given to the job and its occupant. In order to determine these rankings researchers generally rely on **surveys** in which respondents are asked to rank occupations relative to one another. One way to accomplish this is to list a set of occupations, for example 10 or 15 different jobs, and ask respondents to rank the whole series from highest to lowest. An alternative method, known as the method of paired comparisons, asks respondents to compare only two different ones at any one time, but perhaps ask each of them to make many such comparisons over the course of a survey. Using either method, researchers then summarize the responses into a continuous scale of prestige with higher rated jobs at the top and lower ones at the bottom. In general jobs such as religious minister, physician, university professor, and public administrator tend to be near the top of the prestige hierarchy in modern industrialized societies, while jobs as unskilled labor in transportation, manufacturing, and agriculture tend to be near the bottom.

This way of ranking occupations is different from that used in studies of occupational status or class. The measures used in research on status attainment rank jobs according to which job holders have the highest incomes and educational levels. Studies of social class identify jobs according to a theoretically derived schema that relate them to the dominant social order. While all of these methods are related, they do result in varied findings. For example, researchers have found that jobs with higher prestige are more likely to be occupied by people with more education and allow incumbents more control over their work schedule and activities. Prestige is not entirely related to pay, however. Some well paying jobs, such as skilled tradesmen have, tend to fall in the middle of the prestige hierarchy, while some of the highest prestige jobs, such as religious minister, tend to pay very little. For this reasons, prestige is not entirely the same as an occupational status score as measured by standard socioeconomic indices. Many positions ranked highest in terms of class might also rank lower in a prestige scale because, for example, factory owners are held in lower esteem than ministers by most people.

In modern societies, where the labor market has become differentiated and jobs are increasingly becoming more specialized, occupational prestige has been found to relate to two main factors. One is the amount of power or control over individuals allocated to different occupations. In general those positions that grant an individual more power will be more respected. For this reason higher government and managerial positions tend to have more prestige than lower positions in the same organizations, since those in higher positions have more direct authority over subordinates. The second is the amount of control over resources that are considered to be scarce in that society. These resources might be access to capital for investment, concrete skills such as surgery or the creative ability to write novels, or religious skills such as the ability to do missionary work. For this reason bankers, authors, physicians, and ministers all have higher prestige. Research

has shown that in all societies across the globe those people in jobs that involve the use of power or control over scarce resources will have higher prestige than those in other jobs.

See also Social Stratification

OEDIPUS CONFLICT

As used in psychoanalytic **theory**, this Freudian concept or complex is defined as a crisis arising from the intense desire of a young boy for sexual engagement with his mother. Accompanying this powerful yearning is the rivalry or conflict between father and son. The young boy feels threatened by the same-sex parent, recognizes the father might punish him for his incestuous desire, and eventually strives to reduce the conflict.

Sigmund Freud first introduced the Oedipus complex in his *The Interpretation of Dreams* in 1899. The complex is so named because it corresponds to the Greek legend of a Theban hero, Oedipus Rex. As the legend goes, Oedipus unwittingly kills his father and marries his mother. The female parallel to the boy's Oedipus complex is known as the Electra complex, derived from another mythological figure, who assisted with the slaying of her mother.

According to Freudian theory, boys between the ages of three and six years experience the Oedipus crisis during the third stage of personality development, the phallic stage. For this reason, Freud considered the phallic stage the most important in personality development, and Oedipus conflict as a part of normal development in a boy's life. To resolve the jealousy and anger toward his father, the child identifies with his father and strives to be like him. Freud believed the resolution of this conflict is also accompanied by the formation of the **superego**. If a young boy develops a healthy superego during the phallic stage he will then suppress his sexual desire for his mother. However, the development of a functioning superego depends on how the child is treated during the phallic stage. For example, if parents are extremely prohibitive or excessively stimulating, a child may experience permanent trauma and have difficulty distinguishing right from wrong. This trauma can fixate the child in the phallic stage and block the natural progression into Freud's next developmental stage, latency.

OGBURN, WILLIAM FIELDING (1886-1959)

American sociologist and statistician

Sociologist, educator, and statistician William F. Ogburn was born in Butler, Georgia, on June 29, 1886, the son of Charlton Greenwood, a planter and merchant, and Irene Wynne Ogburn. After earning a bachelor's degree at Mercer University in Macon, he went on to Columbia University in New York City for an M.A. (1909) and a Ph.D. (1912) in sociology. From 1912 to 1917, he taught sociology and economics at Reed College in Portland, Oregon, and sociology at the University of

William Fielding Ogburn *(AP/Wide World Photos, Inc.)*

Washington (1917–1918). At that time, he said he turned his attention fully to science, the world of statistics, and change. During World War II, he served in the U.S. Bureau of Labor Statistics and on the National War Labor Board. His work during this period established him as a pioneer in methods of analyzing family budgets and building price indexes.

Ogburn became a professor of sociology at Columbia (1919–1927) and at the University of Chicago, where he spent most of his academic career (1927–1951), sixteen of those years as chairman of the country's largest Department of Sociology. He was frequently called on to serve as a labor mediator, and in 1930 and 1931, he was research director of President Herbert Hoover's Committee on U.S. Social Trends. From this came his two-volume landmark work *Recent Social Trends*. During these early years of his career, Ogburn claimed that he was "much interested in socialism and spent a good deal of time in radical circles." In addition, he was director of the Consumers Advisory Board of the National Recovery Administration (1933) and research consultant of the Science Committee, National Resources Committee (1935–1943). Ogburn served as president of the American Statistical Association and the American Sociological Society. Beginning in 1953, he was also visiting professor of sociology at Florida State University in Tallahassee, where he died on April 27, 1959.

Ogburn coined the term "cultural lag" which is still in use. It was first presented in his most influential work *Social*

Change (1922), which discussed themes that recur throughout his career—the description and **measurement** of tangible aspects of **social change**. Ogburn claimed that social upheaval was unavoidable, the result of differing developments in differing cultures. **Cultural lag**, he said, occurred because human intelligence and capacity for adaptation did not keep pace with the ever occurring technological advancements. This apparent gap between technology developments and social adjustments in laws and customs was used in later years to explain resistances to or difficulties with social change. Ogburn said that cultural lags are generally unnoticed over long periods of history. But sometimes a lag can threaten an entire society. A major invention in industry, for example, could so disrupt the economy of an area or nation that it would threaten the existence of the entire society. From shock waves such as this, a new equilibrium must be established.

Change was Ogburn's great interest, especially as manifested in technology-generated transformations in the traditions, laws, and ethics of society. In 1946, he discussed the growth in the air travel industry and its possible effects, politically and economically, on modern society in *The Social Effects of Aviation*. In addition to *Social Change*, his 1928 work *American Marriage and Family Relationships* focused on family changes, and his 1955 book *Technology and the Changing Family* explored the effects on society, in particular the nuclear family, generated by the machine and scientific discoveries. In 1940, Ogburn collaborated with Meyer Nimkoff in a textbook *Sociology*, which has been revised several times.

Throughout his varied career, Ogburn, always anxious to explore a new avenue, taught classes in several social sciences, including history, political science, and economics. All the major social institutions fascinated him, and he wrote extensively on numerous topics concerning **government**, politics, and the family. Sometimes Ogburn seemed to explore subjects only for his own curiosity at the time, such as a project on the income of baseball players or how the order of birth affects one's personality. His probings were so varied that one of Ogburn's former students, A.J. Jaffe, wrote a tribute to his teacher in an article published in *Science*. Said Jaffe, "Ogburn, in his interests and works, must be called the last of the great social scientists who wished to know it all."

OPEN SOCIETY

Social stratification systems differ in the extent to which ascribed and achieved statuses determine an individual's or group's social position. Sociologists distinguish between these types of stratification systems as either open or closed. This distinction is dependent upon the degree of mobility within that system.

An open system of stratification is one that does not have either formal or ideological barriers to mobility. As such, individuals are assumed to move within the system as a result of their own achievements. Modern industrialized societies are considered open. However, this concept of an open system is

an abstraction, or **ideal type**, that falls at the end of a continuum. Thus, an open stratification system will vary in the extent to which an individual can move up the **social mobility** ladder as a result of his or her own achievements. At the same time, the amount of influence an **ascribed status** has will vary according to the level of openness found in a **society**.

Sociological studies of social mobility identify the level of openness, or fluidity, of a social system to guide research into the causal mechanisms of inequalities in class, **race**, and gender. In addition, an understanding of the level of openness of a society is essential for developing an understanding of the dynamics of economic inequality in any social system. The openness of a stratification system will also reflect the available opportunities for mobility for different groups and individuals. This opportunity structure based upon the type of stratification system can partially explain changes in **status** and economic inequalities over time. Consider, for example, the strides that women have made as the social system has become more open and provided increasing opportunities to them in the labor market. In sum, an open society is a descriptive tool that is employed to describe the level of influence that achieved and ascribed statuses have on a given social position. This device is crucial for any exploration and understanding of stratification and inequalities issues.

OPERATIONALISM

Operationalism (sometimes called operationalization) is a process by which variables are defined as measurable items on a **measurement** instrument. To understand **society**, social scientists often need to measure concepts that are not easily defined or that have several dimensions. Concepts such as compassion, **prejudice**, patriotism, and religiosity are abstract and multidimensional and cannot be objectively observed or measured.

Operationalism involves defining these concepts through a process of conceptualization and creating indicator variables to measure the various aspects of the concept. A researcher wishing to study compassion as a variable must first operationalize the concept. Because there is no universally agreed upon definition for this concept, the researcher must carefully consider which elements of the definition are most appropriate for the research study.

After the concept has been defined, the researcher must specify measurable criteria that indicate varying levels of compassion. If the researcher decides that compassion is to be defined as the willingness to help someone who is perceived to be less fortunate, the researcher should ask the subjects of the study a variety of questions that can generate concrete answers. For example, the researcher may include questions that ask how much money the respondent donated to charity in the previous year and how many hours in the previous month were dedicated to volunteer work.

Using operationalism to measure abstract concepts always involves subjective interpretation, though a researcher can increase objectivity by consulting other researchers and previous research materials to determine definitions and indi-

cator variables. Often it is desirable to use previously created definitions and indicators so that new research can fit into the context of existing literature.

OPERATIONALIZATION

Operationalization is the process of operationalizing a concept which means to create a format for empirical **measurement**. In other words, it is a process by which a concept is precisely defined. For example, in order to test the theory that **juvenile delinquency** leads to adult criminal behavior, we must first define exactly what is meant by each concept. The goal is to work toward a level of understanding that will allow empirical measurement of the concepts. What is meant by juvenile delinquency? How will it be measured? Will different dimensions of the severity and the frequency of offences be considered? In order to create an index of juvenile delinquency that ranges from no delinquency to extremely delinquent, all of these factors must be considered. Analyzing all options that surround our understanding of a concept is called conceptualization.

The point at which conceptualization becomes operationalization remains vague. Moving from the former to the latter is the process of moving from theory to measurement. Theory and measurement in the social sciences must always be considered simultaneously. Theoretical concepts are supposed to be rather general: i.e., ''Juvenile delinquency leads to adult criminal behavior.'' But measurement must be precise. A concept has been operationalized when the researcher has precisely defined it and measured it.

ORAL TRADITIONS

Oral traditions are bits of knowledge, **culture**, and religion that are passed on from one generation to another by oral means. Oral traditions can be songs, stories, plays, poems, and a variety of other types of spoken knowledge. In early societies, oral transmission was the only way to circulate knowledge. Teachers, tribal leaders, and poets were the first to circulate vast amounts of oral knowledge to the people in their villages. Within the **family** group, the elders, who were considered to hold a vast amount of knowledge because of their life experience, were held in high esteem because of their ability to teach these oral traditions.

As alphabets and written languages developed, oral knowledge was transcribed into written form. Though early societies began to develop written language, a vast majority of people in these societies still relied on oral traditions. In many societies, a greater part of the population was illiterate. The written word was reserved for monks, stenographers, and the ruling class. People in the working class had no need for the written word, so they still relied on oral tradition. Because of the vast differences in the literacy levels of the people of these societies, oral **communication** and oral traditions were both relied on for quite some time. These ages of oral and written communication coexisting in **society** spanned from 1000 B.C. to the mid–1400s A.D.

Ancient Greek writers and philosophers debated the importance of oral communication and oral traditions (as do today's thinkers). These philosophers believed in the superiority of oral communication over written communication. They speculated about how important oral communication was and they feared that society would get lost in the mire of written communication, losing appreciation for what is important about oral communication. Socrates (470–399 B.C.) believed that conversations and debates should take place as face-to-face interactions. With face-to-face interaction, one is able to clarify points quickly, the interaction is more personal, and the use of body language increases the effectiveness of communication. Face-to-face interaction also provides the opportunity to elicit spontaneous reactions to the materials presented. His style of communication, called the ''Socratic method,'' is still coveted by universities and law schools as a means of transmitting knowledge.

With the invention of the printing press and movable type during the mid–1400s, written communication became more widespread and more accessible. When the first books were printed, however, they were large, expensive, and took months to illustrate and publish. Because of the labor put into the books, only the wealthy aristocrats could afford to buy them. In time, however, printers became more efficient, books became smaller, and the cost of the books dropped enough that they became affordable to people of all classes. As presses and publishing companies spread throughout Europe, written communication became common.

Oral traditions are still important to many cultures determined to maintain their long-established customs and background. Many cultures whose oral traditions have stood the test of time are today feeling the slow and foreseeable extinction of these traditions. In the American information age, the **Internet** maintains a space where written communication can flourish, but oral communication may perish. Many cultures who still use oral traditions have been working on recording them for fear of losing them forever.

ORGANIZATIONAL SOCIOLOGY

Organizational sociology or the sociology of organizations, also known as organization **theory**, is the multidisciplinary study of the **structure** and dynamics of modern **complex organizations**. Modern complex organizations, like business firms, state agencies, political parties, churches, hospitals, and universities, differ fundamentally from other complex social phenomena such as primary groups, kinship systems, communities, and societies. Complex organizations are more likely than these other social systems to be characterized by a formal structure designed to coordinate and control goal-oriented activities based on pre-determined rules, authority relations, and **division of labor**.

The importance of organizational sociology lies in its unique understanding of the rise and predominance of modern complex organizations. While organizations have always been a feature of human societies, the re-organization of society

during the **Industrial Revolution** in the West stimulated scholarly interest in modern complex organizations. The Industrial Revolution fostered the sociology of organizations by expanding of the scope and power of organizations, which resulted when corporate actors gained legal rights formerly guaranteed only individuals.

Although organization theory and the sociology of organizations are almost indistinguishable, organization theory tends to be more diffuse in scope, encompassing basic and **applied research** by economists, public officials, industrial psychologists, and management and administrative scientists, as well as sociologists. The managerial origins of organization theory reflect the predominance of manufacturing in the nineteenth century. Research by Taylor (1911) and Fayol (1919) focused on the science of management in the factory as did later work by Barnard (1938), Roethlisberger and Dickson (1939), Mayo (1945), and Dalton (1959). Early organizational sociology, on the other hand, paralleled the rise of the modern state. Organizational sociology traces its lineage to Weber and Michels. Marx is included in some versions of this genealogy (Mouzelis 1967).

Weber's (trans. 1946 [1924]) study of organizational authority and power and Michels' (1915) depiction of the iron cage of **bureaucracy** are founding works in organizational sociology. Weber conceived of three ideal types of authority that supported bureaucratic power. These types of authority are referred to as rational-legal, traditional, and charismatic. Rational authority rests on belief in the legality of normative rules and the right of those elevated to authority to issue commands based on those rules. Obedience is to the impersonal order of authority established by the scope of a given office. In contrast, traditional authority gains its legitimacy from established belief in the sanctity of immemorial traditions, while charismatic authority rests on devotion to the exceptional sanctity, heroism or exemplary character of a particular individual. Created through rational-legal authority, modern complex organizations have six chief characteristics: (1) jurisdictional areas are clearly separated, (2) the principle of hierarchy guides the structure of the organization, (3) rules govern all official decisions and actions, (4) all official **property** belongs to the organization, (5) officials are personally free and selected for office based on technical qualifications, (6) employment is a way of making a career.

Weber's emphasis on the components of rational-legal organizational structures defines organizations as deliberate, purposive, goal-oriented, legal entities. In research related to this line of thought, the formal characteristics of an organization are of central interest. For example, Taylor and Fayol, and later Simon (1945), pursued rational-model assumptions in order to understand worker productivity, worker and manager motivation, decision-making processes, and authority structures. A related issue is the bifurcation of social structure within organizations. **Organizational structure** contains two components: a formal structure (i.e., guidelines determining those actions, interactions, and behaviors which ought to be or must be performed) and a behavioral system, often referred to as informal structure. While formal structure specifies impersonal roles, **norms**, and rules for interaction, informal structure depends on the personal characteristics and relations of specific individuals.

The **human relations school**, sometimes called the natural systems model (Scott 1998), investigates the disjuncture between formal and informal structures Important management theorists in this area were Barnard, Roethlisberger and Dickson, Mayo, and Dalton. From a human relations' perspective, organizations are not just tools or instruments for achieving desired ends but social systems in their own right. Natural system theorists developed the idea that individual people inhabit positions in organizations. Organizations must consider individual personalities, preferences, unique skills, **intelligence**, prejudices, beliefs, and sentiments. For example, Mayo's famous study of General Electric's Hawthorne plant revealed the discrepancy between purported organizational structure, and individual workers' interactions and productivity.

In each of these models, spanning the early 1900s through the 1940s, the individual organization served as the analytic focus. In the 1940s, organizational sociology differentiated itself from management science by developing a general theory of organizations. By the 1960s, theories based on Parson's (1951) structural-functionalist perspective began to emphasize the organizational environment as a class of organizations facing similar environmental vulnerabilities. This theoretical innovation suggested that all similar social systems, including those in organizations, are mutually interdependent. Organizations are themselves components of a larger system. In March and Simon's (1958) theory of bounded rationality, Lawrence and Lorsch's (1967) contingency theory, Williamson's (1975) transaction cost theory, organizations adapt to the larger system of changing environmental conditions in different ways. In the first example, contrary to expectations that organizations are guided by rational decision-making, it was discovered that organizations settle for acceptable rather than optimal outcomes in a process called satisficing. In the second example, organizations learn to seal off their technical cores in order to manage environmental uncertainties.

Finally, current organizations models, based on work begun in the seventies, are quite varied. These include Hannan and Freeman's (1997) studies of organizational ecology, Pfeffer and Salancik's (1978) resource dependence theory, and, Meyer and Rowan (1977), and DiMaggio and Powell's (1983) theory of organizational institutionalism, called the new institutionalism. Organizational ecology focuses on populations of organizations in order to understand why there are so many different kinds of organizational forms, while institutional theory focuses on understanding why so many organizations mimic one another's organizational forms. Recent advances include reconciling organizational ecology and new institutionalism, **network theory**, and the burgeoning of a new domain called economic sociology.

ORGANIZATIONAL STRUCTURES

Organizational analysis examines the structures within an organization. These structures are the framework within which an **organization** operates and meets its goals. Some examples of organizational structures are departments, work groups, power distributions, levels of authority, and the politics. Some analyses also examine structurally related aspects of an organization such as its **culture**, networks, and communications. Although size and technology affect the type of organization, three characteristics of organizational structures are complexity, formality, and centralization. Complexity refers to the layers of coordination and authority within an organization. After World War II, new technology and high consumer demand supported the emergence of mass production and large complex bureaucratic organizations. While bureaucracies characterize the military and federal government, large **complex organizations** began to permeate many other social structures such as the media, educational system, and state and local governments. In the 1970s many small organizations closed because they were unable to compete in the market against the resources of larger firms, but since the 1990s computer technology has supported the emergence of smaller Internet-based companies who are able to respond quickly to consumer demand for high tech products.

The level of complexity of an organization, expressed in its differentiation, is usually measured by its **division of labor**. In every organization there is a division of labor that determines task or work assignments. Horizontal differentiation reflects how that work is clustered, and ranking tends to be either high or low. For example, in craft-based, highly skilled technical or professional types of work, employees tend to control various aspects of employment, so the organization has a low degree of differentiation. A high degree of horizontal differentiation is found in organizations that are automated and where separate tasks are performed repetitively by workers.

Vertical differentiation refers to the degree of hierarchical ordering in organizational personnel. Many organizations such as IBM or Kraft dominated the market in the 1970s and maintained large hierarchical organizations with rigid decision-making embedded in the management and supervisory positions. In the 1990s many organizational structures were flat, with less distinct levels of authority. Again, because many supervisory tasks are performed now by computers, access to information and international market demands are requiring employees to work cooperatively to respond more quickly to environmental factors.

Spatial location is another characteristic of complexity that refers to where the workers are physically located and the configuration of operational facilities. At one time all workers were housed in one location, but in 2000, work configurations are much more complex. Many companies have multi-national sites and satellite operations as well as more complex **employment** relationships. For example, in telecommuting arrangements the worker can work from a different off-site location such as home and communicate to the office from his/her computer.

Formalization refers to the rigidity of rules and procedures. Hospitals tend to have very explicit rules for handling patients and a number of outlined procedures for emergency decision-making situations. A less formal structure is guided by fewer or less rigid rules and communications that define what workers do. For example, universities agree upon department curricula, but are less rigid in how course information is communicated in the classroom to students.

Centralization refers to how power is structured within an organization. For example, in a **bureaucracy**, decision-making is limited to a few members of the upper echelon. While technology has increased levels of authority for some tasks, others that require technical skills and expertise tend to allow those workers more independence in their decision-making. Decentralization, the process of distributing decision-making to those with technical skills and expertise, expedites the communications process and reduces response rates to the market.

To understand the complexity, formalization, and centralization of an organization means realizing that organizations are dynamic entities that affect individuals who are in the organization and other organizations. Many factors such as the internal politics and exercise of power within an organization affect strategies and objectives. Furthermore, environmental factors, like globalization, new technology, and competitive action, also influence the structures of an organization and must be considered in an analysis.

ORGANIZATIONS

Organizations incorporate many complex networks of social relations and have a framework that shapes patterns of interaction both formally and informally. Formal organizations are based on structured forms of interaction, which usually consist of formal rules, methods of **communication**, functions, and goals. **Max Weber** developed a typology of organizations from ancient China to modern industrial **society**, providing the foundation for the **sociology** of organizations. In particular, Weber was concerned with what he considered to be the most rational form of organization, the **bureaucracy**, and the authority embedded in it. Weber noted that bureaucracies, prior to industrialization, were large and efficient but were guided by the patrimonial **culture** and the ruling aristocracy. For Weber, only in modern society do formal organizations embody purposeful and rational goals to achieve some outcome. Weber argued that the levels of authority formalized within the bureaucracy ensure its ability to achieve goals. He identified six characteristics of a bureaucracy: specialization of duties or responsibilities, hierarchical reporting structures, formal rules, technical competency, an impersonal approach, and formal written communications system.

Karl Marx also examined contemporary bureaucratic organizations, but his focus was on the inequality and power relations embedded in their infrastructures. In his theory of society Marx argued that the organization of labor reflects an historically specific stage of economic development. For example, in hunting and gathering societies the level of subsistence is minimal, and the division of labor is based on task

assignments for survival. In capitalist societies, the organization of labor is shaped by the drive for capital or profit maximization. Therefore, for Marxists, organizations are examined within the context of the economy so their different forms, whether the decentralized structures of internet-driven corporations or bureaucracies, can be analyzed in terms of their contribution to profit.

A multi-disciplinary effort, however, had emerged in the 1940s at Carnegie Institute of Technology (now Carnegie Mellon University) with an emphasis on the systematic examination of management theories. This school of thought conducted analysis under the direction of James March and Carl Simon. In the 1960s, the sociology of organizations emerged as a formal area of study in sociology with Amitai Etzioni and Richard Scott as key U.S. sociologists. In his work, Etzioni identified three types of organizations: normative, coercive and utilitarian. In normative organizations individuals pursue goals because they perceive them to be worthwhile (e.g., swim teams, hospital volunteers). In coercive organizations, individuals such as prisoners or psychiatric patients are forced to join a group. In utilitarian organizations the motivation for involvement is monetary rewards.

Scott defined organizations as collectivities with fixed boundaries, a normative order, a specific ranked order, and systems of communications and incentives. He also argued that there are three perspectives on organizations: rational, natural, and open systems. In the rational system, the organization is goal oriented with formal rational structures. In the natural system perspective, the common goals of members shape the organization, making it more informal. Open systems refer to interdependent **coalitions** whose continuous exchanges are shaped by environmental factors. Since the 1980s, much literature on organizations is conducted by and in conjunction with management research. Organizational analyses examine the structures, the power relations, the culture, the network of relations and change, whereas organizational theory focuses on inter-organizational relations, effectiveness, and environmental factors. Environment refers to those factors outside the boundaries of an organization that could affect its achievement of specific goals.

Organizations must socialize their members regarding rules of operation and train them to perform organizationally dictated behaviors. This socialization does not mean behavior is determined, but that some exchange or motivation to accept the rules and perform certain tasks exists, such as compensation in **corporate organizations** or social gratification in voluntary organizations. While this area of the discipline focuses on formal organizations, informal organizations are usually briefly mentioned as associations where members interact on a less complex, more collegial basis. These organizations often are informal networks within formal organizations that emerge in response to the rigidity and formality of specific structures.

ORGANIZED CRIME

Generally, organized crime refers to an **organization** with a hierarchical structure that engages in ongoing criminal activity.

Activities include but are not limited to extortion and to providing a forum for illegal goods and services, such as alcohol, drugs, gambling, usury, and **prostitution**. Organized crime suggests an ongoing rapport between the public and the lower echelons of the organization. Organized crime is helped by local police who are corrupt and poor and by political machines.

Before the turn of the century organized crime did not exist. It evolved in the city slum areas in ethnic neighborhoods, especially in New York City, Chicago, and New Orleans, among competing gangs. These gangs supplied and controlled illegal goods and services, such as gambling and racketeering. These services were profitable and the intergroup **competition** became fierce. Old World animosities surfaced between many of these ethnic minorities and were fueled by ethnic and religious conflict.

The turn of the century allowed for the consolidation of small businesses, labor unions, and gangs, particularly during prohibition. Then, syndication of these gangs meant incredible economic profits and increased economic and political power. With interstate and international empires, organized crime infiltrated legitimate businesses and segments of the labor movement. The beginning of the crackdown on organized crime happened after the repeal of prohibition when the national resentment at its corruption and brutality changed history.

Syndicated crime uses legitimate business as a front for its activities and employs legal and tax experts who keep the syndicate in operation. The hierarchical structure is composed of a few different factions. The ''flunkies'' are at the bottom and have daily interaction with the public. The upper echelons of syndicated crime include a few individuals who do not seem to be involved in the organization al all. It is hard to keep track of organized crime because no records are kept, transactions are made in cash, and the practice of nepotism ensures that no one is likely to turn the family in to the authorities. Therefore, the leadership remains free from arrest and conviction. In addition organized crime deals with the maintenance and control of intragroup struggles for power. These attempts to monopolize power between groups that occur within the community instill fear in the local populace. Examples of organized crime include: the Mafia of Sicily, the Tongs of China, the Camorra of nineteenth century Naples, and the Cosa Nostra of the United States.

OWEN, ROBERT (1771-1858)
Welsh reformer, industrialist, and socialist

Robert Owen is considered one of the original socialists. His ideas about cooperation and workers' rights laid the foundation for socialist principles and trade unions and influenced thinkers such as **Karl Marx** and Frederick Engels.

Owen was born May 14, 1771 in Newton, Wales as the sixth of seven children. Beginning at age seven, he educated himself and left home at ten to apprentice with a draper. In 1875, Owen arrived in Manchester, England, which was in the throes of industrial development. At this point, Owen made his

way into business, applying his savings and his textile knowledge to start his own factory. At age twenty, Owen managed a textile mill of five hundred workers and was eventually made a partner.

Soon after, Owen met Anne Caroline Dale, whose father owned the mill in New Lanark, Scotland. Owen and Anne married and Owen and his partners were able to purchase the mill, which employed one thousand workers. Owen and Anne moved to New Lanark in 1800, at which time Owen began to put his theories about human character into practice.

Owen's main premise was that humans are not inherently good or bad but are shaped by their environment and heritage. It would, therefore, follow that, in the right environment, anyone would develop a good character and moral values. Owen's contemporaries believed that the poor were lazy and ignorant and that they always would be. Owen believed, however, that the poor were poor because they were unemployed and uneducated—that better housing, food, and clothing would improve the character of the poor. It was this idea that he put into practice at the New Lanark mill.

Owen's changes included reducing workers' hours, improving company housing, and improving sanitary conditions. He often met with difficulties from his partners but in 1813 entered into a satisfactory partnership with a few benevolent Quakers and the Utilitarian **Jeremy Bentham**. These partners did not hold all Owen's views but agreed that conditions should be improved and allowed Owen to focus on the children employed by the mill. He believed that schooling was necessary not to teach facts and figures but to develop children's character so that they would become well-adjusted adults. He set up a school for children that included play, music, and affection rather than abuse. He also prohibited anyone under ten from working and reduced hours for workers under 18. In 1816, he established the Institution for the Formation of Character, which was used as a school during the day and an **adult education** and community center at night.

New Lanark was soon well known throughout Europe as a model community and enjoyed many visitors. Owen hoped to see his success duplicated across England and campaigned for a bill in 1815 that regulated the **employment** of children in the textile industry. His bill, however, found no supporters. Well respected for his work at New Lanark, he was invited to write a proposal to a government committee that addressed manufacturing issues. This *Report to the Committee for the Relief of the Manufacturing Poor* (1817) laid out Owen's plan to place the unemployed into self-sufficient cooperative villages rather than give them government hand-outs. Like the bill regarding child labor, this report did not persuade the committee. Owen continued to develop his plan, realizing that self-government and equality would be necessary for a cooperative settlement to succeed. He took these ideas to the United States in 1824, where he was invited to lecture on his

Lucky Luciano (handcuffed) was one of the most recognized organized U.S. crime figures of the twentieth century *(AP/Wide World Photos, Inc.)*.

model for self-sufficient cooperative communities. While there, he found a dissatisfied community of Rappites in Harmony, Indiana and purchased the land and village. On May 1, 1825, eight hundred people had arrived to join his model society and New Harmony was established. In less than a year, quarrels among its members and break-away communities led to the failure of the community.

In England, however, the working class was gaining ground. Trade unions were legalized in 1824, and laborers became leaders in their own movement. Workers adopted Owen's ideas as an agenda, forming trade communities and artisan societies. These societies empowered workers and gave them a sense of value. Owen's opinion that labor is a source of wealth and that workers have certain rights greatly contributed to the labor movement and the development of a new working class. Owen did not, however understand or promote class struggle, feeling that a transformation to a cooperative, egalitarian society would be peaceful and natural.

Frederick Engels developed Owen's ideas of cooperation and socialism into a new **civilization** based on industry and workers. He agreed that workers could master their existence and need not toil as slaves. Owen also criticized religion and **marriage**, feeling that these institutions had been forced on mankind to keep them ignorant and enslaved. Engels and Karl Marx agreed that religion would have no place in the new society. They saw the move towards a cooperative society as a natural progression from **capitalism**; however, they believed a revolution was necessary. Robert Owen gave workers confidence and presented ideas for a socialist government. Great thinkers of his time and since were influenced by his ideas, and many of them have been put into practice.

P

PAINE, THOMAS (1737-1809)
American politician and philosopher

Born in Thetford, England, Thomas Paine began life as a corsetmaker, his father's trade. He showed an interest in **philosophy** and science as a young man, and this interest led him to become an influential thinker during the American and French Revolutions. Paine worked as both a corsetmaker and an excise officer in England. He was widowed by his first wife and agreed to a formal separation from his second. Shortly after his separation in 1774, he met Benjamin Franklin in London and sailed to Philadelphia with a letter of introduction to Franklin's son-in-law.

In 1775, Paine became editor of *The Pennsylvania Magazine,* writing poems and articles anonymously. When the Revolutionary War broke out, Paine published *Common Sense* in January of 1776, which called for an American republic and was read widely throughout the American colonies. It was followed by a series of letters supporting American independence and defending *Common Sense* that were published under a pseudonym. Paine joined a militia later that year, acting as an *aide-de-camp* and war correspondent. In December of that year, *The American Crisis, Number 1* was printed to encourage American soldiers following numerous defeats and was followed by more than ten installments throughout the war.

While living in England following the war, Paine closely watched the political climates of both Britain and France. In 1791 he published *The Rights of Man,* a defense of the French Revolution and traveled to Paris. There, he called for Louis XVI to be overthrown. The second part of *The Rights of Man* (1792) included a discussion of republican governments and how the **government** can help the poor. When the French monarchy was overthrown later that year, Paine was granted honorary French citizenship and a seat in the National Convention. Well-loved in France, Paine was at this time summoned to stand trial for libel and sedition in England. He was convicted in absentia in December of 1792 and outlawed in England. Almost a year later, Paine was removed from the National Convention and arrested. Paine remained there until James Monroe, the American minister to France, successfully pleaded for Paine's release. While Paine was in prison, *The Age of Reason,* an explanation of Paine's deist beliefs, was published.

Paine was reinstated to the National Convention in 1794 and fought unsuccessfully for universal suffrage until the convention was dissolved in 1795. Paine criticized leaders in the United States, England, and France until he was hardly welcome in any of these countries. The French threatened to deport him, and when he returned to the United States, old friends refused to see him. He died in New York City in 1809. Paine wrote many essays on **democracy**, universal suffrage, and revolution, shaping the unheard of idea of democracy into the freedom y the citizens of so many countries know today.

PANEL STUDY

Panel studies are longitudinal study designs in which the same group is observed over time. They are designed to assess causation and change. For example, a social researcher might want to study the effects of corporal (physical) punishment of children on their adult relationships. Generating a random sample of adult respondents and asking them about their experiences as children and about their current relationships might be problematic because they may have trouble recalling their experiences as children. Instead, it would be more feasible to follow a group of children through to adulthood, administering a **questionnaire**, and/or conducting interviews with them at different intervals through to **adulthood**.

A researcher could begin by generating a random sample of eight year olds, and asking them about their current experiences regarding corporal punishment. Then, these same children could be contacted and administered another questionnaire when they are about 16 and again when they are

PANIC

Panic is an acute fear reaction marked by loss of self control. It often causes non-rational flight and other irrational behavior. Panic is the antithesis of organized group behavior. Panic may commence within a crowd or group in response to an hysterical belief that the group preserves whatever is perceived to be threatening. The panicked reaction reduces typical social interaction and is related to hysteria and contagion. Feelings of panic can also occur on an individual level and may be associated with psychological and neurochemical conditions.

Mob violence, riots, uncontrolled military aggression, social unrest, and rapacity are sometimes characterized by panic. Sociologists characterize the elements that constitute panic and the conditions that contribute to its occurrence. Some sociologists have identified general structural conduciveness, strain, (hysterical) belief, and actual mobilization as precipitating elements to panic. In order for a panic to occur, fear generated by a threat must become a **generalized belief** within the crowd and communicated to all participants. The group is subsequently mobilized for action, which is typically a flight. Researchers have looked for patterns of **leadership**, mobilization, and communication in the pre-panic state to examine development of panic.

Moral panic refers to a period during which many members of a given society become intensely concerned with a specific perceived threat to such a degree that rational analysis is impossible. The persecution of witches undertaken both in Europe and the United States is an example of moral panic, in which little could alter the course of events once the accusation of witchcraft was made.

Thomas Paine *(The Library of Congress)*

about 24 years old. The successive administrations of the questionnaire are referred to as "panels" or "waves" of the study. Once information gathered in each successive wave of the panel study is collected, the researcher can assess change over time and may be able to explain causal links between past experience and current behavior.

Panel studies are valuable for generating explanations in social research; nonetheless, they contain some inherent drawbacks. Panel studies are extremely expensive because of their ongoing study design. Also, the researcher may realize that the way in which a question was asked in the first wave may not have been the best way in which to ask it, but by the time it is discovered, it is too late to make changes. Between different waves of a panel study, some respondents may die, move, or just decide not to participate in another wave, and of course, this problem multiplies with each additional wave of the study. Because of these potential problems, the first wave of a panel study must be relatively large, which is more expensive and time consuming. Longitudinal studies are inherently time consuming because some amount of time must pass between waves. Regardless of the potential drawbacks of their designs, panel studies are becoming more prominent in social research. Their popularity is attributable to the rich **data** and detailed information that is generated.

PARADIGM

A paradigm is a conceptual tool used to differentiate the theoretical perspectives within a discipline. This term derived from the work of Thomas S. Kuhn, a philosopher of science, who argued that a paradigm is in the general sense a framework, or **model**, that guides the scientific process and research. For Kuhn, paradigm shifts occur when several anomalies develop in a theory that cannot be accounted for within the paradigm. At this point, a new paradigm is developed that solves those problems and offers a new theoretical structure through which to pursue an area of scientific research. Within sociology, paradigms are generally rather self-contained, with their own methods and theory that are used to analyze social phenomena. In sum, the paradigm is a framework used to determine what logical model will be chosen or created to specify the relationships among variables to explain why things are the way they are. It is the perspective from which scientists derive generalizations, theories, and laws about their respective topics of study.

Sociology's three major paradigms are described as functionalist, conflict, and symbolic interactionist. The difference between these paradigms lies in what premises are accepted prior to the development of **theory**. The functionalist

paradigm assumes that there is a general societal consensus about important values and **norms** that are important, that **society** is a whole made up of many integrated and interdependent parts, and that a society will seek stability and avoid conflict between these parts. In this view social arrangements are examined through a holistic and subjective approach in terms of their contribution to meeting the objectives specified by the shared **values** and norms. This paradigm originated primarily in the work of Émile Durkheim and more recently was explored in the work of **Robert K. Merton**.

The conflict paradigm directly contradicts the assumptions made by the functionalist paradigm; it assumes that individuals in society belong to competing groups with conflicting values and goals and that subgroups within society are competing for scarce resources. As a result, and conflict is an expected part of society. This tradition stems from the economic works of Hegel and the sociological insights of **Karl Marx** and Frederich Engels.

Last, the symbolic interactionist paradigm assumes that how people act depends upon how they see and evaluate reality. According to this paradigm, people learn to see reality from others and attempt to find the "meaning" of their own behavior and that of others through interpretation. Because people do not always attach the same "meanings" to the same behaviors, conflicts and misunderstandings arise in society. This paradigmatic view asks what meanings individuals derive from behavior, how meaning is shared or conflicting among members of society, and the consequences of this.

PARENTAL ROLES

To understand parental roles, we must first understand what it means to be a parent. Parents can be one of two types, biological or social. A biological parent is one who has donated either an egg or sperm to the creation of a child. Biological parents sometimes never come into contact with the children they have produced. A man who sells his sperm to a fertility clinic may be the biological father of many children, none of whom he will ever see. By the same token, many women give up their children for **adoption** and never come into contact with them again. A social parent is one who has devoted time, effort, discipline, **love**, and care to a child throughout its lifetime. In these cases, step-mothers, adoptive fathers, foster mothers, aunts, cousins, family friends, or any other range of caregivers can care for children as if they were biologically their own. The role of parenting has been viewed by **family** researchers as social rather than biological. There is no ingrained biological inclination toward one's children and no instinctive knowledge or recognition of one's children. With this social aspect of parenting in mind, the roles of parents can be described.

Today roughly half of American children do not live with one or both of their parents. Twenty-four percent of children are raised by single mothers, this number up from only eight percent in 1960. Three and a half percent are raised by single fathers, up from 1.1 percent in 1960. Fifteen percent live with step-families which is a result of a rising **divorce** rate.

Grandparents, as they begin to live longer, are also playing a larger role in raising children. Traditionally it was common for poor and minority children to be raised by grandparents, but in recent years grandparents caring for grandchildren occurs across racial and economic boundaries and is more common with white Americans.

Parents play a significant role in a child's life. A good parent teaches values highlighting success, independence, goal establishment, responsibility, kindness, and education. The family is a child's primary agent of socialization, and parents are the primary source. Through **socialization** children learn language, manners, beliefs and **values**. Parents are held to a high standard when it comes to socializing their children. Parents are expected to successfully socialize each child they bear, however difficult that task may be.

The roles of mothers and fathers today are different from what they were just two generations ago. In the past roles were clearly defined for both parents. Good mothers were to stay at home and be the primary caretakers for the children. Fathers played the role of breadwinner, decision maker, and disciplinarian. Though fathers did not have much contact with the children during the day, they provided for them in an indirect way through money. In the present day, family structure has changed as a result of a higher divorce rate and altered patterns of **employment**. Married women with children are entering the work force in great numbers, and divorced women are caring for children on their own without fathers. From this, the roles of working mother and single mother are being established.

Many sociologists use **role theory** to describe how families interact with one another and how parental roles are maintained. According to this theory, each family member has a defined role. This role comes with obligations, responsibilities, expectations, and privileges. These role responsibilities are defined by **culture** and differs between societies. Mother and father roles begin to change when the structure of the family changes. For example, a single mother not only has to fulfill her "mother" role but also has to execute the "father" role. In another case, when both parents work full time, who the primary caretaker role goes to is questioned. Changes in role expectations and **norms** change can cause role strain which can eventually lead to change in the structure of roles. For instance, dual income married families have redefined their mother and father roles to accommodate their lifestyle. Parental roles are undoubtedly changing in **American society**, and will continue to change. What will emerge from this change is a new cultural ideal of what is expected of parents in their respective roles.

See also Family Roles; Fatherhood; Motherhood

PARETO, VILFREDO (1848-1923)
*French sociologist, political theorist, and
   economist*

The Italian sociologist, political theorist, and economist Vilfredo Pareto (1848–1923) is chiefly known for his influential

theory of ruling elites and for his equally influential theory that political behavior is essentially irrational. Vilfredo Pareto was born in Paris on July 15, 1848. His father, an aristocratic Genoese, had gone into political exile in France about 1835 because he supported the Mazzinian republican movement. He returned to Piedmont in 1855, where he worked as a civil engineer for the government. Vilfredo followed his father's profession after graduating from the Polytechnic Institute at Turin in 1869. He worked as director of the Rome Railway Company until 1874, when he secured an appointment as managing director of an iron-producing company with offices in Florence.

In 1889 Pareto married a Russian girl, Dina Bakunin, resigned his post with the iron company for a consultancy, and for the next three years wrote and spoke against the protectionist policy of the Italian government domestically and its military policies abroad. His reputation as a rebellious activist led to an intimate acquaintance with the economist Maffeo Pantaleoni. This association led to Pareto's interest in pure economics, a field in which he quickly became proficient and well known. His reputation gained him an appointment in 1893 to the prestigious post of professor of **political economy** at Lausanne University.

In 1894 Pareto published his first noted work *Cours d'économie politique,* which evoked a great deal of commentary from other economists. Two years later he inherited a small fortune from an uncle, a windfall which caused him to think of retiring to pursue research. At this point he began to develop the theories for which he is most famous, elitism and irrationalism in politics.

In his own earlier political career Pareto had been an ardent activist in behalf of **democracy** and free trade, as had been his father before him. The reasons for the marked change in his political outlook have been much disputed, ranging from the neo-Freudian analytical account, to the interpretation which stresses certain developments in his own career, to the explanation which maintains that, quite simply, he changed because of the results of his own vast studies. By the time his next book *The Manual of Political Economy* was published in 1906, his ideas on elites and irrationalism were already well developed. The following year he resigned from his chair of political economy at Lausanne to devote all his energies to researching his theories.

Pareto retired to his villa at Celigny, where he lived a solitary existence except for his 18 Angora cats (the villa was named ''Villa Angora'') and his friend Jane Régis, a woman 30 years younger than he who had joined his household in 1901, when his wife left him. In 1907 he began writing his most famous and quite influential work *The Treatise on Sociology;* he completed it in 1912 and published it in 1916. (The work was published in English translation as *The Mind and Society* in 1935 in a four-volume edition.) In 1923 he secured a **divorce** from his wife and married Jane Régis. Later the same year he died.

Pareto's theory of **elitism** is sometimes simplistically explained on the basis of his aristocratic heritage. However, as recent scholarship has shown, throughout his life and in his published works he often expressed extreme distaste with the titled Italian aristocracy, just as he was anti-socialist, anti-government-interventionist, anti-colonialist, anti-militarist, anti-racialist, and ''anti-anti-Semitic.'' Attracted to fascism when it first came to power in Italy, he later opposed it. He is perhaps best described as an iconoclastic individualist.

The Mind and Society is at one and the same time a debunking of Marxism and of the bourgeois state. Pareto's method of investigation is inductive or positivistic, contemptuously rejecting natural law, metaphysics, and deductive reasoning. On the basis of very extensive historical and empirical studies, Pareto maintained that in reality and inevitably the true form of government in any state is never a monarchy, hereditary aristocracy, or democracy but that always all social organizations, including states, are governed by a ruling elite. This ruling elite, which has greater vitality and usefulness than other elites, dominates them until it in turn is overturned by a more powerful elite—Pareto's theory of ''the circulation of elites.'' Political behavior itself, both of the masses and of the elites, is basically emotional and nonrational. The function of reason is to justify past behavior or to show the way to future goals, which are determined not by reason but by emotional wants.

PARK, ROBERT E. (1864-1944)
American sociologist

Robert E. Park (1864–1944) was a pioneer American sociologist who specialized in the dynamics of urban life, **race** relations, and crowd behavior and was largely responsible for standardizing the field of **sociology** as practiced in the United States. Robert Ezra Park was born on February 14, 1864, near the town of Shickshinny, in Luzerne County, Pennsylvania. After the Civil War his father, a veteran of the war, took the family to live in Red Wing, Minnesota, where Park was to spend the first 18 years of his life. There he got to know Norwegian immigrants struggling to build a new life in a new land and he shared in their adventures. He even briefly encountered Jesse James, who asked him directions to the nearest blacksmith shop while fleeing from a bank robbery (1876).

When Park graduated from high school in 1882, his father decided that Robert was ''not the studious type'' and that no further education was necessary. Robert ran away from home, worked on a railroad gang during the summer, earned fifty dollars, and enrolled at the University of Minnesota as a freshman in engineering. Although he had problems studying he passed his freshman courses, and his father relented and offered to finance further studies. Robert entered the University of Michigan, abandoned his interest in engineering, and majored in philosophy. He took philosophy courses with John Dewey, of whom Park said that studying with him was ''an adventure that was taking us beyond the limits of safe and certified knowledge into the realm of the problematical and unknown.'' Park graduated in 1887 with a bachelor's degree and a Phi Beta Kappa key.

Returning to Red Wing briefly, and inspired by Dewey and by a course in Goethe's *Faust* to seek adventure in the

world, Park became a newspaper reporter, first in Minneapolis, then in Detroit (where he was city editor of two papers), Denver, New York, and Chicago. He spent 11 years learning the reporter's craft and in the process "developed an interest in sociological subjects, based on observations of urban life.

Spurred on by his father, by his 1894 marriage to the artist Clara Cahill, and by Dewey, he decided to return to university life because he "was interested in **communication** and **collective behavior** and wanted to know what the universities had to say about it." He received a master's degree in philosophy from Harvard University (1899) and moved his family to Berlin. He enrolled at the Friedrich-Wilhelm University, where he expanded his interests in the newspaper to the broader concerns of human social life, particularly in its unplanned aspects, such as crowds and public gatherings, crazes and mobs. At the university he was exposed to the writing and lectures of the sociologist **Georg Simmel**; indeed, the course that he took from Simmel was the only course in sociology that Park ever had in his entire life. He received his Ph.D. in philosophy from the University of Heidelberg in 1903, having written a thesis titled "Crowds and Publics: A Methodological and Sociological Investigation," regarded today as a classic study of both collective phenomena and **social change**.

Park returned to Harvard in 1903 and spent a year as assistant in philosophy while he completed his thesis. In 1904 he became secretary of the Congo Reform Association, a group organized in England and dedicated to publicizing atrocities perpetrated against Blacks in what was then the Congo Free State. The organization hoped to bring pressure for reform on King Leopold II of Belgium, who was solely responsible for administration of the area. "To fight such iniquity as this [Park wrote] is a great privilege." He wrote a series of articles for the muckraking periodical *Everybody's Magazine,* which generated considerable public outcry leading eventually (1908) to the formal annexation of the Congo by Belgium and the substitution of parliamentary control for personal rule. With this the Congo Reform Association ceased to function.

In 1905, while working with the association, Park felt himself to be "sick and tired of the academic world" and "wanted to get back into the world of men." Introduced to the noted African American teacher and reformer Booker T. Washington, Park was invited to become a publicist for Washington's Tuskegee Institute in Alabama. Sensing that this might be an opportunity both to help the cause of African Americans and to learn about them and about the South, and in the process "get back into the world," Park accepted the offer. Together they toured Europe (1910) comparing and contrasting the plight of Southern African Americans and European laborers and peasants. In that year, too, he helped organize the National Urban League. Park served Washington as confidant, as well as serving as director of public relations of the institute. He assisted Washington in preparation of the latter's *The Man Farthest Down* (1912) and appears as one of its authors. In 1912 Park organized an International Conference on the Negro at Tuskegee.

As the conference opened, Park had decided to leave Tuskegee in order to spend more time with his family. Attending the conference was the sociologist W. I. Thomas who, after a lengthy correspondence, invited Park to join him on the faculty of the Department of Sociology at the University of Chicago, then one of a few departments of sociology in the United States. Park came to Chicago in 1913 and remained there until 1936, well past his formal retirement in 1933. He served as president of the American Sociological **Society** (now American Sociological Association) in 1925. He was a visiting professor at the University of Hawaii from 1931 to 1933; travelled extensively in China, India, South Africa, the Pacific, and Brazil; and in 1936 joined the faculty of Fisk University, Nashville, Tennessee, and taught intermittently as a visiting professor. He died in Nashville a week short of his eightieth birthday, on February 7, 1944.

During his tenure in the Chicago department, both in his writing and in teaching a generation of students who for the most part themselves became influential sociologists, Park virtually single-handedly shepherded sociology from the ranks of a movement to better the world to the status of a science of social life. First, with his younger colleague Ernest W. Burgess, he tried to define sociology in a way that was more than simply arm-chair theorizing about society and its problems. Their *Introduction to the Science of Sociology* (1921, 1924) presents sociology as both "a point of view and a method for investigating the processes by which individuals are inducted into and induced to cooperate in some sort of permanent corporate existence [called] society." Second, Park tried to make sociology a research-oriented field of study by suggesting a strategy for social research and a laboratory—the city—in which this research could be carried out (see his 1915 article "The City: Suggestions for the Investigation of Human Behavior in the Urban Environment"). He coined the term "human ecology" to suggest that one dimension of sociological study. Finally, he argued that the problems of society could not be understood, let alone ameliorated, without a thoroughly documented awareness of the varieties of social processes that give rise to such problems.

Throughout his work one finds a continuing concern with social transformation and change that characterized his doctoral thesis. Additionally, the notion persists that the sociologist is very much like the reporter. But the sociologist's depiction of "the Big News" differs from the reporter's story in that the sociologist has a set of analytical categories in which to place that story, to establish relations between events over the longer term, and to predict as accurately as evidence might permit on the basis of what has happened in the past what might well happen in the future. His approach to sociology as the outcome of human communication raised the Department of Sociology at Chicago to a pre-eminent level and his views still are influential.

Everett C. Hughes, one of Park's distinguished students, said of his mentor: "Park's genius was to arouse a student's interest in a small project and develop it into a large one, stated in universal terms.... He was a tireless teacher. He insisted that **data** gathered for research should not be used for social casework or individual therapy. He tried to understand and guide his students in their efforts to learn and communicate clearly

what they were learning....[His] teaching always gave the sense of something in the making; he said in a handwritten note, 'Science is not knowledge. It is the pursuit of knowledge.''

PARSIMONY

The principle of parsimony states that the best statistical and theoretical models are those consisting of the fewest possible parameters. In the context of statistical and theoretical **sociology**, parsimony is synonymous with simplicity. Thus, although it may be statistically and theoretically possible to explain various social phenomena in a number of ways, the principle of parsimony calls for the simplest of these explanations. The most parsimonious models are those that not only consist of the fewest statistical variables or theoretical propositions, but that also explain as many social phenomena as possible.

Parsimony is, therefore, best understood specifically in the context of two distinct but interrelated principles, economy and unification. First, statistical and theoretical models can be parsimonious in the sense that they exhibit a certain level of economy, which refers to the orderly arrangement of the fewest possible explanatory parameters. Second, such models can be labeled parsimonious in the sense that they exhibit a certain level of unification, or the extent to which a statistical or theoretical **model** reveals the interrelated or unified significance of a variety of social phenomena.

The significance of parsimony in the social sciences derives from its importance within the natural sciences. Many social scientists assert that statistical and theoretical parsimony should be just as consequential in the field of sociology as it is in such fields as chemistry and physics. In this vein, even though it may be possible to adequately explain a phenomenon in a number of different ways, the simplest of explanations (the one with the fewest variables or propositions) should be selected.

PARSONS, TALCOTT (1902-1979)
American sociologist

American sociologist, Talcott Parsons (1902–1979), analyzed the socialization process to show the relationship between personality and social structure. His work led to the development of a pioneering social theory. Talcott Parsons was born on December 13, 1902, in Colorado Springs, Colorado. He graduated from Amherst College in 1924, where he majored in biology, but decided to do graduate work in economics. In 1924–25 he attended the London School of Economics. He earned his doctorate at Heidelberg University in Germany in 1927. While at Heidelberg, he translated Max Weber's *The Protestant Ethic and the Spirit of Capitalism,* which exercised a great influence upon young American sociologists.

Parsons was an instructor in the department of economics at Harvard University from 1927 to 1931. During this period he studied the works of Alfred Marshall, the great classical

theorist and codiscoverer of the principle of marginal utility; Émile Durkheim, the French sociologist; and Vilfredo Pareto, the Italian sociologist. Parsons' *The Structure of Social Action* (1937) fused the theories of Durkheim, Pareto, and Weber into a single new body of **theory** and shows their relationship to Marshall's type of economic theory. Parsons became a full professor of sociology at Harvard in 1944. He held that position until his retirement in 1973.

The pioneering social theory developed by Parsons is abstract and complex. As a frame of reference for his system, he adopted the social action theory and stressed the structural-functional approach as the only way for sociology to achieve systematic theory. He stated that personality formation develops out of action organized around individuals, while action organized around relations of actors leads to a social system which consists of a network of roles. A third system which is indispensable to the personality system and the social system is the cultural system, which constitutes the standards and channels for guiding action. These three systems interpenetrate one another, and Parsons focused on the analysis of the **socialization** process to show the relationship between personality and the social **structure**.

The areas in which Parsons made contributions included the classification of the role of theory in research; the analysis of institutions; the outline of systematic theory in sociology; the voluntaristic theory of action; the analysis of specific structure and roles, kinship, occupations, and professions; and the analysis of certain modern problems of aggression, fascism, and anti-Semitism. He also made significant scholarly and practical contributions in his writings on the academic profession and on racial and intercultural relations. He was elected president of the American Sociological Association in 1949 and served as secretary from 1960 to 1965.

Parsons died of a stroke on May 8, 1979, while giving a series of lectures in Munich, Germany. The obituary in the *New York Times* the next day described Parsons as ''a towering figure in the social sciences,'' who was responsible for ''the education of three generations of sociologists.''

PARTICIPATORY RESEARCH

Participatory research, sometimes called field research, involves a researcher studying a situation or subject in a unique way. Researchers become part of the group they are studying and at the same time collect **data**. This method of research requires that researchers take an active role in the events taking place. In this situation, researchers have a chance to develop a relationship with those who are being observed, gain knowledge of activities, and view firsthand the thought processes and feelings of those within the group. Some examples of groups that are subject to participatory research are gangs, groups of employees, fraternities, politicians, police officers, and children's playgroups. Information gleaned from observing these diverse groups range from curbing crime to determining the social forces on decision-making to finding out how children learn from one another.

There are three types of participatory research, complete participation, complete observation, and participation/

observation. As a complete participant the researcher is completely immersed in the situation being studied. The researcher must conduct all observations while participating in any and all activities. Conversely, the complete observer does not take part in any activities of the group being studied. Instead the researcher is present for and observes all activities. The participant/observer uses a mixture of the two previous methods. The researcher participates in some activities and simply observes at other times.

The complete participant can become part of the group being studied without the group knowing that he is a researcher. This is called covert observation, and at times this method can allow the researcher to obtain data that would not be available if the subjects knew of his/her status. One disadvantage of covert observation is that the role is often difficult to play, questions asked about the meanings of attitudes and actions may arouse suspicion so much is left up to the researcher's interpretation which could result in biased assumptions.

Results from participatory research in general should be used with caution. Findings are not always generalizable to the public. Information that is obtained is often only applicable to the particular group that has been observed. **Bias** is another concern when using this method of research. The complete participant often does not have time to make notes while participating in group activities, and thus important data may be lost or forgotten. There is also a chance that bias can occur during data collection or data interpretation. Participatory research is often utilized when other means of collecting data are not available, or when intensive knowledge of particular groups and interactions are needed. All **research methods** have advantages and disadvantages and there is always a chance of bias. In general, participatory research is a useful tool for gathering data.

Talcott Parsons *(AP/Wide World Photos, Inc.)*

PATERNALISM

The underlying assumption of paternalism is that management, governmental or industrial, has a social responsibility toward citizens or workers. Few might dispute that concept; however, difficulties arise as to degree of responsibility and its administration. Paternalists not only want to keep people from what they regard as sinful behavior, they intend to see to the health, welfare, and safety of those deemed to be in need. In America, this inclination led to such groups as the Woman's Christian Temperance Union (WCTU) to stamp out saloons, to the Anti-Cigarette Movement, and to the Social Hygiene Movement, which after 1900 tried to eradicate **prostitution** and **pornography**.

Early U.S. industrialists promoted the concept of paternalism. In 1813–1914, Francis Cabot Lowell built a textile mill in Lowell, Massachusetts. He also built boardinghouses for his largely female work force. Each house was run by a woman who saw to the "morality" of the workers, not letting them out after 10 p.m., for instance. In the 1860s, George M. Pullman built a factory to manufacture his train "sleeping cars." In addition, he built the town of Pullman (now part of Chica-

go). The buildings of this paternalistic company-owned town, the subject of much discussion at the time, remain largely unchanged today. When Henry Ford set up his automobile company in 1914, he also established what he called a "sociology" department for his employees. Ford's social workers scheduled regular house calls to help avert troubles on the family scene.

Following the 1933 repeal of Prohibition, American industry became less paternalistic, with a general tendency to assume that a community's welfare should be the responsibility of **government**. Paternalism became prevalent again in the 1960s and 1970s, when anti-war protests, counterculture protestors, and flagrant drug use brought guardians of social responsibility and morality back into the limelight. Twentyfirst century thinking argues that the "new paternalism" applies only to instances of common interests, calling paternalistic programs viable options when there is a conflict in **society** between reason and will, as in an addict who wants to quit but cannot or with programs to stop teenage pregnancies.

PATH ANALYSIS

Path analysis is a statistical technique used to model both the direct and mediated effects of one or more independent vari-

ables upon a dependent variable. A path diagram, which visually represents the causal hypothesis, similar to a flow chart, is usually constructed first. Modified linear regression methods are used to quantify each of the model's parameters. The technique was first developed by geneticist Sewel Wright in 1921 and was imported into the social sciences by Otis D. Duncan in the 1960s.

Herbert Simon and Hubert Blalock developed a earlier version of this kind of causal modeling (Simon-Blalock techniques) which employed just one exogenous and two endogenous variables (i.e. X causes Y which in turn causes Z). While this method is effective in adjudicating between some kinds of hypotheses, it is limited by its inability to include more than three variables.

Path analysis overcomes this difficulty, allowing for both multiple independent and intervening variables. Additionally, path analysis allows one to measure the direct impact of the original **independent variable** on the dependent **variable**, controlling for its impact through the intervening variable(s). Path analysis can also be carried out using more advanced models that include both unmeasured variables and feedback loops.

Duncan and Peter Blau's 1967 *The American Occupational Structure,* which explored occupational mobility for white males, provided the first extended treatment of path analysis in the social sciences. They hypothesized that a father's socio-economic **status** affected his son's occupational attainment primarily through its role in influencing the son's level of educational attainment. Using path analysis, Duncan and Blau largely confirmed this finding, discrediting theories that emphasized the direct transmission of privilege and supporting the hypothesis that education plays a central role in stratification.

PATRIARCHY

Patriarchy is the stratification system by which women are subordinated to men. In patriarchal societies, men have more social power than women, and their activities and desires are considered as superior to those of women. While it initially referred to the status of fathers as the rulers of households, patriarchy has come to be used more generally to refer to men's domination of women. A central concept in feminist **sociology**, it is used as a explanation for sexual violence, the gender wage gap, and other situations in which women are marginalized or oppressed.

Simone De Beauvoir was one of the first social theorists to suggest that women's lower status was not due to biological characteristics but rather social organization and, thus, was not inherently "natural" and could be changed. Feminist theorists have argued that the underpinnings of patriarchy lie in men's control of women's bodies, women's economic dependence on men, and socialization that passes on gender stereotypes used to justify patriarchy.

Some theorists have argued that patriarchy serves to subordinate not just women but some men as well. R.W. Con-

nell conceptualized it as a way hegemonic masculinities are privileged over marginalized masculinities, so that men who are stereotypically masculine (i.e. tough, athletic, in control, and/or heterosexual) have more social power than men who are atypically masculine (i.e. empathetic, weak, dominated, and/or homosexual).

PATTERN VARIABLES

American sociologist **Talcott Parsons** identified the systematic character of social **interaction** and built his social **theory** based on the patterns within social systems. Namely, how an actor responds within a social situation is based on a series of **values** and **norms** that can be identified and often predicted. Therefore, social interaction can be defined within the framework of basic choices, or pattern variables. According to Parsons, within any given social situation, the actor makes four particular decisions that determine all social relationships and **structure** any system of interaction.

Particularism versus universalism determines if the actor judges a person using specific criteria (particularism) or general criteria (universalism). Whereas particularism notices the uniqueness of a person, universalism identifies the person in terms of general categories that contain similar people. For example, a mother may be particularistic with a child, seeing her child as different from other children. However, in some cases, she may view her child universally, for example, placing the child in a general group with other children the same age in order to assess school grades or athletic ability.

Performance versus quality, a notion that Parsons inherited from anthropologist Ralph Linton's use of ascription versus achievement, denotes the choice between evaluating a social object based on what it does (performance) or based on some intrinsic value that is independent of what it achieves or what benefits it provides to the actor (quality). Within the business world, roles are assigned primarily based on performance. Within close relationships, roles tend to be based on quality.

Affective involvement versus affective neutrality distinguishes the level of emotional attachment of the actor. Common to spouses, friends, and other intimate relationships, affective interaction engages the actor's emotions. Contrarily, affective neutrality is social interaction devoid of any emotional attachments. For example, doctors are expected to remain neutrally affective toward their patients.

Specificity versus diffuseness refers to the range of activities and roles that a social relationship encompasses. Specificity describes relationships limited to certain role interactions, such as employer-employee or waitress-customer. The relationship may be extremely important, (employer-employee) or relatively inconsequential (waitress-customer). The criterion is the breadth of roles that the interaction entails. Relationships that account for a wide range of roles and activities, involving the totality of the person, are described as diffuse. This would likely describe members of a close-knit **family**.

The terms and categories first employed by Parsons continue to be used within the language of social scientists. How-

ever, Parsons' overarching social theory lost influence in the 1970s after being criticized for being too theoretically based and not amendable to the predominant empirical slant that dominated American **sociology**.

PAVLOV, IVAN PETROVICH (1849-1936)
Russian physiologist

Ivan Pavlov is best known for his studies on the digestive systems which consequently led to the discovery of conditioned reflexes making it possible to study a purely physical reaction to an outside stimulus. His other major fields of study include research on the cardiovascular and nervous systems. I. M. Sechenov and his 1863 book *Reflexes of the Brain* were strong influences in Pavlov's life. Sechenov hypothesized about physical reflexes and their relation to psychic activity. This idea was the foundation upon which Pavlov based his experiments. Dogs were Pavlov's experimental animals, used in his research on the physiology of digestion that earned him a Nobel Prize in 1904. He noticed that when hungry dogs were presented with the thought of food, provoked by sight, sound, or smell, the dogs would salivate and produce gastric secretions, thus producing a physical response to external stimulus or a conditioned reflex. There was, until Pavlov's experiments, no known scientific explanation for this response.

Pavlov began his experiments on what was previously regarded as a psychic phenomenon from a physiological position. His research had a major effect on the world of **psychology** as well. One experiment performed involved ringing a bell when the food was presented to a dog. This elicited the response of salivation or the ''conditioned reflex.'' If the **variable** of food is removed, the bell is still able to elicit salivation. On the contrary, if the bell is rung too many times and the food is not presented to the dog, the animal will stop salivating at the sound of the bell.

Pavlov's father was the village priest, so his schooling began in the field of theology, but due to his love of science, Pavlov decided that theology was not his true calling and in 1870 he began his education in physiology. By 1875, he received his degree of Candidate of Natural Sciences, and by 1879 he completed his studies at the Academy of Medical Surgery where he was awarded his second gold medal and a fellowship which allowed him to continue his studies.

In 1890 Pavlov was appointed a professor of Pharmacology at the Military Medical Academy, and the very next day after his appointment he was asked to organize and head the Department of Physiology at the Institute of Experimental Medicine. Until 1905, Pavlov did the bulk of his research at the Institute of Experimental Medicine. In 1905 the Physiological Laboratory was opened which allowed him to expand his research there, so that by 1917 he had about forty people working with him in the study of conditioned reflexes. In 1912 he was awarded an honorary doctorate from Cambridge University.

He married Seraphima Vasilievna Karchevskaya on May 1, 1881. She was a devoted and loving wife to him, and

Ivan Pavlov *(Corbis Corporation [Bellevue])*

after a miscarriage with her first pregnancy and a sudden death of their son Wirchik, they had three more sons: Vladimir, Victor, Vsevolod and a daughter: Vera. Ivan was never very concerned with finances, so after many bad decisions with the family's money, Seraphima had to handle the financial responsibilities of the family and most other day-to-day issues since he was not adept in handling these matters. They remained together until Ivan's death on February 27, 1936 in Leningrad.

PEACE

Peace is the absence of violence. Following Johan Galtung, theorists discuss two paradigms of peace research: one based in a negative conceptualization of peace and one based in a positive peace conceptualization. A negative peace is an absence of war or other armed conflict, and thus researchers working in this **paradigm** usually only address direct violence. Negative peace is generally achieved through political and military means. On the other hand, positive peace incorporates negative peace but also includes an absence of any type of exploitation, including indirect cultural or structural violence. Positive peace is created through a combination of political, military, economic and cultural institutions and actions.

Theorists using a positive peace definition, including Galtung and R.J. Rummel, whose conception of a ''just peace'' is similar to Galtung's ''positive peace'', tend to be social critics and assume a more activist stance. These social scientists write about exploitation that continues, even in the absence of war. For instance, sociologists, including Walden Bello, have explored and criticized the United States for its ongoing military and economic imperialism in the Asian Pacific. Others, like Frederick Buttel, look at more indirect exploitation resulting in **poverty** and starvation in developing countries while wealthy countries continue to prosper. Within this paradigm, injustice is the main threat to peace; therefore, any form of injustice must be remedied for a positive peace to be attained.

Social scientists working in a negative peace paradigm focus on empirical predictors and mitigators of armed conflict.

U.S. President Jimmy Carter signs the Mideast Peace Treaty along with Egyptian President Anwar Sadat (left) and Israeli Prime Minister Menachem Begin (right) *(Corbis Corporation [Bellevue]).*

Two main lines of research explore the relationships between **democracy** and peace and that between trade and peace. The democratic peace proposition suggests that democratic states do not wage war with each other. Political scientists Zeev Maoz and Bruce Russett have examined **data** on international conflicts to determine which types of dyads tend not to engage in battle. They have found that **norms** of cooperation dominate when democracies deal with each other, but that confrontation is much more likely in mixed democratic and nondemocratic dyads.

Likewise, researchers have found that dyadic trading partners are much more unlikely to engage in armed conflict than pairs that do not have such a cooperative relationship. Solomon Polachek has theorized that most states cannot produce all the goods and services necessary to maximize their population's standard of living, and therefore trade is a rational means of gaining additional goods and services. Because conflict interferes with trade, the rational state will avoid conflict in favor of trade.

PEARSON, KARL (1857-1936)
English mathematician and professor

Karl Pearson is considered the founder of the science of statistics. In developing ways to analyze and represent scientific observations, he laid the groundwork for the development of the field of statistics in the twentieth century.

Pearson was born in London, England, on March 27, 1857, to William Pearson, a lawyer, and Fanny Smith. At the age of nine, Karl attended the University College School but was forced to withdraw at sixteen because of poor health. After a year of private tutoring, he went to Cambridge, where the distinguished King's College mathematician E. J. Routh met with him each day at 7 a.m. to study papers on advanced topics in applied mathematics. In 1875, he was awarded a scholarship to King's College, where he studied mathematics, philosophy, religion, and literature. At that time, students at King's College were required to attend divinity lectures. Pearson announced that he would not attend the lectures and threatened to leave the college; the requirement was dropped. Attendance at chapel services was also required, but Pearson sought and was granted an exception to the requirement. He later attended chapel services, explaining that it was not the services themselves, but the compulsory attendance to which he objected. He graduated with honors in mathematics in 1879.

After graduation, Pearson traveled in Germany and became interested in German history, religion and folklore. He studied law in London, but returned to Germany several times during the 1880s. He lectured and published articles on Martin Luther, **Baruch Spinoza**, and the Reformation in Germany, and wrote essays and poetry on philosophy, art, science, and religion. Becoming interested in **socialism**, he lectured on **Karl Marx** on Sundays in the Soho district clubs of London. During this period, Pearson edited a book on elasticity as it applies to physical theories and taught mathematics, filling in for professors at Cambridge. In 1884, at age 27, Pearson became the Goldsmid Professor of Applied Mathematics and Mechanics at University College in London.

In 1885, Pearson became interested in the role of women in society. He gave lectures on what was then called "the woman question," advocating the scientific study of questions on sex difference and gender. He married Maria Sharpe in 1890. They had three children, Egon, Sigrid, and Helga. Maria died in 1928, and Pearson married Margaret V. Child, a colleague at University College, the following year.

Pearson was greatly influenced by **Francis Galton** and his 1889 work on heredity, *Natural Inheritance*. Pearson saw that there often may be a connection, or **correlation**, between two events or situations. By making use of the broader concept of correlation, Pearson believed that mathematicians could discover new knowledge in biology and heredity.

A young professor of zoology, W. F. R. Weldon, asked Pearson for help on statistics regarding Darwin's theory of natural selection. From their association came many years of productive research devoted to the development and application of **statistical methods** for the study of problems of heredity and evolution. Pearson became the Gresham College Professor of Geometry in 1891. His lectures for two courses there became the basis for a book *The Grammar of Science* in which he presented his view of the nature, function, and methods of science. He dealt with statistical problems by means of graphs and diagrams and illustrated the concepts with examples from nature and the social sciences. In later lectures, he discussed **probability** and chance, using games such as coin tossing, roulette, and lotteries as examples. He described frequency distributions such as the **normal distribution** (sometimes called the bell curve because its graph resembles the shape of a bell), skewed distributions (for which the graphed design is not symmetrical), and compound distributions (which might result from a mixture of the two).

Pearson introduced the concept of the "standard as a measure of the variance within a population or sample. The standard deviation statistic refers to the average distance from the **mean** score for any score within the data set, and therefore

suggests the average amount of variance to be found within the group for that **variable**. Pearson also formulated a method, known as the chi-square, of measuring the likelihood that an observed relation is in fact due to chance, and used this method to determine the significance of the statistical difference between groups. He also developed the theory of correlation and the concept of **regression**, used to predict the research results. His correlation, also known as the Pearson *r*, is a measure of the strength of the relationship between variables and is his best-known contribution to the field of statistics.

Between 1893 and 1901 Pearson published 35 papers in the *Proceedings* and the *Philosophical Transactions* of the Royal Society, developing new statistical methods to deal with **data** from a wide range of sources. This work formed the basis for much of the later development of the field of statistics. Pearson became the Galton Professor of **Eugenics** in 1911, and headed a new department of applied statistics. He retired in 1933 at age 77, and received an honorary degree from the University of London in 1934. Pearson died on April 27, 1936, in Coldharbour, Surrey.

Pearson produced more than three hundred published works in his lifetime. His research focused on statistical methods in the study of heredity and evolution but dealt with a range of topics, including albinism in people and animals, alcoholism, mental deficiency, tuberculosis, mental illness, and anatomical comparisons in humans and other primates, as well as astronomy, meteorology, stresses in dam construction, inherited traits in poppies, and variance in sparrows' eggs. Pearson was described by G. U. Yule as a poet, essayist, historian, philosopher, and statistician, whose interests seemed limited only by the chance encounters of life. Colleagues remarked on his boundless energy and enthusiasm. Although some saw him as domineering and slow to admit errors, others praised him as an inspiring lecturer and noted his care in acknowledging the contributions of the members of his lab group. For Pearson, scientists were heroes. The walls of his laboratory contained quotations from Plato, Blaise Pascal, Huxley and others, including these words from Roger Bacon: ''He who knows not Mathematics cannot know any other Science, and what is more cannot discover his own Ignorance or find its proper Remedies.''

Peer Group

Strictly speaking, a peer **group** is a collectivity consisting of members who share a common characteristic or are considered equals. However, in sociology the definition has generally come to describe those of a similar age and often goes further to specify adolescent or teen groups whose members are bound by youth **culture**. The majority of peer group formations during this age occurs at school. Such peer groups play an invaluable **role** in the secondary socialization of youth because relationships are formed that are not hierarchically constructed. In addition, peer groups serve as an important means of **socialization** because, as opposed to the family, participation necessitates an active interest in inclusiveness. Peer groups are also important during this stage because they are a voluntary association, allowing greater freedom of choice than adolescents have previously experienced. This freedom of choice becomes more and more true as a person ages. In childhood, peer groups are largely a function of propinquity (geographic closeness); as a child grows into **adolescence** and young **adulthood**, however, peer groups become defined by more specific commonalties, such as activities, interests, symbols, **values**, and styles of dress.

Peer groups share common characteristics with other subcultures, such as the fact that they have their own **norms** and sanctions against deviant behavior. However, what often distinguishes youth peer groups from other subcultures is their high degree of solidarity and a normative system that rejects those of the adult world. This normative system reaches its climax during the teenage years, when peer groups serve as a much stronger socializing agent than families do.

Penology

Penology, or penal science, from the Latin *poena,* meaning pain or suffering, is the study of repressing criminal activity in **society**. Modern penology dates from 1764 and a pamphlet by Cesare Beccaria entitled *Crimes and Punishments.* A 26-year-old lawyer in Milan, Italy, with no experience in criminal law, Beccaria were translated his ideas into several languages, including the first American edition published in 1777. He argued that government policy should seek the greatest good for the greatest number. Any punishment beyond that which achieved the proper purposes of security and order was tyranny. His was a remarkable advance in criminological thought which lashed out against the barbaric punishment practices of the day and became known as the classical school.

Following the classical school, neoclassicism appeared after the French Revolution (1789) and proclaimed natural law, liberty, and legality as the guides for the criminal **justice** system in Europe. Different degrees of legal and moral responsibility concerning crimes were recognized, such as those involving children, the insane or unusual circumstances in which crimes are committed. Next came the so-called positive school in the late nineteenth century, which said that inherited characteristics doom criminals to their acts and, therefore, criminals cannot be held responsible. This position implied that society must protect itself against such people but not inflict punishment upon them.

Penology has always included the policy of inflicting punishment for wrongdoing. It may, however, as in the present accepted sense of the term, also include such measures as education or medical treatment aimed at rehabilitating offenders. This science attempts to delineate the bases for punishment and society's motives behind it, to study penal laws throughout history, and to look at social consequences of punishments inflicted by a system.

In the twentieth and twenty-first centuries, penology often involves psychologists or psychiatrists and incorporates mental studies of the criminal into the diagnosis. The emphasis is on research into what causes **crime** and how society can best protect itself while trying to save or reform criminals.

PERSONALITY AND SOCIAL STRUCTURE

The focus of personality and social **structure** is on the effects of culture, macro-social processes, and social structure on various dimensions of individual functioning. Research includes, but is not limited to, **socialization** processes, elements of cultural influence, and effects of social structural characteristics like social class and occupational characteristics on aspects of conceptions of the self, psychological functioning and cognition, aspirations, attitudes, and meanings.

Personality and social structure is a movement which has its roots in social psychology. The primary concern of this movement is to find a middle ground between the overly individualistic, psychological view of the world and the highly structural, sociological conception. Articles by James House and Melvin Kohn in the late 1970s and early 1980s implored social psychologists to return to a research basis not controlled by the ''structure versus agency'' debate. Researchers and theorists working in personality and social structure focus on the areas in which human personality and social structures intersect and on the outcomes of the intersection.

A prime example of personality and social structure research is the elaborate body of research credited to Kohn and his colleagues on aspects of work. Kohn's work has identified the primary structural aspects of work that have significant effects on psychological aspects of the workers including complexity of the task being done on the job, the degree of self-direction held by the worker, the closeness with which the worker is supervised, the amount of routine in the work, organizational position of the worker, extrinsic risks and rewards and additional job pressures. In each of these occupational situations workers have a degree of agency and the ability to make individual choices to control their activities, although in some cases the ability to choose may be limited to occupational choice. However, structural imperatives affecting the lives of the individual both on the job and away from work exist. In this way Kohn's work indicates the goal of personality and social structure research, to locate the interaction of psychological functioning and social patterns and to make known the processes which are involved in this interaction. Other prominent work in the area of personality and social structure includes Alex Inkeles on **culture**, Sheldon Stryker on **identity**, Ralph Turner on self-concept and roles, Morris Rosenberg on self-esteem, and Glen Elder on socialization over the **life course**.

Although personality and social structure is a relatively recent movement in sociological and social psychological research, the argument has been made that many theories, ideas, and research typically identified as sociological often have strong elements of personality and social structure involved. Any work in which the structures, processes, and cultural elements of society enact some influence on individual functioning is an example of personality and social structure research.

PERSONALITY THEORIES

Personality refers to the relatively distinct and consistent psychological functioning of an individual, such as thinking, feel-ing, and behaving. By studying the combination of cognitive, affective, and behavioral components of an individual's personality, researchers form theories of personality. A wide diversity of personality theories, offering unique and sometimes conflicting paradigms, floods the field of study. Each, however, attempts to answer the three fundamental questions of structure, process, and development: What is personality? In what ways does personality affect behavior? How is personality formed? Based on similarities in approach to these issues, personality theories can be categorized into five main classes, as psychoanalytical, humanistic, behavioristic, social-cognitive, and as trait theories.

Although interest in an individual's psychological functioning dates back centuries to the Greek philosophers, the psychoanalytical approach is the oldest form of the modern personality study. **Sigmund Freud** developed this controversial understanding of personality as the dynamic interplay between opposing instinctual and social influences. The mind, according to Freud, consists of three distinct systems: unconscious (**id**), preconscious (ego), and conscious (**superego**). The id is driven by instinct, the superego responds to social forces and acts to repress the id, and the **ego** remains in constant flux between the two. Because the psyche exists in the midst of constant tension between the id and superego, it develops defense mechanisms, such as repression and **rationalization**, to maintain self-integration and self-identity.

Others, including Alfred Adler and Carl Jung, built on Freud's psychodynamic approach to personality. Although Adler, Jung, and other neo-Freudian thinkers disagreed with Freud and each other in many areas, developed different approaches, and emphasized unique aspects of personality, they still maintained the basic paradigm set out by Freud: personality is a dynamic relationship between complex systems that act on each other, fueled by basic instinctual drives over which the individual has little or no control. Psychoanalytical study tends to focus on explaining neurosis and tracking personality development through various stages from childhood to **adulthood**.

Unlike psychodynamic theories that focus on the unconscious urges that drive the psyche, humanistic theories emphasize the individual's innate desire to achieve self-realization. Whereas the psychodynamic identifies the abnormal human psyche, the humanistic **theory** addresses the normal. Humanistic theorist Carl Rogers believed that ''each person has an inherent tendency to actualize unique potential.'' Reaching this potential is a deliberate act by the individual who gains a clear concept of self through a constant process of interaction with oneself and others. According to Rogers, those who do not progress toward self-actualization are often held back by their tendency to sacrifice their own wisdom and self-understanding for the advice of others. Other theorists that developed approaches to personality that stress the unique and central place of human potential include Abraham Maslow and Rollo May. Both psychoanalytical and humanistic theories have received criticism from more scientifically-minded theorists who contend that these approaches tend to be unsystematic and operate without any quantitative controls.

The behaviorist theory was developed primarily by B. F. Skinner, who stated: ''Personality is acquired and main-

tained through the use of positive and negative reinforcers.'' Unlike many of his contemporaries, Skinner rejected the notion of personality as a phenomenological event. Rather, he held that the internal functions of the mind are not relevant to scientific study; behavior shapes the entire individual, including, though not exclusively, the personality. Positive behavior, which receives positive reinforcement, causes the individual to alter patterns of operation, just as negative behavior, which receives negative reinforcement, also initiates change. As behavior changes, so follows personality. Much more adaptable to a scientific method of study, behaviorism was welcomed by those desiring a more quantitative approach to personality research; however, critics denied the theoretical assumption that the human psyche could be ultimately reduced to observable behavior alone.

The social-cognitive paradigms emphasize interaction between the individual and events. Reality is a subjective experience, dependent on the perceptions of the individual and therefore constructed by an individual's understanding of the external world. George A. Kelly undertook an extreme cognitive approach, claiming that ''all our interpretations of the universe are subject to revision.'' Postulating that the primary determination of behavior rests on the way in which an individual anticipates and interprets events, Kelly created a series of personal constructs to describe how people view reality. His premise was that an individual will develop a life-pattern for anticipating and interpreting the world that will determine behavior and personality. Although Kelly occupies an extreme cognitive position, others, such as Julian Rotter, developed social learning approaches within the social-cognitive school of thought.

Along with social-cognitive approaches, trait theories became the influential personality paradigms of the latter twentieth century. Trait theories assume that personality traits can be quantitatively measured on a scale much in the same way that physical traits, such as height and weight, can be measured. Although they maintain differing opinions on the identification of significant personality characteristics, trait theorists agree on the assumption that personality can be compartmentalized and classified based on a standardized set of traits. Introduced by Gordon W. Allport in the 1930s, trait theory offered a compromise between the extremes of behavioristic and psychoanalytical approaches. According to the theory, traits are observed in behavior but are not reducible to it; they are the underlying triggers that generate specific behavior. Trait theory lends itself to mass **data** collection through questionnaires. Responses are correlated to a quantitative **measurement** scale, which in turn produces a personality profile.

Although there is general consensus that approximately half of an individual's personality can be attributed to heredity, a spirited debate continues over the unknown components of personality. For example, the Five Factor Model (FFM), which emerged during the 1990s, is a development of trait theory in which five characteristics are identified as fundamental dimensions of personality: extraversion-introversion, emotional stability-neuroticism, agreeableness, conscientiousness, and openness or **culture**. Not remarkable as a new approach, the

FFM proponents claim unprecedented consensus among personality theorists, noting that there is widespread agreement that extraversion-introversion and emotional stability-neuroticism are critical concepts of personality study. Even with some agreement pending, the vast sea of personality theories continues to expand as new paradigms and variants of existing paradigms are introduced for scrutiny.

PERSUASION

Persuasion is a form of social **influence** in which an attempt is made to alter the beliefs or attitudes of an individual regarding some issue, person, or situation. Persuasion is accomplished through the use of information, discussion, or argument regarding the topic of interest. However, persuasion does not involve issuing demands or making threats or promises to the target to accomplish the change.

Persuasion typically occurs in one of two ways: through the dissemination of information with the intention of causing critical evaluation or interpretation or the information being given or through the use of peripheral cues such as the source of the information of the characteristics of the situation in question. Generally the former strategy is used when the target of the persuasion has knowledge of the topic, has already settled on an opinion, or has expressed interest in gaining more information, while the latter is effective when the target is uninformed about the topic in question and might be swayed by the words of a celebrity endorser or trustworthy source.

To better evaluate persuasion across various situations, the communicator-persuasion paradigm has been established to highlight how aspects in the communication of a persuasive message interact with one another to influence the level of effectiveness the message will have. The three components encapsulated by this **paradigm** are the source, the message, and the target, each of which will have a resulting effect on the effectiveness of the persuasive message.

The source of the message is vital when speaking to either an informed or uninformed audience. To the uninformed target, the source of the message should ideally be both physically attractive and trustworthy (such is the case with celebrity endorsers for various products). In this scenario the message is coming from a pleasing source, and the information provided can be seen as accurate since the target believes the source can be trusted even if the source has no obvious knowledge about the topic being discussed. To the informed source, attractiveness and trust remain important factors, although attractiveness may be somewhat downgraded here due to the increased focus on information. Expertise in the area is added as a third key aspect of persuasion. When the target already has knowledge the source must be able to demonstrate possession of knowledge for the source to be seen as an effective dispenser of information.

How persuasive the appeal of the message also depends on the target. If the target is knowledgeable a two-sided message (in which multiple sides of an argument are presented to the audience) is used. In doing this the informed target is

shown why the new information is better than the previous way of thought and potentially the appeal of the message is increased. If the target is uninformed a one-sided message (presenting only the persuasive message) is used so that the audience remains uninformed regarding options other than the one being presented. Also, the amount which the persuasive message is discrepant from the currently accepted information must be considered. While the new message must be somewhat discrepant for the possibility for change to exist, there is a critical level above which messages will be considered too discrepant and therefore ignored. For example, people will be more open to a message that those living in **poverty** are victims of bad luck as opposed to a message that those living in poverty are victims of a prejudiced, society who has not given them ample opportunity to succeed. Finally, the message will typically be based on either an emotional or factual appeal. An emotional appeal typically attempts to arouse a drive or desire within the target that will stimulate a change while a factual appeal will likely attempt to resolve or meet a desire already felt by the audience by providing an answer or solution to their concerns.

As is highlighted throughout this paradigm the target is a key factor in deciding the style of message and presentation of materials. The amount of knowledge and involvement with the topic will affect the presentation and strategies used in persuasion of the target. Also the effectiveness of the message may be reduced if the target has been forewarned about the message and has had time to formulate a counter-argument.

PETTY, SIR WILLIAM (1623-1687)
English political economist

Sir William Petty was a sailor, physician, professor, inventor, surveyor, and member of Parliament, as well as a political economist and statistician. He was born in Romsey, Hampshire, England, on May 26, 1623. His father was a clothier, and the family had little money for the boy's education. The details of his early years are sketchy, but Petty was apparently schooled to some degree in the small village. In his writings he remembered his greatest joy as a youth was watching the different artisans—carpenters, watchmaker, blacksmiths—at their work. By the time he was 12 years old, he felt that he could have acquitted himself at any of those trades, so well did he know them by watching. But, instead, at the age of 15 he managed to get aboard a sea vessel heading for Caen in France. Once there, he educated himself in French, Latin, Greek, and mathematics, and also spent time in the navy. About the age of 18, he went to Paris to study anatomy and to read with Thomas Hobbes.

In 1648, Petty went to Oxford, where he taught anatomy to young students. He also taught music at Gresham College in London and was a physician to the British army in Ireland in 1652. Three years later, he completed a survey of Irish lands that had been forfeited in 1641. His next assignment was as commissioner of the distribution of land grants to soldiers, and then as secretary to Henry Cromwell (1657), the lord deputy of Ireland.

Charles II, known as the Merry Monarch, king of England from 1660 to 1685, appointed Petty to be surveyor general of Ireland and during this period, Petty opened quarries, fisheries, and mines and set up ironworks in the country. A sailor at heart, Petty also designed a two-hulled ship in 1662. It sailed well until it was lost during a storm in the Irish Sea some years later.

Petty built a wooden model of his ship, wrote a treastise on ship building, and gave them to the Royal Society of London for the Promotion of Natural Knowledge, of which he was a founder. It is the oldest scientific society in England and one of the oldest in Europe. The Royal Society was granted a charter in 1662 by Charles II, newly restored to the throne, but it received little attention from the crown after that. The idea was for interested members to meet periodically to discuss scientific subjects. This stimulus of free expression would result in international fame for the society by the eighteenth century. Besides Petty, other distinguished members have included inventor Robert Hooke, architect Christopher Wren, physicist Isaac Newton, and astronomer Edmond Halley.

Petty was an originator of political arithmetic, which he called the art of reasoning with figures about things that relate to **government**. He presented *Essays in Political Arithmetick and Political Survey or Anatomy of Ireland* in 1672. In it were calculations and population estimates about social income. Later works *Verbum Sapienti*(1665) and *Quantulumcunque Concerning Money* further developed his ideas on money **theory** and policy.

However, Petty's most significant work is *Treatise of Taxes and Contributions* (1662). In it, he argued that the price of a product depends upon the labor necessary for its production. He favored giving free rein to the natural forces of individual self-interest, but he disagreed with many other liberals by declaring a high level of employment to be a duty of the state.

Sir William Petty, who married Elizabeth Fenton, daughter of an Irish knight, in 1667, died in his home on Piccadilly Street in London, on December 16, 1687. The cause of death was gangrene of the foot, exacerbated by gout. He is buried near his parents in Romsey. Some of his manuscripts can be found in the British Museum and their scope gives an idea of his varied interests and talents, such as expenses of a state and the branches of its revenues, people and religions of the world, growth of London, observations on the births, burials, and marriages of London, Paris, and Dublin, and the commercial world and the great emporium. A collection of his printed works is also housed at Oxford in the library of Brasenose College.

PHENOMENOLOGY

The phenomenological method in **sociology** developed as a response to criticisms and weaknesses found in the positivistic approach to the study of social life. According to the phenomenological sociologist humans create the social world and the social structures that make up that world. Positivistic sociolo-

gy assumes that humans find meaning and agency only through external social forces. The phenomenology school of thought, however, uniquely addresses this positivist assumption arguing instead that human beings create social life through interactions and meaning patterns, which they conceptualize as the life world. For the phenomenologist, agency, or the ability of humans to create social life, is of utmost importance and should be recognized as an integral part of any social science. As such, these social thinkers argue that human beings actively construct social reality. This feature of social life is causally related to the relationship between human actions' dependence upon shared understanding and shared behavioral meanings.

Alfred Schutz, the sociological theorist most frequently associated with phenomenological sociology, was the leading contributor to phenomenology as a sociological **paradigm**. Schutz utilized phenomenological principles to begin assessing much of Max Weber's theoretical insights in the early 1930s. Schutz developed a set of criticisms of Weber's analyses that focused on the ability of humans to create meaning and impute meaning when they reflected upon behaviors they had engaged in, including habitual behaviors.

Contemporary theorists, **Peter Berger** and Thomas Luckmann, have also presented a theoretical **model** of **society** through a phenomenological paradigmatic view. According to Berger and Luckmann, human beings construct social life by objectifying the subjective. In this way, individuals allow the subjective to create **structure** amid social life, producing patterns of social action for individuals in society and, therefore, creating a sense of normalcy to social actions and the larger social life. Thus, **legitimacy** is given to social actions, institutions, and meanings such that they become objectified and real. This objectification allows for the **socialization** of new members in society, therefore, structure is given to society and interactions occur that are meaningful.

The phenomenological school of sociology emphasizes the mechanisms by which reality is constructed, interpreted, and reinterpreted as an ongoing process. Thus, realities depend on the meanings attached to the interactions, situations, and structures granted through the interactions that occur in society by its members. Furthermore, in the phenomenological view, structures, meanings, and the like only exist as realities, or entities, based upon the social and historical processes that have created them and allowed them to be passed on to other members. In essence, phenomenology is an abstraction of awareness concerning the existence of phenomena, sentiments, behaviors, and other social mechanisms.

Phenomenologists tend to oppose the acceptance of unobservable social things developed through speculation. This school of thought tends to justify cognition and action with reference to the ability to sense it through use of the five senses of taste, sight, sound, touch, and smell. In addition, all natural, cultural, and ideal objects of conscious life can be known and studied. Thus, phenomenology is the study of consciousness from the first-person perspective where subjective experience is fundamental to any understanding. Furthermore, assumptions, preconceived notions, and causal ideas are left out of a phenomenological inquiry.

Plato *(The Library of Congress).*

PHILOSOPHY

The term "philosophy" refers to systems of beliefs or ideas about the universe and humankind's place in it. Philosophy as a discipline of thought addresses innumerable questions about the nature of knowledge, understanding, logic, **language**, reality, and **causality**. Philosophical thought attempts to formulate beliefs and claims of knowledge about the world and human experience. Through critical, rational thinking, philosophers attempt to develop systematically a theory of existence (metaphysics), a theory of knowledge (**epistemology**), and a theory of value (ethics).

In *Philosophic Inquiry* (1968), authors Lewis White Beck and Robert L. Holmes offered five common traits that characterize philosophy. First, philosophy requires an inquiring attitude. Unlike learning about facts, dates, and events, philosophical study involves an examination of the perplexing issues of human experience and knowledge and addresses the complexities not necessarily apparent to the casual observer. Second, philosophy is an outgrowth of ordinary reflection. People struggle to understand the meaning of life and one's place in the world. The philosopher approaches these questions systematically, clarifying meanings and analyzing language that defines meaning. As Henry D. Aiken suggested in *Reason and Conduct* (1962), the difference between the ordinary thinker and the philosopher is "not so much a difference in method as a difference in the thoroughness and sensitivity with which it is applied."

The critical role of questions is the third trait of philosophy. All ideas from scientific theories to religious convictions are based on certain assumptions that are accepted as starting points. Philosophy addresses these underlying beliefs to decipher their meaning, impact, and plausibility. For example, if given the question ''Is it just to act in this manner?'', the philosopher begins by examining what is being assumed in the questioner's definition of justice. Fourth, philosophical questions are speculative. Although in recent times, under the influence of science, philosophers have spent increasing time on the critique of logic and the analysis of language, one of the long-standing traditions of philosophical study is speculation. According to Beck and Holmes, the questions asked ''by philosophers have pushed past the established limits of knowledge, speculating about what might lie beyond. By the very nature of such questions they were not capable, at the time they were asked or perhaps in principle, of conclusive verification in experience.'' The last trait of philosophical inquiry concerns the relationship of philosophical questions to decisions about **values**. The goal of philosophy is not facts, but wisdom. Whereas science attempts to provide value-free explanations, philosophy by its very nature ascribes meaning and values to its propositions on the nature of language, truth, and knowledge.

The scope of philosophy is broad, and its study includes many other disciplines such as science, religion, and politics. Over time, these focus areas have often evolved into specialized fields such as the philosophy of religion, the philosophy of law, the philosophy of art, and so on. Still, philosophical study can be divided into three areas: metaphysics, epistemology, and ethics.

Metaphysics, which addresses the none too narrow topic of the general nature of the world, can be divided into ontology (the study of the nature of reality) and cosmology (the study of the structure of the universe, such as time and space). Study is conducted through a number of procedures, including self-contradictions, appearances, and abstractions. Using purely rational arguments, self-contradiction arrives at conclusions by showing that the denial of a statement results in contradictory statements, thus proving the inherent truth of the proposition. In addition, philosophical arguments based on appearance often address that which lies behind the appearance. Plato's theory of Forms suggests that objective universals exist in a world of forms outside the realm of time and space. This explains our ability to recognize similar objects in a state of flux; therefore, in a most simple example, existing along with this large, blue chair and that small, brown chair is the universal Chair that holds the essence of ''chair-ness.'' Metaphysics also delves into the study of abstract relations such as properties, classes, numbers, and propositions.

Epistemology seeks the definition of knowledge by investigating its possibilities, structure, and limits. Whereas metaphysics asks ''what is reality?'', epistemology takes one step back to question the very ability to possess knowledge of reality. Epistemology asks ''what is knowledge?'' Epistemological arguments can be divided into two parts. First, Leibniz defined the first division as the distinction between truths of

reason and truths of **fact**. Not dependent upon the senses for proof, truths of reason are known *a priori*, that is, by pure reason alone. Truths of fact, or *a posteriori* propositions, are based on experience and provable by sensory observation. The second division is between knowledge that is inferred and knowledge that is acquired directly. The age-old problem is how to verify what we experience, what we infer from the experience, and what the true nature of these experiences and inferences is. Because our perceptions are fallible, what we know by inference is fallible. If what we know by inference is questionable, how do we prove that any of our perceptions is correct? In fact, how do we know the world itself is not simply a misperception? How then do we solve the problem of knowledge as experienced or perceived? This is the commission of epistemology.

Ethics, or philosophy of value, is the third major branch of philosophy. It is the rational and critical assessment of human action. Unlike behavior, which can be explained devoid of intent, action denotes an interest in human choice. Thus, in the study of ethics, the ethicist examines the factual basis of behavior and imposes upon it a theory of value including choice, desirability, consequences, and alternatives that give the behavior ethical meaning. Influenced by **Christianity**, the field has been dominated by the study of moral action. The primary question addressed by ethics is whether moral convictions have any validity and, if so, what is the nature of these convictions. Two schools of thought exist: intuitionists and utilitarians. Intuitionists operate on the assumptions that moral traits are *sui generis,* or independent of any actor and that all actions are intrinsically right or wrong. Utilitarians reject the universality of the intuitionists, suggesting that the moral nature of action is determined by outcome, or at least the outcome a rational person could expect to occur.

Because of the complexity of the issues addressed by philosophy and its basic characteristic of pushing the limits of understanding, philosophy is a discipline of conflicting theories. Philosophical debate is, indeed, a creative force in the development of new theories and the rejection of old theories. Because of its involved history, philosophy can only be truly studied and conceptualized by delving into its history and traditions, and the political, social, and historical events that have given rise to the issues and problems that it seeks to address.

PIAGET, JEAN (1896-1980)
Swiss psychologist

The Swiss psychologist and educator Jean Piaget (1896–1980) is famous for his **learning theories** based on identifiable stages in the development of children's **intelligence**. Jean Piaget was born on August 9, 1896, in Neuchâtel, Switzerland, the son of a historian. When he was 11, his notes on a rare part-albino sparrow were published, the first of hundreds of articles and over fifty books. His help in classifying Neuchâtel's natural-history museum collection stimulated his study of mollusks (shellfish). One article, written when he was 15, led to a job offer at Geneva's natural-history museum; he declined in order

to continue his education. At Neuchâtel University he finished natural-science studies in 1916 and earned the doctoral degree for research on mollusks in 1918.

Piaget's godfather introduced him to **philosophy**. Biology (the study of life) was thus merged with **epistemology** (the study of knowledge), both basic to his later learning theories. Work in two psychological laboratories in Zurich introduced him to **psychoanalysis**. In Paris at the Sorbonne he studied abnormal **psychology**, logic, and epistemology, and in 1920 with Théodore Simon in the Binet Laboratory he developed standardized reasoning tests. Piaget thought that these quantitative tests were too rigid and saw that children's incorrect answers better revealed their qualitative thinking at various stages of development. This led to the question that he would spend the rest of his life studying: How do children learn?

After 1921 Piaget was successively director of research, assistant director, and co-director at the Jean Jacques Rousseau Institute, later part of Geneva University, where he was professor of the history of scientific thought (1929–1939). He also taught at universities in Paris, Lausanne, and Neuchâtel; was chairman of the International Bureau of Education; and was a Swiss delegate to UNESCO (United Nations Economic and Scientific Committee). In 1955 he founded the Center for Genetic Epistemology in Geneva with funds from the Rockefeller Foundation and in 1956 he founded and became director of the Institute for Educational Science in Geneva.

In studying children, particularly his own, Piaget found four stages of mental growth. These are a sensory-motor stage, from birth to age 2, when mental structures concentrate on concrete objects; a pre-operational stage, from age 2 to 7, when they learn symbols in **language**, fantasy, play, and dreams; a concrete operational stage, from age 7 to 11, when they master classification, relationships, numbers, and ways of reasoning about them; and a formal operational stage, from age 11, when they begin to master independent thought and other people's thinking.

Piaget believed that children's concepts through at least the first three stages differ from those of adults and are based on actively exploring the environment rather than on language understanding. During these stages children learn naturally without punishment or reward. Piaget saw nature (heredity) and nurture (environment) as related and reciprocal, with neither absolute. He found children's notions about nature neither inherited nor learned but *constructs* of their mental structures and experiences. Mental growth takes place by *integration,* or learning higher ideas by assimilating lower-level ideas, and by *substitution,* or replacing initial explanations of an occurrence or idea with a more reasonable explanation. Children learn in stages in an upward spiral of understanding, with the same problems attacked and resolved more completely at each higher level.

Harvard psychologist Jerome Bruner and others introduced Piaget's ideas to the United States circa 1956, after which the translations of his books into English began. The post-Sputnik (1957) goal of American education, to teach children how to think, evoked further interest in Piaget's ideas. His definable stages of when children's concepts change and ma-

ture, derived from experiments with children, are currently favored over the hitherto dominant stimulus-response theory of behaviorist psychologists, who have studied animal learning. Piaget's theories developed over years as refinements and further explanations and experiments were performed, but these refinements did not alter his basic beliefs or theories.

Piaget received honorary degrees from Oxford and Harvard universities and made many impressive guest appearances at conferences concerning childhood development and learning. He remained an elusive figure, though, preferring to avoid the spotlight. A quieter life allowed him to further develop his theories.

Piaget kept himself to a strict personal schedule that filled his entire day. He awoke every morning at four and wrote at least four publishable pages before teaching classes or attending meetings. After lunch he would take walks and ponder on his interests. "I always like to think on a problem before reading about it," he said. He read extensively in the evening before retiring to bed. Every summer he vacationed in the Alpine Mountains of Europe and wrote extensively.

Piaget died on September 17, 1980, in Geneva, Switzerland and was remembered by the *New York Times* as the man whose theories were "as liberating and revolutionary as Sigmund Freud's earlier insights into the stages of human emotional life. Many have hailed him as one of the country's most creative scientific thinkers."

PIE CHART

A pie chart is a type of graph that is used to display a variable's distribution in terms of the frequencies or percentages of cases that fall within each category of the **variable**. Pie charts are circular (or pie-shaped), and divided into portions or slices representing each variable category. Each portion of the pie contains the total frequency or percentage of cases in a sample or population falling into that particular value of the variable. Pie charts are an effective, precise, and comprehensible means of visually representing **data**.

Pie charts are suitable for displaying distributions of variables that are discrete (whose units are not able to be subdivided) and either nominal or ordinal with respect to their level of **measurement**. Pie charts are thus well suited for displaying categorical data, whose categories do not overlap. To ensure the ease of comprehending the content of a pie chart, these charts are often reserved for displaying the distributions of variables having four or fewer categories or values.

In constructing a pie chart, the size of each portion or slice of the pie graph is proportional to the size of the category being represented. Therefore, the higher the percentage of cases within a given category, the larger the slice is. Because of this relationship between the size of the category and the size of the pie segment, pie charts more commonly display percentages, which facilitate the division of the pie into proportionate segments. The total percentage of all segments should equal one hundred percent.

Because pie charts are used to illustrate differences in the percentages of cases falling within each category of a vari-

Types of families
Composition of families, March 1998

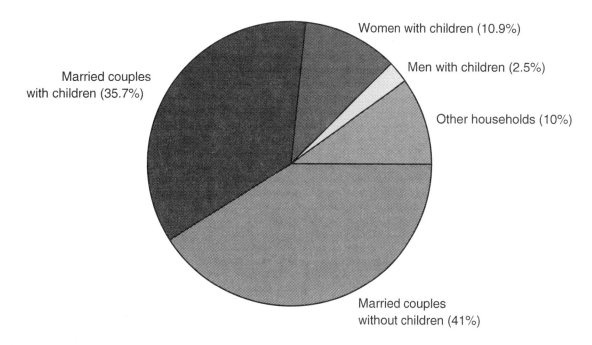

Women with children (10.9%)

Men with children (2.5%)

Married couples with children (35.7%)

Other households (10%)

Married couples without children (41%)

Source: U.S. Census Bureau

A pie chart is a type of circular graph that is used to display a variable's distribution in terms of the frequencies or percentages of cases that fall within each category of the variable. (© *Data Copyrighted by Source. © Graphics Copyrighted by Public Agenda 2000. No reproduction/distribution without permission.*)

able, they are effective tools in showing contrasts between the sizes of different groups or categories within a variable's distribution. Given this utility, pie charts often appear in social science journals; in addition, their use has trickled down into lay materials, such as newspapers.

Pie graphs should include a title which identifies the variable whose distribution is being displayed. The title should also include the source of the data, the total number of cases in the distribution, and if applicable, the year in which the data were collected. Each slice or segment of the pie should be clearly labeled in terms of the category the segment represents, as well as the percentage of cases contained within the segment. These conventions improve the comprehensibility of the chart.

PILOT STUDY

A pilot study is a preliminary study conducted on a small scale that tests the procedures, instruments, and feasibility of a larger project. Its purpose is to identify potential problems that may jeopardize the implementation of, or results generated by, a larger research project. Identifying problems first saves money and time in the long run.

For example, in a project in which a team of social researchers investigated employee theft of patients' belongings in **nursing homes**, researchers included an employees' self-report survey. Prior to disseminating the survey instrument to forty nursing homes across the country, the research team decided to conduct a pilot study to test the survey instrument. Paying respondents ten dollars each, they assembled a small group of nursing home employees from one local nursing home for an afternoon to complete copies of the survey and then to discuss their experiences. The researchers carefully selected participants so that every occupation within the nursing home environment was represented, as were various ages and races of the staff.

After the respondents completed the survey, the session was opened for discussion. Researchers discovered that a few of our questions were unclear to the respondents. They also received a valuable suggestion to ask respondents whether they had ever seen or suspected fellow employees of theft. This information gathered in the larger study proved to be valuable because it may have compensated for inhibitions about self-incrimination. Had the researchers chosen not to conduct the pilot study in the nursing home project, some results generated from the larger project might not have been very useful, and valuable information would have been missed.

Often, especially for telephone **surveys**, pilot studies are conducted by generating a short list of randomly generated telephone numbers in order to contact a small sample of respondents. Then, following the administration of the survey, questions are usually asked about the survey itself. There are many ways in which to conduct pilot studies, but they are always beneficial to the success of a project.

PLURALISM

The term pluralism refers to many individuals or diverse groups within a single **society**. Ethnic pluralism occurs when diverse racial and ethnic groups exist in society each keeping its own **culture** and **identity**. The United States is an example of a pluralist society. However, the United States was once known as a ''melting pot''. This image suggests diverse immigrants blended when they came to the United States, assimilating their new American culture. During the 1960s Civil Rights Movement people began to assert the equal value of difference and the importance of maintaining native ways. The ideal became a mixture of different races, ethnicities, languages, and cultures coexisting peacefully.

Pluralism in religion and politics refers to tolerance within a society for different religions and political parties. Freedom of religion allows U.S. citizens to practice their beliefs without fear of legal reprisal or infringement, so long as the religion does not violate state or federal laws. In the political arena, the pluralist **model** allows interest groups to exert influence. This model assumes that competition between groups creates a certain balance in government. No single group can hold all the power. A few examples of interest groups are the National Rifle Association (NRA), Mothers Against Drunk Driving (MADD), or the **National Organization for Women (NOW)**. These groups mobilize certain sectors of the public and use that support to promote their interests.

POLITICAL CORRECTNESS

Political correctness arose in the United States as a distinctive form of **discourse** specifically intended to counter the historically oppressive character of the English language. The movement toward politically correct speech entailed the efforts of those who sought to challenge dominant interpretations of social reality, which have been traditionally based upon Eurocentric ideas and modes of interaction. In this context, political correctness involves the social construction of more inclusive patterns of speech designed to give voice to the existences and experiences of historically marginalized groups of people.

Social scientists have traced the origins of politically correct speech to the feminist movements of the 1960s. During this politically tumultuous era, many women began to publicly object to the widespread **ideology** that women were in various ways inferior to men. In their efforts to challenge this sexist ideology, numerous feminist communities worked toward the development of non-sexist forms of language. These initial attempts to capsize male-centered discourse, replacing it with patterns of speech less oppressive to women and more inclusive of women's experiences, grew to have an enormous impact upon the pursuit of equality among other oppressed groups as well.

Toward the end of the 1960s and throughout the 1970s the movement toward political correctness in American discourse branched out from the feminist community, similarly giving voice to the existences and experiences of racial and ethnic minorities; gays, lesbians, and bisexuals; elderly people; and people with physical **disabilities**. Politically correct speech thus moved beyond the construction of non-sexist patterns of speech, to include the development of non-racist, non-heterosexist, non-ageist, and non-ableist discourse as well. In these contexts, one of the primary goals of politically correct speech involved an effort to counter the white male power structure of American society. Another important objective of this movement aimed toward revealing the diversity and the value of ideas and experiences among non-dominant Americans.

More recently, however, the term political correctness has taken on a negative connotation. Various groups of conservative and even liberal Americans have interpreted the movement toward politically correct discourse as an attack upon the right to free speech. As a result, the term politically correct is frequently employed as a pejorative label attached to individuals and groups advocating discursive sensitivity to diverse populations. Consequently, because recent criticisms of politically correct speech have become so prevalent, the original intentions of political correctness have been severely obscured.

POLITICAL CULTURE

Political **culture**, the area of intersection between political sociology and **sociology** of culture, refers to collective meanings and symbols attached to politics and political life. The study of political culture as a distinct subject began in the post-World War II period and was originally influenced by **functionalism**. Early concerns in political culture had to do with norms and **values** conducive to **democracy**. One of the classic early studies in the area is Almond and Verba's (1963) study of political culture in five nations that explored attitudes and beliefs to see if they were impediments or preconditions to democratic development. Seymor Martin Lipset's *Political Man* dealt with North American values of achievement and equalitarianism as foundations for democracy.

In recent years, with new conceptions of culture, sociologists have asked about the symbols and meanings attached to political life, political practice, and in particular democracy and civic life. One important influence was that of Jürgen Habermas, whose concept of the public sphere describes democratic deliberation as a potentially emancipatory activity and refers to those spaces of rational deliberation where citizens debate common problems. Margaret Somers, Michael Schudson, Nina Eliasoph, and others have asked a number of questions about public spheres in civic life. Scholars as Robert

Bellah, head of the team of authors that published *Habits of the Heart* in 1989, explored the culture and civic life in the United States and concluded that an individually-oriented culture was eroding the bases for collective life and civic engagement. In a similar vein, Robert Putnam argued that Americans are becoming more self-centered, and community life has ceased to be vital. Other scholars, like Paul Lichterman, argued based on studies of civic groups that the culture of self-improvement that Bellah and his colleagues decried can serve the function of civic engagement.

POLITICAL ECONOMY

Political economy can be approached from two different but similar disciplinary frameworks, the sociological, the economic, or a synthesis of the two. Political economy initially emerged as an area within the social sciences and eventually developed into a sub-field of economics. The concept of political economy grew out of seventeenth century study and explication of European shifts from feudal or pre-capitalist **society** to capitalist and eventually industrialized and highly complex organized economic structures which culminated during the eighteenth and nineteenth centuries. One of the most important figures in the study of political economy and capitalist **structure**, **Adam Smith** remarked that **capitalism** worked as an "invisible hand" in the market, a hand which operates as an autonomous manifestation of capitalist enterprise.

Political economy in economics uses a specific form of analysis to understand the structure of capital, business, and, the production of capital itself. Whereas **sociology** attempts to understand how the results of capital and business production influence the construction of a class divided society. In the United States many scholars have debated about exactly how many classes actually exist, but in general most agree that there are at least three, an upper, middle, and working class (or low-income) structure that separates individuals and groups by economic earnings and **status**.

Many studies of political economy within sociology attempt to focus on class as a macro-level phenomenon that creates wealth as well as poverty in both a domestic and international context. One area of growth from political economy has been World-Systems **theory** based primarily on the work of Immanuel Wallerstein who explored the ways in which class and political economy represent key variables in understanding the development of society.

Many of the debates about political economy in recent years have centered on the intersectionality of class or political economy with other sociological fields such as **race**, gender, and sexuality. These debates often focus on the origins of political economy and the scholarship of **Karl Marx** and Friedrich Engels, perhaps the first scholars to comparatively and comprehensively analyze both capitalism and **communism** as forms of political and economic development and governance. However, many scholars of both **feminism** and critical race studies argue that political economy alone cannot explain the development of society and that Marx and Engels are only useful to a certain degree as neither integrated race or gender into his most fundamental studies.

There has been a turn in the discipline of sociology toward academic work that attempts to make a greater synthesis of variables from theories of political economy, class, race, gender, and sexuality to more comprehensively study society and the behavior of individuals, groups, and organizations. In light of the many newly industrialized countries (i.e., Brazil and Korea) there has been a growth geographically for areas to study in the field political economy. However, while the study of political economy continues to expand in terms of areas and themes to examine, there remain essential principles in the study of class and economics that make oversimplification and reduction of the field impossible.

POLITICAL ORGANIZATION

Political organization is best defined by first explaining its two constituent terms separately. In **sociology**, the word "organization" is defined as a more or less stable pattern of social relationships based on shared social roles, **norms**, meanings, and/or goals. The more formal the organization, the more stable, clearly defined, and/or explicit the social relationships. Politics refers to those social processes and structures through which power is created, organized, distributed and employed. Hence, political organization may be defined broadly as those more or less stable patterns of social relationships through which power is created, organized, distributed, and employed. Thus defined, political organization refers to a wide variety of social structures, prominently including states, parties, and other political associations, and these organizations are of interest to many sociologists.

Perhaps the most prominent form of political organization of interest to sociologists is the state, due primarily to its sheer size, complexity and influence, especially in the modern, industrialized world. Max Weber defined the state as "a human **community** that successfully claims the monopoly of the legitimate use of physical force within a given territory." According to Ralph Miliband, the state is composed of five elements: **government**, administration, military and police, the judiciary, and parliamentary assemblies. As with other forms of political organization, sociologists are most commonly interested in the formation, growth, and decline of states, the relative condition and form of their power, as well as their relations with other parts of society.

After the state, political parties are probably the most prominent form of political organization in modern, democratic societies. Parties may be defined as organizations of people more or less committed to advancing the same political issues and goals, saliently including the election and/or appointment of their candidates to government office. Parties emerged as major political actors in the nineteenth century and have tended to grow in importance with the expansion of **democracy**, universal suffrage, and the political participation of more and more citizens. However, over the last several decades, parties in the United States and elsewhere have been declining. Growing proportions of citizens associate with and participate less and less in political parties due in part to the growth of televised campaigning at the expense of grassroots, face-to-face party organizing.

Over at least the last three decades, there has been growing interest in other, non-party forms of political organization, including social movements and interest groups. **Social movements** are generally a less structured, stable and permanent form of political organization than parties, and they engage their members in less conventional forms of political participation, such as protest demonstrations, consumer boycotts, civil disobedience and political street theater. Recent and more prominent examples of social movements include the anti-war, environmental, women's rights, and gay rights movements. Interest groups typically engage their members in more focused issue campaigns and may seek to influence government policy or elections but do not run their own candidates as parties do. The category of interest groups encompasses a wide array of political organizations, from strictly local, small issue groups to prominent national associations like the Teamsters, the National Rifle Association, and the Christian Coalition.

A growing body of research shows a marked trend in the United Stated, starting in the 1950s, toward a decline in many face-to-face political organizations of ordinary citizens, especially including labor unions and political parties. Simultaneously, researchers have documented an explosion in national ''checkbook membership'' interest groups run by professionals who solicit the money rather than the time and face-to-face participation of their members. The growing professionalization of political organization and the simultaneous decline in face-to-face participation by ordinary citizens have become a growing concern to many sociologists who study the condition of democracy and ''civil society,'' that broad sphere of voluntary and often collective citizen activity separate from the state. Political theorists, from Aristotle to Alexis de Tocqueville to Jürgen Habermas, have long argued that the voluntary, face-to-face political organization of citizens in a democracy is essential to socializing individuals to become alert, public-spirited citizens, and to curbing the power of a potentially despotic state.

POLITICAL PARTY SYSTEMS

Political party systems are those systems in which there is more than one political entity or party. Political parties are a crucial component of democratic and democratically-influenced political systems. They are organizations representing different groups of people in a **society** that facilitate the spread of ideologies and nominate candidates for an election.

There are different types of political party systems, ranging from multi-party to single-party systems. Multi-party systems can have two primary parties that are fairly equal in strength and influence (like the United States); a multiplicity of parties of differing strengths and sizes that form coalitions (like France or Great Britain); or a multiplicity of parties with one being dominant (like many African countries). The things that affect the kind of party system in a county are: its stage in industrialization and development; historical forces; and the social and cultural characteristics of the country.

Political parties can be defined descriptively (office seeking) or normatively (policy seeking). In descriptive terms,

Sen. Albert Gore at the 1992 convention of the Democratic Party—one of two political parties that are fairly equal in strength and influence in the United States *(Corbis Corporation [Bellevue]).*

according to **Max Weber**, political parties are made up of elites and exist to gain power for them. They will ignore the desires and needs of their constituency if it serves their goal of gaining power. The goal of the elites (and thus of the political party) is to gain enough power to rule the state or **government**, if only for a short period. Normatively, political parties are considered representative or educational entities. They are more concerned with following through with the needs and desires of their constituencies.

According to Klaus von Beyme in *Political Parties in Western Democracies* there are three major theories to explain the evolution of political parties: historical crisis situations, modernization, and institutional theories. Crisis theorists claim that it is important developments in history that ultimately lead to one form of government or another. According to the **Social Science Research Council**, there are five kinds of crises: crisis of national **identity**; **legitimacy** of the state; level of political participation; level of distribution of resources; and state integration into society. These theorists claim that it is the sequence in which and extent to which these crises are solved that will affect and determine the evolution of the political system.

Modernization theorists follow the lead of structural functionalists and believe that a certain level of modernization is necessary for political parties to emerge and evolve. This modernization includes efficient and growing transportation and **communication** systems, a middle class, a complex market economy, a public education system, **secularization**, and **urbanization**. In contrast, institutional theorists claim that political parties emerge as a result of the functioning of the representative bodies present in a society (i.e., they emerge out of tension and conflict between different groups). Their emergence is also affected by voting laws and participation.

The most well-respected and influential theory of political party systems is a combination of all three of these theo-

ries—a comparative-historical theory put forth by Seymour Lipset and Stein Rokkan. They claim that the current systems in the Western countries emerged during and after World War I, resulting from mass mobilization and industrialization.

Political sociologists have primarily studied the organizational characteristics of political parties and the institutional components of the systems in which they exist. Areas of interest include: distribution of power between and within the parties and among different constituent groups in the same party and in different parties; the **socioeconomic status** and history of politicians, supporters, and people in interest groups; and the ideas supported or rejected by certain political parties.

In contrast, political scientists focus to a great extent on the role of political parties in society and whether they are open or closed systems. Open systems are pluralist and considered more liberal. They are systems in which interest groups and parties compete for the right to represent certain constituencies that supposedly leads to shared power between many entities. This concept has been critiqued as naïve the groups that dominate the political realm also dominate the economic realm, leading to conflicts of interest that affect national and international policies. Closed systems are those in which certain parties are established and new parties are not able to emerge.

Researchers have identified several things that can affect the strength of a political party system: social cleavages (behavioral, ideological, or positional) and party loyalty. If the cleavages in a society are too deep, it will have repercussions in the political parties, and cause either strict polarization or confusion as to which party to follow.

POLITICAL SCIENCE

Broadly defined, political science is the study of power and the allocation of power in political systems. In assessing power structures, political scientists study components within the political body ranging in scope from individual political behavior to international relations. Often manifested as the study of **government** institutions and policy-making bodies, political science examines how and why political systems originate, develop, and govern in a specific manner. Although political **philosophy** can be traced back to Plato and Aristotle, the modern study of politics, using scientific principles, made its appearance in the United States during the **Industrial Revolution**. Since that time, political science has grown into a diverse field with numerous ideologies, methodologies, and areas of study.

Prior to the Industrial Revolution, the study of politics had depended on a classical ethical philosophy as the basis for knowledge. However, by the middle of the nineteenth century, political scientists, fascinated with the rapidly changing technology and subsequent changes in **society**, began to study existing political structures. Presupposing that some systems of governance, namely democratic, were superior to others, political scientists assumed the task of studying various institutions to determine which would best sustain these superior democratic **values**. The new approach, termed the ''institutional''

period, helped pave the way for political science to emerge as a distinct academic discipline by the end of the nineteenth century.

Political science, as an academic discipline, originated at Columbia University in 1856 when Francis Lieber arrived from Germany to become the first professor of political science. Soon after, through the work of John W. Burgess, Columbia began offering a graduate studies program in the field. By the turn of the century, most major academic institutions had developed political science departments, and in 1903, the American Political Science Association (APSA) was formed. Interdisciplinary conflict arose quickly as the historicolegal approach of institutionalism came under attack. Critics bemoaned the limited scope, calling it conservative, biased, and filled with untested assumptions. The conflict, which could be found in similar forms in all the social sciences at the time, came to a halt with the tragedy of World War II. Following the war, Charles Merriam, who had been an early proponent of a scientific approach to political studies as reflected in his 1925 *New Aspects of Politics*, influenced numerous graduate students and faculty at the University of Chicago, who ultimately carried the new methodology of **behaviorism** across the nation.

In rejecting institutionalism, the behavioralists focused on developing ways to incorporate scientific methods, increase the scope of study, introduce the use of **theory**, omit value statements, and emphasize the analysis of individual political behavior over institutional functioning. This quantitative approach dominated political science from the 1950s until the present day. Based on the crises of the Vietnam War and Watergate, behaviorism did come under fire in the 1970s by political scientists who called for a postbehavior approach that would acknowledge the social scientist's duty to participate in the making of policy decisions. Claiming that behavioralism ignored real-life responsibility in the name of science, postbehaviorists called for an integration of values in political study. The result was a significant growth in the area of policy studies.

The APSA originally delineated the study of political science into six major fields: (1) political theory or political philosophy, (2) comparative government, (3) public administration, (4) constitutional law, (5) international relations, and (6) American national government. However, as academic departments grew, the number of fields and subfields expanded exponentially. By the 1980s, the APSA list totaled 27 areas of teaching and research. With this fragmentation, little consensus exists among scholars about the primary objectives of political study. The most basic conflict concerns what should be studied and why. Whereas some political scientists believe the field should be restricted to the legal and constitutional functions of the government, others opt for a broader vision that includes important social factors, such as **voting behavior** and political parties, which directly affect the government. Still others voice the concerns of the postbehaviorist plea for making and critiquing public policy.

In *Rules and Conflict: An Introduction to Political Life and its Study* (1981), A. Lee Brown, Jr., suggests organizing

the area of inquiry into three basic subfields: spatially identified, activity-based, and theoretical. Spatially identified subfields are characterized by the focus on a particular geographical area. The major areas of inquiry within this subfield are comparative government, comparative politics, area study, and international relations. Whereas comparative government study looks at governmental institutions, comparative politics keys on political processes. Usually, comparative government scholars limit their focus to one or two governmental institutions and are not necessarily truly comparative in method. On the other hand, comparative politics uses such methods as linguistic and statistical analysis to comment on the **correlation** and difference between differing political processes. Area studies are characterized by the specialization of a particular, and often large, geographical area such as the Middle East or Western Europe. Dissimilar to area studies, which deals with political happenings within an area, international relations deals with political happenings between countries.

Activity-based subfields have grown rapidly over the last two decades. The main areas are public policy studies, political **psychology**, political parties and interest groups, and public law. Public policy studies, which merges public administration concerns with political science methodology, concentrates on the administration and implementation of the **rules** of public life. Whereas political psychologists aim at obtaining an understanding of political behavior at the individual level through the study of voting behavior and **public opinion**, students of political parties and interest groups concentrate on political activity on the **group** level. Expanding into the previously untouched areas of study, public law, previously known as constitutional law, addresses an array of issues involved in legal activity, influences, and outcome.

Finally, theoretical political studies can be divided into numerous camps of scholars who employ different theoretical constructs to explain political behavior. Theories tend to be either prescriptive or descriptive. Prescriptive theories offer suggestions based on moral philosophy, and descriptive theories attempt to give an unbiased, scientific description of politics. The subfield can be further divided based on the level of study. Macro theorists seek an explanation of the entire political process. Karl Marx's *Communist Manifesto* is an example of an overarching theory of the political and social development. Although macro-theory was often used, it has been replaced in popularity by micro theory, which attempts to explain the political action of individuals. Falling between the macro and micro levels are midrange theories, which deal with smaller units of study such as political parties, legislatures, and interest groups.

Obviously, political science is a complex and diverse field. The subfields as distinguished by Brown are helpful for sorting through the many areas of study, but the list is not an exhaustive one. As the availability of information continues to increase and the world grows into a complex myriad of political relationships, political scientists have a seemingly inexhaustible resource of research possibilities. Using different theories and methods, political scholars continue to address the questions of political behavior from the individual to the international level.

POLITICAL SOCIOLOGY

Political **sociology** refers to the branch of sociology concerned with the distribution of power in **society**. Whereas political scientists generally focus on political institutions and processes, political sociologists do not *a priori* assume that institutions themselves hold causal primacy. Rather, for political sociologists, political institutions may represent the interests and influences of powerful groups in society who reproduce their own power through them. Political sociologists take as their object of study collective processes and institutions that reflect the social bases of power in Society. Their concerns include the study of political processes, regime types, **social movements**, political behavior and attitudes, the state, revolutions, political **culture**, and the individual experience of politics.

Political sociology began in the World War II period and was influenced by the writings of **Max Weber** and, to a lesser extent, **Karl Marx**. One of the first important debates in political sociology concerned the nature of North American **democracy**. In his book *Who Rules* (1963), Robert Dahl, who studied political processes in New Haven in the 1950s, espoused the view that democracy in North America represented the organized interests of plural pressure groups. C. Wright Mills, who in 1957 wrote *The Power Elite*, presented the opposing view: interlocking elites wielded power by the control of economic, political, and military institutions. These elites, who shared similar backgrounds, were a relatively small group of persons with similar goals who were able to manipulate supposedly democratic processes.

Studies in the early and mid-1960s continued to focus on the nature of democracy and, in particular, the nature of democracy in other industrialized societies. Almond and Verba's early study of **political culture** in five nations explored attitudes and beliefs to see if they were impediments or preconditions to democratic development. Seymor Martin Lipset's work throughout the 1960s sought to understand the preconditions for democracy. In *The First New Nation*, he compared the history of the United States with that of European countries and argued that American history had fostered a set of **values** of achievement and equalitarianism that made for a stable democracy. He found remnants of **elitism** in both France and Germany, which made them, in this view, unstable democracies. **Reinhard Bendix** developed similar arguments in his famous book *Nation-Building and Citizenship* (1964). Much work at this point was largely influenced by **modernization theory** and **functionalism**.

Since the mid-1960s, new critical approaches have developed within political sociology. Political sociologists have felt the influence of Marxist scholarship, on one hand, but also of social struggles of subaltern groups demanding full entitlement and inclusion. As a result scholarship has tended to change its focus to injustice, oppression, and **domination**. Barrington Moore's *Social Origins of Dictatorship and Democracy* (1964) argued that conditions for political developments in the modern era were set by the conflicts between peasants and landlords as agriculture became commercialized. Much work

in the area has taken the form of historical studies with historians like Perry Anderson and E.P. Thompson becoming increasingly influential.

One important area within sociology influenced by Marxist ideas was the study of the State. Whereas scholarship prior to the 1960s tended to view the functioning of the state within industrial democracies as the United States as the expression of the competing groups' interests, scholars began to point at the ways in which they reflected the interests of elites and maintained the conditions necessary for the accumulation of capital. A number of important debates about the form and functioning of the state took place; scholars like Goran Therborn defended the position that members of the ruling class directly controlled state apparatuses, while others like Nikos Poulantzas argued that the actual form of the state in capitalist society was what guaranteed the reproduction of capitalist relations. While no ultimate agreement among scholars was reached, the debates about the nature of the state have continued to be influential in the work of Claus Offe, Theda Skocpol, Thomas Mann, Fred Block, and others.

Political sociologists have also turned their attention to the sources of **social change** and redistribution of power in society, to social movements and revolutions. Students of social movements have looked to the sources of **collective behavior** and the conditions under which social movements might achieve their goals. If an earlier generation of political sociologists looked to psychological explanations for social movements, essentially treating them as expressions of collective irrationality, political sociologists now looked to political opportunities, patterns of resources available, and bases of solidarity. Charles Tilly's *The Vendee* (1964) dealt with patterns of **collective action** in the aftermath of the French Revolution and Theda Skocpol's (1979) *States and Social Revolutions* dealt with the French, Russian, and Chinese revolutions. Both treated structural and institutional factors as central to their explanations. Skocpol, for instance, argued that fiscal pressures on central states from competing foreign powers were a necessary condition for the success of revolutionary movements.

Two important trends have continued to shape Political Sociology since the 1980s. One is the central inclusion of gender to the study of states, social policies, and social movements. Theda Skocpol, Margaret Weir, Ann Orloff, among others have helped bring gender analysis to the analysis of state policies and particularly of the **welfare state**. Another important development is the inclusion of culture to the analysis. Lynn Hunt, Jeffrey Alexander, Bill Sewell, Jr., George Steinmetz, Anne Keane, and Phil Gorsky, among others have brought cultural analyses to the realm of political sociology.

POLYGAMY

Polygamy is the practice of having multiple spouses at one time. This practice is prohibited today by law in the United States and other countries, but many cultures around the world continue to engage in such marriages, and polygamy has existed at one time or another in almost all parts of the world, including the United States. Anthropologist George Murdock even cited it as the preferred form of **marriage** in a study of 565 societies in 1949.

Polygamy is divided into two categories, based on gender: polygyny is defined as one man with multiple wives, and polyandry as one woman with multiple husbands. Through history, polygyny has been the more common by far—a disparity best explained by the ability of a polygynous arrangement to produce far more offspring than a polyandrous one. This distinction explains the fact that within cultures that allow polygamy, the practice is generally reserved for the wealthy and powerful elite with rarely more than 10% of the population engaged in it. Only the elite, it is believed, can provide for multiple spouses and the many children which may result.

Inequality of the sexes within a **culture** is another factor in the existence of polygamous marriages. For example, it may be seen as a man's duty to provide for as many women as he is able or as his right to possess as many as he desires. The wives, though, are sometimes instrumental in arranging subsequent marriages in order to lessen their own responsibilities, and it is common for sisters to marry the same man which allows them to maintain their childhood relationship.

In the United States polygamy has been engaged in from time to time in isolated cases, but the most famous and extensive episode was connected to the nineteenth-century Mormon church. Joseph Smith, the founder of Mormonism, endorsed polygyny as one a divinely inspired tenet. But the practice contributed to the sect's persecution in the East and caused members to migrate to a nearly uninhabited desert region in present-day Utah. There they freely engaged in the practice for some years until pressure from the U.S. government led them to repeal the church sanction as a condition of Utah statehood.

POPPER, SIR KARL RAIMUND (1902-1994)

Austrian philosopher

The Austrian philosopher Sir Karl Raimund Popper (1902–1994) offered an original analysis of scientific research that he also applied to research in history and **philosophy**. Karl Popper was born in Vienna on July 28, 1902, the son of a barrister. He studied mathematics, physics, and philosophy at the University of Vienna. Though not a member of the Vienna Circle, he was in sympathy with some, if not all, of its aims. His first book *The Logic of Scientific Discovery* (1935) was published in a series sponsored by the Circle. In 1937 Popper accepted a post in New Zealand as senior lecturer in philosophy at Canterbury University College in Christchurch.

At the end of World War II, Popper was invited to the London School of Economics as a reader, and in 1949 he was made professor of logic and scientific method. Popper then made numerous visits to the United States as visiting professor and guest lecturer. In 1950 he gave the **William James** Lectures at Harvard University. In 1965 Popper was knighted by Queen Elizabeth II.

Popper's first book laid the foundations for all the rest of his work. It offered an analysis of the procedure to be used

in scientific work and a criterion for the meaning of the statements produced in such work. According to Popper, the researcher should begin by proposing hypotheses. The collection of **data** is guided by a theoretical preconception concerning what is relevant or important. The examination of causal connections between phenomena is also guided by leading hypotheses. Such a hypothesis is scientific only if one can derive from it particular observation statements that, if falsified by the facts, would refute the hypothesis. A statement is meaningful, therefore, if and only if there is a way it can be falsified. Hence the researcher should strive to refute rather than to confirm his hypotheses. Refutation is real advancement because it clears the field of a likely hypothesis.

Popper later applied his analysis of knowledge to theories of society and history. In *The Open Society and Its Enemies* (1945) he attacked Plato, G. W. F. Hegel, and **Karl Marx** as offering untenable totalitarian theories that are easily falsifiable. *The Open Society* is often considered one of Popper's most influential books of this century. It also was responsible for the prevalent use of the term "open society." Critics argue that Popper succeeded in this book and in its sequel *The Poverty of Historicism* (1957) in formulating a deterministic theory about general laws of historical development and then refuting it. A lively controversy ensued on the issue of which philosophers, if any, held the doctrine Popper refuted. Popper found himself embroiled in a decade of polemics, particularly with partisans of Plato. Popper was thus credited with a convincing logical refutation but one misdirected in its targets.

Popper's later works *Objective Knowledge* (1972) and *The Self and Its Brain* (1977) combined his scientific theory with a theory of evolution. In the 1980s, Popper continued to lecture, focusing mainly on questions of evolution and the role of consciousness. Karl Popper died of complications from cancer, pneumonia, and kidney failure on September 17, 1994, at the age of 92.

POPULAR CULTURE

Popular (pop) **culture** charts the unofficial history of a country. Official histories hinge on dates, important personages, and events, but popular culture speaks to the tenor of an era, its obsessions and preferences on the level of the majority of people who do not make the pages of history books. The vehicles of popular culture are many, including music, **television**, film, popular religion, parapsychology and the occult, popular **leisure** activities, sports, food, advertising, folklore and folklife, and genre fiction, such as pulp novels, westerns, and romances.

Any given time period in the twentieth century takes its image from popular culture as much as from major events (themselves part of popular culture). The 1920s call up images of flappers, while the 1950s call up bobby sox, poodle skirts, cars with fins, and the birth of rock and roll. This iconography is shared in the United States, a referent available to anyone, not just the academics; sharing is accomplished through the media, especially as its outlets grow increasingly pervasive in public and private lives. While print, broadcast, and, most re-

In the United States polygamy has been engaged in from time to time in isolated cases *(Corbis Corporation [Bellevue]).*

cently, digital media facilitate the sharing of ideas and icons from coast to coast, they also create popular culture, through movies, television shows, the choice of what is covered as "news," and the like. These ideas are fed into the marketplace, reinforcing their "importance" and attractiveness.

Analyses of popular culture clues researchers in to a society's attitudes on **race**, class, gender and sexuality, especially to views that prevail in but are not explicitly expressed by the populace. Prime-time television, for example, was criticized during the turn of the twentieth century as ghettoizing programs with African-American actors that were targeted toward an African-American audience; the three major networks (ABC, NBC, CBS) generally avoided producing dramas and situation comedies for this audience, while the stations that did program for African-Americans created few programs and placed them on the same evening. In addition, shows that were produced, especially situation comedies (African-American-oriented dramas were even more scarce), were criticized by some members of the black **community** for playing off of (often unflattering) stereotypes. During the 1970 **National Organization for Women (NOW)** documented months worth of television programming, analyzing the representation of women in every advertisement and regular program; again, stereotypes prevailed, and NOW used this information to petition the Federal Communications Commission against renewing broadcast licenses for the large networks, on the basis that the networks were not fulfilling the federal mandate to serve the public interest if they were not serving women's interests.

Every place has its own culture, but American culture enjoys a particularly broad influence. American books, films, and television shows make homes for themselves in countries around the globe, as does American fashion; in some countries, such as the former USSR, American blue jeans, cigarettes, and even used Nike shoes bring high prices in the informal marketplace. Not all countries have welcomed the **hegemony** of American culture with open arms; France is the most vocal critic of the United States "cultural imperialism," considering it a direct threat to the survival of French culture. France legislates "protections" against American cultural in-

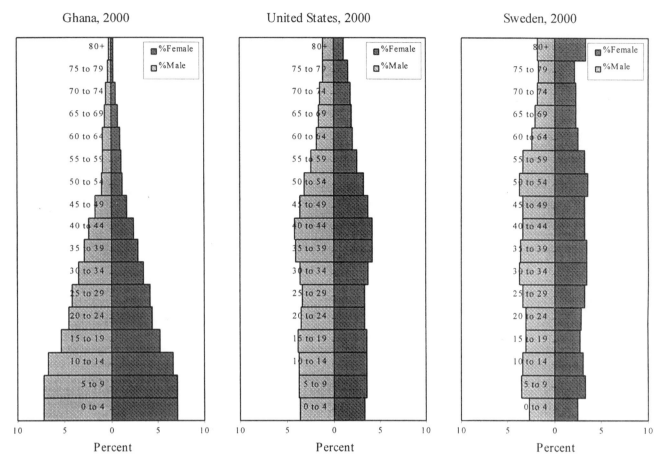

Population pyramids show the proportional size of each age-sex group and can be used to make cross-national comparisons of population structure *(Courtesy of Esther I. Wilder).*

roads by placing quotas on American goods, forbidding the adoption of English words into the French language, and requiring all advertisements to be in French. The French particularly object to the Internet, on which the majority of traffic is in English; as a result, the French were late adopters of the global network (however, a local network, the Minitel, is popular). Even the term ''American pop culture'' is ethnocentric, ignoring non-English speaking residents, Canadians, and Mexicans.

Popular culture is a relatively recent arrival in the academic arena, an outgrowth of folklore, consumer studies, and mass culture studies that is truly interdisciplinary. The *Journal of Popular Culture* was founded in 1967 by Dr. Ray Browne, who founded the Popular Culture Association two years later. Browne created a Master's program at Bowling Green State University in Ohio in 1973, and an undergraduate degree program followed in 1974, under the aegis of the newly-minted Department of Popular Culture; a Ph.D. program in American Studies is also administered through the department. ''American Studies'' is a common moniker for programs covering American pop culture; **cultural studies** and cultural anthropology programs also provide a home for scholars of popular culture.

POPULATION PYRAMID

A *population pyramid*, or age-sex pyramid, is a visual representation of the age and sex distribution of a population. The classic pyramid shape (broad base, narrow apex) represents nations with high fertility and high mortality. Until recently, nearly all nations of the world could be described in this manner. Today, however, the classic pyramid shape accurately represents only those developing countries which maintain high fertility levels.

A population pyramid consists of two vertical histograms placed back to back along a central vertical axis. The number or percentage of males or females in a particular age group is indicated by the width of the appropriate bar. Males are shown to the left of the vertical axis, females to the right. The youngest ages are represented at the bottom of the pyramid and the oldest ages at the top. Five-year age intervals are commonly used, although single years of age (or any other evenly spaced intervals) are also appropriate. Because there are relatively few people at the oldest ages, the uppermost age group is generally open-ended—''65+,'' ''75+,'' or ''85+,'' for example.

Population pyramids can show either percentages (percentage of the population within each age-sex group) or abso-

Much societal debate focuses on whether pornography is harmful in both its production and consumption *(Corbis Corporation [Bellevue]).*

lute numbers (number of people within each age-sex group). In constructing a population pyramid based on percentages, it is important to use the total population—males and females combined—as the base figure for calculating the percentage of males and females in each age group. (Calculating the percentages separately for males and for females may give the misleading impression that the population is divided evenly by sex.) Population pyramids showing the proportional or relative size of each age-sex group can be used to make cross-national comparisons of population structure, especially if the vertical and horizontal scales are constructed identically for each country. However, only pyramids showing absolute numbers can be used to compare the overall size of the population within each age-sex group.

Population pyramids for three nations are shown below. Ghana's pyramid is the classic *expansive type* associated with high-fertility countries. In contrast, the population pyramid for the United States is *constrictive*. The bulge in the middle can be attributed to the baby boom (increased fertility from the mid-1940s to the mid-1960s), and the narrower part below the bulge reflects the fact that fertility has declined considerably since the post-World War II era. Sweden's population is *near stationary*, with both low mortality and low fertility. In a stationary population, the birth rate is equal to the death rate (zero population growth) and the size of the population, as well as its age/sex composition, remains constant over time.

PORNOGRAPHY

Pornography is generally defined as sexually explicit pictorial or written material, conveyed through a number of media: books, magazines, film, video, and, most recently, through a number of digital formats which can be viewed with computers. This definition, however, is so broad that it would include many highly esteemed works of art, classic novels, and much contemporary popular **culture**. Rather than group such valued cultural products with socially condemned pornographic mate-

rials, we attempt to construct borders between sexually explicit materials which contribute to non-sexual social values, such as health education and artistic or literary enrichment, and those which seek only to gratify the sexual appetites of viewers and readers. In cultures where sexual pleasure is defined as a negative aspect of the human experience, pornography is more likely to be illegal, regulated, or socially marginalized.

Much debate focuses on whether pornography is harmful in both its production and in its consumption. Feminist theorists have pointed out gender inequalities embedded within popular pornography: the largest portion of the pornography market is oriented toward the heterosexual male consumer, which means that most pornographic images are of women in sexually suggestive positions and settings. This presentation of the female body for men's sexual pleasure contributes to the sexual objectification of women. Sexual objectification is a social process which dehumanizes women, reduces their social value to nothing more than a sexual gratifier for men. While women are presented as sexual objects in cultural practices which range from advertising to beauty contests, pornography's sexual content makes it a particularly transparent form of sexual objectification.

Anti-pornography activists have also pointed out other ways in which pornography is harmful to women. They claim that women are forced, either physically or through economic hardship, into the pornography industry, where they are expected to endure painful sexual acts and risk contracting sexually transmitted diseases. Moreover, they argue that producing pornography turns this physical violence against female models and actresses into symbolic violence against all women as it is packaged and sold for male consumption. Many attempts have been made to link pornography to other **social problems** such as rape and violence against women. This premise holds that consuming pornography increases sexual **aggression** in males, as it redefines sexuality around male pleasure and ignores women's capacity for sexual pleasure or their humanity.

Critics of the anti-pornography campaigns have responded by demonstrating that the production of sexually explicit materials does not necessarily require these kinds of abuses and gender inequalities. Pointing to the smaller segments of the pornography industry in which women write, direct, and produce pornography, they demonstrate that women can control their working environment and provide comfortable and safe working conditions for actors and models. In addition, gay and lesbian pornography does not follow the problematic formula of male consumption of female sexuality, and the abundance of amateur pornography, in which people make and distribute their own home movies, demonstrates that power differentials between producers and workers can also be decoupled from the creation of sexually explicit materials. The essence of this debate centers on whether the nudity and sexual activities presented in pornographic videos, magazines, websites, and so on, are in themselves potentially harmful to viewers and readers or whether consuming pornographic materials causes people to then act violently or disrespectfully to others. Many studies have attempted to measure these effects, but results have been mixed, and no clear answer has yet emerged.

POSITIVE ASSOCIATION

Positive association refers to one of two possible directions in which two variables can be correlated with one another, the other being a negative relationship. When two variables are correlated, researchers can estimate the extent to which scores on one **variable** move either up or down, in conjunction with a rise or fall in scores on the second variable. A positive association occurs when scores on one variable rise in conjunction with rising scores on the other variable.

To illustrate a **correlation** between two variables, picture a graph in which one variable's scores are listed along the horizontal axis from low to high scores and the other variable's scores appear along the vertical axis in ranked order from lowest scores to highest. Each case is then plotted with a dot that corresponds to each respondent's scores on each of the two variables. Then, a line (called a **regression** line) is fitted to the dots that represents the least squared distance from each dot to the line itself. The **regression line** describes the strength of the relationship among the variables and the direction of the relationship. If the regression line slopes upward from low scores to high scores along the horizontal (or X) axis (something like this: /), then there is a positive relationship between the two variables. When scores along the horizontal axis rise, scores along the vertical axis (or Y axis) rise as well.

Now picture the graph again. Scores along the horizontal (X) axis represent the number of hours a person spends at work, and ranges from zero to sixty hours per week. Scores along the vertical (Y) axis represent income and range from "under $5,000" per year to "$100,00 +" per year. If we plot the average number of hours each person works with each respondent's annual income then fit a regression line that represents the least distance from each dot to the line itself, we would probably find that the line slopes upward from left to right. Thus, the more hours people work, the more money they earn. This association represents a positive relationship between hours worked and income earned.

POSITIVISM

Founded by **Auguste Comte**, Positivism is a philosophical position which holds that knowledge can be ascertained only through scientific study of things which can be observed and measured. It is in opposition to philosophical reasoning (sometimes called "armchair theorizing" because it does not require going out into the world to collect **data**). Therefore, positivism is embedded within empiricism, necessitating the use of data to create empirically grounded laws.

Comte applied positivism to the field of **sociology** (which he is also credited with founding) and argued that sociology can use the same scientific methods that the physical sciences (such as physics and chemistry) use. He also used the term to apply to the historical development of human thought, which evolved from attributing the cause of things to divine beings to recognizing laws inherent in nature that can be identified through the scientific method. Positivism stresses the importance of quantification and **measurement**, applying theoretical concepts to test their **validity**, and the detachment of the observer from the observed. It tends to depend on social structures rather than human motives or desires to explain social phenomena. Positivists use a language of cause and effect, and are generally interested in determining relationships between social phenomena.

Émile Durkheim was also a positivist and focused his work on identifying measurable social concepts (what he termed social facts). One of his most famous works *Suicide* is considered a **model** of early positivist research. He also sought to lay out methods appropriate for sociological inquiry in his book *The Rules of Sociological Method*. Durkheim was influential in the development of early American empirical sociology.

Robert Park and Ernest Burgess have been credited with greatly influencing the continued positivism of sociology in the United States. They stressed the importance of empirical rigor and the systematic observation, recording, and classification of data. Social phenomena that were not measurable were not considered appropriate topics for sociological inquiry. Social facts, according to Park and Burgess, were not linked with **values** or morals (as these were not concepts that lended themselves easily to **operationalization**).

The current conceptualization of positivism assumes a progressive evolution of scientific knowledge which produces increasingly better understanding of society. As methods for observing social phenomena improve, sociologists become more rigorous in their application of the scientific method; as their knowledge accumulates, the discoveries that they make result in more coherent and specific theories. These theories are produced through the same methods used in physical or natural sciences.

Positivism has come under attack in contemporary debates within sociology. First, critics from the Frankfurt School argued that positivism was too concerned with identifying social facts and did not pay enough attention to interpreting those facts, which inhibited true understanding of sociological phenomena. Realists argued that sociologists should be trying to unearth the underlying and sometimes unobservable mechanisms that produce social phenomena. More recently, Jürgen Habermas claimed that the very notion of an apolitical science conducted by detached scientific observers was implausible because attempts to understand **society** are intricately connected to political positions and struggles. Similar criticisms of positivism have come from feminist sociology, which asserts that knowledge itself is situated and not universal or unchanging.

POST COLONIALISM

Postcolonialism is the return in colonial exploitation of a colony that has ostensibly achieved independence. Postcolonialism refers to the period following **decolonization** of second-wave colonies. According to D.K. Fieldhouse in *Colonialism 1870-1945*, the term Postcolonialism came into use around 1950 as

a result of imperial withdrawal of political control in its colonies. The implication of the term is independence was not entirely realized in ex-colonies. Post-colonization refers to the theoretical political independence of a colony. Although the imperial state no longer occupies the role of sole ruler, economically the ex-colony is still held hostage. Superficially, the colony is politically liberated, but economically it is completely tied to the colonial state.

Fieldhouse asserted that **colonialism** made colonies poorer than they had been prior to colonization the following ways: 1) colonization forced peasants to produce unprofitable crops for export to foreign traders and the European metropolis; 2) under colonization natural assets such as minerals were extracted; and 3) the means of production and exchange exclusively fell into the hands of foreigner-European colonials who used their monopolistic power to exploit both the producer and consumer. Furthermore, they transferred the profits overseas instead of reinvesting them in colonies for development of the local economies. At the end of the colonial period, the colonies were reduced to selling their natural resources/raw materials to maintain subsistence. Since the colonies could not afford their own industries, they relied on selling unrefined resources to wealthy industrialized countries, who refined the natural resources, turn them into products or merchandise, and then sold them back to the colonies (the new markets) at rates that were determined by the industry.

Europe was able to maintain economic control in two ways according to Fieldhouse: through large-scale commercial enterprise and by controlling the new rulers in these territories. In these colonies, foreigners owned and controlled the commercial enterprise, the ex-colony only supplied the materials for production and the market for consumption. The second means of control was through manipulation of new rulers in the ex-colonies. Some rulers, in these newly independent colonies, thought it were wise to maintain good relations with the ex-colonial state. In return, some leaders were paid salaries to maintain collaborative relations. This arrangement enabled Europe, in the form of multinational corporations, to retain and expand their activities.

Another important implication of post-colonial relations is the cold war. Although it officially ceased with the dismantling of the USSR in the early 1990s and was primarily an invisible war between two super powers, the United States (defender of **capitalism**) and the USSR (defender of socialism), the Cold War is significant for understanding the war of liberation and the period that followed. Since colonies were possessed by imperialist states, like the United States and those in Europe, support for liberation was primarily provided by states like USSR and Cuba. In Angola and South Africa, for instance, socialist nations like USSR and Cuba helped natives win their liberation from European imperialists. The question under consideration was what was to be the fate of these countries following their liberation. Would they become socialist states (as many did) or would they become capitalist-democracies? This question of outcome was an important factor in Cold War battles. If these countries chose **socialism**, there would be a smaller market in which industrialized-

imperialist states could sell their products; moreover, the world would be sharply divided between socialism and capitalism. The Vietnam War is a good example. France occupied Vietnam for nearly a century and then Japan occupied it during World War II. After the war, France sought to regain colonial control. Just as Vietnam had won its liberation, France called on its ally, the United States, to continue the battle. The United States stepped in but was unable to win. U.S. troops were withdrawn as Vietnam won complete sovereignty over the entire state that had once been split, one part socialist and one part capitalist-democracy, as is Korea today.

POST-INDUSTRIAL SOCIETY

Post-industrial **society** is a macro level theoretical construct that refers to a particular stage of societal development. The concept is most centrally associated with the work of Harvard sociologist **Daniel Bell** and rose to prominence in sociological **discourse** with the publication of Bell's 1973 book *The Coming of Post-Industrial Society: A Venture in Social Forecasting*. The social and political turbulence in the decades following World War II suggested that the United States was undergoing a period of extensive social transition with an uncertain future. Bell's book outlined the key dimensions of **social change** underlying this transition and attempted to forecast the potential consequences and characteristics of the new social **structure** that was likely to emerge.

As a stage of societal development, post-industrial society was contrasted with the earlier stages of pre-industrial society and industrial society. According to Bell, post-industrial society represented ''a continuation of trends unfolding out of industrial society.'' The transition to post- industrial society was primarily centered on five dimensions of social change. The first dimension, the change from a goods-producing to a service economy, was primarily based on growing concentration of **employment** in the service sector of the U.S. economy. However, Bell also argued that the quality of life in post-industrial society would be measured by the consumption of services such as **health care**, education, recreation, and the arts.

The second key dimension of social change, a shift in the occupational distribution of the U.S. **labor force** marked by the growth of a professional and technical classes of workers, was based primarily on shifting worker populations and educational upgrading of the U.S. labor force. Bell contended that this professional and technical *intelligentsia* would rise to dominate the power structure in post-industrial society. Moreover, education and **skill** would provide the primary means for upward mobility in the increasingly meritocratic stratification system.

The third key dimension of social change, the growing centrality of theoretical knowledge as the source of innovation and policy formulation, was based on the extensive growth of science, the scientific U.S. establishment, the importance of scientific research in technological innovations, and in informing public policy decision-making. Interrelated with this shift

was the fourth and fifth dimensions of change which consisted of (a) the growing control by society over technology, in part, through the systematic assessment of the potential future consequences of new technological developments; and (b) the creation of a new intellectual technology for decision- making purposes. Bell was optimistic that regulatory institutions, such as the former Office of Technology Assessment, would grow in importance and be effective in controlling and ameliorating the potential negative consequences of technological change. Moreover, new ''intellectual'' technology such as linear programming, new forms of software, and sets of problem solving rules such as game theory, would increasingly be used to make more effective the judgements by policy makers. Today, an analysis of post-industrial society would indicate that many changes consistent with the concept of post-industrial society have taken place while other changes have not occurred in the manner envisioned by Bell. Nonetheless, the concept of post-industrial society has stimulated substantial debate over the future course of the United States as well as other developed nations.

POSTMODERNISM

Postmodernism, undoubtedly a controversial topic in late twentieth-century sociology, is variously defined and subject to debate. Sociologists have diversely defined postmodernism as a social movement, a state of mind, a cultural logic, an extension of high modernism, and a period in history reflective of the maturing of consumer oriented **capitalism**. Despite little agreement among sociologists, certain characteristics are generally associated with postmodernism: eclecticism, **pluralism**, non-linearity, radical **democracy**, local knowledge, interdisciplinary studies, decentralization, **multiculturalism**, a suspicious view of science, and the play of symbolic meaning in a mass mediated world. Postmodernism is also closely associated with the rise of post-industrial societies driven by the emergence of service-based economies, the development of computerized technologies, the growth of a **consumer culture**, and the expansion of mass mediated cultural systems. In addition, the widespread influence of postmodernism is demonstrated by its penetration of **sociology**, history, philosophy, ethics, aesthetics, literary criticism, art **theory**, geography, religious studies, **feminism**, **cultural studies**, comparative literature, and anthropology.

Sociologists generally agree on two trends within postmodernism. The first is a socially nihilistic trend that emphasizes the collapse of semiotic systems as a result of the mass media proliferation. Here, the focus is on the loss of truth, **progress**, self, and meaning in advanced capitalist societies, all of which results in a generalized social and cultural disorientation and ambivalence. The second is a culturally optimistic trend that celebrates multivocality, pluralism, and multiculturalism. This version of postmodernism embraces a newfound set of cultural opportunities for democratic social transformation, the expression of marginalized voices, and symbolic freedom in self-definition.

One central theme of postmodernism is suspicion of what French sociologist Jean-Francois Lyotard calls *grand narratives*, the predominating epistemological and theoretical frameworks used to make both knowledge and truth claims. Theories or ideologies that claim to have universal application are perceived under postmodernism as reflecting the arrogance of a hegemonic and totalizing world-view. Postmodernists interpret these grand narratives as merely stories and suggest that truth claims cannot be universalized and are more appropriately understood and developed within a local context.

Other postmodernists, like French sociologist Jean Baudrillard, extend these ideas by arguing that not only has truth become localized, but reality itself has become impossible to clearly discern. The focus here is on the semiotic proliferation of symbols that are no longer connected to real objects or events. Social reality becomes inhabited by *simulacra,* simulations of objects that have no true original. This situation results from the ability of mass media to technologically reproduce, and radically recontextualize, social symbols within a mass mediated space, and create objects and experiences that have no basis in the empirical world. In this way, postmodernists argue that meaning in the symbolic world of simulations becomes blurred, and individuals are no longer able to distinguish between empirical **fact** and a mass mediated reality. What is left is an endless play of self and meaning in unbounded and fragmented semiotic systems.

Still other postmodernists emphasize the importance of the cultural movements described by identity politics. Faced with a cultural situation in which traditional distinctions between high and popular **culture** are dissolving, new managerial and service-oriented social classes are emerging, and once marginalized voices are becoming increasingly legitimated, postmodern political movements raise the issue of identity to the forefront. Here, feminist, queer, multicultural, and postcolonial discourses become an essential feature of the postmodern project of pluralism and democracy. The focus in these identity struggles is not to universalize notions of group identity but to deconstruct the definitions of identity, searching for differences and not similarities such that non-hegemonic self-definition can occur. While many sociologists consider postmodernism to be an academic **fad**, a tremendous amount of intellectual energy has been devoted to exploring and elaborating postmodernism. It remains a viable alternative to the more traditional paradigms of sociological theory and **methodology**.

POVERTY

Poverty can be defined in several ways and can mean different things to people of different societies. Absolute poverty is to have inadequate funds to provide a minimum **standard of living** for oneself or one's family. Relative poverty is defined as doing worse off financially than the average person in a given **society**. Persons living in relative poverty may have no car, no **television**, and no toys for their children but have enough **money** for clothing, food and shelter. Relative to the average Americans, they are living poorly. A person or **family** living in absolute poverty, on the other hand, may not have enough

money to pay for the rent or groceries for the month. These different ways of defining poverty are debated by **government** officials and researchers. How poverty is defined is integral to the task of reducing its prevalence in society.

Reports state that most of the poor in the United States and other industrialized nations live in relative poverty. This again can be thought of in terms of not having as much as everyone else. Many poor in developing nations or unindustrialized nations, however, live in absolute poverty. Individuals in absolute poverty are living under life-threatening conditions. Living in absolute poverty means not having enough food to eat, not having shelter, safe water, medical care, or proper clothing.

The United States government has created a numerical poverty line in which to distinguish those who live in poverty. Other nations prefer not to use an exact number but use relative poverty as the estimator of poverty levels. In 1999, the United States government declared a family of four earning $16,897 annually to be living on the poverty threshold. Approximately 14 percent of Americans today live at or below the poverty threshold. Children under the age of 18 are the most likely of all age groups to live in poverty. They comprise twenty percent of the poor in America. Native Americans are the most likely of all ethnic groups to live in poverty (30%), followed by African Americans (27%), Hispanic Americans (27%), Asian Americans (14%), and white Americans (9%). Female-headed households are more likely to be poor than any other **household** type. Those individuals who hold less than a high school diploma are also the most likely to live in poverty (24%) followed by those with a high school diploma (10%), and those who hold a college degree (2%). Clearly there are demographic patterns among the poor. These patterns are used by researchers for help in implementing programs to help the poor.

The **feminization of poverty** refers to the growing and disproportionate number of women living in poverty. As stated above female-headed households live in poverty more often than all other household types. This poverty is most often the result of a change in family composition such as **divorce**, separation, remarriage, **marriage** or birth of a child. These women are categorized as the ''new poor''. They did not necessarily come from a family background of poverty, but their poverty is driven by a series of events in their lives.

The consequences of poverty can be great. Living in poverty means that an individual may always be on the verge of not having enough money to eat, pay rent, or have proper clothing. As a result, children and adults alike may be underfed. Poorer individuals on a strict food budget may opt for cheaper and more filling foods (i.e., rice, potatoes) that may not meet daily nutritional requirements. Prolonged malnourishment can result in serious illnesses such as scurvy and rickets. The poor often do not have adequate medical care and are not able to see physicians when they become ill. The daily stresses of making ends meet also eventually take a toll on individuals' health. This in conjunction with malnutrition and inadequate **health care** is a cause for concern for many people.

In the United States, the federal government has a method through which it distributes food coupons, services, and

Many poor in developing nations or unindustrialized nations live in absolute poverty such as these starving refugees in the Sudan *(Corbis Corporation [Bellevue]).*

money to poor families who apply and show a need. With the food coupons, families can purchase nutritious foods at participating grocery stores. Health care is available for some as well as money for those who are disabled and unable to work. A system of welfare is in place to assist families who do not have an income. There is a continual debate over how much the poor should receive in welfare benefits and if they should receive benefits from the government at all. Reforms to the welfare system in the United States is a continuous process aimed at fine tuning the system that is geared toward assisting those living in poverty.

POWER ELITE

The American sociologist **C. Wright Mills** coined this phrase in his book *The Power Elite* (1956), in which he developed the concept to explain how power was distributed and maintained in the United States. The term refers to the small group of upper class officials who share similar values, backgrounds, and interests and hold the top-ranking positions in business,

government and the military. Together, this group of mainly white, male Anglo-Saxon Protestants makes laws, directs foreign policy, and oversees the direction of the American economy.

There are four mechanisms by which the power elite retains control over American wealth: **socialization**, intermarriage, interlocking directorates, and a revolving door between politics and economics. First, members of the power elite send their children to private schools and universities, after which they join a handful of private clubs such as the Bohemian club of San Francisco. Second, children of the power elite are encouraged to intermarry. Events such as debutante balls where nineteen to twenty-one year olds are presented as officially ready for **marriage** are normal activities for children of the power elite. Third, a small group of people sit on multiple corporate boards and therefore make the major decisions concerning the economy. Finally, a ''revolving door'' exists among the power elite that makes it possible for them to move in and out of jobs in the government, military, or business. A typical example of this phenomenon is Alexander Haig, who retired as a general, went on to hold influential positions in business, served as Secretary of State under Richard Nixon and then ran for president on the Republican ticket in 1988. Discussions of the power elite are important to our understanding of the power **structure** in U.S. **society**.

PRAGMATISM

Pragmatism is a unique school of American philosophical thought. Its approach constitutes the very core of classical American **philosophy**, first conceived of and named at the Cambridge Metaphysical Club, founded by William James and Charles Peirce. Its development coincided with the Progressive Era (1896-1914) in America and was fostered at the University of Michigan and the University of Chicago. Along with James and Peirce, John Dewey and George Herbert Mead are most often associated with pragmatism. Though differences exist between these philosophers, which they themselves considered radical, these men shared a view of what philosophy is and what it should do.

Pragmatism's arguments are situated in certain primary themes. First, pragmatism rejects the arguments of modern philosophy and the **language** and notions central to it. Philosophy, as the pragmatists conceived it, is bound in everyday practice, not the wistful theoretical arguments of European philosophers. Instead of divorcing itself from everyday concerns, pragmatism approaches these as the primary interest of philosophy. Second, the pragmatists had no concern for an infallible truth but instead searched for a ''plural'' one. Instead of absolutist arguments, as philosophy often wishes to postulate, pragmatism pursues a truth bound within everyday concerns and actions. Truths, pragmatism suggests, are real only insofar as they are experienced. Thus, pragmatism searches for an individually based truth, not a metaphysical one. Third, regarding the idea that philosophy can improve the human condition, pragmatists conceived philosophy is useful only if it

can resolve problems. Knowledge, they argued, is a highly practical thing and must be put to use in practical ways to solve problems that affect social conditions. Fourth, and perhaps most important for **sociology**, pragmatists focused on the intersection of **community** and the individual. The individual self is inherently a ''social self'' bound by relations to the social world. This position is a radical departure from more abstract metaphysical accounts of the self. While various pragmatists, such as Charles Cooley, considered this issue, it was Mead who conceptualized it in the greatest detail. Mead argued that the self is developed through social processes or interaction with others and the community. In addition, he suggested the self is implicated by both individual and community. It is a play between **free will** and community needs and demands that determine individual action and interpretation.

Certainly the most important contribution of pragmatism to sociology is its philosophical support of **symbolic interactionism**. The term itself was coined by **Herbert Blumer**, who studied under Mead while a graduate student at the University of Chicago. Symbolic interactionism argues that individuals orient to and act on the meanings they construct through interaction with each other. Everyday sociology argues social life is an ongoing process that is constantly negotiated and ordered by individual interpretation and action. Pragmatism's down-to-earth orientation and focus on individual action are readily apparent in the theory.

Even though its most influential time was certainly the early twentieth century, pragmatism has not disappeared as a school of thought. Pragmatism reemerged in the late twentieth century as an important genre of philosophical and social thought. Philosophers such as Richard Rorty and Cornel West urged others toward a practical philosophy committed to **social change** and a liberal democratic **society**. In what some have termed neo-pragmatism, Rorty and West combined pragmatism with the emerging ideas of **postmodernism** and poststructuralism in their discussions of change, science, and **identity**.

PRAXIS

The concept of praxis was articulated in ''German Ideology'' written by **Karl Marx**. In this essay, Marx presented his theory on the development of historically specific stages of production. He argued that labor is core to the subsistence and social creativity of the individual and **society** and that the organization of that labor correlates to the type of economic structure. The search for profit is the objective of the capitalist stage of development, so workers become alienated from the product of their labor, from themselves, from other workers as they become more physically isolated through the mechanization of production (or in modern society, the introduction of computers), and from their potential. Marx argued that in the final stage of economic and social development the individual is no longer isolated or alienated but becomes empowered not only as an individual, but as an individual with membership in a **community**. Praxis refers to the unity of the individual and the community or what Marx would call the unity of theory and action.

Marx believed that human beings differ from other social animals because they can create in their minds the product of their labor. Human consciousness, then, is not simply an intellectual process. Consciousness is shaped by the dialectic between individuals creating the world in which they live, and individuals being shaped by that world. Praxis allows individuals to pursue those activities that will create personal development and simultaneously transform society. In other words, individuals actively transforms themselves as well as the world. People therefore actively participate in shaping the conditions that will determine their existence.

Marx wanted to interpret the world and to consciously change it. Although the emphasis in the United States on **pragmatism**, a philosophy that distinguishes between rational thought and purpose, and other theoretical perspectives appears to have limited the use of this term, some social scientists include praxis in their research. Embedded in praxis is the notion of action achieved by employing theory and critical methods. Theory is a set of abstract ideas and traditionally not thought of as an active dimension of action. For Marxists, however, theory presents the opportunity to change the world based on knowledge of historically specific issues. As a result, praxis involves the dynamics to distinguish between essence and appearance and to pursue informed committed action and to consciously change the world.

PRAYER

Prayer is the spiritual action directed toward a divine influence (defined by various religions as God, Allah, Yahweh, etc.) by which the one who prays seeks an inward or outward response. The act of prayer has existed since the beginning of recorded history. Throughout history, prayer has been used by individuals, families, states, and nations for innumerable causes, such as to invoke change, provide protection, offer thanksgiving, ensure the defeat of one's enemies, and seek healing. A discussion of the role of prayer in contemporary **society** can be divided into two types: private and public.

Private prayer emphasizes the relationship between an individual and the divine. Many forms of prayer exist. Generally, prayers can be described as inward, upward, or outward. Inward prayer focuses on the needs of the one who prays. Personal concerns, needs, desires, fears, and joys are offered to God. Upward prayer emphasizes the nature of the divine being. It includes praise, adoration, and an enumeration of the superior traits of the divine. Outward prayer is manifest as petitions for others who are in need. Although all major religions include inward, upward, and outward prayers as part of their **belief system**, each group has its particular emphasis and structure for how prayer is used.

Public prayer has been used for the blessing of a nation and the defeat of its enemies for all of history. The United States has a peculiar relationship with public prayer based on its dualistic understanding of separation of church and state and with the generally accepted belief by many of its citizens that the United States is a "Christian nation." From its incep-

Prayer is the spiritual action directed toward a divine influence by which the one who prays seeks an inward or outward response *(AP/ Wide World Photos, Inc.).*

tion, public prayer was used by the U.S. government and its agencies, such as the school. However, as the constitutionality of this practice was questioned, the controversy centered on prayer in schools, at such events as high school graduations and football games. The school prayer dilemma illuminates changes in the social and cultural make-up of the U.S. population.

The dilemma over public prayer in the schools was explored in the case of *Engel v. Vitale*, which came before the U.S. Supreme Court in 1962. When the Board of Education in New Hyde Park, New York, instructed the principal to read a prayer each morning that was written by the New York State Board of Regents, a father of two students, Lawrence Roth, objected to the school board. When his concerns were not heeded, he ran an advertisement in the local newspaper inviting other parents to join him in a lawsuit. Ultimately, five parents suited the school board, but the lower courts supported the recitation of the prayer. The Supreme Court disagreed, with only one justice dissenting. The majority opinion states in part: ''... the constitutional prohibition against laws respecting an establishment of religion must at least mean that in this country it is no part of the business of government to compose official prayers for any group of the American people to recite as a part of a religious program carried on by the government.''

The reaction to the Supreme Court's decision was immediate and strong as the debate over the role of prayer and the very nature of the nation came into question. Christian evangelist Billy Graham called it ''another step toward the **secularization** of the United States,'' and Cardinal Spellman of New York commented he was ''shocked and frightened that the Supreme Court has declared unconstitutional a simple and voluntary declaration of belief in God by public school children. The decision strikes at the very heart of the Godly tradition in which America's children have so long been raised.'' Angry people protested and called for the resignation of the justices. At the same time, the decision found support. Concurring with the court's decision, a *New York Times* editorial noted that those who opposed school prayer were a minority,

but "the Constitution was designed precisely to protect minorities."

After the initial outcry, the public schools adjusted to the new law, although some schools quietly disregarded the Supreme Court's ruling. The controversy entered the courts again in the 1990s. In 1992 the Supreme Court outlawed public prayers at high school graduations, and in 1999 it rejected the legality of student-led prayers before high school football games. Proponents of school prayer periodically make a push for passage of a constitutional amendment allowing school prayer, proceeding as far as a bill through the House of Representatives in June 1998. Believing that school prayer would mark the beginning of the return of the nation to its Christian roots and re-implement moral **values** to society, supporters of school prayer continue their cause. On the other side, opponents recognize religious diversity and the importance of freedom of religion as a constitutional right. Then, too, many want to protect the separation of **church** and state which is fundamental to U.S. government **structure**.

PREDESTINATION

Predestination refers to the religious belief that people's place in the afterlife is determined at or before birth. Predestination is a fundamental belief of the Calvinist **sect** of Protestantism, which **Max Weber** argued was the necessary impetus for the development of **capitalism**. In *The Protestant Ethic and the Spirit of Capitalism,* Max Weber argued that the belief in predestination encouraged the growth of capitalism in Western Europe and North America, while religions without fervent belief in this doctrine did not support the development of capitalism.

While other religions and other sects of Protestantism viewed poverty as an acceptable and pious condition, the Calvinist belief in predestination led its followers to justify their pursuit of economic activities as their religious duty. While the Calvinist interpretation of predestination provided the motivation for commercial success, other Calvinist **values** furthered the development of capitalism. In addition to hard work and economic success, the Calvinists valued thrift, **asceticism**, and sobriety.

While Calvinists worked with religious fervor to prove their favored status through commercial success, their beliefs precluded spending their wealth ostentatiously or frivolously. With no other acceptable uses for their wealth, they reinvested much of it in their commercial enterprises to make these ventures even more profitable and successful, allowing Calvinists to accumulate large amounts of capital.

Calvinism allowed the accumulation of wealth and **property** that brought about the wealthy capitalist class, but Calvinist and other Protestant beliefs also allowed the development of the ideal proletariat. The belief in predestination encouraged those without accumulated wealth to view hard work as a religious obligation. With a class of people with a religious duty to work hard without expectations of earthly reward, capitalists were able to advance their commercial efforts to further advance the growth of capitalism.

PREDICTIVE VALIDITY

Within the assessment of measurement instruments, predictive validity is a specific type of **validity**. Validity is the extent to which an instrument assesses the construct it is intended to measure. If an instrument assesses the construct it is purported to measure, then the instrument is valid. The term, predictive validity, is often used interchangeably with criterion validity or criterion-related validity. Actually, predictive validity is a sub-type of criterion validity, but the terms are often used synonymously.

A measure has predictive validity when it accurately estimates some external criterion. If an instrument has predictive validity, it provides an accurate prediction of the underlying construct or behavior. For example, college entrance exams, which are used to predict performance in college, have predictive validity if students with high scores on the entrance exams also earn high grades in college. This is the more general meaning of predictive validity.

Predictive validity differs from other types of validity in that it is assessed empirically rather than theoretically. To determine the degree to which a measure has predictive validity, the researcher examines the correlation between the score on the measure and the criterion the measure is designed to capture. The **correlation** indicates the correspondence between the measure and the underlying construct. The higher the correlation is, the better the predictive validity.

As a sub-type of criterion validity, predictive validity concerns the relationship between a measure and the underlying criterion, which occurs sometime in the future. The example above is an instance where predictive validity is in question, as performance in college occurs subsequent to the administration of the entrance exam. Predictive validity can thereby be contrasted with concurrent validity, which concerns the relationship between a measure and the underlying criterion, which exists and can be assessed at the same time the measure is administered.

Predictive validity, in either its more general or more specific meanings, is often used in fields such as **psychology** and education but can rarely be assessed in the social sciences. This is because social science variables tend to be abstract (for example, **prejudice**), and the more abstract the construct, the more difficult it is to identify an appropriate criterion against which to compare the measure.

PREJUDICE

Prejudice is the act of judging an individual of a certain **group** based on perceived notions about that particular group. Prejudice is linked to discrimination but prejudice is an **attitude** whereas **discrimination** is the action associated with that attitude. Some people hold prejudices, but may not express them or act on them. In contrast, many people do act on their prejudices in the form of discrimination. Although the term "prejudice" is often linked with interpersonal judgments, it can also apply to any judgment not solely based on reality. In this sense "prejudice" refers to an irrational decision that somehow distorts the information relevant to the judgment made.

In the United States, as in other countries, prejudice exists in many forms. Some theorists, researchers and philosophers believe that no one is truly free of prejudice and people hold prejudices whether consciously or not. Some researchers draw from **evolutionary theory** and suggest that prejudices are an instinctive biological feature and it is this that makes us human. They believe that prejudices people hold against other groups in conjunction with **xenophobia** (fear of strangers/ foreigners) is what enabled *homo sapiens* to survive. Other researchers posit that prejudice is learned throughout childhood from parents during the **socialization** process. Whatever the origins of prejudice, it is plentiful in every **society** and has created a long lasting power struggle between different groups and therefore it merits study.

Prejudice is closely linked to the practice of stereotyping. A stereotype is a generalization of a category of people on the basis of perceived traits or attributes. These traits ascribed to a particular group are not based on personal experience but often on unsubstantiated information. Stereotypes embellish upon characteristics of specific groups. For instance the Native American population has a disproportionate number of individuals suffering from **alcoholism**. Thus one negative **stereotype** of Native Americans is that they abuse alcohol. An individual who has had no contact with Native Americans or their lifestyle may think that all Native Americans abuse alcohol based on this stereotype. Prejudices aimed at Native Americans develop from these negative stereotypes.

Prejudice can target many different populations. Prejudice aimed at ethnic groups is often the result of ethnocentrism. Ethnocentrism is the inclination to believe that one's own **culture**, **ethnicity**, or **race** is superior to all others. With this idea, groups that possess different beliefs and practices are labeled as strange and inferior. Prejudices are not confined to race and ethnicity. They can be directed toward other groups such as homosexuals, the elderly, women, and the disabled. Prejudices can also be aimed at people who live in the south, New Yorkers, blue collar workers, people who live on farms. etc. Almost any group that is differentiated from the whole of the population is likely to have some prejudice directed toward them.

Prejudice influences society in many ways. In a group of studies aimed at measuring prejudice, the effects of prejudice become clear. A group of white students were asked to serve as a jury in a mock rape trial. The rape victim was a nineteen year old white female. The student jurors were given different scenarios and asked to judge whether the rape suspect was guilty or not guilty. In one scenario the alleged rapist was a white man with strong evidence against him (eyewitness and victim identification). In another scenario a white man was the suspect with weak evidence against him (no eyewitness and no victim identification). In the other two scenarios the suspect was African American with strong evidence against him and with weak evidence against him. The results showed that the white student jurors were more likely to blame the African American man regardless of whether the evidence was weak or strong. Similar outcomes have been confirmed in later studies. The results of this study raises many questions regarding the effects of prejudice on the criminal justice system. Continued research investigates these difficult questions.

Prejudice occurs in all societies and is aimed at many different groups. When linked with discrimination problems begin to emerge. **Human rights** can be violated and individuals' lives can be affected. It is important for researchers explore the problem of prejudice and discrimination in order to try to minimize it if not eliminate it from society.

See also Discrimination; Stereotype

PREMARITAL SEXUAL STANDARDS

Premarital sexual standards refers to the normative expectations regarding what is considered ''appropriate'' **sexual behavior** prior to marriage. Premarital sexual standards are highly contextual, depending on historical time period, **culture**, and individual characteristics. The Mangaia in Polynesia expect that male and female adolescents will engage frequently in premarital sexual intercourse and other forms of sexual behavior. However, in the United States, premarital sex has had less acceptance, although it has become increasingly more acceptable over time. These changing premarital sexual standards are dependent upon gender. For example, many contemporary sexual **norms** still use Victorian ideas of sexuality, specifically that women are asexual and men are sexually aggressive or predatory. Consequently, premarital sex is still generally more acceptable for men than for women. Premarital sexual standards can also vary depending on whether the sexual activity is same-sex or different-sex. For example, in ancient Greece it was acceptable for young boys to have sexual intercourse with older men prior to **marriage**, but because sexual intercourse with women was predominantly intended for procreation, men usually did not have female partners until after marriage.

Age of the individuals involved is also a factor of premarital sexual standards. While sexual intercourse before marriage is largely accepted in the United States for people over the age of 18, sexual activity by adolescents is frowned upon, and the occurrence of teenage pregnancy is considered a major social problem. Religious beliefs also have an impact on premarital sexual standards. Many Catholics and conservative Protestants and Jews believe that all sexual intercourse outside of marriage is morally wrong and constitutes sin. However, premarital sexual standards should not be confused with behavior; many people who embrace religious beliefs that sex outside of marriage is a sin still engage in premarital sex.

Many factors are involved in the growing acceptance of premarital sex. The increased effectiveness of contraception and the legalization of abortion have made sex outside of marriage easier to engage in by decreasing the likelihood of unwanted pregnancy. The increased legitimization of female sexuality has made it more accepting for women to accept and initiate sexual contact with men (although same-sex sexuality is still deemed unacceptable by many people). The delay in the age of first marriage is a significant factor in the growing acceptance of premarital sex. From 1975 to 1991, the **mean** age for first marriage increased by 2.8 years for men and 3 years for women. These three additional years before marriage occur

during the age at which premarital sex is most accepted (early twenties) and thus increase the opportunities for premarital sex at a time in which it is the least socially prohibited.

See also Sexual Behavior

PRIMARY DEVIANCE

The concept of primary deviance is derived from the work of sociologists Frank Tannenbaum, Edwin Lemert, Howard Becker, William Chambliss, and Edwin Schur from the 1930s to the 1970s and is associated with the labeling theory. According to this **theory**, society's response to an individual's participation in an act that violates a social norm—known as primary deviance—can put a "label" on that individual which is self-perpetuating. In other words, once an individual commits a deviant act, society's labeling of that individual as "deviant" may cause that person to assume the label to be true and to persist deviant acts, a response referred to as "secondary deviance."

For example, a person who experiments with marijuana in high school, whether because of peer pressure or simple curiosity, has committed an act of primary deviance. This act violates both formal criminal laws and informal norms agreed upon by many teachers, parents, classmates, and **community** members. If the person is caught in the act of primary deviance, he or she will typically be punished in a variety of ways. Punishment might involve an official arrest by police, followed by imprisonment, or more informal types of punishment such as being grounded by parents, shunned by friends, or suspended from school.

According to labeling theorists, this punishment, whether formal or informal, attaches a label to the person. In this example, the label attached to the person may be that of "drug user" or "pot head." Often, individuals will begin to internalize the labels attached to them by the criminal justice system and others, and begin to think of themselves in the same manner. In short, they accept the deviant or criminal label. When this happens, individuals may then continue to commit the same acts that led them to receive the label in the first instance. These continued acts are referred to as acts of secondary deviance. As Tannenbaum describes it, a person with a deviant or criminal label often becomes the person others believe him or her to be.

This approach is in sharp contrast to that of deterrence theorists such as James Q. Wilson, who assert that if primary deviance is initially punished and a negative label is attached, the behavior will typically cease. Labeling theorists argue that the negative label attached to a person after being punished for an act of primary deviance may result in more of the same behavior.

PRIMARY GROUP

Sociologists have long studied the nature of social groups and the level of interaction and meaning associated with **group** membership. According to Charles Horton Cooley, social groups may be understood in terms of the goals of the group and the amount of interpersonal concern that members have for one another. Cooley suggested that there are two types of social groups: primary groups and secondary groups. Secondary groups are large, impersonal social groups in which members share a common goal or activity. Common examples are students in a classroom and employees in an office. Members of secondary groups may interact on a regular basis, but the interaction is instrumental toward accomplishing some common goal. Secondary groups lack a sense of belonging and intimacy among members.

Primary groups, by contrast, are small social groups in which relationships are personal and enduring. Simply being a member of a primary group conveys a sense of belonging and camaraderie. Members of primary groups often spend much time together and develop a genuine bond. Examples of primary groups are families, close friends, close neighbors, and, in some cases, members of community and religious groups.

Cooley suggested that the most important primary group is the family. The **family** is the first social group a child is exposed to and is responsible for the daily care and guardianship of the child. Additionally, the family is typically the main agent of **socialization** for at least the first five years of life. During this time, families must teach **language**, **norms**, **values**, appropriate behaviors, and social **identity**. The family is portrayed as an indispensable group, a group where members genuinely care for one another despite personal differences or disagreements. For example, family reunions bring together a large number of people who interact at varying levels and who may be quite different. Yet, an instant bond usually is conferred on a person simply because they are "family." This example illustrates the power of primary group membership.

Primary groups are most common in agrarian societies where economic conditions necessitate a greater emphasis on family and community social bonds. With the transition to industrial and now post-industrial economies and the advent of more efficient forms of transportation, secondary groups become more common as individuals generally lack the time, patience, and proximity to others needed to foster primary group relationships.

PRIMITIVE SOCIETY

Primitive societies are considered to be the earliest forms of human societies. Societies are often described according to particular characteristics, using a classification system to group them with other similar societies on given traits, such as development in key areas. Researchers can then examine various societies and discuss them as they compare and differ. The word "primitive" denotes an elementary level of technological and social organizational complexity. It also commonly implies a certain "prelogical" mentality associated with this level of technology and organization.

Although "primitive society" is intended to be a nonjudgmental term, many modern researchers favor labels such

as "simple society," "tribal society," or "nonliterate society" instead, but these terms may also carry negative connotations. Such negative ideas are based on the assumption that so-called modern **society** (such as that of the United States and other countries with similar levels of organization and technology) is a superior form of society. As social scientists, though, sociologists seek not to impose their values on other societies, so those who study these societies try to do so on the basis of the traditional societies' own characteristics rather than judging them based on the characteristics of modern or complex forms of society. More neutral terms that are beginning to be used more commonly include "traditional society" and "hunting and gathering society" (which are perceived as less judgmental, yet still describe those societies in terms of particular characteristics).

There are a number of traits which distinguish a traditional society from other forms. **Traditional societies** are the least internally differentiated type. Most members of the group, women, men, and children who are old enough, have similar roles and spend most of their time working toward the same ends (there is typically little specialized **division of labor**). For example, in a traditional society, most people spend a large amount of their time searching for or hunting for necessities, such as collecting water or gathering or hunting food. Members typically have few personal possessions, and there are fewer social inequalities in this type; theirs is thus considered to be the most egalitarian form of society. Traditional societies frequently have no designated ruler and most decisions are made by consensus. The only highly specialized role which often exists in this type of society is that of the shaman, or priest, but despite having a specific role within the group, the shaman also participates in the maintenance of the group along with everyone else.

Since there is no real division of roles, the fundamental organization for this type of society is kinship, or bonding by ancestry or marriage. This organization not only performs the functions expected of the family, but it also fulfills the functions of several other organizations found in more "modern" societies, such as education and **health care**.

Despite media depictions of traditional societies as aggressive, warring tribes, most are peaceful and place a high value on the sharing of resources. Members of these societies are generally nomadic people who move in search of new food sources once one area's supplies are exhausted. The death rates among this form of society are typically high, due to high risks of disease and the destruction or contamination of food sources; the birth rates are also high to compensate for higher death rates.

Often traditional societies lack a form of written language and rely on an oral transmission of history and **culture**. In some non-literate traditional societies a small group of people within the society do possess a form of written **communication** which may create a privileged class of scribes within the group who control the power of defining the culture, and recording it for future members. In these cases, the development of a written language is considered to be a major step in the development of the society, although this again implies a judgment that more developed societies and more literate societies are superior.

Traditional societies were fairly common until a few hundred years ago. Now, however, there are only a few left in existence, such as the aborigines of Australia and some tribes in sub-Saharan Africa. Some formerly traditional societies "evolved" into more modern ones, but some have been driven out of existence by the expansion of modern societies into areas the traditional societies depended on for survival. Others have been purposely eradicated, while still others have simply died out. In recent years there have been movements to try to preserve the few remaining traditional societies, but those movements have met with limited success.

See also Traditional Societies

PRIVATIZATION

Privatization is the transfer of state responsibilities to the private sector of the economy. Privatization may be sudden, involving the transfer of **property** and assets of public corporations, or it may be gradual, in which a **society** sees a decline in state provisions, subsidies, and regulation until all responsibility for the areas once supported by **government** are held by private enterprise. In Britain and Western European, conservative governments made a commitment to privatization during the 1980s. The most aggressive programs were initiated after the fall of the communist governments in Eastern Europe. In America, the 1970s and 1980s marked the beginnings of a move towards privatization, though Peter Drucker used the term in the late 1960s. Privatization was seen as a remedy to America's fiscal problems of the late 1980s, but it was not as strongly accepted as it was in Britain and Europe.

The merits of privatization are hotly debated, but the ultimate decision of whether to privatize revolves around the financing of payment for a good or service and the performance of the provider. The questions that economists and other financial thinkers consider are whether payment should come from individual or collective resources and whether the good or service should be delivered by a governmental or non-governmental **organization**. Often the lines between public and private are blurry at best. Yet proponents of privatization assert the benefits to be had in making public undertakings the responsibility of the private sector, including an increased responsibility for accountability in the individual or collective, granted the ability to work on behalf of public **authority**.

PROBABILITY

Probability is a **measurement** in inferential statistical analysis by which the likelihood of a designated event is determined to occur. It is mathematically defined at a basic level by the expression $p = n/N$, where p represents the probability, n represents the number of possible times a particular outcome can take place, and N represents the total number of outcomes possible. For example, to determine the probability of drawing a queen from a deck of playing cards in one try, n would be four

(the number of queens in the deck) and N would be 52 (the total number of cards in the deck from which to choose). This equation assumes that N outcomes are all equally likely and mutually exclusive. This equation changes when the likelihood of a particular outcome changes based on the frequency in which it has already occurred.

Probability estimates are always represented as a proportion (either as a decimal, fraction, or percentage) and range from 0.00, which is zero likelihood, to 1.00, which is a certainty. Early probability **theory** was developed by the French mathematician, Blaise Pascal, who became interested in probability theory by studying games of chance using six-sided dice. Another development, the Bernoulli distribution, predicted the likelihood of a particular outcome of a dichotomized **variable**. Moreover, the Poisson probability model allows one to predict the number of particular outcomes during a set interval of time.

The mathematical uses of probability generally depend upon or assume the outcomes are random, meaning a pattern cannot be determined even after many repetitions. In sociological research, however, outcomes are assumed to depend upon a set of independent variables that can be measured statistically. Social scientists use the basic concept of probability to determine how these independent variables affect the likelihood of a particular outcome. Many statistical analytic techniques use probability theory, such as logistic regression analysis, which estimates the likelihood of a specific outcome when certain conditions are met. For example, one can use a logistic **regression** to determine the likelihood of a person developing cancer if that person is male or female, a smoker or non-smoker, and regularly exercises or exercises infrequently.

Probability can also be used as a sampling method to increase the fit of an estimate of an outcome based on a sample with the actual number of times an outcome occurs in the population from which the sample was taken. Using probability (or sometimes referred to as random) sampling ensures that the results found in a sample will also be found in the larger population.

PROFESSIONS

The term, professions, refers to middle-class occupational groups that require both intellectual and technical expertise. Traditionally, professions include occupations such as teaching, law, medicine, and the armed services. Professions lay claim to a specified area of knowledge and certain functions within **society**. For example, doctors dominate the medical profession in terms of medical authority. Only doctors can perform certain functions within society such as prescribing drugs. Professions limit access through gatekeeping mechanisms such as educational requirements and licensing. In addition, professions set their own work and ethical standards. If professionals do not adhere to these standards, they risk losing professional membership. For example, the American Bar Association (ABA) sets the education and licensing requirements for lawyers and outlines the profession's ethical standards.

Which occupations qualify as professions is debated within sociology. Many occupations do not fit neatly into ei-

ther professional or non-professional categories. For example, many blue-collar occupations include some aspects of professions. For example, plumbing requires an expertise in a set body of technical knowledge and access to the occupation is limited through apprenticeships and licensing requirements.

Historically, professions have been presented in two ways within sociology, as altruistic and as self-interested. Functionalists have shown professions as serving vital societal functions in the interest of society. This conceptualization presents professions as fulfilling a needed function in society that benefits society at large. For example, doctors are providing the needed service for health care, and patients benefit from the expertise of the medical profession. This altruistic conception of professions can be juxtaposed with an understanding of professions as partially self-interested entities. Professions have an interest in limiting access to its profession ranks and controlling a body of knowledge in order to gain rewards such as lucrative incomes, social esteem, and job autonomy.

The term professionalization refers to the process of occupations claiming the **status** of a profession. Burgeoning professions often have to compete with other occupations for dominance in a specialized area of knowledge and functions within society in the process of gaining professional status. The process of professionalization is in part the elimination of **competition** from outsiders. For example, historically doctors had to compete with many other health professionals such as midwives, pharmacists and abortionists for clients and control over certain practices such as childbirth and abortion procedures.

The process of professionalization can also involve establishing or increasing the standards of professional membership. One aspect of professionalization is the setting of educational requirements including specifying the requisite credentials for a profession such as the mandate of doctors having a medical degree. Randall Collins, a sociologist, found that often educational requirements for an occupation do not the result from need for specific or technical skills. Collins pointed out that many professions that today have long education requirements, including medicine and law, were once apprenticeship based. **Higher education** requirements are primarily to prepare students for social and cultural positions of professional life. Students in higher education pursuing a professional **career** do not learn the needed skills in the classroom, but rather they learn the proper mindset and commitment to middle-class values and work ethic. Not only do credential requirements limit access to the profession, the standard of education credentials is one way for professions to gain social status and legitimacy.

Professions are a vital and fruitful area of sociological research. Future research in this area could include how the booming **internet** and computer industry relates to the concepts of professions. Sociologists can study how and if the new technology occupations such as web programmers seek professional status and whether the increasing amount of public knowledge available on the internet will threaten the monopoly of profession over areas of specialized knowledge.

PROGRESS

Western **civilization** has been driven by the notion of progress for three hundred years. Progress, here, is conceived as the ever-increasingly sophisticated knowledge and improved **quality of life**. Throughout the twentieth century, almost every country in the world has assumed this same notion of progress. In the less developed areas, also known as the Third World, the concept of modernization is seen as identical to progress.

While it is difficult to pinpoint the origin of the concept of progress, it is clear that the idea of a universal history of human progress was developed during the eighteenth century in the writings of Voltaire and Kant. Kant contributed a fully developed notion of humanity heading towards the idea of a universal civil **society**, or a society established on **justice** which is based on maximum individual freedom.

Eighteenth- and nineteenth-century philosophers were caught up with the notion of progress. The notion of heaven after death shifted to an idea of heaven on earth. These early notions were flavored with complete, optimistic faith in the meaning of life and human destiny, meanings colored with religious overtones. Over the next hundred years this shifted to the more recognizable form of the idea of progress that we have today. Progress became less religiously tinged and increasingly logical.

Throughout the twentieth century, theories of progress followed those of the nineteenth century. These theories were increasingly rational, optimistic, and materialistic. **Sociology** added to this bed of progress early functional and post-industrial theories. These theories foresaw a future society based on science, meaning a society which was well-balanced and prosperous. Toward the end of the twentieth century, scholars have seen the end of the theories. These theories have imploded at great cost. Science failed to produce utopia and, moreover, the future is shrouded by environmental doubts.

PROPERTY

Central to a capitalist **society** is property. Property involves socially determined rights over both animate (e.g., pets) and inanimate (e.g., cars) objects. Property can include a variety of things. Owning a home, land, stocks, and other assets (e.g., furniture, paintings, antiques, etc.) are all forms of property. Possession of property confers power, and as a result, property rights shape social relationships. For example, in other times and here and elsewhere people themselves have been considered property. Property is unique compared to other monetary sources. Unlike income, property is wealth. Wealth is not necessarily in monetary form but can be transformed into such. Historically, income has been a more central measure than wealth, but the significance of wealth has been increasing. Patterns of acquisition, distribution, and the consequences of ownership are main concerns in the social sciences. Ownership, control, and transmission of property are key to understanding the dynamics of inequality in society. For instance, in their 1993 book, Black Wealth/White Wealth, Oliver and

Shapiro show that using income as an indicator of racial equality can be misleading and that there is an even more dramatic racial disparity in terms of wealth. Their research illustrates that blacks and whites are similar along a variety of dimensions (e.g., education, size of **household**, occupation, income, etc.) have very different levels of wealth, whites having much more than blacks. One reason why equality in wealth has been much more difficult to achieve than equality in income is that, in general, property **values** appreciate over time. Another related reason is that property accumulates. Last, property is transferred from generation to generation through inheritance. This means that families with property confer this wealth onto their children who benefit from the advantage and then confer it onto their children. Advantage remains in the **family**. Inheritance plays an especially pivotal role in explaining why the disparity in wealth is so great between blacks and whites. Once considered property themselves, blacks historically have been denied access to property. Formal laws were in place to restrict and prevent blacks from having ownership in any form. Without wealth to pass on generation to generation, black families are disadvantaged compared to whites. Any savings that can accumulate is spent on either caring for parents who were not economically prepared for their later years or trying to help children get ahead, such as paying for schooling.

PROPHET

In his 1922 academic paper titled *Wirtschaft und Gesellschaft,* later translated as *Economy and Society: An Outline of Interpretive Sociology* by G. Roth and G. Wittach, German sociologist **Max Weber** defined a prophet to be any "individual bearer of charisma" who by virtue of his or her life mission, "proclaims a religious doctrine or divine commandment." For Weber, it is the "personal call" and revelation of the prophet that distinguishes him or her from a priest, who has authority merely as the "servant of a sacred tradition." Weber also states that prophets have usually arisen from outside the priesthood.

Weber also discusses another significant distinction between *ethical prophecy,* in which the prophet proclaims God's will, and *exemplary prophecy,* whereby the prophet demonstrates by personal example the way to personal salvation. According to Weber, the latter is characteristic of the Far East and the former first appears in the Near East and is associated with the appearance of conceptions of a personal, transcendental, ethical God only in his region.

PROSTITUTION

Prostitution, the exchange of sexual acts for **money**, is called the world's oldest profession, for it continues despite widespread laws which prohibit it. Prostitution occurs in **cities** as well as small towns, in just about all nations of the world. In fact, prostitution is just one segment of the larger sex industry in which customers can, for example, pay for sexy chat over

Prostitutes are socially marginalized, often keeping their occupations secret from others for fear of rejection *(AP/Wide World Photos, Inc.)*.

the phone or on the **internet**, order a lap dance from a stripper in a gentlemen's club, or orchestrate a role-playing session in which the client and the provider pretend to be characters in a sexual fantasy.

Considered by many to be a social problem which needs to be contained if not eradicated, prostitution is often linked to crimes like drug use, petty theft, and assault. Prostitutes are socially marginalized, often keeping their sex work secret from friends, **family**, and potential employers for fear of rejection. For women especially, **society** reserves a special stigma for those who get paid to have sex, defining prostitution as an irreparable fall from female virtue and assuming only the most depraved, desperate women resort to it. In reality, work experiences in the sex industry ranges from sexual slavery in which women who are coerced into prostitution, often have little access to the money they earn and no freedom to find different work to appointment-based services in which women charge high fees, have control over the clients they accept, and can freely move in and out of sex work as they choose. Limiting the definition of prostitution to only the most economically disadvantaged women ignores those women who are financial-

ly successful or those who are supplementing their incomes as they work other jobs, work their way through college, or finance their artistic pursuits. In addition, defining prostitution narrowly ignores the sizable minorities of male prostitutes, women who serve female clients, and transgendered prostitutes, a particularly invisible and outcast population.

Approaches to solving problems of prostitution vary, depending on whether prostitution is defined as a social ill or as a type of work. The former suggests stronger enforcement of criminal codes, crackdowns on international trafficking rings, and sometimes pursuit of criminal penalties against clients as well as prostitutes. The latter suggests decriminalization of prostitution as a minimum step in improving working conditions for all prostitutes, as well as other typical labor demands such as safe working environments, living wages, and the freedom to select or reject clients. For a prostitute working on the street, these demands may be as simple as being allowed to work on streets with better lighting and getting access to emergency assistance. For someone working in a brothel, demands may include limiting the percentage of client fees collected by the establishment or negotiating the maximum number of hours worked each day.

An important policy question regarding prostitution is whether prostitutes should be tested for sexually transmitted infections (STIs), such as AIDS. Many people consider prostitutes to be the source of STIs, spreading disease throughout the population. Administering regular tests to prostitutes would identify infected prostitutes and make them ineligible for sex work, thus protecting clients from contracting STIs. Testing prostitutes and not their clients, however, ignores the fact that prostitutes must contract an STI before they can spread it and is an ineffective means of containing **disease**. Removing infected prostitutes from service sets up a new **cohort** of prostitutes to contract STIs from infected clients, creating a disposable population of sex workers while failing to halt the spread of disease. Testing clients is an impractical alternative, but a third option of providing education regarding STI transmission, lower-risk sexual behaviors, and condom use may prove to be more effective in reducing transmission rates.

PROTEST MOVEMENTS

Protest movements are a form of contentious **collective action**. The groups mounting the protests may in organization and size, but the historical impact of **social movements** on the world remains substantial. For example, the Protestant sect of **Christianity** was formed as a result of Martin Luther's objections to the state of Catholicism and papist rule in the sixteenth century. This sect, one of Christianity's largest, memorializes its origin in its name.

Protest movements mount sustained challenges to the status quo in the attempt to realize a vision shared by its participants; this shared vision is the glue holding disparate individuals together in any given movement. These movements begin their lives as a loose collection of like-minded individuals; single-issue protest movements tend to disband once they realize

their objective, while movements focused on more nebulous goals, such as winning equal treatment under the law for a given **group**, become increasingly institutionalized as they experience successes. Such institutionalization can occur on two levels: within the group itself, as it develops a formal **leadership** and structure; or the movement may become integrated into the mainstream, which can generate a backlash and accusations of co-optation.

The United States was founded by a protest movement, begun when members of a persecuted religious group, the Puritans, left Britain and formed settlements in New England in the seventeenth century. By the eighteenth century, thirteen colonies lined the eastern seaboard, chafing under Britain's rule and, especially, its taxation of the colonies; in April of 1775, the colonies launched a rebellion against British colonial rule, waging the eight year Revolutionary War, until Britain granted them independence. These protestant origins are codified in the First Amendment of the U.S. constitution, which guarantees its citizens the right to mount (peaceful) protests as an exercise of free speech.

The French Revolution, which lasted the ten years between 1789 to 1799, was launched by the lower classes against the ruling classes. The less-wealthy French objected to the dire economic straits in which they found themselves, the strict class **structure** and the monarchy, whose rule was backed by the Divine Right of Kings. This revolution, which rid France of the last vestiges of **feudalism**, inspired Karl Marx's historical **dialectic** of the relationships between classes, leading Marx to propose the inevitability of a proletarian uprising in capitalist societies. Protest movements against the Communist regimes in Eastern Europe, which had cruelly twisted Marx's utopian vision, brought about the fall of the Communist empire in 1989; Eastern and Western Germans celebrated together as they pulled down the Berlin Wall.

Because its Constitution guarantees freedom of speech, the United States has long been a site of protest movements, from abolitionists seeking to end slavery in the nineteenth century, to protests against the Vietnam War in the 1960s and 1970s, to current movements protesting police brutality and lax firearm laws. The U.S. protest movements that left the most lasting impact on the latter half of the twentieth century are the Civil Rights movement and the Women's Movement.

PROTESTANT ETHIC

The Protestant ethic has its origins in Christian **asceticism**, the practice of self-denial and abstinence from worldly comforts and pleasures. Christian asceticism resulted from a belief that self-denial, characterized by self-control, planning, and hard work, ensured salvation. The subject is explored in Max Weber's *The Protestant Ethic and the Spirit of Capitalism* (1904-1905). In this famous work Weber traces the relationship between ascetic Protestantism, especially the doctrine of French theologian John Calvin (1509-1564), and the rise of post-Reformation **capitalism** in Western societies. Weber's work has generated much scholarly debate. For sociologists,

John Calvin introduced the idea of predestination, an ideology espousing that each person's fate in the afterlife was "predestined" by God *(The Library of Congress).*

a part of the debate stems from the idea that the work attempts to refute Marx's claim that major **social change** derives only from economic conditions. Weber's work revealed religion to be a major force in social change. Today, capitalism has developed in many societies independent of religious tenets, but for many post-Reformation Western Europeans and North Americans the rise of capitalism correlated with their Protestant ethic.

Weber rejected alternative explanations for the rise of capitalism in the West in the sixteenth and seventeenth centuries. Some posited that capitalism came to prominence because conditions were favorable for its emergence. To this claim, Weber argued that similar material conditions were in place at other times but capitalism did not arise. Others attributed capitalism to the inherent drive for accumulation. To this claim, Weber argued that, although such an instinct has always existed, it has not always culminated in capitalism. In an effort to address the rise of capitalism, Weber worked to establish causal significance between **religious orientations** and Western capitalism. Weber recognized that capitalism existed in some form in China, India, and during the Middle Ages but argued that it was a different form of capitalism because it lacked the peculiar Protestant ethic. Weber's focus was a specific type of

capitalism which was significantly different from earlier forms of capitalism: rational capitalism. Rational capitalism is relentless in the pursuit of wealth, while it utilizes the most efficient means for acquiring material goods. It is viewed as a means to an end, not as an avenue for obtaining goods or assuring salvation.

Weber began his work by analyzing the relationship between occupation and denominational affiliation. He noted that economic leaders throughout Europe and the United States were disproportionately Protestant. Weber's review of the sixteenth-century Protestant Reformation reveals the uniqueness of the Puritan lifestyle and the consequences for the economic system. Early sixteenth-century Christians held the pursuit of profit to be morally questionable. The Protestant Reformation brought changes that supported the entrepreneurial spirit. Martin Luther, the German theologian who was a catalyst for the Protestant Reformation, taught that God gave each individual a vocation or ''calling'' and expected hard work in efforts to glorify him. Later, French theologian John Calvin introduced the idea of **predestination**, an **ideology** espousing that each person's fate in the afterlife was ''predestined'' by God. The Protestant Reformation discredited the authority of the pope and traditional Catholicism by emphasizing the importance of an individual relationship with God. Early Protestant reformers refuted the role of church hierarchy as an intermediary system between God and believers. But this freedom from the church also raised serious questions. How could people be assured of their place with God? For Catholics, this surety remained in their faithfulness to the church. For Protestants, a break with the church meant that proof of salvation had to come by way of faith and a demonstration of God's redemptive grace in one's life. Such a demonstration of the changed nature of an individual was evidenced in vocational obligations and material success.

The teachings of John Calvin emphasized that some were born to go to heaven, others doomed to hell, and individuals could not know if they were among heaven's elect. This produced much anxiety for Calvinists. As a result of the psychological turmoil produced by the doctrine of predestination, believers began to seek signs of God's grace. Weber suggested that the Protestant ethic characterized by asceticism and hard work provided relief from anxiety about the afterlife. Thus, the assurance of salvation was linked to vocational accountability, and worldly success became the sign of being among the elect. Individuals were persuaded that by working hard, they could uncover the signs of salvation. The money earned from hard work could not be spent for luxuries and so it was invested. This accumulation of wealth led to a surge in production and ultimately contributed to the advent of the **Industrial Revolution**.

PSYCHOANALYSIS

Psychoanalysis was originally introduced by **Sigmund Freud** (1856-1939). Psychoanalysis is a therapeutic approach that attempts to eliminate anxiety by giving the patient insight into unconscious motivation and conflict. Anxiety is a state of tension that moves us into action. There are several types of anxiety; one, neurotic anxiety, is the fear that the our instincts will get out of control and cause difficulty. **Ego** defense mechanisms help alleviate and repress this anxiety by helping the individual cope. The ego defense mechanisms are: repression, denial, reaction formation, projection, displacement, rationalization, sublimation, regression, introjection, identification, compensation, and ritual and undoing.

According to the psychoanalytic perspective, the personality consists of the **id**, ego, and super-ego. Id is present at birth. It is the primary source of psychic energy and the seat of all instincts. It is aimed at reducing tension and acts on the pleasure principle. Ego mediates between the external world and the id and super-ego. It controls consciousness and exercises censorship and is ruled by the reality principle. Superego is a person's moral code. The focus is on right and wrong, and it represents the traditional value and ideals of **society**. It inhibits the id and injects moral standards and strives for perfection.

A significant contribution of the psychoanalytic **model** is the delineation of the stages of psychosocial and psychosexual development from birth through adulthood, all grounded in the first six years of life. The oral stage includes birth to the end of the first grade and is characterized by sucking and familiarizing the infant to the world through oral sensation (child putting toys in the mouth). The anal stage includes ages one to three, and toilet training is considered to be a child's first experience with discipline. The tasks mastered during this stage are learning independence, personal power, and autonomy and learning how to recognize negative feelings. The phallic stage includes ages three to six. Childhood **experimentation** is common, and many attitudes toward sexuality originate in this phase. Children learn moral standards and form attitudes about physical pleasure during this genital stage.

PSYCHOLOGY

Psychology is the scientific study of human behavior and experience. Through systematic observation and research, psychologists attempt to explain how and why human beings act and react to the world around them. The emergence of psychology as an independent scientific discipline rather than a branch of **philosophy** is commonly dated to 1879 when Wilhelm Wundt opened the first psychological laboratory in Leipzig, Germany. As the field of psychology expanded, various schools of thought developed. Although all purported to be based on scientific method, they differed on the matter to be studied, how they defined the goal of psychology, and their research **methodology**.

Wundt and numerous collaborators founded the school of structuralism, which studies the structure of consciousness. Wundt believed that complex mental processes are created by the conscious mind from basic elements, just as compound chemicals are the result of a formulation of simple elements. According to Wundt, the elements of conscious experience

were sensations (sights, sounds, tastes, touches, and smells) and feelings (excitement-calm, pleasure-displeasure, and strain-relaxation). Human experiences elicit various sensations and feelings that are combined and synthesized by the mind to produce a cohesive conscious event. Further, Wundt suggested that these compounds could be reduced to their base elements for the purpose of study and understanding.

The methodology for study employed by Wundt and his followers consisted of introspection. Individuals were asked to examine and report on their personal mental processes. For example, observers would listen to the ticking of a metronome and record in minute detail their reactions to variances in speed, tone, and volume. Introspection required extensive training for the testers and was highly regulated to maintain scientific. Unfortunately for the structuralists, little consensus in results was reached among researchers at different laboratories, and with no verifiable means to settle disputes, introspection lost respect as a scientific methodology. **Structuralism** likewise lost influence with the death of Wundt's former student Edward Titchener in 1927.

The functionalist school emphasized the function of consciousness. The field was most heavily influenced by the work of **Charles Darwin** and his theory of evolution. Darwin argued that animals possess a variety of characteristics, and those animals with characteristics more suited to their environment will reproduce at higher rates, thus passing on the desirable traits to their young. Although the idea that animals developed and changed over time was not original, Darwin's contention that natural selection applied to humans was revolutionary.

The most important functionalist was **William James**, an American-born psychologist and Harvard professor of physiology. Influenced by Darwin, James focused on how humans used their perceptive abilities to function in, and adapt to, their environments. Arguing against the reliance on pure sensation as proposed by the structuralists, James explained consciousness as a continuous flow, hence the phrase, "stream of consciousness." Perceptions are formed based on previous experiences with reoccurring perceptions and experiences becoming habits that need little mental energy to comprehend. James also established an interest in comparative, individual, and developmental study. The functionalist cause was later taken up by James' followers John Dewey and James Angell.

Whereas both the structuralists and the functionalists presupposed that the mind used association as a tool for comprehension, associationists manufactured situations to study the connections of ideas and experiences in the learning process. Associationism was developed by Hermann Ebbinghaus (1850–1909), Ivan Pavlov (1849–1936), and Edward Thorndike (1874–1949). Ebbinghaus engineered the modern study of memory. He tested his own memory systematically and extensively by using nonsense syllables (such as ceg, zut, and pov) to study the factors involved in remembering and forgetting new information. Pavlov, a Russian physiologist, studied the associations in animals between external stimuli and physiological response. In his most famous experiment, he trained dogs to salivate at the sound of a buzzer. By sounding the

Psychoanalysis is a therapeutic approach that attempts to eliminate anxiety by giving the patient insight into unconscious motivation and conflict *(Custom Medical Stock Photo, Inc.)*.

buzzer every time the dogs ate, Pavlov taught them to associate the two events, a process he termed "conditioning." Thorndike also studied animals but focused on the associations between external stimuli and voluntary responses. He developed the "puzzle box," a cage out of which an animal could escape by pulling a loop of string. Thorndike measured the time needed for the animal to escape, using it to indicate learning rate.

In 1913 John Watson (1878-1958) published "Psychology as the Behaviorist Views It" in *The Psychological Review*, thus establishing the school of **behaviorism**. He argued that the study of the unconscious mind was no more than superstitious speculation. It cannot be clearly identified or measured and, thus, is not fit for scientific study. Influenced by Pavlov, Watson suggested that all behavior could be explained as a response to stimuli. The response was either instinctive (as with Pavlov's dogs) or leaned (as with Thorndike's "puzzle box"). Behaviorism marked a major shift in the object of study and methodology from the study of the conscious mind through introspection to the study of behavior through objective analysis. The behaviorist school was quickly accepted as an important contribution and dominated psychological thought during the second half of the twentieth century. Other psychologists who undertook the early behaviorist approach are Edward Tolman (1886–1961), Clark Hull (1884–1952), and B. F. Skinner (1904–).

Originating in Germany, Gestalt psychology had three major proponents: Max Wertheimer (1880–1943), Kurt Koffka (1876–1941), and Wolfgang Kohler (1887–1967). Roughly translated Gestalt means "whole" or "form," thus the word refers to an emphasis on human experience as a unified event. Gestalt psychologists objected to the reduction of phenomena to individual parts and argued that human perception and thought should be addressed holistically. Gestalt psychology rose in popularity before dissolving in the 1930s after its three leaders emigrated to the United States to escape Nazi Germany.

Psychoanalysis provided a unique break from the other schools of thought in that it did not give center stage to the functions of the conscious mind or responses to stimuli. Psy-

choanalytical psychology was established by Sigmund Freud (1856-1939), who believed that much of human behavior was dictated by hidden motives and desires. Therefore, the key to understanding human behavior and thought was the unconscious mind. Psychoanalytical **theory**, which tended to study **abnormal** human activity, was perpetuated by Freudian disciples Carl Gustav Jung (1870-1961) and Alfred Adler (1870-1937).

Numerous new approaches continue to appear on the scene, including the increasingly recognized role of cognitive psychology, which returns to the claim that human mental processes can and should be studied and that human behavior is more than a simple response to stimuli. To understand human phenomena, the manner in which humans perceive, interpret, store, and retrieve information must be studied. Some of these theoretical viewpoints have maintained lasting impact on the field of study, whereas others are now only of historical interest. Nonetheless, modern psychology bears the impress of its predecessors.

PUBLIC AND PRIVATE SPHERES

Classical **liberalism** defines the relationship of the individual to the state through the concept of private and public spheres. The private sphere encompasses all aspects of domestic and personal life; work and political life make up the public sphere. A liberal, democratic government's power extends only so far as the front door of a man's home, at which point the individual becomes sovereign.

John Locke, in England, and **Jean-Jacques Rousseau**, in France, were the leading figures in the introduction of liberal ideas in the nineteenth century. Liberalism champions the right of the individual to pursue his (at the time, only a white male could be a liberal subject) self-interest without government interference, as long as his actions cause no harm to others. The liberal state is marked by guaranteeing to its subjects "freedom from" (government interference) rather than freedom to (take advantage of rights and privileges). This distinction is codified in the U.S. Constitution in the form of the Fourth Amendment, which protects individuals from unwarranted search and seizure, among other impositions.

Women's lives were relegated to an invisible existence in the private sphere. They were considered extensions of either their fathers or husbands from cradle to grave and were not endowed with any right of access to or participation in political or economic life. As women's access to education increased throughout the nineteenth century—primarily to make better companions for their husbands, as noted by **Alexis de Tocqueville** in *Democracy in America*—women began to agitate for the right to vote, arguing for a universal interpretation of the word "man" in the laws of the United States. After almost eighty years of work towards their goal, suffragettes won the right to vote in 1920, with the ratification of the Nineteenth Amendment. This period of political action became known as feminism's "first wave."

The Great Depression brought many women out of their homes and into the world of work, in the attempt to support their families; however, most opportunities open to women at the time mirrored the work they did in their own homes, essentially moving them from their husband or father's domain to the private sphere of a stranger.

World War II brought women out of the realm of "home work" and into work in the public sphere, where they filled assembly lines to produce goods, such as airplanes and munitions, for the war effort. With her boast that "We can do it!", Rosie the Riveter, hair in a kerchief and biceps bulging, is the quintessential female icon of these workers. Once the war had ended and the veterans returned to the United States, women were pushed back into the private sphere, where they remained until the 1963 publication of Betty Friedan's *The Feminine Mystique*, a book often credited with sparking feminism's second wave.

Sounding the battle cry, "the personal is political," second wave feminists fought to collapse the boundaries between the private and public spheres. Modeling their movement on the Civil Rights Movement, these women struggled for equality in the workplace and a recognized, respected voice and place in the polity. The elevation of women's control over their own reproductive systems to a political flashpoint is a prime example of an issue shifting from the private to the public realm; abortion and contraception came out of hiding and into the light of public, political discussion. Women were "granted" the right to have abortions and use contraception not on the basis of a woman's natural claim to control her own body, but on that of the classic liberal barrier between individual privacy and the state.

Other once-private issues brought to the floor by second-wave feminists were met by difficulties predicated on this treasured liberal notion of the split between public and private. As women participated in the consciousness-raising sessions so integral to the second wave, those experiencing spousal physical abuse and rape found that they were not alone, causing feminists to seek state protection from the perpetrators of this violence. Women in abusive situations still do not receive a level of state protection that is sufficient to keep them out of harm's way, largely because of the classic liberal prohibition of state involvement in the home life of its subjects; spousal and acquaintance rape remain more difficult to prove than rape by an unknown assailant, and police departments are notoriously inept at keeping women and children safely separated from their batterers. Women have yet to enjoy the level of privacy and protection enjoyed by the male liberal subject, even within their own homes.

PUBLIC OPINION

Public opinion is most generally and commonly defined as the aggregated opinions, attitudes, preferences and/or **values** of a population on one or more public issues. The term first came to be used at the time of the French Revolution when Louis XVI's finance minister Jacques Necker said that public opinion governed investors' behavior in the money markets of Paris. Since that time, public opinion has become a commonly used term, and its referent has become an increasingly important force in the political life of modern, mass democracies.

Sociologists and political scientists study public opinion in several basic ways. The most common means for gathering public opinion **data** are mail and telephone **surveys** of statistically random samples of a given population. While some researchers are beginning to use the **internet** to gather public opinion data, mail and phone surveys remain the most common methods. Researchers then study the public opinion data as opinions interrelate and as they are distributed among various significant sub-groups in the population, most commonly distinguished by variables such as education, income, occupation, **race**, gender, geographic location, and associational or party affiliations. Other scholars examine the political influence of public opinion on **government**, individuals, and political associations. Still others study how politicians, political groups, and public relations firms manipulate or use public opinion selectively to advance their goals or interests.

The growth in importance of public opinion, especially in the twentieth century, has been tied to the expansion of democratic government, universal suffrage, and the development of statistical sampling techniques in the United States in the 1930s. Statistical sampling has made it possible to more accurately measure and estimate the direction of public opinion, making the technique of keen interest not only to social scientists, but to politicians, marketers, and public relations experts, among many others. Correspondingly, since the 1930s, there has been a sharp rise in the number of private and university opinion research outfits, as well as public relations firms bent on controlling and manipulating public opinion, in the United States and abroad.

While it is commonly claimed that the prominence of public opinion surveys reflects the importance of citizen opinions in democratic regimes, political scholars have questioned both the validity and virtue of this claim. Some critics of public opinion, such as the prominent political scholars Alexis de Tocqueville and Walter Lippmann, have argued that public opinion is most often uninformed, unstable, and prone to irrational fancy and fear, and that government which follows such opinion may be a threat to rather than an instrument of freedom and **democracy**. Indeed, some of the most consistent empirical findings about public opinion are that most citizens of modern, mass democracies are generally uninformed about basic political facts, inattentive to even the most prominent political news, and often harbor intolerant or authoritarian opinions. In part due to these findings, some scholars, such as Seymour Martin Lipset and Joseph Schumpeter, have argued that political decisions are best left to experts and professional politicians while the mass of citizens should (and do) occasionally vote their opinions and preferences through public opinion polls and the ballot box. In contrast to these proponents of so-called ''elite democracy,'' radical democrats, like Jane Mansbridge, Nancy Fraser and Jürgen Habermas, argue for more participatory democracy based on various publics or groups of ordinary citizens engaged in a rational or deliberative formation of public opinion. Radical democrats argue that conventional public opinion is really a collection of private, personal opinions, and citizens can and do form a more informed and tolerant public opinion through sustained and open dialogue on issues of public concern. Such arguments call into serious question the legitimacy and value of the standard, widely used public opinion polls. Taking the argument further, political scholar Benjamin Ginsberg has argued in his book *The Captive Public* that the standard ''mass'' opinion polls serve to extend state power, passify citizens, and limit their participation in democracy by tying citizens directly to the central government rather than to each other, and by channeling their activity into harmless, isolated, and occasional opinion expression rather than collective action potentially threatening to state and business elites.

PUBLIC OWNERSHIP

Public ownership refers to the direct ownership of an economic enterprise by the central **government**. Under public ownership, the government assumes the role of entrepreneur by supplying the capital, determining facilities, managing the affairs of the business including hiring, accounting, and distribution, and setting prices. As the business owner, the government is also the beneficiary of all profits and responsible for meeting all deficits.

If the government assumes ownership of a previously privately owned enterprise, it is called nationalization. For example, after World War II, Britain went through a period of extensive nationalization during which time the ownership of the industries of coal and gas, iron and steel, electricity, and civil aviation were all turned over to the British government. Later, a major **privatization** program reversed the process almost completely. According to research, no inherent level of productivity appears to exist in either private or public enterprise. External factors such as market fluctuations, environmental issues, and shortage of resources more directly impact the economic situation.

Proponents assert that public ownership is necessary to regulate and allocate vital natural resources that, if left unchecked by private ownership, become public utilities monopolies. Advocates also believe public ownership is more efficient, allows for better overall planning and control, and bypasses the social inequalities that result from self-interested private owners. Public ownership is one of the central tenets of **socialism** and **communism**. Marxist ideology maintains that the capitalist system of private ownership places the financial power of the nation in the hands of the industrial elite, who, in order to maintain control over the working class, institute oppressive policies. According to Marxist **theory**, only public ownership can empower the working class and release them from the oppressive control of the capitalists. Opponents of public ownership point to the economic failure of the Soviet Union and the countries of Eastern Europe. Critics also call attention to the government's tendency to create complicated procedures, operate inefficiently, and become encumbered by needless **bureaucracy**.

Although public ownership is often identified politically in association with Marxism, public ownership exists in numerous countries dominated by private ownership. For exam-

ple, various types of transportation, the postal service, and public utilities all have a history of governmental ownership in capitalist countries such as France, West Germany, Canada, and the United States. While some advocate strictly private ownership, and others demand complete public ownership, still others look for an economic balance between public and private ownership.

Q

Qualitative Models

Sociologists remain divided over the appropriate methods for conducting research and gathering **data**. Early researchers, such as Émile Durkheim and **Max Weber** explored different models for such construction of knowledge. Durkheim, in his pioneer work *Le Suicide* developed a large statistical base from which he was able to develop general knowledge of which social conditions were more conducive to individuals becoming suicide victims. Weber, while not completely rejecting Durkheim's statistical model, felt it was essential that a much broader historical knowledge of the society be developed, thus assuring a better basis for understanding and interpretation of the data that had been gathered. Subsequent to their work, repeated efforts have failed to produce a perfect **model** or **paradigm**. Instead, multiple models now serve as guides for the development and presentation of sociological knowledge.

All sociologists, whether relying primarily on statistical or quantitative data, or ethnographic or qualitative data, require models upon which to build their research design and interpret their data. The models, or paradigms, provide standardized patterns that may be used by all researchers. Such models, when properly developed and refined, allow current researchers to build data files that may be utilized far into the future by other social scientists who may wish to re-examine old data in light of new information. With knowledge of the model used in gathering and analyzing the original data, the original data is more easily understood and utilized.

For many years social scientists hoped to develop a single model that would always work perfectly. But many have come to the conclusion that no single model can perform all required functions perfectly all the time. And as of 2000 no single model has been able to adequately capture and analyze data from all sources in a manner that provides satisfactory results under all circumstances. Instead, as a result of the process of searching for a perfect model upon which to base qualitative research, several models have emerged, four of which are commonly used.

The positivist model is not statistically oriented for qualitative purposes, but does seek to capture "real" reality that can be repeatedly tested for verification of its validity. Such verification typically uses quantitative devices, but once the testing has been completed the data may be reviewed and presented in a more qualitative manner. The postpositivist model recognizes that the "real" reality of the Positivist Model may be imperfect but that most of the findings are probably true. Manipulation of data to see if it can be structured to fit the hypothesis being researched may occur, and instead of a single perfect result, multiple conclusions may be reached. The critical theory model relies heavily on the historical realism of the data gathered, requiring complete knowledge of social, political, cultural, economic, ethnic and gender **values** so that those may be compared with the newly gathered data. This comparative dialectical process allows the researcher to develop and refine the findings in lieu of accepting them at their face value. The constructivist model places paramount importance on the **methodology** used in the data gathering process, suggesting that the methodology may affect the nature and content of the data gathered. All data gathered are subject to careful interpretation based on the potential for realities being constructed as a result of the data gathering process.

The positivist and postpositivist models seek to accurately explain the data that has been gathered through the inquiry process. Through such explanation it is believed the researchers, as well as others utilizing their findings, may be able to predict and control future phenomenon of the same type that have been studied. Those who use the critical model hope to critique the subject of study and subsequently engage in processes that would lead to the transformation of the structures to better serve mankind. Finally, the constructivist researcher hopes to understand and reconstruct that which has been observed, leading to a future consensus of what the data have really revealed. Ultimately, through such consensus, the constructivist researcher hopes to advocate and assist in processes leading to positive social change.

QUALITATIVE RESEARCH TECHNIQUES

Qualitative research techniques refer to research methodologies used in the analysis of **data** that is not easily reduced to numbers, i.e. quantified. Qualitative research is concerned with the subjective understanding and interpretation of social behavior. Qualitative researchers seek to understand how social actors use and make sense of their social setting. Some techniques used in qualitative research are historical analysis, interviews, and participant observation. Collectively, these techniques are commonly referred to as field methods. Historical analysis clarifies and interprets archival data, such as birth and death records, minutes of meetings, and newsletters. Personal interviews help researchers to understand the meaning surrounding a social actor's participation in or perceptions of social phenomena. Interviews may be conducted according to structured or unstructured **interview** guidelines. Participant observation is used when an intimate knowledge of some social event is sought. Sometimes the researcher enters the setting where the social behavior under study is being acted out. The researcher may choose to participate completely or act more as an observer. Qualitative research stands in contrast to quantitative research which relies on the statistical analysis of data to interpret social behavior.

Early founders of **sociology** stressed that sociology should model its research techniques along the lines of the natural sciences in order to uncover laws of human behavior. Later, classical sociologist **Max Weber** argued for an **interpretive sociology**. Interpretive sociology emphasized the need of the researcher to understand or interpret the actors' meanings as crucial to providing descriptions and explanations of their social behavior. During the 1960s, much debate developed about appropriate research methodologies for sociology. Quantitative researchers were accused of reducing human behavior to variables and numbers, while qualitative researchers were accused of being nonscientific. Today, both approaches are generally thought to be useful in their attempts to understand social behavior. Both qualitative and quantitative methods may be used in the same research to provide a fuller understanding of social behavior.

QUALITY OF LIFE

Quality of life (QOL) refers to the positive and negative aspects of an individual's life as defined by the individual or measured in relation to social and cultural expectations and definitions. Ultimately, quality of life is concerned with individual human happiness, a topic which has drawn more interest in recent decades. Although historically there has been awareness of and a search for a better QOL, in the past concern was with values of work, **family**, and the way **society** provided for human needs in terms of survival. Concern was directed to the quantities of resources available, both for supplying necessities and for luxuries. Life expectancy, or quantity of life, has increased greatly to an average of 78 years. The problem has now become identifying those things that make life worth living or which contribute quality to our lives.

As a concept, quality of life is defined variously. In general, Ann Bowling referred to it as a ''grade of 'goodness'.'' Quality of life must be measured to have meaning, but ultimately we are measuring those things which contribute to our individual happiness, which is itself highly subjective. We may see various social institutions as enhancing, limiting, or diminishing our happiness, our health, and even our freedom, but often we do not agree on these interpretations.

Quality of life can be measured by **social indicators**, which are quantifiable and reflective of social composition, functioning, and **structure** and can be compared to similar past or future measures. These indicators vary considerably depending upon individual and **group** perception. David Smith, in his 1973 publication *The Geography of Social Well-Being in the United States*, identified six basic life categories for measurement: income, wealth, and **employment**; environment; health; education; social disorganization; and alienation and political participation. These broad categories contain numerous variables. Although useful, Friedman noted that this classification was not comprehensive or adequate. Some categories overlapped, and others proved to be highly complex.

In 1966, the National Aeronautics and Space Administration (NASA) commissioned sociologist R. A. Bauer and colleagues to develop a system of social indicators to measure the social effects of the space program. Interest in such development was growing for use in social planning and policy. By the 1970s and 1980s, applications of social indicators were extended from a narrow reference to social problems to areas of urban planning, **health care**, international development, and quality of life.

Various types of social indicators have been developed to measure different aspects of quality of life. Health indices are often used, such as the McMaster Health Index **Questionnaire**, which uses physical, social, and emotional functions to establish an index of health. Measurements in areas of performance and experience are aggregated into a single value. Indices may also use perceived satisfaction supplemented with an objective-type assessment. QOL may be expressed as the gap between aspirations and reality. Profile indicators, as used in the Nottingham Health Profile, are not aggregated, but quantify and describe various aspects of health such as pain and mobility, producing a health profile.

Although QOL is sometimes perceived in terms of **life expectancy**, assuming that living longer infers better quality, health economists often use quality-adjusted life years (QALYs) for such things as comparing different health services. QALYs go beyond life expectancy by combining both the quality and duration of survival. It is recognized that there are some activities that improve quality but not quantity of life, while others may prolong life but decrease its quality. Although useful in determining allocation of resources and public policy, there are questions about the **methodology** of derivation of QALYs and concerns about the exclusion of political and management issues.

Although the concept of quality of life remains subjective and elusive, after decades of quality-of-life studies, Americans generally have agreed upon a number of general

indicators that influence the quality of their lives. These include financial security, physical and emotional well-being, opportunities and facilities for a good education, and for participation in social and cultural activities. Americans want good jobs, minimal exposure to crime, self-respect and respect from others. There is a growing need for understanding the role of social institutions and the influence of **social policy** in enhancing or diminishing the quality of our lives. The concept of QOL is thus central to the work of many social scientists, as well as policy analysts and other professionals.

QUANTITATIVE RESEARCH TECHNIQUES

Quantitative research techniques are used to generate scientific knowledge about various social phenomena. Quantitative techniques are associated with objectivism and **positivism**. The central notion of quantitative study is that findings emerge from investigation without **bias** from researchers' **values** and ideologies. Quantitative techniques differ from qualitative techniques in that they are more data-centered than individual-centered and are more detached and descriptive than in-depth and probing.

Three main quantitative research techniques are used in the social sciences. The most widely used technique in **sociology** is the survey. **Surveys** are designed to elicit a small amount of information about attitudes and behaviors of individuals from a representative sample of the population. If a sample is representative of the population being studied and researchers are careful in the wording of survey questions, a survey can provide accurate information about a large population. Typically, this information is between 95 and 99 percent accurate. Surveys are ordinarily administered by mail, telephone, face-to-face interviews, or electronic mail and **Internet**.

A second common quantitative technique is the analysis of existing data and secondary **data** analysis. Here, researchers use available data, often from government sources, to investigate various topics. Common types of data are United States **Census** data, **employment**, earnings, and tax data, and Uniform Crime Reports data. This method also involves researchers reanalyzing data from previous major scientific studies. Typically, researchers will apply some new theoretical or statistical strategy in the reanalysis. This method is inexpensive as it saves researchers the time and expense of designing, funding, and conducting an original study. One drawback, however, is that the analysis is limited to what is contained in the original data, and researchers generally cannot correct problems found in the original data collection.

The least commonly used quantitative research technique in sociology is the experiment, although sociologists sometimes use quasi-experimental designs. In a typical experiment, researchers examine the effects of some stimulus on a group of individuals in a controlled setting before and after the stimulus is applied. Experiments ordinarily have a **control group** of individuals who do not receive the treatment to allow for a comparison with the experimental group. Although they differ in exact procedures and content, these four quantitative research techniques are geared toward discovering and verifying scientific knowledge in a systematic and unbiased manner.

QUASI-EXPERIMENTAL RESEARCH DESIGNS

A classical experimental design includes three key sets of components: a pre- and post-test, an independent and **dependent variable**, and both a control and an **experimental group**. In this design, both the **control group** and the experimental group are first measured on the dependent variable. After this comparison, the experimental group is exposed to the independent variable. Following this exposure, both the control and experimental group are again measured on the dependent variable. In this highly controlled research design, any changes between the control and experimental group at the second measurement is attributed to the effects of the **independent variable**. Of course, not all experiments can be conducted in this way. Quasi-experiment is the term used for research that lacks one or more of the aspects of the classical experimental design.

Many times researchers are unable to use a controlled experiment with two identical groups, two points of **data** collection, and the capability to manipulate the independent variable in a way that exposes only one group. Another aspect of the classic experimental design is that the control group and the experimental group are assumed to be equivalent. Randomization is the most efficient way to ensure that these two groups are similar along all dimensions relevant to the study. Quasi-experimental designs also typically characterize any experiment that does not randomly assign subjects to these two groups. These limitations can be due to the topic of study, the context in which the study takes place, or a host of other unique aspects of the research. Most **evaluation research** faces these challenges in design. Evaluation research is **applied research** that examines the real-world effects of a specific social intervention that has been instituted or that is planned to be instituted.

One example of the numerous quasi-experimental designs is the comparison-group quasi-experiment. This design involves two groups and both a pre-test and post-test of each group. What makes this a quasi-experiment is that the two groups are not randomly assigned and the participants have not been consciously matched to one of the two groups. Pre-experimental equivalence cannot be assumed to exist between the two groups. For this reason, there is an experimental group and a comparison group, but they cannot be considered a control group in the strict sense of the term. Take, for instance, a project that is going to study two different teaching styles at the college level. Students are going to self-select classes on the basis of interests and time schedules. The researcher is unable to randomly assign students to the classes; therefore there can be only a comparison group, not a control group.

Another quasi-experimental design, the ''post-test only'' quasi-experiment, lacks a pre-test **measurement**. If a re-

searcher wants to evaluate the effectiveness of a new state-wide educational program that has already been instituted, there is no way to get a measurement of conditions prior to the new program because participants have already been introduced to the change. In this case, the researcher will randomly select participants from the state with the new program for the experimental group and randomly select participants from another state without the new program as the control group. Each group will then be measured along the dependent variable as a post-test. The problem with this design is that certain assumptions have to be made. The researcher assumes that the control group and the experimental group were equivalent before the new program, but there is no pre-test to confirm this assumption. Only by making this assumption can researchers conclude that a difference between the two groups in the post-test represents an effect of the new educational program. While different books refer to these designs by a variety of names, the variations on the classical experiment remain the same. Ultimately, the use of such designs means that researchers must take greater caution in drawing conclusions from the results. Still, these are useful variations on the classical experiment when a complete controlled experiment is not an option.

QUESTIONNAIRE

A questionnaire is one of two types of **survey research** (the other being interviews), in which a sample of respondents are solicited to record their answers to questions on the instrument provided them by the researcher, often distributed as part of a mass mailing. This type of research serves two major purposes: the questionnaire translates the research objectives into specific, standardized questions whose answers will obtain the desired **data**, and it assists in the motivation of the respondent to communicate the desired information.

Several characteristics generally accompany questionnaires. Due to their mass nature, the sample groups to whom questionnaires are sent are often quite large (it is not unusual for over a thousand to be mailed) and an endeavor is made to reach a representative sample (or cross-section) of the population. Questionnaires involve direct interaction between the respondent and the instrument (as opposed to interviews, in which responses are recorded by the interviewer), and are conducted in the natural setting of the interviewees (i.e., filling out the forms in their homes). These characteristics bring both advantages and disadvantages. To their credit, well-sampled questionnaires give the researcher standardized, generalizable data at a relatively low cost. However, response rates for mail questionnaires are notoriously low.

Questionnaires are more than a series of questions mailed to a large number of people, however. Several factors need to be taken into consideration when people undertake this type of research. Researchers should ensure that the language of the questionnaire is as accessible as possible; the vocabulary and syntax of both the cover letter and the instrument itself should offer maximum opportunity for a complete and accurate response. Second, it is important to retain respondents' in-

terest. If the questions seem mundane and monotonous to readers, they will be less inclined to complete it. To combat this problem, the researcher may add filler questions that add some entertainment. A researcher should also keep in mind the degree to which their research may be perceived as socially acceptable. If the questions being asked pertain to particularly sensitive matters, the questionnaire should begin with a series of benign, unobtrusive questions so that respondents are not immediately repelled by the content of the survey. And finally, the researcher should take respondents, frame of reference into account; slang, colloquialisms, and obscure references should be avoided.

QUETELET, ADOLPHE (1796-1874)
Belgian statistician

Lambert Adolphe Jacques Quetelet was one of the individuals most responsible in the ninteenth century for the quantification of in the physical and social sciences. He was born in Ghent on February 22, 1796, and was educated at the Lycee of Ghent. At age 19 he was appointed an instructor in mathematics at the Royal College in Ghent. In 1819 he was the first person to receive a doctorate from the University of Ghent for a dissertation on conic, and in the same year he moved to Brussels to take the chair of mathematics at the Athenaeum. Quetelet was elected to the Belgian Royal Academy in 1820. He married a Mlle. Curtet and they had two children.

In the early stages of his career, however, there was nothing to suggest that Quetelet's fame would spread throughout Europe. In 1824, he spent three months in Paris and learned two things: **probability** and how to run an observatory. As soon as he returned to Belgium, he began to campaign for the construction of a Royal Observatory. Successful in his efforts, Quetelet was appointed director of the Observatory in 1828. At the observatory, he could pursue celestial mechanics in the same manner as Pierre Simon Laplace, whose work he greatly admired.

In 1835, Quetelet published *Sur l'homme et le developement de ses facultés* ("On Man and the Development of his Faculties"). He explores two topics: the importance of gathering quantitative **data** in order to answer questions about human problems and the usefulness of the idea of "l'homme moyen" (the average man). Quetelet reveals a general understanding that the **reliability** of an average increases with the size of the population. What appears to have given the book some of its brilliance was Quetelet's vision of the average as something at which nature is aiming. Deviations from the average were seen as errors, although the notion of deviation as an object of study was familiar to Quetelet. This point also rendered Quetelet's perspective an easy subject for attack by the next generation of statisticians, who recognized the importance of variability in connection with the theory of evolution and other areas. The English statistician **Francis Galton** often criticized Quetelet's focus on the average rather than the deviations.

To some extent, Quetelet's portrayal of social phenomena as expressed in his book reflected the sources of his ap-

proach. On the one hand, he had a law of large numbers that had come down to him from more mathematically-minded statisticians, which indicated that when an experiment was repeated, the outcome is more reliable. On the other hand, he also had a Laplacean view of some deterministic mechanics underlying the phenomena. As a result, in every area Quetelet found the accumulation of data essential for the purpose of recognizing the **normal distribution** underneath. The law of large became the central principle of all science for Quetelet, and at the very least that encouraged him to promote data-gathering in every field.

In 1846, Quetelet published a volume of letters on the theory of probability. He was active in the reform of scientific teaching in Belgium and had become permanent secretary of the Brussels Academy in 1834. He was instrumental in the founding of the Statistical Society of London and was the first foreign member of the American Statistical Association. At a time when statistics began to play a role in settings outside the calculation of annuities and games of chance, Quetelet spoke for the statistical **community**. In addition to his scientific work, he wrote an opera and published poetry and popular essays.

Quetelet died on February 17, 1874, in Belgium. His funeral was distinguished by the presence of many scientists from abroad and his memory was honored by the erection of a monument in Brussels. For someone who seldom used mathematics, Quetelet had acquired quite a reputation as a mathematician. The ''average man'' as Quetelet envisioned may have been a figment of the imagination, but the recognition of the importance of data-gathering was a timely lesson for a scientific **culture** about to undergo a probabilistic revolution.

Lambert Adolphe Jacques Quetelet *(The Library of Congress)*

R

RACE

Traditionally, race has been thought of as a biological concept, specifically, that racial groups differ in terms of genetic, hereditary characteristics. Races were classified on the basis of both phenotypes and genotypes. Phenotypes are obvious physical differences among races such as color of skin, color and texture of hair, bodily proportions. While genotypes are the genetic make-up inherited from one's parents. Racial boundaries, though, based on biological distinctions have proved inconsistent. Interbreeding among humans causes a blending of genetic traits and characteristics. Genetic analysis (e.g., DNA) indicates that on average racial groups share about 99.8% of their genetic material. Most genetic variation has been found to be greater within racial groups than between groups. For example, if we grouped people as carriers of the sickle cell gene, Equatorial Africans, Italians, and Greeks would be of the same race. Obviously, physical distinctions among racial groups do exist; however, they are not distinct but exist in gradations. Skin color, for example, varies among European Americans, African-Americans, and Asian Americans. Therefore, differentiating humans into biologically defined races (e.g., Caucasian, Negroid, and Mongoloid) has been called a "myth" (American Anthropological Association, 1997). Biologically, pure races do not exist among humans.

Biologistic notions of race, then, have been rejected and replaced with the view that race is socially constructed. An important characteristic of this process is the construction or creation of the meaning attached to the idea of race. It is social, that is, it takes place in interaction among individuals and, thus, is conceptualized as the social construction of race. Humans decide that categories of racial groups have certain characteristics or traits that are socially significant (i.e., skin color, bodily proportions, athletic ability, IQ, and so on). In turn, they become socially significant to the extent that we decide they have particular meanings and act on the basis of those meanings. However, beyond the analysis of the meanings attached to race, a growing trend is toward investigations of how these meanings are formulated. Omi and Winant (1994) use the term "racial formation" to describe "the sociohistorical process by which racial categories are created, inhabited, transformed, and destroyed." They further argue that what race means is always subject to change through political struggle.

An often cited example of the politics of racial categories is the one-drop rule of black classification, a classification scheme created during slavery. An individual having any black ancestry was labeled black. This rule established those who were and were not marginalized (slaves and non-slaves). Thus, those in power defined racial categories in certain ways. From the racial formation perspective, these divisions occur through the linkage between social structure and meaning conceptualized as a "racial project." The five white racial projects identified include the following: far right, new right, neoconservative, neoliberal, and abolitionist. Each project articulates a particular set of both racial meanings and racialized social **structure**. According to David Roedinger, a further recent development has been a shift in emphasis from "attacking the concept of race abstractly to the specific need to attack whiteness as a destructive ideology." Thus, today in academia there is a growing trend to include white studies as part of the curriculum.

RADCLIFFE-BROWN, A. R. (1881-1955)
English anthropologist

The English anthropologist A. R. Radcliffe-Brown (1881–1955) pioneered the study of social relations as integrated systems. His analyses of kinship relations in Australia and in Africa have had a powerful influence on modern social anthropology. Alfred Reginald Brown was born in Birmingham, England, in 1881. In 1926 he would add his mother's maiden name to his own, becoming famous as A. R. Radcliffe-Brown. Born into a family of modest means, he left school at

17 to work in the Birmingham library. On the urging of his brother, Brown began premedical studies at the University of Birmingham. Though he had aspired to a degree in the natural sciences, Brown was convinced by a Cambridge tutor to enter Trinity College as a student in the moral sciences. Among his Cambridge teachers was the psychologist W. H. R. Rivers, who had recently returned from the Torres-Strait expedition to Melanesia in the South Pacific—the first major anthropological expedition sponsored by Cambridge.

In 1906–1908 Radcliffe-Brown undertook his first field work in the Andaman Islands in the Indian Ocean, research which led in 1922 to the publication of his classic monograph *The Andaman Islanders*. His other major field research was a survey of different kinship systems among the aboriginal groups of Western Australia, undertaken in 1910–1912.

The rest of his professional life was taken up with teaching and writing theoretical papers. Over the course of three decades, Radcliffe-Brown held major teaching posts at the University of Capetown in South Africa, the University of Sydney in Australia, the University of Chicago in the United States, and Oxford University, where he was appointed to the first professorship in anthropology in 1937. In Sydney he founded the influential journal *Oceania*.

By force of personality and intellect, Radcliffe-Brown shaped the course of British anthropology throughout the decade of the 1940s. Whereas the influence of **Bronislaw Malinowski**, the other important British anthropologist of the time, was to set a high standard of field work and **data** collection, Radcliffe-Brown's influence was more theoretical. Malinowski had argued that cultural institutions had to be understood in relation to the basic human psychological and biological needs they satisfied. Radcliffe-Brown, however, stressed a ''structural-functional'' approach to social analysis which viewed social systems as integrated mechanisms in which all parts function to promote the harmony of the whole.

Here the influence of the great French sociologist Émile Durkheim was evident. Like Durkheim, Radcliffe-Brown thought that social institutions should be studied like any scientific object. The job of the social anthropologist was to describe the anatomy of interdependent social institutions—what he called social structure—and to define the functioning of all parts in relation to the whole. The aim of such analysis is to account for what holds a functioning **society** together.

This approach led Radcliffe-Brown to undertake somewhat abstract and clinical analyses of social institutions in the search for general social laws. Among his most famous analyses is that of ''joking relationships'' in tribal societies. In his famous essay ''On Joking Relationships,'' published originally in 1940, he described an often noticed **custom** whereby certain individuals (often in-laws) are expected to engage in formalized banter. He proposed that one could only understand such strange customs by studying the specific joking relationships in the context of the total patterning of social relations in the society.

This highly formal approach to the study of social customs led Radcliffe-Brown to a number of other famous analyses. His early survey of Western Australian aboriginal societies, for instance, led to the first sophisticated account of complicated aboriginal kinship systems as a set of variations on a few structural themes. He was able to identify a set of relationships between kinship terminologies and **marriage** rules that made sense for the first time of the ''structure'' of aboriginal society. These studies are still the cornerstone of the social anthropology of aboriginal Australia.

In an early paper, ''The Mother's Brother in South Africa,'' published in 1924, Radcliffe-Brown made sense of what had been thought to be isolated and peculiar customs observed in African societies whereby a boy has a special relationship with his maternal uncle (his mother's brother) that is distinct from his relationship with any other uncle or with his own father. Again, by examining this relationship in light of the total abstract pattern of kinship relations and the pattern of relations between different social groups, Radcliffe-Brown was able to show the structural-functional ''logic'' of an apparently irrational custom.

In yet another illuminating analysis, Radcliffe-Brown provided the basis of a coherent explanation of ''totemism''— the set of associations between social groups and species of plants or animals. Radcliffe-Brown argued that totemic beliefs create solidarity between nature and human society. Nature was, through **totemism**, domesticated. Furthermore, Radcliffe-Brown insisted that oppositions between natural species of animals or plants served to symbolize differences between one social **group** and another. This approach to totemism, once again stressing analyzing specific social institutions in relation to their total encompassing social context, was a major advance in the understanding of such beliefs and paved the way for the more modern work of structuralists such as Claude Lévi-Strauss.

Radcliffe-Brown's list of publications is not especially long. Yet in a series of powerfully argued papers he was able to transform the face of anthropology in his time. Throughout his career Radcliffe-Brown insisted that the proper aim of anthropology was the careful comparison of societies and the formulation of general social laws. When he went into anthropology exotic cultures were usually studied as collections of separable customs and cultural anthropology was the history of how such customs were ''diffused'' between cultures by borrowing or conquest. Radcliffe-Brown was a major part of a movement to understand human society as integrated systems, open to scientific analysis. This elegant and often abstract approach to social analysis has had its critics and its defenders. But Radcliffe-Brown's analysis of social patterns left an important mark on all of modern social anthropology.

RADICAL SOCIOLOGY

Radical sociology can be defined by a specific historical movement within the field of sociology that sought to meld social **theory** and practice so that society is both defined and acted upon by the sociologist. Calling sociological study out of the isolated halls of academia, radical sociologists take an explicitly political approach that questions and challenges the social

structures of contemporary **society**. In their efforts to unite the personal and the political, radical sociologists heralded the early anti-establishment work of sociologists C. Wright Mills, who wrote in his 1958 book *The Causes of World War III*, ''We must reveal by our work the meaning of structural trend and historic decisions;... we must reveal the ways in which personal troubles are connected with public issues.''

Modern radical sociology had its beginnings in the United States in the mid-twentieth century as some sociologists reacted to the events of the time, including McCarthyism, the Vietnam War, and the Civil Rights movement. However, the roots of radicalism in social theory can be traced to the origins of sociology as a distinct academic discipline and the early sociologists who shaped the field in a manner that opened the door for contemporary radical sociologists. From the late nineteenth century, when sociology departments began springing up at university campuses, dissenting sociologists have called for a new look at old paradigms. With the onslaught of World War I, repression of dissenters increased, and those who voiced opposing opinions risked their academic career. Before the advent of World War II, organizations began to appear to support and unite individuals, including the formation of the Society for the Psychological Study of Social Issues (SPSSI) in 1936 and the Institute for Propaganda Analysis in 1937. Although the SPSSI gradually aligned with the more conservative American Psychological Association, most formal organizations were short-lived as once again the outbreak of war silenced protesting ideas.

Renewed attempts to organize an alternative vision of sociology appeared during the 1950s. The Society for the Study of **Social Problems** (SSSP), formed in 1951, had a twofold purpose, as stated in its journal *Social Problems*: the ''improvement of the opportunities and working conditions of social scientists'' and the ''protection of freedom of teaching, research, and publication.'' However, McCarthyism suppressed protest and dissent in all aspects of public life, and what protests that did take place (over such matters as the Korean War and school desegregation) did not receive media attention. As the 1950s came to a close, the illusion of a peaceful, stable society began to disintegrate. Although the 1960s and the Kennedy Administration brought new hope to some who foresaw a cleanup of inept government procedures and social neglect, instead the decade was marked by the Bay of Pigs, the Cuban missile crisis, and the assassinations of both President Kennedy and Martin Luther King, Jr. As disillusionment became more prevalent, radicalism entered university campuses through its increasingly politically active student populations. Sociology, as other social sciences, did not remain untouched by the pervasive spirit of the student generation.

Radical sociology as an organized movement had its beginnings in August 1967, at the annual meeting of the American Sociological Association (ASA) in San Francisco. A small group came together to offer a resolution opposing the United States' involvement in Vietnam for adoption by the association, which stated in part: ''As human beings, citizens of the United States and professional sociologists, we deplore and condemn the war in Vietnam as an undertaking which is resulting in the killing of innocent people and the destruction of a country and its **culture**. We also deplore and condemn the consequence of this involvement for our own country.... We therefore demand an immediate end to the bombing of Vietnam and the immediate withdrawal of troops from South Vietnam.'' The debate that ensued was heated and created a rift between the majority of the leadership, who wished to remain silent on the issue in the name of scientific neutrality, and the predominately younger sociologists who believed that a neutral stance was both intellectually questionable and morally wrong.

The ASA executive council responded to the proposal with the statement: ''The ASA should not, as a scientific and professional **organization**, express an official statement on political issues.'' Ultimately, the resolution was sent to the voting membership of the ASA in the form of a mailed ballot, which rejected the proposal. Despite the failure to pass the Vietnam statement, the fact that the discussion had begun gave birth to the radical movement. In the spring of 1968 radical sociologists at the University of Chicago organized the New University Conference (NUC), which brought together many students and professors to discuss strategies for addressing the narrowing climate of academic study.

Within the year, the Chicago radicals joined with others who attended the NUC to form the Sociology Liberation Movement (SLM), which adopted the slogan ''Knowledge for Whom?'' Soon after, the SLM began publishing its radical journal *The Insurgent Sociologist* (now *Critical Sociology*). By the next summer, radical sociologists had organized *ad hoc* ASA committees on both coasts as the Eastern and Western Unions of Radical Sociologists. These groups coordinated their efforts to bring numerous proposals before the ASA meeting in Chicago in 1969. This time, the association members, many of whom regarded the radicals as troublemakers and an embarrassment to the profession, approved various noncontroversial proposals, but once again the voting membership, which was limited by ASA by-laws, rejected any resolution with a clear political message.

The SLM and the Union of Radical Sociologists, along with other organizations such as **Sociologists for Women in Society** and the Association for Humanist Sociology, became influential voices for dissenting sociologists throughout the 1970s. However, by the 1980s, the political and social climate changed once again, and numerous factors contributed to the ebbing influence of the radical movement. First, many radical sociologists were personally burdened with the question: is it possible to be a radical and academic sociologist? Continually critical of the apologetic approach universities often took toward the establishment, many radical sociologists had difficulties finding a comfortable place to expand their ideas. Either they removed themselves from the academic setting or university administrations found reasons for their removal. Second, the academic job market became exceedingly tight, forcing those who wished to maintain their careers to acquiesce to the less political demands of professionalism. Nonetheless, the radical movement leaders acknowledge the continuing work of dissenting sociologists who continue to labor in the fields and wait for the climate to change once again.

RAMADAN

Ramadan, the ninth month of the Muslim calendar, is a month-long holiday of fasting; the mandatory observance of Ramadan is the fourth Pillar of Islam (out of five). The Angel Gabriel brought the Holy Quran to Muhammad during the month of Ramadan; initially, Gabriel commanded Muhammad to read, but when Muhammad said, ''I am not a reader,'' he was given verses to memorize over the course of ten days. Muslims believe that these revelations began on the twenty-seventh night of the month of Ramadan, which is known as the ''Night of Power,'' the night Allah determined the fate of the world for the following year.

Muhammad, born in Mecca in 570 A.D., was called as Allah's Messenger when he was forty. The message he brought to the traditionally polytheistic Arab people introduced the idea of a single god who created and controls the world. The Quran (Koran) lays out the **rules** by which Muslims must live. (''Moslem'' means ''One who gives himself to God.'') The fast of Ramadan is among the dictates of the Quran.

The Five Pillars of the Faith are, in order: *Shahada* (affirmation), which requires Muslims to recite ''There is nothing worthy of worship save Allah, and Muhammad is the Messenger of God''; *Salat* (**prayer**), the duty to pray to Allah five times each day, which must be done facing east, toward Mecca; *Zakat* (almsgiving), which includes helping the needy; *Siyam* (fasting), the duty to keep the Fast of Ramadan; and *Hajj* (pilgrimage), which instructs Muslims to go to Mecca at least once in their lifetime.

The Muslim calendar is based upon the cycles of the moon; the month of Ramadan begins and ends when two reliable men see the first light of the new moon. If the moon is not visible, the fasting will be delayed or prolonged accordingly. The fasting itself lasts from first light to sunset, and is broken with a prayer and a meal, called *iftar*; the definition given for first light is ''when you can distinguish a white thread from a black thread.'' Fasting includes refraining from food and sexual activity. Throughout the month one is to refrain from acting badly towards others, which is expected of Muslims every day but is considered a particular affront during Ramadan.

Fasting serves several purposes. Fasting makes one think. The practice also increases self-discipline, which helps Muslims stay the course the remainder of the year. It underscores dependence upon God, stripping away pretensions and revealing the frail individual. Finally, fasting encourages empathy; only one who has experienced hunger knows what it feels like, so fasting makes Muslims more sensitive to those who are less fortunate. Ramadan is a time to reflect upon one's life and religion. In the evenings, following the *iftar*, families go visiting with friends and relatives, and there is feasting at the end of the fasting.

RATIO

A ratio is a type of descriptive statistic which summarizes how a variable is distributed. Ratios compare two groups in terms of some characteristic. Thus, ratios compare two groups in terms of how frequent they are relative to one another.

In computing a ratio, the number of cases sharing some particular value is divided by the number of cases with another value of the variable in question. The formula used to find a ratio is f_1 / f_2, where f_1 equals the frequency of cases in the first category, and f_2 is the frequency of cases in the second category. Using this formula provides the researcher with a precise and accurate measure of the prevalence of two variable categories.

Although the above formula will produce a single numeric value, ratios are generally expressed using a colon (:) between the numeric value generated with the formula and the number '1'. This expression summarizes the frequency of cases in the first category for every one case in the second category. This convention provides a simple way to interpret ratios.

For example, if a sample consists of 200 women and 100 men, the ratio of women to men is 200 (f_1) divided by 100 (f_2). The value of the ratio in this example is thus 2. Conventionally, this statistic would be expressed by reporting that there is a two to one (2:1) ratio of women to men in the sample. This statistic is easily interpreted, by stating that there are two women for every one man in the sample, or that women outnumber men by a factor of two.

Sometimes the ratio produced is not a whole number. Suppose that a researcher has a sample of 175 women and 125 men. The ratio of women to men is 175/125, or 1.4. This means that there are 1.4 women for every one man. In such cases where the ratio is not a whole number, it is sometimes preferable to multiply the ratio by some factor of 10 in order to produce a whole number for ease of interpretation. In the latter example, 1.4 can be multiplied by ten to get 14, meaning that there are 14 women for every ten men in the sample.

RATIONAL CHOICE THEORY

Rational choice **theory** is based on the assumptions of purposive actors and methodological **individualism**. At the heart of current rational choice theorizing is the idea that individuals are purposive, goal-oriented actors. Individuals are thought to desire or possess hierarchically ordered preferences, known as utilities, and to behave in a way that make obtain them possible. The world, however, is such that these preferences are often scarce, and people must compete for them. Therefore, people must make rational decisions about which preferences they can fulfill and how they can go about obtaining them. Before choosing a particular line of behavior, individuals are thought to weigh the costs and benefits of that action. They must decide on which of a number of actions is the most likely to bring about the desired preference, the costs of each action in regards to lost utilities, and the best way to maximize utilities.

Along with this basic concept of utility maximization is the law of diminishing marginal utility. This law states that any unit of something which satisfies a need or preference and thus

decreases the utility of any further unit of that same preference due to satiation. For example, chocolate is a desire or preference for many people. The promise of a candy bar can get them do things they might not otherwise do. But once they have received and eaten a candy bar, they can become satiated with chocolate so each additional candy bar has less utility because they simplydo not want any more chocolate. This law holds true for any and every type of desired object. Although rational choice theories begin with principles about individuals' efforts to maximize utilities, they go on to explain social structures, **collective behavior**, movements among masses of individuals, and collective decisions or emergent social outcomes that result from individuals each making a particular kind of rational choice.

The second premise of rational choice theory, methodological individualism, is the view that all social phenomena are explicable only in terms of the action of individuals. It should also be noted that the choices that individuals make are constrained by the same social phenomena that emerged from subsequent rational choices of individuals. That is, these constraints on individual decisions are the product of previous rational choices. The social phenomena that arise set the parameters for behavior in the sense that they determine the distribution of the resources among individuals, of opportunities for various lines of behavior, and of the nature of **norms** and obligations in a situation.

Social phenomena can be explained as the aggregate consequence of the purposive action of a large number of individuals. To explain social phenomena it is necessary to account for the circumstances of choice that constitute the environment of action, the strategies that rational actors would pursue in those circumstances, and the aggregate effects of those strategies. Rational choice theorists, such as James Coleman, believed that social theory should focus on social systems but that any and all macro level phenomena should be explicable in terms of individual behavior. Coleman preferred this level of analysis for a couple of reasons. First, is the fact that almost all data are collected at the individual level and then aggregated up to the system level. A second reason is that he believed any ''intervention'' for social change must be made at the individual level.

Rational choice theory has been criticized for its conception of humans as perfectly rational actors. Research and everyday experience tells us that humans do not always act in ways that maximize their goals. Most contemporary rational choice theorists contend that actors are subject to bounded rationality in the sense that they are frequently unable to take account of all the available information, compile exhaustive lists of alternative courses of action, and ascertain the value and **probability** of each possible outcome. Bounded rationality does not imply that actors' decisions are irrational, only that they do not conform to decision making as sketched by perfect **rationality**.

Rational choice theory appears simple and can easily be described with premises of purposive actors and methodological individualism. Despite its seeming simplicity, it generates frequent misunderstandings and criticisms. Nevertheless,

within the last decade, rational choice theories have gained recognition and popularity in the fields of **sociology**, political science, and **philosophy**. They have been used to explain a variety of human behaviors ranging from voting patterns to criminal activity.

RATIONALITY

All of the writings of **Max Weber** are related in some manner to his focus on rationality. While he used the terms rational, rationality, and rationalization somewhat interchangeably, Weber never explicitly defined any of these variations. He did, however, believe that modern **society** was the most rational form of society and examined the economic **structure**, the organizational structure, and the legal structure according to actions, **values**, and organizational characteristics. For example, he argued that the modern legal system is technically superior to other forms of **authority** because it is codified and guided by a set of rules. He believed the economic structure of capitalist countries is superior because it is the most efficient system of production and argued that the most technically superior, administrative, and efficient form of organization, the **bureaucracy**, could also be found in modern industrial society.

In his theory of **rationalization**, Weber focused on the emergence of various forms of interaction conducive to the rationality he found in Western culture. He also did extensive comparisons to examine the cultural and social factors hindering the emergence of rationality in other societies. In China, Weber found large-scale, bureaucratic organizations, but the infrastructures of these bureaucracies were shaped by a patrimonial **culture** and steeped in tradition. Weber argued that factors such as calculability, predictability, technical efficiency and methods of control are some of the characteristics necessary in the process of rationalization. He concluded that preindustrial societies lack the calculated, impersonal means to an end. Only in capitalism is the system of production and the organization of society rational because it embodies the most efficient means to acquire a profit.

Because an important part of his writings consisted of delineating the factors promoting rationalization, Weber also developed a theory on domination. Weber noted that modern society maintains rational/legal structures to ensure the implementation of impersonal, rational methods, whereas the **rules** of traditional society are passed from one generation to the next and are accepted because of their longevity. He believed the rational/legal system was technically superior to other forms of authority, arguing it embodied hierarchical forms of authority, the technical means of administration, and a belief in the rightness of the law.

While Marx focused on the inequality embedded in capitalist structures, Weber was more concerned with the potential of rational structures such a bureaucracy to become too rigid in their rules. Weber noted that the efficiency of large-scale organizations required repetitive tasks that are often impersonal by nature. He argued that, while rational society is the most efficient, it also can restrict creativity and human development.

His concern, commonly known as his theory of the iron cage, was that these organizations would stifle, or cage the human spirit. For Weber, bureaucratic methods and rational principles of organization in capitalist societies could potentially regulate every aspect of social life. Thus, the iron cage represents the rationality embodied in the organization of daily life as well as the potential to stifle human creativity and spontaneity by enslaving its members.

RATIONALIZATION

In contrast with the popular definition of rationalization as justification or explanation, sociologists tend, fundamentally, to understand the concept to mean any process wherein the most efficient means are sought and applied in pursuit of any given end. Rationalization, which received perhaps its most significant development in the work of **Max Weber**, constitutes a central concern in Weber's studies of religion, law, administration and economic life. But, as sociologist Rogers Brubaker indicates, Weber used the concept in many related ways: ''Thus modern **capitalism** is defined by the rational (deliberate and systematic) pursuit of profit through the rational (systematic and calculable) organization of formally free labor through rational (impersonal, purely instrumental) exchange on the market, guided by rational (exact, purely quantitative) accounting procedures and guaranteed by rational (rule-governed, predictable) legal and political systems.'' Similarly, in his famous study *The Protestant Ethic and the Spirit of Capitalism*, Weber sees Protestantism as a rationalizing force in early modern European economic life in as much as the religion promoted various behavioral orientations (e.g., methodical, purposeful, sober, scrupulous and consistent behavior) among its adherents.

Weber made rationalization a historical concept in as much as he identified its bureaucratic form as a key and increasingly prominent feature of social life in modern, industrial societies. Weber credited bureaucracy—that form of rationalization in organizations which prioritizes, among other things, hierarchy, expert knowledge, a precise **division of labor**, and meticulous record keeping in the pursuit of any given end—for spurring tremendous growth in efficiency and productivity in modern organizations, including governments, political parties, and business corporations. However, Weber pessimistically predicted that bureaucratic rationalization would inexorably expand in modern society and, accordingly, that human freedom would become increasingly restricted to an ''iron cage'' of rational action; that power would become increasingly vested in scientists, experts and managers separated from the mass of citizens; that impersonal, dehumanizing exchanges would characterize a growing portion of human interaction; and that modern people would grow more disenchanted with all ideologies and religions which seek to explain the world in coherent, moral terms.

REALISM

Realism, in contrast to **empiricism**, or to post-realist positions in the **philosophy** of science, is a doctrine that maintains that there are real, underlying mechanisms or processes that account for empirical manifestations in the social world. In contrast to empiricism, which maintains that theories need to be based on observable features, realists develop theories based on mechanisms that are not directly observable. The realists maintain that these are real mechanisms and processes that exist independently of the observer. Realists also maintain that causal processes and mechanisms can be identified, while the generally shun the proposition that general laws of human behavior can be derived regardless of context, as understood by the covering-law model.

The development of realism is generally associated with debates within the philosophy of science, and it is generally considered appropriate to describe Weber and Marx as realists. The debate about what sort of science sociology is, or ought to be, dates back to Weber, who argued that intersubjective features of social life called into question the proposition that the epistemology of the natural sciences was transportable to **sociology**. Certain observable features of life in capitalist societies, according to Marx, as alienation or the fetish of commodities, were to be understood by virtue of underlying, and invisible, mechanisms of **capitalism**. More recently, authors like Ray Bashkar, in *A Realist Theory of Science* (1978), have developed a sophisticated set of applications of realist philosophy to social science.

Detractors from realism have included a number of scholars who, instead, subscribe to a doctrine of empiricism. Empiricists maintain that only observable features of social life can form the basis of a science of **society**. Symbolic interactionists, like Blumer, and ethnomethodologists like Garfinkel, have been skeptical of theoretical work divorced from social reality. Post-structuralist critics charge that the discursive construction of science, and of objects of scientific study, call for other methodological stances.

Nonetheless, most of sociology is commonly understood to operate within a realist **paradigm**, often implicitly. Similarly, realist assumptions also underlie the methodologically sophisticated sociology of someone like Pierre Bourdieu maintains that certain regularities in the behavior of persons of similar backgrounds can be understood by the concept of habitus, an unobservable mechanism. Though the habitus cannot be observed, its effects, in the regularity of behavior of persons, are apparent.

RECOVERY PROGRAMS

The first recovery program was established in northern Ohio in 1935; the founder, a man named Bill W., named it *Alcoholics Anonymous* (AA). Since that time, AA has grown into an international organization with a tremendous membership and spawned innumerable other recovery groups, all modeled on the AA **paradigm**. Prior to the inception of AA, alcoholics

went to sanitoria to "dry out," a process that mainly involved keeping alcohol out of their reach; since success hinged upon abstinence and willpower, the recidivism rate was high. Alcoholics Anonymous offered a new way of looking at and treating **alcoholism**: viewing alcoholism as a **disease**, and providing a support group composed of AA members meeting almost anywhere in the United States, should they find themselves with the strong desire to drink. When a person decides to participate in the AA program, he or she becomes familiar with established members, among whom he or she finds a person who agrees to act as a sponsor; the sponsor provides personal support by making themselves available to talk the new member through any sort of crisis and helps the initiate stay on track.

Alcoholics Anonymous is now so ingrained in American **culture** that some of its inspirational aphorisms, such as "one day at a time" (during the recovery process, it is useful not to think of abstinence in a long-term sense but to try getting through each day without drinking), have become common parlance. The phrase used to introduce oneself at meetings, "I am Jane, and I am an alcoholic" (recognizing the problem is the first step), is well-known and appears commonly in the entertainment media. Although AA is a "recovery program," its practitioners hold that alcoholism is a chronic illness from which one never actually recovers; the process of recovery is meant merely to manage the illness of addiction.

Between 1935 and the 1980s a number of other addictions were brought into the light of recovery, including gambling, narcotics, overeating, and shopping. Support groups for the families of addicts, such as Al-Anon, were also established. In the 1980s new addictions and new Twelve-Step groups to deal with them proliferated at a phenomenal rate. Other groups were formed by people uncomfortable with the religious orientation of the steps; these people secularized the steps and otherwise altered them to meet their needs. However, the ubiquity of the AA paradigm remains unchallenged.

The popularity of recovery programs in the 1980s brought psychology to the masses; the intensive self-analysis involved in these programs held great appeal to residents of the "me decade." Within the programs, people talked about their pasts, sometimes discovering traumas from childhood that made their psyches ripe for addiction; parents bore the brunt of the blame for scarring their adult children by not being attentive enough or being too attentive and on down the line to serious offenses such as domestic violence, incest, and their own addictions. Blaming one's parents was so widespread it became a cliché, as did the idea of adults trying to heal their "inner child"; as with AA, some Americans fully embraced the "recovery religion," while those outside of the recovery movement appropriated the terminology for mockery.

Critics of the recovery movement often claim that it has created a society of victims, of people who refuse to take responsibility for their own actions. Other criticisms are directed towards the movement's reliance on religion, their strict rules, the lack of diversity within groups, and the disempowering effect of giving oneself over to the "higher power."

REDLINING

In 1933, the Home Owners' Loan Corporation (HOLC), developed as one of many Depression era federal government programs, was designed for two purposes: to increase **employment** in the construction industry and to make home ownership more widely available. The HOLC was the first government-sponsored program that introduced long-term, self-amoritizing mortgages with uniform payments. It provided low-interest loans so those who had lost their homes through foreclosure could regain their properties. The HOLC also granted funds to help home owners refinance their urban mortgages at risk for default.

HOLC initiated and institutionalized "redlining," a discriminatory practice developed to evaluate the risks possibly associated with giving loans for specific urban neighborhoods. The name for this practice comes from the four-category rating system set up for the purpose of evaluation. The lowest category, areas associated with the highest risk, was outlined in red, hence the label "redlining." Individuals interested in buying property in this category received virtually no HOLC loans. The rating system HOLC instituted systematically undervalued low-income and racially and ethnically diverse neighborhoods. Of most concern to the HOLC were black neighborhoods. Money was completely channeled away from even those areas that looked like they might contain blacks in the future.

This system of simultaneous property evaluation and racial discrimination was soon adopted by private lending institutions. The most unfortunate consequence of redlining is that the system itself ended up producing the very outcomes that it was set up to anticipate and avoid. Refusing loans in minority areas impeded the flow of capital, therefore, making it impossible for owners to sell their homes. This effect provoked a drastic decline in property values and a spiral of disrepair, deterioration, vacancy, and abandonment was set in motion. Douglas Massey and Nancy Denton discuss the conception and perpetuation of redlining in their 1993 book *American Apartheid* which explains process as one of many that contributed to the proliferation of racial residential segregation.

See also Discrimination; Segregation and Desegregation

REDUCTIONISM

Reductionism is an intellectual strategy used to explain some phenomenon. It involves explaining something as the result of a single precipitating factor. In the social sciences, reductionism is negatively viewed.

Marxist theories, for example, are often criticized as economic reductionism. They explain all human relations as resulting from political or economic strife, thus ignoring other important factors. General theories of crime have been criticized as another form of reductionism for attempting to explain all types of **crime** as the result of a small set of factors that relate to only a single facet of experience, such as family relations.

Sociologists typically try to avoid reductionism because of the nature of social phenomena. People are influenced by their entire social, environmental, and biological experiences. Instead, researchers try to identify those factors that have greater influence over a specific phenomenon, such as a behavior. For example, they may try to identify the conditions that are most influential in someone's decision to drive while intoxicated.

A theory might specify that some factors are more influential than others, but research should not exclude other known precipitating factors. That is why social researchers usually test theories by controlling for other known correlates. For instance, when criminologists study criminal behavior, regardless of the theory they are testing, they usually control for the effects of race, age, and sex since research shows that these precipitating factors most strongly predict criminal behavior. By controlling these known factors, researchers aim to identify other, less well-established correlates of criminal behavior. To explain all criminal behavior as the result of age, or sex, alone would be reductionist and would result in a limited understanding of criminal behavior.

REFERENCE GROUP

A reference group is a social group that serves as a point of reference in determining our evaluations or decisions. A reference group was first described by Herbert Hyman in 1942; he refers to the reference group as providing a checkpoint, or standard against which one may measure his own status and role performance. Whenever we attempt to evaluate our appearance, ideas, goals, behaviors, attitudes, and **values**, we automatically refer to the standards of some group of reference. Sometimes in our self examination, we may refer to groups that we belong to such as our **family** and friends, and other times we may refer to groups we do not belong to but have aspirations of joining. We may or may not belong to the reference group, but we use this group as a means of **standardization** for our values, our attitudes, our behaviors, as well as the formation of our **identity**. In fact, we may not even interact directly with our reference group. Reference groups are generalized versions of role models.

Many times reference groups can be groups in which a person aspires to gain or maintain acceptance. For example, a young girl or boy on a Little League team may have the professional baseball team, Texas Rangers or Atlanta Braves, as their reference group. They may watch the professional teams play and interact and attempt to model their own baseball skills and team interactions with those professionals. They are using the Texas Rangers or Atlanta Braves as their reference group. This referencing can be both positive and negative for the young player. The young girl or boy may watch and emulate the professional player's good sportsmanship behaviors, and team spirit as positive behaviors and/or may also attempt to emulate the professional player's temper outbursts and chewing tobacco and spitting tobacco juice out on the fields. These same aspiring baseball players could be the best players in their residing state, yet when they compare themselves to their reference group, Texas Rangers or Atlanta Braves, they may feel inadequate. Medical students may aspire to being accomplished doctors. These students may use the American Medical Association (AMA) as their reference group. They may begin to emulate the patterns of behaviors that they see in hopes of becoming part of that group. Clearly, reference groups have the potential of both positive and negative effects on individuals.

Well-rounded individuals may have numerous reference groups which they emulate to various degrees. the choice of reference groups can change over the life span, especially when we acquire a new status in various types of formal organizations. The selection and de-selection of our reference groups change as we make life changes and attempt to accommodate those changes.

REGRESSION

Regression is a statistical method for determining relationships between two or more pieces of information, called variables, and for showing how important each **variable** is in explaining another. Regression analysis allows researchers to show, for example, that there is a relationship between the two variables: **social support** and self-esteem. Additionally, regression can be used to show how strongly and in what direction social support affects self-esteem and how much self-esteem can be affected by increasing social support. Regression is a particularly powerful tool for sociologists because, unlike chi-square or other measures of association, it does not limit researchers to only two variables. Sociologists can use three or more variables to explain a phenomenon. For example, regression can be used to examine simultaneously the relationship between social support, self-esteem, and education. Furthermore, certain types of regression analysis will tell researchers how adequate their variables are for explaining the phenomenon they are studying. For instance, regression can tell sociologists if education and social support together explain most of or very little of the differences in self-esteem from person to person.

The term regression actually refers to various specific types of regression analysis. Commonly it refers to ordinary least squares (OLS or linear) regression, particularly to multiple regression, a type of OLS regression analysis that is used to analyze several variables at the same time. Multiple regression is the most common type of regression used by sociologists. The term regression is used less often to describe other types of regression analysis such as logit modeling or multinomial logistic regression. When sociologists say that they used regression to statistically analyze their **data**, they probably mean multiple OLS regression. Often sociologists to state first that they used logistic regression, and later they refer to their models as simply regression models.

Many disciplines use regression analysis. Regression, however, is particularly useful for sociologists for several reasons Since regression can be used with several variables, it

suits most social phenomena which are caused by multiple factors. For example, educational attainment is related to income, but income alone will not determine how many years of education a person will eventually complete. Other factors such as parents' education, personal aspirations, and **race** also explain completed years of education. Regression allows sociologists to examine all of these variables together in the same **model**. Furthermore, by putting several variables together, sociologists can also show that some phenomena that are thought to strongly affect a variable actually have no impact on that variable at all.

Another reason that regression is essential to sociological research is that it can be used with nearly all types of data. That is, some social data are categorical, gathered in categories such as male or female or black, white or other. Other data are continuous, which means that there is a wide range of values to describe the phenomena, such as age (which can range from 0 to more than 120) or temperature. While many **statistical methods** can only be used with one type of data or the other, regression can be used with both categorical and continuous variables. Furthermore, other statistical methods offer fewer pieces of information about the variables. Some show only that two variables are related, but they do not show how strongly the variables are related or if they are related in a negative or positive direction. Regression gives researchers more information about the relationship between variables than any other measure of association.

REGRESSION LINE

Sociologists use regression lines for mathematically estimating the relationship between two phenomena. These lines are an essential component of linear regression analysis and the building block of multiple regression which is a statistical technique commonly used in the social sciences. Regression lines reveal approximately how strong a relationship is between two factors and the direction of that relationship. For example, a regression line could show that states' **poverty** levels are closely and negatively related to the percent of people who graduate from high school (see figure below). This means states that have more people living in poverty will also have fewer people who graduate from high school. Using a regression line makes this easier to see.

To obtain a regression line, two factors (called variables) are entered into a graph (called a scatter plot) by drawing points that represent each piece of information at hand. A straight line is then drawn that estimates the pattern of the points. The regression line is the best estimate of the relationship between the variables because it is drawn in such a way that the distance between each point on the scatter plot and line is the smallest possible. A line drawn anywhere else would be further away from at least some of the points. Once a regression line is drawn, the equation for that line can be used to mathematically estimate the relationship between the two variables.

Regression lines are a valuable tool in **sociology** because they can be used to tell if two variables are related. If the points on the scatter plot are not very close to the regression line, there is probably no relationship between the variables. On the other hand, if the plots are close to the line, social scientists can then use the line to predict how changes in one factor might impact the other. Using the example above, sociologists could use the regression line, for instance, to estimate how much high school graduation rates would increase if poverty could be reduced by twenty percent by lowering unemployment or improving government assistance.

RELATIVE DEPRIVATION

The theory of relative deprivation describes the frustration or resentment felt by those whose life expectations are not fulfilled. James C. Davies, the author of the theory, pointed out that extreme **poverty** alone does not lead people to protest. However when living standards are rising, expectations rise, and these expectations are disappointed, protests and even revolutions are possible.

Relative deprivation can also be created by the close interaction of rich and poor. Among groups constantly faced with the difference between their own situation and that of more privileged groups, relative deprivation is often acute. Thus, a child growing up poor in a rich neighborhood would be likely to suffer more relative deprivation than he or she would experience in a more modest neighborhood. If you consider relative deprivation on a world scale, the concept becomes even clearer. A moderately successful farming family in rural Indonesia may be more satisfied with their socioeconomic position than a working class French family with ten times the income, who cannot afford the vacations or modern cars that most French people enjoy.

In the late twentieth century, the reach of radio and **television** into even the most isolated communities has increased the level of relative deprivation experienced by citizens of poor countries. Many economic migrants to Europe and the United States are led to risk everything in search of the wealthy suburban life portrayed by imported television programs.

As an explanation of the **alienation** and resentment felt by the disadvantaged, relative deprivation has been explored by those seeking to understand social movements, revolutions, and mass emigrations. It is also frequently used to explain vandalism, robbery, truancy, and other rebellious activities by disadvantaged groups.

RELATIVISM

The concept of ''relativism'' can be applied in two separate senses, epistemological and ethical. Epistemological relativism is the assertion that there is no absolute truth. Protagoras offered the first documented proposition of this view when he said: ''Man is the measure of all things; of what is, and of what is not.'' Here, Protagoras argued that what a person believes is true for him or her. There is no absolute truth against which

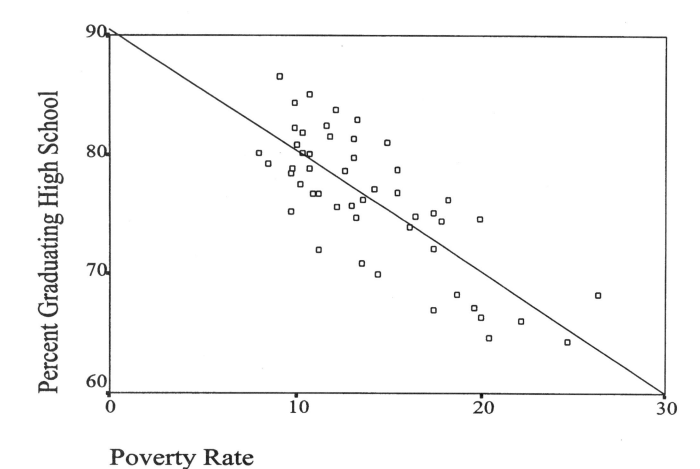

Sociologists use regression lines for mathematically estimating the relationship between two phenomena, such as high school graduation and poverty rates *(Courtesy of Stephanie A. Bohon).*

individual beliefs may be judged. If man is the measure, then each man is the measure of truth for himself. Modern proponents of epistemological relativism are **Michel Foucault** and Richard Rorty.

More specifically related to **sociology** is ethical or moral relativism, the view that there is no universal sense of **morality** or no absolute standpoint from which to make moral judgments. Proponents of ethical relativism cite various anthropological evidence of diverse customs and **mores** in separate social systems. Some theorists claim that this cultural variation is equivalent to 'incommensurability,' or complete lack of shared concepts. These claims ignore, however, some basic human **values** shared cross-culturally: the tendencies to condemn a leader who exploits his people and turn to an impartial arbitrator to judge disputes. A fundamental inconsistency in the assertion of moral relativism must also be pointed out. If the lack of an absolute morality is taken as support for tolerating all cultural diversity, then this attitude must be universally approvable and, therefore, constitute a moral absolute. It remains, then, for sociological and anthropological research to determine the limits of cultural diversity and for philosophical analysis to assess the implications of this variation.

RELIABILITY

Reliability is the ability of a test to yield the same results each time the test is repeated. A bathroom scale is a good example of a reliable testing instrument. Each time an individual steps on the scale, an accurate body weight is shown. An individual can step on the scale one hundred times in a day and yield the exact same results. **Measurement** techniques of collecting data are evaluated on the basis of reliability.

If a researcher asks twenty people about their average yearly food expenditures and then asks the same questions again one month later, the answers should be about the same. If the answers are not the same, then the test is not reliable. Either the measurement technique was not used properly, or the questions were not clear.

Subject matter affects reliability of measurement techniques. Supposedly neutral subjects will be easier to measure than those which seem incriminating. **Data** on a subject like food expenditures are relatively easy to get. When people are faced with answering questions on topics like sexual behavior, sexual orientation, or prejudice, however, they may be less reliable in their responses. Techniques can be modified to compensate for subjects which are more challenging.

Reliability is closely linked to, but not the same as, **validity**. Take the example of the bathroom scale. A man can get the same reading each time he steps on the scale. But if he has set the scale at a negative number give him more self esteem, then the test is not valid because the scale is not displaying the correct weight. Thus, a test can be reliable but not valid.

Reliability can be ensured using different means. Test-retest reliability is one way to help ensure accurate information is gathered. With this method, the same measurement is taken twice. If it is found that information gathered on the second try is different from the first trial, then the method of acquiring the data may need to be reevaluated. Reliability can also be achieved through an inter-item method. Questions or items are asked several different ways to ensure the correct measurement. For example, if items tapping feelings of depression are measured through a series of questions, one question may reappear in different forms. Another way to avoid unreliable testing measures is to use already established measures. To measure attitudes toward political tolerance, one may want to follow the method of Samuel Stouffer (1955) or other researchers who have done reliable and valid studies on the same topic.

Measurement unreliability can also be introduced by research workers. After the data are collected from **surveys**, the data must be coded and put into a computer in order for statistical tests to be run. If workers are coding or entering information incorrectly, unreliability will occur. Workers who act as interviewers can also add to unreliable measurement if they do not carefully record answers to **interview** questions appropriately. In order to keep this from happening, research workers can be trained more thoroughly and offered practice sessions before actual data collection takes place. Another solution is for the researcher to take a small subsample and compare that data with data collected from workers. If there is a difference in information, then unreliable measurements may have been used.

RELIGION, POLITICS, AND WAR

The relationship between religion, politics, and **war** varies depending on both the nature of the religious **community** and the system of government under which religion exists. According to Barry S. Turner in *Religion and Social Theory* (1991), one of the main determinants in the connection between religion and politics is the dynamics in the relationship between a society's majority and minority religious traditions. ''In this respect,'' wrote Turner, ''we can conceptualise a social continuum between monopolistic religious frames (Italy) to pluralistic situations where there is no established church (America)....'' Duopolies, which exist at the center of the continuum, are socio-religious structures in which two religious traditions exert equal influence, and thus Turner concluded that the ''nature of church/state relations and consequently the character of political opposition will vary considerably according to the overall context of religious monopoly, duopoly or *laissez-faire.*

Along with the internal religious structure, the formal and informal relationships between the government body and religious groups affect the impact of religion on the **nation-state**. Although it can be argued, based on numerous factors such as economics and **culture**, that each case is unique, it is possible to define the connection between religion and politics using three general categories: theocracy/caesaropapism, two-powers, and strict separation. In the theocracy/caesaropapism **model**, the state does not exist as a distinct entity. Rather, the religious leader (theocratic) or ruler (caesarpapist) assumes complete and absolute **authority**, which is believed to be based on the authority of a divine will. No distinction is made between the religious and the political because all matters are seen as issues of religious or divine significance. Although most theocractic and caesaropapist models are found in societies dominated by a single religious group, the model can be applied to secular foundations, such as Lenin's rule based on communist ideology. Ideology replaces the divine as the absolute authority.

The two-powers model presupposes a separation of power between religion and the state. Oftentimes within such a system, the state will award one particular religious **institution** an approved position as the national religion. In return, that religion supports the rule of the government. The history of modified theocracy has been identified with the Israelites' time of exile in Babylon during the sixth century B.C. According to ancient tradition, God had always been associated with a particular nation-state; if the nation-state was conquered, that nation-state's God was also conquered. During their time of exile, the Hebrews continued to worship Yahweh, despite their absence from their homeland. In so doing, they introduced into history the concept that religion can exist without a direct and total connection to the nation-state. Other examples of modified theocracies include most medieval European societies, which were characterized by strong Catholic control and the early Massachusetts Bay Colony which was dominated by a Puritan **belief system**.

The strict separation model lies at the other end of the continuum from the theocracy/caesaropapist model. In this case, no connection exists between the state and the religious institutions. Such situations are manifested within totalitarian regimes, which may completely outlaw any religious activity or within societies of religious freedom, such as the United States. Complete separation is more theoretical than realized as most complex societies struggle to maintain a balance between the arenas of power and authority. Typically, the religious establishment is seen as responsible for the soul, and the political establishment is seen as responsible for the body. As Ronald L. Johnstone noted in *Religion in Society* (1992), ''Certainly *partial separation* is the most sociologically sound option. Inasmuch as both religion and politics are social institutions and consist of subgroups, **norms**, and people, they interact with one another; they sometimes overlap in their functions; they often involve the same people; they seek commitment and involvement from the same people.''

Radical **religious movements** often exist as a reaction to the perceived or real movement towards **secularization**, which is advocated by the nation-state as a means to limit and marginalize religious authority within the society. Fundamentalism,

understood in a global manner, arises when rapid social changes occur over which the religious community feels as if it has no power or authority. In *Religion and Politics in Comparative Perspective* (1992), Bronislaw Misztal and Anson Shupe suggested that fundamental groups are led by prophetic leaders, who are characterized by three common traits. First, prophets of the movement issue a call to a return to a previous, now abandoned, religious tradition. Second, they portray the **society** as gone astray and bring the villains under conviction for their wrongdoings. Finally, the prophets identify the current social situation with both the previous mythic tradition and with the modern circumstances, thus linking the divine calling of the movement.

Religious reaction to war policies is predominantly determined by the relationship between the religious institution and the nation-state. If the threat is perceived as external, religion may be claimed as a means to justify war as protection for the religion. If the threat is felt to be from within, and the religious community feels ostracized or oppressed, the response may likely be in opposition to the nation-state's war policy. Although the religious aspects of society interact with the political world in a widely complex manner, since the 1960s most sociologists have advocated an approach of religion and politics that acknowledges a world-system affected by numerous factors, including economic and cultural dimensions. Understanding the impact of religion and politics and the impact of politics on religion must be viewed from a wide perspective of the entire social system.

RELIGIOUS MOVEMENTS

Religious movements exist because religious beliefs and organizations are changing entities. These movements arise from and reflect the necessary change that religion can inspire, since religion in turn reflects the changes of the larger **society**, particularly in its political, environmental, or economic contexts. Religious movements are a subset of social movements, or attempts, to facilitate change in society.

The development of new religious movements increased in the United States during the late 1960s and early 1970s, when the developing counterculture youth explored various and eclectic religious paradigms. This change increase in developing religious movements was also assisted when the repeal of certain U.S. legislation made it easier for Eastern gurus to come to the United States and spread their teachings. This was followed by an increase in the establishment of religious groups and cults. In previous U.S. history, such a phenomenon had taken place in the nineteenth century, when many groups, including Christian Scientists, Mormons, Seventh-Day Adventists, and Jehovah's Witnesses, were formed.

Many sociologists have contributed to the study of religious movements. Charles Y. Clock (1973), **Max Weber** (1958), and Ernest Troeltsch (1960), for example, developed the idea of a **sect**, or an entity that breaks away from the **church** following dissent. According to these theorists, sects eventually end up resembling the churches that they originally

left. H. Richard Niebuhr (1929) elaborated on the idea of sects, claiming that sects drew membership mostly from the lower classes. Benton Johnson (1961) argued that sects eventually conferred middle class **values** (since the middle class was the dominant societal class) on their members. Norman Cohn's thesis was similar; he claimed (in *Pursuit of the Millennium*) that the religious movements in the eleventh and sixteenth centuries targeted and drew upon those who lived on the fringe of society. Virginia H. Hine (1974) postulated that religious movements increased in intensity during periods of increased social change and chaos. Weston La Barre (1972) took the concept further, stating that religion in general had its origins in cultural upheaval.

Social science **theory** denotes three general types of religious movements. Endogenous religious movements originate by trying to change the character of an existing religion. Such action can result in a large schism, or the separation of a religious organization into two independent parts. The Reformation of the sixteenth century is the result of such a schism, and it ended with the split of Protestants from Roman Catholics. Exogenous movements seek to change the environment in which a religious organization exists. These movements may be perceived as, or occur at the same time as, a complementary social movement. In such a movement, churches may claim that God supports them in their attempt to modify or change these external conditions. The Islamic Jihad (or Holy War) of the 1980s was an example of such a movement. Finally, a generative religious movement seeks to form an entirely new religion. These new religions are unique to the **culture** in which they appear, though they may have existed elsewhere. Generally, they are considered cults. The Hare Krishna religion is an example; it appeared in the United States for the first time in the 1960s but was based on ancient Hindu beliefs that originated in India.

Religious movements remained active into the 1990s, often reflecting societal trends and issues. The religions that formed from these movements ranged from extremely isolated to those that eventually came closer to the mainstream. The Heaven's Gate **cult** believed that the world had become so evil that they needed to operate in total separation and isolation. Its thirty-nine members committed **suicide** together. On the other hand, the Unification Church, formed by a religious movement and espousing conservative beliefs, gained credibility when it took control of the prominent newspaper, the *Washington Post*. Some twentieth century U.S. religious movements, such as fundamentalism, have been a strong influence on the perception that people have of certain political issues. The rise of U.S. sects that combine religious and militia or survivalist practices has, in some cases, roused anti-government sentiments, according to Michael Barkun of Syracuse University. These groups point to Biblical prediction of the end of time. Religious movements in the United States have also spawned white supremacist cults. Such groups believe that Caucasians have achieved salvation from their God and that groups such as African Americans, Jews, and gays and lesbians are damned. Religious movements in the United States have also spawned groups that form with an environmental concern in

mind. Such groups draw on the commonalties between religion and the environment and actions that can be taken to benefit both.

RELIGIOUS ORIENTATIONS

Religious orientations are belief systems that help people explain the world around them, cognitively and emotionally. The assumptions and beliefs present in any religious orientation help people make sense of life and the human condition. They are particularly important in helping people make sense of the existence of **evil** and pain in the world and learn how to deal with it in themselves and in others. The central components of a religious orientation are an individual's assumptions and beliefs about the meaning of life, the existence of good and evil, life after death, truth, human existence, and ideas about the existence of a particular deity.

In addition to offering an explanation for evil, religious orientations provide ways of reacting to it. One historical response has been the condemnation, and even death, of someone considered to be evil (e.g., the persecution and murder of ''witches''). Other responses have been personal repentance for evil deeds, conversion to a new or different orientations, or the forgiving and support someone who has committed an evil act. Religious orientations also provide ways to achieve personal salvation. Historically, people would pay large sums of money to the Church to try to buy salvation. Today, people will pray, do **community** service, donate money to their religious group or institution, or preach their beliefs to others, all in an effort to achieve eternal salvation.

There have been many sociological conceptions of religious orientations. Many of the early conceptualizations are now considered reductionist and simplistic. One of the first, posited by Émile Durkheim (1912), viewed religion as a functional social **institution**. He saw it as a system of rituals and beliefs that bonds people together in social groups through its reference to sacred issues. This view has been criticized as too inclusive, since all social groups help bond people together. The second, following ideas of Max Weber, saw religion as a system of answers to broad human questions and problems— birth, death, pain, illness—that helps make sense of the world. Thus, religion is the response to those things that we cannot control and usually do not understand. This view has been criticized for being too broad, implying that all humans have a religious orientation because we are all concerned about the broad issues at some level. In contrast, **Karl Marx** assumed that religion was simply a manifestation of class struggles. According to John Fenton, these authors assumed that religion would disappear as a social institution once people recognized what it actually was—a **belief system** with no basis in reality, which was a theoretically and methodologically limiting perspective.

Current researchers take a less reductionist view and believe that studying religious orientations is important because they often reflect the worldview of an individual or group. Research has focused on two aspects of religious orientations: the subjective (what the symbolism of religious orientations mean

The Hare Krishna movement initially appeared in the United States in the 1960s but was based on ancient Hindu beliefs that originated in India *(Archive Photos, Inc.)*.

to individual people) and, more recently, on the tangible results of this symbolism, such as language, rituals, gestures, and broad discourse, which centers on the group and community, or social aspects.

Empirical evidence has shown that family influences are critical in determining one's religious orientation, although they are not the only factor. The family is in turn affected by other social institutions such as the economy, education, **race**, and gender. Thus, recent research has focused on the intricate processes linking religious orientation and other social institutions. Part of this study has been examining those social institutions that provide the financial, knowledge, **leadership**, and physical resources necessary to maintain religious orientations.

People normally do not self-create a religious orientation, but choose to identify with a pre-existing one. Historically, people would identify with one particular religious orientation. But in recent years, as people are exposed to more different religious orientations, they are combining various components from different orientations, making their belief systems more individualized and personal (Roof and McKinney 1987). This is due in large part to the growing pluralist nature of religion. In most industrialized and democratic countries, there is rarely one dominant religion, rather, there is a broad spectrum of choices. This has led to both an in-

creased questioning of certain beliefs in specific orientations and a greater commitment to the beliefs of these orientations. Some researchers claim that this plurality has led to an increased polarity between orientations that are more progressive and liberal and those that are more fundamentalist and conservative, creating intense and sociologically interesting tensions (Wuthnow 1988).

REMARRIAGE

As the **divorce** rate increases, it seems that **marriage** would be less and less common. In actuality, a terminated marriage does not necessarily destroy the idea of marriage. Divorce leaves individuals in a grieving period. Despite obstacles, the idea of marriage holds enough allure that almost three-fourths of divorced individuals remarry within three years. One-fourth remarry within little more than a year. It seems that the spouse or the relationship is considered at fault more than the institution, and so marriage is still a goal for many divorcés. In fact, about one-third of all marriages are either a second or third marriage for one of the spouses. Some appeal remains even after a second divorce, although the number of people who marry more than twice is small.

The number of widowed people who remarry is smaller than the number of remarriages among divorced persons, but they do account for many remarriages. Widows and widowers are likely to remarry if their marriages were happy; however, the rate of remarriage decreases with age. The younger the widowed person, the more likely they are to remarry. Widowers are also more likely to remarry than widows and reenter marriage sooner than women. Age is a factor for divorced persons: the younger they are, the more likely they are to remarry. A woman married and divorced at a young age is more likely to remarry than an older divorcees. It remains, at all ages, more likely for men to remarry than women. In addition to age, **race** is a factor in whether an individuals remarry following divorce. Almost three-quarters of white women remarry, while fewer than half of African-American divorcees remarry. Hispanic women rarely remarry. Moreover, white women remarry more quickly than other racial groups. Socioeconomic standings also factor into remarriages: affluent men remarry more often than those less well off, while affluent women marry less often than women in lower socioeconomic statuses.

Children play a large part in whether a person remarries, and greatly affect the remarriage itself. Women without children, for example, remarry more often than women with children. Women with three or more children, however, remarry least often. The presence of children in a second or third marriage increases the possibility of dealing with former spouses, which may cause strain. It also creates a unique relationship—that of stepparent and stepchild. This relationship creates serious concerns: How much parenting is too much from a stepparent? How much is enough? Often this tenuous relationship affects that of the husband and wife and the overall quality of the marriage. Moreover, the presence of a stepparent is often seen as a threat to the birth parent, who may try to restrict a former spouse's contact with their children.

Other factors affecting the quality of a remarriage include economics. Most divorces leave individuals in a financial strain. When they enter another marriage, especially one with children, that strain increases. Very often people in a second marriage are still focused on the results of their divorce or the aftermath of their first marriage and cannot properly focus on their current marriage. Moreover, divorced persons do not always completely severe emotional, romantic, or even sexual ties with their first spouse, making it difficult for the second marriage to develop. Despite these factors, there is, however, no significant difference in the satisfaction of individuals in the first marriage and those in a second or third marriage.

It is estimated that close to sixty percent of remarriages will end in divorce, and remarriages end more quickly than first marriages. A remarriage in which both spouses are remarried is more likely to fail than those in which only one spouse is remarried. Following a second divorce, individuals are less likely to marry again.

There are differing theories on how the increased divorce rate will affect the rate of multiple marriages. Sociologists speculate that marriage will eventually be perceived not as a permanent state but as a series of relationships. This change would reduce the strain on second marriages and remove the stigma of divorce, encouraging individuals to marry and divorce repeatedly. For some, marriage and divorce will become a process just as dating is a process now, a way to move from one romantic relationship to another. Other sociologists expect that the remarriage rate will not increase but remain steady as divorced individuals, especially those who have been married more than once, choose cohabitation over marriage. This is already true of older widowed persons. In either case, the allure of marriage will fade for those who marry more than once, and **society** will have to come to terms with a new kind of family group and a variant definition of marriage.

See also Divorce

REPLICATION

The term, replication, refers to two essentially different concepts in the sociological context. First, replication refers to repeating a research study to confirm results and minimize error. Second, replication is a possible description of the relationship among variables in the elaboration **model**.

While it may seem a waste of time and resources, replication can greatly increase the worth of an experiment or research effort. Replication refers to the duplication of a previous study or multiple implementations of research instrument within the same study. Even the most extensive research efforts have limitations that can be addressed by replication. Of course, no study can be exactly duplicated. If nothing else, the passage of time and the disseminated knowledge of the previous study will make the replication study somewhat different. Rather than trying for a perfect re-creation of a previous research effort, replication studies seek to target particular aspects of previous studies.

Studies employing literal replication use the same methods and instruments of the original study to confirm and strengthen conclusions. Theoretical replication uses different methods and instruments but seeks to replicate the original study by testing the same theory used by or developed by the original study. Both literal and theoretical replication can be used either within a single study or in follow-up studies. When replication is used in a single study and results are consistent, literal replication can increase the **reliability** of the measurement instrument. Theoretical replication can boost the **validity** of a single study if the results obtained from each method or instrument all support the underlying theory.

In follow-up studies, literal replication can help determine whether the results of the original research are limited to a specific time, population, or circumstances, or whether the results have the robustness to be applicable in a variety of situations. Literal replication in follow-up studies can provide important verification of or reveal significant limitations of previous research.

In **sociology**, the term, replication, also refers to a possible outcome of the elaboration model. As the name implies, this model seeks to elaborate on the relationship between two variables by controlling for a third variable. Replication occurs when the third **variable** is added to the model and the original relationship retains its strength for all levels or categories of the third variable. For example, a researcher who finds a strong relationship between **poverty** and **crime** may decide to see if this relationship persists when a person's **race** is taken into account. If the original relationship between poverty and crime persists at about the same level of strength for all races, the elaboration model has produced replication. The relationship between crime and poverty in this case can be called a direct relationship.

RESEARCH HYPOTHESIS

In order to test research **data**, researchers make statements about the relationship they believe exists between variables in the analysis. Researchers can then conduct statistical tests on the statements and determine whether the hypotheses are supported. Hypotheses generally fall into two categories, research hypotheses and null hypotheses.

The research hypothesis, sometimes referred to as the alternative hypothesis, is the hypothesis of a statistical test which states what relationship researchers expect to find between the variables, and it is symbolized by H_1. If researchers have reasons for doing so, the research hypothesis may also state a direction of the relationship. For example, if researchers want to test whether a relationship exists between the variables female literacy rate for a country and the country's infant mortality rate, the research hypothesis might state that "the female literacy rate of a country and the country's infant mortality rate are related," or the research hypothesis may state a particular direction for the relationship: "As the female literacy rate of a country rises, the country's rate of infant mortality drops." This is complemented by and contradictory to the **null hypoth-**

esis, which states that the variables do not have a relationship. The null hypothesis is not the conclusion researchers expect to find, but it is what they test.

The research hypothesis is framed either according to an existing theoretical framework or to past research (or to both). The specific form of the research hypothesis varies according to the nature of the statistical test, but it is always expressed in terms of population parameters. Researchers express their hypotheses in terms of populations because they are interested in making statements about populations rather than about individuals.

Researchers test the research hypothesis by a type of proof by contradiction. Rather than looking for data to support the research hypothesis, researchers indirectly test this hypothesis by finding sufficient data to disprove the null hypothesis (or to disprove a non-relationship, thereby supporting the presence of a true relationship). Researchers may be able to find evidence to support the research hypothesis, yet for the variables to have no real relationship with one another. Therefore, researchers must attempt to support or disprove the lack of a relationship in order to make a statement about the relationship. Through this process researchers can determine the likelihood of the research hypothesis being correct or of the relationship between the variables being real.

RESEARCH METHODS

Research methods are a **group** of methodologies or formalized instructions on how to conduct research. Research methods provide a set of recipes for the scientist. In the social sciences, research methods are used to "tell about society" (Howard Becker, 1986). As a whole, research methods are designed so that scientists can identify patterns and relationships, test and redefine theories, make predictions, interpret culturally or historically significant events, explore diversity, give voice, and advance new theories. All research methods use a specialized language consisting of statements that explore relationships between variables.

There are two main families of research methods. The first are *qualitative* methods, those based on descriptions or words and are often referred to as **data** enhancers. Qualitative methods usually study single subjects or small groups of people in great detail. *Quantitative* methods use numeric data and are often referred to as data condensers since they may examine many subjects. Statistical inferences require quantitative methods.

Much debate occurs over which method is more scientific. A researcher must defer to his or her research questions to determine whether a qualitative or quantitative research method is more appropriate. The study of the lifestyles of a group of crack cocaine users will be better served with qualitative methods than quantitative ones, since the human aspect is important in determining results that will speak to the proposed question. A study comparing the poverty rates among American cities is best addressed by quantitative methods since there will be many subjects and rates will be calculated.

Tackling a research question involves going through a number of different scientific steps. These steps differ accord-

ing to the research question and the **methodology** chosen. The first step in social research is always isolating an idea, which is followed by conceptualizing or specifying the research questions. This step can be followed by establishing a theoretical framework and by reviewing the literature. Next comes the specification of the research which may also include **variable operationalization**. The specification of the research methodology dictates the way data are collected, how they will be analyzed, and also the way they are disseminated.

The most widely employed research methods in the social sciences are: experiments, **survey research**, field research, and unobtrusive research. Each of these methods has numerous specific methodologies. Experiments in social research most often happen in the social world and are, therefore, not as tightly controlled as experiments conducted in a laboratory. The comparison of offenders placed in different types of post-incarceration monitoring programs is an example of a social experiment. In this case, there is a naturally occurring control group—those offenders who are assigned to regular probation—and an **experimental group** consisting of those offenders who participate in alternative probation programs. Comparison of recidivism rates can be made to determine the effectiveness of the treatment variable. The one element of experimental research that is often difficult to achieve in social experiments is the random assignment of subjects. Data from experiments are usually quantitative.

Survey research is the most popular research methodology and can be conducted in person, on-line, by telephone, or by mail. There are advantages of each type of survey methodology. Survey research can yield either quantitative data or qualitative data, depending on whether questions are open or close-ended.

Field research typically yields qualitative data and methodologies can range from complete observation—where the researcher does not become involved in the social setting being studied, nor does he or she inform the subjects they are being studied—to complete participation where the researcher is involved and does make the purpose of the research known. Another family of research methodologies are unobtrusive research methods that can yield either qualitative or quantitative data. Examples of unobtrusive research methodologies are **content analysis**, analysis of existing statistics, and historical/comparative research.

The type of research method chosen dictates whether the research will be approached from an inductive or deductive standpoint. An inductive approach involves observing phenomena and then arriving at a theoretical explanation for that behavior. Induction works from the specific and goes to the general. By contrast, deductive approaches begin with a general theoretical premise and then the researcher looks for evidence to back up or refute the theory. Deduction works from the general to the specific. To illustrate, suppose a researcher observed a group of 11-year-olds smoking marijuana at school. After much observation, the researcher proposes that these kids smoked because they were not receiving enough attention from their teacher. This is an inductive approach. If the researcher had come to the school with the lack of teacher at-

tention theory and then began to observe the group of 11-year-olds, he or she would be employing a deductive technique. Research methods in the social sciences typically use a mixture of induction and deduction.

RESERVATIONS AND LAND TRUSTS

The term, reservations, when used in reference to land, generally conjures up an association with American Indians, who were relocated to reservations on land west of the Mississippi beginning in the 1800s. President Andrew Jackson initiated the Indian Removal Act in 1830, giving himself the power to negotiate treaties with American Indian tribes; Jackson wanted tribes east of the Mississippi to trade their land for land in the western Indian Territories, freeing up eastern property for expansion by white settlers. The majority of Indians were forcibly relocated. One of the more horrifying episodes occured when the Cherokee were forced to walk the one-thousand mile to Oklahoma, with massive loss of life (4,000 people). The path the Cherokee took became known as The Trail of Tears.

The treaty that resulted in the relocation of the Cherokee from the southeastern United States, the Treaty of New Echota, was achieved in an underhanded manner; the six men who signed the treaty were not representatives of the government of the Cherokee Nation, which had 15,000 members. The Cherokees contested the treaty in the Supreme Court, which ruled against them. Many of the treaties made by the government with American Indian tribes were suspect and left the Indians at a disadvantage every time. This treatment was simply part of the continuum of abuses heaped upon Indians by the United States government, which began with the smallpox-infected blankets given to the Indians by the European ''discoverers'' of the New World.

The government treated tribes as sovereign nations because treaties can only be made between two governments. Through the treaties, Indians ceded their homelands in trades that reserved Western land for tribal resettlement. The government holds Indian land in trust; this relationship is based on a portion of English law holding that the Crown holds title to newly-discovered lands, but that the native residents are entitled to continue living there as compensation; the native peoples, however, are not entitled to continue living in their ancestral homes. This trust is overseen by the Bureau of Indian Affairs (BIA), now part of the Department of the Interior; the conditions of the trust are not codified and are described by the BIA itself as something that cannot be ''precisely defined.'' Furthermore, this vagueness can lead to ''misunderstandings'' between both parties.

In practice, the tribes govern themselves on their reservations, but the United States government controls the land and its use. The purpose of a trust is to protect and preserve both **money** and property. The BIA is responsible for managing reservation lands, and any monies made off of the use of those lands; throughout its history, however, the BIA has taken advantage of its position, selling resources—including minerals, oil, and timber—at below-market prices and renting land

to off-reservation farmers at deep discounts, costing the tribes millions of dollars in missed income. American Indian tribes are now taking more control of their land and resources, while trying to reform the BIA into an advocate for the tribes rather than an opponent.

The **poverty** and **unemployment** rates on American Indian reservations are among the highest in the nation, and the rate of **alcoholism** is epidemic. Young American Indians are often faced with a choice of staying in the depressed economy of the reservation or moving off of the ''res'' and leaving behind their families and their **culture**. A number of tribes, however, have improved their economic situation by building casinos on their lands, which is an especially canny move in states that ban gambling; since the tribes are sovereign governments that negotiate with the federal, rather than the state, government, they have the latitude to run casinos and high-stakes bingo games.

Land trusts (conservancies) also exist outside of the federal government and Indian reservations. One common motive behind setting up land trusts is ecological conservation. Land trusts are generally local or national nonprofit organizations that acquire land for a specific purpose. Individuals who donate land to a trust can take the cost off their taxes as a charitable deduction. Landowners may make an outright gift of their land; make arrangements for a future gift of land; enter into a covenant with a conservancy, promising to follow the wishes of the conservancy in using the land; or grant the conservancy an easement, in which the landowner continues to hold the title; but agree not to exercise certain rights, such as building on or selling the land, or limiting agricultural pursuits to a specified section of the property. Government-run reservations do take one other form: military. These large tracts of land, such as Fort Bragg in North Carolina, include army bases, training camps, and shooting ranges.

RESPONSE RATE

The response rate is a number that represents the number of respondents who participate in a study compared to the number of potential subjects. The formula, a/b, is usually represented as a percentage (where a = participants, and b = potential subjects). Although the formula for calculating the response rate appears simple, it can be complicated. Many factors must be taken into account in determining the number of potential subjects. Let us say that a researcher conducts a random telephone survey of the general population. Participants must be 18 years old and older. A computer program is usually used to randomly generate telephone numbers for **survey research**. The researcher specifies the area code and the prefixes he/she wants to be contacted, and then the computer program compiles a list of all of the possible four-digit sequences of numbers that can follow the prefixes that have been identified. Within the sampling frame (the list of phone numbers), there will be several working residential phone numbers. However, there are usually also some disconnected and business or non-residential phone numbers and fax machine numbers in the

list. Many companies that compile and sell these lists try to identify unusable numbers and eliminate them from the lists; however, some remain. These numbers are omitted in the process of calling and are not usually calculated into the response rate. In the process of surveying, the researcher will also encounter answering machines, busy phones, and people who cannot be included in the sample, such as those who are under 18 and are home unattended by adults. These numbers are also excluded from calculation of the response rate.

Potential subjects only include the number of phone numbers called in which someone was contacted who could potentially participate in the study and either chose to or not to participate. Participants are those who chose to participate in the study, and do so. In a mail survey, potential subjects include the number of **surveys** mailed out, and participants include only the number sent back in and completed.

In sociological research, a typical response rate is about 80 percent, but expected response rates depend on the methods employed and on the type of information gathered. When more sensitive information is gathered from respondents, like health status or self-incriminating information response rates will be much lower. Alternatively, when the topic of study is intriguing, fun, easy to talk about, or non-threatening, then response rates are typically much higher.

RETIREMENT

Retirement, which refers to the practice of withdrawing, usually in later life, from active **employment**, developed significantly during the twentieth century when economic conditions and dramatically increased lifespans in industrial societies made it necessary to create appropriate policies for elderly workers. More than merely an organic response to the inevitability of human aging, retirement restructured traditional job distributions and created age-based policies that excluded groups from paid employment but also qualified them for other income.

In pre-industrial societies, retirement contracts allowed heads of households to transfer legal title to an heir in exchange for some means of economic support. By the late 1800s, when changes in the **structure** of American capitalism had contributed to the trend away from small-scale businesses toward larger-scale corporate organizations, many businesses had adopted informal retirement policies to exclude older workers from the workforce. In general, the skills of older workers were increasingly devalued; employment rates of men aged 65 fell from 80.6 percent in 1870 to 60.2 percent in 1920. In the view of William Graebner employers during this period viewed retirement policies as an egalitarian method of dealing with superannuated workers, making age-based dismissal routine and enabling employers to tailor the composition of the workforce to favor efficient younger workers. Pension plans, the first of which was offered by the American Express Company in 1875 to selected categories of workers, helped to legitimize the process of superannuating employees.

Until the passage of the Social Security Act of 1935, however, the vast majority of workers in the United States

John Rother is chief lobbyist for the American Association for Retired Persons, which seeks to improve every aspect of living for older people, both working and retired *(AP/Wide World Photos, Inc.)*.

were without pension coverage. The Civil Service Retirement Act of 1920 gave benefits to retired federal civilian employees, and the Revenue Act of 1921 created tax exemptions designed to encourage businesses to create private pension plans. But 85 percent of the workforce lacked coverage. At the same time, new technologies that increased productivity contributed to labor surpluses that exacerbated cyclical economic crises. **Poverty** and **unemployment** among the elderly became a critical problem during the Great Depression, when unemployment rates for workers aged 65 and older soared above 50 percent. In 1934, President Franklin D. Roosevelt created the Committee on Economic Security (CES) to make policy recommendations to deal with this crisis. Its plan, voted into law in 1935 as the Social Security Act, aimed to reduce unemployment by removing older workers from the workforce, thereby creating more employment opportunities for younger workers. According to Graebner, Social Security was more a program of old-age relief than of retirement, but it did legitimate age as a criterion for job competition.

After World War II, when the American economy expanded rapidly, private pension plans proliferated. In 1930, only four million workers were covered by pension plans; by 1960, that number soared to ten million and eventually grew to twenty million. Though improved since the origins of Social Security, pension rates remained relatively low. In 1960, 35.2 percent of Americans over age 65 lived in poverty, compared to 22.4 percent of the general population; for elderly white women and blacks, poverty was the norm. Social research at this time began to emphasize the benefits of retirement. Elaine

Cummings and William E. Henry, for example, argued in *Growing Old: The Process of Disengagement* that withdrawal from active participation in economic and social affairs was a natural and beneficial process.

During the 1970s, significant amendments to the Social Security Act benefits structure resulted in substantial improvement in both labor force participation rates and poverty rates among the elderly. Private pension plans also improved, and retirement came to be seen as a legitimate **status** that workers of average income could afford to choose. Indeed, significant numbers began to take early retirement options.

Economists have tended to consider retirement as an individual decision based a cost-benefits analysis. Sociologists have generally shared this individualistic view but have also emphasized the effects of occupational stratification structures on decisions about retirement. Some positions are structured to protect older workers through seniority measures but may at the same time facilitate early retirement through various incentives. In this view, retirement is "embedded" in both **career** behavior and in general macroeconomic conditions.

Data that distinguish between retired and disabled older workers reveal patterns of retirement based on occupational category. Statistics reported by Mark D. Hayward, Melissa A. Hardy, and William R. Grady show that workers in **professions**, management, and sales generally delay retirement; blue-collar workers tend to take earlier retirement; clerical workers move relatively quickly into both retirement and disability; and service workers have high rates of disability, as well as high death rates out of employment.

The status of retirement improved significantly in the last decades of the twentieth century. Once considered a means of financially maintaining elderly persons in the brief period between the cessation of gainful employment and death, retirement came to be seen as a distinct phase of life to be actively enjoyed as a "reward" after employment. By the 1980s and 1990s, those who retired at age 65 could reasonably expect a decade or more of relatively good health and increasingly used those years in pursuit of **leisure** activities. Retirement communities featuring leisure amenities became popular, at first in Florida and Arizona and later throughout the United States, leading to significant demographic shifts. Patterns of spending among the retired population also affected several economic sectors, particularly travel and service industries.

By 2000, retirees in the United States wielded considerable economic and political power. The American Association of Retired Persons, which lobbies for the interests of elders, numbered more than thirty million. As the retirement population continues to grow with the influx of **aging** "baby boomers" and early retirees, changes in labor structures and consumption patterns are likely to become more pronounced.

REVERSE DISCRIMINATION

Reverse **discrimination** is the term critics of **affirmative action** used to refer to government policies designed to remedy historical effects of past discrimination. In the United States, affirmative action began during the administration of President Lyndon B. Johnson after the Civil Rights Act of 1964 removed the legal basis for racial discrimination. Johnson insisted that legal protection for civil rights were insufficient to guarantee equality of opportunity for African Americans when more than two centuries of segregation and racist attitudes had deprived them of access to good education and jobs, hampering their ability to develop the skills necessary to compete. Believing remedial action was necessary, he issued an executive order in 1965 authorizing affirmative action policies. These were designed to give minorities and women preferences in hiring, job promotions, admission to colleges and universities, and awarding of government contracts and other social benefits. Affirmative action policies recognize the categories of **race**, gender, **ethnicity**, religion, and age.

Under affirmative action, businesses that received federal funds were prohibited from using biased job-aptitude tests to discriminate against African American applicants. The Office of Federal Contract Compliance and the Equal Employment Opportunity Commission (EEOC) monitored facilitation of affirmative action policies and programs. Designed primarily to remedy the injustices of slavery and racial segregation against African Americans, affirmative action policies were also expanded to include women, American Indians, Hispanics, and other minorities.

Many analysts consider affirmative action policies to be among the most effective of the civil rights programs adopted in the 1960s. Affirmative action undoubtedly improved economic conditions for African Americans and other groups. Access to **higher education** and jobs contributed to tripling the size of the black middle class from 1960 to 1976. According to U.S. **Census data** published in the late 1990s, the percentage of black males earning $50,000 or more was 7.5 percent; the percentage of black females earning that amount was 3.7 percent. Data published in 1999 indicated that, by 1998, African Americans controlled almost $500 billion in buying power. Affirmative action policies also resulted in more proportional representation of minority groups among the professions and a more diverse workforce in all sectors.

But affirmative action was controversial from the beginning, and by the late 1970s white plaintiffs began to bring legal challenges against what they called "reverse discrimination." The basis for their argument was the contention that the Civil Rights Act of 1964 prohibited discrimination against individuals, not groups, and that affirmative action policies constituted reverse discrimination. The most significant reverse discrimination challenge occurred in *Regents of the University of California v. Bakke* (1978). In this case, the U.S. Supreme Court ruled that the University of California at Davis Medical School's "set-aside" policy, which reserved sixteen places each year for minority applicants, violated the equal protection clause of the of the U.S. Constitution. The Court found that "Preferring members of any one group for no reason other than race or ethnic origin is discrimination for its own sake. This the Constitution forbids." The Court did acknowledge, however, that affirmative action was permissible if past discrimination had existed and if minority **status** was but one of several considerations in the admissions process.

For this Hindu worshiper, the ritual of bathing at the temple serves as an integral and central aspect of everyday social life and interpersonal encounters *(Corbis Corporation [Bellevue])*.

After *Bakke*, the Supreme Court exercised increasing caution in considering charges of reverse discrimination, upholding some affirmative action policies but condemning others. In 1968, the Court rebuffed by a six to three majority the Reagan administration's argument that racial preferences should never be used except to redress actual victims of discrimination, stating that race should not be an automatic remedy but that race-conscious remedies "may be appropriate where necessary to dissipate the lingering effects of pervasive discrimination." Nevertheless, by the late 1980s, the Court began handing down decisions that gave much greater weight to reverse discrimination claims. In 1989, the Court limited states' use of racial preference policies, and in *Adarand Constructors v. Pena* (1995), it ruled federal affirmative action programs unconstitutional unless they fulfilled a "compelling governmental interest." In Canada, the policy of equal treatment shifted by the 1990s toward an emphasis on affirmative action policies, despite widespread opposition. Though activists in Britain have advocated for positive discrimination policies, they remain unlawful under current Sex Discrimination and Race Relations Acts.

RITUAL

The notion of ritual is prominent in **sociological theory** and research. While the study of rituals is more commonly associated with anthropological investigations or research into religious beliefs and practices, sociological accounts give ritual a much broader focus. For sociologists rituals are an integral and central aspect of everyday social life and interpersonal encounters.

Both anthropology and religious studies have focused on rituals as patterned, often stereotyped, sequences of behavior that mark political, social or personal transitions and express important cultural **values**. Arnold Van Gennep's work *The Rites of Passage* (1909) is a classic example. Van Gennep explores initiation ceremonies that mark the rites of passage from one social position to another in a cross-cultural context. The ritual practices that represent the transition from **adolescence** to **adulthood** are among the most common examples and exist in nearly every **culture**.

Sociologists, however, have emphasized a much broader definition of ritual. Building upon Émile Durkheim's classic work *The Elementary Forms of the Religious Life* (1912) ritual is understood as that set of practices which distinguishes beliefs about the sacred from those about the profane. For Durkheim, rituals are not necessarily stereotyped sequences of behavior. Instead, rituals can be loosely organized and spontaneous sequences of action. Durkheim's definition is important because a ritual has the ability to charge an interaction, group, or social **symbol** with a magical or sacred significance. Such rituals designate for the group those people, objects, or events which are protected by a sacred energy and are not to be defiled or profaned. While Durkheim focused explicitly on the ritual activities that surround the totems of aboriginal cultures, his definition of ritual also applies to political rallies, sporting events, military conflicts, and legal proceedings of contemporary societies. This more expansive definition allowed Durkheim to argue that the worship of the sacred through rituals is, in a very significant respect, the worship of social groups themselves. When individuals worship a sacred object, Durkheim argued, they are also reaffirming the sacredness of their own **society** and the sets of prescriptive and proscriptive social **norms** that circumscribe that object. This position applies uniformly to religious symbols, political flags, military insignia, and sport team emblems.

Durkheim's study of ritual has been most thoroughly expanded by American sociologist **Erving Goffman** in his work *Interaction Ritual: Essays on Face-to-Face Behavior* (1967). Here, Goffman argued that the sacred significance identified by Durkheim in his study of rituals is present in everyday interactions. All interactions, Goffman argued, are rituals in the sense that they attempt to maintain the sacredness of the group. The sacredness of group continuity is illustrated by the fact that individuals do not typically seek to embarrass others when mistakes have been made in ordinary interactions. Instead, participants usually allow individuals to repair their mistakes (pausing to allow individuals remember what they were going to say if they have forgotten, for example) and often will assist them in the process (by reminding them). Through these and similar examples, Goffman argues that social interactions are ritual ceremonies whereby the participants worship the group and the social self as an object of sacred reverence.

The American sociologist Randall Collins expanded both Durkheim's and Goffman's notion of ritual with his theory of "interaction ritual chains," most systematically described in his work *Theoretical Sociology* (1988). Collins argued that for the social rituals described by Durkheim and Goffman to occur four conditions must be present. First, the group must be assembled in a face-to-face situation. Second, the group must have a common focus of attention. Third, the group should have a common emotional mood. Finally, there should be a social or physical boundary between the group participants and non-participants. When all these conditions are satisfied a social ritual can emerge. The result of such a ritual is the production of social symbols that are endowed with a sacred-like significance. Most important, these symbols are charged with what Collins' calls "emotional energy." It is this emotional energy which provides the special or sacred quality to the symbols, social bonds, and group encounters that individuals experience in their everyday lives. The investigation of rituals, particularly through the works of Durkheim, Goffman, and Collins, has been historically prominent within **sociology** and is one of the most promising avenue of theory and research in the discipline.

ROLE

Role, a concept that is used widely in **sociology** and social psychology, is generally defined as that set of behaviors, rights, and obligations that are culturally defined and expected of individuals as they inhabit given social positions. Ralph Linton's classic work *The Study of Man* (1936) provides the basis for this definition by suggesting that a role is the expected behavior attached to a given social position or status. For instance, if one has the social position of "mother" there are specific role expectations, rights and obligations that accompany the performance of the "mother role." Linking together statuses and roles into vast social networks forms the foundation for social **structure**.

Perhaps the most influential and creative use of the concept of role in sociology comes from Erving Goffman's (1922-1982) dramaturgical theory developed in his work *The Presentation of Self in Everyday Life* (1959). Here, Goffman used the metaphor of the stage to suggest that all of social life is like the theater. Some individuals are actors playing roles in a structured social script, while others are audience members for these performances. Sometimes individuals are both performer and audience. Goffman argued that in the course of everyday life these actors are either "front-stage" to a role and engaged in a role-performance or are "back-stage" to a role and preparing for their upcoming performance. In Goffman's work, social life is described as consisting of the movement of individuals from one role to another.

In addition to Goffman's dramaturgical approach, sociologists have developed a rich vocabulary for the description of roles, largely through the functional work of Robert Merton's (1910-) *Social Theory and Social Structure* (1949). While social actors can engage in *role-playing* or *role-performances* as described by Goffman, Merton suggested that in each of these performances every individual has a *role-set* that consists of the rights, obligations, and expected behaviors which accompany the role. Merton focused on the process of *role-acquisition* by which individuals adopt specific roles as their own. In this process, often times the given elements of a single role-set are perceived as inconsistent and produce *role-strain*. The classic example of role-strain is the shop floor supervisor who must be both friendly towards and give orders to the workers being supervised. In addition, there may be incompatibility between the role-sets of two separate roles, pro-

ducing *role-conflict*. Role-conflict occurs, for example, when students bring their children into a classroom lecture and must juggle simultaneously the responsibilities of being student and parent. Also, individuals may engage in *role-distancing* when they find that they are uncomfortable playing aspects of a specific role and, subsequently, subjectively detach themselves from the role because it violates their sense of self-identity. For example, a professor may use slang in the classroom in order to relate more directly to students; a surgeon may tell jokes at the operating table, or a service worker may accomplish a job with an excessively nonchalant attitude.

The concept of role has also played an important part in the development of symbolic interaction. Following the works of **George Herbert Mead** (1863-1931), symbolic interactionists have emphasized the importance of *role-taking* and *role-making* in the development of the self and in the processes of social interaction. When an individuals engage in role-taking, they adopt the perspective of another and evaluate their sense of self and their proposed courses of action as they might be seen through others' eyes. This symbolic interaction view of role is distinct from both its dramaturgical and functional uses. Whereas the latter tend to focus exclusively on individual action in **conformity** to a predetermined set of roles, interactionists emphasize the fluid and dynamic process of adopting roles and negotiating role definitions. While the sociological interest in roles reached its peak in the 1950s and 1960s, significant interest still remains in the analysis of **gender roles**, occupational roles, familial roles, and the dynamic processes of role-taking.

Role Conflict

Role conflict is the individual experience of dealing with conflicting or competing roles or identities within one person. It occurs when one person is fulfilling more than one role, and the expectations or demands on one's time and energy for those roles are not compatible. This term originated in a combination of **role theory** and social **psychology** (symbolic interactionism). In general, role theorists contend that individuals occupy certain positions (or roles) in **society** and that there are expectations that go along with those roles. As individuals, we 'play' these roles. Many different people can occupy the same role (there are millions of students) and one person can occupy several roles (A parent can be a friend and an employee). Although we have some agency to adapt the role and how we act in it, there are social forces that make some components of that role similar for everyone. Role theorists study the structural and social elements that combine to create certain roles. Symbolic interactionists, meanwhile, focus on how individuals subjectively interpret their experience in given roles and how they choose to change or not change those roles.

Taking from both of these perspectives, researchers of role conflict focus on the subjective interpretation and definition of one's experience in roles that conflict (or expectations that conflict). In their 1964 book *Organizational Stress:*

Studies in Role Conflict and Ambiguity, Robert Kahn, et al. were the first researchers to present this concept in an organized and methodical manner. They concentrated on roles in the work place, an area that has expanded into its own specialty in **sociology**. According to Kahn, there are four types of role conflicts: 1) intersender conflict, when conflicting demands are made by two people with the same amount of power; 2) intrasender conflict, when one person makes several conflicting demands; 3) interrole conflict, when two or more roles present conflicting demands; and 4) person-role conflict, when the demands of a role conflict with the personal beliefs of an individual. There can also be role overload, when one or more roles demand so much that the individual becomes overwhelmed.

There are two components to role conflict: the personal, subjective experience (what the individual thinks is expected) and the objective, environmental experience (what the demander thinks is expected). Research has shown that although there may be conflicting environmental pressures in place, not everyone subjectively experiences role conflict. Some people ignore or integrate opposing demands. Likewise, there may be a subjective experience of role conflict when no external pressures are being applied. A person may feel that he is being pulled in different directions when there is no objective evidence of such demands. These differences are explained by looking at the three factors between those sending the messages and those receiving them: 1) organizational factors, which are size, management, and power hierarchy in an organization; 2) interpersonal factors, which is the actual relationship between those sending and receiving messages; and 3) personality factors, which are the individual beliefs and characteristics of those sending and receiving messages. These three elements determine whether an individual will experience role conflict.

Much role conflict research has focused on the areas of work and family, which appear to be two of the most conflicting institutions in our society. Women have been shown to experience more role conflict in modern society than men, partly because their roles in both work and **family** are changing so quickly. They often experience conflicts between being a parent (women are still primarily responsible for house-work and **child care**) and being a worker (women are increasingly responsible for financially supporting themselves and often a family). Some recent research has expanded on the changing nature of **gender roles** and is focusing on 'role ambiguity' and how this relates to role conflict. When people are unsure what their roles are, they tend to experience more role conflict than they would under normal circumstances. This research is also being used to examine marital satisfaction, work satisfaction, and interpersonal satisfaction in general.

See also Status-Conflict

Role Theory

The exploration of roles has been a continuing preoccupation of sociological theory. Many theories developed towards an understanding of roles in contemporary societies explore so-

cial roles at both the collective and the individual levels. Versions of role **theory** which emphasize the collective level have a more social structural orientation, while those which focus on the individual level are oriented towards the situational processes of social interaction.

Structural role theory is indebted to the classic works *Who Shall Survive* (1934) by sociologist Jacob Moreno and *The Study of Man* (1936) by anthropologist Ralph Linton. In these books, roles are defined as the behavioral complement of a social status since every status has a set of expected role behaviors that the individuals who occupy that status are expected to meet. Since both Moreno's and Linton's work, structural role theory has expanded at both the macro and micro levels. At the macro-level structural role theory has been developed by functional theories of social **structure**, building primarily on the works of American sociologists **Talcott Parsons** and Robert Merton. In these theories the social world is conceptualized as a series of vast networks of interrelated statuses and roles. These networks form the essential basis of social structure and provide the scaffolding on which both formal organizations and social systems are constructed. At the micro-level, on the other hand, structural role theory has been advanced by the dramaturgical theories of **Erving Goffman**. Here, social life is conceptualized using the metaphor of the stage. Individuals are viewed as actors performing the respective roles assigned to them by the structured, social script that is dictated by the situation. The basic premise of these versions of structural role theory is that the behavior of individual actors is guided by a set of prescriptive and proscriptive expectations, and they are evaluated according to how well their performances conform to these expectations.

While structural role theory emphasizes the structure within which roles are embedded and enacted, an interactionist version of role theory is more actor oriented. It attempts to answer the criticisms levied against the more structural versions of role theory. These criticisms challenge structural role theory on the grounds that it tends to conceptualize actors as the overly conformist dupes of social structure. Whereas the focus of structural role theory is on the **conformity** of actors to imposed and structured expectations, interactional role theory emphasizes the dynamic process of social interaction in the creation and manipulation of roles. The most recognized proponent of interactional role theory is American sociologist Ralph Turner whose role theory emphasizing process is based upon the premise that individuals do not merely conform to predetermined social roles, but instead they creatively enact them and often use them as resources in social interaction. Turner argued that while structural role theories focus on the more conformist routine of *role-playing*, interactional theories emphasize the imaginative process of *role-making*. Turner suggested that what is interpreted as a set of scripted expectations by structural role theory is actually a norm of consistency which is negotiated and interpreted by individuals in social situations. This norm of consistency is an implicit part of all social interaction and makes role performances a tentative and interpretive, as opposed to structured and conformist, process.

Since Turner's work, there has been little theoretical development in role theory. Not much effort has been directed towards constructing a well-developed synthesis of the structural and interactional versions of role theory. However, much empirical work has been devoted to exploring the means by which roles are differentiated, allocated, and acquired, as well as the importance role plays in the development and transformation of self-identity. With this in mind there is agreement that role theory remains a viable theoretical framework in **sociology** and that it offers a unique means by which the micro and macro levels of social reality can be theoretically linked.

ROSSI, ALICE S. (1922-)
American educator and author

Alice S. Rossi has spent her teaching and writing career studying social change and the **life course**, with emphasis on women's and family issues. She was born in New York City on September 24, 1922, and was educated there as well. The daughter of William A. and Emma Winkler Schaerr, she graduated from Brooklyn College in 1947. She withdrew from studies during World War II, 1942-46, to join the war effort. Her duties included employment in the War Manpower Commission and the lend-lease program, a system by which the United States aided its allies with war materials. Other duties included work as an air force base special order clerk. She married her second husband, Peter Henry Rossi, in 1951. They have three children, Peter, Kristin, and Nina. Rossi returned to college and earned a Ph.D. from Columbia University, New York City, in 1957.

While pursuing her doctorate, Rossi spent time as a research associate at Cornell University, 1951-52, and Harvard University, 1952-55. Her full-time teaching career began in 1959, as a lecturer at University College, the University of Chicago. She remained in Chicago until 1967, becoming a research associate in the departments of anthropology and **sociology**, 1961-64, then in the university's National Opinion Research Center and the Committee on Human Development, 1964-67. From 1967-69, she was a research associate on the staff of Johns Hopkins University in Baltimore, Maryland, in the Department of Social Relations. Rossi's next post was as associate professor at Goucher College in Baltimore, where she was named professor and chairperson in the Department of Sociology and Anthropology in 1971. In 1974, she became a professor of sociology in the Department of Sociology and Social and Demographic Research Institute at the University of Massachusetts, Amherst. Rossi held that position until 1991 when she retired and was named professor emerita.

In addition to her teaching career, Rossi is the author or editor of numerous publications. She contributes to such journals as the *American Journal of Psychiatry, American Sociological Review*, and *Atlantic Monthly*. In 1995, her book on *Sexuality Across the Life Course* was published by the University of Chicago Press. It is intended for those seeking a sociological perspective on sexuality over the life span. The contributed articles emphasize sexuality in the middle life years and include chapters on African-American men and women, which have often been lacking in studies of this type.

Both in her teaching career and authorship, Rossi is noted for her studies of women and women's issues. She was

a founder and member of the governing board of the National Organization for Women, 1966-70; president of Sociologists for Women in Society, 1971-72; and National Commissioner, by presidential appointment, on the National Commission for the Observance of the International Women's Year, 1977-78. She is also a member of the National Abortion Rights Action League and the **Family Planning** Federation of America. Her writings concerning women's issues include: "Women in Science: Why So Few?" in *Science*, 1965; "Abortion and Social Change" in *Dissent*, 1969; "Job **Discrimination** and What Women Can Do About It" in *Atlantic Monthly*, 1970; "Feminists in Politics: A Panel Analysis of the first National Women's Conference, *Academic Press*, 1982; and *The Fertile Years: From Menarche Through Menopause,* Harvard University Press, 2000.

Throughout her career, Rossi has received many awards and honors. They include: the Career Development Award, National Institute on Mental Health, 1965-67, 1967-69; Ford Foundation Faculty Fellowship, 1976; Rockefeller Foundation Research Competition Award, 1987-88; the William J. Goode Book Award for *Of Human Bonding: Parent-Child Relations Across the Life Course*, 1991; Award for Distinguished Research on the Family, American Sociological Association, 1996; and the Ernest Burgess Award for Distinguished Research on the Family, National Council on Family Relations, 1996. She holds honorary degrees from Towson State College (now University), Baltimore, 1973; Rutgers University,1975; Simmons College, Boston, 1977; Goucher College, 1982; and Northwestern University, Evanston, Illinois, 1984. In addition, she was the chair of the board of directors, **Social Science Research Council**, 1971-1974; president of the American Sociological Association, 1982-1983; member of the National Advisory Council, National Institute on **Aging**, 1985-1989; and a member of the advisory council on women's health, the New England Research Institute, 1994-1997.

ROSSI, PETER HENRY (1921-)
American educator and author

Peter Henry Rossi has spent his academic career studying prison reform, urban discontent, social programs, and most notably, the homeless in America. He was born in New York City on December 27, 1921, to Peter M. and Elizabeth Porcelli Rossi. In 1943, he received a B.S. degree from City College (now City College of the City University of New York, or CUNY). During World War II, his education was put on hold while he served in the U.S.Army, reaching the rating of technical sergeant before his discharge in 1945. His first marriage, to Norma Westen in 1942, ended in divorce, and in 1951, he married Alice Schaerr. They have three children, Peter, Kristin, and Nina.

Rossi continued his education at Columbia University in New York City where he earned a Ph.D. and was also an instructor in **sociology** and a research associate, 1950-1951. From there, he joined the faculty at Harvard University as an assistant professor of sociology, 1951-1955. From 1955-1957,

Rossi was a professor of sociology at the University of Chicago, and beginning in 1960, he became a director of the National Opinion Research Center. He was named professor of sociology at John Hopkins University in 1967, leaving in 1974 for the same post at the University of Massachusetts, Amherst, where he remained until 1992. He then became the S.A. Rice Professor Emeritus of Sociology and Director Emeritus, Social and Demographic Research Institute, University of Massachusetts, and Faculty Research Associate, Chapin Hall Center for Children, University of Chicago.

Rossi is best known for his studies of the homeless, most notably his book *Down and Out in America: The Origins of Homelessness,* 1989. Before its publication, during the winter of 1985-86, he conducted a survey in which he counted the number of homeless people in Chicago. Accompanied by a team during the nighttime hours, he took sample blocks and counted those in and out of shelters. In addition to a number, Rossi wanted to know the makeup of the people who constituted the homeless in America. He determined, in general, that they were young, an average of about 34 years old, unemployed for about four years, and, for various reasons, had been to leave the homes of their parents with whom they had lived. Rossi's survey and consequent book led to efforts by the Department of Public Welfare in Chicago to assist the homeless financially.

In addition to the homeless, Rossi studied **crime** and the U.S. prison system. He believes that crime is underreported. Financed by the Kennedy Crime Commission, he led a new approach to counting the number of crimes by interviewing people in an effort to discover those who are victims. The Department of Justice took over this project, and it became an annual survey that ran for 15 years.

Rossi and his wife, Alice S. Rossi, coauthored a book in 1990 entitled *Of Human Bonding: Parent-Child Relations Across the Life Course.* Beginning with Alice rossi's idea of studying the core family relationship in those years between the time when the children leave home and the parents become very old, the authors drew on their childhood experiences spent in ethnic communities in New York City and on their own early family life. They discovered that little was known about these critical years in a family relationship. The idea developed into a research project funded by the National Institute on **Aging**. During some four years of **data** collection, they used Peter Rossi's factorial survey method to analyze and measure complex judgments.

For his work in sociology, Rossi has received many honors. They include: the Myrdal Award of the **Evaluation Research** Society for contributions to this field; the Lazarsfeld Award of the American Sociological Association for contributions to **community** studies and the Distinguished Career Award for the Practice of Sociology, both by the American Sociological Association, of which he is a past president and secretary. In addition, he served as editor of the American Journal of Sociology and Social Science Research and is a fellow of the American Academy of Arts and Sciences and the American Association for the Advancement of Science. Rossi's publications include 40 books and more than 225 articles in professional journals.

Jean-Jacques Rousseau

ROUSSEAU, JEAN JACQUES (1712-1778)
French philosopher, author, and composer

The Swiss-born philosopher and political theorist, Jean Jacques Rousseau ranks as one of the greatest figures of the French Enlightenment. Yet Jean Jacques Rousseau the man and his writings constitute a problem for anyone who wants to grasp to understand his life and work. One interpreter has called Rousseau ''an irresponsible writer with a fatal gift for epigram.'' He has been variously called the founder of the romantic movement in literature and the intellectual father of the French Revolution, among other labels. Rousseau is a contradiction, a severe moralist who lived a dangerously ''relaxed'' life, a misanthrope who loved humanity.

Three major periods characterize Rousseau's life. The first (1712–1750) culminated in the succès de scandale of his *Discours sur les sciences et les arts*. The second (1750–1762) saw the publication of his closely related major works: *La Nouvelle Héloïse* (1761), *L'Émile* (1762), and *Du contrat social* (1762). The last period (1762–1778) found Rousseau an outcast, hounded from country to country, his books condemned and burned.

Rousseau was the second child of Suzanne Bernard and Isaac Rousseau, a man less wellborn than she. Jean Jacques was born on June 28, 1712, at Geneva, Switzerland. Nine days later his mother died. Trained in the piano, Rousseau devel-

oped a scheme for musical notation (1743) as *Dissertation sur la musique moderne,,* but his interest in music spurred him to write two operas—*Les Muses galantes* (1742) and *Le Devin du village* (1752)—and permitted him to write articles on music for Denis Diderot's *Encyclopédie; the Lettre sur la musique française*. Rousseau spent the years before his success with his first *Discours* in Paris, living from hand to mouth the life of a struggling intellectual. In March 1745 Rousseau began a liaison with Thérèse Le Vasseur, a 24-year-old maid at Rousseau's lodgings. She remained with him for the rest of his life—as mistress, housekeeper, mother of their five children, and finally, in 1768, as his wife. Not an educated woman, she nonetheless possessed the uncommon quality of being able to offer stability to a man of volatile intensity.

By 1749 he won a prize with his *Discours sur les sciences et les arts* and became ''l'homme du jour.'' His famous rhetorical ''attack'' on **civilization** called forth 68 articles defending the arts and sciences. This essay sounded one of his essential themes; the arts and sciences, instead of liberating men and increasing their happiness, have for the most part shackled men further. The **social order** of civilized **society**, wrote Rousseau, introduced inequality and unhappiness. This social order rests upon private property.

Rousseau's novel *La Nouvelle Héloïse* (1761) attempted to portray tragedy that foolish education and arbitrary social conventions work among sensitive creatures. Rousseau's two other major treatises—*L'Émile ou de l'éducation* (1762) and *Du contrat social* (1762)—undertook the more difficult task of constructing an education and a social order that would enable men to be natural and free. The originality of the novel won it hostile reviews, but its romantic eroticism made it immensely popular with the public. It remained a best seller until the French Revolution.

The overarching spirit is best sensed in opposition to John Locke's essay on education. Locke taught that a man should be educated to the station for which he is intended. Rousseau, on the other hand, advocated one education for all. Man should be educated to be a man, not to be a doctor, lawyer, or priest. Nor is a child merely a little man; he is, rather, a developing creature, with passions and powers that vary according to his stage of development. What must be avoided at all costs is the master-slave mode of instruction. *Du contrat social,* attempted to spell out the social relation that a properly educated man—a free man—bears to other free men. This treatise is fired by a great passion for humanity. The liberating fervor of the work, however, is easily caught in the key notions of popular sovereignty and general will. **Government** is not to be confused with sovereignty of the people or with the social order that is created by the **social contract**. The government is an intermediary set up between the people as law followers and the people as law creators, the sovereignty. Furthermore, the government is an instrument created by the citizens through their **collective action** expressed in the general will. The purpose of this instrument is to serve the people.

Forced into exile and moving several times, Rousseau came under the good offices of the Scottish philosopher **David Hume** who invited Rousseau to settle at Wotton, Derbyshire,

England, in 1766. Hume managed to obtain from George III a yearly pension for Rousseau. But Rousseau, falsely believing Hume to be in league with his Parisian and Genevan enemies, not only refused the pension but also openly broke with the philosopher. Henceforth, Rousseau's sense of persecution became ever more intense. Rousseau returned to France in June 1767. Wandering from place to place, he at last settled in 1770 in Paris. There he made a living, as he often had in the past, by copying music. By December 1770 the *Confessions,* was completed.

In May 1778 Rousseau accepted Marquis de Giradin's hospitality at Ermenonville near Paris. There, with Thérèse at his bedside, he died on July 2, 1778, probably from uremia. From birth he had suffered from a bladder deformation. From 1748 onward his condition had grown worse. His adoption of the Armenian mode of dress was due to the embarrassment caused by this affliction, and it is not unlikely that much of his suspicious irritability can be traced to the same malady.

ROUTINIZATION

In the late nineteenth century, **Max Weber** explored the dynamics of power and **domination**. The concept of routinization came out of his study of legitimate domination and **authority**. For Weber, there were three main bases from which to legitimate certain claims to power over others. These bases were: traditional, rational-legal, and charismatic. With traditional authority, leaders hold traditionally sanctioned positions that have power in their continuity over time. An example of traditional authority is a monarchy because individuals become leaders based on birthright, a **ritual** solidified over generations. Rational-legal authority is supported through an agreed upon set of rules and procedures. The election of a president is an example of this type of authority. Charismatic authority is based on the unique personality characteristics of a specific leader. Common examples of leaders who had authority based on **charisma** are Hitler and Gandhi. Charismatic leaders are anomalies. They do not ascend to positions of leadership on the basis of tradition or in some legal process of which they are a part. For this reason, charismatic authority has a character opposite to routine structures. Great **social change** is possible with charismatic leadership because the novelty of it is so powerful. However, charismatic authority is inherently unstable because the foundation of power is in the personality characteristics of a particular individual rather than in the position the individual actually holds. This means that when the leader is no longer in power, the authority is gone as well. In order to stabilize charismatic authority, it must be transformed into one of the other two types of leadership. In other words, charismatic authority becomes routinized, changed into either traditionalized or legalized authority. This change can happen a number of ways. One way is to establish a notion of charisma as a quality transmitted by blood. Making charisma hereditary transforms authority from charismatic to traditional. Another way to routinize charisma is to establish a set of prerequisites for leadership, such as specific types of training or tests of eli-

gibility. The creation of **rules** and procedures transforms authority from charismatic to rational-legal. In taking a cross-cultural look at authority and leadership, Weber saw a number of ways in which societies routinized charisma. No matter which method is employed, it is certain that the question of who is to succeed is an important one and how it is decided undoubtedly affects future social relationships.

ROWNTREE, BENJAMIN SEEBOHM (1871-1954)
English sociologist

Although a wealthy manufacturer and chairman of Rowntree, a chocolate-making company, Benjamin Seebohm Rowntree is best known for his exhaustive, fact-based studies of **poverty** in his native city of York. His reputation among sociologists comes out of the research he did for his best-known work *Poverty: A Study of Town Life* (1901). Expanding on the empirical studies performed by Charles Booth in London, Rowntree developed a methodology that involved gathering **data** from an entire population, rather than from select groups. Moreover, he developed specific criteria for defining poverty. Still, his **methodology** outlasted the categorizing. That is to say, while his use of direct interviews and detailed data collection was the basis for much subsequent British **empirical sociology**, he himself disavowed the distinctions he had made in his book between "primary" and "secondary" as overly precise and difficult to maintain empirically.

Rowntree was born in York in 1871 and studied chemistry at Owens College, Manchester. At eighteen, he joined the family firm of H.I. Rowntree & Co. When the company became publicly traded in 1897, he continued on as a member of the management team, becoming the first Labour Director. Even before taking on that position, however, he instituted several major reforms, including the establishment of the eight-hour workday in 1896. "More a philanthropist than a capitalist," in one description of him, Rowntree was heavily influenced by his Quaker upbringing. In the years that followed, he set in motion other progressive measures, which included a pension scheme in 1906, a five-day work week and work councils in 1919, the establishment of a psychology department in 1922, and a profit-sharing plan in 1923. From 1923 until his retirement in 1941, he served as the company's chairman of the board.

Both his philanthropic concerns and research interests are said to have first been prompted by his visits to impoverished Newcastle-upon-Tyne in 1895 and his reading of Booth. Interested in finding out if poverty in York was as bad as Booth's description of it in London, he conducted extensive research for the previously-mentioned *Poverty*. The book caught on with both the scholarly **community** and the public, heightening interest in the problems of the poor. Still, Rowntree did not want to sensationalize the issue or exaggerate the problem of poverty in England. Thus, he established strict criteria for defining poverty, estimating precisely what was necessary to keep a person out of abject poverty. Ironically,

this estimate was used by many manufacturers to set the lowest possible minimum wage, which engendered antagonism toward Rowntree among many in the labor movement.

His later studies on poverty—specifically, the Second York Survey which was published as *Poverty and Progress* in 1941—were far more sophisticated, taking into account many more aspects of life than simple necessities and thereby giving a more nuanced picture of the life of the poor. In all of his work, Rowntree avoided broad theorizing and *a priori* reasoning, preferring instead to use vivid **case studies** to make his point, probably the most important factor behind his contemporary popularity.

His interest in social issues and his fame as a researcher and writer led Rowntree to a brief flirtation with politics. He advised Labour Prime Minister Lloyd George in the 1920s and 1930s on issues of **unemployment**, housing, and agriculture but quickly grew disillusioned with the compromises inherent in politics. At the same time, he attempted to serve as a mediator in strikes, where he had some success. But his reserved academic temperament was not suited to the task, and he soon gave up these endeavors as well. In later years, he served on the board of a number of philanthropies, including the Outward Bound Trust. Rowntree died at the age of 83 in 1954.

RULES

Socially defined, rules are those specifications of regularities within social relationships that allow for understandable social interaction, regardless of the social actor's cognitive awareness that a rule is being followed. Within the social sciences, a variety of theoretical approaches have been employed to define rules. The basic division comes between those who understand rules as controlling and guiding social behavior within social institutions and those who understand rules as having their genesis within the social community and whose meanings are dependent on being embedded within a specific social context.

The first approach is based on an empiricist version of the social sciences mostly clearly delineated by sociologist **Talcott Parsons**. According to Parsons, rules and **norms** function to regulate the social environment by providing the means by which behavioral choices can be made and allow for the understanding of the behavior of others. From this assumption Parsons builds a conceptual framework that links the social system that contains the rules to the social action that employs the rules. The resulting **structure** of social systems and subsystems is based on Parsons' assertion that rules are systematic in nature.

The second conceptualization of a rule, developed by Peter Winch, is built largely on the work of philosopher Ludwig Wittgenstein. Winch suggests that human behavior is given meaning by following socially created rules. Rules do not exist outside the social context in which they are created and acted out. Thus Winch argues against any **correlation** between rules and universal laws or generalized concepts and, conversely, he denies that rules, and thus behavior and **lan-**

guage, can be private in nature. He writes in *The Idea of a Social Science* (1958): "It is only in a situation in which it makes sense to suppose that somebody else could in principle discover the rule that I am following that I can intelligibly be said to follow a rule at all."

RURAL SOCIOLOGY

Rural sociology had its beginning in United States the during the last two decades of the nineteenth century when it was first introduced into college curriculum at the University of Chicago and Columbia University, with the University of Michigan, Michigan State University, and the University of North Dakota creating study programs by the turn of the century. From these efforts, an entirely new field of social science emerged, which focused on the social organization and social processes of geographical locations where the population is both sparse and low-density. In the United States, rural sociology dominates the study of rural and agricultural America. As the field has expanded internationally into both developed and underdeveloped countries, other fields with various emphases have emerged, including peasant studies and development studies. Common to all, however, is an interest in the organization, character, and function of the social, cultural, and political aspects of rural life.

The changes brought on by the post-Civil War industrialization of the United States prompted the interest in the study of rural **society**. As the population of rural areas decreased due to large-scale migration to the cities, poverty, injustice, and poor living conditions were often found in the population-depleted rural areas. Subsequently, two polarizing views of rural life were formed that continue to dominate the field to this day. One tradition glorifies rural society and looks upon the effects of industrialization as the cause of society's ruination. This tradition, first made popular by Ferdinand Tönnies and later by Robert Redfield and other Tönnies followers, produced the stereotype of rural American as characterized by harmony and stability. The other tradition, often supported by industrialists, considered rural life to be undeveloped and backwards and understood the advanced technology of the urban areas to create a superior way of life.

Based on these contradictory understandings of rural society, rural sociology expanded rapidly during the first forty years of the twentieth century. The Populist movement developed as a means to voice the concerns of those who considered rural society a viable way of life. At the same time, the Country Life movement was also established, which sought social, cultural, and moral reforms in country living to assist in the **progress** of rural society. Whereas the Populist movement blamed industrialization for the plight of the rural population, the Country Life movement believed that rural folk simply needed assistance in acquiring the more desirable social and economic structures found in the urban settings. In 1908, President Theodore Roosevelt created the Commission on Country Life, which supported the agenda of the Country Life movement. In 1914, the Cooperative Extension Service was created

and charged with modernizing rural areas. In 1925, with the passage of the Purnell Act, which provided research support and assistance to agricultural-based studies, colleges and universities began creating departments of rural sociology separate from their departments of sociology.

The organization of the field of rural sociology also developed. In 1913, the first textbook on the subject, *Constructive Rural Sociology* by John M. Gillette, was published. In 1916, with George E. Vincent of the University of Chicago serving as the president of the American Sociology Society (ASS; now the American Sociological Association), the ASS chose ''The Sociology of Rural Life'' as the theme for its annual conference. By the end of the 1930s, the journal *Rural Sociology* had been created, and rural sociologists had separated from the ASS to form the Rural Sociological Society. The institutionalization of rural sociology resulted in certain alignments of resources that have influenced the direction of rural studies. First, rural sociologists received financial support from the federal government during the depression of the 1930s to research the effects of various federal programs aimed at modernizing rural life. Second, rural sociologists moved away from the field of sociology and aligned themselves more closely with agricultural departments and cooperative extension programs, both very interested in the advancing technology of agricultural methods. The result was the alignment of most resources and programs with the paradigm of social and technological modernization of rural areas with preservationists playing the role of antagonists.

The complexity of the field of rural sociology increased dramatically after World War II when the study of rural societies became international. By 1970, the study of rural sociology had spread into more than one hundred countries. Accompanying this expansion was the proliferation of research information; however, the body of research as a whole lacked adequate organization to be easily accessible. The problem was not addressed until 1970, when T. Lynn Smith and Paul E. Zopf, Jr. published *Principles of Inductive Rural Sociology*. Smith and Zopf delineated nine important differences between rural and urban societies: occupation, size of **community**, population density, environment (physical, biological, and sociocultural), degree of social differential, degree of **social stratification**, degree of social mobility, social interaction, and **social solidarity**. Drawing on the research of earlier rural sociologists, they suggested that, compared to urban societies, rural societies had lesser degrees of social differentiation, social stratification, social mobility, and social interaction.

In 1990 Guy M. Robinson published *Conflict and Change in the Countryside: Rural Society, Economy, and Planning in the Developed World*, in which he compares 23 rural communities in developed countries. In his study, he refutes the **stereotype** of rural society as being predictably unchanging and harmonious. He also addresses the difficulties in the international comparative study of rural life. For example, depending on the make-up of the country, some consider a population of two hundred or less as rural, and others define rural as ten thousand or fewer. Also, depending on the location, the social and economic character of the community is widely divergent, resulting in difference in social, political, and religious concerns. Nonetheless, the body of available information on rural life both in the United States and internationally has grown dramatically as rural sociologists address a growing number of issues, including the future of rural life, the introduction of mass agricultural production alongside the family farm, the role of women, and the emergence of the service industry in rural America. In researching these and other concerns, rural sociologists continue to remain basically divided between conflicting paradigms of modernization and preservation.

S

Sacred and Profane

The dichotomy of the sacred and the profane was first articulated by French sociologist Émile Durkheim (1858–1917) in his book *Elementary Forms of Religious Life*. Durkheim defined the profane as that which belongs to the everyday, ordinary life. The sacred, on the other hand, is that which is set apart from this everyday life. This separation typically involves attention to the supernatural, to which the natural response includes feelings of awe and respect, perhaps even fear. The term ''sacred'' does not simply refer to beings labeled as deities, but to any objects, words, or actions that elicit such a response in a person.

Durkheim's concepts of the sacred and the profane come from his conceptualization of the origin, components, and purposes of religion. For Durkheim, religion does not come from a supernatural being or entity. Rather religion arises from the **society** itself, as a representation of what he called the collective conscience (or group mind) of the society. Therefore the roots of religion are in the **structure** of the society. A given society has particular needs and must find ways to meet those needs. Religion is one significant way a society meets many needs. For example, members of a society need reasons to conform to the standards and expectations of the society, and religion offers such reasons: members of a society are told they should not steal from others, not simply because it is illegal, but because it is morally wrong according to the standards of the society's religious perspectives. Further, it may be deemed illegal because it is believed to be immoral from a particular religious standpoint. Thus members are less likely to steal from others, not simply because they may be caught and punished, but also (and perhaps more significantly) because they believe it is wrong to do so.

Similarly, religion offers answers to questions all societies must confront, such as reasons and justifications for weather patterns (droughts and floods), geological and astronomical phenomena (earthquakes and eclipses), social inequalities (**gender roles**, race-based slavery, and age-related restrictions), and even suffering and death. According to Durkheim, society creates religion by differentiating between things which are sacred and those which are profane. While there are other significant elements in a given religion, the distinction between that which is sacred and that which is profane is essential to something being labeled a religion.

Durkheim considered religion to be a system of unique and coherent sets of sacred elements. The beliefs, creeds, myths, and legends associated with a religion are representations that express the nature of that religion's sacred elements as well as their relationship to the profane. Religions also develop a system of rites which are the **rules** of conduct that prescribe how people are to behave regarding the sacred.

The sacred and the profane are not merely opposing aspects of the same quality, such as good and **evil** or pure and impure. According to Durkheim the distinction between the sacred and the profane is absolute, and the two have no common ground. They cannot exist in the same time and space, and it is therefore necessary to set aside definite times and places for the sacred in which nothing profane can be included. This separation is achieved through a system of prohibitions against the profane in the presence of the sacred.

Durkheim also does not conceptualize the sacred and profane as having a hierarchical relationship with each other. The sacred is not superior in power or in character to the profane on the merits of its sacredness, nor is the profane necessarily inferior. Within sacredness and profanity, however, there can be levels; one element may be more or less sacred (or profane) than another.

Even though the realms of the sacred and the profane are completely segregated and isolated from each other, people are not constrained to one or the other. People are capable of passing between the two worlds of sacred and profane; however, as sacred and profane are opposing concepts, one cannot belong to one without fully leaving the other. The rites of passage found in many cultures demonstrate the duality of these ideas. Passage from the profane to the sacred is seen as a total metamorphosis, not merely the cultivation of characteristics already

Claude-Henri Saint-Simon *(Corbis Corporation [Bellevue])*

present within a person. The person is often considered to have been transformed into a completely different person. The Fundamentalist Christian concept of being "born again" is a classic example of such a transformation, a demarcation of differences before and after an experience viewed as a significant change of life.

SAINT-SIMON, CLAUDE-HENRI DE ROUVROY, COMTE (1760-1825)
French social theorist

Claude-Henri de Rouvroy, Comte de Saint-Simon, is perhaps best known as the author of *The New Christianity*, published in the year of his death, 1825. Having spent many years studying the potential of science and the need for a new rationally-based **leadership** for society, Saint-Simon focused on theology. Religion, he said, offered the best hope for the poor. The precepts of **Christianity** should serve as a guide by which society works to improve as quickly and effectively as possible the lot of its less fortunate members, he argued. It was this idea that led to the subsequent movement that came to be known as Saint-Simonianism, which began soon after his death. During the 1830 "July Revolution," Saint-Simonians issued proclamations demanding common ownership of **property**, the abolition of inheritance, and the enfranchisement of women.

Both **Thomas Carlyle** and **Friedrich Engels** claimed a debt to Saint-Simon, and his ideas have indeed influenced much subsequent Marxist, socialist, and reform capitalist thinking.

Saint-Simon was born in Paris in 1760 to an aristocratic family that had fallen on hard times. His uncle had served at the court of Louis XIV and his memoirs of his life there is a French classic. Saint-Simon himself claimed descent from Charlemagne. Educated in a haphazard fashion by private tutors, Saint-Simon entered military service in 1777 and was sent to aid anti-British revolutionary forces in North America. He was present as a captain of artillery at the British surrender at Yorktown in 1781. Returning to his homeland, Saint-Simon made a fortune speculating in former religious and royal lands nationalized by the government during the French Revolution, although he was also jailed during the Reign of Terror in 1794. With his newly-minted wealth, Saint-Simon lived a life of excess and splendor for a time but soon spent himself into bankruptcy. At that point he turned to the study of science, enrolling briefly at the prestigious École Polytechnique and meeting with the greatest scientists of his day. Still, he never truly escaped from poverty, a fact which led him to such despair that he attempted to end his own life in 1823 but only succeeded in putting out an eye.

His first published writings *Letters of an Inhabitant of Geneva to His Contemporaries* (1803) was not so much a work of science as a study of science's role in society. Specifically, he advocated that scientists should assume the role of priests and that they should be subsidized in this endeavor by the wealthy. In later writings such as *On the Reorganization of European Society* (1814) and *Industry* (1816-18, co-written with **Auguste Comte**), Saint-Simon laid out a series of simple ideas about social organization. Reacting to the violence of the French Revolution and the dictatorial militarism of Napoleon, he advocated **science and technology** as solutions to the world's problems. In doing so, he anticipated the **Industrial Revolution** and a future political order dominated by businessmen and technocrats. His ideas on social and economic planning greatly influenced future Marxists, while his analysis of the looming industrial order would have an enormous influence on all of the social sciences.

SAMPLING

A sample is a subset of individuals or units taken from a population. The aim of sampling is to create a group that, when analyzed, produces results representative of the population. Probably the most widely known use of sampling in the United States are the political polls conducted by the Gallup organization. Gallup polls a sample of one thousand adult Americans about their political affiliations. The technique that Gallup employs allows them to state that the political affiliations of the sample are representative of the entire population or are generalizable to the population.

Sampling can be either random (**probability**) or non-random (non-probability). Probability or random samples are chosen on the basis that each person in the population has an

equal chance of being selected in the sample. Because of this principle, probability samples are more representative of the population than non-probability samples. Probability samples begin with a sampling frame which is a list of the accessible population that may be included in the sample. There are a number of different types of probability samples. Simple random sampling can be conducted by drawing a predetermined number of names out of a hat. A second way to conduct a simple random sample is to assign each subject in the sampling fame a number and then use a computer generated table of random numbers. The computer generated random numbers are then matched up with the numbers on the sampling frame to produce the sample. A slightly different method of obtaining a random sample is the use of systematic sampling. This method involves choosing every *n*th person on the sampling frame to arrive at a predetermined sample size. For example if we have a sampling frame with four hundred names and require a sample size of forty, we would choose every tenth person. It is important when using systematic random sampling to be aware of any patterns in the sampling frame. For example, every ninth house may be situated on a corner lot and thus may be the most expensive house on the block. Subtle patterns like this can affect generalizability of results.

A stratified sample is a way to ensure a greater degree of representativeness of certain groups. The researcher first divides the sampling frame into strata or groups. For example, suppose a researcher wanted to sample freshmen and seniors at a particular university. First, he or she would divide the sampling frame into four strata—freshmen, sophomores, juniors and seniors. Then the researcher samples from the strata using either systematic or simple random sampling. In this example, the researcher would sample from the freshmen and senior strata. The sample in this case is stratified by class year.

In some research situations, it is impractical or impossible to obtain a sampling frame of the target population. In such situations, researchers can use cluster sampling. If, for example, a researcher wanted a sample of all church-goers in the United States, compiling a list of these people would be impractical. Instead, the researcher could obtain a list of churches. The churches would be clusters or units from which the sampling elements are derived. The next step is to take a random sample of the churches, then a list of church-going families could be obtained from those churches. This list of families is the second cluster. A random sample of families could then be obtained, followed by random sampling of individuals within those families. This example involves several stages of sampling and is known collectively as multi-stage cluster sampling.

In the above multi-stage cluster sampling example, and in other types of sampling, often the last sampling unit is the **household** or **family**. A researcher must consider possible sources of **bias** when sampling households. For example, who in the household should be chosen? Bias can be introduced if a researcher interviews during regular working hours or if the researcher selects the person who answers the door.

Researchers often use non-probability sampling when resources are scarce or it is difficult to obtain a sampling frame. In convenience or haphazard, a researcher chooses a sample simply because the subjects are convenient or known to the researcher, for example, sampling the first one hundred people who walked out of a professional basketball game. Another example is a professor who uses his or her class as a sample. The researcher must be careful when discussing results from a convenience sample, since they are not likely to be indicative of the population.

A second type of non-probability sampling is purposive or judgmental which involves choosing a sample based on the researcher's knowledge of the research question, the population, and possible subjects. A third type is snowball sampling. Often subjects in a sample are connected to each other by common characteristics. A researcher studies one person and then asks that person to refer him or her to another suitable person. This process continues, or snowballs, until the researcher has a large enough sample. This method is usually done in qualitative fieldwork and is especially useful in the study of illegal activity. A fourth commonly used method of non-probability sampling is quota sampling, used when certain quotas of groups are needed in the sample because of the research question. For example, a sample may need to be fifty percent African American and fifty percent white. The sample is collected based on these quotas.

Given the nature of probability **theory**, the larger a sample is, the more likely it is to be representative of the population. Heterogenous populations require larger samples than homogenous populations given their larger variability. A researcher uses **inferential statistics** to infer results from the sample to the population.

SAMPLING ERROR

Sampling error, sometimes referred to as sample selection **bias**, represents the degree to which a study has or has not been able to reproduce the characteristics of the population of interest. Since sociological research gains its impetus from the extent to which the characteristics of a limited number of cases reflect those of a much larger population, the degree to which sample and population match is of paramount importance. While a distinction is made between sampling error and sampling bias (Sudman 1976), both refer to error that appears in the process of selecting a sample for study.

Most error in statistics is comprised of a random component and a systematic component. Sampling error refers to the random component. Random sampling error occurs when chance differences arise between the population and the sample. This source of error can be quantified and corrected. Increasing the size of the sample decreases random error. Sampling bias or systematic sampling error reflects the failure of researchers to select the sample from an appropriate sample frame and to conduct selection without accidentally favoring any one sample member over another. The sample frame is the list of members in the population of interest from which the sample is to be drawn. Incomplete or limited frames result in error which cannot be altered once the sample has been deter-

mined. A classic example in the sociological literature is the *Literary Digest*'s presidential election poll of 1936. *The Literary Digest* had correctly predicted the outcome of previous elections. But in the 1936 presidential election, it mistakenly predicted Republican Alf Landon would win over Democrat Franklin Roosevelt. The failure of the Literary Digest's poll is attributed to a misconceived sample frame. The list of sample respondents was taken from telephone directories and club membership lists. The list biased the sample towards affluent respondents, who were more likely to vote for Landon and less likely to vote for Roosevelt.

Sampling bias also results when selection of sample members is not random. All population members must have a calculable **probability** of appearing in the sample. If a sample members' probability of selection is unknown, usually because of an incomplete or misconceived sample frame, the sample will not be representative. Some population members will have no chance of appearing in the sample, and others will have too great a chance of appearing. Consequently, statements about the population will be fundamentally incorrect.

SANCTION

Sanctions, a means of control external to the individual, are responses to social behaviors and attitudes with the intention to enforce conformity to socially approved standards or **norms**. Sanctions can be positive or negative. Behaviors and attitudes that conform to social norms are reinforced with positive sanctions, encouraging continued **conformity**. Behaviors and attitudes that are not aligned with social norms are considered deviant and are responded to with negative sanctions to punish and discourage such actions. What is considered to be a positive or negative sanction may vary with **culture**. Sanctions can also be formal or informal. Formal sanctions would be those responses enforced by laws, regulations, or policies created around common perceptions of what is appropriate. Someone who breaks into a residence and steals another's possessions will be arrested. A cashier at a super market who, despite store policy, is unfriendly and rude to customers may be fired. These are examples of negative formal sanctions. A reward for turning in lost property or getting a raise for always having a positive attitude at work are examples of positive formal sanctions. Informal sanctions do not have legal backing but can be just as powerful and persuasive. If someone makes racist or sexist remarks in a speech, the audience may express disapproval to the speaker or leave. This is a negative informal sanction. A positive informal sanction would be applause to reward a good speech. Often, it is only the anticipation of certain sanctions that is necessary in order to encourage socially appropriate actions. The majority of people do not commit crimes perhaps because of a fear of being arrested, a fear of letting family members down, a fear of losing friends, or a combination of all these negative sanctions. At the same time, you might find that negative sanctions and positive sanctions may exist for the same action. It is important to understand in these cases which sanctions are the most influential in order to understand why

people act in a certain way. For example, a teenager who is more concerned with impressing his or her friends than with the possibility of arrest may engage in criminal behavior. We constantly engage in actions that are shaped by norms. We need only reflect on our day to create a list of the norms we followed or broke and the sanctions that we faced because of the choices we made.

SAPIR, EDWARD (1884-1939)
American anthropologist, linguist, and poet

Edward Sapir was a linguist dedicated to the investigation of the languages of native North America. Sapir played a major role in the formulation of the "culture and personality" field, and was recognized for his work in linguistics and its formal application to **culture**. Edward Sapir was born in 1884 in Lauenburg, Germany to Eva Seagal and Jacob David Sapir. The family moved to the United States when Sapir was five, and he grew up in New York City. Sapir received his B.A., M.A., and Ph.D. from Columbia University, where he studied with Franz Boas. His studies led to a fascination with the Amerindian languages and their grammars, and he helped Boas to record these languages before they became extinct. His fieldwork included an analysis of the languages of the Chinook, Takelma, Yana, Ute and Southern Paiute. In 1910, Sapir was made the director of the anthropological division of the Geological Survey of Canada and remained in that position until 1925. During this time, he primarily worked with the languages of the Nootka of Vancouver Island. Sapir then moved on to teach at the University of Chicago (1925–1931) and at Yale University (1931–1939). Also a poet, Sapir published over two hundred poems and one volume of poetry during the course of his career.

Sapir is perhaps most well known for the linguistic **theory**, the Sapir-Whorf hypothesis. Sapir began working with Benjamin Lee Whorf in the early 1930s, developing a systematic approach to his own studies of the interrelationship between **psychology** and **language**. The hypothesis developed by Sapir and Whorf suggests that language shapes the way we think about the world. The most noted examples of this theory are the Eskimo language, which has over one hundred words for snow, each describing a different real-world situation; or the Hanunoo, who have 92 different names for rice. The hypothesis suggests that in instances such as these, language allows for the description of real-life differences because those differences are important to the culture. This hypothesis holds some truth but can lead to **relativism**. Theorists also point out that there are common linguistic features where words are invented to describe reality (for example, the word "microwave" was created to describe the phenomenon and did not mark the invention of the ovens themselves). In spite of a lack of empirical research into these views, Sapir and Whorf were critical in heightening interest in the field of comparative linguistics and helped to promote the field of psycholinguistics.

SARTRE, JEAN-PAUL (1905-1980)
French philosopher and writer

The French philosopher and man of letters Jean Paul Sartre (1905–1980) ranks as the most versatile writer and as the dominant influence in three decades of French intellectual life. Jean Paul Sartre was born in Paris on June 21, 1905. His father, a naval officer, died while on a tour of duty in Indochina before Sartre was two years old. His mother belonged to the Alsatian Schweitzer family and was a first cousin to Albert Schweitzer. The young widow returned to her parents' house, where she and her son were treated as "the children." In the first volume of his autobiography *The Words* (1964), Sartre describes his unnatural childhood as a spoiled and precocious boy. Lacking any companions his own age, the child found "friends" exclusively in books. Reading and writing thus became his twin passions. "It was in books that I encountered the universe."

Sartre entered the École Normale Supérieure in 1924 and after one failure received first place in the *agrégation* of **philosophy** in 1929. The novelist Simone de Beauvoir finished second that year, and the two formed an intimate bond that endured thereafter. After completing compulsory military service, Sartre took a teaching job at a lycée in Le Havre. There he wrote his first novel *Nausea* (1938), which some critics have called the century's most influential French novel.

From 1933 to 1935 Sartre was a research student at the Institut Français in Berlin and in Freiburg. He discovered the works of Edmund Husserl and Martin Heidegger and began to **phenomenology** into his thought. A series of works on the modalities of consciousness poured from Sartre's pen: two works on imagination, one on self-consciousness, and one on emotions. He also produced a volume of short stories, *The Wall* (1939).

Sartre returned to Paris to teach in a lycée and to continue his writing, but World War II intervened. He served briefly in the army on the Eastern front and was taken prisoner. After nine months he secured his release and returned to teaching in Paris, where he became active in the Resistance. During this period he wrote his first major work in philosophy, *Being and Nothingness: An Essay in Phenomenological Ontology* (1943).

After the war Sartre abandoned teaching, determined to support himself by writing. He was also determined that his writing and thinking should be *engagé*. Intellectuals, he thought, must take a public stand on every great question of their day. He thus became fundamentally a moralist, both in his philosophical and literary works.

Sartre had turned to playwriting and eventually produced a series of theatrical successes which are essentially dramatizations of ideas, although they contain some finely drawn characters and lively plots. The first two, *The Flies* and *No Exit,* were produced in occupied Paris. They were followed by *Dirty Hands* (1948), usually considered his best play; *The Devil and the Good Lord* (1957), a blasphemous, anti-Christian tirade; and *The Prisoners of Altona* (1960), which combined convincing character portrayal with telling social criticism. Sartre also wrote a number of comedies: *The Respectful Prostitute* (1946), *Kean* (1954), and *Nekrassov* (1956), which the critic Henry Peyre claimed "reveals him as the best comic talent of our times."

Jean-Paul Sartre *(Editions Gallimard)*

During this same period Sartre also wrote a three-volume novel *The Roads to Freedom* (1945–1949); a treatise on committed literature; lengthy studies of Charles Baudelaire and Jean Genet; and a prodigious number of reviews and criticisms. He also edited *Les temps modernes.*

Though never a member of the Communist party, Sartre usually sympathized with the political views of the far left. Whatever the political issue, he was quick to publish his opinions, often combining them with public acts of protest.

In 1960 Sartre returned to philosophy, publishing the first volume of his *Critique of Dialectical Reason*. It represented essentially a modification of his existentialism by Marxist ideas. The drift of Sartre's earlier work was toward a sense of the futility of life. In *Being and Nothingness* he declared man to be "a useless passion," condemned to exercise a meaningless freedom. But after World War II his new interest in social and political questions and his rapprochement with Marxist thought led him to more optimistic and activist views.

Sartre has always been a controversial yet respected individual. In 1964, Sartre was awarded but refused to accept the Nobel Prize in literature. Sartre suffered from detrimental health throughout the 1970s. He died of a lung ailment in 1980.

Arthur Schopenhauer *(New York Public Library Picture Collection)*

SCHOPENHAUER, ARTHUR (1788-1860)
German philosopher

The German philosopher Arthur Schopenhauer (1788–1860), whose pessimistic **philosophy** was widely known in the late nineteenth century in Europe and the United States, held that ultimate reality was nothing but senseless striving or will, having no divine origin and no historical end. Arthur Schopenhauer was born in Danzig on February 22, 1788. His father, a successful Dutch businessman, had a taste for urbane living, travel, and bourgeois culture, while his mother aspired to the more exotic culture of writers and nonconformists. When Schopenhauer was five, Danzig, formerly a free mercantile city, was annexed by Poland. As a consequence, his **family** moved to Hamburg, Germany, in search of a more congenial setting for his father's business. In 1797 Schopenhauer was sent to stay with a family in France, returning to Hamburg after two years to enter a private school. Later he became interested in literature, earning the disapproval of his father, who nonetheless gave him the choice of pursuing serious literary studies or traveling with the family for two years. Schopenhauer chose to travel.

His voyages over, Schopenhauer took a job as a clerk in a Hamburg merchant's office. That year, 1805, his father died, apparently a suicide. The mercantile world held only drudgery for young Schopenhauer, whose ambitions and de-

sires were both unfocused and frustrated. Feeling constrained by a promise to his father, Schopenhauer remained at work until 1807, when he joyfully resigned in order to study Greek and Latin in a school at Gotha. Having enraged an unsympathetic instructor, he transferred to a school in Weimar, where his mother had already established herself as mistress of a literary salon frequented by Goethe and other notables. But Schopenhauer had earlier quarreled with his mother, whom he thought too free with her ideas and her favors. He therefore resided with his mentor, the philologist Franz Passow, who paid his tuition. Schopenhauer's studies went well, and in 1809, on acquiring a handsome legacy, he enrolled at the University of Göttingen. He studied mostly the sciences and medicine but eventually turned to philosophy.

Schopenhauer's new passion for philosophy led him to the University of Berlin, where he hoped to cull the wisdom of **Johann Gottlieb Fichte**, then the foremost philosopher in Germany. He was disappointed in Fichte but remained at the university until 1813, when Prussia mobilized to expel the French after Napoleon's defeat. Seeing the dangers of staying in Berlin and having no heart for nationalistic fervor, Schopenhauer sought refuge in Rudolstadt. There he completed his doctoral dissertation, which he submitted successfully to the University of Jena. He published the dissertation at his own expense and then returned to Weimar. He met Goethe, who seemed sympathetic to his thinking. One fruit of their conversations was Schopenhauer's brief study *Über das Sehn und die Farben* (1816; *On Vision and Colors*).

Schopenhauer's unhappy relations with his mother finally terminated in open hostility, and he moved to Dresden. By this time the central and simple idea of his philosophy had taken hold in his mind. The principal source of this idea was his own experience and moods, but the expression of it owed much to the philosophies of Plato and **Immanuel Kant** and the mystical literature of India. He foresaw that his reflections would eventually lift him above the absurd stresses and conflicts of his life, and he thought that ultimately his writings would usher in a new era not only in philosophy but also in human history. Whereas former philosophies had been parceled into schools and special problems, his own, as he envisaged it, would be a single, simple fabric. The simplest expression of this potent idea is probably the very title of the book he wrote at Dresden, *Die Welt als Wille und Vorstellung* (*The World as Will and Idea*). The world is necessarily present to a subject that perceives it; thus the world is "idea" or "representation." Yet the world is not created or constructed by the subject or the mind; its own nature is will, or blind striving. "My body and my will are one," and in the final analysis one person's will is indistinguishable from every other form of willing.

The book was printed by a reluctant publisher in 1818 and failed to gain public recognition. Nevertheless, with two books to his credit, Schopenhauer was given a lectureship in philosophy at the University of Berlin. At that time G. W. F. Hegel was the center of attention, and Schopenhauer decided to compete with him by lecturing at the same hour. But he addressed an empty room, and shortly his academic career was over.

In 1831 cholera was epidemic in Berlin, and Schopenhauer fled to Frankfurt, where he stayed for the rest of his life. In 1836 he published a study of contemporary science, *Über den Willen in der Natur* (*On the Will in Nature*), showing that his philosophy was consistent with the sciences. In 1839 he won a prize from the Norwegian Scientific Society for an essay on freedom of the will. To this essay he added another, publishing them in 1841 as "Die Beiden Grundprobleme der Ethik" ("The Two Fundamental Problems of Ethics"). During these years he revised and augmented the text of *The World as Will and Idea*, which was republished in 1844 with fifty new chapters. In 1847 he republished his dissertation *Über die vierfache Wurzel des Satzes vom zureichenden Grunde* (*On the Fourfold Root of the Principle of Sufficient Reason*). By now he was attracting some notice, but the fame he had predicted for himself was still only a dream. Schopenhauer's style of life in his Frankfurt years has always both fascinated and puzzled his admirers. Though he wrote about the ultimate value of negating the will, he displayed unusual willfulness; though he extolled tranquility, he was always energetic; though he wrote savage diatribes against women, he could not forgo female company.

At last, in 1851, Schopenhauer published the book that brought him fame and followers. Titled *Parerga und Paralipomena*, it was a collection of highly polished, insightful essays and aphorisms. Its style was probably the chief reason for the book's immediate success. Yet the ideas were important too, particularly the notion that will was primary over intellect. The pessimism that follows from such a notion was already in vogue, and Schopenhauer became its voice. Another reason for his fame was surely his appeal to the inner experience of moods and feelings, in contrast to the more traditional appeals to history, reason, **authority**, and objective evidence. His philosophy takes its source in "the selfsame unchangeable being which is before us." Life is all suffering, he said, but it can be reflected upon, and then it will be seen to be "nothing." Schopenhauer died on September 21, 1860. By then he had countless followers, and he was idolized as a kind of savior.

SCHUTZ, ALFRED (1899-1959)
Austrian philosopher and sociologist

Vienna-born philosopher Alfred Schutz developed **phenomenology**, the study of the development of human consciousness and self-awareness into a sociological science. He was born on April 13, 1899, after the death of his father, Alfred. His mother, Johanna Fialla Schutz, married her husband's brother, Otto, a bank executive. During his school years, Schutz became interested in literature, music, and art. He graduated from Esterhazy Gymnasium and was drafted into the Austrian army at age 18. During World War I, he served on the Italian front.

After the war, Schutz entered the University of Vienna and studied law under Hans Kelsen, an Austrian and later American legal philosopher and teacher who formulated what is called the "pure theory" of law, meaning that law itself should be logically self-supporting. Schutz also studied eco-

nomics under another Austrian-American, Ludwig von Mises, known for his contribution to liberalism in economic **theory** and his belief in the power of consumers. Schutz earned an LL.D. degree in international law, and in 1921, he became executive secretary of the Austrian Banker's Association. In 1926, he married Ilse Heim; they had two children.

Schutz joined the private banking firm of Reitler and Company in 1929 and remained there until his **retirement** in 1958. During those years, he devoted most of his evening free time to the social sciences. He became intensely interested in the theoretical aspects of human actions and relationships which led to the theories of German sociologist **Max Weber** and others. Weber is best known for his thesis of the "Protestant Ethic," relating protestantism to capitalism. When he found Weber's theories inadequate, he turned to Henri-Louis Bergson, a French philosopher noted for what he called a process philosophy, which rejected static **values** for values of change, motion, and evolution. Still searching for adequate self-understanding, Schutz eventually was led to the theories of German phenomenolgoist Edmund Husserl (1859-1938). Schutz came to regard himself as a close follower of Husserl and went briefly to Freiburg, Germany, to work with the older man.

The philosophical movement called phenomenology has been regarded as the direct investigation and description of phenomena as experienced consciously, as free as possible from preconceptions and presuppositions. It has gone through many changes since Husserl's theories, but most phenomenologists adhere to his watchword, translated as the phrase "to the things themselves," through which Husserl advocates bracketing our human presuppositions in order to directly experience things as they exist independently in the world. Schutz's first work on the subject is entitled *The Meaningful Structure of the Social World,* 1932. Called by some a masterpiece on the subject, it shows how actions become meaningful when projected and interpreted in relation to causes and purposes. It investigates how the self relates to others, to close associates who act upon one another directly, and to contemporaries who act indirectly. It is also concerned with scientific investigation of the socio-historical cultural world.

In 1938 when Hitler invaded Austria, Schutz and his family left for Paris and then immigrated to New York City, where his company had moved its headquarters. With other emigres and American followers of Husserl's theories, Schutz founded the journal *Philosophy and Phenomenological Research,* in 1940. For nearly the next twenty years, Schutz was a banker by day and phenomenologist by night. He blended his insights of American social science and **philosophy** into his theories nurtured in Vienna. He also was a part-time lecturer, then professor at the Graduate Faculty of Political and Social Sciences, the New School for Social Research in New York City. In addition to his teachings in the social sciences, he studied, taught, and wrote about music, **race** relations, technology, reality and relevance, and literature. Alfred Schutz died in New York City on May 20, 1959.

Although he made numerous contributions to scientific journals, Schutz is best known for his four posthumous (1962,

1964, 1966, 1996) volumes of *Collected Papers*. The English translation of his *Sinnhafte Aufbau, The Phenomenology of the Social World,* appeared in 1967. A final statement of his theories appeared in two volumes *The Structures of the Life-World* (1973, 1983), completed after his death by Thomas Luckmann. Copies of Schutz's papers are found in the Center for Advanced Research in phenomenology, Florida, Atlantic University, in Boca Raton.

SCHWARTZ, PEPPER (1945-)
American educator and author

Noted for her publications and lectures on human sexuality, Pepper Schwartz is a frequent guest and host on local and network television shows in the Seattle, Washington, area. She was born in Chicago on May 11, 1945, to Julius J. and Gertrude Puris Schwartz. She attended undergraduate school at Washington University in St. Louis, where she was Woodrow Wilson Fellow. Schwartz earned a B.A. in 1968 and an M.A. in 1970. She married John A. Strait in 1970, was divorced, and married Arthur M. Skolnik in 1982. They have two children, Cooper and Ryder, and live on a horse and llama ranch in Snoqualmie, Washington.

Schwartz continued her studies at Yale University, earning a Ph.D. in sociology, 1974. She began her teaching career in 1972 as an associate sociology professor, University of Washington, Seattle, becoming professor of psychiatry and behavioral science in 1988. UW's Department of **Sociology** was established in the 1920s. Today, Schwartz teaches classes in the family, gender and sexuality, changing patterns of family organization, and sociology of families.

Beginning in 1971, Schwartz began her studies in human sexuality with the publication of *A Student's Guide to Sex on Campus*. This was followed by *Women at Yale* with Janet Lever and *Sociological Perspectives on Female Sexuality* with Judith Long Laws. Since then, her many books and articles on the subject explore such issues as: *The Gender of Sexuality*, *Bisexuality* with Philip Blumstein and Jane Adams, *Everything You Know About Love and Sex Is Wrong,* 2000, and *201 Questions to Ask Your Kids/201 Questions to Ask Your Parents,*, 2001. For several years, she wrote a monthly column with Dr. Janet Lever on sex and health for and a weekly column for Microsoft's *One Click Away* called "Sex.net with Dr. Pepper." She contributes to numerous **internet** sites and is the author of a bi-monthly column for *American Baby Magazine*. In addition, she was a news staff member for 12 years at KIRO-Rv (Seattle).

One of Schwartz's most distinguished works is *American Couples: Money, Work, Sex,* written with Philip Blumstein. The culmination of the authors' life-long interest in the nature of relationship, this study attempts to put the American couple in perspective by using 20 actual case histories, five married, five cohabiting, five lesbian, and five gay male couples. Although the authors explore every aspect of these peoples' lives, they concentrate on money, work, and sex since these three are such critical issues in any relationship. A total

of 22,000 questionnaires were mailed initially. The final selections, gathering and sorting of **data**, took years and the work of many people. A basic finding emerged that despite the enormous changes that have occurred in America since its founding, the American couple—and its family—has remained remarkably stable.

Schwartz has served on the board of directors of the National Abortion Rights Action League and the Anti-Defamation League and has been a consultant to many national organizations. She is a member of the National Assembly for Policy Research and Development, National Woman's Resource Center, Council for Woman's Equality, American Sociological Association, Washington State Government Commission on Venereal Disease (1974-77), and National Institute of Mental Health review committee. She received the Matrix Award for Achievement in Education and the International Women's Forum Award in Career Achievement in the State of Washington. Schwartz was named Outstanding Young Woman of the Future, *Time-Life*, 1981. She has appeared as an authority on the NBC network show "Some Thoughts on Being Single," 1984, and on ABC's "After the Sexual Revolution," 1986. In 1984, Schwartz was appointed to President Ronald Reagan's roundtable on the family. She appeared as a member of the Women in the '90s Conference Report, a panel discussion sponsored by the *Ladies Home Journal*entitled "Decade of Decisions: What's next for Women?"

SCIENCE AND TECHNOLOGY

Science and technology, viewed from a sociological perspective, is understood as a specialized field of study, sometimes referred to as a subfield of the sociology of knowledge that examines the normative and institutional basis of the development of scientific and technological knowledge. Originating in the United States in the twentieth century, especially through the work of American sociologist Robert Merton, the **sociology** of science addresses various aspects of science and technology at different levels, including the social organization of the field of science, the interplay between scientists and scholars from other disciplines, and the impact of social issues and public policy on scientific research.

The development of modern science along with the rise of capitalism gave scientists strong incentives for understanding and discovering new knowledge as a means of both economic and social **progress**. In his book *The Sociology of Science* (1970), first published in 1942, Merton suggested that a normative structure for scientific study emerged, characterized by four identifiable **norms**. First, all scientific contributions are examined for merit, independent of the scientist. This norm of universalism deems factors such as the religion, **race**, or nationality of the scientist irrelevant. Second, disclosure of knowledge is required. This norm of **communism** suggests that scientists have a responsibility to share discoveries with the public and other scientists. In turn, they are rewarded by receiving recognition and credit from their peers and **society**. Third, although not bound to altruism, scientists are expected

to act independently of financial gain. This norm of disinterest-edness creates an environment in which private gain for scientific contributions is not acceptable. Finally, Merton added the norm of organized skepticism, which not only permits but expects that challenges will be made to claims of knowledge.

Merton's understanding of the social processes within the scientific community as functional interactions dominated the field of sociology of science, as other theorists either expanded Merton's ideas or reacted against them. Ian Mitroff accepted Merton's basis of normative structures but argued in his 1974 article "Norms and Counternorms in a Select Group of Scientists: A Case Study in the Ambivalence of Scientist," which appeared in *American Sociological Review,* that a parallel set of norms also exists that is exactly opposite of those described by Merton. Based on interview **data**, Mitroff suggested that sometimes such criteria as personal merit and emotional commitment are viable considerations that can contribute to scientific development. In "Interpretation and the Use of Rules: The Case of Norms in Science," appearing in *Science and Social Structure: A Festschrift for Robert K. Merton* (1980; edited by T. F. Gieryn), Michael J. Mulkay challenged Merton's positivist assumptions, arguing that scientific study is not an autonomous endeavor, guided by universal norms, but is subject to numerous external influences, cultural circumstances, and personal desires.

Stuart S. Blume, editor of *Perspectives in the Sociology of Science* (1977), suggested in his introduction that two general reactions developed against Merton's understanding of science: externalist and cognitive. Following Mulkay's lead, the externalist **paradigm** rejects the notion that science can be studied as a closed system that is not subject to external influences. Instead, externalists attempt to view science completely, or at least to a large extent, through the influences of outside factors. For example, externalist **theory** may suggest that scientific research priorities are based on dual pressures from the cultural environment of its host community and from political pressure placed upon it in most large industrialized countries.

According to Blume, three focal points serve to validate the externalist approach. The first focal point is upon the reward system in science. Merton's norms suggest that scientists are motivated by recognition of scientific discovery. Blume noted that studies have provided evidence that a system of stratification exists within the scientific **community** so that merit is not doled out equally. Such external factors as prejudices, personal loyalties, personal preferences, and professional or personal affiliations determine the awarding of scientific merit. The second focal point is found in the diversity of social demands placed upon an individual scientist. In particular, Blume noted the links between scientists and political influence. In highly institutionalized industrial societies, scientific work is closely connected with political goals. Scientists may use their recognition or merit as a means to further or establish a particular political agenda. The third focal point concerns the evolution of the institutionalization of science. Blume referred to this phenomenon as politicization and unionization, reflected in a movement during the 1970s toward the development of political goals and a unionized structure within professional scientific organizations.

The cognitive approach challenges the epistemological presuppositions of Merton's version of science. Whereas Merton assumed the **validity** of the logical empiricist tradition, which proposed that timeless, universal, and logical rules of the universe exist and simply need to be discovered, cognitive theory suggests that the discovery of knowledge is a socially bound activity. Historian Thomas S. Kuhn published *The Structure of Scientific Revolutions* in 1962, in which he argued that scientific theories, standards, and formulations were not universal but varied over time. He divided science into two categories: normal and revolutionary. Normal science is governed by paradigms in which scientists search for answers to puzzles of nature based on shared values, presuppositions, and experimental **methodology**. In revolutionary science, disconfirming evidence that arises in normal science provokes a scientist or group of scientists to propose an entirely new paradigm, which even if evidentially proven is often resisted by the scientific community. Using the Copernican Revolution as an example, Kuhn suggested that social factors, not scientific discovery itself, determine the survival of these new paradigms. Cognitive theorists built on Kuhn's work to create theories that dictated the need to examine the social, structural, and intellectual, or cognitive, factors impacting the scientific community.

Blume defines the two general approaches of externalism and cognitivism: "Very broadly, in the first case focus is upon the relations between internal and external structural factors, in the second upon the relations between internal structural and cognitive factors." As science and technology continue to delve into new areas such as genetic reproduction, the advancement of computer technology, and **disease** research, **sociology of science** will continue to be challenged to understand and address how these developments affect society and, in turn, how society affects scientific knowledge.

SCIENTIFIC EXPLANATION

A scientific explanation is an attempt to describe why some situation or phenomenon is the way that it is according to a particular **paradigm** within which the investigator is working. It is a researcher's conclusions of a study. The way these results were determined will be different depending on how the research question is asked which is directly drawn from the theory that the researcher is using in the study. Thus, slightly different theories can lead to different explanations of the same phenomenon without contradicting one another or being wrong *per se.* That is not to say that all results from scientific studies are in agreement or are never wrong.

Science has historically been thought of as a rigorous and systemic process of examination which is joined with meticulous, logical thinking in order to provide a new insight or type of knowledge. Scientific explanations take many forms; each form answers different types of questions. Some explanations may be nomothetic in nature. This refers to the traditional **model** of physics in which general laws are found to describe particular observations. These observations are factors, which

necessarily follow from general, causal laws. That is to say, one agent caused a reaction in another object or individual. This same reaction will occur every single time that process is repeated. For example, when dropped, an apple will always fall to the ground.

Other explanations may be ideographic, when limited generalizations are used to describe a particular observation or sequence of observations. The descriptions are symbolic representations, which both provide an understanding of a different social reality and furnish an informal model of organization. In general, this type of explanation attempts to find or gain an understanding of how a system, phenomenon, or situation works, or did work at some point.

Yet another type of explanation may be critical of an observation which serves to illuminate an underlying nature of the object, suggest how the object can be modified or changed, and describe the possible after effects of the change. A critical explanation views laws as constantly shifting and malleable, in contrast to a nomothetic explanation, in which laws are considered fixed. Policy researchers, among other types of inquiry, frequently employ this model of explanation in their work.

SCIENTIFIC MANAGEMENT

Scientific Management is a theory of work which sought to make industrial labor more efficient. It was developed by Frederick William Taylor and, therefore, is sometimes referred to as Taylorism. Taylor believed that workers could (and should) be treated as extensions of industrial machinery and their movements regimented in the same way machines could be calibrated to perform operations in a specific and consistent manner. Scientific management requires the detailed study of a particular task, breaking the task down into essential steps, and then regimenting those steps specifically.

The intent of scientific management is to increase the efficiency of a worker by eliminating all unnecessary movement and requiring the consistent repetition of movement so that it can be performed with greater speed and accuracy. Scientific management was applied primarily to factory line work, but it can also be applied to any job task that involves repetition of movement, little or no analytic or evaluative effort, and produces many products when performed more quickly.

In his book *Labor and Monopoly Capital,* Harry Braverman specified that scientific management is "a science of the management of others' work under capitalist conditions" (1974:90). It is a way for capitalist management to control the bodily movements (and thus control the bodies) of workers. While certain control over workers was commonly practiced before Taylor developed his theory (such as requiring workers to perform their work in a specified location, the factory, and dictating how long the work day would be), scientific management went much further by dictating how the work was to be performed. Taylor justified this level of control by pointing out the greater efficiency obtained through scientific management. He believed it could be used to extract a "fair" amount of work from the worker, defining fair as the physiological maximum.

Scientific management coincided (and supported) the scientific-technological revolution, which involved increased use of technology in the manufacturing of goods. It also comprised the separation of mental work from physical labor, so that workers were not expected to think about the work they were doing (and in fact, were actively encouraged not to think). Scientific management fit well into this new schema of the labor process, as it treated physical tasks as a process that could be analyzed and regimented scientifically and made mental work unnecessary and even inefficient.

Taylor faced intense resistance from workers when trying to implement scientific management. Because it resulted in increased output, it undermined the output-control mechanisms workers used as a leverage against the demands of management. It also required maintaining an often grueling level of speed, and many workers argued that it was not physically possible for most humans to maintain machine-like movements as rapidly as Taylor demanded. And because scientific management eliminated thought in the labor process, it often resulted in making labor more tedious to workers. However, the resistance of workers was not enough to dissuade factory owners, who implemented scientific management throughout the industrialized nations (particularly the United States, Great Britain, and Germany).

SECONDARY ANALYSIS

Secondary analysis is an unobtrusive research **methodology** that utilizes existing **data** to study research questions that differ from the original work. The researcher does not design a sampling methodology, nor does he or she actually collect data. Instead, the researcher relies on the data collection expertise of another researcher and analyzes data that have already been collected. Secondary data analysis is usually of a quantitative nature, although existing qualitative data can also be analyzed. With the advent of computerized databases, there is a wealth of data available for researchers to analyze. A quick tour of the Inter-University Consortium for Political and Social Research (ICPSR) housed on the University of Michigan homepage reveals the wide range of data collected by various government and private agencies available for secondary analysis. A database of qualitative data called Qualidata, is maintained by the British based Economic and Social Research Council (ESCR).

The most famous and one of the first studies to utilize existing data was Émile Durkheim's study titled *Suicide.* In this study, Durkheim took the suicide rates collected by government agencies of a number of different European countries and analyzed them to determine how social integration— through religious affiliation—affected suicide rates. He discovered that those individuals involved in religious groups that were based on collectiveness had lower suicide rates than those individuals whose religions idealized **individualism**. This landmark study established the legitimacy of secondary data analysis.

The main advantage of secondary analysis is that the researcher saves time and resources by not having to design a

sampling method and collect data. In the past, such a shortcut may have been viewed by sociologists as substandard research, but with increasingly sophisticated analysis techniques and up-to-date data, secondary data analysis has the potential to address pressing social issues. Some branches of government, for example, the Department of Justice, even fund secondary data analysis of their data sets. Often an existing data set will be much larger than the data set an individual researcher could have collected, and existing data may be collected by experts in sampling and survey implementation.

The biggest drawback to using secondary analysis is limitations on validity. The researcher has to carefully consider whether the data really measure the research questions posed. In cases where the data do not quite fit the research questions, different measures of the same variables can be used to help bolster **validity**. Additionally, a researcher may combine one existing data set with another.

One of the first steps a researcher should take when undergoing a quantitative secondary analysis is to use scatterplots of variables to identify outlying or deviant cases and possible miscoded data. Miscoded data and deviant cases can threaten **reliability**. Obvious coding errors and unlikely deviant cases can be replaced with **mean values** to avoid affecting all data analysis.

A potential problem with using secondary data occurs when collection agencies have made corrections to the data. Mistakes in the data are usually brought to light by a researcher conducting secondary analysis who identifies a problem in the data and alerts the principal investigator. Changes may then be made to the data set. Such changes are usually reported in the abstract of data sets and can affect test-retest reliability. Many data sets are longitudinal which means that data are collected from the same group of participants over a number of years. A researcher using longitudinal data must be mindful of attrition rates, as subjects who remain in studies may have similar characteristics.

Although sociologists normally view secondary data analysis as quantitative, qualitative secondary analysis can also be conducted. Some research questions are better addressed by qualitative data. Like quantitative secondary analysis, the issue of validity is of great concern in qualitative secondary analysis. In addition, qualitative analysis is more likely to initiate ethical issues, particularly that of informed consent. A researcher must consider whether re-analyzing qualitative data violates any part of the confidentiality agreement between the original researcher and the subjects. The researcher who conducts secondary analysis on qualitative data must also be mindful of the relationship between the original researcher and the subjects. Because of the nature of qualitative research, the original researcher may bring subjectivity into the discourse.

One of the most recognizable secondary data analyses in modern society is the FBI Uniform Crime Reports (UCR). The FBI tabulates data sent in from the some 17,000 police agencies across the country and produces crime rates and trends for the entire nation. The media may conduct their own analyses of these data, as may various politicians, since the crime platform has become an important one. Thus, secondary data analysis can sometimes be used as a tool for arranging data to support particular perspectives. Research ethics in secondary analysis should therefore be closely followed.

Secondary Deviance

Secondary deviance is one of two major concepts in labeling theory. This **theory** emphasizes the importance of societal reactions to offenders and the offenders' **self-concept** in the commission of deviant and criminal acts. Work on secondary deviance may be found in the writings of sociologists such as Frank Tannenbaum, Edwin Lemert, Howard Becker, William Chambliss, and Edwin Schur who worked primarily between the 1930s and the 1970s.

To understand what secondary deviance is, it is first important to understand primary deviance. **Primary deviance** is an initial act that violates some societal norm and/or criminal law. Reasons for this act may include a breakdown of social controls, peer influence, and financial strain. If caught in the initial act of deviance, individuals are typically punished either formally or informally, and this punishment attaches a deviant label. This label acts as a stigma or ''tag'' that brands the person and shapes his or her reputation. In other words, the person is seen as a deviant or criminal in the eyes of others. A negative label is often difficult to resist, and in many cases people continue to repeat the same behaviors because they cannot resist the label. This repeated behavior is known as secondary deviance.

This process is epitomized in William Chambliss's well-known article ''The Saints and the Roughnecks,'' in which he contrasts a wealthy, high-status group of young boys known as the Saints with a poor, disadvantaged group of boys known as the Roughnecks. Chambliss details how, when the Roughnecks committed petty thefts and acts of vandalism (primary deviance), they received negative labels of ''troublemakers'' and ''deviants.'' These negative labels, along with their poor social positions, combined to define the boys as deviant by teachers, police, and **community** members. Because they had difficulty resisting the powerful labels placed on them, the Roughnecks continued to engage in the same acts (secondary deviance) that led to their receiving the negative labels in the first instance.

This research details how punishment and labeling of individuals may actually lead to more of the same behavior rather than less, as deterrence theorists such as James Q. Wilson argue. **Labeling theory** thus has important policy implications as it calls for a less stigmatizing and less punitive approach to dealing with offenders, especially juveniles.

Secondary Group

A social **group** consists of two or more people interacting with one another. Members of a social group tend to share interests and experiences and are inclined to think of themselves as

''we'' while still keeping their own identity. A secondary group is a social group that is large, anonymous, formal, impersonal, and serves a purpose, usually the completion of a task or specific goal. Primary groups have face-to-face interactions, long lasting relationships, and emotional intimacy; they **influence** individuals and shape their self-identity. An example of a **primary group** is a **family**; a secondary group could be college students in a General **Sociology** course.

In this secondary group example, the bond between classmates is weak, especially in a large class. The students may or may not communicate with each other outside of class and may or may not continue interacting after the class has ended. This group is brought together for a common goal, members feel a sense of unity, and have the common interest of sociology. Other examples of secondary groups are teachers, nurses, citizens of New York City, or members of a Rotary Club.

As societies become more complex, secondary groups have more influence on behavior. For example, in the small kinships typical of hunting and gathering societies, the focus is on the family as a primary group. Secondary groups are not needed. As societies became larger and more industrialized, secondary groups appear in the form of peer groups, work groups, neighborhoods, and educational groups.

If individuals lack a primary group, have weak ties to their primary group, or are under stress, secondary groups can take on primary group characteristics. A child from a broken, abusive home may turn to a gang for those connections the family cannot provide. Neighbors may over time become intimate and dependent on one another and in a sense become family. In catastrophes, survivors may bond and become more intimate.

Secondary State

A secondary state is an area that exists on the periphery of a primary state and is involuntarily taken over, in part or in full, to enhance the resource and power bases of the primary state. Often referred to as a ''colony,'' it is usually the result of **imperialism**. A secondary state is less formed and less autonomous than a primary state. It does not rise out of a pristine state, meaning it is already in existence when the primary state intrudes and is altered by the introduction of new, more dominant, social, political, or economic elements.

The two primary theories of secondary state development agree that the goal of intrusion and **domination** is to access the capital and resources of a region, for use by the more dominant state. They also agree that the dominant state will politically and economically reorganize the secondary state for the benefit of the dominant, rather than the local, state. The two theories differ on the degree to which they think the dominant state exploits and reorganizes the secondary state.

According to Price (1978), secondary states are a result of the capture, domination, and reorganization of a region by a foreign agent, for the purpose of taking all the capital and labor of that region for its own benefit. In these cases, a domi-

nant state would conquer an area; organize it to maximize resource extraction; reconstruct all existing social institutions; and allow the colony to grow only in ways and to the extent that it would benefit the dominant state. In this scenario, dominant states often used extreme and extensive military domination to attain their aims, sometimes decimating indigenous populations. The Inca **civilization** is often used as example.

In contrast, Thapar (1981) believes there can be a limited domination of secondary states. She claims that not all primary states maximize exploitation. Rather, they reconstruct the social, economic, and political systems already in place only to the extent needed to develop control over the resources of the region. There is still domination, but a complete reorganization and redistribution of resources is not necessary. The Aztec **culture** is often used as an example.

Much research regarding secondary states is historical. Many were formed during time periods when imperialist empires were rising and falling. In modern times, some entities originally considered secondary states have taken on primary importance and have played pivotal roles in international politics.

See also Imperialism

Sect

Sects are relatively small religious groups which have separated from an established religion to return their **group** to what the members believe to be the initial basis of the faith. Sect members often believe that the established religion has changed and moved their doctrines away from the ''true meaning'' of the faith. For this reason, sects tend to shun mainstream beliefs although long-term survival of a sect can lead to increased acceptance of and by **society**. Disputes with societal **values** can lead to the sect to withdraw from society (i.e. Quakers/Society of Friends) or to attempt to change society through evangelical means (i.e. Jehovah's Witnesses).

The categorization of religious organizations was developed in the 1910s by Troeltsch and revised by Weber in the 1920s. In this typology of organization, sects demonstrate less organization than most groups, small but zealous memberships, relatively informal religious services, and clergy with minimal training. In the 1950s, Wilson delineated four subtypes based on indifference to mainstream social values: conversionist, introversionist, revolutionary, and gnostic.

Individual membership within religious sects is typically based on acceptance of a specific dogma of the faith. Because sects tend to arise from canonic disputes with established faiths, sect members often exhibit intense religious fervor and loyalty, adopting radical views toward most aspects of government and society.

As sects are often small in membership and somewhat controversial in beliefs, they may be confused with cults. However, while cults tend to represent a revolutionary innovation regarding religious doctrine, sects are focused on reestablishing the purity of a specific doctrine within an existing faith. For example, the Amish way of life was a response to the dis-

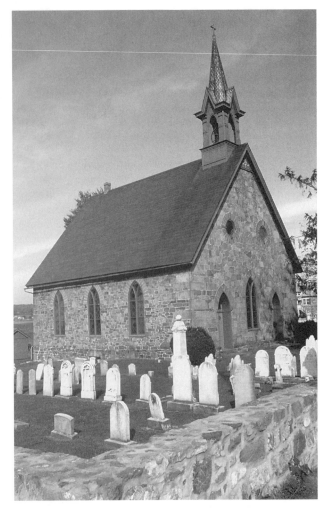

The Amish way of life was a response to the dissatisfaction many Mennonites felt towards the use of technology and worldly goods *(Corbis Corporation [Bellevue]).*

satisfaction many Mennonites felt with the use of technology and worldly goods within their community. The dissatisfied Mennonites separated from the original group in order to establish communities in which modern advances would not interfere with the practice of their true, communal Christian faith.

SECTOR THEORY

Sector **theory** states that **cities** grow outward in wedge-shaped sectors from their center. Each defined wedge is characterized by a different economic activity. Sector theory is a **model** of land use and urban growth first proposed by Henry Hoyt, a land economist, in *The Structure and Growth of Residential Neighborhoods in American Cities* (1939). It is one of the theories in Urban Ecology, the study of the link between the physical and social dimensions of cities, which looks at and helps explain why cities are located where they are and why they develop the way they do.

Previous to Hoyt's proposition, the *concentric circle* model was the most popular model of urban expansion. Theorists believed that each city was made up a series of concentric rings, with the poorest section in the inner city and the more prosperous areas in the outlying areas. Cities were supposedly comprised of a central business district, surrounded by successive zones devoted to light manufacturing, worker's homes, high-class apartment buildings, single-family homes, and finally a commuter zone.

The most valuable and novel addition of sector theory was the concept of orientation. Hoyt believed that the circle concept was too simplistic. He proposed that early in a city's development, one sector of town would get established as the good side and another as the bad side. The projected goodness or badness of these sectors persisted as a city spread out from the center. The result was wedge-shaped, high- and low-rent districts extending from downtown out into what became known as the suburbs.

Hoyt believed that sectored urban expansion had several characteristics: high-income parts of an urban area are located in sectors that extend outward along established major transportation routes; there is a tendency for cities to develop toward higher elevations; expansion occurs toward the homes and neighborhoods of **community** leaders; and there is a tendency for growth of a city to continue in one direction for an extended period of time.

A third important model of urban expansion was *multiple-nuclei theory.* Modern, industrial cities supposedly consisted of several nuclei (centers), around which different kinds of economic and social activities cluster. Although all three of these classic theoretical models have merit, none were able to predict or explain the rapid growth of urban areas that resulted from the extensive use of cars and the complex web of roads and highways covering the country.

SECULARIZATION

Secularization refers to a process by which religion and religious belief become less influential in modern societies. Through this process, ''secular'' forces come to control aspects of **society** that previously were under religious authority. The term originated in eighteenth-century Europe, when nation-states began taking over lands controlled by the Catholic Church. Social theorists of that era interpreted this development as an indicator of social evolution. However, secularization as a specific **sociological theory** did not emerge until the twentieth century.

Peter L. Berger is often credited as the key sociologist to develop a theory of secularization. In his book *The Sacred Canopy: Elements of a Sociological Theory of Religion* (1967), Berger described religion as a cohesive moral order that is socially organized and sustained by representations of ''the sacred.'' Religion allows followers to make sense of events by providing credible structures of meaning. Those parts not otherwise understandable are interpreted through religious frames. However, in contemporary modern societies

(characterized by **rationality**, **bureaucracy**, and technology), the power of religion comes under a secular assault. What used to be mysterious is demystified through the techniques and conclusions of science and technology; supernatural beliefs are no longer as widely depended upon as they once were.

Berger theorized that under the secular conditions of modern society, strong religious traditions serve as sacred canopies, insulating believers from those aspects of society that threaten their religious beliefs. But, as secularization proceeds, the canopy is penetrated. Sociologists who study various forms of religious fundamentalism use secularization theory to explain fundamentalism as a reaction formation against the modern secular state.

Not all sociologists who study religion agree with secularization theory. Some argue that secularization focuses too much attention on formal religious institutions without accounting for the influence of less formalized religious belief. They point to new **religious movements**, **civil religion**, and the development of alternatives to formal religion (such as humanism) all of which serve functions previously provided by institutional religion.

Still others, such as **Andrew Greeley**, argue that secularization has not eroded formal religious authority at all. Over a twenty-year research career, using survey **data** spanning several decades, Greeley (a priest and sociologist) has consistently failed to find significant decreases in religious behavior despite marked increases in indicators of modernity. Accordingly, Greeley and others argue that secularization theory should be dismissed as untenable; traditional religious authority is still strong. Secularization theory today continues to be an issue of lively debate among sociologists who study religion.

SEGREGATION AND DESEGREGATION

Segregation is the practice, by law or **custom**, of separating groups spatially according to **race**, class, or **ethnicity**. In South Africa, the apartheid system kept the black population in physically isolated areas; in the United States, racial segregation began after the end of slavery, when new laws barred blacks from many occupations, restricted voting rights, and designated separate public facilities for black and white populations.

In the antebellum South, whites and blacks often lived together closely. This contact, however, was rigidly controlled; slaves were expected to show subservience in all interactions with whites. The Emancipation Proclamation and ratification of the Thirteenth Amendment, in outlawing slavery, removed the basis for the traditional dynamic based on white superiority. Almost immediately, whites enacted Black Codes, which forbade African Americans from entering many occupations and **professions**, regulated their movements, denied their right to vote, banned interracial **marriage**, and even outlawed insulting speech toward whites. Separate criminal codes were also established, setting harsher punishments for African Americans. So severe were the Black Codes that pressure from Northerners forced their eventual repeal.

The Black Codes were replaced by less obvious yet equally discriminatory ''Jim Crow'' laws, which prohibited

African Americans from using white railroad accommodations and excluded them from transport, hotels, restaurants, parks, theaters, schools, and even telephone booths and white elevators in public buildings. When a group of African Americans in 1891 challenged the transportation law requiring ''equal but separate accommodations for the white and colored races'' on railroad travel, the case went to the Supreme Court, which ruled in *Plessy v. Ferguson* (1896) that the separate but equal provision did not violate the Constitution. Until 1954, separate but equal stood as law.

Segregation existed somewhat differently in the North, to which, by the early 1900s, increasing numbers of African Americans moved in search of improved economic opportunities. Seen as a threat to white labor, especially since massive immigration from Europe had flooded the unskilled labor market, blacks were excluded from many jobs and were refused such economic supports as business loans or home mortgages. As a result, they remained isolated in impoverished areas. Though blacks were not technically barred from attending white schools or using white facilities, patterns of residential segregation created a segregated educational system.

Different conditions in the North and South led to different kinds of social organization among African American communities. Though the biracial system in the South kept many African Americans impoverished and disenfranchised, it also created conditions that facilitated the development of a strong black middle class and cultural institutions. Black schools and especially the black church enabled the development of African American leadership, and became the base of the Civil Rights Movement. In the North, however, the black middle class was less cohesive and lacked strong institutional support; schools, for example, were run by white teachers and administrators and did not foster racial pride as many did in the South. For Northern blacks, then, civil rights issues focused on **discrimination** and unequal access rather than formal desegregation. In the South, the Civil Rights Movement focused primarily on ending segregation.

The Civil Rights Movement emerged in the 1950s, when the number of middle-class and skilled blacks was almost forty percent of the Southern black population. The earliest victory came in 1954, when the U.S. Supreme Court ruled in *Brown v. Board of Education*, that racially ''separate educational facilities are inherently unequal.'' The following year, the Court ordered state and local governments to ''effectuate a transition to a racially nondiscriminatory school system... with all deliberate speed.'' School systems reacted with such violence that federal military protection was often necessary to ensure the safety of black children attempting to integrate white schools. School desegregation was an equally volatile issue in the North, where in many cities National Guard troops protected black students bused into white neighborhood schools. Court-ordered desegregation prompted ''white flight'' from public schools in many areas, as families with the financial resources to do so enrolled their children in private schools or moved to mostly-white suburban school districts.

The effort to abolish other forms of segregation, initiated in 1955 when seamstress Rosa Parks refused to relinquish

Prior to the Civil Rights Act of 1964, blacks were continually denied the same access to public accommodations as whites *(The Library of Congress)*.

her seat in the white section of a Montgomery bus, continued through the 1960s. The movement was led by Dr. Martin Luther King, Jr., who developed a philosophy of nonviolent activism based on principles of Christian belief and the passive resistance teachings of Indian independence leader Mahatma Gandhi and American philosopher Henry David Thoreau. Under King's Southern Christian Leadership Conference, and later, the Student Nonviolent Coordinating Committee and the Congress of Racial Equality, civil rights workers participated in marches, boycotts, and sit-ins to prompt legislative reform. Activists in the South were often beaten, jailed, or even killed, circumstances that helped to galvanize support among white liberals in the North, some of whom joined the movement. In 1964, passage of the Civil Rights Act banned segregation and discrimination in employment, housing, and other areas.

Changes in practice, however, lagged far behind legislative reform. Despite passage of the Voting Rights Act in 1965 and the Civil Rights Act of 1968, conditions for blacks were slow to improve. By the late 1960s, many younger African Americans abandoned the pacifist tactics of Civil Rights leaders and embraced the **Black Power Movement**, which rejected the **values** of white society, scorned integration as an ideal, and advocated violent confrontation.

The results of desegregation remain controversial. After integration, public schools failed to improve educational outcomes for African American students, who by the 1980s averaged two to three years behind standard grade levels in all basic subjects. This circumstance, many argue, is associated with teachers' low expectations for black students and has prompted research into the desirability of Afrocentric curricula and pedagogies for African American students, which have been effected in newly-formed charter schools. Integration, William J. Wilson has argued, also exacerbated the deterioration of black community structure as access to **higher education** and jobs prompted relatively affluent African Americans to abandon inner cities and the black institutions they supported.

SELECTIVE INCENTIVES

The concept of selective incentives was developed by Mancur Olson in *The Logic of Collective Action* (1965) to explain how actors solve the free rider problem. Olson's starting point is the notion of collective or public goods, such as public parks or clean air. By definition, those who do not pay for or contribute

to such goods cannot be excluded or kept from sharing in them. Rational actors, Olson concluded, will refuse to contribute to a collective good because they can benefit from it without bearing any of the costs of providing it. In short, rational actors take a ''free ride'' at the expense of others. Free riding does not necessarily imply a lack of altruism; free riders may simply conclude that their contribution is too negligible to be worthwhile.

How then, Olson asks, are public goods possible? Olson identifies two means by which rational actors can be made to contribute to a public good. On the one hand, actors may be forced to do so. Unions, for example, may coerce workers into paying dues through compulsory membership (the closed shop) or through threats of violence against free-riding strikebreakers (scabs). On the other hand, contributors may be provided with separate incentives in addition to the public good itself from which free riders cannot benefit. These incentives are selective insofar as those who do not contribute can be treated differently from those who do. Unions, for example, may provide noncollective goods to members, such as insurance benefits or seniority privileges.

The concept of selective incentives leads to a number of sociological insights. For example, Olson pointed out, neither capitalists nor workers will engage in **collective action** to pursue their class interests if the individual members of the class act rationally. For the same reason, shared interests or grievances are not sufficient to lead individuals to form pressure groups. However, Olson is careful to point out that selective incentives only become important in large, ''latent'' groups in which free riding does not significantly affect other members. Moreover, although selective incentives need not be economic or material, Olson also cautioned that they are less likely to be important for noneconomic or affective groups such as mass movements and families. To assume the need for selective incentives for all forms of collective action, Olson noted, is to define all action as rational, thereby presupposing what must be established beforehand.

SELF CONCEPT

Self concept refers to the totality of an individual's thoughts and feeling about him/herself as a physical, spiritual, and moral being. This concept entails a sense that the individual is both continuous and somewhat consistent in attitudes, identities, beliefs, motivations, experiences, emotions, and evaluative components. Self concept is reliant on the development of self and reflexivity so that an individual can place him/herself in the position of others and see him/herself as others do. This process allows individuals to claim more accurate versions of self concepts and to engage in impression management in order to portray and protect identities.

Little research on self concept and **identity** existed prior to the mid-1960s because the dominant theories in both **psychology** and **sociology** found little use for the study of individuals' conceptions of themselves. Psychology was dominated by **behaviorism** which conisdered most behavior as learned responses and had little use for the study of underlying conceptions of self. At the same time most sociological work was based in structural **functionalism** which viewed human behavior as primarily controlled by the **structure** of society. Therefore, only since competing paradigms have arisen in these fields has the study of self concept and identity become a research focus.

The study of self concept has developed primarily along two, often intersecting, paths. Psychologically much work has been done regarding self esteem, self efficacy, self cognition, and several other aspects of psychological functioning that indicate how the self concept is affecting the individual and how the individual is working to protect his/her self-concept. Sociological work has focused on social structural influences on self concept and associated identities through roles, role expectations, and **group** memberships. However, as many researchers work in the personality and social structural tradition, the two agendas often cross and add to each other's work.

Recently in sociological literature, self concept has become synonymous with identity. Self concept is often conceptualized as an organization of various identities and attributes which develop through social interaction. Sheldon Stryker developed the dominant theory of identity using a structural symbolic interactionist approach. According to Stryker, self concept consists of a hierarchy of all the identities held by an individual. Here the content and organization of the self concept is important. Stryker holds the more important a given identity is to the self concept, the more likely the individual is to be committed to that identity, have behaviors and attitudes affected by the expectations of that concept, and look for instances in which to enact that aspect of self concept. The sum of personal self perceptions are organized and function across various situations to present a consistent picture of the individual. Other prominent work regarding self concept includes Ralph Turner's analysis of roles on self concept; Morris Rosenberg's work in identity, self esteem, and efficacy; Peter Burke's cybernetic identity **model**; and Viktor Gecas' summary works on various motivational and causal aspects of self concept.

SELF-FULFILLING OR SELF-DEFEATING PROPHECY

A self-fulfilling prophecy refers to the phenomenon of something coming true simply because one believe's that it will. It suggests that people's beliefs can shape their choices and the outcomes of their actions. The principles of self-fulfilling prophecy are that we form certain expectations of people or events; these expectations are communicated by direct or indirect social cues; people respond to the cues by adjusting their behavior to correspond with the expectations; and the ultimate result is that the original prediction comes true. Self-defeating prophecy suggests that an expectation or prediction will bring on behavior or results opposite of what was expected or desired.

The concepts were developed by **Robert K. Merton**. He wanted to explain how a belief or expectation, correct or incor-

rect, could bring about a desired or expected outcome. He primarily studied deviants and whether or not deviant behavior was a result of expectations; whether negative opinions or expectations would bring about negative behavior or results. He believed that labeling someone deviant, whether or not that person was actually deviant, would eventually bring about deviant behavior.

There are two kinds of self-fulfilling prophecy: the Pygmalion effect is when one person has expectations of another, changes her behavior in accordance with these expectations, and the object of the expectations then also changes her behavior as a result. The second kind is when a prediction is made about actions or opinions and people individually change their actions to agree with the original prediction.

The theory of self-fulfilling prophecy is used extensively in education research. In general, research has shown that high expectations result in higher performance, and low expectations result in lower performance. Research has found that children internalize expectations from others—those who are treated as intelligent and capable will excel in school, whereas those who are treated as unintelligent or untalented will fulfill such low expectations. By labeling students, then, the teacher's need to simplify his or her classroom experience by categorizing students, may have caused unintended results.

In contrast, a self-destroying prophecy is one in which the original prediction does not occur because someone has made the prediction. It is a form of risk management, whereby people internalize warnings about disastrous consequences to a particular action and do not engage in that action. Thus, the risks are prevented and do not become a reality.

SELF-HELP GROUPS

Self-help groups, also sometimes called support groups, are groups that include two or more people who share the same social situation, social problem, or **health care** problem. People who belong to self-help groups meet on a regular basis in churches, **community** centers, schools, or hospitals. These groups tend to be free of charge, are member-run, are confidential, and are usually open to anyone who shares the same problem or concern or is associated with or related to those with the problem or concern.

Self-help groups provide emotional, practical, or intellectual support for members dealing with their particular life situations. Members share personal information, offer suggestions for others, and provide insights gained through first-hand experience with similar situations. Groups help people learn to deal with their problems by developing coping strategies, offering a forum to share issues or concerns, and allowing them to help others through their own sharing. Although many self-help groups are small and community-oriented, they can also be connected to national organizations that offer support through advice hotlines or newsletters, or by giving organizational assistance or advice.

Extensive research in **sociology**, social **psychology**, and social work has shown that self-help groups are effective in helping many people. Those who join self-help groups are often able to overcome emotional or physical ailments, show more and faster improvement than those not in such groups, tend to be more self-motivated to deal with their problems or illness, and have lower levels of anxiety and depression about their problems. Self-help groups have also been shown to improve health conditions and prevent problems associated with chronic physical and mental illnesses.

Self-help groups often extend and expand the effectiveness of the health and mental **health care systems** because they are able to reach people who do not have the resources, information, or desire to seek help from the formal medical systems. This fact has led to research on self-help groups that has defined them as emergent **social movements**. Recent research has estimated that there are currently over six million Americans actively in self-help groups. Other research indicated that over fifteen million Americans have participated in at least one group at some point in their lives. This research, however, does not endorse replacing medical or psychiatric treatment with self-help groups. Most researchers advocate a combination of professional and self-help treatments, particularly for those with biologically-based illnesses.

Although self-help groups are not supported or endorsed by many medical practitioners, several federal agencies have begun supporting and cooperating with some of the national-level self-help organizations, including the National Center for Education in Maternal and Child Health, the Office of the Surgeon General, and the National Institute of Mental Health (NIMH). In 1988, the Surgeon General's Office assisted in the formation of the National Council on Self-Help and Public Health, and the NIMH has funded several mental health research centers to evaluate the effectiveness of self-help groups.

The most well-known type of self-help group are twelve-step programs such as Alcoholics Anonymous (AA), Codependents Anonymous, Adult Children of Alcoholics, Narcotics Anonymous, Smokers Anonymous, etc. But there are currently over 500,000 self-help groups in the United States for everything from childhood diabetes to weight loss to ethnic and racial integration issues to battering and spousal abuse. Self-help groups have been found to be particularly effective in helping people deal with loss and bereavement and with maintaining recovery from alcohol and other drug-related addictions. For example, AA has been studied extensively over several decades and has been shown to be highly effective in helping people maintain long-term sobriety and in preventing relapse.

Self-help groups can be particularly helpful for those dealing with physically or emotionally traumatic or socially humiliating experiences, such as **incest**, spousal abuse, rape, or hate-related incidents such as gay-bashing or racially-motivated crimes. These groups provide a safe, supportive, and understanding environment for people to deal with these issues. A major criticism of self-help groups, however, is that they can replace an addiction to someone or something with an addiction to the group. They can also take on a 'cultish' quality, and the people involved sometimes distance themselves from everyone and everything in their lives not related to the group.

Demographically, serial murders may cover a span of several states, such as with serial killer Ted Bundy *(AP/Wide World Photos, Inc.)*.

SERIAL KILLER

The term "serial" refers to a consistency in pattern, meaning more than one occurrence of behavior. The term "killer" refers to a person who killer another human being. A serial killer commits murder; that is, the person unlawfully kills another. To qualify as a serial murder, two or more murders must take place as a reflection of a series of murders committed by one or more associated murderers over a period of time. When multiple murders take place simultaneously, this is a mass murder, not to be confused with serial murder. Demographically, serial murders can occur in a specific location, such as in the case of the "Southside Slayer," who is believed to have killed at least 12 women in the Los Angeles area over a period of time, and "The Boston Strangler," or the serial murders may cover a span of several states, such as with serial killer, Ted Bundy. Most serial killers are male, usually Caucasian, and the victims are usually strangers within the same **race** of the killer. Most serial killers act alone in committing the murders. The motive for serial murders is usually not material gain but is believed to be associated with the desire to control the victim. The "Black Widow" murders are an exception, in that the killer is typically female and kills family members, and financial gain may be the motive in many of these types of murders. The victims of serial murder can be children, adults, or elderly, may be male or female, may be wealthy or poor, can be any race or religion and present an array of physical traits.

SEX DIFFERENCES

Sex differences occur on a biological level and on a social level. Biologically, men possess the chromosomes XY; women possess the chromosomes XX. A fetus is sexually biopotential, neither male nor female, until the sixth week of development. During this sixth week, a sequence of events initiate genital differentiation. Females and males at birth have different internal and external genitalia as well as different

hormones (androgens for men and estrogens for women). Aside from the chromosomal differences, there are also noticeable physical differences between the sexes. As they develop, males on average tend to be larger and heavier than females, tend to have more pronounced facial and body hair, tougher skin, and larger bones and muscles.

Aside from these biological differences, social differences between the sexes are culturally induced. Traditionally, men in many societies are expected to be assertive, tough, decisive, independent, competitive, and provide for their families. Traditionally, women are expected to be emotional, intuitive, sensitive, caring, cooperative, and provide care for children. In prehistoric **hunter-gatherer** societies, **division of labor** was sex-linked. Men were the hunters; women gathered food and cared for the children. Nursing infants or caring for small children, women were unable to take part in a hunt that took men away from camp. Men without these responibilities took part in large scale hunting expeditions. These different jobs encouraged diverse sets of traits for men and women. Men needed to be brave, daring, and aggressive; conversely, women needed to be nurturing, compassionate, and caring. The sexual division of labor facilitated survival. Patterns in masculine and feminine traits illustrated by both the hunter-gatherer societies are visible in societies throughout the world today.

Researchers question the extent to which biology determines social sexual differences. Among many studies, one followed the development a boy whose penis was destroyed in a circumcision accident. His sex was reassigned, and he was reared as a girl. Subsequently, the child rejected his female socialization and developed emotional problems because of gender identity conflicts. The result was another sex reassignment at the age of 14 after the child was informed of what had happened to him as a baby. Some researchers assert that because the child was biologically a male and exposed to male hormones in the womb, he could never successfully be socialized as a female. Much more research is needed in this area to explore the extent to which biology dictates **sexual behavior**.

Anthropologists study sex roles in diverse societies. Margaret Mead, in the 1920s and 1930s, visited several societies in New Guinea. She hypothesized that if gender differences are biological, people in every **society** should classify "masculine" and "feminine" in a similar manner. If gender differences are created through **socialization**, then these ideas should differ. Mead found through observation that there are indeed cultural differences in the conception of what is masculine and feminine. Regarding biological or social factors in sex differences, researchers continue to gather **data** in order to increase our understanding.

SEXUAL BEHAVIOR

Sexual behavior includes any and all sexual activities and expressions of sexuality. Sexual behavior consists of, but is not limited to the following: celibacy, erotic dreams, fantasies, masturbation, sexual expression, touching, kissing, oral-genital stimulation, and coitus.

Celibacy is the choice that a physically mature person makes to abstain from sexual behavior. There are two degrees of celibacy. In complete celibacy, the individual does not masturbate or have intimate relations with a partner. In partial celibacy, one does not engage in sexual activities with a partner but does masturbate. This lifestyle often is closely aligned with religious doctrine. Indeed, many religious groups require a vow of celibacy from their clergy or devotees. While the period of celibacy may end at **marriage** for the followers of the faith, it may extend throughout the clergy member's lifetime.

Erotic dreams and nocturnal emissions (also known as nocturnal orgasms or ''wet dreams'') occur without conscious direction. Dream content varies greatly from person to person and dream to dream. Containing either logical or seemingly random images, erotic dreams may be a method of exploring various facets of experiences, emotions, and desires. The subconscious nature of erotic dreams differs them from erotic fantasies, which often occur during conscious daydreams, masturbation, or sexual activity with a partner. The content varies greatly. These fantasies perform many functions. They facilitate arousal and allow individuals to imagine activities in which they do not engage. Fantasies help people explore their sexuality, rehearse potentially new sexual experiences, and relieve gender-role expectations. The most commonly reported erotic fantasy focuses on sexual activities with a loved one. Other common fantasies include: sexual encounters with strangers, sexual acts with more than one member of the opposite sex, **taboo** sexual activity, forcing sexual activities on a partner, being coerced into performing sexual acts, and homosexual behavior.

Masturbation is the stimulation of one's own erogenous zones for the purpose of creating sexual pleasure. People masturbate for the pleasure of sexual arousal and orgasm. Throughout Judeo-Christian history, masturbation has been viewed as a social problem deserving admonition. Judeo-Christian doctrine contends that procreation is the only legitimate purpose for engaging sexual activities. Since masturbation cannot lead to conception, it was condemned. Tissot popularized the so-called negative effects of ''self-abuse'' in the mid-eighteenth century. He believed that the loss of semen was debilitating and could lead to blindness and death. This view influenced the dominant belief about masturbation in the West until the mid-twentieth century. In contemporary Western society there are conflicting views of masturbation. In the medical community masturbation is widely considered to be harmless, but many religious groups that contend that it is ''morally unacceptable.''

Sexual expression is the context and meaning of sexual interactions between people. It is the relational aspect of sexual activity where partners reveal or demonstrate the affective or emotional aspects of sexuality. Not infrequently this exchange is the context for sexual activity.

Touch is one of the five basic senses. Sexual touching is frequently considered pleasurable for both the partner being touched and the one doing the touching. While the entire body is responsive to touch, some areas are more sensitive than others. These areas vary from person to person. For example, some people of both sexes report that their nipples are especially sensitive to touch, while others may find it unpleasant.

Kissing is an extremely common sexual activity. The mouth and lips are wrought with erogenous, pleasure-inducing nerve endings that often lead to sexual pleasure when stimulated. All areas of the body are potential sites for kissing. Activities such as licking, nibbling, sucking, and gentle biting are variations of kisses. While light kissing without the use of the tongue is often affectionate, deep kissing with tongue, also known as French or soul kissing, is regularly more intense and passionate. Oral-genital stimulation includes fellatio (oral stimulation of the penis and scrotum), cunnilingus (oral stimulation of the female genitals), and analingus (oral stimulation of the rectum and anal region).

Coitus or sexual intercourse includes both vaginal and anal penetration. Coitus also includes interfermoral intercourse, the act of the penis being moved between the gripped thighs of a partner. It further may include the rubbing together of two females' genitals as is frequently done between lesbian partners. Oral-genital sex and anal stimulation of any variety is considered by a minority of people to be a homosexual activity regardless of the sex of the partners. These activities are loosely referred to as sodomy. Despite the prominence of these behaviors there are legal sanctions against these activities throughout most of the United States. Other qualms about these activities are based on the notions that it is unsanitary or that genitals are unattractive.

Paraphilias, formerly referred to as deviant, **abnormal**, and perverted behaviors, are more uncommon forms of sexual expression. These forms of expression are also known as atypical sexual behaviors. There are two types of paraphilias: coercive and non-coercive. The key distinguishing characteristic between them is in the use of force or pressure. Coercive paraphilias include exhibitionism and peeping. Non-coercive paraphilias are comprised of fetishism, transvestism, sadism, and masochism.

SEXUAL HARASSMENT

The term ''sexual harassment'' first came into use in 1975 at a time when more and more women were in the work force voicing their complaints of unwanted sexual pressures in the workplace. While commonly associated with the workplace, sexual harassment includes any sexual comments, gestures, or physical advances that are unwanted in any setting. Schools are also a common venue for such actions. The victim does not need to be in a subordinate position to the executor in order for an act (or set of acts) to be considered sexual harassment. Unwanted sexual acts of coworkers or fellow students are considered sexual harassment in the same way as acts perpetrated by superiors, such as bosses or teachers.

Sexual harassment can occur in two ways. First, there is *quid pro quo* sexual harassment, the type directed at a particular individual. In this case, certain outcomes are presented as contingent on specific sexual acts. These outcomes can be explicitly stated or implied and include both threats of negative repercussions if the person does not comply (e.g. demotion, lowered grade) and guarantees of positive repercussions if the

person does comply (e.g. promotion, raise, better grade). The second type, hostile environment sexual harassment, is directed at no one in specific, rather at a group. In this case, the environment is sexualized in a way that is uncomfortable, intimidating, offensive, and/or threatening. An example would be a work environment in which one's coworkers have pornographic images on the walls. Any unwanted sexual gestures, comments, or advances also contribute to the overall atmosphere. A hostile environment can be created deliberately or unintentionally.

SEXUAL VIOLENCE AND ABUSE

Sexual violence and abuse includes a range of sexually coercive behaviors such as rape and other nonconsensual touching of a sexual nature, child molestation, exposing oneself or ''flashing,'' **sexual harassment**, and the mutilation of genitalia (of which female circumcision is often considered to be a part). While not universal, **pornography** is considered by some people to be a form of sexual violence, in that it presents sexualized images of women that can be perceived as degrading or dehumanizing and thus promotes more tactile forms of violence. Also, the actual women appearing in pornographic materials are sometimes sexually exploited as part of their work (although some feminist scholars see work in the pornography industry as a legitimate and empowering occupational choice for women, partly because their pay is comparable to or greater than men's pay).

While there is evidence that it has existed in many cultures from an early time, sexual violence and abuse did not receive much attention from sociologists until the women's movement in the 1970s gained entry into academic sociology. Before that time, sexual violence was not treated by most sociologists as an appropriate topic for sociological inquiry. Susan Brownmiller's book *Against Our Will: Men, Women, and Rape*, published in 1976, is credited with being one of the first attempts at treating sexual violence as a social rather than a personal problem and with framing it within the context of women's oppression.

After *Against Our Will*, other pivotal works followed that broadened the sociological understanding of sexual violence and abuse within the growing fields of gender and feminist theory. Nearly all research to date on sexual violence has conceptualized it as a form of male violence against women and children. Andrea Dworkin, an early theorist and activist in the area of sexual violence, is most noted for her efforts to enact legislation holding pornography purveyors responsible for violence that their material allegedly encourages. She suggested that sexual violence is part of the system of male supremacy and that sexual violence can be ended by deconstructing men's power over women. Catherine MacKinnon is attributed with constructing the legal argument that workplace sexual harassment is a form of sex **discrimination**. She contended that it was part of a larger system of sexual violence against women, using heterosexual relations to maintain male **domination**.

Various causes of sexual violence and abuse have been identified. A relatively small set of researchers have proposed biological or evolutionary roots that precondition men to committing sexual violence against women. Most researchers, however, assert that social conditions exist which give rise to sexual violence, specifically that it is a byproduct of sexism and patriarchy. Dworkin contended that men are socialized to believe they have the right to rape women and children, which serves to maintain both their power as men and to position themselves above other men. Micro-level analysis has identified particular characteristics in men that indicate a proclivity to rape (see the work of Neil Malamuth for examples). While some of this research, as well as conventional wisdom, supports the idea that men who commit sexual violence are deviants, researchers from feminist and **men's studies** orientations insist that these men have successfully learned the lessons of a woman-hating culture.

Most sociological research on sexual violence is conducted from a feminist orientation and has had an activist agenda. These researchers want to raise the public's awareness of sexual violence, improve the way individuals and key institutions (such as **law enforcement** agencies and the courts) treat victims of sexual violence and to decrease the incidence of sexual violence. Research with an activist agenda has been criticized on the assumption that the results of such research are not reliable because the purpose of conducting it is more political than scientific. However, these criticisms have come from a positivist orientation, which itself has been called into question for not recognizing the political nature of knowledge.

SEXUALLY TRANSMITTED DISEASES

The phrase ''sexually transmitted diseases'' refers to any one of several types of diseases that may be passed from one partner to another through sexual contact. In recent years there has been an increasing rate of sexually transmitted diseases (STDs) among those between fifteen and twenty-nine years of age. Many factors influence the rate of STDs including increased numbers of sexual partners, use of hormonal birth control rather than condoms, and unknowingly infected partners who show no symptoms and pass the disease along.

There is a social stigmatism associated with contracting an STD. There is a common perception that those who have an STD are ''dirty'' or are sexually promiscuous. This stigmatism undoubtably fosters feelings of guilt and shame associated with having an STD which may prevent some people from seeking adequate medical care even when they suspect a condition. By ignoring the presence of a **disease**, many people unwittingly help maintain STDs' continued prevalence.

There are four varieties of STDs: bacterial infections, viral infections, vaginal infections, and ectoparasitic infections. The most common varieties of bacterial infections are chlamydia, gonorrhea, and syphilis. Chlamydia, caused by chlamydia trachomatis, is one of the most commonplace and destructive of all STDs. There are two main types of chlamydia, both of which are transmitted through direct sexual contact. These are infections of the lower reproductive system and the more invasive infections of the upper reproductive tract.

Chlamydia infection is the cause of trachoma, which is the world's foremost cause of preventable blindness. Gonorrhea is caused by the gonococcus bacterium. The initial symptoms of a gonorrhea infection are usually evidenced by men and may go undetected by women. Infected men tend to experience a discharge and burning while urinating. Syphilis, caused by the treponema virus, is passed from a syphilis lesion through the mucus membranes or breaks in the skin.

The most common forms of viral STDs are genital herpes, hepatitis, and the human papilloma virus. There are no cures for these STDs. Genital herpes is caused by the herpes simplex virus. It is primarily transmitted through genital-genital contact or oral-genital contact. Initial exposure may produce episodes of painful blisters, which become ulcerous, and finally crust over. Hepatitis A and B are both transmittable through sexual contact. Oral to anal contact is the primary form of transmission of Hepatitis A. Hepatitis B is commonly passed through blood, blood products, vaginal secretions, and saliva. Hepatitis attacks the liver. The human papilloma virus causes genital and anal warts. It is transmitted through sexual skin-to-skin contact.

The most common varieties of vaginal infections are: bacterial vaginosis, candidiasis, and trichmoniasis. Bacterial vaginosis, also known as a bacterial infection, may be transmitted sexually but is not necessarily acquired through sexual activity. Candidiasis, or a yeast infection, may be passed to a partner by sexual contact but may also occur spontaneously. It is caused by the candida albicans organism which is normally present in the vagina but may overgrow into an infection under certain conditions. Trichmoniasis is caused by the trichomonas vaginalis organism. While this is a normally occurring organism in the body, the primary route for transmission is sexual contact. These three vaginal infections are easily treated.

Ectoparasitic infections are caused by parasitic organisms that live on the skin of humans and other animals. Scabies and pubic lice are two common forms of ectoparasites. Scabies are a type of parasitic mite that searches for food on the skin of its host organism. Pubic lice, also known as ''crabs,'' are parasites that take nourishment from the small blood vessels in the genital area of its host.

SHOCKLEY, WILLIAM (1910-1989)
English physicist

Physicist William Shockley shared the 1956 Nobel Prize in physics for inventing the transistor. He was also involved in the controversial topic of the genetic basis of **intelligence**. William Shockley was a physicist whose work in the development of the transistor led to a Nobel Prize. Shockley shared the 1956 Nobel Prize in physics with John Bardeen and Walter Brattain, both of whom collaborated with him on developing the point contact transistor. Later, Shockley became involved in a controversial topic for which he had no special training, but in which he became avidly interested: the genetic basis of intelligence. During the 1960s, he argued, in a series of articles and

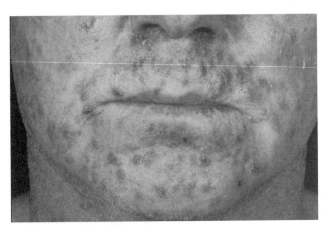

Syphilis, caused by the treponema virus, is passed from a syphilis lesion through the mucus membranes or breaks in the skin (*Custom Medical Stock Photo, Inc.*).

speeches, that people of African descent have a genetically inferior mental capacity when compared to those with Caucasian ancestry. This hypothesis became the subject of intense and acrimonious debate.

William Bradford Shockley was born in London, England, on February 13, 1910, to William Hillman Shockley, an American mining engineer, and May (Bradford) Shockley, a mineral surveyor. The Shockleys, living in London on a business assignment when William was born, returned to California in 1913. Shockley was home schooled until he had reached the age of eight.

Shockley's interest in physics developed early, inspired in part by a neighbor who taught the subject at Stanford and by his own parents' encouragement. He earned a bachelor's degree in physics at Caltech in 1932. Offered a teaching fellowship at the Massachusetts Institute of Technology (MIT), Shockley taught while working on his doctoral dissertation, ''Calculations of Wave Functions for Electrons in Sodium Chloride Crystals,'' for which he was awarded his Ph.D. in 1936. This research in solid-state physics led to his interest in the transistor field.

Shockley accepted an offer to work at the Bell Telephone Laboratories in Murray Hill, New Jersey, where he worked with Clinton Davisson, who was to win the 1937 Nobel Prize in physics for proving Louis Victor de Broglie's theory that electrons assumed the characteristics of waves. Shockley's first assignment at Bell was the development of a new type of vacuum tube that would serve as an amplifier. Soon he began to think of a radically new approach to the transmission of electrical signals using solid-state components rather than conventional vacuum tubes. By 1939, Shockley was experimenting with semiconducting materials to achieve that transition.

In 1940, war was imminent, and Shockley soon became involved in military research. In 1942, he became research director of the U.S. Navy's Anti-Submarine Warfare Operations Research Group at Columbia University, and served as a consultant to the Secretary of War from 1944 to 1945. In 1945, Shockley returned to Bell Labs as director of its research pro-

William Shockley *(The Library of Congress)*

gram on solid-state physics. Together with John Bardeen, a theoretical physicist, and Walter Brattain, an experimental physicist, Shockley returned to his study of semiconductors as a means of amplification.

By 1947, Bardeen and Brattain had learned enough about semiconductors to make another attempt at building a device. This time they were successful. Their device consisted of a piece of germanium with two gold contacts on one side and a tungsten contact on the opposite side. When an electrical current was fed into one of the gold contacts, it appeared in a greatly amplified form on the other side. The device was given the name transistor (for *trans* fer re *sistor*). More specifically, it was referred to as a point contact transistor because of the three metal contacts used in it.

The first announcement of the transistor appeared in a short article in the July 1, 1948, edition of the *New York Times*. Few readers had the vaguest notion of the impact the fingernail-sized device would have on the world. A few months later, Shockley proposed a modification, now called the junction transistor, which he found that it worked much better than did its point contact predecessor. In 1956, the Nobel Prize for physics was awarded jointly to Shockley, Bardeen, and Brattain for their development of the transistor.

Shockley left Bell Labs in 1954 (some sources say 1955). In the decade that followed, he served as director of research for the Weapons Systems Evaluation Group of the De-

partment of Defense, and as visiting professor at Caltech in 1954–1955. He then founded the Shockley Transistor Corporation to turn his work on the development of the transistor to commercial advantage. Shockley Transistor was later incorporated into Beckman Instruments, Inc., and then into Clevite Transistor in 1960. The company went out of business in 1968.

In 1963, Shockley embarked on a new career, accepting an appointment at Stanford University as its first Alexander M. Poniatoff Professor of Engineering and Applied Science. Here he became interested in genetics and the origins of human intelligence, in particular, the relationship between **race** and the Intelligence Quotient (IQ). Although he had no background in **psychology**, genetics, or any related field, Shockley began to read on these topics and formulate his own hypotheses. Using **data** taken primarily from U.S. Army pre-induction IQ tests, Shockley came to the conclusion that the genetic component of a person's intelligence was based on racial heritage. He ignited further controversy with his suggestion that inferior individuals (those whose IQ numbered below 100) be paid to undergo voluntary sterilization. The social implications of Shockley's theories were, and still are, profound.

During his life, Shockley was awarded many honors, including the U.S. Medal of Merit in 1946, the Morris E. Liebmann Award of the Institute of Radio Engineers in 1951, the Comstock Prize of the National Academy of Sciences in 1954, and the Institute of Electrical and Electronics Gold Medal in 1972 and its Medal of Honor in 1980. He was named to the National Inventor's Hall of Fame in 1974. Shockley remained at Stanford until retirement in 1975, when he was appointed Emeritus Professor of Electrical Engineering. In 1933, Shockley had married Jean Alberta Bailey, with whom he had three children, Alison, William, and Richard. After their 1955 divorce, Shockley married Emily I. Lanning. He died in San Francisco on August 11, 1989, of prostate cancer.

SIGNIFICANT OTHER

The term significant other is derived from the late 1920s work of George Herbert Mead (1863-1931) on the genesis of the self. According to Mead, the self is developed through reflexivity or the ability of an individual to ''take the role of the other'' and see him/herself through the eyes of that person. Through ''taking the role of the other,'' an individual learns what is expected of him/her from the perspective of that person and can alter behavior accordingly to fit these expectations. Although reflexivity, once developed, is used in every social **interaction**, Mead indicates that not every ''other'' encountered has equal ability to influence the behavior, attitudes, and decisions made by the individual. Those who have increased influence are termed significant others.

Significant others are those individuals or groups who exercise a strong influence over the formations of one's self in early life and the shaping and adjustment of one's behavior in later life. Typically, significant others are those individuals to whom a person would have the most interest in appeasing especially those in control of rewards (i.e. teachers, employ-

ers), those to whom the person has an emotional connection (i.e. parent or spouse), or shares a common interest (i.e. friends, teammates). These also tend to be people with whom the individual will spend most time. As the individual works to fulfill the expectations of these significant others, the expectations of each will alter the behaviors, beliefs, and attitudes of the individual. In popular use, ''significant other'' has been adopted as a generic term indicating a long-term romantic relationship.

SIMMEL, GEORG (1858-1918)
German sociologist

The German sociologist and philosopher Georg Simmel (1858–1918) wrote important studies of urban **sociology**, social **conflict theory**, and small-group relationships. Georg Simmel was born on March 1, 1858, in Berlin, the youngest of seven children. His father was a prosperous Jewish businessman who became a Roman Catholic. His mother, also of Jewish forebears, was a Lutheran. Georg was baptized a Lutheran but later withdrew from that Church, although he always retained a philosophical interest in religion.

His father died when Georg was very young. A family friend and music publisher became his guardian and left him an inheritance when he died which enabled Simmel to pursue a scholarly career for many years without a salaried position. He studied history and **philosophy** at the University of Berlin, earning a doctoral degree in 1881. He was a lecturer at the University of Berlin from 1885 to 1900 and professor extraordinary until 1914. He then accepted his only salaried professorship at the provincial University of Strassburg. There he died on September 26, 1918.

Simmel's wide interests in philosophy, sociology, art, and religion contrasted sharply with those of his more narrowly disciplined colleagues. Eschewing pure philosophy, he preferred to apply it functionally as the philosophy of **culture**, of money, of the sexes, of religion, and of art. Similarly in sociology, the field of his lasting renown, he favored isolating multiple factors. In 1910 he helped found the German Sociological Association. His sociological writings were on **alienation** and on urban stresses and strains; his philosophical writings foreshadowed modern existentialism.

Although a popular and even brilliant lecturer, academic advancement eluded Simmel. The reasons for this include prewar Germany's latent anti-Semitism, the unorthodox variety of subjects he pursued rather than following a more acceptable narrow discipline, and perhaps jealousy at his sparkling originality. Ortega y Gasset compared him to a philosophical squirrel, gracefully acrobatic in leaping from one branch of knowledge to another. Unable or unwilling to develop consistent sociological or philosophical systems, Simmel founded no school and left few disciples. ''I know that I shall die without intellectual heirs,'' he wrote in his diary. ''My legacy will be, as it were, in cash, distributed to many heirs, each transforming his part into use conformed to *his* nature....'' This diffusion occurred, and his ideas have since pervaded sociological thought.

His insightful writings still stimulate while more systematic contemporaries are less read. **Robert K. Merton** called Simmel a ''man of innumerable seminal ideas.''

SKEWED DISTRIBUTION

The word ''skew'' originates from the Middle English word ''skewen'' which means to escape or run sideways. Skewness is a measure of the asymmetric distribution of observations around a sample **mean**. A distribution is skewed if one of its tails is longer than the other. Skewness occurs when the mean (the arithmetic average of all observations in the distribution) and the median (the middle observation of the distribution) for the same distribution have different values. When a mean is larger than its associated **median**, the distribution is positively skewed. The visual result is a distribution with the bulk of observations on the left and a long tail of outliers stretching to the right. When a mean is smaller than its median, the distribution is negatively skewed. This distribution has the bulk of observations on the right and a long tail of outliers stretching to the left. When the difference between the mean and the median is zero, the distribution is perfectly symmetrical and there is no skew. It is important to consider the skewness of a distribution when tests are being used which are sensitive to normality assumptions. When these assumptions are violated, skewed **data** can often be transformed, through Log techniques, for example, to reduce the effects of the violations.

SKILL

Skill is a term commonly used to denote a wide variety of meanings. Employed most broadly, skill can simply be applied to any situation that requires a learned or inherent talent. In a technical sense, skill is often defined as a combination of the tacit knowledge and training that provide a worker with the tools necessary to successfully complete a particular job. Although no consensus exists on the definition, there are three basic paradigms for understanding the term depending upon its application to an occupation, a person, or as a socially constructed concept.

Within the context of a job or occupation, skill refers to the qualities needed to successfully perform the duties of that particular position. In other words, it defines the objective requirements of a job, including such components as mechanical or technical complexity, the level of independence or supervision involved, the amount of time needed to learn the job, and the amount of training or schooling necessary.

When applied to a person, skill refers not to what the job requires, but rather what qualifications the worker brings to his or her occupation. Originating in the field of social **psychology**, personal skill can connote acquired skills or tacit knowledge. In other words, skill is a combination of learning and natural aptitude. The fields of capabilities to which the term skill is applied include: cognitive ability (capacity to reason, calculate, remember, and so on), manual dexterity, physical

ability, and social abilities, including expertise in interpersonal **communication**, leadership, and teamwork. A skilled worker is one who would be expensive for a business to replace.

An understanding of skill as a social construct involves the incongruous nature of the two previous definitions of skill. Namely, skill as applied to a job may not be equivalent to the skills brought to it by a person. On one hand, some occupations that require high levels of skill may not have co-existing high rates of pay or **status**. On the other hand, certain jobs that require little skill have elevated pay rates due to such factors as the efforts of labor unions, job regulations, and **custom**. Officially categorized by the U.S. Census Bureau as ''skilled,'' ''semi-skilled,'' and ''unskilled,'' jobs are commonly referred to by these socially constructed labels even though the label applied may not correctly describe the occupation. For example, women have traditionally been paid at a lower rate than men, and even if the job is technically advanced, their work is often seen as less skilled. Other jobs, such as traditional farming, may require numerous, wide-ranging skills, but maintain the status of unskilled labor.

The historical evaluation of skill has centered on the disappearance of highly skilled crafts since the late nineteenth century when the Industrial Revolution instigated the development of assembly lines and automation. Numerous socioeconomic theories suggest that the technological advances made during the twentieth century all contributed to the reduction in the need for skilled workers, leading to the deskilling of the workforce. Proposing a Marxist perspective, Harry Braverman offered the most comprehensive analysis of deskilling in *Labour and Monopoly Capital: The Degradation of Work in the 20th Century* (1974). According to Braverman, the capitalist system creates an imbalance in economic power that capitalist industrialists wish to maintain. As a result, capitalists continually strive to achieve their production goals based on the lowest level of skill possible. In this way, not only do they control costs by offering low pay for low skill jobs, but they also retain control over the working class.

Critics of this Marxist interpretation have noted that Braverman does not address the socially constructed nature of the definition of skill, relying completely on an individualistic and stagnant notion of skill. For Braverman, workers possess certain skills and jobs require certain skills. When the skills needed for the job are reduced, so is the worker's ability to function at a skill level higher than the job now required. Others argue that skill and demand for skill fluctuate with the ebb and flow of the economy. In volatile markets, industry demands skilled workers who can adjust quickly to changes and shifts in production. In stable markets, production is consistent and unchanging, thereby requiring unskilled workers to perform routine tasks.

SKINNER, BURRHUS FREDERIC (1904-1990)

American psychologist

The American experimental psychologist Burrhus Frederic Skinner (1904—1990) became the chief exponent of that form of **behaviorism** known as operationism, or operant behaviorism. Born in Susquehanna, Ohio, B. F. Skinner attended Hamilton College. He then went to Harvard, where he received a master's degree in 1930 and a doctorate in experimental **psychology** in 1931. In 1936 he began teaching at the University of Minnesota, the same year he married Yvonne Blue; they had two daughters.

In Skinner's first book *Behavior of Organisms* (1938), he ''clung doggedly to the term *reflex,* thus allowing his immediate psychological roots in classical or early behaviorism.'' A Guggenheim fellowship enabled him to begin writing *Verbal Behavior* in 1941. He continued on the fellowship through 1945, finishing most of the manuscript. In 1947 he gave a course at Columbia University and the **William James** Lecture at Harvard, both based on *Verbal Behavior* which, however, he put off publishing for twenty years. *Walden Two* (1948) described his notions on a feasible design for (utopian) **community** living.

In 1954 Skinner became chairman of the Department of Psychology at Indiana University and published ''Are Theories of Learning Necessary?'' Conferences begun at Indiana culminated in 1958 in a new journal *Journal of the Experimental Analysis of Behavior.*

Toward the end of World War II, with the birth of his second child, Skinner built an air crib for baby care in which the infant, instead of staying in a tight crib wrapped in layers of cloth, can lie with only a diaper on in an enclosed space which is temperature-controlled and plastic-sheeted, thus allowing the child greater freedom of movement. Many babies are now raised in this way.

During the 1950s, stimulated by an interest in psychopharmacology, Skinner studied operant behavior of psychotics at the Metropolitan State Hospital in Waltham, Massachusetts. For his systematic experiments on this type of behavior, Skinner designed his famous Skinner box, a compartment in which a rat, by pressing a bar, learns to repeat the act because each time he does so a pellet of food is received as a reward. Skinner demonstrated that when these reinforcements accompany or follow certain specific behavior, learning occurs in the experimental animal. Such a response, reinforced by food or other means, is called operant behavior and is distinguished from respondent behavior, which is elicited by a stimulus. Skinner's main concern in studying operant behavior and its parameters was neither ''with the causal continuity between stimulus and response, nor with the intervening variables, but simply with the **correlation** between stimulus (S) and response (R).''

Skinner's books *Verbal Behavior* (1957), while omitting the citation of experimental evidence for its assertions, gives a highly objective functional account of **language**, with the basic unit of analysis being the verbal operant. He explains how differential social reinforcement from other members of the speech community forms, strengthens, or weakens dependency relations between stimulus variables and verbal responses. Included also are discussions of how listener ''belief'' is fortified by reinforced responses to a speaker's words; how the metaphorical expressions of a speaker reflect the kinds of stimuli which control his behavior; how and why it is that we cease verbalizing; suggestions regarding the nature of aphasia; and logical and scientific verbal behavior.

In *Schedules of Reinforcement* (1957) Skinner and his coauthors reported on a research program that was "designed to evaluate the extent to which an organism's own behavior enters into the determination of its subsequent behavior." They demonstrated that response rates, temporal patterns of rates, and patterning of rate in the temporal vicinity of the reinforcer are dependent upon the schedule of reinforcement. No detailed quantitative laws emerge, however, from their seventy thousand hours of **data** gathering. *Schedules* is suggestive regarding the power of the operant as a tool to investigate psychopharmacological and neurophysiological problems.

Skinner acknowledged Roger Bacon as an influence on his thinking and formulating. Skinner said that he emulated him because Bacon rejected verbal authority; studied and asked questions of phenomena rather than of those who had studied the phenomena; classified in order to reveal properties; recognized that **experimentation** included all contingencies, whereas mere observation overstresses stimuli; and realized that if nature can be commanded, it must also be obeyed.

Critics of operationism maintained that it disregarded problems such as motives, personality, thought, and purpose or greatly diminished their relevance or importance. Although Skinner dealt with complex psychological problems, his mode of treatment of these problems was criticized as having been seriously limited. His basic behaviorist viewpoint itself has been questioned recently, in part because it rejects consciousness. The concept of consciousness cannot be omitted from psychology without a serious loss in explaining much that man does—since the viewpoint is completely indifferent to introspection.

On August 18, 1990, Skinner died and was buried at the Mt. Auburn Cemetary in Massachussetts. He left behind many distinctive awards and achievements. In 1968 he was awarded the National Medal of Science, in 1971 he was honored with the Joseph P. Kennedy, Jr. Foundation Award, and in 1985 was given the Albert Einstein School of Medicine award for excellence in psychiatry. Skinner continued to write throughout his later years, authoring such works as *Enjoy Old Age* (1983), *Upon Further Reflection* (1986), and *Recent Issues in the Analysis of Behavior*.

SLAVERY AND INVOLUNTARY SERVITUDE

Slavery, the condition of one person owning another, has been abolished by most modern societies, but it predates recorded history and has existed in nearly all parts of the world. Involuntary servitude is still a problem, and though it is more prevalent in Third World countries, it occasionally surfaces in the United States.

The term "slavery" often refers to a large system, endorsed by the law of the land, in which people are in permanent bondage for no other reason than their **race**, class, **ethnicity**, or nationality. The Hebrews of ancient Egypt and the Africans of colonial America are the most famous examples of slavery. The term also applies, however, to a more class-

B.F. Skinner *(The Library of Congress)*

oriented system, such as existed in ancient Rome and Greece. A person could become a slave through capture in battle, inability to repay a debt, or numerous other conditions. Once enslaved, that person was completely at the mercy of his owner and any children he had would be born slaves, as well. It was often possible, though, to earn or purchase one's freedom and, once free, to gain permanent status for oneself and one's descendants as freemen.

In the Roman Empire, slavery grew in significance. As the military conquered new **territory**, they made slaves of captured soldiers and civilians. Their labor freed manpower, and the military grew more powerful. This cycle was common to all the great powers of the time. By the Middle Ages, the great classical empires were gone, and the rulers no longer had the power to control vast numbers of slaves. Also, **Christianity** and **Islam** were growing in influence; while not denouncing the practice, these religions instructed owners to treat slaves more kindly. Gradually, slavery dwindled, replaced by serfdom which saw laborers attached to the land. They were still virtually slaves, but in a somewhat less oppressive **society**.

In the fifteenth century, a number of events drastically altered slavery in the West. The great sea explorations of this period claimed vast new territories for Europe and discovered a flourishing slave trade in Africa which provided the labor to work these new lands. Much of the new territory was severe in climate, and Africans were seen as better adapted to work

With slave traders and buyers gathered, a group of Africans disembarks from a slave ship *(The Library of Congress)*.

in these conditions. Of course, they were also viewed as more expendable. Initially, settlers in the Americas, half of whom were indentured servants themselves, lived fairly simple lives and kept few slaves, if any. The expansion of agriculture into cash crops such as sugar and coffee, however, brought huge numbers of slaves into the West Indies. In 1793 the cotton gin created a similar **culture** in the United States. By 1850, forty percent of the population in the American South was slave.

Even as the South was being transformed into a slave society, abolitionist sentiment was sweeping Europe and the northern United States. The late eighteenth century brought the first large-scale movement, ever, to end the ancient practice. The cultural shift, worldwide, was remarkably swift; by the early 1800s slavery was banned on most of the European continent and in the northern United States. Even so, it took an act of war—the Emancipation Proclamation—to begin the end of slavery in America. President Abraham Lincoln signed the document, in 1863, to weaken the rebelling Confederate States of America. The official end did not come until 1865 with the passage of the Thirteenth Amendment to the constitution.

Brazil, in 1888, was the last nation in the western hemisphere to abolish slavery. Gradually, Asia and Africa followed

suit, and when Saudi Arabia ended the practice in 1962, slavery was officially banned in every nation on the globe. Still, forms of the practice, particularly debt servitude, continue in many places. Organizations such as the United Nations and Amnesty International are active in putting an end to these last vestiges.

Slavery has always required outsiders to fill the role of chattel in a society. The greater the difference of owner and owned, the easier it is to maintain a sense of contempt for the slave class and to break the spirit of the slave. Africans, in the United States, were visibly different and marked as outsiders, even in the North. The combination of overt racism and instinctive contempt for a person who had once been property made freedom a very difficult proposition. In many cases, the roles of whites and blacks in the South remained virtually unchanged. The difficulty of the transition had been predicted by the founding fathers, and to some degree, had been the rationale for keeping the system in place. George Washington and Thomas Jefferson, among others, had hoped for an eventual **abolition**, but chose not to actively pursue it.

It is impossible to judge the effect of the history of slavery on today's culture or to draw a line between the race-based class **structure** that followed abolition and simple, crude racism. It is clear, however, that the end of systemic slavery, worldwide, is a remarkable event. The ease with which persons of the past could dismiss others as less than human no longer exists.

SMALL, ALBION WOODBURY (1854-1926)

American sociologist and educator

The American sociologist and educator Albion Woodbury Small (1854–1926) was instrumental in founding and developing the profession of **sociology** in the United States. Albion Small was born in Buckfield, Maine, on May 11, 1854. Though trained as a minister at the Newton Theological Institution (1876–1879), he pursued wider interests at the universities of Leipzig and Berlin (1879–1881), particularly in **political economy**. Thereafter, until 1889, he taught at Colby College in Maine and embarked on advanced studies in economics and history at Johns Hopkins University. After selection as president of Colby College, he was chosen in 1892 to found a department of sociology at the new University of Chicago. During his tenure at Chicago, Small built the leading department of sociology in the United States, helped in founding the American Sociological Society (of which he was president in 1912 and 1913), and was the first editor of the *American Journal of Sociology*.

Small's teaching and writings were animated by the desire to demonstrate the distinctive nature of the young discipline of sociology, as well as to indicate the interrelations among various social sciences. His first major book *General Sociology* (1905) viewed the subject matter of sociology as the processes by which various group interests clash and become resolved through accommodations and social innovation. In

this work, he summarized and creatively interpreted the writings of Ludwig Gumplowicz and Gustave Ratzenhofer for the first time in English. Further interpretations of European thinkers were included in *Adam Smith and Modern Sociology* (1907) where Small tried to demonstrate the moral and philosophical undergirding of Smith's famous *Wealth of Nations; The Cameralists* (1909), an extremely detailed review of the social theory underlying the public economic policies of Germany from the sixteenth through the nineteenth century; and *Origins of Sociology* (1924), a highly erudite reconstruction of German academic controversies that seemed to Small to provide the foundation of modern methodology in social science.

The best summary of Small's overall thinking is contained in *The Meaning of Social Science* (1910), where the thrust of his *General Sociology* is clarified in surprisingly modern terms. Essentially, social science—including sociology—studies continuing processes through which men form, implement, and change valuations of their experiences. Human behavior derives meaning from these valuations, and both **values** and behavior are simultaneously patterned in the individual (as personality) and in **society** (through groups and organizations).

Small retired from the university in 1924. He died in Chicago on March 24, 1926. Although his ideas were largely derivative, his contribution to American sociology is incontestable.

SMELSER, NEIL JOSEPH (1930-)
American sociologist

Neil Joseph Smelser has been an influential mind in the study of collective behavior for four decades. In 1956, he published *Economy and Society* with **Talcott Parsons** and in 1959, *Social Change in the Industrial Revolution*, a historically-oriented piece of research on Victorian Britain. Since the publication of his *Theory of Collective Behavior* in 1963, a highly theoretical exploration of the nature and causes of **collective behavior**, Smelser has pushed for objective consideration of the social sciences. His two most influential works have been *Theory of Collective Behavior* and *The Handbook of Economic Sociology*, which he edited with Richard Swedberg, published in 1988.

Smelser's work is highly definitional, seeking exact specification of the components of social action, whether that action be collective behavior or economic behavior. Smelser sought ways that a sociological perspective might assist in our explanation and understanding of these phenomena. In his *Theory of Collective Behavior*, Smelser explores components of social action, particularly those that influence collective behavior as a response to structural strain, including the creation of generalized beliefs and the development of belief into action. Smelser's areas of interest range from collective behavior to the varied areas of the **sociology** of education, historical sociology, social **theory** and **economic sociology**.

Smelser was born in 1930 in Kahoka, Missouri, the son of Joseph Nelson, a teacher, and Susie (Hess) Smelser. He married Helen Thelma Margolis in 1954 and they had two children, Eric Jonathan and Tina Rachel, before divorcing in 1965. Smelser married Sharin Fateley in 1967, and fathered two children, Joseph Neil and Sarah Joanne. Smelser attended Harvard University, where as a freshman in 1948 he was greatly influenced by Gordon Allport in a course on Social Relations. He graduated from Harvard (*summa cum laude*) in 1952, was a Rhodes scholar at Oxford University in England where received a second B.A. in 1954, and an M.A. in 1959. He returned to Harvard for his Ph.D. in 1958, and completed a postgraduate position at the San Francisco Psychoanalytic Institute in 1971.

From 1959 to 1961 Smelser was a member of the Center for Integrated Social Science Theory at the University of California, Berkeley. He served as a member of a counsel to the **American Sociological Association (ASA)** from 1968 to 1971 and again from 1973 until 1975. He served as vice president to the ASA from 1971 to 1973. Smelser's academic career flourished at the University of California, Berkeley, which he joined as an assistant professor in 1958. In 1968 he became an associate professor and began a full professorship, 1962–72. He served as Assistant to the Chancellor for Educational Development, 1966–68, and University Professor of Sociology, 1972–94. In 1994 he became Director of the Center for Advanced Study in the Behavioral Sciences located in Stanford, California.

SMITH, ADAM (1723-1790)
Scottish economist

The Scottish economist and moral philosopher Adam Smith (1723–1790) believed that in a laissez-faire economy the impulse of self-interest would work toward the public welfare. Adam Smith was born on June 5, 1723, at Kirkcaldy. His father had died two months before his birth, and a strong and lifelong attachment developed between him and his mother. As an infant, Smith was kidnapped, but he was soon rescued. At the age of fourteen he enrolled in the University of Glasgow, where he remained for three years. The lectures of Francis Hutcheson exerted a strong influence on him. In 1740 he transferred to Balliol College, Oxford, where he remained for almost seven years, receiving the bachelor of arts degree in 1744. Returning then to Kirkcaldy, he devoted himself to his studies and gave a series of lectures on English literature. In 1748 he moved to Edinburgh, where he became a friend of **David Hume** whose skepticism he did not share.

In 1751 Smith became professor of logic at the University of Glasgow and the following year professor of moral **philosophy**. Eight years later he published his *Theory of Moral Sentiments*. Smith's central notion in this work is that moral principles have social feeling or sympathy as their basis. Sympathy is a common or analogous feeling that an individual may have with the affections or feelings of another person. The source of this fellow feeling is not so much one's observation of the expressed emotion of another person as one's thought of the situation that the other person confronts. Sympathy usu-

Adam Smith *(The Library of Congress)*

ally requires knowledge of the cause of the emotion to be shared. If one approves of another's passions as suitable to their objects, he thereby sympathizes with that person.

Sympathy is the basis for one's judging of the appropriateness and merit of the feelings and actions issuing from these feelings. If the affections of the person involved in a situation are analogous to the emotions of the spectator, then those affections are appropriate. The merit of a feeling or an action flowing from a feeling is its worthiness of reward. If a feeling or an action is worthy of reward, it has moral merit. One's awareness of merit derives from one's sympathy with the gratitude of the person benefited by the action. One's sense of merit, then, is a derivative of the feeling of gratitude which is manifested in the situation by the person who has been helped.

Smith warns that each person must exercise impartiality of judgment in relation to his own feelings and behavior. Well aware of the human tendency to overlook one's own moral failings and the self-deceit in which individuals often engage, Smith argues that each person must scrutinize his own feelings and behavior with the same strictness he employs when considering those of others. Such an impartial appraisal is possible because a person's conscience enables him to compare his own feelings with those of others. Conscience and sympathy, then, working together provide moral guidance for man so that the individual can control his own feelings and have a sensibility for the affections of others.

In 1764 Smith resigned his professorship to take up duties as a traveling tutor for the young Duke of Buccleuch and his brother. Carrying out this responsibility, he spent two years on the Continent. In Toulouse he began writing his best-known work *An Inquiry into the Nature and Causes of the Wealth of Nations.* While in Paris he met Denis Diderot, Claude Adrien Helvétius, Baron Paul d'Holbach, François Quesnay, A.R.J. Turgot, and Jacques Necker. These thinkers doubtless had some influence on him. His life abroad came to an abrupt end when one of his charges was killed.

Smith then settled in Kirkcaldy with his mother. He continued to work on *The Wealth of Nations,* which was finally published in 1776. His mother died at the age of ninety and Smith was grief-stricken. In 1778 he was made customs commissioner, and in 1784 he became a fellow of the Royal **Society** of Edinburgh. Smith apparently spent some time in London, where he became a friend of Benjamin Franklin. On his deathbed he demanded that most of his manuscript writings be destroyed. He died on July 17, 1790.

The Wealth of Nations, easily the best known of Smith's writings, is a mixture of descriptions, historical accounts, and recommendations. The wealth of a nation, Smith insists, is to be gauged by the number and variety of consumable goods it can command. Free trade is essential for the maximum development of wealth for any nation because through such trade a variety of goods becomes possible.

Smith assumes that if each person pursues his own interest the general welfare of all will be fostered. He objects to governmental control, although he acknowledges that some restrictions are required. The capitalist invariably produces and sells consumable goods in order to meet the greatest needs of the people. In so fulfilling his own interest, the capitalist automatically promotes the general welfare. In the economic sphere, says Smith, the individual acts in terms of his own interest rather than in terms of sympathy. Thus, Smith made no attempt to bring into harmony his economic and moral theories.

SOCIAL ACTOR

The term "social actor" can be essentially defined as an agent of any social system. More specifically, social actors are motivated to achieve goals or "ends" defined by their social system. Several sociological theorists have used the term social actor as one aspect or component of their theories, which typically explain social behavior and systems. Talcott Parsons and **Erving Goffman** are the most notable sociologists to incorporate the social actor in their explanations of both **culture** and **society**.

As used in Parson's theory of social action, social actors are individuals with minds and consciousness who are capable of making decisions. However, the actors are not entirely free to make their own choices because they are constrained by cultural entities such as **norms** and **values**. Parsons maintained that norms, values, ideas, and situations govern the social actor's individual choice in the cultural system.

Goffman's dramaturgy compares daily life with a social actor's theatrical presentation. Members of the actor's audi-

ence judge the performance with the actor attempting to play roles as well as possible. The objective for the actor is impression management in all social situations. For example, people change their actions based on the audience and are constantly engaged in impression management as they adopt different roles to suit the social situation in which they find themselves.

SOCIAL CHANGE

Social change is variation in social life over time. Interest in social change has itself varied across time. Classical sociologists conceived of social change as historical and uniform, in broad abstractions that appealed to ideals. But their accounts and their prescriptions differed in which aspects of social life they deemed most important. Karl Marx focused on economic structures, foresaw class struggles, and ultimately expected revolution. Émile Durkheim focused on functional processes, described a shift from mechanical to organic solidarity, and hoped for professional associations as a stalwart to **anomie**. **Max Weber** focused on competing status types and the rise of the **Protestant ethic**, feared an iron cage of **rationality**, and anticipated turns to other forms of **authority**.

Reacting to industrialization and liberalization, historic shifts that seemed to replicate across societies, the earliest conceptions of social change were linear and evolutionary. Ferdinand Tönnies discussed a shift from *gemeinchaft* to *gesellschaft*. The social dynamics of **Auguste Comte** involved three stages of development in societal knowledge. (Arnold Lenski later offered four forms of social organization but took account of diversity within societies and increasing over time.) Others sociologists have focused on particular thresholds of change. Thomas Malthus identified a conflict between arithmetic growth in resources and geometric growth in population, and Marx wrote about conflicts between classes as well as pressures of the capitalist system upon itself. **Herbert Spencer** (1820-1903) used a metaphor of **society** as an organism, explicitly theorizing evolutionary changes based on population growth and structural differentiation. Some changes are commonly deemed evolutionary, such as scientific knowledge and role specialization. Recent interest has returned to evolutionary explanations, including attention to organizational fit and adaptiveness. Other patterns of change have also been identified. Cyclical patterns were identified by Arnold Toynbee, to address the rise and fall of civilizations, and **Pitirim Sorokin**, theorizing a pendulum of three mentalities.

Some, including Marx and Comte, saw social change as a process of progress. Others, such as Weber and **Jean-Jacques Rousseau**, saw change as a worrisome regression. Functional perspectives, such as those of **Talcott Parsons** and Neil Smelser, conceived of change as unpatterned deviations from a norm of equilibrium. For them, change is undesirable and problematic. For conflict theorists, including Marx, equilibrium is undesirable; change comes from the force of internal contradictions and may either correct or exacerbate inequalities. It is, therefore, revolutionary rather than evolutionary.

Social change is now generally understood as continual (if not continuous) and persistent (if not constant), episodic in some ways but continuous in others. However, the process, pace, and pattern of ubiquitous social change have received less recent attention than the substance of change itself. Early sociologists' attention to actual changes focused on historical events or developments (such as the **Industrial Revolution**, **democracy**, and Christianity) and structural aspects (such as class stratification, status arrangements, and the size and constitution of **family** groups). Later usage of the phrase became focused on the substance of change, including technology (such as travel, power, medicine, and computing), **demography** (including life expectancy and birth, death, and marital rates), **culture** (such as ideas about the status of women, children, and minorities), behavior (including **suicide**, crime, and **marriage**), and relationships (as in organizations or among scientists). Recent interest has returned to social **structure**, from feminist critiques of knowledge production to postmodern claims such as the end of history.

Social change is also now understood to vary in speed (or rate) and significance, both across societies and within them. But a focus on substance and sources often isolates social change as either cause or effect rather than a complex process or set of processes. Many indicators of social change can be seen as either causes of or responses to social change. Civil rights legislation responded to a social movement strengthened by a host of factors, but that legislation also altered relationships that spurred other social changes. Social change is also reciprocal. New technologies (as well as theories and organizational forms) effect social change, but they also emerge from social changes, enabled by new resources, demands, and conflicts. Sociology itself both emerged in response to social changes and has effected social change as well, from early Marxist governments to expert testimony on sampling in the **census**. Social change is thus best understood not as the cause or effect of societal and structural conditions but as variation in those conditions themselves.

Sources of social change include both governments (in legislation, redistribution, or declarations of **war**) and individuals (as in social movements, crime, or suicide), as well as **inventions**. Even early sociologists noted the influence of technological inventions, such as guns, machinery, railroads, cars, computers, and a host of **communication** technologies including the printing press, telegraph, telephone, **television**, and **Internet**. Social change is also generated by scientific inventions (as in medicine or **sociology**) and innovation in organizational form (from kibbutz to matrix corporations), sometimes called mutations. Diffusion is at least as important as invention. William Ogburn identified a **cultural lag** of technological change spreading through society. Other sources of change include geographical and ecological variations, as well as environmental events (such as drought).

SOCIAL COHESION

Social cohesion is a sense of connectedness, commonality, or we-ness that binds people together in a certain group, **culture**, or **society**. It is the presence of and collective understanding

of certain common patterns of social **interaction** and a core set of collective **values** or beliefs. The cohesion is developed through a sense of trust and mutual loyalties, marked by the ability of groups to engage in cooperative and **collective action**.

There are several conceptions of social cohesion and how it emerges or dissipates. The differences between these theories center on the meaning of human interactions, what values are important, and how these values are developed and maintained. The three major sociological conceptualizations of social cohesion were developed by Ferdinand Tönnies, Émile Durkheim, and **Talcott Parsons**.

Tönnies developed the notions of *gemeinschaft* and *gesellschaft. Gemeinschaft* is **social solidarity** (cohesion) based on tight social networks and daily personal interactions; people are bonded together by common experiences, sentiments, values, collective **identity**, and senses of place and purpose. *Gesellschaft*, on the other hand, is social solidarity characterized by **individualism**, isolation, normlessness, heterogeneity, and superficial relationships; in this case, people are bonded by formal authority.

Émile Durkheim conceived the ideas of *mechanical* and *organic solidarity,* both rooted in his ideas about the **division of labor**. For Durkheim, the division of labor was not only economic, but was also the basis of solidarity and **morality** in a society. Mechanical solidarity is when people hold common values, beliefs, and experiences and are thus able to cooperate. Organic solidarity is when there is a complex division of labor and established economic and legal systems; social integration is maintained by interdependence and a collective conscience that comes from shared principles and expectations.

Finally, Talcott Parsons developed the *theory of normative integration,* similar to gemeinschaft and mechanical solidarity. He believed that a society's **norms**, values, sanctions, roles, and behaviors are institutionalized and individually internalized, thus creating social cohesion. Many argue that the possible level of normative integration of a society decreases with its size, complexity, and diversity.

Political **community** and solidarity are important components in all conceptions of social cohesion. Thus, key concepts for social cohesion are citizenship and social participation; political, social, cultural, and economic integration; and effective conflict resolution. Some theorists see the major threats to its development and maintenance as the global economic and political restructuring that has resulted in lessened loyalty to specific countries.

SOCIAL COMPARISON THEORY

Social comparison **theory** posits that when there are no objective standards for comparison, we will use others in our environment to develop judgments about and estimates of our own self-worth. We compare ourselves to others using our beliefs about their abilities and opinions. The ultimate goal is to maintain or increase our positive self-conception, often by feeling equal to or better than the people with whom we are comparing

ourselves. Social comparison can result in an increase, decrease, or maintenance of self-conception. If we do not feel equal to or better than others, the negative self-evaluation can change from adjusting our attitudes or actions. Festinger, the original proponent of this theory, believed that people have a need to be correct, so they constantly need to compare themselves to others and reaffirm that what they are doing or thinking is right.

People can evaluate themselves on two scales in comparison to other people: good/bad or correct/incorrect. People usually want to move in the direction of what they consider socially good or correct. When we can choose between comparing ourselves to similar or dissimilar people, we are more likely to choose those similar to us, otherwise the comparisons have no meaning. We can compare ourselves with those we consider above, below, or at our level (of whatever criteria we choose). Research has shown that **self-concept** suffers the most when we do not measure up to people we consider below ourselves. On the other hand, when we compare ourselves to those above us and do not measure up, there is an impulse to compare ourselves to those below us, so as to balance out the effect, and make the overall result an increased or neutral self-conception.

This theory has been used extensively in research on school children—how they form their individual and collective identities, and how teachers encourage or dissuade students from developing their individual abilities. Tajfel expanded on Festinger's theory by studying intragroup and intergroup interactions. He found that social comparisons between groups are used to develop and distinguish the uniqueness of each group, rather than to conform or to develop a commonality, as is done on the individual level. This theory does not, however, explain why people change their opinions or actions to conform. Thus, Festinger developed the theory of cognitive dissonance, positing that people are more influenced by a need to be consistent than they are by a need to be correct.

See also Self-Concept

SOCIAL CONSTRUCTION OF REALITY

Social Construction of Reality was introduced by **Peter Berger** and Thomas Luckmann in their book *The Social Construction of Reality: A Treatise in the Sociology of Knowledge* (1966). Heavily influenced by the work of **Alfred Schutz**, Émile Durkheim, and George Herbert Mead, Berger and Luckmann theorized that what people think of as the reality of everyday life is created through human action, and is not something that exists independent of human actors.

Berger and Luckmann explained that a process called *typification* occurs in which people classify one another as belonging to certain groups. Eventually, those typifications become common to the society as a whole and, while not necessarily shared by all members within the society, are acknowledged by most people. These typifications become objectified through language, so that they are considered

"common knowledge" and seemingly existing external to human agents. As more and more people treat the objectified typifications as real, an objective reality is formed and acted upon as if it has always existed in this same fashion. Subsequent generations inherit this objective reality, further institutionalizing the objective reality and making it more resistant to change.

Berger and Luckmann used the social construction of reality to explain the institutionalized roles people have and the meaning they ascribe to these roles. Although the roots of social constructionism precede the publication of their book, Berger and Luckmann influenced the development of these theories. However, only the general principle of the social construction of reality is commonly used by other social scientists; the details of Berger and Luckmann's theory are rarely referred to current social constructionist work. The concept is used heavily by symbolic interactionists, who focus on the meanings people attach to everyday social **interaction**.

SOCIAL CONTRACT

Social contract theories emerged during the Enlightenment in the seventeenth and eighteenth centuries. Philosophers such as **Thomas Hobbes**, John Locke, and Jean-Jacques Rousseau questioned why individuals accepted the political authority of those who ruled. While each philosopher attached a different meaning or intent to the social contract, all believed the nature of human beings was core to its acceptance. From the perspective of Hobbes who wrote the *Leviathan* in 1651, **human nature** reflects the greed and selfish behavior of individuals. He argued that conflicting self-interests produced a state of **war** in nature. The role of **society**, therefore, is to establish control over the individual. Hobbes argued that this control could only be enforced through the agreement of individuals to relinquish their liberty in exchange for protection. In essence, this exchange between government authority and the individual is a social contract. During the time in which Hobbes wrote, the **authority** of society was embedded in the sovereignty whose power, he argued, was absolute.

Locke argued another dimension of the social contract. In *Two Treatises of Government* (1690) Locke wrote that there are two aspects of nature: the rights of the individual and the notion of property. From his perspective, the individual accepted authority in civil society not only in exchange for protection but to ensure the protection of individual property. In an effort to prevent the absolute concentration of power, Locke argued that the different elements of **government** need to work cooperatively and not separately to protect the two dimensions of the social contract.

Rousseau argued in *Social Contract* (1762) that individuals were not at war with nature. Rather, in nature humans were good and creative but only through society could they achieve **morality** and a sense of obligation or duty to the **community**. In essence, the social contract is designed to regulate social **interaction** based on the common good. The government, therefore, must embody the general will of society, rather than some divine right of kings, to achieve political association with its individuals.

Today, contemporary social contract **theory** argues that human rights are based on mutually beneficial agreements. Social contract is often used within the context of **political organizations** such as the Libertarians who argue that the Constitution embodies the social contract agreements of American society when it was formed. Some social scientists have used the term within the context of **employment** arrangements, defining the social contract as a rational arrangement between the employer who maintains authority and establishes rules over the individuals within an organization in exchange for agreed upon wages. Some social scientists have further argued that inclusion of personal development and resource programs for employees in need of some assistance to deal with personal or family issues embodies the principles of developing mutually beneficial benefits. Within this context, however, the emergence of flexible workplace contracts and increased job insecurity of the 1990s suggested a weakening of a social contract between employers and their workers.

SOCIAL CONTROL

Social control is conventionally understood as the capacity of a society to regulate itself according to established principles and **values**. It is a pervasive system of social processes that generate **conformity**. Social control typically refers to an amorphous character of a **society** or **organization** rather than mechanisms or instances of a utilitarian strategy. It typically refers to ideological rather than physical constraint. Although the source, nature, and extent of control mechanisms may attend negative connotations, human and other social groups seek the stability and predictability that social control systems are understood to provide. However, consensus is not always an ideal, and social control can become oppressive. Labeling theorists even argue that labels are imposed by the powerful upon the powerless. And conflict theorists often regard social control pejoratively, questioning the existence of normative consensus.

Classical usage of social control was not in reference to conformity or management but an abstracted political concern for social **mores** following revolutions and industrialization. As a response to **Karl Marx**, visions of norms and social control provided an alternate basis for **social order**. Conformity could be understood as generated and maintained by social life, apart from economic **structure**. Prohibitions could be understood not as superstructural elements of the ownership of production, but as the flesh of social order itself. Émile Durkheim emphasized the restraint achieved through moral education, through its engagement with (socially constructed) individuals. **Sigmund Freud** looked to identification with others and their commonalties, filtered by psychological processes. Even contemporaneously, social control is broadly conceived as maintaining social order, including for example physicians as social control agents through vaccination and public health protection.

Social control is conventionally seen as a capacity, not unlike power or **status**, rather than a behavior. And this capaci-

ty is said to be more or less present, weaker or stronger. Edward A. Ross, for example, considered prerequisites for control and foundations for order. Law is one mechanism towards this capacity, not merely through sanctions but also the force of law (Roscoe Pound). And even prestige systems enhance this capacity (William J. Goode). Social control **theory** attempts to demonstrate that mechanisms of social control operate as a cohesive whole. While the principles of that coherence change over time, understanding both the mechanisms of control and the processes of change helps one understand larger social processes and mechanisms. And a weakening of social control can lead to social conflict or disintegration (**Morris Janowitz**). However, although it may contribute to order and affect organization, social control is not synonymous with social order or organization.

Usage of the term, social control, is particularly American, and particularly during the 1920 and 1930s, to address the assimilation of immigrants as well as **deviance** and criminality. (This same period experienced popular xenophobia and an academic focus on structural facts.) Rather than emphasizing power and divisive struggles, as earlier European **sociology** had, social control theory purports to address consensus and **socialization** processes. But while **norms** are both prescriptive and proscriptive, social control is understood to respond to deviance, as an abstract, generic, and continuous barrier. Systems theorists and functionalists regard some level of conformity as requisite to social order and see deviance as weakness in (rather than absence of) social control. A lack of functioning norms of restraint may lead to (or itself be) anomic and alienating. Interactionists and phenomenologists argue that social order is generated through informal relations and see social control in the microsociological engagement with contingencies. Deviance is here viewed as an interaction between the supposed deviant and societal norms. But while often portrayed as deterministic, social control is not purely external. Norms of behavior are communicated for the purpose of maximizing conformity, but they are also internalized and then acted upon without need for explicit sanction. **Talcott Parsons**, drawing on Mead and other interactionists, contended that social control emerges from (and is constituted by) individuals labeling their own behavior, witnessing their own lives as others see them. Such understandings, like learning and sanctions, come particularly from and within primary groups (Charles H. Cooley). Conformity is understood to be generated through socialization as well as sanctions, and social control (like social structure) is generated through these interactions. Social control may be informal, as children learn, deviants are labeled, and gossip informs others. It is also formal, as when institutionalized in law or bureaucratic procedure which compel behavioral patterns and respond to deviations. In either case, norms are identified by conflicts and internalized by participants.

Alexis de Toqueville noticed that in the United States, commonality of beliefs and values was achieved through associations. However, there is often conflict between the informal or local norms of constituent groups and the formal and institutional norms of society, as between organized crime and law.

Social control may be weaker or problematic where individuals have conflicting value commitments. Conflict also ensues where there is a cultural lag between laws and popular mores. Such conflicts may generate substantial social change. But accounts of such conflicts are typically *ad hoc,* and largely psychological. Political attention is paid to the **legitimacy** of those who engage in social control, and pragmatic attention is paid to the effectiveness of mechanisms of social control. But social control itself remains typically abstract and generic.

Contemporary usage involves an emphasis on social control not directly as a means of maintaining conformity, but of managing deviance. Social control cannot eliminate deviance. Indeed, from the functional perspective, deviance is normal and itself is part of the social control apparatus. However, crime may be reducible, and criminal populations may be managed, as through rehabilitation. Meanwhile, state controls paradoxically increase deviance both because new behavior is defined as deviant and because the relationship between state and citizenry shifts in status and tone. Some controls perpetuate further deviance, such as occurs in systematic collusion between prison guards and prisoners. As a consequence of these understandings, social control during the 1960s shifted, in both theory and practice, from maintaining conformity to managing **marginality**. The criminal **justice** system expanded greatly, with an emphasis on rehabilitation efforts and new restrictions on the death penalty. Meanwhile, communes were illustrating the significance of social control: those that eschewed **authority** encountered rampant deviance and withered, while those that established leaders and enforcement maintained social order for much longer, as some even still do.

Empirical **data** have been mounted in the name of social control, but conventional usage has not employed particularly effective theory. Like power or **morality**, social control is often conceptualized and less often measured. Its use has remained classical and has provided little success in illuminating social structure, stratification, or **social change**. With regard to structure, social control has typically meant something uniform across a **group** or society, something imbued within the collectivity rather than varying within it. (White collar crime, for example, attracts a different response than murder, and murderers are handled variably depending on their status and relationship to the victim and accusers.) With regard to stratification, social control has typically referred to something authoritative (if not authoritarian) and suppressive (if not oppressive); less attention has been paid to conformity and regularity generated from lower status individuals or by equals. With regard to social change, social control has conventionally been assessed as present or absent, weak or strong, potential or unattainable, but without testable accounts of the conditions conducive to any of these. Sanctions do not account for varieties of behavior, including deviance itself. Sanctions (and inducements) are neither automatic nor absolute, and so their presence, enactment, and force must be accounted. Conventional understandings of social control do not explain the appearance of or variation in social control.

Recent work has taken a different approach, recognizing that social control varies. The strategy follows from cross-

cultural studies extended from Durkheim's work on law, such as Karl N. Llewellyn and E. Adamson Hoebel's focus on actual conflicts in order to understand and generalize about conflict patterns among the Cheyenne, and Max Gluckman's **correlation** of relationships among adversaries with the outcome of court cases in Zambia. Contemporary evidence on the structural dependence of law comes from variations in the behavior of police (Wayne LeFave, Donald Black), sentencing (Henry P. Luunsdgaarde), and other legal officials (Malcom M. Feeley). While much evidence concerns formal means of handling conflicts, primarily law, conflict management is also informal. Indeed, most conflicts are handled informally (Stewart Macauley). Here, too, the supporting evidence suggests structural variation: grievance expressions of all types (and not just in legal form) are structurally dependent.

The strategy invented by Donald Black goes further and explicitly treats social control as a **dependent variable**. It considers variation in the labeling process itself, asking not who violates **rules** or what response violations incur, but whose deviations attract response and even who is said to deviate. Variation in labeling (i.e. the distribution of expressions of grievances) is conceptualized as the behavior of social control. Labeling is no longer the explanation of deviance, but the very means for observing it. Conflict itself is reconceptualized, not as something endemic and abstract but as something observable any time someone labels someone else's conduct as wrong. Each such empirical event is conceptually an instance of moral life, the handling of a grievance locally structured by participants, partisans, and settlement agents. And Black's theory of social control (the theory of conflict management) predicts and explains variation in these processes. It predicts the circumstances (the social conditions) under which social control occurs, including the quantity, form, and style of those behaviors. It specifies where, for example, there is more legal behavior, legal behavior rather than avoidance, and penal responses rather than compensatory responses. The theory orders social facts, describing patterns of social life through a scientific approach to moral life. Black's **model** orders diverse findings from formal as well as informal, explicit and even covert conflict management within the context of particular settings.

This fruitful approach has been employed to account for diverse behavior in diverse settings, including the handling of disputes among executives (Calvin Morrill), within nonhierarchical corporations (James Tucker), among the mentally ill (Allan Horwitz), and among children in a day-care center (M. P. Baumgartner). It has also been employed to account for a variety of forms of social control, from suburban toleration (M. P. Baumgartner) to collective violence (Roberta Senechal de la Roche).

SOCIAL DARWINISM

Darwinism is an **evolutionary theory** of biology presented by Charles Darwin in 1859 in *On The Origin of the Species by Means of Natural Selection*. Drawing on his observations of species living on an isolated island, Darwin tried to account for the fact that the population of certain species of birds and animals remained stable over time even though their rates of reproduction were greater than necessary for population stability. Darwin postulated that since there were more members than were necessary to maintain the population rate, there must be a systematic method of selection which determinedwhich members of the species would survive to propagate offspring and which would see their lineage die out. Darwin theorized that this method of selection must be based upon the level of environmental adaptability of the individual members of the species. The strongest and most adaptable members of the species—more able to survive in the natural environment—would be the most likely to survive to maturity, attract and protect mates, and pass on their genes. By this mechanism, the species as a whole evolved, as each succeeding generation carried on only the strongest traits from the previous generation.

Darwinism appealed to many sociological thinkers of the time period because they were already using an organic analogy as their theoretical model of **society**, which viewed society as composed of an interrelated series of functions that together made up a systematic whole, similar to the organs and muscles of the human body. As a result, Darwinism was readily adapted to the organic **model** of society, creating a theory of social evolutionism called Social Darwinism.

The earliest and most prominent proponent of Social Darwinism was the British sociologist **Herbert Spencer**. Spencer developed his model of social evolutionism prior to Darwin's work on species evolution, but Darwin's work served to both legitimate and invigorate Spencer's ideas. In his work, Spencer coined the phrase ''survival of the fittest,'' suggesting that humans followed an evolutionary model similar to Darwin's. Spencer believed human society evolved from simple structural forms to more complex ones through the process of role specialization—what later sociologists would label the division of labor. Just as Darwin believed that the strongest members of a species served to make the species as a whole better through their superior adaptability, Spencer believed that the strongest members of society made society better by being more fit or able to fulfill the more specialized needs of an increasingly complex society.

Social Darwinism had several important implications. First, it implied that any societal **structure** that existed was a result of a natural process of selection and was hence both inevitable and good. Second, it linked strength and ability with social outcome, thereby justifying social stratification. Finally, it implied that aggressive human competition was good since it would benefit society as a whole.

These ideas had a particularly powerful impact in the United States and Britain, where they were used to justify the quickly escalating levels of **social inequality** being created by the rapidly developing capitalist political economy. Social Darwinism allowed the elite of society to feel that their wealth and **status** were deserved because they were the strongest and best, the ones responsible for the continued evolution of society. Conversely, disadvantaged groups such as the poor, ethnic and racial minorities, and the handicapped were further stig-

matized by being labeled as the weak, expendable elements of society. In the most modest form of this view of the disadvantaged, Social Darwinists such as Spencer advocated a laissez-faire approach by the government regarding the advantage of the upper classes over the weaker elements of society. These moderates argued that ameliorative efforts for these groups in the form of alms or social welfare would only artificially sustain the perpetuation of the weak members of human society, thereby stunting the evolution of the society as a whole. More extreme Social Darwinists, such as the Eugenics Society, called for active involvement in preventing the propagation of what they viewed as the inferior members of human society by advocating such policies as forced sterilization or imprisonment of the poor.

Social Darwinism is now viewed as a discredited theory. In its absolute emphasis on the influence of natural selection on life outcomes, Social Darwinism ignored the immense impact social environment has on an individual's life course. For both sociologists and biologists today, the question is not whether people's lives are shaped by nature or by nurture but rather what the confluence of these forces is in shaping life outcomes.

SOCIAL DISTANCE

Social distance can be defined in two ways. First, social distance refers to the actual physical distance that people maintain from one another when interacting in social situations. This type of social distance is culturally determined. In American **culture**, three to four feet of physical distance is common for people engaging in conversation. If one individual breaches that unspoken distance by moving closer, the other individual generally will move away. In many Middle Eastern cultures people commonly stand closer during conversation.

Social distance can also be defined as the distance people of one group feel from another **group**. In this instance distance based on difference and membership issues. Thus, social distance is based on the idea that all people are part of an ingroup and are wary and distrustful of those who are part of the outgroup. Ingroups contain people who are of the same **race**, ethnicity, religion, sexual orientation, or social class. Individuals feel a sense of belonging and loyalty within their ingroups. Everyone who is not part of the ingroup is considered part of the outgroup. Social distance is connected to levels of familiarity and **prejudice**. Though social distance can be associated with all categories of difference, much social research focuses on race and ethnicity.

The term social distance was coined by **Robert Park** in 1924 and then expanded by Emory Bogardus in 1925. Bogardus created a social distance scale, which today is commonly referred to as the Bogardus Scale. This scale asks people how willing they are to enter into a certain social situations with someone not of their race or **ethnicity**. The situations include marriage, sharing a social club, residing in the same neighborhood, and sharing employment in an occupation. Bogardus also asked questions about different races and ethnici-

ties and whether individuals are willing to grant citizenship to outsiders, allow them in as visitors only, or exclude them altogether. This scale has been modified several times by other individuals in this field, but it still serves as a measure of attitudes toward acceptance and levels of prejudice.

SOCIAL EQUILIBRIUM

Functionalist **theory** defines social equilibrium as sustaining boundaries in which a social system maintains patterns relative to its environment. Economist Alfred Marshall and sociologist **Herbert Spencer** began to apply the concept of equilibrium to societies in the late 1800s in an effort to systematize the social sciences. In 1916, Vito Pareto described a social system in equilibrium, stating that equilibrium was achieved if a system, when subjected to an unusual and artificial modification, reacts to restore itself to its normal state. **Talcott Parsons** and Edward Shils worked with this theory in the 1950s, and established a theoretical system that identified the relationships between variables. Parsons, in particular, asserted that a social system never fully reaches equilibrium but that all social systems approximate a state of equilibrium. Yet equilibrium was roundly debated, and **Pitirim Sorokin** claimed that equilibrium cannot be applied to human **society**, since societies are made up of individuals who do not make mechanistic responses but act irrationally.

Equilibrium may be described as stable and unstable. Static equilibrium is stable in that its structure is fixed, as is the relationship of the social system to the environment. Activity does not alter the relationship between variables in the system. In dynamic equilibrium, or moving equilibrium, activity initiates change; however this change does not alter the relationships between variables in the system. When it does, the system tends to correct itself, and so it is also considered stable. If equilibrium is unstable, even small changes create chain reactions which lead to the destruction of the system or to the creation of a new balance.

SOCIAL FACT

French sociologist Émile Durkheim (1858–1917) identified social facts as human phenomena that exist independently of individual psychology. Social facts include (but are not limited to) laws, languages, norms, ethical conventions, and aggregate population trends (such as suicide rates). Durkheim argued that these subjects should be treated as phenomena containing properties and characteristics of their own. His view differentiates social facts from phenomena studied by psychologists. Social facts exist independently of the consciousness or will of any particular individual. For instance, laws are created by individual human beings, but legal codes are social facts. Legal structure precedes individuals' births and exist after their deaths. As such, legal structure is a social fact that can be treated on its own.

Social facts are the product of **group** life. They cannot be understood or studied if divorced from that context.

Durkheim also differentiated social facts from terminology used by other sociologists or social philosophers of his era. Unlike a social current or a **mores**, a social fact conveys the extent to which it is observable and measurable. Whereas a current is not necessarily tangible, a social fact is. Durkheim argued that the rigorous analysis of social facts would establish **sociology** as a science on par with biology, chemistry, and physics.

The most famous application of social facts is Durkheim's 1897 analysis of European **suicide** statistics. We generally think of suicide as an intensely individualistic act, the product of individual psychic breakdown. But Durkheim argued differently. He showed that the annual rate of suicide for any given country was stable from one year to the next. But when he compared annual rates for different countries, he found significant differences. Since suicide is a premeditated act by definition, Durkheim argued that the cross national patterns were due to factors beyond individual **psychology**. This sociological examination of suicide rates as social facts led him to his classic theoretical statement on **anomie**. Today, more than 100 years later, Durkheim's study on suicide continues to be read as an exemplary example of sociological thinking and research. The examination of social facts, particularly as they can be represented through statistical indices, dominated sociology for much of the twentieth century.

SOCIAL FORECASTING

Social forecasting, according to sociologist **Daniel Bell** is an attempt to outline the probabilities that certain social phenomenon will occur or will not occur under a specific set of circumstances. These probabilities are only considered within the realm of the possible when there are regularities or repetition of specific phenomenon. The forecasted social phenomenon are more likely to occur when trends can be charted statistically or articulated as historical movements and when the researcher can count on a high degree of **rationality**, rather than affective decision making, from the actors involved. For example, a researcher can forecast possible population changes over time given a certain set of circumstances based on how the population has changed over time and providing that all of the actors involved act in a rational manner.

That is not to say that forecasters are absolutely accurate. These conditions are, in fact, very hard to come by and isolate in the social sciences. Therefore, social forecasters are often limited to spelling out the restrictions within which particular policy decisions can be made effective, or more effective, instead of being able to foresee the actual results of one adopted policy change versus another. Social forecasting is in contrast to the discredited practice of social prediction. Social prediction endeavored to formalize the rules of the prediction of outcomes as they pertain to specific social conditions.

SOCIAL GERONTOLOGY

Social **gerontology** is the study of the many effects of **aging** on society and, conversely, the impact of **society** on aging.

This study encompasses the social factors that affect the aged and the social functions and consequences of the aging process, including the impact on the **family**, the **community**, the economy, the political process, and the **health care** system. By addressing the historical, cultural, physiological, and social issues of aging, social gerontologists address a broad range of topics concerning the later years.

According to the 1990 National Center for Health Care Statistics, more than 30 million Americans are 65 years or older. Equaling 13 percent of the population, this number is expected to grow to 20 percent, or 59 million, by the year 2025. With the increase in **life expectancy** due to better health care, the number of elderly 85 years or older will rise to between 11 and 18 million by 2050. Globally, the United Nations Secretariat estimates that one out of every seven people worldwide will be 65 years or older by 2025. Of this number, an estimated 72 percent of the world's elderly will reside in developing countries. These numbers suggest the need for continued study of the complex issues that affect the elderly, including social policies, health care concerns, economic conditions, and **quality of life**.

Social gerontology, a term coined by sociologist Clark Tibbitts in 1954, is a twentieth century phenomenon. With the passage of the Social Security Act of 1935, social scientists became interested in the personal and social transitions brought on by the aging process. In the 1940s and 1950s, several organizations supported research into social gerontology, including the Rockefeller Foundation and the National Institutes of Mental Health. The development of the Gerontological Society of America also increased interest and support for research, along with the National Institute on Aging, which funds a wide range of health-related studies. Traditionally, social gerontology operated from a **paradigm** that depicted old age as a time of great loss and deprivation. This concern was reflected in the early studies, which focused primarily on issues such as problems of **social integration**, negative effects of the aging process, poor health care or **long-term care**, and age **discrimination**.

Although current researchers acknowledge the presence of a higher rate of illness, disability, and social isolation, empirical **data** have shown that the majority of elderly Americans live self-sufficient, well-adjusted lives. From this perspective, the elderly do not dread the aging process but anticipate the benefits of **retirement**. With the benefits of Social Security, Medicare, and **Medicaid**, the aged are less likely to experience **poverty** than the general population. New theories combating negative stereotypes and ageism (the discrimination against people due to age) appeared during the 1960s. Sociologists Elaine Cumming and William Henry offered the theory of disengagement in *Growing Old* (1961). According to Cumming and Henry, as people age, they voluntarily withdraw from society as their energy levels decrease and their expectations of death increase. An inevitable process, disengagement is seen as a positive means of transition for the aged, and a healthy means of creating room in society for new generations. Exactly opposite the disengagement theory, the activity theory, offered by sociologist Robert Havighurst, suggests that the level of adjustment and quality of life that the elderly experience is

directly proportional to their continued social involvement. Based on activity theory, numerous programs for the elderly emerged, such as recreational events, tours, and senior centers. Both disengagement and activity theories have been criticized for their generalized approach that fails to account for differing experiences among the elderly.

In response to the limitations of disengagement and activity theories, new approaches have been tested. The approach of symbolic interactionists stresses the interaction between the aged and their environment and others, suggesting this interaction is a determining factor in the aging experience. Social **exchange theory**, drawing from behavioral **psychology** and economics, addresses the ability of the elderly to access power and resources compared to other age groups. Finally, political economic theorists, taking a macro perspective, deal with the issues relevant to aging and social policies.

Social gerontology is a broad ranging area of study. Although an incomplete list, major research areas include (1) age stratification, (2) status of old age, (3) life-course experiences, (4) well-being, and (5) environment and aging. Age stratification refers to the socially defined categories of age groups into separate, meaningful entities, which is useful in assessing the role of age in the organization of society. The assessment of status in old age is formulated on studies of social, political, and environmental conditions that produce the class designated as elderly. Old age as a continuation of life-course experiences focuses on the effects of early life events, such as economic status and educational levels, as determining factors in later years. Studies of well-being, or life satisfaction, have been popular since the 1950s. Combating the negative image of aging, well-being studies have supported the theory that most older adults are satisfied, with satisfaction based on the availability of resources and an accessible social structure. Finally, environment and aging studies are based on the social and physical context of later life. With the "graying" of the United States and the world on the rise, social gerontology will remain a field of interest to both social scientists and policymakers as the effects of the increased population of elderly bear more heavily on the social, economic, and political conditions of the future.

SOCIAL INDICATORS

Social indicators are aggregate **data** that describe the status of society. Social indicators usually attempt to assess well-being, quality of life, or **standard of living** in a **society**, country, or **community**. Social indicators address social welfare issues such as health and illness, social mobility, the environment, income and **poverty**, public safety and **crime**, and education.

Social indicators are derived from economic indicators such as Gross Domestic Product (GDP), Gross National Product (GNP), and Consumer Price Index (CPI). While these economic indicators have become important in their own right, their original purpose was to "indicate" the status of an entire nation's economy. Prior to the 1960s, these economic indicators also served as social indicators. The popularity of devel-

opment **theory** and its modernization thesis reinforced the belief that underdeveloped countries needed to modernize to become richer and that increasing a country's wealth (as measured by GNP or GDP calculated on a per capita basis) would translate directly into a higher standard of living.

However, GNP and GDP were not successful as social indicators because these measures neglected issues of distribution, non-market transactions, and appropriate pricing. The limitations of economic indicators as predictors of standard of living and **quality of life** prompted the beginning of the social indicators movement in the 1960s. In the 1960s, domestic social problems in the United States became an increasingly important issue, creating the need for appropriate statistics and information. The recent rise in the popularity of economic indicators made researchers feel that similar information could be obtained through the development of social indicators. Social indicators were developed to supplement economic indicators by addressing quality of life, standard of living, equity, and other social considerations such as crime and pollution.

Raymond Bauer is often credited as the "father" of the social indicators movement. In 1962, the National Aeronautical and Space Agency (NASA) commissioned a study to determine how its space program might affect American society. Little direct information about the possible effects of the space program was available, but Bauer and his colleagues were able to amass a large amount of information about the current status of society. They shifted the focus of their research to assessing social conditions in general, and their results were published in 1966 Bauer's book *Social Indicators*. Here, Bauer and his colleagues emphasized the importance of accurate statistics and pointed out that many existing statistics were so misleading that they were worse than no information at all.

The use of social indicators became increasingly popular until the mid-1970s. Social indicators were adopted early by the Organization for Economic Co-operation and Development (OECD) and the United Nations (UN), and these organizations have used them extensively. The popularity of social indicators leveled off and began declining in the 1980s. The publication of Britain's *Social Trends* ended in 1982 and the U.S. Center for Co-ordination of Research on Social Indicators closed in 1983. While social indicators continued to be used in specialized reports, they have ceased being used as comprehensive and all-encompassing descriptions of social life. One area in which social indicators remain important, however, is in local and community studies, where they are sometimes called local indicators.

There are several types of social indicators, usually based on various dichotomies. Some popular **typologies** are: (1) direct vs. indirect indicators, (2) input vs. output indicators, and (3) objective vs. subjective indicators. Quality of life indicators are a specific type of indicator that can be further classified based on these dichotomies. Quality of life indicators have a specific direction that is universally perceived as desirable.

Indicators have a variety of uses. Most researchers agree that primary functions of social indicators are: (1) descriptive reports of the status of society, (2) analytical studies of **social change**, and (3) forecasts. Some researchers feel the use of so-

cial indicators can be expanded to include other functions: (1) evaluating social programs, (2) setting goals and priorities, and (3) developing a system of social accounts.

SOCIAL INEQUALITY

Social inequality is differential access to social resources by members of a **society** or **group**. Social resources can include wealth, **status**, and power. All existent societies exhibit social inequality to some degree or another; however, whether or not social inequality is an inevitable component of society is a point highly debated within the discipline of **sociology**.

Conflict theorists, drawing on the ideas of **Karl Marx**, argue that, while social inequality is in evidence in all modern societies, it is not an inevitable component of all societies. Marx argued that it was the economic structure of modern societies—specifically capitalism—and not the inherent nature of man's needs that created social inequality. To Marx, social inequality as created by exploitive **capitalism** was an unsustainable social force that would result in societal conflict and, under the right conditions, societal transformation. Marx believed that **communism**, a societal form in which individuals were not separated by artificial societal inequality, was a potential outcome of this societal conflict. Marx's communist society was one in which man's inherent needs and desires were grounded in self-fulfilling creativity, not in materialistic pursuit of goods as in a capitalist society. Hence, individuals in Marx's communist society would not be engaged in a struggle to acquire, but in a quest for personal creative fulfillment through complementary rather than competitive social interaction. As a result, social inequality would not be possible since social resources would not be conceptualized as private commodities, but rather as social goods crafted for the use and benefit of all.

Modern conflict theorists have extended Marx's ideas beyond the economic realm. The prominent British sociologist Ralf Dahrendorf noted that social classes in modern society are not based exclusively on economic relations and, as such, social class might better be understood as differences in authority relationships (*Class and Class Conflict In Industrial Society*, 1959). According to this theory, social inequality arises based upon differential standing in the social spheres of **authority**, which include the economic sphere as well the legislative and judicial spheres. Authority relationships also arise within social classes in the form of age, gender, and ethnic conflicts. The result of all of these conflicts is a high level of social inequality that, as Marx stated, leads to a fundamentally unstable social system. Both Dahrendorf and Marx argue, then, that social inequality is a function of particular forms of social **structure** and is not inherent in all forms of social structure. Furthermore, the existence of social inequality creates more and more social instability because those who benefit from it use their disproportionate power to ensure that the pattern of social inequality is maintained or, more often, enlarged in their favor.

In contrast to conflict theorists, functionalist theorists believe that social inequality is inevitable and inherent in any society. Functionalists argued that no society has ever been totally unstratified or totally classless for the simple reason that there is always a necessary degree of specialization within a society. For example, even the smallest hunting and gathering society needs a form of **leadership** to organize the group's activities, to settle disputes, and to divide the spoils of the hunt in a way that does not create conflict among the group. **Kingsley Davis** and Wilbert Moore argued that social inequality in the form of stratification is inevitable because these specialized roles carry with them onerous burdens of responsibility and often daunting investments because of thetime and money invested in acquiring the necessary tools or education to perform the job. As a result, society needs to have a way to motivate the best people to take on the burdens of training for and filling these positions and to ensure that those who do properly execute the functions of the positions once theyare filled. Social inequality in the form of differential rewards and access to resources serves to fulfill this purpose. Hence, functionalists argue that social inequality is not only inherent to society but is, in fact, beneficial to society since it ensures that the most important and most difficult jobs are executed in a socially beneficial manner.

Although there have been attempts to bridge these two perspectives, such as the sociocultural evolutionary work of **Gerhard Lenski**, these two dominant paradigms in the field remain largely polarized.

SOCIAL INTEGRATION

Social integration refers to the effect of the quantity and quality of the social bonds between and among individuals in **society**. It is assumed that the more numerous the social bonds, the more tightly integrated the society. Social integration has long been a central theme in **sociology**. From Émile Durkheim's *Suicide* in which he identified higher levels of **suicide** among groups with lower levels of social integration, to more recent demographic studies of **community** attachment in the modern metropolis, sociologists understand that social behavior is affected by social structure in many ways.

Durkheim made significant contributions to the field through his analyses of the modernizing world and its effect on social integration. In *The Division of Labor in Society* Durkheim explored the transition from mechanical to organic solidarity (which idealized the transition from pre-industrialization to industrialization) and addressed the degree of differentiation in society. Durkheim suggested that this transition increased physical interdependence at the cost of decreasing social contact and loosening social integration.

Social integration remains a prominent theme in **demography**, particularly in studies of **urbanization**, in **social network analysis**, and in other social sciences. Studies of urbanization have explored the question of whether increasing urbanization has negatively affected social integration by weakening an individual's ties to the community. The results have been contradictory. Some sociologists contend that urbanization has led to a decline in social ties, while others suggest that the nature and **structure** of social ties have changed without necessarily having a detrimental effect on social integration.

SOCIAL MOBILITY

Social mobility is the movement of individuals or groups either upward or downward within a social **status** system. Social mobility can be measured in two ways. Mobility as measured over the course of an individual's adult life is intragenerational mobility. Mobility as measured by comparing the status attainment of an individual with that of their parents is intergenerational attainment.

Every **society** has a different level of social mobility. Closed societies—those that assign status based largely upon the inherent unchangeable, ascriptive characteristics of an individual, such as **family** background, religion, race, and gender—tend to have low levels of social mobility. The most extreme example of this type of social system is a caste system. In a caste system an individual's lifelong social status is based almost entirely upon the ascriptive characteristics with which he or she was born. Open societies—those that assign status based primarily on achieved characteristics such as education, marital status, and occupational attainment—tend to have higher levels of social mobility. The most extreme example of this type of society would be a pure **meritocracy**, in which individuals' **status attainment** is based exclusively upon their own efforts and abilities.

Social mobility became an important sub-field of **sociology** mostly because of the rise to prominence in the 1950s and 1960s of the influential status attainment approach. Still a main theoretical approach of researchers in the United States, the status attainment approach to social mobility attempts to measure social mobility through the use of indexes of occupational prestige or **socioeconomic status**. The methodological assumption of this approach is that dissimilar occupations can be arrayed together hierarchically based upon consensual societal perceptions of their status. Social mobility is then determined by measuring a person's movement within these prestige scales.

Peter Blau and Otis Duncan wrote one of the most important works in this field, *The American Occupational Structure*, in 1967. In it, Blau and Duncan determined that while the United States did have social mobility, it tended to be low-level social mobility. Most people tended to stay either in the same rank or in one rank above the status rank of their parents, and many people actually ended up in a lower status rank than their parents. Their findings showed that even in the most open societies, such as the United States, ascriptive characteristics still play an important part in determining social mobility. Later status attainment research supported their findings by revealing that whites and men are more likely to achieve social mobility than blacks and women, respectively. However, most status attainment theorists have also tended to conclude that over time modern democracies were moving toward greater degrees of social mobility. This trend has happened partly because ascriptive characteristics have becomeless salient as a basis of social mobility because **discrimination** based on **race** and sex has been outlawed and also becausenew pathways to social mobility have opened up, such as wide-scale availability of **higher education** and the introduction of new occupational industries such as internet-based technology.

In the 1970s, European theorists began to criticize the status attainment approach for ignoring the impact of class on social mobility. Rather than examine consensual perceptions of occupational status, European class theorists preferred to focus on the social **structure** of class, creating comparative groups based upon whether or not individuals shared social positions with similar market and occupational conditions. Using this approach, class analysts concluded that, contrary to the findings of status attainment theorists, there was in **fact** little to no change occurring in patterns of social mobility. Class analysis showed that the class structure of such open societies as the United States and Britain was actually highly rigid and not very open to social mobility. Similarly, class analysts also argued there had been no consistent rise in the emphasis on meritocracy as the basis of social mobility.

The fact that American and European theorists take different approaches and arrive at diametrically opposed interpretations of social mobility reflects the larger theoretical divisions that divide American and European sociologists in many sociological sub-fields. In fact, both approaches have come under criticism by feminists and other groups for inadequately addressing the importance of **identity** factors such as gender and race. These vigorous debates surrounding social mobility reveal both its high level of importance in society and the fundamentally complex nature of determining the social processes that create and transform class and status within a society.

SOCIAL MOVEMENTS

Social movements are systemic group mobilizations aimed at modifying or overthrowing the existing policies or social structures of a **society**. Social movements are distinguished from more general forms of collective behavior such as riots, fads, and crowd behavior, by the organized and sustained nature of their activities. For much of the early history of **sociology**, social movement participation was seen as a pathological phenomenon. In fact, for most of the first half of the twentieth century, **mass society theory** was the dominant theory of social movements. Mass society theory argued that social movements arose out of social disorganization due to widespread changes in the social order, such as economic cycles or political upheaval. These social changes were seen as creating widespread **anomie**, social isolation, and disaffection by dislodging large numbers of people from the social communities in which they had been embedded. These disaffected people were then subject to being "swept up" by charismatic leaders into social movements. In the late 1950s and 1960s these ideas were refined by the new theoretical concept of discontent in the form of **relative deprivation**. Relative deprivation theorists, such as Ted Gurr, argued that while social disorganization lead people to feel freer to protest, whether they actually did depended on their perceptions of whether they were unjustly deprived of social opportunities or outcomes compared to other groups (*Why Men Rebel*, 1970).

With the extraordinary amount of social activism that arose in the 1960s and early 1970s, social movement theory

took in a new direction. Social movements, like the student, civil rights, women's, and environmental movements, appeared to be of a new type that could not adequately be explained by discontent or breakdown theories. These new movements drew their members not from the disaffected segments of society but from those with stable, quite often upper middle class, backgrounds. In addition, many participants were active in movements that did not benefit them directly, such as white northern students working to increase southern black political participation or men advocating for women's rights. As a result of the perceived inability of existing theory to account adequately for these new social movements, two streams of social mobility theory were formed.

In the United States in the early 1970s resource mobilization theory challenged discontent theories on the grounds that while discontent is an ever-present social phenomenon, social movements are not. Resource mobilization theorists thereby claimed that discontent alone was not sufficient to form social movements, arguing instead that social movements only arise when a society has sufficient levels of civic freedom and resources to support them. Rooted in rational choice perspectives of social action, resource mobilization theory was hence primarily concerned with the process of how a social movement, as an organization, develops and acquires resources. In an important statement of the theory, Mayer Zald and John McCarthy conceptualized all the social movements of a society as together forming a social movement industry (*The Dynamics of Social Movements*, 1979). Within this social movement industry any particular social movements must compete with all the other social movements to acquire control of available social resources, such as commitments of time, money, and labor and control of symbols and media representations. This competition takes place both between movements sharing similar ideologies and between movements with different ideologies. Mobilization and participation in a social movement is hence viewed as a recruitment problem in which individuals weigh the costs and benefits of action before deciding on their level of involvement. As a result, the key issue for social movements is one of effective organization, resource management, and **communication** between supporters, opponents, and the bystander public.

Simultaneous with the development of resource mobilization theory in the United States, theorists in Europe developed a competing **model** of social movement analysis called new social movement theory. These theorists, such as Alan Touraine, argue that the key distinction of the new kinds of social movements is that they are social movements based upon issues of identity, ideology, **culture**, and class. They maintain that new social movement participation is driven in part by the alienating forces of modernization and hence serve as a critical new form of **identity** construction in a disaffected world.

As tools for analyzing social movements, discontent, resource mobilization, and new social movement theory are often complimentary as they emphasize different aspects of the social movement problem, conflict, structural conditions, and socio-psychological issues, respectively.

The **Suffragist** movement of the early twentieth century lobbied for the right to vote for women *(Corbis Corporation [Bellevue])*.

SOCIAL NETWORK ANALYSIS

Based on graph theory techniques of sociometry developed by J. L. Moreno in the 1940s, social network analysis is a theoretical approach that emphasizes the study of social relationships connecting individuals and groups within a **society** as a result of their participation in patterned social structures. A network consists of all the individuals or groups connected by the specified social relationships. To examine the **structure** of a network, a sociomatrix, a table detailing the patterns of relationship between all the individuals or groups within the network, is formed. From this sociomatrix, a pictorial representation of the network, called a sociogram, can be produced. Each individual or **group** within a network is called a node and is represented visually in the sociogram by a point. If two nodes are connected by the social relationship in question, they are said to have a tie, represented by a line connecting the two nodes.

Network theory was developed as a direct response to two main approaches to social analysis. Network **theory** rejected atomistic approaches which emphasized analysis of the decision-making process of actors without concern for the social relationships in which they were embedded. Network theorists

felt atomistic approaches were micro and placed far too little emphasis on the large influence social structures have on individual behavior. Network theory also criticized the theoretical approaches emphasizing the role of internalization of **norms** and **values** in determining actors' behavioral orientations. These normative approaches were perceived by network theorists as being too removed from the actual reality of social **interaction**. Network theorists wanted to emphasize actual patterns of behavior rather than actors' socially influenced perceptions or attitudes about which behaviors were appropriate or inappropriate.

Early network research focused on basic structural analysis, such as determining the actual patterns of social relationships between nodes and recognizing clusters of ties that represented cliques within the larger network. However, by the late 1950s, network theory had developed more sophisticated approaches, and researchers began to focus on processes of interaction within the network, such as cohesion, balance, and bridging. Cohesion is the process through which such strong ties as cliques are formed and strengthened within the network. Balance is the process through which such highly cohesive groups can polarize. Bridging examines the impact when two members of separate cliques within the network share a tie, thereby creating a resource pathway between cliques. As they were concerned with the stability of the network and its ability to allow resources to flow between its nodes, these areas of study all reflected a growing emphasis on deep structural forces.

In the 1960s, Harrison White took this deep structural focus even further in the form of structural equivalence. Structural equivalence uses a technique called blockmodelling to create analytical reference groups out of actors in the network that share the same structural position within the network. By examining these structural equivalent groups rather than individual actors themselves, structural equivalence allows for the study of patterned relations of stratification and group processes.

The power of network theory is that its concern for structure and resource flow often reveals new ways of examining social relationships hidden by more traditional methods of social analysis. One important example is Mark Grannovetter's analysis of the social importance of bridges (*Getting a Job*, 1973). Traditionally, sociologists believed that strong ties, such as **family** and friends, were the most important type of social ties for getting resources, like information about job opportunities. By examining the flow of resources within a network, Granovetter's network research revealed that in fact in certain situations weak ties such as acquaintances and friends of friends are sometimes the most useful ties. Whereas strong ties usually share similar resources and hence access to similar information, weak ties serve as bridges to new cliques within a network and hence new pathways to resources, such as information about job opportunities. By expanding the reach of sociological analysis in these ways, network theory has helped to reinvigorate many areas of sociological research.

SOCIAL ORDER

The question of how and why societies hold together or how the social order is maintained is central to **sociology**. There are basically two types of explanations of the social order that can be linked to Émile Durkheim and **Karl Marx**. According to Durkheim, in *The Division of Labor and Society*, social order is developed not by self-interest, but because of collective **norms**. Simultaneously opposing a centralized state, he thought that a **society** might best be ordered by the **division of labor** into groupings, each which relate the individual to the **government** in a specific way. Durkheim sought a combination of **individualism** and collectivism to ensure a stable social order.

Durkheim's notion of order is also tied to the work of Talcott Parsons and the functionalists. Parsons specifically addressed Durkheim's view in his 1937 *The Structure of Social Action*. This book asked the question: why is society ordered instead of involved in a Hobbesian war? In this book, he argued that the participation in a social order was voluntary, not the result of necessity, **coercion**, or self-interest. According to **functionalism**, societies cohere because they have shared norms and values. Thus, according to them, the social order is fairly stable.

According to Marxist **theory** people obey the social order because they are constrained by those in power. Social order is the upshot of the balance of power between powerful and weaker groups. In short, people adhere to social norms because they have little opportunity to do otherwise. The social order is very precariously maintained because the lower classes will eventually unify and overthrow the existing social order.

Explanations of social order tend to be macro-theories that focus on society as the **unit of analysis**. That is not to say that these are the areas to which the problem of social order is addressed. On the micro-level, symbolic interactionists, dramaturgists, and ethnomethodologists have different understandings of how the social order is reproduced during **interaction** on the interpersonal level.

SOCIAL ORGANIZATION

A social **organization** can be characterized as any relatively stable structure or pattern within a **society**. The term also refers to the process of creating and maintaining this structure or pattern. Used in its most general sense, the term overlaps with social structure and social order.

Social organizations exist primarily in two forms: formal organizations and informal organizations. A formal organization is a group established and maintained for the purpose of meeting a set of specific, stated goals. This type of organization is ordered by a formal set of rules and guidelines with a distinct hierarchy of authority and a specific division of labor. Membership in these organizations is often restricted. Examples of formal organizations include corporations, schools, churches, the military, and labor unions. Relationships within

these organizations tend to be formal and are typically ordered according to preestablished guidelines. Formal organizations tend to exist for many years and give those who participate in them a sense of membership, as well as providing their members with norms, values, and roles. These organizations allow people who have little else in common to work together for common goals by providing organization, stability, and focus to group experiences.

A specific type of formal organization is a **bureaucracy**. Max Weber defined a bureaucracy as a specific type of formal organization which directs the efforts of the people involved primarily through impersonal written rules and a hierarchical arrangement of the organization's parts based on the ideas of authority and the **division of labor**. The hierarchy can be conceptualized as a pyramid in which the authority increases and the number of people decreases as one moves up the levels. Succession is not determined by the office-holders themselves but rather by an official policy set forth in the official written documents. Further, even though there may be promotions and evaluations, the office is often held for life (or for as long as the office-holder desires), and there is usually a fixed salary and a pension. For example, once they are hired for a job, government employees such as division heads and support staff (but typically not elected officials) may hold the job for the remainder of their working lives.

The activities of a bureaucracy are divided into several units, each with a specific focus to meet a certain need. Each unit is responsible for meeting its own goals as a way of meeting the goals of the organization. For example, a corporation may be divided into sales, manufacturing, research, product development, and marketing. While there is still a clear interconnectedness between the units, as well as overarching common interests and agendas, each unit is focused on a distinct goal in the process of furthering the overall goals of the corporation; without a part of the corporation, the entire corporation and its goals suffer.

In a bureaucracy the authority of the position resides with the position itself, rather than within the specific person filling the job. For example, the president of the United States has the same authority regardless of who holds the office, and once another person moves into that office, the authority of the position transfers to that person. The hierarchy usually works as a chain of command. Each level of authority answers to the level above it and is responsible for both its own responsibilities and for those who are under it as well. The members of the president's cabinet answer to the president for their actions as well as for the actions of their departments.

The second type of social organization, informal organizations, do not have the same level of structure as formal organizations. While they are generally focused on a set of central ideas or goals, they do not have the same sort of formal procedures to meet those goals. Examples of informal organizations include families, neighborhoods, and peer groups. Social relationships within these organizations are typically unstructured and spontaneous and have more general goals and roles. Informal organizations do not have the preestablished written rules, and most of the organizational guidelines are developed out of

a general understanding. For example, a **family** may have the goal of caring for its members, but they do so through less formal means, authority resides with specific people in the family, and they have no formalized written procedure for making decisions (i.e., they do not form an advisory committee, consult the regulations handbook, request bids for work to be done, hold meetings following particular procedures, and replace members as necessary).

SOCIAL PERCEPTION

Social perception refers to the way in which humans construct an understanding of the social world using **data** and information gathered through sensory experience. Individuals collect information about the people, objects, and situations surrounding them through visual, auditory, olfactory, tactile, and other sensory means. This information is processed to allow individuals to form attitudes and impressions about the world in which they live. Social psychological study of social perception has produced several theories regarding how information is processed and stored by humans, as well as studies of how social perception allows individuals to function effectively in social settings.

The study of social perception typically involves examination of social interaction and how individuals' perceptions of the people and scenarios surrounding them will affect the style and quality of the **interaction**. As the sensory data are collected, they are immediately categorized by individuals in order to allow them to create a reliable and predictable situation in which they feel a measure of understanding and increased comfort. Individuals use well-organized structures of cognitions, known as schemas, to categorize the sensory data and place the information into an appropriate category for what is being experienced. Schemas classify information about individuals (how we categorize ourselves), their group memberships (expected behaviors or **values** from a member of a certain group), their roles (expectations of someone holding a certain role), and events surrounding the interaction (for example, scripts which people generally follow in a certain situation, such as ordering in a restaurant) to accurately place individuals so that they may use the schema in order to make general judgements about what can be expected of the subject, their attributes, and their intentions. Schemas are interrelated so that various pieces of information can be used to construct a more complete picture of the subject. Take, for example, an eight year old boy named Kyle. Schemas can refer to the person in his entirety, allowing for comparison between Kyle and others. Another schema classifies Kyle by various attributes others know of him (short, young, Jewish, American). Another classifies Kyle in terms of the relations he holds with others (son of Gerald and Sheila, brother or Ike, friend of Stan). Each of these classifications could affect the way Kyle is perceived, especially due to the attributes of those with whom he has relationships. If his father is a lawyer, this piece of information places Gerald in a schema about lawyers, and since his relationship to Kyle is so close, it could also change the expecta-

tions we have of Kyle (since he is the son of a lawyer). This interrelation of the types of schemas help to build the cognitive structure by which individuals process sensory information and use it during interactions.

Schemas also help set our expectations for people and can affect the way we perceive and attribute behavior in various people. Attribution refers to the process by which we infer the causes of another's behavior. Observation of another's behavior serves as the sensory data which are analyzed in the attribution process. The observer then attempts to infer why the person behaved as he or she did by considering his or her intentions, motives, abilities, physical and psychological traits, and situational pressures. Generally, behavior is due in part to the individual's disposition (internal drive) or results from the situation faced by the individual (environmental or external factors). Traits held by the individual performing the action may affect where the action is attributed. For example, if an individual believes that by nature, Irish people are prone to violent behavior and then observes an Irish man standing over a fallen person, he is likely to assume that the Irish man is acting aggressively and not attempting to help or show concern for the fallen person. Similarity to the observer is also likely to affect attribution. Individuals are more likely to assume that those similar to them act in positive ways due to internal traits and in negative ways due to circumstances. For those dissimilar to the observer, the attribution pattern is often inversed (negative behaviors are internal, positive are environmental). In this way, perception and attribution can be altered by the process of categorization which makes interaction easier. However, it is worth noting that social psychologists believe that, in most cases, observers commit the fundamental attribution error, namely, the underestimation of the situational impact on behavior accompanied by overestimation of dispositional factors.

SOCIAL PHILOSOPHY

Social **philosophy** is not specifically defined within the field of contemporary sociology. On one hand, social philosophy can refer to the ontological explanation of the social world. Namely, social philosophy explains the existence of social structures and the **interaction** between these structures and individuals within the **society**, creating a conceptual theory of society. On the other hand, social philosophy also includes a **methodology** that addresses the normative study of social action and individual behavior within society. Whereas the ontological approach focuses on the concept of society, the methodological approach to social philosophy concerns the ability of **sociology** to discern particular knowledge that can be counted as fact regarding the characteristics and attributes of social action within a society.

Assuming social philosophy as an ontological endeavor involves examining the assumptions that create the theoretical base for social study. The two factors around which social theory can be formed are interaction and aggregation. Interaction refers to the social interaction between individuals that results in the formation of numerous types of relationships, which necessarily involve issues of **communication**, collaboration, exchange, and all other collective behaviors. Aggregation is associated with how and to what extent individuals exhibit group behavior through shared **values**, actions, and attitudes that result in the creation of social institutions.

Interaction theories are distinguished by the division between atomists and non-atomists who fundamentally disagree on the relation between social interaction and individuals. Atomists defend the idea that individuals and their characteristics are formed independent of society. Society is secondary to the individual. Contrarily, non-atomists deny the concept of self-made individuals, asserting instead that it is only through social interaction that individuals and their specific traits are created. According to *The Oxford Companion to Philosophy* (1995; edited by Ted Honderich), ''The non-atomist holds that the same sort of social dependence governs the ability of an individual to reason and think: the ability, as we may take it, not just to have beliefs and desires, but to act with a view to having rational beliefs and desires. The atomist denies this, maintaining the view that all that is involved in reason and thought, all that is non-causally required for their appearance, is available to the individual outside society.'' The atomist perspective has been prevalent in British and American social thought, while the non-atomist view has been primarily located in France and Germany.

Social aggregation is also separated by two fundamental approaches: individualism and holism. The individualist, like the atomist, maintains the primacy of the individual. Accordingly, the individualist believes that all social institutions can be reduced to those individuals who combine to create the social grouping. No social **institution** exists independent of the individuals who compose it. On the other hand, holism theory suggests that social entities are not reducible to individuals but exist independent of each individual's beliefs, purposes, and actions. Understanding social interaction and social aggregation affects formulation of a social philosophy that identifies a conceptual understanding of society.

Social philosophy as methodology addresses the social scientist's claim to knowledge and the nature of that knowledge. Dealing with such issues as universality and neutrality, social scientists have long been concerned with presenting knowledge as empirically substantiated. Sociology grew out of a tradition that believed that social science could be tied to the same laws as natural science. The social reality, just like physical reality, was not created but discovered. Other schools of thought emerged that challenged naturalism. Sociologists began to argue that no judgments can be rendered value-free and, further, that universal laws do not dictate human interaction because, unlike activities of nature, social action requires **intentionality**. Whereas natural phenomena can be explained by causal relationships, social phenomena must necessarily account for the intentions of the social actors involved.

The social philosophical influences on the field of sociology have been diverse. In the United States, **symbolic interactionism** and British logical positivism resided with the influences of European philosophy reflected in the sociological

work of European-trained sociologists **Talcott Parsons**, Paul Lazarsfeld, and Robert Merton. Other perspectives emerged that both supported and challenged the traditional schools of thought. In the late 1960s and early 1970s **Thomas Kuhn** and Michael Polanyi both argued against the natural model, suggesting a link between sociology and artistic values. Around the same time, Alfred Schutz proposed a phenomenological **model** for social assessment, later taken up in the work of **Peter Berger** and Thomas Luckmann. In the 1980s, Jürgen Habermas made the most significant contributions to the philosophical underpinnings of sociology. Habermas' postmodernist approach stressed **rationality** as the standard by which social action could be judged. In each philosophical approach, the scholars attempt to define society and understand how and to what extent social knowledge can be attained and confirmed.

SOCIAL POLICY

Government organizations coordinate federal, state, and local services. They also have decision-making responsibilities with regard to recognizing and dealing with social issues. Social policy, therefore, embodies decisions that have intended consequences or unintended outcomes for certain groups of individuals. Social policy involves two dimensions. The first is the decision-making process that identifies some particular social issue and who is affected. The second aspect of social policy involves the outcome of the decision to implement some program or action and how its impact will be measured. While social policies traditionally tend to be associated with social welfare efforts, in the 1990s, other issues affecting marginalized groups in the United States often are included in policy considerations. For example, recent social science research has been conducted on the emergence of contingent **employment** among low skilled workers, many of whom are single female parents. The intent of the researchers is to create interest in developing social policies to ensure the fair treatment of women in the **labor force** by highlighting the social implications of a highly disposable, uninsured, low paid female workforce.

Historically, welfare services emerged during the Roosevelt administration, which established both social security and a welfare program called Aid to Dependent Children. During the Johnson administration social programs such as **Medicare**, **Medicaid**, and public housing were implemented. Many, in fact, refer to these efforts during the 1960s as the "War on Poverty". Today, the United States provides additional social policy programs including childcare and head start programs, nutrition and lunch programs, public housing, and medical and disability programs.

Political influence affects the decision-making actions of politicians to recognize, develop, or maintain policies on certain social issues. The intent of social policy is to help individuals who are not able to provide or are in need of supplemental assistance for themselves or their families. The effectiveness of social policy reflects the types of strategies developed to improve the social conditions of these individuals. Because social policy programs require public funding, many

evaluations focus on the positive and negative outcomes of social reform and the intended and unintended results of policy making. Recent reports on the inadequacies of the welfare system and fraudulent claims by recipients have received much attention and support many recent policy revisions.

Social policy tends to fall into three areas: social provisions, social services, and social action. Social provisions refer to supplements designed to help the individual or **family** in the provision of everyday life such as housing, public assistance, and medical services. **Social services** are sources of assistance designed to alter behaviors or actions that our **society** has deemed unsafe or undesirable. Although much criticism has been voiced about the issue of control by social service agencies, their methods of intervention, and efforts to enforce change, the focus of social services is to provide resources and actions that will empower the individual in his or her future decision-making.

Social action focuses on institutional changes. Efforts to bring about institutional changes affect the individual, but group efforts to improve the social conditions of children in educational organizations may also bring about positive changes for the **organization** such as improved communications. While community involvement does not always result in consensus or resolution, it can sometimes encourage individuals and institutions to work cooperatively to resolve **social problems**.

SOCIAL PROBLEMS

Crime, **poverty**, AIDS, drug and alcohol abuse, **divorce**, abortion, and unemployment are all conditions most people would agree are social problems. However, can divorce be considered problematic for the women and children escaping an abusive husband? Is abortion wrong for the victim of rape? Was AIDS considered a social problem in the 1950s? These questions suggest there are no absolute definitions of what constitutes a social problem. Definitions always include value judgments. As a result, how social problems are defined vary both within and across societies and historical periods.

All social problems begin with an objective condition that can be observed and measured. However, considering social problems in terms of their objective conditions alone remains incomplete. Social problems also have a subjective element. **Herbert Blumer** stated (1971): "knowledge of the objective make-up of the social problem area is of significance only to the extent that the knowledge enters into the process of collective definition which determines the fate of social problems." In other words, members of **society** must see and define a social condition as a problem in society. Combining both objective and subjective elements, Mooney, Knox, and Schacht (2000) defined a social problem as a "social condition that a segment of society views as harmful and in need of remedy."

Sociologists use three main theories, structural-functionalism, conflict theory, and symbolic-interactionism, to study social problems. Each theory has its own view of how

society works and existent social problems. Structural-Functionalists view society as a system of interconnected parts that work together in harmony to maintain a state of social stability, integration, and cohesion for society as a whole. The society's parts are social structures. Social structures are primarily composed of the major social institutions. They include the family, education, religion, medicine, the economy, and politics. These social structures or institutions persist because they fulfill different needs or functions. The **family** is functional for society to the extent that it provides its members with emotional and material support, reproduces and socializes children, and confers social **status**. But some families are dysfunctional because they interfere with the performance of functions typically served by the family (i.e., abusive families). According to structural-functionalists, then, social problems exist when any part of society becomes dysfunctional and prevents society from having its needs met.

In contrast, conflict theorists see pervasive tension and conflict among social parts with inequality as the driving force behind the conflict. The two main branches of **conflict theory** are Marxist and Modern. Marxist theorists argue that conflict is a result of class inequality inherent in the capitalist system. **Capitalism** is beneficial for the upper classes, but translates into a lack of resources (i.e., wealth, power, prestige, etc.) for the lower classes. For example, poverty is associated with lack of medical care, lower educational achievement, and higher crime rates. Modern conflict theorists argue that conflict occurs because groups in society have opposing interests and **values**. For example, Pro-life activists value the life of unborn embryos and fetuses whereas Pro-choice activists value the right of women to control their own body and reproductive decisions. Vested interest groups are those that benefit from existing social arrangements. Thus, from the conflict perspective, social problems occur when a group believes either their sufficient share of resources or interests are not being met.

Finally, symbolic-interactionists focus on how society is created, maintained, and changed through social interaction. Humans interact through the use of symbols such as words, facial expressions, and body language or gestures that have meaning for ourselves and others. By using symbolic gestures we show how we intend to act toward others. Similarly, by reading the symbolic gestures of others, we get an idea of how they will behave. This capability allows individuals to coordinate their behavior. A central premise of symbolic-interactionism is that interaction is always situated. We can construct a definition or interpretation of others' actions and respond to those actions based on situations in which we find ourselves. Our interpretations are mediated by symbolic gestures. We respond to our situation based on the meanings we attach to people and events rather than actual physical objects or actions. In other words, the definition of a situation is subjective; it is based on an individual's viewpoint. As a result, symbolic-interactionists maintain that social problems exist when a given social condition is defined or labeled as such by members of society.

Social Psychology

Social **psychology** developed during the early 1900s as an attempt to bridge both sociological and psychological theories. Whereas traditional sociological and psychological explanations tended to exclude one another, social psychological **theory** endeavors to incorporate both perspectives. In other words, social psychologists, regardless of their sociological or psychological orientations, assert viability in both approaches. That is, sociological and psychological theories are unique explanatory paradigms that have the capacity to complement one another. One prominent body of sociological social psychology is termed social **structure** and personality theory. As the name suggests, this theory is concerned with the relationship between social structure and individual psychological processes. Social structure and personality theory is deemed social psychological because it involves the examination of both sociological and psychological processes. That is, whereas social structure is generally associated with **sociology**, personality is mainly held to be the domain of psychology.

James House, an influential exponent of social structure and personality theory, was particularly interested in the relationships among such macro-social structures as societies and communities, social processes like industrialization, and psychological and behavioral processes (namely, personality). More specifically, he argued that social structure may be defined as patterns of interpersonal relationships, whereas **culture** can be characterized as the content of these relationships. House's work succeeded in bridging both sociological and psychological phenomena.

Social psychological theory generally concerns itself with both society's effect upon the individual and the individual's influence on **society**. By virtue of these theoretical interests, social psychological explanations typically derive from both microscopic (pertains to individual behavior) and macroscopic (refers to the behavior of larger groups of individuals) levels of analyses. So, social psychological explanations attempt to account for both individual and structural phenomena.

Social psychological theories, more specifically, consider how individuals and the societies that influence them affect individuals' thoughts, emotions, and behavior. This focus appears to imply that social psychological theory is reciprocal in nature. In fact, it is argued that the primary goal of social psychology is to articulate this reciprocal influence and that this ability solidifies its theoretical importance. In short, it is largely through the accomplishments of social psychology that we may view human behavior of individuals within a social context.

Social Resources Theory

Social Resources **Theory** proposes that the access to and use of personal and social resources can lead to higher **socioeconomic status**. This theory also states that the access to and use of personal and social resources is at least partly determined by one's position in the hierarchical structure of **society** (the

strength of one's social position) and one's ability to create and use weak tie networks. Thus, one's social status is in great part determined by one's level of social capital. Ultimately, we use social and personal resources to attain or enhance our social status.

Resources are both material and symbolic and are important because of their value in certain social contexts. Personal resources are those belonging to an individual, which include ascribed statuses and achieved statuses such as **race**, gender, age, education level, religion, and family resources. The individual possesses these resources and has control over their use. Social resources are those embedded in one's social network and available through social ties. The individual does not directly possess these resources. Social capital is defined as the amount of economic, cultural, social, and symbolic capital one has as an individual in combination with the extent, strength, and diversity of one's social network. It can be conceived of as the value of an individual's social relationships— how much this network can buy or get an individual, or it can be considered the extent to which one has the social and economic tools to navigate any individual or structural constraints that may be presented in opposition to one's goals.

Social resources theory states that one's success in life is due primarily to one's support system (i.e., social network). There are at least four kinds of support that we get from other people, to varying degrees: emotional, material (financial, good and services), information, and companionship. According to Nan Lin, the strength of social ties is related to the kinds of support and resources we need from and provide to other people. Strong ties are close, intimate ones with people who are similar to ourselves. We tend to get all four kinds of support from our close ties, some more than others. Weak ties are less emotional, can be with people with whom we have little in common, and are found in broad social networks. We often get material and informational support from these ties. Thus, one needs both strong and weak ties to perform instrumental actions, actions motivated by the need or desire to get valued resources (getting a job, buying a house, dating, or looking for a business partner) because these social tasks require a broad and diverse social network. However, one can rely solely on one's strong ties for expressive actions, actions motivated by the need or desire to keep valued resources (having an intimate relationship, being friends, sharing life experiences), because of the increased intimacy and emotional trust that is needed for these social actions.

Lin proposed three general hypotheses about the use of social resources: the social resources hypothesis, which states that people are able to more successfully perform instrumental actions if they have access to social resources; the strength-of-position hypothesis, which states that the position in society into which one is born will have a strong effect on access to resources; and the strength-of-ties hypothesis, which states that the more weak ties an individual has, the more able that person is to take advantage of social resources.

In terms of professional rewards, Lin's research based in this theory has shown that social resources (social capital) adds to one's attained statuses such as **career** status, level of authority, and degree of power in certain segments of the economy. Social capital has also been shown to add to one's financial earnings in these attained statuses. This is in part due to the fact that extensive social networks (including both strong and weak ties) give people better opportunities. Some research, however, has found that weak ties become less valuable as one ascends the hierarchical ladder. On the more personal and emotional level, research has shown that close, homophilous social relationships are crucial to one's psychological health and well-being because they provide the trust and intimacy necessary to deal with stressful situations. This theory also states that caregivers with a large, strong social support network are able maintain their own health while also caring for others.

SOCIAL SCIENCE RESEARCH COUNCIL (SSRC)

The Social Science Research Council (SSRC) is the preeminent sponsor of interdisciplinary research in the social sciences. Founded in 1923, the non-profit SSRC works to advance research through conferences and workshops and by funding fellowships and grants both to graduate students and more advanced researchers. Since the Cold War, the council has maintained an international focus, with over half of its 1998 budget geared towards research outside North America. SSRC funds over ten million dollars in research annually.

The SSRC functions primarily as a conduit between foundations and government with resources devoted to the social sciences and researchers working in academia. During the last ten years, the SSRC received major support from such foundations as the Ford Foundation, John D. and Catherine T. MacArthur Foundation, and the Andrew W. Mellon Foundation, and from governmental sources like National Science Foundation, the United States Information Agency, and the National Endowment for the Humanities.

An annual average of 2,000 people participate in 80-90 conferences, workshops and other activities funded by the SSRC. Additionally, the SSRC has funded graduate student pre-dissertation and dissertation work through programs such as its International Predissertation Fellowship Program, Sexuality Research Fellowship Program, and Areas Studies Programs. In addition, the Council publishes *Items & Issues,* its quarterly newsletter.

In 1923, members representing the American Political Science Association, the American Sociological Society, the American Economic Association, and the American Historical Association, met to discuss strategies for collaborative work on fundamental interdisciplinary research. Joined by American Statistical Association, the American Psychological Association, and the American Anthropological Association, they incorporated as the SSRC in 1924. Funding came primarily from the Rockefeller Foundations in this early phase. Some initial projects included lobbying congress to allow the Library of Congress to publish an annual index of state laws and working with the National Research Council to study the social aspects

of human migration. In the mid-1920s the Council began to sponsor annual conferences to bring together prominent researchers working on similar topics but in different fields, researchers not ordinarily in contact with one another.

Out of these early meetings came two polices that would both formally and informally guide the SSRC over the next seventy-five years. First, they would only fund projects that involved more than one discipline. While not opposing traditional disciplinary work, they thought that the greatest potential for the social sciences was in interdisciplinary work. Furthermore, they felt that this kind of research would not grow organically; it needed to be specifically nurtured. Second, the SSRC would put emphasis on funding work that was in the planning stages rather than on research that had already begun. During the 1930s, the SSRC added a focus on developing solutions to current social problems to its mission. The SSRC's committee on Social Security played a prominent role in the development of President Roosevelt's program of the same name. During this period, the SSRC also began funding the training of specific researchers. These programs, now embodied in the SSRC's support of pre-dissertation, dissertation, and post-doctoral fellows, primarily target the development of individual researchers, with the specific content of the endeavors coming secondary.

In the 1950s, the SSRC initiated a number of committees that focused on specific global regions, including Eastern Europe, the Middle East, and Africa. One of its most prodigious committees from this era was the Committee on Comparative Politics which helped sponsor more than 30 conferences and workshops and initiated over 300 reports in its twenty-year history.

Over the years, a number of prominent academics have been associated with the SSRC, including Clifford Geertz, V.O. Key, Jr., Frank Knight, Neil Smelser, C. Vann Woodward, Robert Dahl, Paul Lazarsfeld, Robert Merton, Samuel Huntington, and Marshall Shulman.

The SSRC is governed by a board of directors including representatives of the seven founding disciplines, eight members elected at large, and the organization's president. All of these members are traditionally academics. Craig Calhoun, a **sociology** professor at New York University, was named SSRC's most recent president in the spring of 1999. The SSRC is headquartered in New York City.

SOCIAL SECURITY SYSTEM

Social Security, the United States' version of social insurance, established by President Franklin Delano Roosevelt in 1935, has grown to the status of the primary shibboleth of American politics. Social insurance programs were first adapted in European countries at the end of the nineteenth century. The United States developed its Social Security program in response to the Great Depression, the effects of which did not abate as expected and to the large demographic shifts which changed the **structure** of American social life.

The **Industrial Revolution** sparked these changes. Prior to the Industrial Revolution, farms provided the main mode of

employment, and **capitalism** operated on a localized scale; rather than providing cheap labor for capitalist industries, workers owned their means of production and profited directly from their labor. Americans were more likely to live in small towns, with and/or nearby their extended families. This arrangement made caretaking of the elderly or disabled a shared experience and lessened the economic impact of a lost wage-earner. As industrialization progressed, people abandoned agriculture and small towns in favor of **cities** and factory work. Consequently, the nuclear family became the dominant **paradigm**, and those unable to work—the elderly—were left behind. Additionally, due to advances in medical knowledge, people were living longer, creating a large population of the elderly where a small population had existed previously.

President Roosevelt, making note of these changes in a message to Congress on June 8, 1934, announced his plans for building a Social Security program. He signed the completed bill on August 14, 1935. Social Security was established with two titles: Title I, ''Grants to states for old-Age Assistance,'' provided for state-based welfare programs for the elderly; Title II, ''Federal Old-Age Benefits,'' established the federal pension program funded by payroll taxes that remains the backbone of Social Security today. Under Title II, workers contribute, via payroll taxes, to a joint federal fund. Upon retirement, originally set at age sixty-five, the worker is entitled to a monthly check from the government, the amount of which is determined by the individual's lifetime contributions to the fund.

The Social Security program has gone through a number of changes since its inception, including the extension of entitlements to the primary earner's dependents, the addition of disability as a state qualifying for aid prior to **retirement**, automatic cost-of-living adjustments, provisions for early retirement (sixty-two years of age) with diminished benefits, and the institution of the **Medicare** program, which provides health insurance to the majority of the over-65 population. A new program, Supplemental Security Income (SSI), was established in the 1970s to take control of benefit distribution to needy aged, blind, and disabled individuals.

The Social Security program works as long as there are more workers paying into the fund than there are people receiving funds. In the past, this was not a problem, since the average person's **life expectancy** was seventy-five years. However, a new demographic shift became apparent in the last decades of the twentieth century: life expectancies saw substantial growth, thanks again to medical progress, while the country's birth rate diminished. As a result, the entrance of the Baby Boom generation into their retirement years is expected by some to bankrupt the Social Security fund. This problem could be addressed in a number of ways, such as using the federal budget surplus to supplement the fund, creating special savings accounts for individuals to add to their Social Security contributions, using federal funds to match contributions to such accounts in lieu of Social Security, investing existing funds in the stock market, or allowing workers to invest the part of their pay that would have gone into Social Security into the stock market for themselves.

Changing Social Security is a politically tricky endeavor. Due to the contributory aspect, Americans see Social Se-

curity as an absolute entitlement, and for currently-retired or nearly-retired Americans, it is often the main source of income. Americans over the age of sixty-five vote in larger numbers than any other age group and are represented by an extremely powerful lobbying organization, the American Association of Retired Persons. Politicians up for re-election, especially presidential candidates, regularly make the preservation of Social Security an integral part of their platform, in efforts to win the support of this very valuable voting block. In Congress, reforms to Social Security can be impossible to pass, since legislators fear backlash from their constituents. This catch-22, between the need for reform and the desire for re-election, earned Social Security its nickname: the third rail of American politics.

SOCIAL SERVICES

Social services, also called welfare services, are any publicly or privately funded aids to people or groups who are disadvantaged or in some way vulnerable. The term, **social work**, although sometimes used in this context as well, is generally employed when discussing the people who render these services. In some countries, a distinction is made between social services and welfare services. ''Social'' refers to such areas as education and **health care**, and ''welfare'' indicates aid for those in need, such as the poor or disabled.

In Europe, recognition of the need for private charity dates back at least to the Elizabethan Poor Laws of 1601. These laws, administered by leaders of the local parishes, gave relief to the sick, elderly, and poor infants. Late in the eighteenth century, the poor laws were replaced by a system that gave allowances to workers who made what was considered to be below a living wage. However, sustained welfare programs did not develop until late in the nineteenth century, in such urban centers as London and New York City, and it was not until the 1930s and 1940s that a comprehensive system of public social services was instituted. Today, such services are basically concerned with these majors area: **family** and child welfare, programs for youth, aid to the elderly, and welfare of the sick, disabled, and mentally ill.

Social services for the family are performed with the idea that the family unit is the best environment to promote social welfare. Support may include financial aid where needed and personal assistance such as marriage counseling and **family planning**, in addition to prenatal, maternal, and infant care programs. In those families who are burdened with chronic illness or like dependencies, ''home-help'' or ''homemaker'' services give household assistance. All such programs aim to strengthen the family relationship.

Child welfare is the focal point of all family welfare programs, with the aim of rendering such services within the family unit and setting. Besides family economic and health-care programs, child welfare services are especially concerned with the programs and conditions of malnutrition and widespread disease. In the late twentieth century, as more and more mothers entered or re-entered the workforce, **child care** extended to babysitting services and day-care programs.

Care of the child in need must include those in situations outside the usual family unit. The special needs of unwed mothers and their infants must be addressed, as well as the problems of children from broken or abusive families. Where appropriate, social services may, with the cooperation of legal agencies, carry out arrangements for **adoption**. Foster homes and institutional care, on a temporary or permanent basis, are provided by child welfare services to those whose home lives have been disrupted by **divorce**, abuse, or other misfortunes.

Most social services for youth are adult-supervised activities, such as scouting or athletic events, as well as personal guidance, rehabilitation, and counseling services for troubled youngsters. Scout groups, 4-H clubs, religious youth organizations, and Outward Bound programs are examples in the United States. Youth groups may be organized on a local basis depending on need. All are aimed at helping troubled or otherwise disadvantaged young people find the path to responsible **adulthood**.

The elderly comprise the largest single group using social services worldwide. Services for the elderly include visiting nurse aid, transportation, home meal delivery, reduced-costs medical supplies, and visits by ''friends'' to shut-ins or the lonely. Entertainment in the form of crafts or outings may be found at senior centers in most local centers across the country. These centers are often the site for social services to local groups based on religion, race, or language. For those elderly who are unable to care for themselves, nursing homes, which are funded by various methods, give medical and custodial care.

Much of the need for social welfare stems from illness and disability, which may profoundly affect the family unit with loss of income and emotional stress. Social programs may provide educational and counseling services to family members, psychiatric help to patients, and the establishment of half-way houses or sheltered workshops to ease the path back into the workforce for those who have suffered severe illness or **disabilities**.

Today's social focus on the mentally ill in **society** is more and more directed away from the hospital setting and toward keeping the person in the family unit or organizing local hostels that give supervision and support. Voluntary agencies and local authorities contribute both staff and volunteers for these programs. Treatment is aimed at keeping the mentally ill out of hospitals whenever possible.

SOCIAL SOLIDARITY

Social solidarity is the extent to which there is interdependence within a **society** given its social **structure**. Émile Durkheim is the most famous sociological thinker to examine issues of social solidarity. His primary empirical question was, ''What is the basis of social solidarity?''.

Durkheim published *The Division of Labor in Society* in 1893, which attempted to develop an explanation and description of the elements that create social solidarity. Durkheim asserted that the social structure, or the **division of labor**, and

occupational fragmentation would solidify society because within this structure people develop a reliance upon one another.

Durkheim described two types of social solidarity that have existed in societies, **mechanical and organic solidarity**. Mechanical solidarity is manifested in the primitive, non-industrial society. It is characterized by a simple division of labor, and individuals in it are basically alike sharing what Durkheim called the **collective conscience**, or shared ideas, **values**, and norms.

Organic solidarity, on the other hand, exists in modern industrialized society, which Durkheim argued was complicated by the division of labor. Within this society individuals are dependent upon one another but their interests are divergent. Durkheim said that individuals substitute the invisible collective conscience of this type of solidarity with a visible representation of it. This visible part can be represented with something like the law. According to Durkheim the role of these visible representations of the collective conscience is to produce social solidarity.

Each type of solidarity Durkheim described was also tied to specific consequences for a social structure. In a society governed by mechanical solidarity Durkheim saw the law, or visible manifestation of the collective conscience, as repressive, as aiming to punish. Furthermore, organic solidarity is characterized by use of restitutive laws. These laws seek to restore and make people in a society whole again. Where repressive laws shock the collective conscience, restitutive laws affect the individual conscience. Thus, the type of social solidarity in a society is directly tied to the type of collective conscience of that society. In sum, social solidarity is the glue that holds a group of individuals together and binds their common existence. This glue, however, as noted by Durkheim, may come in different forms and as such has different consequences for the individuals of a given social structure.

SOCIAL STATISTICS

Social statistics are mathematical procedures used to analyze and understand data obtained through social research. While the procedures in social statistics are largely mathematical, social statistics emphasize logic and reasoning rather than mathematical **theory** and processes.

Most research **measurement** instruments provide raw numerical **data** for social scientists to analyze and interpret. Because looking at hundreds or thousands of individual cases is time consuming and confusing, researchers use social statistics to create aggregate data from individual measurement responses. The purpose of social statistics is to assimilate large amounts of data to condense research results in an easily understood format. Often, this format is something as simple as a percentage or **mean**, though more elaborate and complex analyses are available.

There are two basic classifications of social statistics: descriptive and inferential. **Descriptive statistics** can reduce data so that they can be readily used or interpreted. Descriptive statistics can also measure associations between or among variables by calculating correlations or using regression models that predict variation of a **dependent variable** based on one or more independent variables. Other descriptive statistics allow path analyses and time series analyses that can help determine if there is a causative relationship between variables.

Inferential statistics take descriptive statistics based on sample data to estimate the characteristics of the population the sample represents. Often, researchers collect data from only a sample of a population because of limited time and resources and because inferential statistics can allow precise estimates of a population from sample data. However, even when samples are perfectly random, there is always a chance that the sample does not accurately represent the population it was drawn from. While extremely unlikely, choosing 1,000 U.S. residents at random could result, for example, in an all-female sample. Inferential statistics, therefore, are always based on probability. Though social scientists can be highly confident about generalizing research results to describe a population, they can never be absolutely certain.

SOCIAL STRATIFICATION

Social stratification refers to a system of divisions in **society** which has a number of characteristics. Stratification implies a series of layers, or strata. In the 1950s, a functional approach to stratification pervaded in the social sciences. The functional perspective saw society as an organism with several different parts, each with an equally important role to play. From this view, stratification yielded a benign, yet necessary, set of distinctions between certain groups of people. This approach gave way to a conflict perspective of stratification.

A conflict theorist sees society as a hierarchy of layers. Within each strata, the elite shrinks so that at the top, only a few are able to dominate everyone else. A conflict perspective does not see social stratification as harmonious. Instead, the conflict theorist sees social stratification serving the sole purpose of maintaining advantages for those in the upper strata through oppression and exploitation of those in lower strata. As a result, social stratification is now equated with the study of social inequality which signifies that divisions in society are inherently unequal and involve active **domination** and subordination due to systematic inequalities in social processes and social relationships.

Studies of social stratification generally work toward four related goals. First, they attempt to understand the factors contributing to the formation of class and status structures and their differentiation found cross-culturally and cross-historically. Every society has certain individuals, a set of social positions, and certain goods or rewards that are deemed valuable. Inequality is produced through mechanisms which unevenly distribute rewards across existing jobs, occupations, and social roles and then matches certain individuals to these positions. Individuals in valued positions gain access to rewards, resources, and the resulting power that are allocated to those positions.

Second, studies of social stratification attempt to understand how class and status boundaries and inequalities of con-

dition, opportunities, and outcomes are maintained and perpetuated. Several types of resources advantage those who possess them and disadvantage those who lack them. These include economic resources such as income, wealth, and **property**; political assets such as leadership and **authority**; cultural resources such as knowledge of proper language and etiquette codes; social resources such as people networks, social ties, and memberships in clubs and associations; and human resources, such as work expertise and formal education. Since those in more highly valued positions have greater possession of and control over these resources, others are excluded from the benefits they provide and remain unable to become upwardly mobile. Social and institutional processes help perpetuate inequality.

Researchers of social stratification are also interested in the patterns of advantage and disadvantage. What ascribed characteristics of individuals help determine where they will be in society and what resources and opportunities they will have? What patterns do we see within and between strata? Studies of economic class stratification are the most numerous and have the longest histories, but several other dimensions of difference have been recognized as contributing to social stratification and inequality. These other dimensions include but are not limited to gender, **race**, sexual orientation, religion, physical ability, and age. Not only has research on social stratification expanded the number of dimensions of inequality that are considered, but it has also made efforts to study the intersections of these various dimensions of inequality.

Also, research on social stratification attempts to understand its consequences, how much and in what ways certain class and status systems guide social action. How are the patterns in behavior, attitudes, and lifestyle shaped by the locations in society of certain groups of people? How often and under what conditions is upward mobility possible? Which boundaries are most permeable and which are most rigid? What types of social and institutional forces affect opportunities for transcending barriers between strata? Social stratification research is continually exploring these questions and trying to articulate new questions of interest.

SOCIAL SUPPORT

Social support refers to the functions that significant others such as family members, friends, and co-workers perform on behalf of an individual in need of assistance. Social support is a mediator within the **stress** process, which is to say that, in the research, social support has deomonstrated the potential to influence or change the effects of stressors. As a result, support from others has been found to have beneficial effects upon individuals' physical and psychological well-being. Within the sociological study of stress, social support is considered to be a coping resource. People draw upon the assistance of others when undesirable events, strains, or problems arise. More specifically, social support is a social (as opposed to personal) coping resource, as it involves one's ties to others and social interaction between the provider and the recipient of support.

Of the psychosocial resources sociologists are interested in, social support has received the most attention and investigation.

Perhaps the considerable attention results from the fact that the study of social support can be traced to one of the earliest empirical works within sociology: Durkheim's *Suicide*. This work, published in the late 1800s, documented variations in suicide rates by gender, marital status, and religion, where men, the unmarried, and Protestants were more likely (relative to women, married people, and Catholics, respectively) to kill themselves. Durkheim explained all three of these patterns with one factor: **social integration**. Women, those who are married, and Catholics had stronger ties to the larger **society**, and he believed these ties acted as a deterrent to suicide. This early work spurred the ongoing interest within sociology of how connection to others benefits well-being.

Building on Durkheim's work, sociologists have identified a number of different types of social support. Emotional support refers to providing another with comfort, care, and concern to another. Conversely, instrumental support involves the provision of more practical assistance. Instrumental support can be further divided into two sub-types: cognitive support and material support. Cognitive support pertains to information, knowledge, and advice that may be offered to someone in need, while material support includes supplying others with products, physical items, or services intended to solve specific kinds of problems. These different types of support tend to be closely related.

Social support can also be distinguished in terms of whether it is perceived or received. Perceived social support refers to the sense that one has others to turn to in times of need, while received support is assistance that is actually obtained from others. Most sociological research has examined the effects of perceived support and suggests that the perception that support is available if needed appears to have a much greater influence upon well-being than does received support.

As part of the body of research rooted within the stress process paradigm, sociologists have found that social support is positively associated with physical and psychological health. Individuals who report having at least one person to turn to when faced with a problem also tend to report better physical and mental well-being. In addition, those who report a high sense of social support tend to be better able to adjust when stressors such as losing one's spouse or job are experienced.

Social support has been shown to have a direct as well as a buffering effect upon well-being. First, researchers have demonstrated that social support directly contributes to well-being, and this direct effect operates even when stressors are not being experienced. The sense of having others to provide assistance if needed thus provides beneficial effects for health. In addition to this direct effect, social support also has a buffering effect, as support acts to decrease the negative influence of stressors upon physical and psychological health outcomes. In this way, social support buffers the harmful effects of stress-inducing events and strains upon well-being.

While sociologists have theorized a great deal about exactly why social support influences mental and physical health,

the exact mechanisms through which social support benefits well-being remain unclear. While very few studies have empirically tested possible mechanisms, sociologists believe that social support benefits health through changing harmful behaviors, restoring self-esteem, and/or providing a sense of calm. These explanations, though tentative, offer behavioral, psychological, and physiological reasons for the benefits of social support.

Sociologists have found that the distribution of social support varies across different groups, divided on the basis of marital status, gender, age, and **socioeconomic status**. Studies indicate that married people and women tend to report higher levels of perceived social support, compared to non-married people and men. Sociological research also suggests that perceived support decreases with age and increases with socioeconomic status.

SOCIAL WORK

Social work generally means the activities of those who carry out a country's social service or welfare programs. In the late nineteenth century, the need for **social services** began to be seriously considered, especially in Great Britain, Germany, and the United States. In such cities as London, New York City, and Boston, charity organization societies were founded to develop a system of social services. This activity led to the founding of schools of social work. As more and more nations during the twentieth century recognized their responsibility to provide aid, social work became an organized profession whose goals are to improve **society** through administrating programs to citizens who are ill, disadvantaged, elderly, too young to care for themselves, or in financial or other need.

In both the United States and Great Britain, the so-called settlement movement drew voluntary workers interested in easing the suffering of society's poor and disadvantaged. The leader in settlement work was Samuel A. Barnett, who, in 1884, founded Toynbee Hall, named after social reformer Arnold Toynbee. Barnett and his wife invited Oxford and Cambridge students to spend holidays in this neighborhood house in a depressed area of London so that they might learn about social conditions. From this, Toynbee Hall became a center for improving conditions and welfare in the neighborhood. During a European trip, American **Jane Addams** visited Toynbee Hall. Upon her return, she and partner Ellen Gates Starr founded **Hull House** in Chicago, one of the first social settlements in North America. Among its services were a day nursery, boarding rooms for working girls, a gymnasium, educational courses, and classes in arts and crafts. In addition, Hull House became a training school for social workers.

Today, the duties of social workers include community assistance at many levels, social care assistants, helpers in the home, day-care supervisors, those who deliver in-home meals, and a variety of therapists and psychologists. Probation officers are social workers with a special link to the court system. Social workers go to homes and schools, work in hospitals and local service centers, provide counseling, and may have exclusive authority for placing children in **foster care** or adopting families.

Social casework, an important part of the job for social workers, stems from the medical almoners as far back as the thirteenth century. Almoners were designated officers responsible for giving alms to the poor. They were generally connected with a religious institution. The office of grand almoner was established in France in 1486 and abolished in 1870. The office still exists in Great Britain where the high almoner distributes royal alms on Maundy, or Holy, Thursday, the Thursday before Easter. Modern casework requires the social worker to give counseling services to the individual or **family** in need or distress, to ascertain the type of service needed by the person or persons, and to see that the service is adequately provided.

There is great diversity in the training and careers of social workers. Therapists and psychologists involved in social work acquire the same general education as those outside the field. In such countries as the United States, Great Britain, Canada, and Japan, the would-be social worker may earn bachelor, master, and doctorate degrees in the field at schools within the higher education system. In other nations, France and Sweden, for instance, the aspiring social worker attends an institution outside the regular college/university system. And just as there is much diversity in their training, so there is great diversity and complexity in the roles that social workers play in the community. As modern society accepts more responsibility for the welfare of its needy, ill, or otherwise disadvantaged citizens, so the role of the social worker has broadened in scope and responsibility. In large cities such as New York City, with a broad and varied population, one social worker within the system may have almost total responsibility for the guidance and welfare of a child as he or she progresses through infant, youth, and adult programs.

In the United States, as well as some European and Asian nations, formal voluntary and private social agencies receive direct or indirect grants from the government. Most of these agencies are registered as charities (voluntary) and companies (private). They have paid career staff who must work within the statutes of the city, state, etc. Even with government backing, these agencies could not cope with the overwhelming demand for services were it not for the informal care that is given by neighborhood and community organizations. Professional staff often train these informal-care workers.

SOCIALISM

Socialism is a political and economic system in which the distribution and use of property and capital are determined by the common good and individual rights must be subordinated to this cause. The term was first applied in Great Britain and France in the 1820s, and in 1841 the followers of Robert Owen officially adopted the name of Socialists. The socialist movement, however, had been under way in France since the end of the eighteenth century when François-Noël Babeuf had organized the "Conspiracy of Equals" only to be executed by the ruling Directory.

Socialist **theory** is historically linked to many Utopian writers, going back as far as Plato and, later, Sir Thomas More.

The idea that humankind has always been moving toward a point in which the world's wealth will be shared and everyone will be free from want has been a seductive one for thousands of years. In addition, a strong tradition of essentially socialist thought exists within many Christian denominations. Jesus' teachings were often interpreted as a call to share with one's neighbor, and churches had long been active in **community** service and, in some cases, renunciation of personal accumulation of wealth. But with the French Revolution organized movements began to implement these theories in a broad political context.

The **Industrial Revolution** in the early nineteenth century swelled the ranks of socialist theorists. As the formerly voiceless lower classes began to move from the countryside into the **cities**, they began to feel a sense of power in their numbers. Here was a large, receptive audience for the ideas of radical political thinkers. Technology was increasing food production and distribution; it became possible to foresee a day in which there would be enough for everyone and competing for land and food would no longer be required. The average worker still had little **leisure** time and faced extreme hardships, but a new way of life seemed inevitable.

This new **idealism** of technology as the liberator of the proletariat formed much of the basis for the *Communist Manifesto*, written in 1848 by **Karl Marx** and **Friedrich Engels**, which greatly altered the existing ideas about socialism. This document split from the Utopian version of socialism as the ideal **society** and argued that it was merely the inevitable result of class struggle through the ages, culminating in the Industrial Revolution.

The political revolution envisioned by Marx and Engels failed to take hold, but socialism had made inroads into every industrialized nation and was a major political force from that time. Marx's writings inspired the creation of the Social Democratic Party which became immensely powerful in Europe. The party, and its many offshoots, believed in democratic elections and won power in several European countries after World War I, which saw the end of monarchies in Germany and Austria-Hungary. At the same time, however, Russia was seized by a communist totalitarian regime which took socialist ideas to anti-democratic extremes and heightened fear of all leftist politics in the democratic nations. Under **communism** the state was the sole holder of property, and individual rights were not merely downgraded but abolished. The state became all, and in most places, even religion was banned.

In the United States the Socialist Party also reached its peak around the time of WWI. During the war, measures were taken to silence Socialists who tended to be against the war effort. These measures, along with post-war prosperity, lessened the party's influence until the Great Depression of the 1930s. Democratic President Franklin Roosevelt's New Deal borrowed a great many socialist principles to bring the country out of the depression. The government regulated the economy in new ways and implemented strong measures to cut **unemployment** and fight **poverty**. These measures were supported during such dire circumstances, but the idea of a truly socialist government was not acceptable to the American people. When the

Eugene V. Debs and the American Socialist Party attained great popularity around the time of WWI *(The Library of Congress).*

economy recovered, capitalism ruled once more. Nevertheless, such measures as Social Security, unemployment insurance, and federally-insured bank deposits survived and became an almost universally accepted part of American life, even as the Cold War against communism dragged on.

In the 1980s and 1990s the Soviet bloc of Eastern Europe was broken, and **capitalism** also made strong inroads into China. Communism was discredited as untenable as well as immoral. Capitalism, as much as **democracy**, was seen as the victor in the Cold War which was a simultaneous blow to socialist ideals. Socialist parties survive, and even hold power, in much of Europe, but their policies are much less sweeping than those developed by the first theorists. Socialism, in most places, has been diluted to programs that benefit everyone, including the wealthy, such as social security and **medicare**, or to the fulfilling of the most basic needs of food, shelter, and **employment**. The capitalist ideal of free markets and limitless accumulation of wealth is, if anything, stronger worldwide than in the infancy of socialism. This capitalism has a new face, though, in the opportunity now available to the proletariat of two hundred years ago.

SOCIALIZATION

Socialization is a lifelong process by which individuals learn attitudes, values, and behaviors appropriate to social life. Socialization ensures the acquisition and internalization of **norms**, which serves two functions: individuals develop a social **identity**, and social continuity is maintained from one generation to the next. Despite emphasizing certain societal patterns, socialization is a unique experience for each individual that is affected by one's family, peers, school, **race**, class, gender and myriad other social factors.

In 1919, Edward Ross wrote, "the socializing process is that growth in the closeness and extent of similarity which multiplies sympathies, promotes cooperation, and makes for harmony among men." The structural-functionalist perspective argues that socialization primarily entails the learning of

social norms. Parsons and Bales (1955) argued that socialization involves both integration and differentiation. This view is less popular in **sociology**, however, than the symbolic interactionist argument that maintains (largely from the writings of G. H. Mead) that the self is developed in the context of personal interaction and that individuals' self-perceptions are largely based on how they believe themselves to be viewed by others.

Socialization is acquired through several different agents. The first, known as primary socialization, is predominantly associated with childhood and includes **family** members, most notably parents. During this time basic notions of **values**, beliefs, manners, public behavior, and self-conceptions are acquired, and gender and age roles are also learned. The second means of socialization is secondary socialization, a period whose beginning is most often associated with school and is largely influenced by peer groups and continues throughout **adulthood**. During this time knowledge and skills are acquired, along with new understanding of the social world. Socialization is a fluid, constantly evolving process; no definitive age or event marks its beginning or end.

Socializing Agents

Socialization is an ongoing process. We are socialized in a variety of settings and by a variety of people, in both intentional and unintentional ways, and with both specific and general goals. The different individuals and groups by which we are socialized are considered agents of socialization. In very early childhood, parents, siblings, other relatives or caretakers are the primary agents of socialization. As children age, they may start to spend more time with other children. Peers are another set of socializing agents. Once children enter school, this new context opens the door for other groups of people who **influence** development. Teachers and classmates become new agents of socialization. Later in life the workplace becomes a context of socialization. Here fellow employees, employers, customers, and clients all become socializing agents. If individuals get married, their spouses and in-laws are socializing agents. If individuals become parents, their children become agents of socialization. All forms of the media, although unique in that there is not an actual person or **group** of people with whom to interact, are socializing agents. These contexts and agents of socialization are overlapping rather than mutually exclusive. Parents and the media may be socializing agents throughout life whereas elementary school teachers or a boss at a first job will have only temporary effects. Peer groups change as people age and navigate different life transitions. Socializing agents are also intersecting. Parents and teachers may guide each others' influences through communication. Parents may also monitor or control what children are exposed to through the media or with which friends they are allowed to interact. It is also important to note that the influences of socializing agents may sometimes be complementary and may sometimes be competing. For example, school-age children may feel competing pressures from parents and peers. Additionally, socializing agents do not all have the same intensity

of influence, and the amount of influence they do have may be different for different individuals depending on circumstances. A last important aspect of socialization is that just as people are socialized by socializing agents, they simultaneously socialize these socializing agents. Children socialize their parents as parents socialize them. People socialize their friends as they are socialized by them. Thus, socialization, with the exception of the media, is a reciprocal process.

Society

Although used quite regularly in discussions of the state, structure, individual behavior, and **sociology** in general, the term ''society'' rarely is defined or used in a consistent fashion. Generally society refers to a group of people who share a common **culture**, occupy a particular region or area, identify themselves as a unified entity, and live relatively independent of groups outside of the social area. Society also refers to the boundaries of nation-states which separate one group from another. Societies are the largest types of human groupings and typically arise on the basis of common heritage or a shared culture and are maintained and reinforced through consistent, sustained patterns of social interaction among the members.

Because of the lack of a consistent, reified usage of this term, society is often used as an abstract categorization that refers in a general way to some complex organization (**American society**, post-modern society). Although this may be the most consistent of use of the term, it also tends to be quite problematic. These utilizations of 'society' fail to recognize the complex diversity that often exists within these organizations. The rampant use of the abstract definition also leads to claims that society is actually a useless term that has only been sustained to refer to aspects of social life that we either do not or wish not to fully understand.

The concept that society may be an entity apart from the state emerged when thinkers such as **John Locke** began to differentiate between laws of nature, laws of the **church**, and laws enacted through contracts formed with the state. Later romantic philosophers began to stress the integrated whole of society. This conceptualization saw society less as an individualized, rational contract among persons and more as an integrated, organic being which envelopes the practices, **norms**, culture and traditions of the entire group. Sociologically these conceptions of society served as influences on the development of functionalist work on society.

During the mid–1800s, **Karl Marx** wrote about society as constantly evolving and developing through the interrelations among the elements of society. For Marx, all social behavior must be considered in relation to the machination of change within the social setting as well as to the efforts of individuals in meeting their basic material needs. This primary economic goal is made problematic by the division of individuals into social classes and the exploitation of the workers by the wealthy. In this way, society exists within the relations among social groups and is based upon inevitable historical change and economic competition. Marx's work serves as the basis for many **conflict theory** perspectives on society within sociology.

With the dawn of sociology as a discipline, early sociologists began to study society as an independent reality that exists and has an impact on lesser structures within the social system. Within this **paradigm**, Émile Durkheim wrote of society as more than simply an intricately woven collection of individual ideas. Durkheim conceived as society as *sui generis* (loosely translated as "something in and of itself"), or consisting of a set of external, constraining independent forces, known as social facts, which exist independent of the wishes of individuals within the group.

Max Weber based his conception of society on the social relationships that are prerequisites for the existence of **social order**. Weber saw relationships among society members taking either a rational orientation toward an individualized society or a more communal orientation that would result in communal attitudes and solidarity among the members.

George Herbert Mead viewed society as a social process arising through interaction. Mead developed a theory of how the self develops socially in individuals. Here, society is a symbolic process that arises through the adoption of socially learned roles and identities. In Mead's society as process, people adopt roles, understand the expectations which others within the social group have for someone holding a particular role, and act to conform to those expectations thereby reinforcing the expectations. This, in turn, transforms others' expectations into actual aspects of society. Mead's work is considered the benchmark work in symbolic interactionist theory.

During the twentieth century, these conceptualizations have evolved and changed form, but nearly all still exist in some way. Generally, sociologists view society as being inseparable from the culture it supports. Society consists of the structures of society (patterns of social behavior) which give rise to social institutions. These institutions meet the needs of individuals living in the society, thereby allowing the patterned behavior to continue and the society to survive.

SOCIETY FOR APPLIED SOCIOLOGY (SAS)

The Society for Applied Sociology (SAS) is an international professional organization dedicated to the advancement of applied sociological knowledge in a wide variety of settings. Founded in 1978, SAS is regarded by sociologists as the authority on harnessing sociological knowledge for practical use. In order to improve global communication among applied sociologists, one of the principal aims of the SAS is to provide a forum for sociologists and others interested in applying sociological knowledge. SAS welcomes applied sociologists from all walks of life, from the undergraduate or graduate student enrolled in **sociology** programs to academic or professional social scientists. The SAS hosts an annual conference to provide an opportunity for applied sociologists to present research to colleagues in an informal setting. Presentations typically involve didactic seminars, thematic speakers and panels, professional development workshops, and organized critical social issues sessions.

SAS publications include a newsletter *The Useful Sociologist* distributed three times a year to members and a professional magazine *Social Insight: Knowledge at Work* produced annually to reach professionals and students inside and outside sociology. Innovative applications of sociological knowledge designed to produce positive **social change** and groundbreaking training techniques for applied researchers are captured in the *Journal of Applied Sociology,* a professional journal published yearly.

SAS is an association comprised of more than 500 leading social researchers representing all 50 states and 14 countries worldwide. A board of directors governs SAS, with elected officers for the positions of president, president elect, vice-president, vice-president elect, secretary, treasurer, and six members-at-large. Members of SAS strive to enhance the understanding of the interrelationship between sociological knowledge and sociological practice, and to increase the usefulness and effectiveness of applied sociological research and training.

SOCIOBIOLOGY

Sociobiology is one of many theories, or frameworks of thought, used to describe human behavior in **society**. Sociobiology is a recent social theory introduced by Edward O. Wilson (1929-) in the mid-1970s. Wilson is a biologist and an ethologist (one who studies animal groups in their natural environment) educated at the University of Alabama and Harvard University. He has extensively researched ants and other social insects, applying the results of his research to humans and other animals and creating the **theory** of sociobiology. His theory was first introduced in 1975 with the publication of *Sociobiology: The New Synthesis.*

Sociobiology joins aspects of biological theory and sociological theory to create a separate theory that attempts to explains human behavior. Sociobiologists see a parallel between human behavior and animal behavior. It is through studying animal behavior that studies of human behavior can be enriched. Sociobiology in general has not been well received among sociologists. The theory has had better reception among psychologists, biologists, and some anthropologists. **Sociology** has a passing interest in the theory, but in general does not view it as a compelling answer to the question of what drives human behavior. This is not to say that no sociologists favor the theory, but the majority of sociologists find other theories more suitable for explaining human behavior.

Sociobiology is a theoretical framework which considers biology to be the fundamental cause of human behavior and it is this that affects how we establish **culture**. Sociobiology systematically studies human behavior in biological terms. Sociobiologists use theories of evolution and natural selection to draw conclusions about behavior. The theory views biological traits as having the primary influence on behavior. Wilson believes that humans are born with traits and characteristics which profoundly influence behavior. **Courtship** rituals, sexual unions, collective actions and even the psychological foundations of behavior are addressed by this theory.

Courtship rituals, for example, are explained differently by sociologists and biologists. Many non-human animals con-

duct highly ritualized ceremonies in order to attract mates. These can take the form of a dance, a colorful display of feathers, or a mating song. Sociobiologists argue that humans too perform their own brand of courtship rituals. Eye contact, flirting, touching, and laughing constitute part of our mating **ritual**. Humans of all races, ethnicities and cultures conduct mating rituals that are similar. The explanation for this, in sociobiological terms, is that humans are equipped with instincts that drive courtship behavior.

The ongoing debate between nature and nurture in regard to behavior is also known as biology versus **socialization**. The debate centers on whether human behaviors are governed strictly by genetic makeup or by environment and learned behavior. Humans are genetically programmed to have a particular hair, eye, and skin color, why then can they not be programmed to have traits that govern behavior? Take the example of a person who commits crimes in society. Does an individual's genes (nature) predispose him or her to commit crimes, or is it his or her upbringing and socialization process in society (nurture)? The discipline of sociology generally sides with the nurture portion of the debate. Most sociologists believe that it is largely socialization and environment which dictate behaviors. Proponents of sociobiology, however, generally claim that nature primarily dictates human behavior. Not enough is known about biology or behavior to provide conclusive evidence to answer this important question.

SOCIOCULTURAL ANTHROPOLOGY

Sociocultural anthropology is a subfield of anthropology. It is the comparative study of the social, symbolic, and material lives of human societies and cultures. Broadly taken, it is the study of the human condition. The other three subfields of anthropology are physical or biological anthropology, prehistoric archaeology, and linguistic anthropology.

Sociocultural anthropology is a combination of **sociology**, anthropology, and **cultural studies**. Sociologists tend to study larger, modern societies, whereas anthropologists tend to study smaller, pre-industrial societies. Sociology is usually considered a science because it uses both quantitative and qualitative methods, whereas sociocultural anthropology has not traditionally been considered a science because it relied on supposedly non-scientific methods (ethnography and ethnology). Combining the two disciplines involves using diverse **research methods** to increase our understanding of human behavior.

Sociocultural anthropologists originally developed the term ''culture,'' the central concept in anthropology. **Culture** is the learned and shared behaviors, beliefs, knowledge, rituals, customs, and **values** of a group of people. Culture is learned, based on symbols, constantly adaptive, and is not the same as nature (i.e., each culture has its own ways of adapting to natural needs—the processes of eating, mating, clothing and sheltering oneself differ from culture to culture). Sociocultural anthropologists strive to maintain a high level of **cultural relativism** (judging a culture by its own standards and on its own merits) and avoid ethnocentrism (judging a culture by one's own cultural standards, not the standards of that culture).

Sociocultural anthropologists research diverse topics. They traditionally focused on small, non-Western cultures, and between the late nineteenth century and the mid-twentieth centuries, most anthropological studies looked at the diversity of human life before Europeanization. Cultures, kinship groups and systems, legal and political systems, different conceptions and forms of **deviance**, and various rituals were the major topics investigated. Among the ritualized behaviors studied has been music, dance, religion, witchcraft and magic in different societies and ethnic groups, and the development of mythologies and other ideas about supernatural phenomena. In addition, they have studied courting, mating, **marriage**, and sexual patterns.

But in recent decades, the research has expanded to include the customs, cultures, and social lives of people in large, modern **cities**. Research has begun to include issues such as the social organization of economics, poverty, gender, and race/ethnicity in industrialized countries; law and social change in modern societies; life in urban centers; and the impacts of **divorce** and separation on different cultures. Researchers also concentrate on topics such as **health care**, environmental issues and safety, education, and the development of megalopolises.

There are currently three major debates in sociocultural anthropology: biological **determinism** vs. cultural constructionism; emics (how members of a culture view their culture) vs. etics (how outsiders see a culture); and individual agency vs. structurism. Although these issues do divide the discipline to some extent, most researchers agree that these are the most important topics to study.

Although anthropology has not traditionally been considered a 'science', there are specific research methods associated with it. The primary ones are **ethnography** (a firsthand, detailed description of a culture based on personal observation) and ethnology (a **cross-cultural analysis** of a specific topic in several cultures, using ethnographic research techniques). These methods are also known as participant observation, a process through which researchers become intimately involved in the lives of the people they are studying. Researchers live with their subjects, get to know them personally, participate in group life, and spend anywhere from weeks to years studying the details of their day-to-day lives. Along with this formal and informal observation, researchers often use extensive, usually unstructured, interviews with individuals of the group, information from which is combined with field notes taken by the researcher.

However, as research has extended to complex, industrialized societies, sociocultural anthropologists have begun to use other, more structured methods. Many of these have come from increased integration with the fields of sociology and **psychology**. These methods include more structured interviews with larger samples; complex psychological tests that focus on discerning the cultural and individual aspects of personality; and the use of more qualitative surveys, analyzed by computer applications, to examine the more objective aspects of societies and cultures. Historically, sociocultural anthropologists worked alone in the field, but these expanded research

SOCIOECONOMIC STATUS

Socioeconomic **status** refers to any measure that takes into consideration combinations of indicators including education, income, and occupation. These measures can be used to classify individuals, families, and households. Socioeconomic status is a commonly used measure in the social sciences. Such a measure has also become a standard control **variable** in research spanning all areas. It attempts to mark not only economic status but also social standing, hence the term socioeconomic status. While commonly used interchangeably with occupational prestige, the two measures are computed differently and are connected to entirely distinct dimensions. Thus, the two concepts are not always positively correlated. Individuals can have low socioeconomic status but be in jobs evaluated highly. Conversely, individuals can have high socioeconomic status and be in jobs considered low in terms of prestige. Another difference between the two concepts is that socioeconomic status can characterize multiple units of analysis such as individuals, families, and households. **Occupational prestige** characterizes individuals.

It is important to note that socioeconomic status is always a composite of two or more indicators. Education, income, and occupation are the three variables from which these combinations are created. Socioeconomic status requires a combination of variables because these variables can vary from one another. Therefore, no one variable can represent socioeconomic status. For example, college professors make relatively little money compared to other occupations (ex., computer programmer). Yet, to be a college professor, one must first earn a Ph.D. A computer programmer may only need a Bachelor's degree to find a well-paying job. The college professor and the computer programmer are both white-collar workers. Therefore, labeling these two individuals solely according to a typology of occupations makes them appear quite similar. However, labeling them according to either level of education or income causes their relative positions to shift, the college professor being ranked higher with respect to education and the computer programmer ranked higher with respect to income. Examples of how these indicators vary from one another are not hard to find. Using only one of the three indicators to compare individuals, families, or households gives a false representation. Combining indicators and providing each individual with a composite score that takes the three variables into account is much more useful.

SOCIOLINGUISTICS

Sociolinguistics is the systematic study of **language** as a social phenomenon. A largely interdisciplinary field, social linguistics, which has been traditionally associated with anthropology, has come under the influence of such fields as communication **theory**, urban studies, social **psychology**, and sociology. Although linguistics as a social concept was addressed by several early sociologists such as **George Herbert Mead** and linguists including Antoine Meillet, during the first half of the twentieth century the social sciences and linguistics remained distinctly separate areas of study. Linguistics was based on understanding language as a code, a concept introduced by Chomsky. The role of the linguist was to decipher the code through the use of grammatical rules. A pure form of language, or idealized language, was understood to be within the muddle language used in everyday life. A growing interest in the social aspects of language on the part of both social scientists and linguists during the 1960s resulted in a new approach that subsequently became known as sociolinguistics. Sociolinguists wished to account for the social and cultural rules applied to language, thus accounting for the actual speaker, rather than an idealized form, as the primary giver of meaning.

Sociolinguistic study attempts to answer numerous questions regarding the relationship between language and **society**. In the introduction to *Sociolinguistics: A Reader* (1997), Nikolas Coupland and Adam Jaworski suggested a variety of main concerns addressed within the broad field of social linguistics, including: How are forms of speech and patterns of communication distributed across time and space? How do individuals and social groups define themselves in and through language? How do communities differ in the ''ways of speaking'' they have adopted? And how is language involved in social conflicts and tensions? In the study of society's impact on language and language's impact on society, a variety of theoretical and methodological differences exist.

In his highly regarded book *Sociolinguistic Patterns* (1972), William Labov addressed the term, sociolinguistics, as redundant, saying, ''I have resisted the term *sociolinguistics* for many years, since it implies that there can be a successful linguistic theory or practice which is not social.'' According to Dell Hymes in *Foundations in Sociolinguistics: An Ethnographic Approach* (1974), no single definition of sociolinguistics will satisfy the multiple manners in which it is interpreted by social scientists. Hymes suggested that the field can be categorized based on the starting assumption that sociolinguistics is defined as either ''(1) the social as well as the linguistic; (2) socially realistic linguistics; [or] (3) socially constituted linguistics.''

Defined as ''the social as well as the linguistic,'' sociolinguistics is conceived as an application-based method that tends to lack theoretical goals. For example, social linguistics can be used to study the role of language and the use of language in **social problems** and issues. Seen as dealing with concerns beyond the scope of traditional linguists, such an approach poses no challenge to the theory-laden field of general linguistics. The second conceptualization of sociolinguistics as ''socially realistic linguistic'' begins from the same theoretical foundation as normal linguistics. Often asking the same questions, socially realistic linguistics adds to and challenges existing linguistic study. ''Socially constituted linguistics'' is

theoretically unique from the previous two orientations and from normal linguistics. Whereas linguistics most often employs a structuralist perspective that begins with language structure and moves to meaning, socially constituted linguistics is underwritten by an interactionist perspective that moves from referential meaning based on social and cultural context to language structure. Hymes argues that only sociolinguistics defined as socially constituted can fully address the complex interplay between language and its use.

Sociolinguists are concerned with studying the use of language within groups. However, the outcome of such studies differs depending on what is understood to be the primary unit within groups. Micro-sociolinguists begin from the theoretical basis that the individual is the defining unit of all groups. Groups, in fact, are social constructs populated by individuals. Therefore, drawing heavily from psychology and **social psychology**, micro-sociolinguists focus on the individual's speech act, accounting for variables such as status, attitude, goal, and intimacy between the speaker and listener. Macro-sociolinguists consider the social **group**, rather than the individual, as the primary unit. Accordingly, macro-sociolinguists study the distribution of differences within language use across such social variables as age, **ethnicity**, sex, education, and so on. Seeking the **correlation** between social demographics and speech patterns, macro-level social linguistics is influenced by sociological theory and **methodology**. Micro-level sociolinguistical studies has increased tremendously since the beginning of the 1970s. Macro-level also has seen growth but at a slower rate. Remaining for sociolinguists are many theoretical and methodological questions that have yet to be fully understood and explained.

Sociological Theory

Like the physical sciences, **sociology** strives for scientific explorations, descriptions, explanations, and predictions about the phenomenal processes that occur in the world around us. Sociological investigations focus on developing systematic understandings of the structures and processes of human social life. These investigations include the study of human behavior and action, social interaction, group dynamics, the principles of social organization and integration, social and cultural differences, inter-group conflict, and geo-political struggles and transformations. Sociological **theory** is the guiding framework for investigations into these social phenomena.

Sociological theory can be characterized by four fundamental attributes. First, it is a set of abstract statements about the relationships among social phenomena. These statements are often written in the form of propositions. For example, one abstract proposition might read: The more frequently individuals interact with one another, the more that solidarity will develop among them. Second, these statements are testable through the application of the scientific method and are subject to empirical scrutiny. For instance, in the example above, the two concepts, the ''frequency of interaction'' and the ''degree of solidarity'' can both be measured, and the extent of their re-

lationship empirically determined with a specified degree of accuracy. Third, each tradition of sociological theory embodies a set of epistemological assumptions about the social world. While some theories might give priority to social interaction or **social solidarity**, as in the example above, others might emphasize economic, gender, or ethnic differences among individuals in producing social solidarity. Still others might focus on the effects of social structures or social organizations on social interaction and group life. Finally, sociological theories are intended to reflect the search for social patterns and the regularities that occur in the social world. Thus, following the example above, sociologists guided by their theories would explore the patterned relationships that occur between social interaction and social solidarity. In short, sociological theory can be defined as a set of abstract, testable statements that embody a set of epistemological assumptions and seek to illuminate the patterns of the social world.

Four distinct, yet often overlapping, traditions of theory have emerged within sociology. The first cohesive body of sociological theory was functionalism. Functional theories emerged from the collective works of August Comte (1798-1857), Émile Durkheim (1858-1917), **Herbert Spencer** (1820-1903), and later Talcott Parsons (1902-1979). Very generally, these functional theories focused on the forces of cohesion and systemic integration within societies. **Functionalism** was the dominant theoretical perspective until the 1960s when the interests of sociology turned more towards exploring conflict, inequality, revolution, and the dynamics of social interaction. Here, the more marginalized traditions of **conflict theory**, symbolic interaction, and social **exchange theory** became prominent. Conflict theories, inspired by the works of **Karl Marx** (1818-1883) and **Max Weber** (1864-1920), sought to explain the systems of inequality, oppression, discrimination, power disparity, and exploitation that develop within and between societies. Following the work of **George Herbert Mead** (1863-1931), the tradition of symbolic interaction emerged as a micro-level alternative to the more macro-level functional and conflict theories. It emphasized the negotiation of meaning, the emergence of the social self, the dynamics of interaction, and the relevance of **language** and symbols in social life. Finally, social exchange theory developed from the theories of Georg Simmel (1858-1918) exploring the effects of the exchange of resources between individuals and groups. Exchange theories endeavored to explain the importance of commitment, reciprocity, social **status**, and power in social relationships. The development of each of these four traditions continues today and within the discipline no one tradition dominates.

The development of these sociological theories typically occurs at three different **levels of analysis**: the micro-level, the macro-level, and the meso-level. Micro-sociological theories focus on encounters between individuals or among small groups. These theories typically emphasize the situational factors that drive social interaction, the negotiation of meaning, the expression and communication of emotions, self-based processes, and the dynamics of social groups. Macro-sociological theories are oriented towards societal-level phenomena and focus on the integration, change, and conflict that

occur at the societal and inter-societal level. Some macro-theoretical approaches attempt to describe the internal dynamics of societal cohesion and conflict, while others emphasize the patterns of warfare, exploitation, trade, and communication that occur between nation-states. Still other macro-level theories focus on social revolutions, state-breakdowns, and the collapse of complex societies. Finally, meso-sociological theories are commonly referred to as "theories of the middle range," focus on social phenomena that are not reducible to the dynamics of social situations and are not broad enough to explain macro-level or societal phenomenon. Instead, meso-level theories focus on large-scale social aggregates such as formal organizations, systems of stratification, and social institutions like law, the **family** and religion.

One enduring problem within sociological theory is developing a link between the micro and macro levels of theory. A debate has generated many theoretical models—Anthony Giddens' structuration theory and Pierre Bourdieu's theory of habitus and field are two widely used, contemporary examples—but there is little agreement about how to establish a micro-to-macro link.

Some debate in sociology concerns whether sociological theories should be strictly oriented towards scientific approaches. Feminist, critical, and postmodern theories have all posed specific challenges to the legitimacy of scientific approaches in sociology. These traditions of theory generally reflect attempts to explore the **domination**, oppression, and subjugation of marginalized social groups like women, ethnic minorities, citizens of non-industrial nations, and those without economic or political power. These traditions of theory have more humanistic, as opposed to scientific, concerns and are often referred to as "social theories" and not as "sociological theories" proper. While some overlap between both sociological and social theories exist, they are clearly divided in their perceptions of the role of the scientific method in investigating the social world.

SOCIOLOGISTS FOR WOMEN IN SOCIETY (SWS)

Sociologists for Women in Society (SWS) is an international organization of national and international sociologists, social scientists, and students whose goal is to promote and disseminate research about women in society as well as to maximize the effectiveness of and professional opportunities for women in **sociology**. SWS is dedicated to exploring the contributions which sociology can, does, and should make to the investigation of an improvement in the **status** of women in all societies.

SWS promotes the special needs of women in sociology to professional organizations, especially the **American Sociological Association (ASA)**, and has organized a job market service to bring together applicants and potential employers. SWS established a committee on **discrimination** to offer advice, organizational support and financial aid to women who pursue cases charging sex discrimination in the workplace.

SWS publishes the quarterly journal *Gender and Society and Network News*, a quarterly newsletter to members. SWS

maintains a website: (www.socwomen.org). As a service to the social science **community**, SWS sponsors an annual Feminist Lectureship and several awards honoring new feminist scholarship, including the Rosenblum Scholarship for the Study of Women and Cancer. SWS supports an ASA minority scholarship. SWS meets twice annually, once concurrent to the ASA conference in August and once each winter.

As a watchdog to the ASA, the **organization** has promoted services for women such as childcare during annual meetings, assistance in publishing articles, the establishment of the Sex and Gender section of the ASA, and the inclusion of feminists (both male and female) on the editorial boards of social science journals. From its beginnings in 1970 as a counter-convention to the dominant organization for sociologists, SWS now has about one thousand members and twenty local affiliated groups.

SOCIOLOGY

Sociology is the social science which studies human behavior in society. Sociology seeks to understand patterns of behavior within **society**, and how culture and social institutions shape human behavior. Economics, political science, anthropology, and **psychology** are also social sciences. Each of these focuses on human behavior and how it is related to society. Economists seek to understand production and distribution of goods and services. Political scientists center their attention on **government** and politics. Anthropologists focus on understanding **culture** in variously defined and developed societies. Psychologists seek to understand mental processes and problems of individuals how people cope in relationships. Sociologists explore the social consequences of politics, government, and distribution of goods and services. Sociologists wish to understand how culture dictates daily interactions and how people adjust to difficulties of life. Sociology combines all of the disciplines together, and studies human behavior on a large scale.

Sociologists follow the scientific method when doing research, just as physicists and chemists do. The goals of scientific research include explaining why phenomena occur, making generalizations from individual cases and using data collected from wider groups. Most important, sociologists try to understand the social fabric in order to predict and perhaps improve the future.

The science of sociology developed out of the pervasive social changes of the **Industrial Revolution**. The actual term "sociology" was originally coined by Auguste Comte (1798-1857) who was interested in applying scientific method to the study of society. Comte wished to study society not to fix what was wrong but to learn about it. Comte's ideas came from a time when people were beginning to accept **positivism** (belief in scientific explanations instead of theological or metaphysical ones). Comte believed that society operates according to particular laws, just as the physical world operates according to laws of gravity and nature.

From Comte's basic idea of social research, three men made their contribution to **sociological theory**. **Karl Marx**

(1818-1883), Émile Durkheim (1858-1917), and **Max Weber** (1864-1920) constructed theories to explain how and why society functions. These theories have been drawn from extensively and continuously over the years. These theorists laid the framework for the entire discipline of sociology. New theories have sprung forth from their work, but current research confirms their approaches.

Several women and minorities have made their names in sociology as well. **Jane Addams** (1860-1935) was the first and only sociologist to be awarded the Nobel Peace Prize (1931) for her work with **urban sociology**. Addams also established a center for reform in Chicago where sociologists worked on problems using sociological **theory** and the scientific method. **Harriet Martineau** (1802-1876) contributed to the field of sociology by translating Comte's writings from French to English. She also worked to eliminate slavery and advance the position of women. W. E. B. Du Bois (1868-1963), an African American, recognized racial inequality, spoke out against it, and became a founding member of the National Association for the Advancement of Colored People (NAACP). Du Bois also established the nation's second Department of Sociology at Atlanta University (the first Department of Sociology was at the University of Chicago). Sociologists research religious cults, domestic violence, **race** relations, and **poverty**. They may specialize in **criminology**, **social psychology**, work, organizations, or inequalities related to race, class, and gender. An especially new area in sociology is the study of behavior patterns linked to computers and the **internet**.

In **applied sociology**, the scientific method is combined with social theory to provide solutions for problems. For example, if a city wanted a new type of water treatment center that would benefit the public but would required increased taxes for residents, sociologists might be employed to find out how individuals feel about the new plan. Sociologists use surveys, interviews, and existing **data** to find answers.

Sociology of Development

Sociology of development, or the sociology of economic change, is concerned with the social and economic transformations associated with industrialization in the Third World. After World War II, sociologists in this area explored the preconditions to successful industrialization in these nations and the impact of industrialization. Some early work in the field was strongly influenced by **functionalism**, and developed in the context of the Cold War. This early work, known as the modernization school, posits that all nations follow similar paths to economic development. W. W. Rostow's (1950) book on stages of development argued that some nations have yet to reach the take-off stage, where industrialization, urbanization, and rapid cultural change transform them. As with all modernization scholarship, it was assumed that the impact of industrialization was largely positive, and the preconditions for it were greater contact with the cultural values and economic expertise of advanced countries. In this case, it was also assumed that economic development would accompany modernizing social, cultural, and political transformations.

Developed in the 1960s, **dependency theory** represents a challenge to modernization **theory**. Influenced by **Marxist sociology**, and inspired by the apparent successes of socialist experiments like those in Cuba and in Tanzania, these scholars pointed to the negative impact of the relationship between industrialized nations and the Third World. Dependency scholars argued that because of the external ties of Third World nations that made them dependent on industrialized nations for capital, advanced technology, and expertise, these nations would remain in a state of underdevelopment, or stunted economic and social growth. This state of development would be one marked by poverty, continued dependence on international finance, and an export-oriented economy based on cash crops or basic manufactured goods. It was also pointed out that local elites tied to international capital, like large land-owners, benefited from this process and wielded strong influence over local government to facilitate it. Largely associated with scholars as Paul Baran, Andre Gunther Frank, Theotonio dos Santos, and Samir Amin, dependency theory also posited negative impacts of dependent industrialization, for example, high inequality between workers linked to foreign-owned industries and those in traditional sectors of the economy. Dependency scholars also pointed to other kinds of impacts like an uneven urban system that facilitated the export of goods to the industrialized world. Dependency theory varied in its predictions about the future of these nations. Some more extreme versions, as posited by Gunther Frank (1967), predicted that Third World nations would never develop any substantial industrialization, while others, like Amin (1981), pointed to highly uneven patterns of industrialization.

Dependency theory has been criticized for having a static **model** of the relationships between countries, as well as having been inattentive to local outcomes. Scholars have begun to point to countries like Brazil and Mexico that exhibit characteristics of both the industrialized world and the underdeveloped world. Also, several scholars have pointed to the success of East Asian countries in industrializing as a way to call into question some of the assumptions of dependency theory. These scholars, like Peter Evans and others, have pointed to the role of the state in creating conditions for successful development. It was argued that the role of strong states in countries like Korea and Taiwan fostered development by creating incentives for local industry.

Dependency theory has been replaced by other research agendas as the dominant **paradigm** in field. Recent changes in the world economy, for example, the rise of export-processing zones and the mobility of capital, have called into question the usefulness of dependency theory. **World-systems theory**, first advanced by **Immanuel Wallerstein** (1974), is more attentive to the impacts of globalization on all countries. This kind of analysis points, for example, to the interrelationship of changes in industry throughout the global economic system. Scholars now tend to consider the impact of the de-industrialization of North American **cities** as part of the same process that causes the impact of industrialization in Third World. Other elements introduced to the analysis of development as a result of this global perspective are the analysis of factors leading to the emigration

from Third World countries and the impact of their remittances in the development of sending countries. Saskia Sassen (1993), for example, argued that investment in Third World countries tends to provoke a migratory reflex from those countries to the country of origin of the investment.

More recent work in the sociology of development has also tended to call into question some fundamental assumptions in the field. Arturo Escobar (1994)and others have pointed to the assumption about the desirability of progress that underlies modernization and dependency scholarship alike. Industrialization and Western-style development are assumed to be inherently desirable to persons in all nations. Scholarship in this vein has searched for alternative ways of thinking about development and **progress** that revalues local and traditional wisdom. Greater attention has been given to the ecological impact of industrialization and the search for sustainable forms of development.

Scholars like Maria Meies (1992) have also begun to point to the absence of gender analysis within the sociology of development. These scholars have argued the role of women in development has been crucial in providing specific kinds of labor, as in the export processing zones, and has long been ignored by the scholarship. It has also been argued that women have suffered from the negative impact of development by, for example, retaining responsibility for traditional household duties while providing cheap exploited labor in nascent industries.

SOCIOLOGY OF EDUCATION

Education has long been of interest to various scholars. History, philosophy, and **psychology** have all made education and schooling major subjects of study. **Sociology** has also contributed greatly to our understanding of education. The production and management of knowledge, the **social control** of children, and **socialization** are part of a child's education, and thus education is a robust topic for sociological study. Many influential names in sociology have addressed education and schooling in their work.

Émile Durkheim contributed the most to the sociology of education. Durkheim believed that every **society** needed a certain level of homogeneity in order to survive. In simple societies, one major source of that homogeneity was religion, which bonded people together through a set of shared rituals and beliefs. Durkheim argued that education was the functional equivalent of religion in the modern world in that it provided a source of social solidarity in complex societies. In *The Development of Education Systems,* he perceived that the point of schooling in the modern world was not just to present a set of facts to students. Rather, education was designed to provide a ''deep-lying disposition'' of the soul that would shape the direction of student development and instill in students the attitudes appropriate for social life in their society. As part of his larger work analyzing the transition to modern society, Durkheim believed that the demand for education would increase as the **division of labor** in a society demanded occupa-

tional specialization. Although in the latter half of the twentieth century the focus of the sociology of education shifted somewhat, the influence of these earlier studies is still evident.

One line of scholarship that has been influential in the sociology of education, that of **functionalism**, has grown directly out of Durkheim's observations about education and **social solidarity**. Advocates of this school of thought study the ways in which education transmits socially accepted **norms** and values to younger generations. Beyond that, schools also manage the ''official knowledge'' of the society. Schools then are where children in a given society learn what it means to be a member of that society. Indeed, particularly in the United States, the history of public education is full of pronouncements about the way schools could overcome the particularism of the immigrant's home culture and thus turn the immigrants into Americans. The **concept** of civic or citizenship education depends upon the ability of the school to inculcate certain values. Whereas families were primarily responsible for the reproduction of society in their children in earlier times, the highly differentiated societies of the modern world needed a more consistent and regulated source of socialization. In providing children with a common framework and experience, schooling assures continuity between a society's past and its future. Although functionalism as a theory went through a period of crisis after the 1950s, many insights from scholars who embraced this theory are still influential in the sociology of education.

If the functional perspective argues that schooling is necessary for solidarity, the social control perspective argues that schooling is a means of managing the lower classes. Influenced by Marxian theory, this body of scholarship holds that the higher strata of society benefits from schooling by teaching the lower classes that their position of privilege in society is legitimate. By instilling the idea that hard work is the means to social mobility, the schools serve the interest of the higher class by teaching students to be good workers. In fact, one major topics of investigation in the sociology of education is the link between education and inequality. Although perhaps counter-intuitive, a number of studies have contested the notion that education is the prime determinant of **social mobility**. Though controversial, the work of Christopher Jencks and his colleagues has been particularly influential in this regard. In both *Inequality* from 1972, and *Who Gets Ahead?* from 1979, Jencks argued that education was not the only, or even the most important, determinant of economic success in America.

Another scholar who has looked at the relationship between class position and education is the influential French sociologist **Pierre Bourdieu**. He held that schooling contributes to the creation of ''cultural capital,'' which serves the interest of the upper classes by setting up boundaries between themselves and the lower classes. These boundaries consist of manners of speech and conduct that help members of one class to identify one another and limit access to their ranks to insiders. This entire body of work questions the often taken for granted notion that schools provide a means by which the disadvantaged can improve their class standing.

The sociology of education is not limited to questions about the way schools relate to society. Other sociological

studies of education have looked at the teaching profession. A number of studies have tried to document the characteristics of effective teaching. Class size, the importance of teacher training and certification, and parental participation have all been suggested as possible contributors to the overall effectiveness of teaching. Scholars have also looked at the social **organization** of the schools. For instance, authority relationships, social interaction between teachers and students, and the evolution of teacher and student subcultures, and school life outside the classroom have also been recent topics of study.

THE SOCIOLOGY OF EMOTIONS

During the 1970s, the sociology of emotions surfaced in response to a sociology that had become primarily concerned with individuals' cognitive and rational processes. Whereas sociological theories such as rational choice and exchange describe individuals and/or social actors as rational profit seekers that behave in terms of rewards and costs, emotion **theory** argues that while social behavior may, to a degree, result from individuals' cognitive and rational processes, emotional experiences are important for sociological explanations.

Arlie Hochschild, often considered to be the founder of the sociology of emotions, focused on emotion work and/or emotional labor. Emotion work occurs when forces, external of the individual, compel that individual to manipulate or ''manage'' their emotional experience. For example, certain social situations invariably require individuals to overcome such feelings as sadness and disappointment. Hochschild's book *The Managed Heart: Commercialization of Human Feeling* examines how individuals endeavor to manage the intensity and/or quality of their emotions. For example, regarding flight attendants, Hochschild argued, in order to maintain a demeanor that appeared consistent with passenger expectations, airlines actually required fight attendants to manage their emotions. Hochschild's work is important for the discipline of sociology because it intimately associates emotional experience with social behavior.

The sociology of emotions typically examines how individuals' emotional experience may be both the cause and effect of social behavior. On the one hand, some sociologists argue that emotions are experienced intrapersonally and then interpreted. In other words, given bodily sensations associated with emotions, individuals attempt to determine the cause of their emotions. Other sociologists, however, maintain that emotions are socially constructed. That is, interpretations and descriptions of emotional experience are not realized physiologically but rather socially. Despite these differences, most sociologists explore how such emotions as **love** and hate, embarrassment and disappointment are experienced and managed in everyday life.

The sociology of emotions is considered an important body of theory because it essentially contextualizes emotional experience. That is, emotion theory systematically articulates the ways in which our emotional experience may be both the cause and effect of social behavior. The sociology of emo-

tions' most notable contribution is the understanding that emotional experience, once considered entirely intrapersonal, may now be conceived of as an interpersonal phenomenon.

SOCIOLOGY OF HEALTH AND MEDICINE

The sociology of health and medicine is a relatively recent addition to the sociological fields of study. In the nineteenth and early twentieth centuries, writings and research in the field of medicine were thought to be the province of medical practitioners and biological scientists. The major focus of the medical field was on **disease** and infection caused by microorganisms. Sociologist William Cockerham noted some early work on the relationship of social factors to disease, such as that by McIntire, Blackwell, and Stern. McIntire, in fact, first used the term *medical sociology* in an article in 1894. Still, it was not sociologists who first discussed the social factors related to medicine but physicians themselves.

Rudolph Virchow, the nineteenth-century physician and recognized founder of modern pathology, actually argued that an epidemic of typhus fever in 1847 was due primarily to poor social and economic conditions. He sought improved living conditions for the poor as a means of prevention and argued against the idea of *biomedical reductionism*, or the attempt to reduce the cause of every disease to a biological source.

Medical sociology, as a subspecialty of the field of sociology, did not emerge until the 1940s. With World War II government funding became available for sociomedical research. Funding and support were generated by a number of postwar factors, such as changes in mortality and morbidity, the rise of preventive medicine, the establishment of modern psychiatry, and numerous administrative needs.

In The American Sociological Society (renamed the American Sociological Association [ASA] in 1959), the Committee on Certification in Medical Sociology, formed in 1955, described medical sociology as a subfield which places health and disease in a social, cultural, and behavioral context. The focus was on specifically related topics such as distribution of diseases among various populations, a range of specific health and illness behaviors, attitudes and beliefs, the study of structure and organization of medical occupations and professions, the relationships of medicine to other social institutions, and the contribution of social factors to the origins of disease, with application of a diversity of perspectives, theories, and methodologies. Although the definition was broad, the title of Medical Sociology was retained by the ASA, due mostly to the fact that it was traditional and widely recognized.

By the 1950s, a debate had arisen among sociologists as to whether the professional role should focus on the academically oriented development of theory and method or take an applied direction, making practical contributions to medical practice and the field of medicine. Summarizing the distinction, sociologist Robert Straus coined the terms *sociology of medicine* to describe the former, and *sociology in medicine* for the latter. Sociology in medicine focused on information directly relevant to care of patients or to public health issues. Re-

searchers in this area found **employment** in medical schools, nursing schools, teaching hospitals, public health agencies, and other health organizations. From applied work within the medical field these sociologists gained much acceptance and credibility. Engagement in the sociology of medicine involved researching and analyzing the medical environment from a sociological perspective, generally by academic professors and researchers in sociology departments of colleges and universities. David Mechanic described the sociology of medicine as "testing sociological hypotheses, using medicine as an arena for studying basic issues in **social stratification**, power and influence, **social organization**, socialization, and the broad context of social values."

This academic orientation was strongly reinforced in 1951 when Talcott Parsons published *The Social System*. The work was highly theoretical and presented Parsons' conception of the *sick role*. He had analyzed the function of medicine in society, identifying illness as a form of **deviance** and linking medicine to the function of **social control**. This connection was accomplished through the physician's diagnosis, which labeled and thus legitimized the patient's ailment. Physicians thus became agents of social control. Although strongly criticized, Parsons' work had the impact of providing a broad theoretical base which gave impetus to the early development and intellectual recognition of the subdiscipline of medical sociology.

The theoretical and applied areas of medical sociology, while competitive at first, began to converge. Sociologists working in both areas received the same training, and the theoretical foundations of the subdiscipline were present in both. In addition, research into increasingly broad and complex topics, such as **health care** reform, required a broader view which encompassed numerous areas of social structure, power, political and economic issues, as well as human attitudes, perceptions, and behaviors.

Areas in which medical sociology can make valuable contributions include, for example, unmet needs in the field of health care, **social change** effects on the health **professions**, medical care effects on the **quality of life**, and the relationships of social networks and health status. More sociological research is needed with regard to public policy, and it is estimated that policy-oriented research will become much more important as the issues become more complex. Medical sociologists Pescosolido and Kronenfeld have argued that since the social and socio-medical landscape has changed, people must have an understanding of that landscape, including social institutions, the systems of stratification, and the nature of communities.

Cockerham noted that "At present, medical sociologists constitute the largest and one of the most active groups of people doing sociological work in the United States and Western Europe." In addition, medical sociology is the second largest section of the American Sociological Association. Approximately one out of ten American sociologists is a medical sociologist. "Medical sociology" is now used interchangeably with such terms as "sociology of health, healing, and illness." Significantly, this expansion of terminology also reflects the growth and development of the field, and the connections of medicine and medical care to broader social concerns and issues.

SOCIOLOGY OF HOUSING

Sociology of housing is a subfield of sociology that examines the social implications and effects of housing patterns, including such areas as housing tenure, demographics, homeownership, availability, and public housing. Sociology of housing concerns itself with three major areas: the social setting and values that determine housing choices and preferences, the ways in which housing allows for or limits opportunities for social relationships and personal happiness, and issues that determine housing satisfaction.

An interest in housing, particularly on the impact of housing policies, arose in the years following World War II. In the early years of the development of the sociology of housing, from the 1940s to the 1970s, social scientists focused primarily on the rapid expansion of public housing for the economically underprivileged. Through social research, sociologists of housing quickly discovered that the definition of adequate housing was dependent on more than adequate shelter. In *Housing and the Urban Poor: A Critical Analysis of Federal Housing Policy* (1974), A.P. Solomon writes that "experience demonstrates that, by itself, a sound physical structure does not constitute a suitable living environment. Clean surroundings, playing space for children, personal safety and security, and access to work and shopping areas represent only a few of the many prerequisites for an acceptable home and neighborhood." Such realizations impacted the federal government's development of large, densely populated high-rise public housing projects.

During the 1970s sociology of housing broadened its scope to include more research on single family, detached homes. According to Donald L. Foley in "The Sociology of Housing" (*Annual Review of Sociology,* 1980), "Homeownership has several social implications—e.g. it serves as an investment that eases one's financial burden in later years; it furnishes symbolic evidence of social **status**; it encourages the private pursuit of one's activities; it permits one to make independent decisions about one's house and its furnishings; and it fosters an identification with one's own home."

As the subjects of interest addressed by sociology of housing scholars has expanded, the methodological approaches have ranged from the Marxist perspective to an analysis of housing functions within a capitalist **society**. Also, the number of specialized fields has grown. The sociology of architecture, environmental psychology, and, to a lesser extent, **environmental sociology** all emerged as a means to examine the factors related to the subject of design. Other areas of focus include housing situations of the poor, ethnic minorities, women, the physically disabled, and the elderly. Often research is conducted by government agencies in order to provide information necessary to create or reform public policy.

SOCIOLOGY OF KNOWLEDGE

The Sociology of Knowledge is a broad sub-field within sociology dealing with the social character of knowledge. Its boundaries are not always distinct, as it occasionally overlaps with the sociologies of science, medicine, culture, and religion. Moreover, questions of the field's primary focus changed dramatically over time, as different epistemological debates within sociology arose.

Many early theorists in sociology were interested in the social aspects of knowledge. **Auguste Comte**, generally considered to be the father of sociology, was interested in the connection between types of knowledge and science. Karl Marx was also engaged in the debate about how knowledge is developed, particularly how social class impacted knowledge. His theory of **ideology** identified a relationship between social class and the development of knowledge that increased the power of particular classes.

Karl Mannheim, however, was one of the first major theorists (if not the first) to focus exclusively on the sociology of knowledge. He conceptualized the sociology of knowledge as the study of the relationships between ideology and social **group** and how knowledge was determined. He used Marxist ideological analysis as his starting point but extended Marxist theory by including social groupings other than class (a theory detailed in his book *Ideology and Utopia* 1936). Any group of people with a collective interest, Mannheim argued, will consciously or unconsciously develop ideas that further their collective interest and increase or maintain the group's power. However, Mannheim did not believe knowledge was relative. He supported a positivist conception of knowledge, and he saw intellectuals as a group independent of the interests of other groups. In Mannheim's theory, intellectuals remained removed from self-interest; therefore, they could produce objective, scientific knowledge and mediate the conflicting knowledge claims of other groups. He asserted that once scientific knowledge was established, it functioned independently of history or **culture**.

Another theoretical tradition influenced by Marx was critical theory. Critical theorists from the Frankfort school at the beginning of 1900s argued in support of a type of rationalism that was dialectical rather than linear. Critical theory is often contrasted with **positivism**, which uses an empirical approach to knowledge. Many early epistemological debates in sociology centered on the contention over **empiricism** versus rationalism.

After the mid-1930s, there was a period of time in which few additions were made to the sociology of knowledge. A possible exception is selected work by **Pitirim Sorokin**, although it seems to have little lasting impact. In the late 1950s, the **sociology of science** emerged which addressed the production of scientific knowledge. Early contributors were **Robert K. Merton** ("Priorities in Scientific Discovery, 1957 and *The Sociology of Science*, 1973), **Thomas Kuhn** (*Structure of Scientific Revolutions*, 1962) and **Peter Berger** and Thomas Luckmann (*The Social Construction of Reality*, 1966). The combining of the sociology of knowledge with the sociology of science continues in the growing fields of the sociology of scientific knowledge (SSK) and science and technology studies (STS). The subsuming of the sociology of knowledge with the study of **science and technology** is reflected in the organization of the American Sociological Association, which groups the study of knowledge and science together in the Science, Knowledge, and Technology section (SKAT).

Much of the work now in the study of science and knowledge uses a constructivist approach, which contends that "truth" is constructed rather than being absolute and unchanging throughout history. The constructivist approach remains popular in the sociology of knowledge, although supporters of the approach are still engaged in somewhat contentious battles with defenders of positivism.

Other contributions to the sociology of knowledge that rely heavily on **constructivism** have come from feminist and **race** theorists, who have continued the Marxist tradition of connecting the content of knowledge and ways of acquiring or developing it to social position. These theorists have demonstrated that social stratification has produced a stratified knowledge system in which some ways of knowing are privileged over others. For example, feminist sociologists have argued that the way that men produce knowledge is generally considered "better" than the way women produce knowledge, and thus the content of men's knowledge is privileged over women's knowledge. Dorothy Smith, who is credited with developing **standpoint theory**, showed how women's experiences have been devalued as common or base, and thus the knowledge gained from those experiences is devalued. However, Smith contends that women's common or "everyday" experiences produce valuable knowledge that only women have direct access through by virtue of their subordinate position to men (this theory is detailed in her book *The Everyday World as Problematic*, 1987). Patricia Hill Collins used positionality as a conceptual platform as well, and argued that black women can, by virtue of their gender and race, produce knowledge that white women and black cannot. Once this knowledge is recorded, however, it can be accessed by anyone regardless of social position (this theory is described in her book *Black Feminist Thought*, 1990).

SOCIOLOGY OF LAW

Sociology of law, also called legal sociology and sociolegal studies, refers to the macrostructural and microstructural study of the social context, development, and function of law. Unlike many subfields of sociology, sociolegal studies did not develop from the field of sociology. Rather, it had its roots in the intellectual development of the **philosophy** of law. In the late 1920s and early 1930s law professors at Columbia and Harvard first attempted to introduce social science **theory** to legal problems. However, the experimental approach did not gain widespread support and was soon abandoned.

The interdisciplinary study of law and sociology received new interest after World War II when the Ford Foundation supplied the Law School at the University of Chicago with

funding for the interdisciplinary study of three specific issues: the jury system, the tax system, and commercial arbitration. Although only the study of the jury system produced noteworthy results, the experience set the precedent for the **methodology** of interdisciplinarian study between the social sciences and law. Legal experts were expected to set the questions of study and dictate the purposeful use of the study's results. Social scientists became artisans, creating the **data** collection system, determining validity, and interpreting data.

Although work between legal scholars and sociologists has continued, the relationship has sometimes been strained. Because there is no consensus on a theory of **society** and law, debate is ongoing regarding the basis and emphasis of empirical study. This debate has been shaped by several sociologists who addressed the relation between society and the legal system, including Karl Marx, Émile Durkheim, and **Max Weber**. Each offered a unique perspective on the interplay of the macrostructural elements of society and law.

Developed outside the realm of legal study, the Marxist theory of law emphasized the legal system as a component of the capitalist superstructure. Because Marx understood all societal relations to be dominated by class conflict, he viewed law as an oppressive tool that the upper class used to maintain power. By institutionalizing legal oppression, the upper class was able to create a false justification for the unfair treatment of the working class. The Marxian perspective of law, prominent during the 1970s, was used to examine class and **race** bias in civil and criminal cases.

Émile Durkheim believed that the institution of law differed depending on the primary dynamic of society as a whole. Using his concept of **division of labor**, he argued that societies that were bonded by mechanical solidarity would impose primarily repressive laws and societies bonded by organic solidarity would employ primarily laws of restitution. Thus, for Durkheim, the nature of the legal system is determined by the collective conscience of the society. Accordingly, whereas simple societies can operate sufficiently with relatively few laws, industrial societies are so structurally complex that the need for laws, especially criminal laws, increases.

Max Weber identified three types of legitimate **authority**: charismatic, traditional, and rational-legal. Like Durkheim, Weber believed that more complex societies required more complex legal structures, namely a higher level rational-legal system. Drawing his conclusions from the study of the historical development of legal **rationality** in Western **civilization**, he argued that **capitalism** and legality were closely aligned. In fact, the development of rational law was a precondition for the modern development of a capitalist society. According to Weber, the character of capitalism inherently promotes coercive domination under the law, a necessary component of the capitalist-legal relationship.

The emphasis in sociology of law has been primarily on theory, not method. Because of the overarching complex interactions between the legal system and other social structures, creating empirical studies that can produce verifiable quantitative measurements becomes a major undertaking in which researchers disagree over theory and methodology. Also, the sociology of law tends to embrace various specialized studies by legal experts and social scientists, from such subfields as labor law, criminal law, family law, and comparative law. Few social scientists actually attempt to study the whole legal system. Thus, even though sociology of law is, in its broadest definition, a macrostructurally-based endeavor, most empirical studies of contemporary sociolegal issues have taken place on the microstructural level.

Modern trends in empirical sociological studies of the legal system include attention to jury studies and legal access. Over the last forty years, many jury studies have been conducted by sociologists in which methodologies have varied greatly. During the 1960s and 1970s many jury studies were simulated. In some cases mock juries listened to tapes or read manuscripts from actual trials. Attempting to obtain more **realism**, some studies staged mock trials, complete with courtroom, lawyers, and defendant. By the end of the twentieth century, studies had begun using ''shadow jurors,'' a second jury that sits in on an actual trial and decides the case. Even though the decision has no bearing on the defendant's verdict, results can be used for comparison and study. Although considered a superior empirical method, shadow juries have been relatively rare due to lack of support from the legal community.

The debate over the ability of the legal system to provide equal access to the law has interested sociologists of law for years. The answer has important theoretical implications. If the law does not distribute level access across all social structures, then it can be argued that the legal system is oppressive. However, if access is equal, then the opposite can be argued: the legal system is fair and just, even if particular laws may be unjust.

Recently, small survey studies have become more common than institutional analyses. Both jury studies and legal access research point to the increasing use of microstructural studies by sociologists of law. Although the contemporary sociological study of law was initiated by the legal profession, the field has gradually shifted with social scientists now taking the lead. The field is still fragmented; however, sociolegal researchers have begun to develop more quantitative methodologies and to employ greater use of behavioral analysis.

SOCIOLOGY OF RELIGION

Sociology of religion is defined as the scientific study of religions and pseudo-religions, including all associations, institutions, organizations, and practices found within each. It is not, per se, the study of the origins of a religion or belief. In general, the sociology of religion is concerned with the study of cultural systems that generate in an actor a comprehensive understanding of meaning and significance within a total order of existence that can be seen as sacred, complete, and transcendent. In other words, religion provides a comprehensive way in which to view and understand reality and one's placement within it. This is accomplished through an arrangement of symbols, things deemed either sacred or profane which communicate meaning that are then reified. These symbols repre-

sent models or suggestions of behavior that, within a cultural context, furnish both design and motivation to being. This symbolic system further offers templates for action, thought, and reaction for various situations.

Religion seems to be a universal feature in human cultures. This includes the large, organized faiths such as **Judaism** or **Christianity**, **ancestor worship**, and even thought-systems such as fascism or **capitalism**. These possibilities are limited by the myriad number of ways that exists to understand and explain existence. There is a tendency within sociology to define religion both inclusively and functionally. Since the specifics of any religion can widely differ from another religion, studies of these structures tend to focus on function rather than substance of the particular practice. That is not to say that the specific practices are not studied by social scientists.

Religion is often studied in relation to its social environ. This is necessary because there are so many variations worldwide in religious practice, and there must be something to account for these differences other than random chance. Furthermore, the abstraction of a **belief system** from its social setting would remove many opportunities for insight that would otherwise be apparent within the cultural context. That is to say, the practice of dunking people in water makes no sense without the context of a baptism. Accepting the fact that religious symbols have meaning within their context, the following question is thus asked: Under what social conditions does this **symbol** have a particular definition?

The sociology of religion can be seen as a reaction against the nineteenth century positivist theories, which were primarily focused on the emergence of religions. These positivists, furthermore, attempted to explain religion with rational and individualistic assumptions. According to these early positivists, religion was an erroneous belief system that would fade away when science and scientific thought became widespread throughout the **society**. Positivists held that religion was indeed irrational.

The study of religion sociologically was historically couched as the struggle between the sacred and the secular, or even the irrational versus the rational. Later, scholarship in the field advanced the notion that **rationality** itself, as a generalized system of strongly related means and goals, was an integral part of many modern religions. This is the case even more often in heterogeneous societies. That is to say that religious structures often incorporate an explanatory logic, which proscribes affective behavior for adherents of the faith. Religion, here, therefore cultivates rational affective reactions. Thus, some religions generate their own form of rationality. Religions, by more contemporary standards, are viewed as both products and generators of society. Here, religion is seen as a response to the human need for meaning and placement within one's social world.

In general, there are two opposing schools of thought within the sociology of religion. The first was led by Émile Durkheim and the second by **Max Weber**. While Durkheim's work concentrated on the general functions of religion relative to **social integration**, Weber was primarily focused on the comparative investigation of the compulsion for salvation and various problems of theodicy, including interpretations of moral problems like death or **evil**.

While having once been widely held as the theoretical core of the discipline due to its focus on such wide ranging topics as symbolism, the nature of rationality, and the overall nature of the **social order**, the sociology of religion has lost its place as the analytical cornerstone of sociology. This may be, in part, due to the increasingly narrow focus of many of the researchers in this field. For example, many social scientists study recruitment processes within religious organizations while forgoing a more comparative approach. While the scientific study of religion may have lost its prominence within the discipline, it is still holds a unique position with the field of sociology.

Sociology of Science

The Sociology of Science is a sub-field within sociology that deals with the social organization of scientific activities, products, contexts, and scientific systems of belief. It is related to the sociology of knowledge, in that it often focuses on the way scientific knowledge is produced. The sociology of science was developed in the United States, where Robert K. Merton is generally regarded as the founder. With the publication of his ''Priorities in Scientific Discovery'' in 1957, the field began to come together as a coherent specialty. He later published *The Sociology of Science* in 1973, a compilation of his work on the impact modernity had on the development of science. It presented what came to be known as the Merton thesis, that the establishment of science (particularly in the Western **civilization**) was a consequence of Protestantism.

The publication of Thomas Kuhn's *Structure of Scientific Revolutions* in 1962 furthered Merton's efforts to develop coherency in the sociology of science. It also provided a new direction for the area. Kuhn was one of the first theorists to challenge Karl Mannheim's assertion that once scientific knowledge was established, it functioned independently of history or **culture**. Kuhn argued that science was divided into periods of ''normal science'' (when there is consensus through most of the scientific community about how science should be practiced), and **paradigm** shifts (when there is conflict in the scientific community over **theory**, methods, instruments, and standards of evaluation). Thinking of science in terms of shifting paradigms challenged the progressive and idealistic conception of science that dominated previous to the late 1950s.

In the 1970s the sociology of scientific knowledge (SSK), derived mostly from **British sociology**, extended Kuhn's interpretation of the history of science by claiming that science, like all human enterprises, is socially constructed. It focused on questions surrounding the nature or character of science, what constitutes scientific knowledge, and how the criteria for scientific knowledge are determined. Theorists in the sociology of scientific knowledge examine, among other things, the **norms** that scientists claim to follow, whether they actually follow those norms, and the practices that scientists engage in as a way to legitimize the knowledge they create.

Also related is **science and technology** studies (commonly referred to STS), which was influenced by the sociolo-

gy of scientific knowledge. Like SSK, it draws heavily from constructivist theory by examining the way scientific facts and the veracity of those facts are constructed. It also challenges the notion that science produces a form of knowledge that is somehow superior to other types of knowledge systems. Within STS a group of studies emerged called laboratory studies (among which the work of Bruno Latour and Steven Woolgar is most notable). Laboratory studies, using mostly ethnographic methods, examines the activities in laboratories of physical, chemical, biological, and sometimes social scientists. STS has become policy-oriented in recent years, responding to concerns over scientific funding, the direction that science and technological advancement should take, and the education of scientists.

Continued conflict occurs between supporters of positivist theories of science (depending heavily on Merton, as well as more classical theorists) and the supporters of STS and SSK theories. Critics of the ''science as socially constructed'' approach perceive the work coming out of STS and SSK to be too relativistic and thus not meaningful. If scientific work is shown to be contextually-dependent and not absolute, then how can we ever know truth? Supporters of STS and SSK respond by explaining that there are many truths to know, and the practice of science allows us access to some of them. It is only through the authority that our **society** gives science and scientists that scientific knowledge is viewed as absolute truth.

But these conflicts may be more than ideological or theoretical differences. Thomas Gieryn called such conflicts the ''science wars,'' and contended that they are really struggles over boundaries. According to Gieryn, supporters of positivist science are shoring up the boundaries of science against attack, and they interpret constructivist views of science as attacks. By recognizing that scientific knowledge is, like all forms of knowledge, socially located and socially constructed, SSK and STS research calls into question the authority of science that privileges the knowledge it produces over other types of knowledge. This could ultimately weaken the legitimacy of science and call its importance into question. On the other hand, supporters of **positivism** perceive supporters of **constructivism** as doing ''bad'' science. The ''science wars'' are likely to persist within the sociology of science as science and technology continues to be an important part of our lives.

SOCIOLOGY OF SPORT

Sociology of Sport is both a context for understanding basic sociological principles and a fertile field for study. Its focus includes, but is not limited to, history of sports, adaptation, **aging** and sports, athletes' rights, coaching, **culture**, disability issues, drugs, economics of athletics, ethics, fans/spectators, **feminism**, gambling, gay games, hegemonic ideals, international sports, media coverage, politics and sports, **socialization**, as subcultures, Title IX, violence, and youth sports. Sociology of Sport grew from exploration of a range of topics such as Susan Cahn's *Coming on Strong: Sexuality and Gender in Twentieth-Century Women's Sports*; Harry Edwards research about low

graduation rates for athletes, institutional responsibility, and racism in athletics; and Michael Messner's focus on sports and masculinity. In response to the growing body of literature, Andrew Yiannakis and Susan Greendorfer cofounded the *North American Society for the Sociology of Sport (NASSS)* and developed a webpage to provide links to a variety of information including lists of experts in the field, graduate programs, journals, and listserves. The American Sociological Association publishes *Syllabi and Instructional Materials for Teaching the Sociology of Sport*.

The use of **leisure** time activity is a cultural universal, that is, it is found in all cultures. Often the activity parallels or reflects values in the economy of the culture. For example, in the capitalist United States sports involve either individual or team competition and results in clear winners or losers. It is a *meritocratic system* rewarding mental and physical vigor stemming from individual talent, ability, and application. By contrast, leisure activity in foraging economies is more likely to reflect cooperative efforts with everyone winning or playing until each person wins.

Thornstein Veblen's *The Theory of the Leisure Class* discusses athletic competition as parallel to kings showing their wealth and power by equipping and supporting strategists, leaders, and soldiers for battle. Veblen also draws parallels between the pageantry surrounding athletic competition and royalty sending knights off to battle. Conflict theory and **critical theory** see sports as a means of diverting attention and support away from **social problems** while promoting **false consciousness** that identifies with sports teams or players instead of the oppressed. In these views, athletics are seen as perpetuating and reflecting hegemonic beliefs about class, race, and gender. They also discuss issues surrounding the perception that athletics is a better option than education for those wanting to escape **poverty**. In addition, there are concerns about the power associated with contracts and parallels between this activity and slavery. Functionalist **theory** sees sports as manifest functions such as entertaining; alleviating tension; representing the collective consciousness; generating income, opportunity, and good will. It sees sports as economically advantageous for players, teams, institutions, and communities. Latent functions can include job creation. Dysfunctions include injuries/death, violence, **drug abuse**, loss of **identity**.

Symbolic Interactionist theorists see athletics in general and team spirit and paraphernalia as promoting hegemonic **morality**, group solidarity, nationalism, and identity for the players and fans. Symbolic Interactionists study the social construction of status as ''star athlete'' or as ''non-athlete''. The process of becoming an athlete sometimes involves adopting **norms** of subjugation to authoritarian coaches, teamwork, tattoos, hairstyles, uniform, contests for position, and argot (jargon) associated with in-group solidarity. Glamorized images of athletes provide for their potential as either positive or negative role models. Enough players earn huge incomes to highlight the potential to get rich through sports. Athletes are faced with role engulfment (social demands that insulate the athlete from traditional expectations and relationships). In some ways it gives the athletes extreme freedom from traditional norms,

but it also can cause isolation that is exacerbated when star status ends. Symbolic Interactional so studies the development of a coach like Bobby Knight and Bear Bryant as more prominent than the institution.

There is special emphasis on opportunities for athletic competition for individuals with physical or mental challenges. *Special Olympics* creates a niche for participants and their families. The Wheelchair Olympics brings major competition among well-trained dedicated athletes. Athletes continue to face issues such as the use of golf carts for the mobility challenged.

Minority studies views sports as reflecting capital logic (for profit maximization), **race** logic, and sex logic (to promote race and gender hierarchies). These terms refer to the ''logic'' or basis for decisions that are rooted in racist and patriarchal ideologies and stereotypes about class, race, and sex. They are used to give legitimacy to essentially racist, classist, or sexist positions. For example, until recently, positions of quarterbacks and coaches were generally only given to white males because they were seen as better leaders and strategists. Professional sports do not subsidize the education for the college players even though they draw heavily from the risks and perseverance of the scholar-athletes. Racial and ethic stereotypes are also seen in caricatures for logos and mascots. The Cleveland Indians, Washington Red Skins, and Atlanta Braves are subjects of debate. The transparency of sports as reinforcement of inequality is exemplified by the Olympic committee refusal to allow American Jews to compete in the 1936 Olympics to avoid offending Hitler, the debate over medals won by Jim Thorpe, and more recent examples of segregated golf courses.

Feminist writers focus on the polemics of athletic builds and images of ''femininity''. For example, female body builders resort to breast implants to replace body fat carefully eliminated by hours of exercise. Traditionally male sports relegate women to the sidelines with the role of cheerleaders but ignore the athletic ability, training, and practice required for cheerleading. Lack of professional opportunities, media support, public interest, and funding continue to be areas of concern for female athletes.

Title IX is intended to provide opportunities for female athletes; it created contempt for female sports as colleges and universities eliminate male swimming and soccer teams to even the positions and comply with the regulation. Arguments for Title IX as implemented are that they ensure equal opportunity and pay for women's sports and will strengthen their position in society. Arguments against it are that football teams have so many positions that the majority of women's positions are used to balance the opportunities provided by a single male sport. Many feel that football teams should be excluded from Title IX consideration and instead categorized as training camps for professional teams rather than on par, with other college sports with the possible exception of basketball.

SOCIOLOGY OF THE BUILT ENVIRONMENT

The **sociology** of the built environment, a late twentieth-century development in the field, considers the interrelation-

ship of several subdisciplines previously regarded as separate, including **urban sociology**, city planning, and the sociology of architectural movements. Sociologists who study the built environment focus on the forms of individual buildings and on the patterns of structures that characterize towns and **cities** as both distinct artifacts and as expressions of cultural **values**.

The sociology of the built environment is closely related to cultural and social geography, which are concerned with the spatial aspects of culture. American geographer Carl O. Sauer was particularly influential in integrating anthropological and sociological concepts and theories into geographic study. Sauer emphasized both the effect of the natural environment on human societies and the impact of human activity on the environment. While cultural geography tends to focus on **traditional societies**, such as the American Indian cultures in which Sauer specialized, social geography concentrates more on urban problems and their spatial aspects.

Among the theoretical issues of interest in the field are the relationship of the built environment to the commodification of space; the ways in which urban design and planning reflect cultural **identity** and goals; and the conflict between opposing approaches to design, planning, and architectural movements. More concretely, the sociology of the built environment considers such matters as how infrastructure, including road systems, bridges, and other structures, contribute to settlement patterns and patterns of consumption; how it affects patterns of work and the distribution of energy and materials; how it contributes to land-use planning; and how it contributes to matters of public health and community.

Questions of cultural identity and goals are frequently related to the impact of tourism, especially in older cities. Critics have argued that tourists, as ''consumers'' of the built environment, often have a negative effect on the cities they visit and contribute to contested views of history as symbolized in buildings and other structures. Analysts have repeatedly identified tourism, with its internationalizing and homogenizing influences, as a threat to the build environment's capacity to express national identity. They also argue that, in general, tourists engage only superficially with the historic, cultural, and social meanings of the built environment.

The relationship between the built environment, settlement patterns, and land-use issues has also received attention. In the United States, expansion of infrastructure since the 1950s has made possible the rapid flight of middle-class families from urban areas to outlying suburbs. This **suburbanization**, still rampant by the early 2000s, contributed significantly to urban decline and has been associated with the reluctance of business to reinvest in inner city areas. Suburbanization also changed patterns of social **interaction**. Suburban areas became known as ''bedroom communities'' because many residents worked elsewhere and only returned to their homes in the evenings. With few opportunities for neighbors to interact, families in suburbs became more isolated than had been true for earlier generations. The huge growth of suburbs also created a dependence on the automobile; the resulting automobile **culture**, in turn, fueled increased expansion of highways as well as extensive pollution.

Suburbanization is also associated with other negative environmental impacts. Between 1970 and 1990, when the re-

gional population of Los Angeles grew 45 percent, the developed area tripled. By the 1970s, more than a third of the surface area in Los Angeles was devoted to freeways, driveways, streets, and parking lots. The built environment in Los Angeles, argues urban theorist Mike Davis in *Ecology of Fear: Los Angeles and the Imagination of Disaster*, is characterized by inappropriate land use in geographic areas unsuitable for development, a dynamic that contributes significantly to the increase in frequency and scale of natural disasters such as brush fires. Financial losses associated with fires, earthquakes, and other disasters have also skyrocketed, he points out, because the wealthy population has increased in disaster-prone environments ill-suited to the scale of building. Insurance arrangements and political commitment to rebuilding these areas, in his view, further exacerbate the negative environmental impact of human manipulation of space in Los Angeles.

Davis also argues that Los Angeles's built environment creates conditions that physically isolate groups according to wealth and **status**. Planning decisions and development patterns have pushed low-income populations into undesirable locations underserved by businesses and city agencies and far from lucrative jobs. "Videotape surveillance zones," such as that established in Hollywood's Yucca Street neighborhood, the **privatization** of public space, such as sidewalks and shopping malls, and the proliferation of gated communities are examples of what Davis called the city's "spatial apartheid." He cites police representation on many urban and suburban planning boards as further evidence of repressive environmental measures against targeted populations; in one case, an affluent suburb decided to ban alleys as a "crime prevention measure," based on police advice.

Continued population growth, migration, and **urbanization** across the globe will contribute to significant growth in the built environment. The sociological study of the built environment enables specialists to study how economic, demographic, and cultural issues affect and are affected by human manipulation of the environment.

SOCIOLOGY OF THE FAMILY

Sociology of the family examines the ways in which social forces shape family life. Prior to 1960 family sociologists typically employed a functionalist perspective in their analysis of the family. The family was narrowly conceptualized as a nuclear household, consisting primarily of a married couple with children. In 1949 sociologist George Murdock defined the family as follows: "a social group characterized by common residence, economic co-operation, and reproduction. It includes adults of both sexes, at least two of whom maintain a socially approved sexual relationship, and one or more children, own or adopted, of the sexually cohabiting adults." During the first part of the twentieth century this and similar other definitions of "the family" formed the primary foundation upon which sociological theorizing and research on family life was based.

During the 1960s, however, many sociologists began to assert that the functionalist approach to family life contained an inherent bias. Functionalist analyses restricted the examination of families to nuclear household arrangements, which most typified white heterosexual middle-class families. Relations of "economic co-operation" in these families most often consisted of a male head of household, who was likely to be the primary breadwinner, and his typically unemployed spouse. Deviations from this gendered economic ideal were often identified as dysfunctional and pathological. As such, functionalist family sociologists effectively disregarded a wide range of families whose experiences departed from this white heterosexual middle-class norm.

In an effort to counter biased functionalist analyses of family life, contemporary social scientists employ a constructivist approach in their examination of families. This perspective places the various forms of family life in specific cultural and historical contexts, thus challenging the universalistic claims of the functionalist approach. Furthermore, the constructivist perspective on families more accurately reveals the historical and contemporary diversity of family forms.

This more inclusive perspective on families has thus moved family sociology beyond Murdock's restrictive definition of the family. Contemporary family sociologists have sought to reveal the complex ways in which **race**, ethnicity, class, and gender inform the structure of family life. In addition, family researchers have disputed the traditional notion that only married couples with children may be called families. In this vein, much of contemporary sociological research on family forms has sought to legitimate the family structures characteristic of singlehood, unmarried **cohabitation**, single parenthood, and gay/lesbian/bisexual family arrangements. Furthermore, current trends of **divorce** and remarriage have had a monumental impact upon family arrangements.

Consequently, more recent sociological research on families explores the experiences of those who have traditionally been oppressed or stigmatized for not conforming to the white heterosexual middle-class nuclear family norm. Such research has given voice and validation to individuals and groups whose family lives had previously been considered dysfunctional or pathological. Furthermore, contemporary family sociology has functioned to demystify popular and political rhetoric that posits a current societal departure from "family values." Critical analyses of family life reveal that these politicized "family values" in actuality represent a popularized ideal that is really achieved only by a limited few.

Research on family diversity has unraveled many stereotypes that were traditionally held about "the family." Most importantly, this research has challenged the notion that such a thing as "the family" actually exists. Referring to "*the family*" in effect asserts that there is some universal family form within **society**. However, as family sociologists have begun to explore the multitude of family forms that have endured throughout society, both historically and in the present, diversity rather than universality has prevailed.

Social scientists who have studied the diverse family arrangements of various racial and ethnic groups have highlighted the ways in which fictive kin arrangements, filial piety, and **extended family** formation contribute to a variety of racial-

ethnic family structures. Sociologists employing a gender perspective illustrate the manner in which race, **ethnicity**, and class have influenced the gendered structure of family forms. Racial, ethnic, and class backgrounds have historically had a consequential impact upon the roles women play in their families, especially in terms of their economic contribution to families. Women from poor and working-class families have historically been more likely to work in the labor market out of economic necessity. Moreover, women of color have historically been more likely to live within poor and working-class families.

Contemporary family researchers challenging the traditional belief in the inseparability of heterosexual union and family formation depict the variety of family arrangements among gay, lesbian, and bisexual communities. Gay, lesbian, and bisexual men and women have increasingly formed families with children through **adoption**, artificial insemination, and natural reproductive means. Fictive kin arrangements among gay, lesbian, and bisexual men and women are extremely common as well. Moreover, the traditional prejudicial belief that gay, lesbian, and bisexual men and women are somehow rejecting their families of origin negates the continued significance of these families, which do not automatically disappear from the lives of those who are gay, lesbian or bisexual.

Divorce, **remarriage**, and the increase in never married individuals and couples (with or without children) has had an enormous impact upon family formation. While these family forms have borne the brunt of avowedly conservative ''family values'' proponents, the increasing and even highly prevalent existence of divorced, remarried, and never married families attests to their legitimacy. Furthermore, interethnic and interracial families have increasingly added to the diversity of family forms in contemporary times.

While the newer, more inclusive perspectives on family studies have functioned first and foremost to explore and validate the family experiences of individuals and groups ignored by the functionalist perspective on family life, contemporary sociologists have by no means abandoned their examination of heterosexual white-middle class nuclear families. More recently, however, family researchers have developed a greater tendency to illuminate the social, cultural, and political significance of **heterosexuality**, marital status, whiteness, middle-class status, and various gender considerations within these families. In the same manner that race, class, gender, sexuality, and marital status inform the lives and experiences of oppressed groups within society, so too are the lives and experiences of the privileged shaped by these systems of inequality.

SOCIOLOGY OF WORK

The **sociology** of work emerged as an area study in the early twentieth century. The sociologists contributing to this effort were from the University of Chicago, the leading force in social theory during this time, and included Everett Hughes, Robert Parks, and others. A significant factor in the development of this study was that the discipline now had its stronghold in the United States, where the dominant intellectual **discourse** on theory was shaped by the logic of science. Unlike the European tradition of grand theory in which work would be analyzed within the historical context of the division of labor and its relationship to social, political and economic factors, work was now being defined in terms of **employment**, an outcome of the industrialization process. Consequently, under the influence of **the Chicago school**, the sociology of work emerged as a systematic classification of employment into occupational categories.

The sociology of work was driven by the desire to understand the many social changes, including **poverty**, **crime**, and clashing cultural differences among immigrant populations, occurring during this time of rapid industrialization and growth of monopoly capital. Its subjects related to the dominance of manufacturing positions in the goods producing sector and the respective relationship of the factory worker, and an emerging, distinct segment of higher skilled positions performed by a professional worker. For Hughes and others, the focus of analysis was always on the individual's relationship to the occupational structure. These early sociologists hoped to develop scientific reforms to improve the lives of urban workers and their families.

The historical formation of this work as an area of study is relevant because theoretical perspectives have variously defined the meaning of work. Even the classical theorists, Émile Durkheim, **Karl Marx** and Max Weber, integrated the concept of work with their theories about social structure and processes, but they interpreted work's meaning and significance in different ways. For Durkheim, the study of **society** required analyzing the division of labor and its relationship to moral society. His focus on the increasing specialization of the **division of labor** in modern society greatly influenced subsequent efforts, particularly in functionalist theory which dominated the sociology of work paradigm between 1940 and 1960. Functionalist theory developed quantitative techniques, influenced by the **methodology** of Durkheim and the cause and effect approach of Weber, to examine issues of **social mobility**, stratification theory, and social **status**. The major contributors in this phase of the sociology of work included Parsons, Davis, and Moore, and others. They studied occupations as part of a social system, which needed to be understood within the context of traditional economic theory based on a system of rewards and scarcity of resources.

Marx, on the other hand, developed a theory of labor as opposed to work to emphasize the distinctions between paid wages of capitalist society and the concept of labor as a material and intellectual product of human creativity and cooperation. Contemporary Marxist and feminist theory emerged during the late 1960s as the influence of **functionalism** declined. The shift again corresponds to interest in the changing economic structures as the tertiary sector became dominant, women began to enter the labor market in greater numbers and the political climate was confrontational. Many studies focused on wage and occupational inequalities. Most contemporary Marxists discussed labor and the mechanisms of control.

Some topics explored are union struggles, transnational corporate power, **alienation** of workers, loss of worker control, and deskilling. Some feminist topics are changing **gender roles**, unpaid labor, the dual roles of women, work and **family**, wage differentials. Contributions from theorists of color focused on marginalized roles, occupational segregation, oppression, cultural **identity**, **unemployment**, **urbanization** and wage differentials.

These highlight how theory influences focus and intent of discourse. Factors such as major transformations of the **labor force** created by historically specific economic shifts in demand and technological innovation contribute to the subjects sociologists choose to study. Currently a proliferation of literature in the sociology of work covers almost every aspect of work, including worker attitudes, job satisfaction, the labor process, global restructuring, worker demographics, technology, occupational segments, and the workplace organization. The mainstream perspective continues to examine occupational structure, whether at micro level (social psychological) or macro (structural) levels to understand relationships and changes in the division of labor. Alternative perspectives have introduced many topics, particularly as postmodern interpretations have given voice to marginalized issues. These studies capture the fluidity of global capitalist production and reflect the emerging shift from classifications and the structural constraints of boundaries.

SOROKIN, PITIRIM A. (1889-1968)
American sociologist

American sociologist, social critic, and educator Pitirim A. Sorokin (1889–1968) was a leading exponent of the importance of **values** and broad knowledge in an era dominated by science and power. Pitirim Sorokin was born in the village of Turya, Russia, on January 21, 1889. His training was concentrated at the University of St. Petersburg, though he also studied at the Psycho-Neurological Institute in the same city. From 1914 to 1916 he taught at the institute and then at the university, where he was a professor of sociology from 1919 to 1922.

After serving as secretary to Kerensky, Sorokin was forced to leave the country by the Soviet government. A brief period in Czechoslovakia was followed by several lectureships in the United States, where he was appointed professor of sociology at the University of Minnesota (1924–1930). Sorokin founded the Department of Sociology at Harvard University, where he remained until his retirement in 1959. He was elected president of the American Sociological Association (1965) and continued to attend professional meetings all over the world until 1968.

Sorokin's massive publication list and personal influence encompassed many areas. During the Minnesota period, he was interested in social class, social change, and rural community life. The key works of that period were *Social Mobility* (1927) and *Contemporary Sociological Theories* (1928). In the former he distinguished vertical and horizontal forms of mobility and showed the importance of institutional channels as

mechanisms of mobility. The latter work provided a unique and critical summary of numerous sociological theories, with particular emphasis on the shortcomings of nonhuman and excessively abstract explanations.

Though Sorokin and his associates cumulated and ordered a considerable body of material on rural-urban contrasts (*Principles of Rural-Urban Sociology,* 1929; *A Systematic Source Book in Rural Sociology,* 1930-1932), **social change** and its consequences came to be his major focus for many years. After analyzing the causes of revolution in *The Sociology of Revolution* (1925), he began the imposing four-volume study called *Social and Cultural Dynamics* (1937–1941). This work revolved around the controversial thesis that genuine change is traceable to basic cultural presuppositions which undergird each major social institution, and that these presuppositions change because each type apprehends only a portion of complex societal experience. Sorokin therefore posited a series of varyingly recurrent cycles in social change, from ideational (religious-intuitional) to sensate (objective-materialistic) to idealistic (a mixture of the preceding types).

From this standpoint, Sorokin criticized the application of natural science viewpoints to social science, first in *Sociocultural Causality, Space, and Time* (1943) and with gusto in *Fads and Foibles in Modern Sociology* (1956). In a related vein, he wrote as a sociological Jeremiah against the excesses of modern sensate culture—especially in such books as *The Crisis of Our Age* (1941), *Man and Society in Calamity* (1942), *The Reconstruction of Humanity* (1948), and *SOS: The Meaning of Our Crisis* (1951).

As an antidote, Sorokin's last two decades of life were devoted to the cause of **altruism** and **love**, for which he established a research institute at Harvard. Some results of this interest were published in *Altruistic Love* (1950), *Forms and Techniques of Altruistic and Spiritual Growth* (1954), and *The Ways and Power of Love* (1954). However, Sorokin's fame rests on his scholarship and encouragement of **sociological theory**. His final work *Sociological Theories of Today* (1966) was a detailed critique of trends in sociology since 1925. He died at Winchester, Massachusetts, on February 10, 1968.

SPENCER, HERBERT (1820-1903)
English economist and philosopher

Herbert Spencer was an English philosopher, scientist, engineer, and political economist. In his day his works were important in popularizing the concept of evolution and played an important part in the development of economics, political science, biology, and **philosophy**.

Herbert Spencer was born in Derby on April 27, 1820. His childhood, described in *An Autobiography* (1904), reflected the attitudes of a **family** which was known on both sides to include religious nonconformists, social critics, and rebels. Spencer's father, a teacher, and an uncle saw that he received a highly individualized education that emphasized the family traditions of dissent and independence of thought. He was particularly instructed in the study of nature and the fundamentals of science, neglecting such traditional subjects as history.

Herbert Spencer *(The Library of Congress)*

Spencer initially followed up the scientific interests encouraged by his father and studied engineering. For a few years, until 1841, he practiced the profession of civil engineer as an employee of the London and Birmingham Railway. His interest in evolution is said to have arisen from the examination of fossils that came from the rail-road cuts.

Spencer left the railroad to take up a literary career and to follow up some of his scientific interests. He began by contributing to *The Non-Conformist,* writing a series of letters called *The Proper Sphere of Government.* This was his first major work and contained his basic concepts of **individualism** and laissez-faire, which were to be later developed more fully in his *Social Statics* (1850) and other works. Especially stressed were the right of the individual and the ideal of noninterference on the part of the state. He also foreshadowed some of his later ideas on evolution and spoke of society as an individual organism.

The concept of organic evolution was elaborated fully for the first time in his famous essay "The Developmental Hypothesis," published in the *Leader* in 1852. In a series of articles and writings Spencer gradually refined his concept of organic and inorganic evolution and popularized the term itself. Particularly in "Progress: Its Law and Cause," an essay published in 1857, he extended the idea of evolutionary **progress** to human **society** as well as to the animal and physical worlds. All nature moves from the simple to the complex. This fundamental law is seen in the evolution of human society as it is seen in the geological transformation of the earth and in the origin and development of plant and animal species.

Natural selection, as described by **Charles Darwin** in the *Origin of Species* (1859), completed Spencer's evolutionary system by providing the mechanism by which organic evolution occurred. Spencer enthusiastically elaborated on Darwin's process of natural selection, applying it to human society, and made his own contribution in the notion of "survival of the fittest." From the beginning Spencer applied his harsh dictum to human society, races, and the state—judging them in the process: "If they are sufficiently complete to live, they do live, and it is well they should live. If they are not sufficiently complete to live, they die, and it is best they should die."

Spencer systematically tried to establish the basis of a scientific study of education, **psychology, sociology**, and ethics from an evolutionary point of view. Although many of his specific ideas are no longer fashionable, Spencer helped establish the separate existence of sociology as a social science. His idea of evolutionary progress, from the simple to the complex, provided a conceptual framework that was productive and that justifies granting to him the title father of comparative sociology. His views concerning a science of sociology are elaborated in two major works *Descriptive Sociology* (published in 17 volumes, 1873–1934) and *The Study of Sociology* (1873).

Spencer was particularly influential in the United States until the turn of the century. According to **William Graham Sumner**, who used *The Study of Sociology* as a text in the first sociology course offered in an American university, it was Spencer's work which established sociology as a separate, legitimate field in its own right. Spencer's demand that historians present the "natural history of society," in order to furnish data for a comparative sociology, is also credited with inspiring James Harvey Robinson and the others involved in the writing of the New History in the United States.

Social philosophy in the latter part of the nineteenth century in the United States was dominated by Spencer. His ideas of laissez-faire and the survival of the fittest by natural selection complemented an age of rapid expansion and ruthless business **competition**. Spencer provided businessmen with the reassuring notion that what they were doing was not just ruthless self-interest but was a natural law operating in nature and human society. Not only was competition in harmony with nature, but it was also in the interest of the general welfare and progress. **Social Darwinism**, or Spencerism, became a total view of life which justified opposition to social reform on the basis that reform interfered with the operation of the natural law of survival of the fittest.

Spencer visited the United States in 1882 and was much impressed by what he observed on a triumphal tour. He prophetically saw in the industrial might of the United States the seeds of world power. He admired the American industrialists and became a close friend of the great industrialist and steel baron Andrew Carnegie.

By the 1880s and 1890s Spencer had become a universally recognized philosopher and scientist. His books were

published widely and his ideas commanded a great deal of respect and attention. His *Principles of Biology* was a standard text at Oxford. At Harvard, **William James** used his *Principles of Psychology* as a textbook.

Although some of Spencer's more extreme formulations of laissez-faire were abandoned fairly rapidly, even in the United States, he continues to exert an influence as long as competition, the profit motive, and individualism are held as positive social **values**. His indirect influence on psychology, sociology, and history is too strong to be denied, even when his philosophical system as a whole has been discarded. He is a giant in the intellectual history of the ninteenth century.

Spencer spent his last years continuing his work and avoiding the honors and positions that were offered to him by a long list of colleges and universities. He died at Brighton on December 8, 1903.

SPENGLER, OSWALD ARNOLD GOTTFRIED (1880-1936)

German philosopher

The fame of German philosopher Oswald Spengler rests entirely upon his two-volume study *Der Untergang des Abendlandes* (1918–922) or *The Decline of the West, 1926–928*. It is a major contribution to social **theory**. Spengler was born in Blankenburg, Germany, on May 29, 1880, the son of a postal worker and the only surviving son among four children. The family moved to Halle, where Spengler attended a classical high school then universities in Munich and Berlin before returning to the University of Halle, where he earned a doctorate in 1904. His major subjects were mathematics and the sciences. Spengler taught at Saarbrücken, Düsseldorf, and Hamburg, before moving to Munich in 1911 after a small inheritance from his mother's estate allowed him to become a private scholar. Spengler was never in good health—he had a heart condition and suffered from headaches—so he was exempt from military service.

With the outbreak of World War I, Spengler's financial fortunes suffered a relapse since his inheritance had been largely in foreign securities. Living in a dreary slum, he began work on *The Decline*. Despite hardships, he was driven by what he considered to be a great idea building within him. Originally, he planned to call his work ''Conservative and Liberal,'' and it was to concern only Germany. But as the years passed and Spengler grew more and more frightened by what he considered his country's fatal foreign policy decisions, his scope expanded to include not only Germany but the entire Western world. The final title came from a bookstore window where he saw a publication on the fall of the ancient world. The first volume was finished in 1917, but was turned down by the leading German publishing houses. Finally, Spengler found publisher Wilhelm Braumuller of Vienna. The first volume, with a print run of only 1,500 copies, was published in 1918 and the second in 1922. It sold 100,000 copies within a few years.

The Decline was Spengler's doomsday scenario regarding the future of **civilization**. Although it drew criticism from

Oswald Spengler *(Corbis Corporation [Bellevue])*

scholars for its unorthodox methods and errors of fact, it exerted enormous influence and appeal. It is a study of the **philosophy** of history. The literary style is extravagant and cluttered, but its ideas portray the author as a nationalist who also sees himself as an artist. Spengler was convinced that most civilizations pass through life cycles and that historians can predict the duration and meaning of the yet-to-come stages in Western history. One **culture** can never transfer its spirit to another culture. At first, a culture is aristocratic, according to Spengler, influenced by the presence of brave warriors or priests. As a culture matures, it is influenced by urban growth, social classes, intellectualization, and the growing importance of money. During this state, the culture begins to lose its creativity, resulting in a shallow existence called civilization. To Spengler, Western culture had already passed through its creative stage and had entered a period of reflection and reliance on material comforts. He listed some of the symptoms of a decadent civilization as **democracy**, humanitarianism, and pacifism. Spengler concluded that at this stage, the future held only a period of decline for the West. *The Decline of the West* catapulted Spengler into instant stardom. Defeated and humiliated in World War I, Germany's national conservatives hailed him as their political prophet. Suffering from inflation and revolution, Germans were encouraged by Spengler's conviction that the

Baruch Spinoza

war's victors, especially the arrogant United States, might also be doomed to decline.

Then he devoted himself to critical writings against the Weimar Republic, then in power. Ironically, Spengler, himself a racist and admirer of authoritarian rules, regarded the emerging Nazis with distrust. Yet, they regarded him as an intellectual **prophet** mainly because in *The Decline*, Spengler, although predicting Western civilization's fall, formulated a means to save it. Known as Prussian **Socialism**, Spengler's ideas appealed to the Nazi's National Socialism, and Hitler granted Spengler an interview in 1933. But when *Hour of Decision* was published later that year, Spengler was no longer in favor because of the book's critical tone against the party. He was condemned by the Nazis and lived in relative isolation until his death in Munich on May 8, 1936.

SPINOZA, BARUCH (1632-1677)
Dutch philosopher

The Dutch philosopher Baruch Spinoza ranks as a major thinker in the rationalist tradition, and his *Ethics* is a classic of Western **philosophy**. His writings express the crucial issues of metaphysics more clearly than in any thinker since Plato.

Baruch, or Benedict, Spinoza was born on November 24, 1632, in Amsterdam, where his Jewish family settled after fleeing Portugal. Little is known about his early education except that the young Spinoza showed a facility for languages and eventually mastered Spanish, Portuguese, Dutch, Hebrew, Latin, Greek, and German. In 1656 Spinoza was expelled by his congregation on charges of atheism.

For the next four years Spinoza worked as a teacher in a private academy in Amsterdam and his interests in mathematics, physics, and politics developed. From 1660 to 1663 he lived near Leiden wrote *Principles of Cartesianism*, *Short Treatise on God, Man and His Well-Being*, and the first book of *Ethics*.

Spinoza then moved to a suburb of The Hague, where he worked as a lens grinder. The *Ethics* was completed between 1670 and 1675. In 1670 he anonymously published some these writings and corresponded with various scientists and philosophers, particularly Henry Oldenburg, the first secretary of the British Royal Society, and Gottfried Wilhelm von Leibniz. Spinoza died in The Hague on February 20, 1677, of consumption aggravated by inhaling dust while polishing lenses.

Rationalism, the name ascribed to a movement of thought that originated in the seventeenth century, is usually associated with the names of René Descartes, Leibniz, and Spinoza. The point of departure for all rationalists is subjectivity. Descartes, initially a highly original mathematical physicist, generalized from his conception of the method of mathematical reasoning and believed that its proper application might guarantee local certitude in all areas of knowledge. The justification of his theory of reasoning led Descartes to several metaphysical commitments concerning the nature of reality.

Descartes maintained that God was a supreme rationalist who had created an orderly universe that could be known by following the clear and distinct ideas of reason. Descartes separated the mind as a free spiritual power from the physical world of determined mechanical relations. With this step a set of contradictory dualisms between subject and object, thought and extension, spirit and nature, God and world, and freedom and necessity were bequeathed to philosophy. In *René Descartes' Principles of Philosophy* (1663), Spinoza pointed out that Descartes's errors resulted from his inability to follow the metaphysical implications of the logic of rationalism, especially with respect to the notion of substance. Spinoza's *Ethics* consists of five books. The central concern of the treatise is to move from a consideration of God to the realization of human freedom by an analysis of knowledge and passion and their conflict.

Spinoza resolved to seek true happiness and joy "after experience had taught me that all the usual surroundings of social life are vain and futile." Men everywhere esteem "riches, fame, and the pleasures of sense," but their pursuit seems to diminish rather than to enhance men's lives through frustration or overindulgence. The only remedy for the wretchedness of life is to improve or literally "cure" the mind. In a striking passage Spinoza wrote: "All these evils seem to have arisen from the fact that happiness or unhappiness is made wholly to depend on the quality of the object which we love. When a

thing is not loved, no quarrels will arise concerning it—no sadness will be felt if it perishes—no envy if it is possessed by another—no fear, no hatred, in short no disturbances of the mind.'' The ultimate aim of philosophic knowledge is what Spinoza called a ''synoptic intuition'' of all reality as a deductive system. And this is why the *Ethics* begins with a consideration of God as substance. In Spinoza's view the task is not so much to explain God as to understand what it means to be a man. As a rationalist, Spinoza aimed at nothing less than total certitude, and the clearest way was to utilize deductive reasoning. But the content of the system is such that the truth of each proposition depends, in part, on its necessary connection with the others.

The first book of the *Ethics* draws out the implications of one of the central assumptions of the Western metaphysical tradition: that the intrinsic order of nature is an effect of an ordering mind, God. The startling conclusion that Spinoza draws is that the words nature, substance, and God are interchangeable. Spinoza's argument is conducted *a priori*, or without appeal to experience, and its truth or falsity rests on what the concept of substance entails logically. Accordingly, God exists by definition, or negatively one must posit a reason for the nonexistence of such a being and again only God would suffice.

The second book of *Ethics* examines the nature and origin of the mind. An infinite substance possesses infinite attributes, but the mind perceives only two: thought and extension. Yet the relation between mind and matter is not dualistic but one of **identity**, for ''thinking substance and extended substance is one and the same substance comprehended now under this and now under that attribute.'' To understand this doctrine, sometimes referred to as ''psychophysical parallelism,'' the mind must overcome its reliance on sense knowledge (''opinion'') and even advance beyond scientific understanding (''adequate ideas'') of cause-and-effect relations to a synoptic vision (''intuition'') of the complete system of reality. In this perspective the mind of man is an individually existing modification of infinite **intelligence**, the body is the object of that idea, and the two are like different sides of a coin. With this understanding of man's place in nature, Spinoza took up the questions of moral life. The issue is life itself: one is either ensnared in ''human bondage,'' prey to the whims of desire or external persons or objects, or one achieves the freedom that Spinoza calls ''blessedness'' and that is virtue's own reward.

STAGES OF DEVELOPMENT

The evolutionary concept that societies must pass through certain fixed stages of development in a progression toward modernization, a notion that has its theoretical roots in the nineteenth-century work of Herbert Spencer and Émile Durkheim, became very popular among economists during the middle of the twentieth century. The originator of this theory of development was economist W. W. Rostow, who argued in his well-known book *The Stages of Economic Growth: A Non-*

Communist Manifesto (1960) that all societies necessarily moved through five stages of growth. Rostow's stages outlined the manner in which undeveloped countries would, through imitation of advanced societies, catch up economically to the Western world, and ultimately, all societies would reach an advanced stage of self-sustaining economic growth. In describing his stages of growth, Rostow noted: ''These stages are not merely descriptive.... They have an inner logic and continuity. They have an analytic bone-structure, rooted in a dynamic theory of production.''

Rostow lays a clear claim early in *The Stages of Economic Growth*: ''It is possible to identify all societies, in their economic dimensions, as lying within one of five categories: the traditional society, the preconditions for take-off, the take-off, the drive to maturity, and the age of high mass-consumption.'' Traditional **society** is characterized by a pre-Newtonian understanding of **science and technology**. Due to the lack of modern methods, means of economic production are limited. Although the society is not stagnant, the changes and improvements that occur are limited. Traditional economies are agriculturally based, and a majority of resources and time are allocated to the agricultural system. According to Rostow, the social **structure** existed in a dualistic balance between what he termed ''long-run fatalism'' and ''short-run options.'' Namely, over the course of time, one does not expect any better life for one's children than what was experienced by one's parents (long-run). At the same time, it is assumed that the improvement of the quality of life is a worthwhile and desirable goal (short-run). **Social mobility** is limited by the influential position of family relationships, and political control is centered in the regional power of landowners. Within the category of traditional societies, Rostow placed the dynasties of China, the civilizations of the Middle East, medieval Europe, and those post-Newtonian societies that have remained untouched by scientific innovation.

The second stage is the period in which the preconditions for take-off are developed. As modern science is introduced into society, new production methods spur the development of agriculture and industry. Rostow noted that technology is often brought to the traditional society by an outside, sometimes hostile, force. However, regardless of the means of transmission, once the ideas of scientific modernization exist within the society, the process of incorporating them into common life is established. Subsequently, an ideology develops that considers economic progress as innately good. Based on national pride, private profit, or social concern, a new mentality emerges that drives the economy forward. A critical shift toward take-off occurs when regionalism is replaced by an effective central **government** that fosters new feelings of nationalism.

When a society advances to Rostow's third stage, the take-off, he said that it has come ''to the great watershed in the life of modern societies.'' Dominant in the take-off society is the normalcy of growth. The bonds of ''long-run fatalism'' are shrugged off, and improvement and expansion are expected and often eagerly anticipated. The economic basis for the country shifts away from agriculture to manufacturing, but the

scientific advancement of agricultural production remains vital to a rapidly increasing economy. Now, no longer are mere individuals investing capital to spur the economic system, but a politically powerful group takes control of the society's economic future. It is the potent combination of technological advances and this shift in power that catapults a society into the take-off stage, which produces marked and rapid expansion of the economy.

Following take-off, the next stage, the drive to maturity, is a long process of sustained, if not steady, economic progress. During this period, which Rostow estimates at to last between forty and sixty years, society continues to advance through improvements in technology and production techniques. Whereas the take-off period is initially created by a small number of high-achieving economic endeavors, during the drive to maturity, the society develops a complex and diversified system of economic structures, which results in an increase in exports and a decrease on the dependence on imports. Rostow defined the drive to the maturity stage as "the stage in which an economy demonstrates that it has the technological and entrepreneurial skills to produce not everything, but anything that it chooses to produce."

Finally, a society reaches the pinnacle stage of the age of high mass-consumption in which, upon reaching maturity, the economy makes a shift toward durable consumer goods and the service industry. According to Rostow, two noticeable changes occur: the earning power of a majority of the population exceeds what is required to provide basic food and shelter, and the makeup of the workforce moves decidedly toward skilled labor. As the spending power of a large number of people increases, the economy and social goals become centered on the consumption desires of the population. In this post-maturity stage, technological advancements cease to hold primary importance, and capital is funneled into welfare and social programs.

After Rostow proposed his five stages, numerous variations of modernization theory appeared. Although different in form, they all shared the assumptions that (1) societies pass through various stages, (2) each stage is characterized by unique social and cultural forms, (3) currently undeveloped countries will eventually achieve the economic growth level of Western Europe and North American countries, and (4) Western technology is the driving force in the evolutionary movement of economic development. Dominating economic development theory during the 1960s, the stage **model** came under attack during the 1970s. Criticized for the complete lack of attention to international relations, its ethnocentric concept of equating "modern" exclusively with Western **culture**, its failure to account for the contemporary situation of undeveloped Third World countries, and its inability to account for variations to the deterministic movement through stages, the stage development model was replaced by other theories such as **dependency theory**, world-systems, and new-Marxist interpretations. Although stage development theory has been abandoned by contemporary economists, the underlying concepts still influence public policy and international relations.

STANDARD OF LIVING

Standard of living is a conceptual tool used to describe the minimum necessities that must be met to maintain an individual in a given social position. In the social sciences the aspirations of an individual are strongly influenced by the consumption pattern of that individual's peers, thus a person's standard of living changes as his income and interactions change. In sum, a standard of living is an analytic tool concerning what money can buy and how much money is necessary to buy the essentials given a particular level of consumption and social position.

The most frequent measurement device for standard of living has been the development of a budget that approximates the income necessary for a given social position and consumption pattern. These constructs outline costs associated with food, housing, and other consumable items for a given social location. Criticism of these guidelines, however, has arisen over their arbitrariness. The standard of living concept is used in research on economic growth, international affairs, inequality, labor supply and consumption. For the sociologist the standard of living affects future welfare, socialization, inequality and industrialization and as such is crucial to the study of society.

STANDARDIZATION

Standardization is a mathematical process that allows direct comparison between two or more groups or populations. Measurement **data** are often standardized so that resulting numbers are set to the same scale. In data analysis, standardization can be fairly simple and straightforward or fairly complex.

Perhaps the simplest type of standardization is the calculation of percentages or rates. While raw numbers are useful information, standardization often allows a useful context or perspective for these numbers. The utility of standardization can best be communicated by example. If Country A has 2 million people in **poverty** and Country B has 4 million in poverty, we know that Country B has more poverty than Country A. However, without standardizing these results, we do not know which country has the biggest poverty problem relative to its population. While Country B has twice as many people in poverty as Country A, Country B's 4 million impoverished residents may only account for 10% of its population whereas Country A may have 25% of its population in poverty. This example illustrates that standardization allows more comparable data than do raw numbers by taking into account other factors and data.

This type of standardization is common. In addition to simply calculating percentages, standardization can take the form of rates, such as per capita or for some standard number of people. Social scientists sometimes calculate a nation's Gross National Product (GNP) on a per capita basis to standardize this measure because differences among raw calculated GNPs do not account for each nation's population size. In its *Uniform Crime Report,* the FBI reports crimes per 100,000 people for **cities**, states, and counties so that **crime** rates can be easily compared.

Percentile rankings, such as those on standardized tests, are another method of standardization. Computations in percentile rankings are based on the tendency of measurements to be normally distributed about their means, represented by the normal curve, also called a bell curve or standardized curve. If the **mean** and standard deviation of measurement data are known, statistical methods can determine the percent of the population above and below an individual measurement and provide a percentile ranking. This can account for variations and fluctuations in measurements among populations and can be used to compare individual cases based on their respective rankings in each of their own populations. The height measurements of men and women are an example. A six-foot tall woman may be taller relative to the female population than a man of the same height relative to the male population. In this case, standardization allows a more objective comparison by accounting for inherent variations among populations.

Statistics themselves are also standardized to allow easier understanding and analysis of measurement data. Often, standardization involves re-calculating observations based on how many standard deviations they are from the mean, resulting in a standardized z score. This simplifies the process of analyzing the distribution of measurement data and allows easy identification of extreme and influential cases. In multiple **regression**, for example, standardized residuals (score variations not explained by the regression **model**) allow easier evaluation of the model and identification of outliers. In many statistical procedures (including some parts of multiple regression), results are standardized on a scale of 1 to 1 so that their relative strength can be identified.

STANDPOINT THEORY

Standpoint **theory**, a type of **grounded theory**, is most frequently used by feminists because it acknowledges the perspective or viewpoint of the writers of an **ethnography** in terms of where they are in the system. The rationale for standpoint theory is that dominant group members develop and define theories, applications, and realities. In the process they elevate their own rationales and attributes and diminish those of minorities. This tendency leads to distortion of knowledge for both dominant and minority groups. Even so-called "objective" quantitative research is flawed by interpretations based on dominant group ideology. There is no such thing as "value free" research because topic, theoretical framework, research design, and interpretation are all influenced by the researchers' views. Standpoint theorists use qualitative research methods to understand experiences of mothering, **sexual harassment**, career development, sexual assault, **pornography**, **prostitution**, and abuse in order to expose inequality in patriarchal institutions. They feel that this provides insight into the complexity of minority experience.

Standpoint theorists believe that the people who experience discrimination (such as that based on **race**, **ethnicity**, sex, and sexual orientation) experience two realities. They develop survival skills in order to negotiate, work with, and accommodate the dominant group while they simultaneously function within another reality of imposed limitations on expectations and opportunities. The dual emphasis gives minorities a deeper, more complete understanding of how **society** functions. For example, **Patricia Hill Collins** identifies three assumptions of family studies that have been less applicable to black families. These include the idea that mothering occurs within a private, nuclear family with the mother totally responsible for child-rearing, sex-role segregation, and economic dependency on men that makes stay at home motherhood an ideal.

Karl Marx and Friedrich Engels are credited with developing a framework for the process involved in **division of labor** that creates. Feminist writers feel that by substituting the term "women" for "proletariat" then one can understand a *gendering of awareness* that accompanies division of labor. Gender struggle parallels class struggle. Symbolic interaction is incorporated in standpoint theory to describe the fact that males and females construct and internalize through negotiating different material, social, and symbolic expectation. Noted architects of standpoint theory include Julia Wood, Sandra Harding, Patricia Hill Collins, Nancy Hartsock, Mary Forman, and Mary Swigonski.

STANTON, ELIZABETH CADY (1815-1902)
American writer and women's rights activist

The writer and reformer Elizabeth Cady Stanton (1815–1902) was perhaps the most gifted and versatile feminist leader in American history. Elizabeth Cady was born in Johnstown, New York, on November 12, 1815. The daughter of a judge, she became a feminist while still a child after hearing her father inform abused women that they had no legal alternative but to endure mistreatment by their husbands and fathers. She had the best education then available to women. While completing her studies at the Troy Female Seminary, she experienced a nervous collapse on hearing the great revivalist James Finney preach; henceforth she had an intense hostility toward organized religion.

In 1840 Elizabeth Cady married the abolitionist leader Henry B. Stanton. Although he sympathized with her ambitions, he was not wealthy, and she remained home with her five children for many years. All the same, she was able to do some writing and speaking for the feminist cause. In 1848 she organized America's first woman's-rights convention, held in Seneca Falls, New York, where the Stantons resided. She also composed a declaration of principles, which described the history of mankind as one of "repeated injuries and usurpations on the part of man toward woman, having in direct object the establishment of an absolute tyranny over her." Despite opposition, she persuaded the convention to approve a resolution calling for women's suffrage.

During the Civil War, Stanton and her friend and ally Susan B. Anthony created the National Woman's Loyal League to build support for what became the Thirteenth Amendment to the Constitution. Once the slaves were free, the

Elizabeth Cady Stanton *(National Archives and Records Administration)*

two worked to ensure that women would be enfranchised along with the freedmen. However, their work was seen as a threat to the black franchise. If the struggle to enfranchise black males was associated with votes for women, it was thought, neither black men nor women of any color would get the vote. But this opposition only made the Stantonites more stubborn. Their campaign finally divided the women's suffrage movement into two camps: their own New York-based band of uncompromising radicals, the National Woman Suffrage Association, and a more conservative group, the American Woman Suffrage Association, which was centered in Boston and accepted the primacy of black suffrage. There were several ideological differences between the two organizations, and a good deal of personal animosity developed. By 1890, however, these were overcome, and the two organizations merged into the National American Woman Suffrage Association with Stanton as president.

Although Stanton remained active into old age, she was less concerned with suffrage and more interested in divorce re-

form and other matters during her last years. A fluent and witty writer, she collaborated with Anthony and Matilda Gage on the first three volumes of the massive *History of Woman Suffrage* and edited *The Woman's Bible*. Mrs. Stanton also wrote articles on a variety of subjects for the best contemporary magazines. She died on October 26, 1902, in New York City.

STATE THEORY

Three major theoretical schools offer different perspectives on the nature of the state and the role of various social classes in state formation and policy development. The pluralist perspective on the state, which dominates mainstream Western liberal thought, holds that the state is an aggregate set of institutions that stand above and between interest groups and social classes, mediating more or less equally their interests. In this view, state policy is a collective consensus of **public opinion** imposed on the political arena by these competing groups; the state is simply an arbiter of those competing voices. Pluralists argue that relevant interest groups and political parties protect the interest of the populace by representing those interests in the decision-making process, negotiating for those interests, and in influencing state policy-makers. In this view, the state represents a multitude of social, political, and interest groups, who individually and collectively influence state policy and shape the actions of state institutions. Those various interests are institutionalized within state and **political organizations** such that they ensure a stable pattern of interaction. These interactions create a degree of competition among social actors who constitute the political realm over which the state mediates.

Two major variants of Marxist thought have, since around 1970, focused renewed attention on the role of the state in capitalist **society**, both rejecting the claims of the pluralists. Numerous scholars have contributed to the development of these two variants of state **theory**, which represent the "cleavage" inherent in Marx's own perspective of the state. First, the structuralist view holds that the state acts, not on behalf of the interests of particular class interests, but in the general interests of capital, protecting the institutions of the state and relationships of state manager that are necessitated by capitalism and capitalist class rule. Second, the instrumentalist perspective attributes to the relationship between the capitalist or ruling class and the state mechanism an essential instrumental character, contending that the state is an instrument of the capitalist class in promoting its own interest, resulting in state action being both shaped and constrained by dominant economic agents within society.

C. Wright Mills and Ralph Miliband are frequently credited with launching contemporary critiques of the pluralist view of the state and refocusing discussions on its instrumental nature. Placing particular emphasis on the role that capitalists play in influencing political outcomes, partially by its staffing of the state apparatus, Miliband cited comparative **data** that demonstrate the homogeneous class background of state elites. G. William Domhoff cited similar data in asserting that a small

social upper class rooted in the ownership and control of a corporate community is involved in the policy-planning network and exercises great power in both political parties, thus dominating federal policy decisions. Domhoff, like Mills, viewed the upper class as an institutional network, controlled by families who share a high degree of social cohesion through shared memberships, intermarriages, and residential proximity, including corporate interests, government (political and military) elites, and conservative intellectuals, who together combine to help shape federal state policy.

Because state elites are concerned with the reproduction of the capitalist state, the ruling class is not only able to influence the state but are obligated to become politically active in order to defend their particular class interests. However, state theorists from the structuralist school argue that the capitalist state does not directly represent the dominant class's economic interests, but their political interests act as the organizing agent of their political struggle. Fred Block agreed that those who run the state are more likely to reject policy alternatives that conflict with the logic of capitalism.

Theda Skocpol and her associates reinvigorated the structural view, arguing that the state is autonomous in the mechanisms it institutes in insuring political order and promoting national economic development. Skocpol proposed two separate aspects of state **autonomy**: states as organizations and states as actors. In the first cases, states are organizations that claim control over territories and people so that they may formulate policy and pursue goals that are not simply reflective of the interests of particular social groups or classes. In this view, states are seen as composed of structures and activities that influence the formation of groups and the political demands imposed by particular sectors of society. Skocpol and others who argued that the state is relatively autonomous, denied that it is reflective of the goals of any particular class or fraction of class and that state leaders are recruited or closely allied with particular classes within society.

Block advanced an alternative structuralist view of the capitalist state, which attempts to resolve the structure-instrumental debate over the role of the state. He proposed that the state is primarily structural and that the consciousness of the capitalist class plays a secondary role in its functioning. He argued that a sharp **division of labor** exists between those dedicated to the accumulation of wealth and state managers who are interested in expanding their own power. While this division of labor creates a difference in worldviews between elites and state managers, it occurs within a structural framework which ensures that, despite the division of labor, state managers tend to act in the general interests of capital.

STATELESS SOCIETIES

The term stateless **society** refers to disparate or fragmented societies without a centralized state power. Governmental tasks are carried out by individuals as an adjunct to their position and status as members of kinship or descent groups. These forms of society can achieve coherence, sustain existence, even conduct warfare without clearly differentiated state forms, either because they are small enough to require no differentiated machinery or because they possess a complex segmentary structure.

Oftentimes, the term is incorrectly used to describe states that do have a recognized ruler of some sort but do not have a clearly demarcated state structure per se. For example, a state that lacks any leader or heads of state at all is said to be a stateless society, but one with a chieftain is not.

STATISTICAL INFERENCE

Statistical inference is the process of drawing a conclusion about a population on the basis of statistics generated within a sample selected from that population. Researchers infer about population parameters, based on their analyses of sample statistics. Making inferences from sample results is preferable to examining the entire population because it is expensive as well as difficult to collect **data** from all elements within a population. Using the laws of **probability**, social science researchers are able to generalize findings generated within randomly selected samples to the population from which the sample was drawn.

The process of statistical inference is in direct contrast to the other major purpose of statistics—the description and summary of data collected from a sample or population. Instead, the function of statistical inference is to test hypotheses about whether a relationship between variables or a difference in some **variable** between groups exists in the population. These hypothesis tests allow researchers to conclude, with a known risk of error, that the results found within a sample are not due to random chance but are due to a real relationship or difference that exists in the population.

Statistical inference relies on the use of probability samples, which are also called random samples. Probability samples are selected using the technique of EPSEM, which stands for ''Equal Probability of Selection Method''. Hence, each element in the population has the same chance of being selected into the sample. Probability samples help to ensure that the sample is representative of the population, and representativeness in the sample is necessary for inferring results generated within the sample back to the population from which the sample was drawn. Analyzing probability samples selected using EPSEM techniques reduces **sampling error**, as does the use of large samples (i.e. those with 100 or more cases). In sum, researchers' confidence in the inferences they make about a population based on results found in a sample drawn from that population increases with the use of probability samples of large size.

Statistical inference is used to test hypotheses about relationships or differences between groups that may exist in some population. These hypotheses are tested using sample data, and based on probability **theory**, the results found in the sample are inferred back to the population. There is always a risk of error in terms of drawing an incorrect conclusion about what is truly occurring within the population. However, this

risk of error is known and kept low, as it is set by the researcher prior to beginning the statistical analyses. In the social sciences, the risk of error (alpha) is conventionally set at 0.05. This means that there is only a 5% risk of concluding that the results found in the sample reflect true relationships or differences in the population when in fact the results obtained within the sample were merely due to random chance or sampling error.

For instance, a researcher interested in **race** and educational attainment might draw a random sample of U.S. adults in order to determine (depending on the level at which the variables are measured) whether race and educational attainment are related in some way or independent of one another, or if the average educational attainment significantly differs among racial groups. After analyzing the data collected from the sample, the researcher may find that, on average, the educational attainment of the white respondents is higher than that of the African American respondents in the sample. Using the laws of probability, the researcher can infer those results to the populations (all white U.S. adults and all black U.S. adults) from which the samples were drawn. If the researcher has followed convention and set the risk of error at 0.05, there is only a 5% chance that the observed difference in educational attainment between whites and African Americans in the sample does not truly exist in the populations of all white and African American adults in the United States.

The process of statistical inference thus permits researchers in the social sciences to generalize sample findings to the population from which the sample was drawn. Because statistical inference is predicated on the laws of probability, the risk of drawing an erroneous conclusion is known, and small. In addition, statistical inference allows the testing of hypotheses using sample data, which is less expensive, and more quickly and easily obtained than is data from an entire population. Statistical inference processes are thus efficient, economical, and frequently used within social science research.

STATISTICAL METHODS

Statistical methods are specific processes by which mathematical equations are applied to **data** that has been compiled in a systematic, scientific, and logical way. The term, **methodology**, refers to the scientific procedure by which **theory**, logic, and the scientific method are employed in the research process. The methodology of a research inquiry follows several basic steps, creating a study design, collecting data, and interpreting the collected data. These steps follow the basic scientific method used by all researchers in scientific disciplines. In creating a study design, the researcher must first choose an area of research or specify a research topic. This topic should be one that is significant and relevant to the scientific discipline.

The next step in the research process is the collection of data. Data can be collected through observation, experiments, **surveys**, or case studies. Experiments are usually completed in a situations where observations and conditions are clearly controlled. Surveys can be done as interviews, phone conversations, or paper surveys. Surveys are designed to take a small sample from the larger population and use that to gauge the characteristics of the entire population. Great care is taken in selecting the sample to ensure that it is random and unbiased. **Case studies** are designed to study an event over a long period of time.

The final stage is the data analysis stage. Statistical tests, or analyses, are applied to the data and then used to interpret the data. Statistical tests are the actual mathematical processes that are applied to the data that has been collected. Through mathematical calculations, the data is transformed into useable information. Preliminary descriptive statistical tests, including the **mean**, **median**, mode, and range of a particular set of data, are conducted to find out some basic information about the sample.

Other statistical tests are performed on the data to find out answers to the questions posed by the research inquiry. Some common statistical tests include **measures of central tendency**, measures of variability, tests for the normality of the distribution, and tests for skewed distributions. Other more in depth statistical tests include **regression** analysis, factor analysis, and cross-tabulations. Each of these statistical tests is used to answer questions about the data collected and how different variables may interact with one another.

Many statistical tests are based on the assumption that the distribution of the data is "normal". A **normal distribution** occurs when individual data points plotted on a grid take the shape of a bell curve. If data is clustered around the center of the distribution the bell shape is achieved. In measuring the central tendency of the data, researchers are looking for a point where the data is clustered to find out what is average or typical for that data. In measuring the variability of the data, researchers aim to find out whether the data is spread out uniformly through the distribution or if there is a great deal of variability (large gaps or clusters in the spread of the data throughout the distribution). Testing for a **skewed distribution**, when the bulk of the variables cluster toward one end of the distribution, is a useful statistical test.

STATISTICAL PACKAGE FOR THE SOCIAL SCIENCES (SPSS)

The Statistical Package for the Social Sciences (SPSS) is a software package designed to aid social scientists in performing quantitative statistical analyses. The original software was created by three Stanford University graduate students in the late 1960s. Since then, because of the capabilities and availability of more powerful computers, SPSS and similar software packages have made new and more complex **data** analyses possible. While SPSS was originally created to run from mainframe computers at universities, it is currently available for both the Windows and Macintosh platforms and can be run on home machines. SPSS is currently owned, developed, and marketed by SPSS, Inc.

There are several components to the software, including a base program which is capable of basic statistical analyses

as well as a number of different add-on modules for specific purposes (such as one for advanced multivariate analyses and another for business related analyses). Data can be entered by the researcher directly into SPSS, and various existing data sets are available from many sources. Additionally, data from other spreadsheets can often be used with SPSS without being reentered, either by copying and pasting directly into SPSS or saved as files which are readable by SPSS (such as.csv, or so-called comma delimited files); SPSS-generated files can also be saved in common spreadsheet formats so the data can be read by other programs.

After entering or loading data into the software, researchers can use SPSS to generate analyses quickly and to perform various tests and computations much more easily (and possibly more accurately) than by hand. Once data is entered into the program, most analyses are simply a matter of a few mouse clicks. SPSS is capable of many types of statistical analysis, from the basic (such as frequencies, means, and standard deviations) to the complex (such as multi-level multivariate analyses and logistic regressions). SPSS also enables researchers to generate and edit various types of graphs of data.

STATISTICAL SIGNIFICANCE

Statistical significance involves testing whether a relationship found in analyzing inferential statistical **data** is the result of chance, rather than reflecting an association that exists in the population from which the sample was drawn. The conventional social science criterion is that if this probability, or p-value, is less than 5%, than the finding is statistical significant. Finding that an association is statistical significant is important evidence in supporting a hypothesis.

The p-value of a relationship is highly related to both the size of the sample, and the magnitude of effect. Larger samples increase the probability that an effect will be found significant because of a greater probability that the sample will accurately reflect the population from which it was drawn. Relationships that are large in magnitude are more likely to be statistically significant because the **probability** of a large effect being a result of chance is much less than that of a small effect. Additionally, discussions of statistical significance are all based upon the fact that samples, no matter what size, should be representative of the population they are drawn from.

A Type I error is committed when a relationship that does not exist in the sample's population is found statistically significant in the sample. A Type II error is the reverse, when an association that exists in the population is not found to be significant in the sample. Type I errors are considered to be more serious. It should be noted that statistical significance does not **mean** that the observed relationship is significant in the traditional sense of the word. There are many relationships that are either unimportant sociologically or of a small magnitude that are technically statistically significant but do little to advance the social sciences.

STATISTICAL VALIDITY

Validity is a fundamental concern in the social sciences. The general principle of validity refers to the extent to which statements about empirical phenomena are correct, as judged by evaluation of the methods that produce statements about empirical phenomena are adequate means of **measurement**. There are generally three types of validity: measurement, causal, and external. Measurement and causal validity (or **internal validity**) have a statistical basis. Measurement validity expresses the degree to which measures of social processes correspond to a hypothesized underlying phenomenon. Causal validity focuses on whether causation can be established unambiguously. External validity addresses the question whether conclusions drawn from empirical **data** generalize to the population of interest.

Establishing causal validity is more difficult than assessing measurement validity. Experiments are optimal settings for determining causal relations. However, in the social sciences, even experiments may fail to meet the rigorous criteria for showing causation.

Measurement validity rests on the issue of alignment of measures of social phenomena with the theoretical construct they are intended to measure. Schutt (1998) offers three basic approaches for examining measurement validity: content, criterion and construct.

Content validity depends on the extent to which measures of a concept seem appropriate. Often referred to as **face validity**, this approach initiates a series of questions researchers must first ask with respect to measurement of their variables. For example, the question ''How much did you drink last week?'' may appear a valid measure of frequency of drinking, but it is known that people who drink heavily underreport their drinking. As such, the measure is not a completely valid one since it does not uncover the underlying behavior.

Criterion validity compares the measures of a concept with either more direct measures or measures that have already been validated. Self-reports, for instance, are used in the social sciences to capture individual behavior but they require comparison with other criterion measures such as direct observation in order to be valid. The criterion measure, against which the measure of interest is compared, may be measured at any time concurrent with or subsequent to, the measure being validated.

Construct validity compares the measures of a concept to other social phenomena expected to correlate with the measures. This approach is usually undertaken when no other criterion for validation is present. For example, past research shows that substance abuse should be related to medical, legal, familial, and occupational, problems. A substance abuse construct is said to be valid when this is true. Unfortunately, construct validity too closely resembles tests of substantive hypotheses.

Content, criterion and construct validity are usually developed in conjunction with analyses designed to ascertain **reliability**. Reliability differs from validity insofar as it addresses measurement consistency rather than measurement accuracy.

STATISTICS AND STATISTICAL ANALYSIS

Statistical analysis is the process of examining **data** numerically to determine the distribution of a particular **variable** (referred to as descriptive statistics) or to assess the relationship between two or more variables (called inferential statistics). Statistics are the numerical representations of such analyses. Data (or the singular datum) are pieces of information that serve as the basic units for drawing conclusions about particular phenomenon. Data can be collected by a number of methods, but in statistical analysis they must be transferable to a numeric form.

Univariate analysis involves the examination of one variable, and multivariate analysis involves the examination of two or more variables. Most statistical analyses are multivariate and inferential and are designed to determine whether a relationship exists between variables in a sample (the actual data being analyzed) and whether that relationship likely exists in the population (the entire group from which the sample was taken). Determining whether the relationship exists in the population is called testing for **statistical significance** and requires taking a random sample from the population and running a specific analysis to determine significance.

Statistical analysis is a quantitative method of analysis. Quantitative methods predominate the field of **sociology**, as they allow researchers to make broad generalizations and make specific statements about social phenomena that is popular with policy makers and funding agencies. With the introduction of computer-based analysis procdures, statistical analysis can be implemented with relative ease and speed, making it more accessible to a greater number of social scientists.

STATUS

Status has long been used to denote a person or group's prestige or position as defined by law or **custom**. Status defines who a person is (e.g. doctor, American, woman, child), and expectations and beliefs are attached to any given status. A person or **group** never has just one status, and status is always defined in relation to other actors with different statuses.

Status is not a direct function of an individual or group's characteristics (e.g. age, gender, **race**, **intelligence**, income, **property**, education, occupation, leisure and consumption habits, etc.) but rather the social interpretation of those characteristics. Accordingly, skin pigmentation or income may carry different meanings and thus signal different status depending on the period, place, and social groups in which one lives. Since the status ascribed to a characteristic may vary across time, space and social group, and since different statuses sometimes conflict, these conditions may lead to what sociologists call "status ambiguity," or uncertainty and stress about what status should hold sway in any given situation. For instance, a female lawyer and a male client may struggle over whether their competing lawyer-client and female-male status relations should guide their interaction.

Since the birth of **sociology** as a discipline in the late 1800s, status has remained a staple concept at least in part be-cause of its power and prevalence in social life. Status shapes human behavior from the most fleeting to the most enduring, the smallest to the largest scale, the most mundane to the most peculiar.

Max Weber was one of the earliest and best known scholars to develop sociology's concept of status, which he sometimes also called "honor." In contrast to **Karl Marx**, who explained power squarely in terms of social class, Weber understood power more complexly in terms of "party" (i.e. organization), class, and status. Weber recognized that status, class and party often cohere, but he argued that these forms of power are analytically if not also sometimes empirically distinct. For instance, college professors have relatively little class power but typically enjoy substantial status.

More currently, status figures saliently in the works of prominent sociologists like **Pierre Bourdieu** and Michelle Lamont, who demonstrate how status, as expressed notably through talk and consumption practices, is used to establish distinctions and "symbolic boundaries" between people and to thus perpetuate class inequality.

STATUS ATTAINMENT

Research on **status** attainment examines which jobs individuals obtain, a theme common to studies of **social stratification**. The basic theory guiding this research is that in a modern capitalist industrial **society** people compete for jobs in a labor market rather than obtaining them through inheritance or assignment. The primary aim of status attainment research is to assess which attributes of individuals are most important in determining who gets better jobs in different labor markets and in different countries. To make this determination most researchers generally use survey **data** to examine a representative samples of workers and statistically control for both individual characteristics and labor market attributes. The main points of contention are how to measure the quality of jobs and which attributes of individuals and labor markets should be studied in explaining status attainment.

One dominant perspective in status attainment research comes from Peter M. Blau (1918–) and **Otis Dudley Duncan** (1921–)in their book *The American Occupational Structure,* (1967). Blau and Duncan categorized occupations along one continuous scale, which they labeled a scale of occupational status. To construct this index the authors examined the average educational attainment and average pay levels of men in different jobs, as measured in "Occupational Change in a Generation" survey conducted by the U.S. Bureau of the Census in 1962 and made an index that maximized the **correlation** of these two variables. The argument for doing so was that these features made the highest ranked jobs good ones to have and thus most desired by people in the **labor force**. They then examined how different qualities of respondents in the survey were related to who got the better jobs. These features included their educational level, first job, and paternal occupational status and educational level. The primary finding was that educational attainment was the key effect in obtaining a higher status

job in modern industrial society. While paternal status has an effect, it mainly operated through education. That is, high status fathers were able to help their sons attain a high status by making sure they got a good education.

This way of studying status attainment has been expanded since the publication of *The American Occupational Structure*. The measure of quality of jobs, or index of occupational status, has been updated to reflect the current composition of the labor market, since jobs disappear, new ones come into existence, and the status of some jobs changes over time. In addition different versions for men and women have been formulated, as well as versions for different countries and an international one for use in comparing modern industrial societies. Researchers have also examined additional features of workers in the labor market. In addition to expanding the analysis to include women and the effect of gender on status attainment, other variables meant to measure **intelligence**, aspirations, **race** and **ethnicity**, and school quality have been examined. Studies have also included situational variables to measure differences across region, industry, labor market segment, or the ethnic enclave in which a person works. Finally, attempts have been made to incorporate the new theoretical innovations of social capital and cultural capital. The first argues that connections, or network ties, between people and their **family**, friends, and acquaintances are important in determining what type of job a worker is able to find. The second argues that different aspects of upbringing, such as attendance at cultural events like the symphony or the ballet, having parents who owned a lot of books, or reading the newspaper every day are important for determining future job status. As with mobility research, although these factors have influence, the main finding of the importance of education in status attainment in modern industrial societies has not changed.

This tradition of research has been critiqued in two ways. One regards the measure of occupations, as many researchers believe that a single continuous measure of occupational quality is too simple and that instead there should be categories of jobs that relate in a non-linear fashion to each other. The second critique regards the **measurement** of individual attributes that contribute to future status. In particular, some argue that many measures are relatively crude, in particular features such as intelligence level, aspirations, and social and **cultural capital**. Much of the current work in status attainment focuses on how to improve this research to address these criticisms better.

See also Social Stratification

STATUS CONFLICT

Status conflict is when people experience conflict or contradiction between the many different statuses they hold in their lives. This can also be referred to as status strain or role conflict.

There are two sociological definitions of status: prestige, as theorized by **Max Weber**; or a position held by a person in a particular social system, which is the more common usage of the word. Each status is assigned a label. Statuses are relational, meaning they have no inherent meaning; a particular status does not mean anything without being in relation to other statuses (e.g., husband does not exist or make sense without being in relation to wife; there is no sense to employer without employees). Statuses do, however, exist independent of the individuals occupying them. The status of teacher exists even if there is no one in a specific teaching position. Individual people are associated with specific statuses only through their participation in and interaction with a given social system and their association with a certain label. Statuses locate social position's in the complex network of social interactions and relationships.

For each status, there are corresponding role expectations. These are the socially agreed-upon actions and beliefs of a given status. All the statuses we occupy are known as our status set. This set is comprised of all the statuses with which we are associated by others or ourselves. Although statuses can be considered objective entities, independent of the individuals occupying them, the experience of occupying a status is completely subjective and profoundly affects the thoughts, behaviors, attitudes, and experiences of individuals.

In a normal social situation, one status is dominant; this is the manifest status and is the status with which one is most closely identified. The other statuses that fall to the background are latent statuses. The latent statuses can come to the forefront in an emergency situation, at a moment's notice (e.g., in the middle of teaching class, a professor gets a call that her mother is sick and her manifest status changes from being a professor to being a daughter) or can emerge during the course of a normal day (an employee can become a father when he picks his daughter up at school).

There is status conflict or strain when one or more latent status comes to the forefront (becoming a multiple manifest status), when two or more statuses conflict in their demands, when people disagree on the nature of or expectations associated with a status, or when one status prevents an individual from fulfilling the expectations of another status. Ultimately, this means that one person cannot fulfill all of the role expectations of the several statuses all at once (e.g., being a full-time executive and a full-time father). This is different from compound status, which is when two or more statuses are combined successfully (e.g., being a policewoman).

There are several ways to alleviate the strain caused by status conflict. The first is to push one status from a manifest to a latent position. The individual can then focus on one status at a time, although it may entail a violation of the expectations of one status in favor of another. Second, one can abandon one of the statuses completely (e.g., choosing to be a parent rather than an executive). Third is status segregation, when statuses are sometimes manifest and sometimes latent, depending on the situation. Last is status distance, when people emotionally separate themselves from a disagreeable part of one status, dissociating from the negative aspects, lessening the repercussions of status conflict.

Research has shown that today, women usually experience a higher level of status conflict than men. This is because

of the superior position men hold interpersonally and institutionally in our **culture**. There are certain statuses that are viewed as conflicting with being a woman because of beliefs about women's intellectual, emotional, or psychological weaknesses. The statuses that most often conflict for women are those of spouse or parent and worker, mostly because women are still primarily responsible for the care work provided in the home and **family**. There is, however, an increasing number of men who experience these conflicts as well, as more men take on caretaking responsibilities.

STATUS CONSISTENCY AND INCONSISTENCY

Status consistency and inconsistency is a **model** for explaining political attitudes and behavior and **social change** more generally. The model was developed by Leonard Broom, James Geschwender, **Gerhard Lenski**, **Pitirim Sorokin**, and others in the 1940s and 1950s as an alternative to Marxist conceptions of class conflict. Building on Max Weber's distinction between social classes and status groups, the model assumes that complex, modern societies are stratified along several related but distinct hierarchies rather than in a single unidimensional hierarchy. Lenski, for example, identified four social hierarchies: income, occupation, education, and **ethnicity**. Broom, following **W. Lloyd Warner** and Leo Srole, examined ethnicity, occupation, social class, and residence. Individuals whose standing is consistently high or low across these various hierarchies are said to have a consistent or ''crystallized'' status. Conversely, individuals whose standing is higher in one or more of these hierarchies than their standing in others are said to have a discrepant or inconsistent status.

The model hypothesizes that individuals with low status consistency (and, Broom adds, awareness of it) are subject to psychological pressures that make them more likely to support social change. In Geschwender's formulation, status inconsistents experience a gap between desires or expectations, on the one hand, and actual circumstances, on the other hand. When actual circumstances are better than those believed to be proper, this gap is experienced as guilt. When actual circumstances are worse than those believed to be proper, the gap takes the form of anger. Moreover, Broom argues, because status inconsistency heightens one's social visibility, it may generate psychological effects (such as **prejudice**) in others as well. These psychological pressures, according to the model, lead status inconsistents to adopt coping responses, particularly efforts to change **society** through protest or revolution. Geschwender traces rightist movements to a combination of high ethnic status with low levels of occupation or income; leftist movements are said to stem from a combination of high educational level with a low level of occupation or income. The timing and intensity of protest is accounted for by the intensity of the psychological states generated by status inconsistency.

The status inconsistency model has been criticized for placing too much emphasis on psychological discontent while neglecting resources and political context. Moreover, critics

have argued, proponents of the status inconsistency model view protest as a way of coping with psychological distress rather than a rational means of attaining political goals.

STATUS GROUP

The concept of status group refers to a social group in which membership is based upon the shared social esteem of group members. This concept was first introduced by **Max Weber** in his the three-volume *Economy and Society*, first published in Germany in 1921. Weber developed the concept of status group in an effort to move beyond the narrow Marxian focus upon economic class-consciousness as the principal foundation of group solidarity. Weber suggested that in addition to class membership, other social indicators such as educational attainment, heredity, and political power provided similar foundations for collective group affiliation.

Therefore, while Karl Marx's examination of social group membership rested solely upon a person's relationship to the means of production within society, Weber's concept of status group illuminated various other avenues for the formation of group solidarity. Furthermore, while Marxian analyses identified **property** ownership, or lack thereof, as the primary source of group privilege or disadvantage within a **society**, Weber's augmented analysis distinguished social prestige and style of life as similar foundations for the existence of group privilege or disadvantage.

Weber identified four specific status characteristics of that are common among status group members. These status characteristics reveal the boundaries of social intercourse that are common within effectively solidified status groups. First, members of a particular status group tend toward the practice of endogamy. **Marriage** outside of tightly bounded status groups is uncommon. Second, social activities tend to include only those who are clearly identified as members of the status group. Third, status groups tend to exhibit a preference for particular modes of acquisition, thereby denigrating others. And finally, status groups tend to share and uphold clearly defined ''status conventions,'' traditions or modes of interaction that are embraced as indicative of status group membership.

Weber's notion of status group has thus functioned to illuminate the various ways in which bounded social communities are formed. Moving beyond Marx's singular focus upon economic class, Weber's concept of status group reveals the ways in which other **social indicators** contribute to the formation of group solidarity within industrialized societies. Furthermore, because it is not limited to the analysis of economic class membership in capitalist societies, Weber's more inclusive examination of social groups has provided a useful concept for the analysis of group formation in pre-industrial and non-capitalist societies as well.

STATUS SYMBOLS

A status is a place within the social **structure** that is linked to a set of expected behaviors and roles. A status may be ascribed

when a person is born into a particular status such as one's gender or **race**. On the other hand a status may be achieved, as in occupational status, parental status, and/or marital status. A **symbol** is a visible sign, which represents or suggests something else by reason of relationship, association, convention, or accidental resemblance and has cultural significance. The symbol itself is significant because it may convey shared emotions, information or feeling, and may function for **social cohesion** and commitment or may represent social conflicts.

Status symbols are those items that designate an individual's statuses by sight and hearing cues. These symbols provide some of the information that individuals use to know the expectations for interacting with others. Examples of status symbols include uniforms, jewelry such as wedding rings, and other external items. These status symbols allow individuals to feel more comfortable interacting because each status is accompanied with certain expectations about how the incumbent is supposed to behave and how others are to behave toward the incumbent. In other words, when an individual has an idea as to the status of another, the first person can develop expectations about the interaction itself, how the other will act, how they should act, and then perform.

STEREOTYPE

A stereotype is a generalization of a category of people on the basis of perceived traits or attributes. These traits attributed to particular groups are based on received, often prejudiced information rather than on personal experience. Stereotypes reduce and exaggerate characteristics of particular groups and often carry negative connotations. It may be safe to say that stereotypes, like caricatures, reduce people to a simple set of traits, and it is this reduction and not necessarily the traits themselves which prevent those who accept stereotypes for seeing more comprehensively. The elderly, women, minorities, teachers, homosexual men, and politicians, are all groups that have a stereotype surrounding them. The elderly move slowly, women are emotional, minorities do not speak English well, teachers are upstanding citizens, homosexual men are airline stewards and hairdressers, politicians are crooked. In fact, every individual can be stereotyped in some way, by age, **race**, body size, physical attractiveness, disability, speaking mannerism, etc. The potential for reducing someone to less than all he or she is, is always present.

Once a stereotype of a **group** is formed and learned, many people tend to accept it as fact. Individuals then used these "facts" to make generalizations about all individuals within those groups. For example, our **culture** assigns goodness to beautiful people and assumes unattractive people, often those with a foreign accent, are **evil**. For example, Ursula of the *Little Mermaid* is an evil character in the story, this quality being highlighted by her foreign accent. Negative stereotypes are the foundation for **prejudice** and **discrimination**. Prejudice is a judgment or **attitude** about a particular group who has been negatively stereotyped, and discrimination is the action taken on the basis of those prejudices. So-called positive stereotypes are also limiting and damaging.

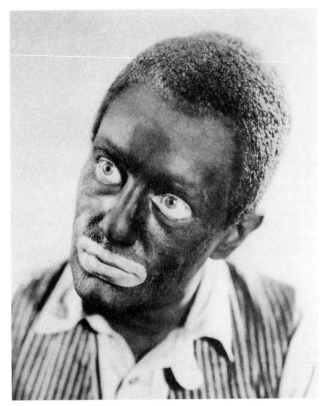

White actors of the past oftentimes portrayed the "blackface" stereotype, which exaggerated characteristics of African Americans and carried negative connotations *(Corbis Corporation [Bellevue]).*

Stereotypes create **social inequality** and social discrimination in the following way. When a particular group is labeled, this label follows it and can affect a range of activities for the group. The point is the process of stereotyping simplifies and thus makes "understandable" what people in fact do not know. The process also perpetuates old, mostly unexamined beliefs, like that wealthy people are better than poor people or that newly weds are happy or that good politicians are handsome men. In short, stereotypes are convenient simplistic ways of handling poorly complex topics.

STOUFFER, SAMUEL A. (1900-1960)
American sociologist and statistician

Samuel A. Stouffer (1900–1960) was an American sociologist and statistician. He was among the leaders in applying rigorous **methodology** to sociological investigations. Samuel Stouffer was born in Sac City, Iowa, on June 6, 1900. After receiving a bachelor's degree at Morningside College in Iowa (1921), he took graduate work at Harvard University and then at the University of Chicago, where he obtained a doctorate in **sociology** (1930). He taught at the universities of Chicago and Wisconsin and worked with several governmental agencies during the 1930s. During World War II he was director of the professional staff of the Information and Education Depart-

Samuel A. Stouffer *(The Library of Congress)*

ment of the War Department. In that position, he directed an important series of studies on attitudes of servicemen. In 1946 he went to Harvard, where he was director of the Laboratory of Social Relations and professor of sociology until his death on August 24, 1960.

Stouffer's work was marked by a dominant interest in the use of varied research techniques, rather than a sustained focus on one or two topical areas in sociology. His doctoral dissertation dealt with the relative merits of the case-study method and the statistical approach. In the 1930s he critically reviewed **data** on **marriage** in his *Research Memorandum on the Family in the Depression* (1937), and he began to investigate the area of opinion research and mass communications, incorporating his findings in a chapter of Paul F. Lazarsfeld's *Radio and the Printed Page* (1940).

A sophisticated use of **statistical methods** by Stouffer was first widely recognized in his analysis of factors in migration (1940). He theorized that the number of migrants between two communities not only was influenced by the opportunities at the receiving **community**, but was modified or reduced by the presence of opportunities between home community and potential destination. By ingenious use of local rental data, he

was able to obtain enough confirmation to stimulate several comparable studies of this basic problem that accurately described and partially explained migrant patterns in the United States.

Stouffer's stature as a research sociologist rests on his experience with **survey research** techniques, which came to fruition in studies on attitudes and difficulties of American military men during World War II. These were published in four volumes known as *The American Soldier* (1949–1950), with Stouffer as leading researcher, editor, or contributor. Stouffer and his associates not only developed useful research techniques (such as scalogram analysis), but demonstrated the importance of relativity in people's judgments of both their rewarding and frustrating social experiences.

In the last decade of his career, Stouffer turned to the study of attitudes in situations of conflicting **values** and roles. He became interested in the actual barriers to educational advancement and mobility among youngsters and, more generally, in the study of the compromises made by people faced by inconsistent moral directives. His major work in this area was the national survey on differences in tolerance of nonconformity, published as *Communism, Conformity, and Civil Liberties* (1955). Stouffer was able to show that tolerance was connected with education, urban residence, and personal optimism.

STRESS

Stress is a term commonly used in everyday **language**, but within sociology, it refers specifically to an internal state of arousal that results from a discrepancy between the demands placed upon an individual and his/her resources for meeting those demands. The sociological investigation of stress builds upon the work of physiologist Walter Cannon, especially his concept of homeostasis and the fight or flight reaction, as well as the research of endocrinologist Hans Selye, who focused on the physiological response to stress, called the general **adaptation** syndrome.

The sociological approach to studying stress, however, focuses less upon physiology and more upon the social patterning of stress and its outcomes. Focusing on what is often called social stress, sociologists are interested in how the **structure** of **society** places differential demands upon people, how individuals cope with stressors, and the results of experiencing stress. These three elements form the basis of the stress process, developed by Leonard Pearlin and others in the early 1980s, which dominates the sociological study of stress. The three components of the stress process are: stressors, mediators, and outcomes.

Stressors are the demands or social factors that bring about feelings of stress and consequently require individuals to modify their behavioral patterns. Stressors are thus distinguished from stress, in that stressors are external circumstances that bring about stress, the internal arousal of the individual. Sociologists argue that stressors are the result of broad social forces, such that sources of stress are unequally distributed across various groups within society.

Pearlin differentiated between two types of stressors: life events and chronic strains. Life events include specific instances of short duration that the individual perceives as stressful, such as the death of a loved one, retirement, or getting fired. The study of life events dominated the early study of stress, following Holmes and Rahe's development in 1967 of the Social Readjustment Rating Scale. Within this **paradigm**, it was believed that all life changes, whether perceived as positive or negative, have potentially deleterious effects. However, recent research indicates that feelings of stress are more likely to be the result of events that are uncontrollable, unscheduled, and undesirable.

Chronic strains are problems, threats, or conflicts which are relatively enduring in duration, and often arise within individuals' social roles, such as spouse, parent, or employee. Research suggests that chronic strains are better predictors of health problems than are life events. Strong empirical evidence exists that suggests that social arrangements have a substantial impact upon people's physical and psychological well-being.

Pearlin contends that many stressors, such as getting a **divorce**, are often misidentified as life events when in fact they are not one-time occurrences but ongoing strains. This overlap suggests that life events and strains interact within stressful circumstances and cause role strain, or the problems individuals experience in carrying out their normal social roles. Common types of role strain include role overload (when the demands of a particular role exceed one's ability to meet them), **role conflict** (when the demands of two or more roles occupied by the individual are at odds and cannot both be met), and role captivity (when an individual occupies a role against his/her wishes, such as a reluctant retiree).

The second component of the stress process are mediators, or resources individuals use in modifying the effects of stressors they experience. Within sociology, the most commonly identified mediators are coping strategies, social support, mastery, and self-esteem. Coping refers to any action people take to avoid or decrease the impact of stressors. **Social support** includes the functions performed on behalf of an individual by significant others. Mastery is the extent to which an individual perceives a sense of control over his/her life, and self-esteem refers to an overall evaluation of oneself. Each of these mediators has been shown, in varying degrees, to modify the potentially harmful effects of stressors.

The final component are outcomes, or the manifestations of experiencing stress. Sociologists working within the stress paradigm focus on both physical outcomes, such as coronary heart disease, as well as psychological health problems, such as **alcoholism**. A major interest within the sociological study of stress pertains to psychological distress, or the subclinical experience of symptoms of depression and anxiety in the general population. Sociologists have documented numerous patterns linking people's location within society to this stress outcome. For example, rates of psychological distress are higher among African Americans, those in lower social classes, and women, compared to whites, those in higher social classes, and men, respectively. These patterns of social stress clearly illustrate the link between social structure and the individual.

STRUCTURAL LAG

Structural lag refers to the gap in the social **structure** that occurs when members of a **society** begin to fulfill new demographic positions, but society has failed to keep pace and construct meaningful roles for them. For example, people today are living longer and remaining healthy to an older age. Such elderly people, however, are generally bereft of educational and employment opportunities, and few meaningful roles in the structure of society have emerged to fill this gap.

The concept of structural lag depends upon the theoretical framework of **structuralism**. This framework mandates that the structures of society have priority over individuals. That is, the patterns and interrelationships among members of a society predominate over the individual. Roles of social actors, in this framework, are defined with respect to those of others. Structural lag, then, takes place when an individual occupies a position for which few interrelationships have been clearly defined. For a structuralist, this state brings about a lack of meaning, since meaning is centered not at the individual, but at the relationships between individuals. Given the example above, the elderly person occupying a new demographic position is left without a concrete and meaningful place in the social structure.

The notion of structural lag is similar to William Ogburn's concept of **cultural lag**. By cultural lag, Ogburn meant that there is often times a rupture between the moral and legal institutions and the technical courses of the society. This break occurs when the technological advancements move faster than the morals and laws within a given society. The **culture** lags, then, when it does not develop a moral consciousness sufficient to deal with its technical capabilities just as the social structure lags when it does not develop suitable places for given individuals within the structure of society.

STRUCTURALISM

The term ''structuralism'' requires a general explanation of the types of **sociological theory** that have developed. Sociological theory may be divided into two broad classes of general theory, both of which are related directly to the level at which a member of **society** complies with behaviors that are considered the society's **norms**. Norms are the behaviors in which members of a society engage that are considered acceptable. The two classes of general theory are called **normative theory** and non-normative theory. Stated simply, normative theory explains how members of a society ought to behave if the members are to accomplish certain results. Conversely, non-normative theory focuses directly on how the members of a society actually do behave. Clearly, these theories are very one sided and are strikingly different in their approaches to explaining in sociological terms the processes by which a society functions. Structuralism is one of the three main kinds of non-normative general theory.

Within structural theory, all social action and function is derived from and based upon the many institutions or struc-

tures that comprise a society. The function of each **structure** is essential to the overall successful operation of the society. And while each structure performs an individual and separate function, each of varying importance, those structures are, within the society, permanently and irrevocably inter-linked and connected. Each of the individual institutions or structures operates under a specific rule, or set of rules, and maintenance of the rules that assure proper function of each structure is so important that individuals who fail to conform to the rules, or break them, are typically punished. In addition, and as part of structural theory, these individual structures and their specific rules, are closely linked as elements within the overall structure of the greater social system.

According to structural theory, the links, or bonds, between the individual structures are so tight that if one individual structure changes, that change will inevitably cause change at some level in all other social structures. In that regard, the processes by which society functions as theorized under structuralism might be explained by using a mathematical equation as an analogy. Such an equation would involve interspersing sociological terms in conjunction with the mathematical figures that would normally appear.

Equations consist of a number of variables. Each **variable** taken separately stands for something specific. But as part of an equation each variable, operating in conjunction with all other variables, produces something larger. Consider the following example in which social functions are shown in parentheses with mathematical functions: $X(\text{people}) + Y(\text{need for beliefs}) + Z(\text{leaders}) = K(\text{religion})$. If, within that sample equation, you substitute $M(\text{need for healing})$ for $Y(\text{need for beliefs})$ the product of the equation becomes something quite different: $X(\text{people}) + M(\text{need for healing}) + Z(\text{leaders}) = H(\text{medical practice})$. So it is within sociological structuralism. Unfortunately for those who subscribe to structural theories, most sociologists now believe that the functioning of society may not be explained through such simple mathematically-based concepts. As a result, structural theories, while considered interesting, are now generally held to be useful only in conjunction with other functional, interactionist or psychological theories, and not as the grand general theory capable of explaining all social function and behavior that was once envisioned.

STRUCTURE

Structure is most frequently used in the phrase social structure, an overused but undertested idea about some identified network of social positions, relationships, and/or behaviors. The phrase is used to describe how constituent participants engage each other in patterned ways. It also explains how those participants generate social life **sui generis**, and how that structure itself is engaged and generated by the activities of participants. The concept of structuration highlights this duality, that structure is both the medium and the outcome (**Anthony Giddens**).

Social structure sometimes refers to a set of elements such as norms, statuses, roles, groups, organizations, and institutions and sometimes refers to underlying **values** or arrange-

ments, as in Marxian work. It is sometimes appropriated to emphasize or assert the significance of particular institutions or fields of action, such as the **family** (George Peter Murdock), in accounting for other institutions or aspects of social life. It sometimes means something general and abstract, such as a system of expectations (Fred E. Katz), a system of **marriage** rules (Levi-Strauss), or an integration of **status** and class analysis (Dahrendorf). Sometimes it means something local and particular, as in the social structure of an Italian-American slum (William Foote Whyte) or Chicago neighborhoods (Park, Harrison White). Other times, it refers to the characteristics of an individual case, from simplistic conceptions of dyads (Georg Simmell) to multidimensional scientific models (Donald Black). The phrase has been so variously conceptualized and operationalized that it has lost cohesive meaning and become merely an analytical tool (Raymond Firth) or metaphor (W.H. Sewell), although sometimes used with important effect. In most cases, structure means something more than the sum of the parts and refers in some way to a whole.

The concept of structure is also appropriated for particular interests and subdisciplines, including political structures, property structures, authority structures, occupational structures, and gender structures. In each case (except perhaps the last), structure is typically intended as something distinct from system, as being a categorical or diagrammatic arrangement rather than a particular enunciation of such an arrangement. Structure is also distinct from organization and stratification, although each may be part of structure.

For Simmell, small groups replicate larger structures, even when in opposition to them. Organization **theory** distinguishes formal structures, which are diagrammatic, and informal structures, the behavioral patterns which deviate from bureaucratic procedures. The very presence of deviation, the concession that structural ideas may have limited explanatory success, raised concerns that structural accounts not be presented as deterministic.

Structure implies consistency and order, stability in lieu of contingency. As such, its use in theoretical work engages forceful generalities about networks or patterns which can be discussed abstractly yet appear to have an air of certainty and specificity. It is often portrayed as an overarching and somewhat static framework, akin to the ironwork framework within a skyscraper. Any emphasis on consistent order, however, attracts the rebuke of those interested in contingency and indeterminacy. Conceptions of structure are cited as being too rigid to account for empirical reality and criticized for not recognizing the efficacy of individual action and in not accounting for social change because structures are presumed to be self-reproducing and without variation. But structures can be instable and their effects contingent upon individual action, historical and environmental circumstance, and more.

Structural explanations need not imply empirical stasis. A structure may be stable enough to allow description or comparison, without being so rigid that it cannot change. The patterns available for comparison may be consistent without particular instances compared needing to remain permanent. Thus, while there is not yet a cohesive structural theory which internally accounts for change, such a theory is not inconceivable. Indeed, it may already exist and yet not be fully explored.

Structural accounts also need not exclude the potential for actor autonomy and human agency to elect from among options, but they do limit those options, place burdens on others, and explain certain patterns and probabilities. Marxist thought sees structures as essentially dichotomous, with cohesiveness and **convergence** to the interests and behavior within each class. But for Marx, interests are subordinated to and disentanglable from structures: The means of production determines both. By contrast, Berger and Luckman do not see structure as determined simultaneously within individual interests, but structure and individual behavior as mutually constituted. Shared conceptions guide individual behavior but only to the extent that they are individually interpreted and employed.

Exclusively structuralist positions may be limited, implying that the future is entirely contained within current facts. Structures are primary only in theory. Effectively conceptualized, they help us understand empirical facts (whether by explanation or through interpretation). Such understanding can be accepted *ceteris parabus,* recognizing that other variations matter. Indeed, whether structures have empirical primacy cannot be discovered without comparing structural theories to other accounts. In that sense, structural accounts may be a crucial resource in the case for agency or they may be its demise.

Structuralism refers not to structural analyses themselves, although it is employed in their rejection, but to the extreme cases (such as Foucault and Althusser) that leave no room for either **autonomy** or construction and interpret social history and processes as the exclusive result of structures. Individual behavior as the consequence of social structures is useful in explanation but is clearly not absolute. The most revolutionary conception of structure is not even interested in individual behavior, but only in the purely social behavior that occurs between individuals (Donald Black).

STRUCTURE AND AGENCY

Modern **sociological theory** has always addressed both human agency and social **structure**. Agency refers to the ability of humans to act willfully in a social context, and structure refers to the context of social institutions, rules, expectations, and conventions which surround that action. Some modern theories, such as **symbolic interactionism**, have focused on the way actions shape or create structure, while other theories, such as structural functionalism, have focused on the way social structures shape or determine actions. In the 1980s and 1990s, a movement emerged in Europe to develop a **theory** that could integrate agency and structure so as to give equal importance to each.

This movement is similar to a contemporary effort in the United States to develop sociological theory that accounts for micro levels of analysis, such as individual beliefs, and macro **levels of analysis**, such as legal systems. Agency is usually thought of as an individual phenomenon, and structure is usually thought of as a large-scale social phenomenon. However, according to George Ritzer, agency is not limited to the micro level but can be characteristic of large groups. Structure can also be found in small group interactions as well as in larger phenomena such as societies as a whole.

Anthony Giddens, Margaret Archer, **Pierre Bourdieu**, and Jürgen Habermas are major theorists associated with the theoretical integration of agency and structure. Giddens, a British sociologist and director of the London School of Economics, took a dialectical approach to the integration. Dialectical thinking involves synthesizing two seemingly opposing viewpoints into a coherent argument. Many earlier theories asserted one of two mutually exclusive viewpoints: that human agency determined social structure or vice versa. Giddens treated agency and structure as two sides of the same coin. He also saw them as two parts of a single process. Agency has always been viewed as a process, but Giddens argued that social structure is also dynamic. This view rendered obsolete the question about which determines the other.

Archer, a sociologist at the University of Warwick in England, believed that agency and structure must be conceptualized separately to best understand their relationship. She also distinguished between **culture** and structure and argued that culture has the greater impact on social action. According to Ritzer, Archer accepted that the cultural system is a product of human agency but stated that, once created, this system is capable of elaborating itself and can constrain action.

Bourdieu, a French social scientist, described the relationship between agency and structure in terms of subjective mental structures (*habitus*) and objective social phenomena (*field*). Ritzer states that habitus refers to the psychological structure through which individuals understand **society**, and field refers to the relationships between the actual social phenomena individuals experience. The field can be construed as structure, and the habitus is the mental framework through which individuals exercise agency. Bourdieu, like Giddens, took a dialectical approach to the relationship: an individual's habitus determines an individual's perception of her or his field, but the field shapes the development of the habitus.

Habermas, a German philosopher and sociologist, described human agency as taking place within the ''life-world.'' According to Ritzer, the life-world is where humans interact and communicate, and the social system develops from the activities in this world. However, in an argument similar to Archer's, Habermas concluded that this system develops a structure of its own that can eventually come to dominate the life-world.

These abstract and complex theories of agency and structure have not had a direct and significant impact on the world outside academia. However, as with most sociological topics, they underlie many areas of society. The concepts of agency and structure are analogous to the concepts of free will and **determinism**. They also underlie American party politics. Some would argue that the Republican Party's beliefs are founded on the idea that humans have agency regardless of social structure and that the government should not create programs such as welfare because individuals are responsible for their own actions. It could also be argued that Democrats believe that social structure can inhibit the opportunities of individuals and that the government has a responsibility to assist these people.

STRUCTURED CODING

Structured coding is used in social **survey research** as a method of questionnaire design that limits the number of possible responses. Closed questions allow respondents to select from a list of possibilities. A simple example is a question that asks the participant to check a box according to gender: male or female. Each response has a particular code assigned for later tally of results. Open-ended questions, which allow individuals to write down their responses, may also employ structured coding. Unlike closed questions, open-ended questions are coded after the results are collected and the information is examined. As Jonathan Silvey explains in *Deciphering Data* (1975), "In a pre-coded **questionnaire**, all the possible answers to a question are listed, so that the interviewer (or the respondent, when a self-administered questionnaire has been used) has only to check off the appropriate categories. But if there are open-ended questions (those not supplied with a selection of pre-coded answers), a systematic way of classifying the responses must be created and adhered to rigidly."

The classification system used in coding is called the coding frame. This provides the basic structure for research development by assigning importance to some factors and disregarding others. The researcher's priorities are manifest within the construction of the coding frame, which usually features both attributes, such as marital status, and measured factors, such as income. The presupposition in the quantitative analysis of qualitative information is that all social research is based on the study of variables. Only through comparative analysis can these variables be identified and assessed. By assigning numeric codes to **data**, the information can be adequately compartmentalized to provide comparative study.

Researchers should be aware of certain problems that can arise in structured coding. First, questions must be as clear as possible and focus on only one dimension of a particular topic so that all respondents understand the question within the same frame of reference. Second, the list of answers provided for closed questions must be exhaustive. Unlisted replies either frustrate the participant or skew the results by not offering appropriate choices. The addition of the "other" category does little to help in assessment. Third, when coding open-ended responses, the coding process becomes much more arbitrary and difficult to manage. For the data to be valuable, an adequate coding frame must be in place, which is governed by specific rules for coding open-ended responses.

STUDENT MOVEMENTS

Student movements are **protest movements**, or forms of contentious collective action, driven by university students. The atmosphere created by the student movements in the 1960s and early 1970s is almost synonymous with public memories of that period. The seeds of these movements were planted by the Civil Rights Movement in the 1960s, during Freedom Summer, when both whites and African-Americans held voter registration drives in the deep south, and the founding of the Student Nonviolent Coordinating Committee (SNCC) at a conference of sit-in leaders held at the traditionally black Shaw University in Raleigh, North Carolina.

Sociologist Doug McAdam surveyed the (now-adult) students who were accepted to participate in Freedom Summer about their involvement in politics in the intervening twenty years; he found that individuals who actually attended Freedom Summer were more likely to remain involved with political and social movements than were those who were accepted but did not attend. Involvement in student movements politicized the actors; participants in Freedom Summer went on to work in the Free Speech, anti-Vietnam, and Women's Movements, and formed organizations such as Students for a Democratic Society.

Students adopted as their own the tactics of the Civil Rights Movement, including boycotts, sit-ins, and marches. They also occupied the offices of university officials and sometimes entire buildings, in the effort to make themselves heard. Some groups used guerrilla theater to educate the public. The students often clashed with police as well as university administrations, leading to arrests and, on occasion, violence.

The Free Speech Movement (FSM) at the University of California at Berkeley closely followed this pattern. Students returning to the University in 1964, immediately following their participation in Freedom Summer, found themselves, along with all other student groups, prohibited from passing out political information from tables set up in the area traditionally used for that purpose. This initial prohibition, and the response of the University administration to student protest of the new rule, galvanized the students and faculty at the campus. Over a three-month period, students persisted in asserting their right to political speech; the University administration retaliated by suspending and otherwise disciplining various participants. The administration building was the site of several sit-ins, both inside and out; at one point, eight hundred people occupied the building overnight. Police arrested the occupying students, which touched off more protests, and the graduate teaching assistants went on strike. Ultimately, a new acting chancellor reinstated the students' rights to political speech on campus. The FSM was the first demonstration of the power university students could exercise.

Students for a Democratic Society (SDS) was another **organization** formed in the crucible of Freedom Summer. Considered the vanguard of the New Left, SDS continued its involvement with the Civil Rights Movement and later became active in the anti-war movement. After internal strife caused the group to disband, the quasi-terrorist underground group, the Weathermen, formed.

Students were the bedrock of the anti-war movement. Protests were held across the country throughout the late 1960s, and a huge demonstration was staged at the 1968 Democratic convention in Chicago, which ended with police throwing tear gas into the crowd and beating and arresting many participants. A similar scene was played out in the protests against the World Trade Organization (WTO) in the spring of 2000.

The most notorious violent incident involving a student protest about Vietnam occurred at Kent State University, in

Ohio. President Richard Nixon ordered the invasion of Cambodia in April of 1970, in an attempt to cut off Vietnamese supply lines. This action set off a renewed round of anti-war protests on college campuses; at Kent State, the protesters burned down the campus ROTC building. Governor Jim Rhodes mobilized the National Guard, which shot into a crowd of protesters on May 4, killing four and wounding nine other unarmed students. Student activism is not limited to the United States. French students staged protests for education reforms in May 1968 and patterned their tactics after those used by American students. In the summer of 1989, Chinese students at Beijing University created a pro-democracy movement and occupied Tienanmen Square alongside other Beijing residents in protest of the authoritarianism and corruption of the Communist Party. The political events of the late-twentieth century demonstrate the power of media in political activism. The television news media disseminates tactical information and garners support for the protesters who stage their demonstrations with full awareness of the media's place in their movement, choreographing their activities with an eye towards being visually newsworthy.

SUBCULTURES

The term, subculture, refers to a **group** of people who hold different values and views from the dominant **culture** but remain a part of the larger culture. Such groups have some degree of permanence and may operate as sub-societies, for example, immigrant groups. Immigrants are often distinguished from the dominant culture by dress, religion, food, language, and geographical concentration. The behavioral **norms** of the group are passed on from one generation to the next. Immigrant groups, like other subcultures, vary in their separateness from the dominant culture. They can be quite distinct from **society** and operate entirely independently with their own social institutions, such as schools, banks, and churches. In the United States, this independence from the dominant culture can be seen in numerous Chinatowns, little Italys, and other ethnic neighborhoods. Other immigrant groups remain distinct from the dominant culture but may not be separated to the same degree.

Other subcultures are less distinct from the dominant culture but still have unique **values** and behaviors that separate them as a group. People are united through art, sexual orientation, music, occupations, and sports. The fitness craze that began in the 1980s spawned a large subculture of road runners. These people are avid runners who log anywhere from 25 to 120 miles per week depending on their level of involvement. As a whole, the group has similar beliefs about nutrition, health, and general fitness; has subcultural heroes; and members often date each other. In other facets of their lives, runners are integrated into the dominant culture.

In modern organic societies, social relationships are complex and people may belong to several subcultures. Many people belong to occupational subcultures that have their own specialty languages as are found in medical fields and in the

Certain societal subcultures, such as skinheads, hold beliefs that challenge the dominant culture (*Corbis Corporation [Bellevue]*).

computing industry. This language is referred to as an *argot*. People may also belong to subcultures temporarily. Fans of popular music groups frequently join subcultures for limited periods of time. The alternative rock group The Cure has a following of male and female youth who dress in black and wear black lipstick and pale makeup in the style of the lead singer, Robert Smith. Youth do not stay avid fans forever but tend to drift in and out of the subculture. It is the subculture that has permanence, not its members.

One of the first and most important sociological theories explaining subcultures was advanced by Albert Cohen (1955). Studying a group of male youths, Cohen proposed that youths join subcultures because of lack of self-esteem and social **status**. Belonging to a group gives each member **identity** and importance. Adherence to the subculture's values and beliefs is an affirmation of identity. The Straight Edge subculture, for example, founded in 1982 by youth fans of the punk rock group, Minor Threat, shuns the use of drugs and alcohol, casual sex, and popular rock music. The group values health, advocates vegetarian diet, and are avid fans of hard-core music—a by-product of punk rock. This subculture's positive values and

beliefs are quite different from those held by many American youth.

An example of a long-standing subculture, the police are part of the dominant culture, but at the same time they hold different values and beliefs about society. Police culture is characterized by an "us against them" mentality, where "them" refers to citizens, thinking which may derive from police overexposure to certain parts of society. Prominent criminologist John Van Maanen proposed that police subculture has a set way of viewing people: police view people as suspicious, resistant to **authority**, and ignorant. According to Van Maanen, this **belief system** pervades the police subculture. Police have an argot which allows them to communicate in terms can only be they understand.

SUBJECTIVISM

Subjectivism is the philosophical view that reality is determined by our subjective experience. The subject matter of **sociology** for subjectivists is feelings, **values**, goals, and emotions of social actors, not concrete observable phenomena. Subjectivism asserts that the goal of sociology is to understand the meanings of events which can be accomplished by reconstructing reality as it appears to the actors. **Herbert Blumer**, for instance, argues that every person has a different perspective in any given situation and that one's perception is constantly being redefined. Understanding the meanings people attach to their behaviors is the primary subject matter of sociology.

Subjectivists, including Herbert Blumer and **Max Weber**, contend that the social world has no reality outside of that given to it by individuals. Reality is created only when objects are defined and labeled. Reality and social facts are socially constructed. In addition, Blumer says that we are constantly in a process of defining and redefining "social objects."

The focus of study for subjectivism is on individuals and individual activities. To understand **society** and human action, subjectivists study language, self, personality formation, and other mental phenomena. The emphasis is on human agency and action, not on structure. Macroscopic phenomena are explained by the **interaction** among individuals.

Subjectivists see life as an ongoing process of interpretation and action. To them the world is dynamic, not static like the objectivists see it. They see humans as active participants in their actions. They do not agree with objectivists that people are determined by their past or position in the social structure. Through the course of defining the situation people make choices on how to act. Subjectivists reject **positivism**. If we are to recreate reality by understanding what it means to the participants, then we cannot be detached neutral observers. To truly understand social phenomena we must experience the reality of the situation as seen by those participating in it.

The philosophical tenets of subjectivism suggest that qualitative methods should be used when conducting research. Reality is subjective and multiple; therefore, one has to use methods that show how the actors view their world which involves participant observation, interviews and **life histories**. It often involves thick descriptions so that the researcher can become a part of the world they are studying. Subjectivism has allowed sociologists to move away from pure quantitative methods and has helped us understand the world through the eyes of the participants.

SUBURBANIZATION

Suburbanization is the result of the migration of the (mainly white) middle and upper-middle classes from faltering city centers to the periphery, where these exurbanites live in settlements that allow residents to work in the **cities** and reside in areas perceived to offer a better way of life.

As World War II drew to a close, veterans began to move their young families to the suburbs, enticed by housing developments built to benefit this population financially. The most famous of these is Levittown, a suburb of New York City located on Long Island. Levittown, a planned **community** that grew to over 17,000 homes between 1946 and 1951, is the paradigmatic example of suburban life in the last half of the twentieth century, characterized by racial uniformity and the uniformity of houses differing in color only; implicit in mass migration to the suburbs is the desire to escape the dangers of increasingly desegregated central cities. African-Americans were discouraged from moving into suburban communities, sometimes subtly but often overtly; the original sale agreements for homes in Levittown stipulated that the owners could not resell to non-caucasians. Eventually, non-caucasians came to live in Levittown and the similar suburbs encroaching upon the American landscape, often triggering another cycle of the "white flight" that brought people out of the cities initially.

The growth of the highway system in the United States facilitated suburban expansion and shaped the suburban lifestyle. Suburbanites commuted to the city by car or public transportation, and day-to-day life was transacted on a terrain unfriendly to pedestrians: neighborhoods often lacked sidewalks, and commercial areas were not integrated with residential areas. Two-car families became the norm in these places because access to the outside world depended upon access to personal transportation; although suburban wives rarely worked outside of the home in the 1950s and early 1960s, these women needed their own cars (the "family car") to do shopping and other errands, and to ferry their children and those of their friends around in carpools, while their husbands worked. The suburban lifestyle was instrumental in the birth of America's car **culture**, as was the post-war prosperity that made suburban living and car ownership readily available to the middle class. Ironically, now that cars are known to be a severe drain upon the environment, some developers are attempting to plan "mixed-use" communities, interspersing commercial and residential structures in an attempt to wean people from dependence upon their vehicles.

The suburbs also changed the shape of local commerce; large grocery stores and shopping malls, built at the edges of suburban areas, drained customers away from "Main Street" (e.g. locally-owned businesses) with the lure of consumer con-

venience. The last few decades of the twentieth century saw the advent of "big-box" and "category killer" stores; these large, warehouse-like structures offered to fill shoppers' needs at a lower price than their smaller competitors, who cannot take advantage of the bulk discount available to these nation-wide chains. Some stores offered everything under one roof, from food to clothing to appliances, while category killers might, for example, sell everything a person would need to build a home, thus saving contractors and homeowners alike from making separate trips to a hardware store, a lumberyard, an appliance store, and a plant nursery when working on home improvement projects.

Concentrations of these nationwide store chains are accessible just off of the highway, where they are joined by fast-food and themed restaurant chains, in cities all across the United States. Contractors build large office parks in these outposts to house mega-corporations that have relocated from the central cities, furthering suburban growth. These commercial agglomerations are known as **edge cities**. The proliferation of edge cities allows American consumers living in states as different as New Jersey and Oklahoma to buy the same clothing, eat the same food, and work in a similar environment.

Some western cities, such as Los Angeles and Phoenix, developed more recently than their eastern counterparts and, as a result, bear more resemblance to large agglomerations of suburbs than to the more traditional urban/suburban layout; this decentralization is becoming a common feature of large metropolitan areas in the twenty-first century. The suburbs may not be the wonderland promoted by developers like William Levitt, but the suburban dream remains strong in the American psyche. Across the country, developers are building ever-larger housing developments, featuring increasingly large, ornate houses built for the prosperous, contemporary **family**.

Sui Generis

Sui generis is a phrase used by Émile Durkheim (1858-1917) to describe social phenomena that emerge as a social reality in and of themselves. For Durkheim the study of **society** was to be concerned primarily with *sui generis* phenomena which emerge from the **collective action** of individuals. Durkheim applied this phrase in his first sociological work *Suicide: A Study in Sociology* (1897) where he argued that **suicide** was not merely the product of the psychopathology of individuals but resulted from a set of complex social forces external to individuals. Durkheim contended that social phenomena like suicide constituted an emergent reality *sui generis* and could not be understood as the simple, collective aggregate of individual acts. In this sense Durkheim wrote: "If... the suicides committed in a given society during a given period of time are taken as whole, it appears that this total is not simply a sum of independent units, a collective total, but is itself a new fact *sui generis,* with its own unity, individuality and consequently its own nature"(46). For Durkheim, society formed a social whole, the dynamics of which could not be reduced to the sum of its individual parts.

Durkheim later expanded this notion of social reality as *sui generis* in his work *The Rules of Sociological Method* (1938) where he argued that sociological investigations should necessarily focus on the *social facts* which are external and constraining to individuals. These social facts have an objective facticity as things in and of themselves and thus can be subject to sociological analysis. The more contemporary studies of the emergent properties of social interaction, **collective behavior**, social structure, and institutional formation are undertaken in the spirit of Durkheim's notion of social reality as *sui generis* the more we will be able to explore social forces and their effects as a measurable reality.

Suicide

Suicide became a topic of sociological inquiry with Émile Durkheim's classic study of it, published in the late nineteenth century. He defined it as "death resulting directly or indirectly from a positive or negative act of the victim himself, which he knows will produce this result." While suicide thus appears as the most personal, the most intimate, and the most intensely individual of acts, Durkheim showed that the suicide rate has all the characteristics of a social fact. Rather than explain the rise and fall of suicide rates by reference to the properties or characteristics of the individuals who commit such acts, Durkheim brilliantly demonstrated that the suicide rate is an emergent property of the victims' social organization. Durkheim's study of suicide is also notable for its early and pioneering use of statistics in sociological research and analysis.

Durkheim's analysis of suicide can be conceptualized in terms of two axes: the degree of social *integration* and the degree of social *regulation*. When either becomes insufficient or excessive, the suicide rate rises as a result. For example, Durkheim found through statistical comparison that suicide rates are relatively high for Protestants, lower for Catholics, and lowest for Jews. The differences, Durkheim argued, cannot be accounted for by a religion's minority status or by doctrinal differences. Rather, the cause lies in the greater degree of **social integration** within the Catholic and Jewish communities, which are less individualistic and more cohesive than the Protestant church. For similar reasons, he argued, suicide rates are reduced by family ties and the strong collective sentiments roused by "great social disturbances." Because Durkheim saw these types of suicides as "springing from excessive individualism," he labeled them *egoistic*. However, an excessive degree of social integration can also raise the suicide rate. This kind of suicide, which Durkheim labeled *altruistic*, accounts for the higher suicide rate among soldiers than civilians.

"But **society** is not only something attracting the sentiments and activities of individuals with unequal force," Durkheim noted; "it is also a power controlling them." When this controlling power is too weak, the result is *anomic* suicide. It is this lack of social regulation, Durkheim argued, that accounts for increased suicide rates during economic crises (which give rise to economic **anomie**) and among divorced

An insufficient degree of social integration may explain the 1978 mass suicide of the occult group led by Jim Jones *(Corbis Corporation [Bellevue])*.

persons (who find themselves in a state of "conjugal ano-mie"). Conversely, an excessive degree of social regulation results in a kind of suicide that Durkheim terms *fatalistic*. While he did not discuss it at length, he referred to this fourth and final type of suicide in a footnote. The two axes of social integration and social regulation thus yield a four—fold typol-ogy of suicides.

Subsequent sociological studies of suicide have tended to confirm the broad outlines of Durkheim's basic arguments. In *Suicide in London* (1955), for example, Peter Sainsbury also found a **correlation** between suicide rates and social disorgani-zation. More recent work, however, has questioned Durkheim's reliance on official statistics and his assumption that the interpretation and classification of deaths is unproble-matic. In *The Social Meanings of Suicide* (1967), Jack Douglas argue that the lower rate of suicide Durkheim found among Catholics has less to do with their degree of social integration than the stigma of suicide among Catholics, which led the fam-ilies of suicides to press officials into misclassifying their deaths as accidental.

SUMNER, WILLIAM GRAHAM (1840-1910)
American clergyman and professor

Best known for his encyclopedic book *Folkways* (1906), Wil-liam Graham Sumner was a founding father of American soci-ology. He explored the foundations of social history and laws of social change from the perspectives of **social Darwinism**, classical economics, and scientific **positivism**. Trained for the ministry at Yale, Sumner gravitated to economics and social science through graduate study in Germany and England. As a sociologist, his teaching and writing pushed American social science to abandon philosophical pursuits and embrace inves-tigation of empirical facts. According to his contemporary, Robert E. Park, "the effect of his researches was to lay a foun-dation for more realistic, more objective, and more systemic studies in the field of **human nature** and **society** than had exist-ed up until that time."

William's parents emphasized the value of sobriety, self-reliance, and personal responsibility. This childhood em-phasis later led him to embrace classical economic doctrine, including laissez-fare policies of market regulation. Sumner's education trained him in inductive **empiricism**. This approach

involves generalizing concepts based on the observation of particulars. That, along with his exposure to German historicism, led Sumner to spend his professional career seeking laws of history through observation of societal indicators. For Sumner, the key to ensuring social **progress** involved developing a critical understanding of the laws that direct it.

Following formal study, Sumner spent two years tutoring at Yale and four years as a clergyman in the Episcopal Church. He returned to Yale in 1872 to occupy a chair in Social Science where he remained until his death in 1910. While he was one of the institution's most popular teachers, he was also the most controversial. Sumner insisted on avoiding philosophical speculation where the studies of scientific fact were possible. This insistence put him at odds with an academic **culture** that was strongly committed to metaphysical inquiry. The issue came to a head when Yale's president, Noah Porter, demanded that Sumner refrain from using Herbert Spencer's controversial textbooks. Though Sumner agreed to use other texts, he publicly criticized Porter's logic as antagonistic to progressive thinking. For Sumner, societies progress and regress according to scientific laws and principles. Accordingly only those disciplines that use the scientific method could hope to seek truth.

Sumner's general **philosophy** was anchored in **evolutionary theory**. He believed that all social behavior conforms to natural law. Building on the thought of **Thomas Malthus** and David Ricardo, he suggested that a man to land ratio is at the heart of societal evolution. Like **Herbert Spencer**, he argued that human beings struggle against one another and nature to secure scarce resources. As population density increases the availability of those resources decreases, which forces **adaptation**. Those with superior **intelligence**, virtue, and efficiency will adapt and reap the rewards of nature. But those with weaker constitutions will be forced to relocate if they are to survive. At the time Sumner wrote, thousands of **poverty** stricken immigrants were entering the United States from southern and eastern Europe providing evidence for his assertions.

Evolutionary **theory** informed Sumner's public writing and lectures between 1875 and 1890. He believed that trade unions, charity, and other forms of social welfare prevent nature from bearing its course and ultimately lead to societal regression. Sumner's fears were anchored in his understanding of human **free will**. Human beings, he reasoned, have full license to ignore natural law despite their best interests. After nearly twenty years of intense writing, teaching, and lecturing about the impending dangers, Sumner experienced a nervous breakdown. He took a brief sabbatical and shifted his focus from the future to the past. The product of this research was his monumental book *Folkways*.

In the work, Sumner argued that human groups develop constellations of habits and **norms** that coincide with their environmental realities. Folkways are designated as those informal group habits that emerge through trial and error. In contrast, *mores* are institutionalized norms that nearly all members of the group abide. Sumner maintained his pessimism about society's future. His research suggested that inherited **folkways** tend to suspend the potential for progress. Yet, he held hope that this fate could be avoided through the scientific study of social laws. With such knowledge, lawmakers and administrators could shape the **mores** to ensure a progressive future.

Sumner spent the final years of his life helping to build the American Sociological Society (now the American Sociological Association). He was the body's first Vice President and later became President in the final year of his life. He died in 1910, just four years after the publication of *Folkways*. His main influence on the field of **sociology** was to anchor it as a scientific discipline.

SUPERCITY

Supercity is sometimes understood loosely as any megalopolis. Defined in a narrower sense, supercity is a descriptive term applied to certain cities that have overcome the challenges of urban sprawl and offer unique advantages and opportunities to residents and visitors. McKinley Conway, an aeronautical engineer and author of numerous books on economic development, writes in ''The Great Cities of the Future'' (*The Futurist*, June-July 1999): ''Many urban areas offer a high **quality of life**. They earn high marks when measured by the usual economic and **social indicators**. Yet, some cities rise above the others, achieving distinction on a higher plane. They are world-class cities that enjoy a special image in the eyes of billions of people.'' Conway defines a supercity as any urban area that has three characteristics: 1) a population of more than one million; 2) sustainable capability to meet its residents' physical and social needs, including shelter, food, safety, health, transportation, and education; and 3) a healthy and dynamic economic structure that is inviting to economic investors so that an adequate number of jobs and public funds are produced.

The establishment of an adequate infrastructure is vital to the success of large cities. Conway names 10 elements of the infrastructure he deems particularly important: water supply, international airport, access to the hinterlands, domed stadium, technology center, communications center, public transportation, waste disposal, green infrastructure, and new political mechanisms. In March 2000, the World Development Federation, an international **organization** of economists involved in large-scale development projects, listed 10 cities chosen as most likely to attain the **status** of supercity. They are: Bangalore, India; Wuhan, China; Istanbul, Turkey; Shanghai, China; Bangkok, Thailand; Denver, Colorado; Atlanta, Georgia; Cancun-Tulum, Mexico; Madrid, Spain; and Vancouver, British Columbia.

SUPEREGO

Three concepts were central to Sigmund Freud's (1856-1939) psychoanalysis, a term that refers to a psychological **theory** of development and a method of treatment. These three concepts

are *id*, *ego*, and *superego*. The **id**, ego, and superego are considered interrelated components of the psyche and are, therefore, key to his **model** of the self. Freud, a pioneer in the study of the human mind, was one of the first to give attention to the role of the unconscious. The id represents our biologically inherited instincts and impulses. It is the source of drives demanding immediate satisfaction and is, for the most part, unconscious. Freud saw the id as mostly preoccupied with the drive for **aggression** and the drive for sex, termed the libido. He felt that all other drives could be traced back to these two fundamental impulses. In contrast to these most inherent impulses exists the superego. This component of the psyche represents the **norms** and **values** deemed appropriate by **society**. These social standards and expectations are primarily transferred to us from our parents and internalized through this learning process, through socialization. Freud conceptualizes the superego as in direct contradiction to the id. The purpose of the superego is to hold back the id's need for expression. Because the id and the superego represent conflicting messages for guiding subsequent action, the **ego** must mediate these presumably incompatible demands, while at the same time trying to find socially acceptable ways for expressing the id's desires.

SURVEY RESEARCH

Survey research is used to measure attitudes and behaviors about a wide range of social issues. The survey, the most widely used quantitative research technique in the discipline of **sociology**, is based on the major premises of objectivism and **positivism**. **Surveys** permit researchers to collect a small amount of information about a large group of individuals that is often representative of the target population.

Surveys allow researchers to determine major trends and distributions in attitudes and behaviors in **cities**, counties, states, and even entire nations. For example, a survey allows researchers to determine that 98 percent of North Americans have at least one television set, that 31 percent attend a religious service weekly or biweekly, and that 47 percent of people identify with the Democratic Party.

Once researchers have decided on a topic for investigation and have chosen the survey as the research tool, the next step is to select a target population of individuals to receive the survey. Common groups of interest for surveys include residents of a specific city, county, state, or nation, and members of governmental, political, or **corporate organizations**. Due to the mathematical nature of sampling, it is not necessary to survey every person in a target population to get an overall view of attitudes and behaviors. In fact, to be representative, a scientifically drawn sample only requires a small percentage of the target population. For example, a representative sample of the 274 million persons in the United States only requires approximately 1200 completed surveys to produce estimates of attitudes and behaviors that are accurate within 3 percent.

Once the sample has been selected, researchers must then focus on construction of the **questionnaire**. The main goal is to write questions that are clear, unbiased, and mean the same thing to all respondents. The idea is that respondents will then select the answer to each question that is true for them. Surveys typically have multiple choice questions where respondents simply check a box to record their answers. These are referred to as closed-ended or forced-choice questions. These types of questions are the simplest for researchers to record and tally. Sometimes, however, respondents will be asked open-ended questions to which they are asked to respond in a few sentences. These questions are more time-consuming to enter into the computer and more difficult to analyze but provide information that may not be gleaned from forced-choice questions.

After the survey questionnaire has been finalized, it will then be administered to the sample. The four most common survey types are mail, telephone, interview, and electronic mail or **Internet**. Mail surveys are the most common. In this instance, the survey and instructions are mailed to everyone in the sample, and recipients are asked to fill out the survey and return it in the enclosed self-addressed, stamped envelope. For telephone surveys, individuals in the sample are called by interviewers to complete the survey by telephone. Interview surveys are conducted with individuals in their households or at a research center. In this case, researchers make arrangements with individuals in the sample to complete a questionnaire in person by having the researchers read the questions to respondents to get their answers. Finally, in the past few years, researchers have begun sending individuals questionnaires through an electronic mail message or through a message directing them to go to an Internet site to complete a survey. Each survey type has unique advantages and disadvantages; researchers choose the type of survey based on issues such as time, cost, desired **response rate**, and questionnaire content.

Overall, survey research has several advantages. Surveys are a quick and efficient means of gauging attitudes and behaviors of large population segments. Due to the uniform and standardized nature of surveys, researchers can quickly record and analyze survey **data** with both simple and more complex statistical techniques. Surveys also provide data on individual and societal change. For example, the General Social Survey, conducted since 1972 by the National Opinion Research Center, provides important data that allows researchers to detect shifts in individual attitudes and behaviors over time.

Survey research is not, however, the only or necessarily the best method of obtaining good data on individual attitudes and behaviors. Surveys have several limitations, and researchers often choose to use other quantitative methods such as analysis of existing data and secondary data analysis, and qualitative methods, such as in-depth interviews, participant observation, and focus groups.

SURVEYS

The survey is one of the most common research tools in the social sciences, especially in the discipline of **sociology**. Sur-

veys provide a method whereby researchers can obtain a small amount of information about a large number of individuals. Sociologists generally survey random samples of persons who are representative of a target population (e.g., city, county, state, nation).

The four most common types of surveys are mail surveys, telephone surveys, interview surveys, and electronic mail or **Internet** surveys. Mail surveys are most common. In a typical mail survey, researchers construct a questionnaire about selected social issues, select a representative sample of some target population, and then mail the survey to those individuals. Good mail surveys include a cover letter explaining the purpose of the survey, an assurance of confidentiality, a request that the respondent complete the questionnaire, and a self-addressed, stamped envelope for return. Mail surveys are relatively inexpensive, quick, less intrusive, and best suited for asking questions about sensitive issues. However, they sometimes produce low response rates and do not work well when dealing with complicated social issues.

The telephone survey is the second most common survey type. For telephone surveys, researchers use random-digit dialing techniques to select samples of individuals to be called at home to complete questionnaires. Telephone surveys provide the fastest means of collecting good **data** but are often expensive, especially when a large staff of interviewers is used and long-distance calls are made.

Another common type of survey is the **interview** survey in which a researcher selects a sample of residents in a particular area and conducts the survey in person. This method typically produces high response rates and allows researchers to answer questions from respondents. Yet, this method is expensive, time-consuming, and interviewers may **bias** the answers of respondents through their reading style and body language.

In recent years, researchers have begun conducting surveys via electronic mail and the Internet. With this method, samples of individuals are sent a **questionnaire** through an electronic mail message or are asked to visit a site on the Internet where a questionnaire is located. Many considerations still surround when it is appropriate to use this method and how confidentiality of respondents can be assured. Regardless of the type used, however, scientific surveys provide an excellent source of data on individual attitudes and behaviors.

See also Questionnaire

SWEEZY, PAUL MARLOR (1910-)
American editor and economist

In his ninth decade of life, Paul M. Sweezy continued to be involved in the publication of the *Monthly Review,* an independent socialist journal he founded with Leo Huberman in 1949. Through his analysis of economics, history, and political systems, Sweezy has made a lasting contribution to Marxian thought in the United States. His role as editor of the *Monthly Review* has been continually intertwined with active participation in numerous political movements. As an adamant support-

er of socialism, Sweezy has influenced economic and political thought for over fifty years through his writing and his personal commitment to the cause.

Sweezy was born on April 10, 1910, in New York City to Everett, an executive at J. P. Morgan's bank, and Caroline (Wilson) Sweezy. He was educated at Philips Exeter Academy and Harvard University, graduating in 1931. He spent the next two years studying at the London School of Economics, where he was first introduced to Marxism. He returned to Harvard in 1936 to attend graduate school and received his doctorate in 1937. His dissertation *Monopoly and Competition in the English Coal Trade, 1550-1850* was published in 1938.

Already working as an instructor of economics during his graduate studies, upon completion of his academic work, Sweezy joined the Economics Department at Harvard fulltime, being promoted to assistant professor of economics in 1940. During the next two years he was involved in the creation of the Harvard Teachers Union and published his first major book *The Theory of Capitalist Development: Principles of Marxian Political Economy* (1942). In 1942, he joined the Army's research unit of the Office of Strategic Services, the organization that served as the precursor to the Central Intelligence Agency.

After completing his service of duty in the fall of 1945, Sweezy returned to the United States and, convinced that he would not be offered a tenured position at Harvard, he resigned from the faculty. After receiving a grant in 1946 from the Social Sciences Research Council, Sweezy moved to New Hampshire and began work on his next book, *Socialism* (1949). In the same year as that publication, Sweezy joined fellow socialist Leo Huberman to found the *Monthly Review* to promote socialist ideas in the United States. For the next fifty years, Sweezy and his co-editors (when Huberman died in 1968, his positions was filled by Harry Magdoff) wrote the review of the month. In 2000, with Sweezy reaching his ninetieth birthday and Magdoff in his advanced eighties, the two senior editors finally withdrew from their roles as managing editors.

In 1948 Sweezy became active in the presidential campaign of the Progressive Party candidate Henry Wallace. Melding his leadership in the pro-New Deal and anti-Cold War platform with his support of **socialism** in the midst of the McCarthy era, Sweezy drew the attention of those seeking out ''subversive'' activities. After addressing the University of New Hampshire as a guest lecturer on the topic of **communism**, Sweezy was subpoenaed in January 1954 by New Hampshire Attorney General's Office, which investigated ''un-American'' activities. Upon refusing to answer questions regarding his and others' roles in the Progressive Party, the contents of his New Hampshire speech, and his beliefs about communism, Sweezy was found guilty of contempt. Most of those previously indicted had pleaded the Fifth Amendment, which provides for safety from self-incrimination. However, Sweezy maintained his silence based upon the First Amendment right to free speech.

After Sweezy's case had finally worked its way through the appeals process, it came before the U. S. Supreme Court

in 1957. Once again taking up the First Amendment, Sweezy addressed the high court: ''If the very first principle of the American constitutional form of government is political freedom—which I take to include freedoms of speech, press, assembly, and association—then I do not see how it can be denied that these investigations are a grave danger to all that Americans have always claimed to cherish. No rights are genuine if a person, for exercising them, can be hauled up before some tribunal and forced under penalties of perjury and contempt to account for his ideas and conduct.'' Considered a landmark case in the area of academic freedom, the Supreme Court overturned the New Hampshire verdict.

Along with his responsibilities at the *Monthly Review*, Sweezy wrote numerous books and served as editor and co-editor of a variety of publications, all published from 1950 by Monthly Review Press. His major works include: *Cuba: Anatomy of a Revolution* (1960, with Huberman), *Monopoly Capital* (1966, with Paul A. Baran), *On the Transition to Socialism* (1972, with Charles Bettelheim), *The Dynamics of U.S. Capitalism* (1972), *The End of Prosperity* (1977, with Magdoff), *Post-Revolutionary Society* (1980), and *The Deepening Crisis of American Capitalism* (1981).

SYMBOL

Symbols are either objects or behaviors that are representative of something else. Not intrinsically related to their referents, symbols are correlated to their referents by socially agreed-upon constructs. That is, the definition and subsequent interpretation of a given symbol is accomplished and/or determined socially. The connection between a symbol and its referent is largely predicated upon the association of attributed characteristics. For example, ''the golden arches'' may be associated with or symbolic of McDonald's or simply fast food.

Symbols may be physical objects, words, or behavior. A crown is symbolic of royalty. Words are symbolic of their referents. Actions may also be symbolic. For instance, a grin may be symbolic of one's amusement. In psychoanalysis, symbols may be understood to represent repressed unconscious desires.

The symbolic interactionist Joel Charon argued that symbols are social objects used by individuals for representation and **communication**. That is, individuals may use objects, words, and actions to represent a status or state of mind. Similarly, individuals may use symbols to communicate thoughts, feelings, or intentions.

The recognition of symbols is important for **sociology** because they are socially constructed. That is, societies construct or create symbolic meaning. Symbols are intelligible because they are conventional or agreed upon. Indeed, symbols facilitate interpersonal communication; consequently, symbols ensure one form of social **interaction**.

SYMBOLIC INTERACTIONISM

Symbolic interactionism is often referred to as the first sociological social **psychology**. During the early 1920s, symbolic interactionism developed, for the most part, in response to Watsonian **behaviorism**. Symbolic interactionists, moreover, regarded the behaviorist stimulus/response **model** as a too simplistic conception of humanity. Whereas behaviorists see human behavior as merely a reaction to various stimuli, symbolic interactionists view individual action as the result of much more dynamic processes.

George Herbert Mead is commonly held to be the founder of symbolic interactionism. Mead's contribution to symbolic interactionism rests mostly on the analysis presented in his book *Mind, Self and Society* published posthumously in the form of notes collected by a few of his students. In *Mind, Self and Society*, Mead developed his notion of the self that is the product of social interaction. In fact, Mead advanced the argument that the self is both the cause and effect of **society**. In other words, Mead saw social **structure** as a social process. Moreover, individuals are born into a preexisting social structure, socialized primarily through education, and are thus compelled to participate in social institutions, such as the **community**, thereby contributing to a social structure that is essentially fluid.

Symbolic interactionism emphasizes cognitive processes, such as thinking and reasoning, and social interaction. The basic premise of symbolic interactionism is that society and the individuals that comprise it are products of interpersonal communication. In fact, individuals succeed in interpersonal communication to the extent that the actors involved attribute similar meanings to objects. Symbolic Interactionism, therefore, seeks to explain social behavior as the consequent of the meanings attributed, by individuals, during social interaction. For symbolic interactionists, meanings are not inherent in any particular social situation but emerge during social interaction.

Symbolic interactionists stress the dynamic, interpretive, and constructive capacities of individuals. More specifically, symbolic interactionists contend that individuals have the capacity for thought; it is this capacity for thought that is shaped by social interaction. During social interaction, it is argued that individuals take the role of the other, which involves the reflexive understanding and/or interpretation of the symbols used by others.

Symbolic interactionism is an important body of sociological theory for two main reasons. First, symbolic interactionism successfully challenged the more simplistic explanations of social behavior, such as behaviorism. Second, symbolic interactionism established that individuals may be thought of as both the cause and effect of a larger social structure.

SYSTEMS THEORY

Systems **theory**, or general systems theory, is an analytic approach to understanding the general or common properties and characteristics of goal-seeking systems of all types. Systems are generally composed of interrelated parts or elements, directed to a particular purpose or goal. The primary model for systems is mechanical and sometimes biological. However, the concept can be applied and used to analyze many types of systems, including social systems.

Systems theory derives from a functionalist view of social structures. Analysis is focused on the unity and preservation of the system, or society, how different structures are coordinated and integrated, and how elements of the system respond and adapt to change. **Auguste Comte**, writing in the early nineteenth century, expressed this view when he stated that ''sociology consists in the investigation of the laws of action and reaction of the different parts of the social system.''

The view of **society**, or the social system, as a living organism was present in early **sociology**. The ideas of social **structure** and function were noted in **Herbert Spencer** and Émile Durkheim and later in the work of Talcott Parsons. They were ultimately concerned with analyzing the ways in which social structures were coordinated and integrated to preserve society as a complete system.

A social system could be seen as composed of a set of social institutions, or sub-systems. These subsystems could comprise units as small as villages, street gangs or even families. Social systems themselves were viewed as networks, or as an organism, composed of numerous connected parts, or elements, all of which contributed to the functioning of the system as a whole. This perspective is known as **functionalism**, or social systems theory.

Systems have various common properties which include goal orientation, or organization, for a purpose such as in the educational system or the health care system. Systems are also composed of elements that are interrelated, so that when there is a change in one part of the system, some or all of the other parts are affected. The elements of the system, organized for a definite purpose, tend toward maintaining *homeostasis*, or balance, through exchange with the outer environment (an open system) and adaptation to change. Those elements of the system which no longer serve a role or function disappear, while new elements required for adaptation to change are ac- quired. Systems can be human constructions, such as systems of **government**, or natural, like the solar system. Systems theory, therefore, essentially involves the study of how systems interact with an environment and how they adapt in order to maintain function and survive.

Systems theory was quite opular in the 1950s and 1960s and was widely applied. **Talcott Parsons**, working with theorists in both physical and social sciences, developed a **model** of the ''social system,'' as well as what he termed ''action systems.'' Parsons saw social systems as tending to preserve their boundaries to differentiate themselves from other social systems or from the external environment, and to preserve the integrity and unity of the system as a whole. Parsons' action systems could be seen to be modeled after a law of physics. He stated that ''a given process of [social] action will continue unchanged in rate and direction unless impeded or deflected by opposing motivational forces.'' These models were the core of Parsons' theoretical perspective of structural functionalism. Parsons hoped to use ''general systems theory'' to integrate the study of various social sciences such as anthropology, economics, and **political science**, but this hope was never realized.

The functionalist approach was extremely influential but has since been criticized as too abstract and too narrow in conception, as not taking into account individual and group behavioral influences. Another criticism is that functions can be invented for practically any element, which may then be used to justify its existence. In addition, according to Alex Inkeles, the perspective is sometimes taken as the ''master key to sociology.'' Nevertheless, functionalism or systems theory has been quite influential in the social sciences and has contributed much to sociological thought and research. Inkeles observed, ''every sociologist to a degree is something of a structural-functionalist.'' The social systems view as predominated in American sociology for most of the latter half of the twentieth century and is used in many types of sociological analysis.

T

TABOO

Taboo is a term of Polynesian origin brought back from Tonga in 1771 by Captain James Cook. Religions that were considered primitive, such as totemic religions, were differentiated from Judeo-Christian religions because of the reliance upon a system of strictures to structure the lives of worshippers. However, all religions and all cultures have their own taboos and laws.

Taboos are proscriptions about behavior for those who would be devout or successful; breaking a taboo, in some religious practices, would bring divine retribution (regardless of the exact nature of the divine) on the perpetrator. The targets of taboos can be sacred or profane, imbued with a sense of the clean and the unclean; for example, inter-caste fraternization is forbidden to Hindus in India, as touching between members of two classes defiles the higher-caste individual. Cows are sacred animals to Hindus (hence the term "sacred cow"), and as a result, there is a taboo against harming one. In some cultures, women who are menstruating are thought to be so unclean that they must withdraw from the **community** every month and they are not permitted to prepare food or to touch males.

The best-known work on the subject is Sigmund Freud's *Totem and Taboo*, published in 1913. Freud wrote that "In the beginning was the Deed". The "deed" he referred to is the first time (in truly prehistoric terms) a **group** of sons murdered and ate their father (they identified with their father by ingesting him) because he was monopolizing all of the women. In the wake of their guilt, they initiated the first two taboos: the totem animal representing the father may not be killed, and due to the close relationship, the sons could not take up with their father's women; the former created religion, and the latter an idea of kinship to support the taboo against incest—thus preventing the murderous brothers from perpetrating violence amongst themselves out of their desire for their father's women. The **incest** taboo remains one of the most prevalent cross-cultural restrictions.

This "origin story" parallels that of *Oedipus Rex;* Oedipus kills his father and marries his mother, despite several efforts to circumvent the prophesied tragedy, blinding himself when he discovers what he has done. Freud's interpretation of Sophocles' play solidified into his theory of the "Oedipus complex": very young boys want to kill their fathers out of jealousy over their mothers, but boys normally grow out of this stage as they age and identify more with their fathers; the outcome of the Oedipal stage permanently shapes an individual's psyche.

Freud believed that societies create taboos to keep people from doing that which they truly—albeit unconsciously—desire. However, taboos also keep societies stratified and compliant by designating who is permitted to take which actions, and by imbuing these laws with religious value to prevent people from questioning their place as dictated by these strictures. **Secularization** has changed most taboos into laws, as has happened with many of the Ten Commandments, and the number of legally prohibited acts far outnumber the two original taboos; retribution by the state has replaced that of the divine.

TABULA RASA

The principle of *tabula rasa*, also referred to as the "blank slate" or "white paper" thesis, states that human consciousness is constructed exclusively within the context of what is learned in the social environment. This principle is based upon the thinking and writings of John Locke, who stated that the mind is like a blank slate. Locke argued that the contents of the mind are written on it by experience, as if written on a piece of white paper.

The tabula rasa thesis arose in direct opposition to arguments that link social behavior to **human nature**. Such arguments assume that all humans possess certain fundamental behavioral proclivities and that these behavioral tendencies are present within individuals from birth. The principle of tabula

rasa rejects the notion that behavioral tendencies exist at any innate level. However, while the tabula rasa thesis does not negate the existence of behavioral tendencies, such tendencies are explained solely within the context of environmental learning and experience. The controversy arising from these divergent currents of social thought has been referred to as the nature versus nurture debate.

In the discipline of **sociology** the tabula rasa thesis is best illustrated in the analysis of **socialization**. Socialization involves the processes through which individuals learn the **norms**, **values**, and acceptable behaviors specific to the cultures and societies in which they live. According to strict socialization theorists, biology plays no role whatsoever in the structure of the mind. The experience of socialization provides the sole framework within which human consciousness is formed. Therefore, within the field of sociology, the principle of tabula rasa exists as the cornerstone of socialization analyses.

TAKING THE ROLE OF THE OTHER

''Taking the role of the other'' describes the development of the self by evaluating oneself from the perspective of another person. This concept evolved from the early twentieth-century writings of two important early American theorists often associated with the symbolic interactionist school, **George Herbert Mead** and **Charles Horton Cooley**.

Both Cooley and Mead explained the development of the self as a process of evaluating oneself from the perspective of one or more other people. Cooley's concept of the ''looking-glass self'' consists of taking the role of another person to understand how we appear to others. By doing this, we can imagine how others judge us and change our behavior and thoughts accordingly.

Mead believed that the mind and self are developed through symbolic interaction. He emphasized the importance of play in the development of a child's mind and self. When children play, they take on isolated roles such as a cowboy or a nurse. When they participate in games, however, children must be able to take the role of every other person in the game and know the relationship between the roles. Mead believed that this skill is carried into adult life, when one constructs the self by taking the role of the ''generalized other.'' In doing this, individuals appraise themselves in terms of the prevailing attitude of the **community**. For instance, when choosing a major in college or considering possible careers, they would likely consider the attitude of the community toward majors or careers under their consideration.

''Taking the role of the other'' is still an important and useful sociological concept. It is a major theme in one of the most famous works in sociology, Erving Goffman's *Presentation of Self in Everyday Life* (1959). Goffman presents social interaction as analogous to a theatrical play. In **society**, the self is strategically constructed for an ''audience'' by assuming the eyes and attitude of the audience and directing them upon oneself.

TARDE, JEAN GABRIEL (1843-1904)
French philosopher and sociologist

The French philosopher and sociologist Jean Gabriel Tarde (1843–1904) made important contributions to general social **theory** and to the study of collective behavior, **public opinion**, and personal influence. Jean Gabriel Tarde was born in Sarlat, the son of a military officer and judge. His father died when he was seven, and Jean Gabriel was raised by his mother. He attended a Jesuit school in Sarlat, obtaining a classical training, and read law in Toulouse and then Paris. From 1869 to 1894 he held several legal posts near Sarlat. Only after Tarde's mother died did he agree to leave Sarlat, and he accepted a position as director of criminal statistics at the Ministry of Justice in Paris. After 1894 he lectured in numerous peripheral institutions outside the university, and from 1900 until his death he held the chair of modern **philosophy** at the Collège de France.

In the last two years of his life Tarde confronted personally his rival Émile Durkheim in debate in Paris, climaxing a series of published exchanges in earlier years. Durkheim was the leading representative of **sociology** inside the French university system. His sociology embodied the rationality and impersonal discipline characteristic of university thinkers of the Third Republic. Tarde, in contrast, maintained a more supple and individualistic approach to social theory. Nevertheless, the two men were in agreement on fundamental conceptions.

These core elements of Tarde's thought constitute three interrelated processes. Tarde saw ''invention'' as the ultimate source of all human innovation and **progress**. The expansion of a given sector of society—economy, science, literature—is a function of the number and quality of creative ideas developed in that sector. Invention finds its source in creative associations in the minds of gifted individuals. Tarde stressed, however, the social factors leading to invention. A necessary rigidity of class lines insulates an elite from the populace; greater **communication** among creative individuals leads to mutual stimulation; cultural **values**, such as the adventurousness of the Spanish explorers in the Golden Age, could bring about discovery.

Many **inventions**, however, are not immediately accepted, hence the need to analyze the process of ''imitation,'' through which certain creative ideas are diffused throughout a **society**. Tarde codified his ideas in what he called the laws of imitation. For example, the inventions most easily imitated are similar to those already institutionalized, and imitation tends to descend from social superior to social inferior.

The third process, ''opposition,'' takes place when conflicting inventions encounter one another. These oppositions may be associated with social groups—nations, states, regions, social classes—or they may remain largely inside the minds of individuals. Such oppositions can generate invention in a creative mind, beginning again the threefold processes.

Tarde was firmly convinced of the necessity for quantifying his basic concepts and processes, and he sought to measure intensities of various opinions. He thus anticipated subsequent work on **attitude measurement**. He also urged the collection of information on industrial production, strikes, **crime** rates, church attendance, voting, and similar actions in order to gauge shifts in public opinion.

Tarde held that an elite was necessary to govern society and to maintain creative innovation, basic cultural patterns, and a minimal social and political stability. Crime, mental illness, and social **deviance** in general were seen by Tarde as frequent results of the disintegration of traditional elites. Migration, **social mobility**, and contact with deviant subcultures also further the tendencies toward deviance.

In opposition to Gustave Le Bon, who analyzed modern society in terms of crowds, Tarde emphasized the importance of the public. Crowds depend on physical proximity; publics derive from shared experiences of their members, who may not be in immediate physical proximity. Trade unions, political parties, and churches all support different publics, and Tarde saw these overlapping but distinct publics as major sources of flexibility in modern industrial societies.

Such technological developments as the telegraph, the telephone, mass-produced books, and the railroad were important in effecting the emergence of modern publics, but to newspapers fell a particularly crucial and independent role. Newspapers helped create public opinions and reinforce group loyalties. Unlike most later mass-society critics, Tarde was more optimistic about these developments for the maintenance of individual **autonomy**. This perspective derived in part from a greater emphasis on interpersonal contacts in channeling ideas and opinions in conjunction with the mass media. In this emphasis on personal contacts, Tarde anticipated subsequent work on the effects of mass communications.

Tarde had almost no immediate followers in France, with the exception of certain criminologists. In the United States, however, he exercised considerable influence on social psychologists, anthropologists, and sociologists.

TAUTOLOGY

A tautology is the needless repetition of the same idea, circular reasoning, also known as ''begging the question.'' Tautological statements are true by definition and, therefore, are unfalsifiable. For example, the statement, ''fifty percent of lawyers graduate in the bottom half of their class'', is a tautological statement. Half is, by definition, fifty percent. The conclusion is thus a restatement of an original premise. In sociology, explanations that situate their effects within the location of the institution that they seek to describe tend toward circular reasoning, in other words, describing an outcome in terms of its process to explain itself. Some initial functional anthropologists, including Bonislaw Malinoski, were likely to argue that all customs must have a function because they exist. They would not exist unless they served some function.

TELEOLOGY

Teleology is a form of reasoning that can occur in one of two ways. It can take the form of an explanation in which the end result of some phenomenon is attributed to the process constructed to achieve that result, and it occurs when something is explained by the function that it fulfills. Teleological reasoning is often described as circular.

Television programming relays numerous messages about cultural norms and expectations, as well as taking part in the actual production of culture *(Corbis Corporation [Bellevue])*.

Examples work best to describe teleology, and a common one is the question, ''Which came first, the chicken or the egg?'' The question cannot be answered because in one sense, eggs (the end result) must be hatched by chickens (the process), and in another sense, chickens (the end result) must be hatched from eggs (the process). **Functionalism** is inherently teleological because it assumes that all parts of **society** function to maintain the whole of society. Therefore, society is because society does, or more succinctly put, society exists as it does because each part of it exists as it does.

Sociologists view teleological reasoning as inherently problematic because it fails to identify causal mechanisms. Instead, the use of teleological reasoning can only identify consequences that result from their own consequences. At best, it describes processes but fails to explain them.

TELEVISION

Television is an electronic device by which images and sounds are transmitted to receivers that project the image onto a screen and reproduce the sound. The first television system was demonstrated in 1926 in England, but televisions were not common households items in the United States until the 1950s.

Sociological research on television has focused on the effects it has on people as a form of media. Television programming relays numerous messages about cultural **norms** and expectations, and takes part in the actual production of **culture**. People have clearly been affected by the images they see on television, as was the case when footage from the **war** in Vietnam contributed to turning public opinion against U.S. involvement in the war. A popular area of study through the 1980s and 1990s in the United States and Canada was the effect of depictions of violence, particular how those depictions affected children. The questions this research attempted to answer centered on whether depictions of violence caused people (particularly children) to be more violent or to be more accepting of violence. The results examining behavior were mixed,

but there were indications that attitudes toward violence were related to watching television violence. This was particularly true for violence against women, in which men repeatedly watching depictions of sexual violence against women became less disturbed by the depictions and began to see the depictions as less violent and more acceptable to the women at whom the violence was directed.

As the content of television programming has changed, so has the interests of social researchers. A concern that developed in the mid to late-1990s was the blurring of entertainment and information-dissemination, which came to be called ''reality television.'' This includes television shows which display footage of actual police work, court proceedings, and home video which occasionally exhibits people engaged in dangerous or illegal activities. Researchers (as well as media watchdog groups and activists) have sometimes found this type of television programming problematic, because while such programs purport to present reality, the actual depictions do not always tell the whole story of an event and can lead people to develop skewed perceptions of the world.

Because so many homes in the United States (as well as in other industrialized countries) have televisions, and television viewing is a major activity, the effects of the programming content have the potential to be widespread and have a tremendous impact on **popular culture**. Television can be both a reflection and a reproducer of culture, which complicates efforts to determine a causal direction in identified relationships between television viewing and attitudes or behavior.

TERRITORY

Territory is a particular geographic area or region of land and water under the control of a person or **group**. It is one's **property**, province, domain, or sphere of interest or action for which one is responsible. It can be a tangible or a conceptual control or responsibility. A territory can be owned officially and legally or by **common law**, which is by unofficial residence on the land or by mutual understanding and agreement. Territories are usually vigorously defended from outsiders. Problems arise when more than one person or entity claims ownership of a particular territory.

A more formal understanding of the concept refers to an area under the formal control and/or jurisdiction of an authorized, recognized political entity, namely a state, nation, or **government**. In this context, parts of the United States were considered territories before they became official states. They were part of the country, but not participating, voting entities. There were two stages to a territory. First, it was considered an unorganized territory and was governed by a judge. It then became an organized territory and was ruled by an assigned governor or other official. It could elect its own legislature, and had a non-voting member in the Congress of the federal government. The last two territories to become states were Hawaii and Alaska.

Giddens distinguishes two kinds of territories: those of pre-industrial empires and those of the modern **nation-state**.

Pre-industrial empires had loosely defined frontiers and lacked clarity in boundaries between territories. Disputes over borders were vague and the marking of borders changed a great deal. Modern nation-states, on the other hand, have much more clearly defined borders demarcating their territory from that of other nation-states. These borders are usually highly administered and protected by police or military forces from invasion. They can been determined from the many maps that are created. This enhanced clarity of borders shows the increased control over time and space held by modern governments and states.

In current times, ''territory'' can also refer to a region covered by a salesperson, agent, or serviceperson. These agents are supposed to restrict themselves to their own territory, and there are social and legal sanctions for encroaching on another person's territory. In many ways, these territories can be analogized to the more formalized political territories. Moreover, the emergence of cyberspace has further expanded the concept of territories as companies and individuals make territorial claims in this new frontier.

TERRORISM

The word ''terrorism'' originated during the Reign of Terror in revolutionary France in the late eighteenth century. The Oxford English Dictionary first defined terrorism as ''government by intimidation as carried out by the party in power in France during the Revolution of 1789-1797.'' However, the existence of terrorist groups has been traced back to as early as the first century with the Zealots-Sicarii. Using primitive weapons to attack their victims, the Zealots-Sicarii, a Jewish religious **group**, had a profound influence on the area they inhabited, the area known today as Israel. In the twelfth and thirteenth centuries, the Assassins, or Ismailis, a group of Islamist extremists, existed targeting prominent religious and political leaders of **Islam**.

While there is no single definition for the word today, many sources rely on the definition used by the Federal Bureau of Investigation. The FBI defines terrorism as, ''the unlawful use of force or violence against persons or **property** to intimidate or coerce a **Government**, the civilian population, or any segment thereof, in furtherance of political or social objectives.'' The FBI further defines terrorism as either domestic, ''involving groups or individuals who are based and operate entirely within the United States and Puerto Rico without foreign direction and whose acts are directed at elements of the U.S. Government or population'' or international where the individual or group committing the violence or unlawfully using force ''has some connection to a foreign power or whose activities transcend national boundaries.'' Terrorist acts include: armed attack, arson, assault, bombing, hijacking, kidnapping, and vandalism. A twentieth-century phenomenon of terrorism is that it commonly targets random victims.

While the United States has experienced numerous acts of terrorism, both domestic and international, the number of terrorist incidents in this country has been relatively few in

The United States has experienced numerous acts of terrorism, such as the kidnapping of U.S. embassy hostages by Iranian terrorists in 1979 *(Corbis Corporation [Bellevue])*.

comparison with other countries. One of the first significant incidents of terrorism in America was the bombing of the World Trade Center in New York on February 26, 1993. The explosion left six dead and thousands injured. Though this incident is quite significant as an act of terrorism, the number of casualties that resulted pales in comparison with that of the terrorist bombing of the Alfred P. Murrah Federal Building in Oklahoma City on April 19, 1995. Almost 170 people, including many children, died as a result of this bombing.

Numerous terrorist groups continue to exist today in the United States. While the **ideology** of these groups vary, for example some are religious while others are secular, they all employ terroristic methods to seek the attention to communicate with their intended audience.

TEST-RETEST METHOD

The test-retest method is one means of assessing a measure's reliability. **Reliability** is the degree to which a measure produces similarity in scores over repeated applications, or the amount of stability in results for some measurement instrument. The test-retest method is a simple way of determining how reliable or stable a measure is.

In this method, the same test is administered at two different time periods to the same subjects. The **correlation** between the measure's results among subjects at Time 1 and Time 2 indicates the measure's reliability. The higher the correlation between scores at Times 1 and 2, the greater the reliability. If the scores at Time 1 and Time 2 are identical, the resulting correlation of 1.00 indicates the measure is perfectly reliable. The correlation produced using the test-retest method allows the researcher to quantify the extent to which the measure delivers consistent results across multiple administrations.

Despite its ease of use, the test-retest method has a number of drawbacks. First, it is often impossible and/or costly for researchers to administer the measure at more than one point in time. Second, the correlation coefficient generated by the test-retest method may underestimate the instrument's reliability if the underlying construct being measured changes between administrations. Reliability coefficients may be low only because of some event or external factor that happens between Times 1 and 2 and does not necessarily **mean** that the measure is unreliable. To minimize this problem, the amount of time between administrations should be relatively short.

Third, reactivity can lead to decreased reliability estimates in that being sensitized to the concept being measured may produce a change in scores at Time 2 that is solely due to exposure at Time 1. Change in scores from Time 1 to Time 2 is merely due to increased sensitivity to the construct. This may, however, be incorrectly interpreted as lower agreement between administrations of the instrument, as the low correlation does not necessarily mean that the measure is unreliable.

Finally, memory may lead to an overestimation of a measure's reliability when the test-retest method is used. Subjects can often recall their responses from Time 1, and they may simply restate these same responses at Time 2. This is one potential drawback of keeping the time interval between administrations short, as the reliability coefficient may be artificially inflated due to memory.

See also Reliability

THEORY

Theory is a set of assumptions used in the process of interpreting and understanding phenomena. In each discipline theories are constructed to systematically explain important principles and relationships between phenomena. The roots of theory can be traced to the Greek philosophers Socrates, Plato, and Aristotle, and to a lesser extent to mathematicians such as Pythagoras. Science was not a component of early theory, since philosophical **discourse** encompassed traditional wisdom, abstraction, and common sense logic.

Because theory is a framework that guides respective inquiry, articulating the historical context of its relationship to **philosophy** and science is helpful in understanding its development. For example, emerging scientific discoveries beginning in the 1600s and ending with the Enlightenment (1700s) were instrumental in shaping philosophical discourse. Francis Bacon, **Thomas Hobbes**, and John Locke argued the importance of scientific logic and the need to ground the knowledge-building process of theory in empirical research.

The magnitude of scientific discoveries during the nineteenth century further shaped conceptions of the physical universe, strengthening the belief that science could systematically explain the laws of nature. Western philosophical discourse also began to argue that laws of nature existed for the social world. As advancements in chemistry, electromagnetism, and physics produced systematic data, disciplines such as **sociology** emerged to study social life scientifically.

By mid-century, grand economic and social theories (in works by Adam Smith, Karl Marx, Émile Durkheim) attempted to explain changing social conditions using historical **data**, or public records to support their inquiries. The cause and effect approach of **Max Weber** and his theory of **rationality** as well as economic models driven by rational choice embodied the dominant sentiment in the late 1800s that theory, rationalism, and positivistic science would reveal universal knowledge.

Two factors altered this relationship. In the twentieth century scientists became aware of the physical limitations of science and introduced probability into their calculations. Second, the emergence of genetics encouraged philosophical debate about the ethics of altering nature. As academic discourse in the social sciences shifted from Europe to the United States, disagreements between the physical and social sciences, micro and macro perspectives, and qualitative versus quantitative methodologies emerged. Discussions on the exclusion of marginalized perspectives from mainstream theory also surfaced and continue to encourage epistemological debates about the impact of standpoint on the process of inquiry and theoretical explanation. Since the 1980s, the integration of various theoretical perspectives, the inclusion of cultural diversity, increasing awareness of international issues, and escalating concerns about biogentics have encouraged many to become skeptical of universal truths and to revisit the philosophical aspects of theory as it relates to the human condition.

THOMAS, WILLIAM ISAAC (1863-1947)
American professor of sociology

William Isaac Thomas was a main contributor to **the Chicago School** of sociological thought, which is at the root of American **sociology**. He is recognized, along with **Talcott Parsons** and George Mead, as a founder of symbolic interactionism. Thomas, along with co-author Florian Znaniecki, published *The Polish Peasant in Europe and America* in 1918, a five-volume tome that was probably his most famous work. *The Polish Peasant* examines how immigrants adjusted to a new **culture** and what social factors affected the process. Thomas refused to see people as completely controlled by external social forces. While external controls provided the actor with a range of socially structured choices, the influence of these was important only to the extent that they were subjectively experienced. His concept of *attitude* as a predisposition of an individual to act in relation to social **values**, rather than as a purely psychical state, formed the rudiments of a social **psychology**. Patterns of an individual's attitudes made up a *social personality,* which helped sociologists ascertain theories of motivation.

Together, Thomas and Znaniecki emphasized the importance of incorporating both objective and subjective **data** into sociological study and stressed the interdependence of fact-gathering and **theory**. This study led to Thomas' notion of the *definition of the situation,* which meant that human actors, faced with an identical situation, reacted to it differently based on how each individual interpreted meanings through the filter of perceptual experience. An individual's **definition of the situ-**

ation was recognized as a link between subjective experience and responsive action. Social actors should be conceived of as in constant, reciprocal interaction with cultural forces and institutions. Thomas applied these ideas in the form of *situational analysis* to works such as *Old World Traits Transplanted* (1921), *The Unadjusted Girl* (1923), and *The Child in America* (1928).

Thomas criticized theories of racial and sexual differences. In *Sex and Society* (1907), for example, he disavowed biological theories of difference and stressed the interrelation between self and society. His development and use of **typologies** demonstrated his belief that there were greater differences within the races and sexes than between them. Thomas' methodological insights, applied in his work on immigrants and prostitutes, were subsequently used in studies of deviant behavior. His main career concern was with issues of **social control** and **social change** as a function of modernization and industrialization. He felt that traditional ways of social control no longer operated effectively and that sociology could be used to help identify the factors that affected social disorganization.

Thomas was born in Russell County, Virginia, on August 13, 1863. His father, Thaddeus Peter Thomas, was a rural farmer and a Methodist preacher with an intellectual bent. Young Thomas received his bachelor's degree at the University of Tennessee in 1884, where he discovered a love for academics. After teaching courses in foreign languages and natural history, Thomas studied in Germany from 1888 to 1889. It was there that his interests turned to ethnography. As soon as they became available, he enrolled in graduate courses at the first American Department of Sociology at the University of Chicago. He received his doctorate in 1896, began teaching there, and was awarded full professorship in 1910. Thomas married Harriet Park in 1888 and had five children, but only two survived into adulthood.

In 1918, Thomas was caught in a scandal that ended his career at the University of Chicago. He was charged with a violation of the Mann Act, which forbade transport of young women across state lines for 'immoral purposes.' He was caught in a hotel with the young wife of an army officer and arrested. The charges were eventually dropped, but he was fired from his position. Although Thomas was known for his flamboyant and unconventional ways with women, recent scholarship suggests that the arrest may have been more political than moral, due to his and Harriet's involvement with the pacifist movement at a time of war. In addition, his interest in social reform and women's issues such as suffrage and sexual freedom may have contributed to his ostracism from the Chicago School. Thomas moved to New York and then New Haven, continued his research and taught part-time, but his career as a professor never recovered. He was, however, elected to the presidency of the American Sociological Association in 1926. Thomas and Harriet divorced in 1934, and he married Dorothy Swaine in 1935. He died on December 5, 1947, at the age of 84 while living in Berkeley, California.

TIME SERIES ANALYSIS

Time series analysis is a technique employed for the analysis of data that consists of sequences of measurements that follow ordered, non-random variation at equally spaced time intervals. This procedure is employed in analysis of **census data** and other sociological and demographic data as well as in the fields of economics, the physical sciences, and business. While basic statistical analysis assumes the independence of individual cases in a random sample, time series data analysis is based on the assumption that groups of cases are related to each other in that they represent consecutive measurements of a phenomenon affecting a particular **variable** over fixed periods of time.

Time series analysis has two primary goals: to identify and describe the phenomena acting throughout the time period on which the data is collected, and to make predictions about future values of the time series variable. Analysis of the phenomena attempts to identify and describe regularly occurring patterns of change by which future values can be estimated.

In a similar fashion to other analyses, time series analysis assumes that data consist of regularly occurring identifiable patterns as well as some random noise. Trend and cyclical components are the most basic classes of pattern that describe most time series data. Trends are general systematic, linear, or non-linear changes over time. Trends do not repeat themselves (at least within the time frame under study) unlike cyclical patterns, which repeat themselves. Seasonal patterns are similar to cyclical patterns, but they tend to be shorter and fall into more identifiable, systematic intervals. Cyclical components usually have a longer duration that varies from cycle to cycle. Both cyclical and trend components may coexist within a single data set and are customarily combined in different forms within the trend-cycle component. For example, a demographer may identify overall population growth in a city during a ten-year period, with more births in the autumn months each year than in the summer months.

Patterned components may combine in an additive or multiplicative fashion. In the example above, with more births occurring in the autumn, the effect of the season is additive, and we could add x number of births to the average each autumn, or subtract y number from the average for months in which there are typically fewer births. However, in years in which the overall number of births in all months is greater, the seasonal affect is multiplicative. The number of births in the autumn can be figured by multiplying the average births times the overall percentage increase in addition to adding the usual season effect.

Most techniques employ some method of filtering out noise that might obscure time series patterns of variability. A technique often used to reduce the effects of noise, smoothing, may assist in revealing trends more clearly as well as their seasonal and cyclic components. Smoothing techniques fall into two distinct categories: averaging methods and exponential smoothing methods. There are several types of each method.

Research questions in **sociology** frequently ask whether outside events affected subsequent observations of the phenomenon under study. A researcher may be interested in the

Alexis de Tocqueville *(The Library of Congress)*

results of a particular government policy designed to reduce teen pregnancy, for example. The study design might include time series analysis of birth rates among teens over time and analyze changes in the patterns of births, with particular attention to changes that might occur after the policy had time to produce an effect. Time series analysis enables this type of research focus, to which other types of statistical analysis are ill-suited.

TOCQUEVILLE, ALEXIS CHARLES HENRI MAURICE CLÉREL DE (1805-1859)
French politician and writer

The French statesman and writer Alexis Charles Henri Maurice Clérel de Tocqueville (1805–1859) was the author of *Democracy in America*, the first classic commentary on American government written by a foreigner. Alexis de Tocqueville was born in Paris on July 29, 1805, of an aristocratic Norman family. He studied law in Paris (1823–1826) and then was appointed an assistant magistrate at Versailles (1827).

The July 1830 Revolution which, with middle-class support, put Louis Philippe on the throne, required a loyalty oath of Tocqueville as a civil servant. He was suspect because his aristocratic family opposed the new order and was demoted to

a minor judgeship without pay. Tocqueville and another magistrate, Gustave de Beaumont, asked to study prison reform in America, then an interest of the French government. Granted permission but not funds (their families paid their expenses), Tocqueville and Beaumont spent from May 1831 to February 1832 in the United States. Their travel and interviews resulted in *On the Penitentiary System in the United States and Its Application in France* (1832). Then followed Tocqueville's famous *Democracy in America* (volume 1, 1835; volume 2, 1840), an immediate best seller. By 1850 it had run through 13 editions.

Tocqueville was elected to the Chamber of Deputies in 1839. He opposed King Louis Philippe but after the Revolution of 1848 again served as a deputy. Tocqueville was foreign minister for a few months in 1849 and retired from public affairs at the end of 1851. During his last years he wrote *The Old Regime and the French Revolution* (1856). He died in Cannes on April 16, 1859.

Despite his aristocratic upbringing, Tocqueville believed that the spread of **democracy** was inevitable. By analyzing American democracy, he thought to help France avoid America's faults and emulate its successes. Chief among his many insights was to see equality of social conditions as the heart of American democracy. He noted that although the majority could produce tyranny its wide property distribution and inherent **conservatism** made for stability. American literature, then still under European influence, he felt would become independent in idiom and deal with plain people rather than the upper classes. The American zeal for change he connected with a restless search for the ideal. Noting the permissiveness of democracy toward religion, he anticipated denominational growth. Discerning natural hostility to the military, he foresaw an adverse effect of prolonged war on **American society**. He anticipated that democracy would emancipate women and alter the relationship of parents to children. He saw danger in the dominance of American politics by lawyers.

Though his work has been criticized for some biases, errors, omissions, and pessimism, Tocqueville's perceptive insights have been continually quoted. He ranks as a keen observer of U.S. democracy and as a major prophet of modern societies' trends.

TÖNNIES, FERDINAND (1855-1936)
German sociologist

The German sociologist Ferdinand Tönnies (1855–1936) pioneered sociology as an academic discipline of rigorously scientific character on a broad base of original studies in the history of ideas, **epistemology**, political science, economics, and social anthropology.

Ferdinand Tönnies was born on July 26, 1855, on a farm homestead in the North Frisian peninsula of Eiderstedt, then still under Danish sovereignty. One of seven children, he received his high school education in Husum where he became deeply attached to the novelist and poet Theodor Storm. After studying classics at different German universities and taking

his doctoral degree in 1877, Tönnies turned to **philosophy**, history, biology, **psychology**, economics, and ethnology as his ideas on scientific sociology began to take shape.

In Berlin in 1876 Tönnies began at the suggestion of his lifelong friend Friedrich Paulsen a study of the much-neglected philosophy of Thomas Hobbes. On his first of many journeys to England and also to France, Tönnies discovered in 1878 several original manuscripts by Hobbes, essential to better appreciation of his system of ideas and natural-law **theory**. In his first account (1879–1881) Tönnies argued the significance of Hobbes in the scientific revolution of the seventeenth century. Continuing his documentation, he published the standard monograph on Hobbes's life and works in 1896 (3d ed. repr. 1971).

Beginning to lecture at the University of Kiel in 1882, at first on philosophy and **government** but soon extending his academic work to empirical social research and **statistical methods**, Tönnies devoted the next six years to working out his own social theory. His world-famous treatise *Community and Society* (1887) found little response in the intellectual climate of the Germany of Kaiser William II. The various schools of historicism disfavored the development of rigorously scientific social theory, and political practice in the Bismarck era refused to solve the pressing social problems of a rapidly growing industrial economy but fought the labor movement by legislation and police action even after 1890.

A clash with the Prussian university administration over Tönnies's connection with the German branch of the Ethical **Culture** movement and his outspoken reports on the Hamburg longshoremen's strike (1896–1897) made him suspect of radicalism if not socialist leanings; what promised to be the brilliant career of a gifted scholar was nipped in the bud. Yet, unremitting work on theoretical problems between 1894 and 1913, informed reviews of the growing world literature in the field, and prominent participation in the Verein für Sozialpolitik (Association for Social Politics) and the Gesellschaft für Soziale Reform (Society for Social Reform) increased Tönnies's reputation inside and outside Germany, creating an unusually wide disparity between scholarly stature and status in academic life. The external conflict was resolved in 1909 by his appointment to a full professorship in political economy at Kiel, which for the father of five young children also meant relief from financial stress.

The early masterpiece had clearly been a first decisive step toward the systematic development of the new social science. As Tönnies's plans for this elaboration were frustrated at the most productive time of life, only a few papers of theoretical importance stem from the period before World War I. At the same time, he became involved in a fierce battle against social Darwinism, adopted in imperial Germany as apologetics for a conservative outlook.

Of two new projects formed in 1907, a critique of **public opinion** and a study in social history, one was completed only in 1922, the other introduced by the volume *The Spirit of the Modern Age* in 1935. With **Max Weber** and others Tönnies had founded the German Sociological Association in 1909 and, as its subdivision, the Statistical Association (1911). He had failed, however, to complete his systematic sociology.

After World War I, with prospects more favorable to social science and its academic recognition in the Weimar Republic, *Community and Society* went through several new editions. Now in his sixties, Tönnies carried out his design of a systematic sociology. The theoretical parts on social units, **values**, **norms**, and action patterns in the *Introduction to Sociology* (1931) were supplemented by three volumes of collected studies and critiques and by a series of papers on his empirical research. He reestablished the Sociological Association, remaining its president until 1933.

The bulk of his published work bears out a distinction Tönnies had proposed in 1908 between pure, applied, and **empirical sociology**. In line with the scientific principles of both Galileo and Hobbes, pure sociology, including the fundamental concepts of **community** and society, relates to abstract constructions appertaining to human relationships; from these, more specific theories are deducible in **applied sociology**, with emphasis on interaction of economic, political, and cultural conditions in the modern age; they, in turn, serve as guidelines in inductive empirical research. Tönnies kept strictly separate from this threefold scientific endeavor what he called practical sociology; this, comprising social policies and **social work**, presents, in a complete system, technologies based on the scientific insights of the three sections of the system.

Tönnies acted on this solution also of the value problem. He relentlessly exposed the neoromanticism of the 1920s, just as his earlier critique of romanticism had been the cornerstone of the theory of *Community and Society*. But in 1933 he was deprived as ''politically unreliable'' of his status as professor emeritus. His death on April 9, 1936, spared him from being witness to the worst excesses of the Nazi dictatorship and from further indignities.

TOTAL INSTITUTION

Total institutions are residential establishments designed to break down prior **socialization** and instill a new set of **norms**, **values**, and beliefs. Some total institutions, such as prisons, set out to ''repair'' faulty or deviant socialization, while others, such as the military, merely replace a workable but obsolete socialization with the norms, values, and beliefs of a new subculture. Some total institutions, such as religious seminaries, are designed as temporary quarters, resocializing and then releasing inmates into the world; others, such as convents, expect a lifelong tenure.

Erving Goffman, who coined the term in a 1961 study of mental hospitals, noted that total institutions have four essential characteristics. First, there is an overriding, tightly-scheduled plan: every detail of the inmate's life, from the number of hours allotted to sleep to the number of weekly telephone calls, is determined in advance, meticulously scheduled, and monitored. Inmates live under constant surveillance, requiring permission to leave the grounds or even to leave the room. Information is strictly controlled: outside reading material, radio and TV programs, and even casual conversation with other inmates may be forbidden. Finally, total institutions

practice violate the boundary of the self, a depersonalization that can be minor and mostly symbolic (cutting the hair of Catholic seminarians), or destructive and traumatic (using assigned prisoner numbers instead of names).

Sociologists have eagerly applied the concept of total institutions to their analyses of prisons, **nursing homes**, boarding schools, boot camp, and convents; more creatively, they have found elements in industrial firms, doctoral programs, the homes of domestic abuse victims, the professional lives of waiters, and the plantation economy of colonial Malaysia. Goffman indicated that the total institution is an Weberian **ideal type**: all schools, churches, jobs, political parties, organizations, and clubs, even those as innocuous and voluntary as a Tuesday Night Poetry **Society**, require a greater or lesser degree of resocialization, and therefore institute a greater or lesser degree of scheduling, surveillance, information control, and depersonalization.

TOTALITARIANISM

Totalitarianism is an extreme political system in which all institutions are under the control of the ruling body or, less frequently, an individual. It is a twentieth-century variation on ancient forms of absolute authoritarian rule. Unlike these authoritarian governments of past centuries, totalitarian regimes can use technology, education, the media, and other modern advancements to maintain a firmer grip on **society**. This control is often manifested by way of suspending free elections, banning oppositional political parties, and limiting individual freedoms of speech, assembly, and so forth.

This form of rule is not necessarily imposed on the people but can appeal to their desire for a more controlled and ordered society. The Nazi Party in Germany, for instance, achieved a great level of public support for their totalitarian policies. Disastrous economic conditions and strong nationalist tendencies outweighed the desire for personal freedoms in the minds of many Germans. Likewise, many communist governments have enjoyed wide support, particularly if their rule is seen as a temporary step toward better conditions.

This irony, that supposedly opposite ideologies like **communism** and fascism can equally embrace totalitarian policies, is an indication of the contempt such a system has for people or their ideas. In environments of fervent nationalism or severe economic distress a nation may turn toward the strongest leader they see, but they rarely choose to live under such conditions for long. And, unfortunately, they normally find that regimes given such sweeping power are loath to surrender it if and when outside threats diminish. For this reason, most totalitarian nations attempt to isolate themselves from the free world in order to maintain a sense of paranoia among their citizens and, even more importantly, to suppress the ideal of freedom as it is practiced by democracies. This strategy is a difficult one to implement in the twenty-first century, however. The ability to control the media—so important to Hitler, Mussolini, and Stalin—has been virtually eliminated by satellites, computers, and other modern communications systems. In the

Camboidian leader Pol Pot and the Khmer Rouge Party that he led symbolized totalitarianism—an extremist political system in which institutions are under the control of an individual and/or ruling body *(Corbis Corporation [Bellevue]).*

twenty-first century, few totalitarian regimes remain. Most have found it necessary to ease restrictions, to some degree, in order to compete economically and to maintain power over people who are ever more aware of the basic freedoms they are lacking.

TOTEMISM

The term "totemism" which derives from the Ojibwa (Algonkian) word *ototeman*, refers to the practice by which human groups identify a symbolic relationships with natural objects such as animals and plants. A classic example of totemism is a clan's belief that a particular animal is its mythological ancestor, but totemism includes a wide variety of beliefs and practices. Totemism has been a central element in the social and religious organizations of many traditional cultures.

Totemism has been found to exist in societies that are divided into distinct clans, each of which is identified with a

specific animate or inanimate species such as a feared or re-spected hunted animal, an edible plant, or any food staple. To-tems are often closely connected with creation legends and instituted **morality**. Taboos and rituals around totems pertain to contact with the totemic entity, **marriage** outside the totemic group, and procreation.

Anthropologists and sociologists have espoused various theories of totemism and its origins. Ethnologist John Fergu-son McLennan wrote the first significant theoretical work on the subject, *The Worship of Animals and Plants* (1869). McLennan argued that all human societies had gone through totemistic stages in their early development. Anthropologist E. B. Tylor rejected this view, arguing that totemism was not sim-ply animal or plant worship but expressed the human need to classify the world. In the first comprehensive study of the sub-ject, *Totemism and Exogamy* (1910), Sir James Frazier theo-rized that totemism evolved from interpretations of conception and childbirth.

Totemistic **theory** received much critical attention dur-ing the early twentieth century. Ethnologist Alexander Gol-denweiser, finding distinct phenomena in totemism, rejected the concept of totemism as a unity. Ethnologist Richard Thurn-wald argued that totemism expressed a specific way of think-ing about the natural environment and went on to develop a **psychology** of totemism. Other ethnologists who contributed to theories of totemism were **Franz Boas**, Fritz Graeb-ner,Bernhard Ankermann, and Wilhelm Schmidt.

The most influential critic of totemism was ethnologist Claude Levi-Strauss. In *Totemism*, (1963) he expanded on the ideas of social anthropologist A.R. Radcliffe-Brown, who had argued for a structural understanding of totemism based on in-terrelationships and antitheses. Levi-Strauss theorized that to-temism was based on antithetical thinking and concluded that totemistic thought provided a means through which groups structured social differences on the basis of distinctions be-tween classes of animals and man.

TOYNBEE, ARNOLD JOSEPH (1889-1975)

English historian

A controversial historian, Arnold Joseph Toynbee is best known for his 12-volume work entitled *A Study of History* (1934–1961). He was born in London on April 14, 1889, into a scholarly, upper middle class family. His Uncle Arnold was a well-known English economist who wrote a history of Brit-ain's **Industrial Revolution** in 1884. Toynbee's father, Harry, was a social worker and his mother, Edith, was one of the few women of the Victorian Era with a college degree. Wrote Toynbee some years later, ''I am an historian because my mother was one.''

Toynbee was educated at Balliol College, Oxford, earn-ing a degree in the classics in 1911. His interest in Greek and Latin led him to the British Archeological School in Athens for a short time. He walked about the Greek countryside con-stantly. ''Few men knew Greece so well as Arnold Toynbee,'' claimed an article in the *Times Literary Supplement*.

Arnold Joseph Toynbee *(The Library of Congress)*

In 1912, Toynbee returned to Balliol College where he became a tutor and fellow in ancient history. With poor health keeping him from the military, he worked for the intelligence department of the British Foreign Office in 1915 and served as a delegate to the Paris Peace Conference in 1919 after World War I. By then, Toynbee was a published author of such works as *Greek Policy since 1882* (1914) and *The Murderous Tyranny of the Turks* (1917), recognized as authorities on cur-rent events in those two countries. With the war over, Toynbee returned to teaching, this time as professor of Byzantine and modern Greek studies at the University of London (1919–1921). His *The Western Question in Greece and Turkey* was published in 1922 as a result of his work as a correspon-dent for the *Manchester Guardian* (1921–1922) during the Greco-Turkish War. In 1925, he became research professor of international history at the London School of Economics and director of studies at the Royal Institute of International Af-fairs in London.

Toynbee began his massive *A Study of History* in 1922, and the first three volumes appeared by 1934. The second three volumes were published in 1939, another four in 1954, an atlas in 1959, and a final volume in 1961. The first ten volumes ex-amine the rise and fall of civilizations throughout human histo-ry. Toynbee concluded that successful civilizations excelled under the leadership of creative minorities made up of elite

leaders. They fell when leaders were no longer creative, which allowed militarism, nationalism, and tyranny to take over. The death of **civilization** was not, inevitable, however, according to Toynbee; since it could continue to respond successfully to new challenges. Arguing that his conclusions were reached from empirical evidence, Toynbee laid out the stages of a civilization, including growth, dissolution, a troubled time, the universal state, and, finally, a collapse that led to rebirth.

Toynbee's work brought him success and intellectual acclaim, but he was not without severe critics. Historians argued that his view of the rise and fall of civilizations relies too much on religion as a reviving force. His conclusions, it was said, were more those of a Christian moralist than a historian, and there were objections to his use of myths, to which he gave the same value as historical **data**. Toynbee's final volume *Reconsiderations* was an attempt to answer those criticisms.

After World War II, Toynbee shifted his interest from history to religion with such publications as *Historians Approach to Religion* (1956). In 1966, he published *Change and Habit: The Challenge of Our Time* in which he predicted that China would become the unifier of the world if the United States and the Soviet Union could not maintain world order.

Toynbee suffered a stroke in 1974 and died the following year in York, England, on October 22. Since his death, critics have taken a gentler view of his master work. Some argue that even with its faults, *A Study of History* has detailed a set of meaningful characteristics concerning major civilizations. Toynbee has at least forced historians to think about the problems of world history and to debate these issues among themselves. Said Peter Gay in the *New Republic,* Arnold Toynbee was "a type we can ill afford to lose—a superficial but thoroughly learned eclectic."

TRADITIONAL SOCIETIES

"Traditional society" is an expression used to describe all non-industrialized societies, generally referring to those that are rural. The term traditional **society** is frequently placed in opposition to modern, capitalist, industrial, or urbanized society, and is presumed to be resistant to change when compared with these latter societies.

The term, however, is no longer preferred by most sociologists. It is used to describe numerous types of societies, such as agrarian, hunter-gatherer, or non-industrial groups, and so is difficult to use clearly. Although the term is associated with the lack of change (or the strict adherence to tradition), it is not the case that no change occurs in societies described as traditional. Moreover, the term "traditional society" is commonly associated with **modernization theory**, a viewpoint critiqued for over-simplification of the differences between so-called traditional and modern societies. Such simplifications have tended to lead to romantic notions of traditional societies and the past in general that are not supported by factual evidence.

In addition, the term "traditional society" may be confused with the use of tradition in a society. For example, Japan

is often contrasted with Western societies as being more traditional. In this case, however, political motivations prompted the establishment of supposed traditions in the nineteenth century in the hope of establishing a national **identity**. What is termed a traditional society, then, may instead be invention, the new incorporation of ideas for new uses. Furthermore, contrasting Japanese and Western societies in this way ignores the extent to which traditions and innovations in the past are incorporated into all societies; there is no sharp break between the so-called traditional and modern societies. It is instead likely that Japan's implementation of historical elements is more apparent to Westerner's because of their Eurocentric attitude and that societies in the West reatin traditional elements to a similar extent.

The use of the term "traditional society," though waning in recent times, is an important aspect of sociological thought. It captures the tendency to revere the past and something wholly different than the "modern" present. The limited use of this term in contemporary times indicates a growing concern for the multiplicity within in all societies and cultures. Sociologists today are less likely to apply blanket terms to a large number of individual entities without exploring the implications of this use or carefully enumerating the differences that exist. Such is the case with "traditional societies;" while it can meaningfully apply to a society that incorporates elements of the past into its present state, manifold differences between separate traditional societies exist and are warranting greater attention.

TRANSNATIONAL CORPORATIONS

Transnational corporations (TNCs) are large corporate conglomerates which own and control assets in multiple countries. Corporate expansion in the world market is often viewed as a recent byproduct of global economy. However, U.S. industries began building alternative production sites outside national boundaries during the 1950s to secure cheaper sources of labor and develop alternative sites for production in case of labor disputes. In recent reports from the United Nations (1995, 1997) transnational corporations are estimated to control two-thirds of the world's trade and create eighty percent of foreign market revenues.

The economic contributions of TNCs in industrialized countries including the United States, Great Britain, Japan, and Germany have been noted by both economists and social scientists. In fact, much recent prosperity has been attributed to the strong performance of TNCs in the world market. *The World Investment Report* of 1997 ranked U.S. transnational corporations first in international assets and in investment returns. Escalating awareness of **human rights** violations by TNCs in developing countries and environmental devastation that has polluted and destroyed local habitats, however, is encouraging public debate about issues of social responsibility and public monitoring of TNCs.

In 1992, the UN was persuaded to terminate its efforts to develop a uniform code of international business conduct

and to serve as a regulatory watchdog over TNCs. These events occurred during the Bush administration at a time when the government was attempting to help U.S. business recover from the slow growth and strong **competition** of the l980s. Recent public concern over TNC actions prompted President Clinton to introduce a voluntary program developed by the U.S. Department of Commerce entitled, ''Model Business Principles'' (1997). Its intent was to encourage TNCs to attach a product label that would identify the location of manufacture. Few companies have complied, although some TNCs do attempt to establish linkage with consumers through their responses to **community** needs or to help during natural disasters.

The term multinational corporation (MNC) emerged in the 1980s and is often used interchangeably with TNC. Multinational corporations (MNCs) generally are described as nationally-based firms. Much current literature examines the social repercussions and growing fiscal and political power of these multi-layered organizations.

Technology has contributed to the growth of TNCs as well as provided them with some degree of ambiguity and fluidity. For example, many TNCs have such complex organizational structures and diverse holdings they frequently have multiple international headquarters. TNCs product offerings may or may not be related, while organizations may be streamlined but are not necessarily integrated. Successful TNCs rely on complex strategies that often obscure their size, worldwide presence, holdings, or intentions. By acquiring a vast array of service organizations to control the production and distribution of products, including the ownership or use of raw materials in many developing countries as well as the acquisition rights of intellectual **property**, TNCs can ensure the flow and accumulation of capital between national borders with little monitoring or repercussions.

While globalization is a complex process, the shift to an international economic system is based on uneven development. Profit making relies on securing labor, raw materials, and other elements of production at lower costs, while also locating new markets for product consumption. The successful growth of many TNCs, such as IBM, General Motors, and Levi-Strauss, has offset their declining domestic revenues and enhanced the position of the United States in the world market. Yet, from the perspective of developing countries, most jobs are low skilled, and residents seldom benefit from the technology deployed or the products made to be sold elsewhere.

Today, over 30,000 TNCs control approximately 90,000 affiliates based in industrialized countries, while there are also over 3000 TNCs with 100,000-plus affiliates based in developing countries. For many, these facts exacerbate the crises already facing developing countries. The depletion of natural resources by TNCs retards the economic growth of developing countries and affects their ecological life systems. The development of a low skilled workforce enables the higher skilled, better paying positions to become available to workers in the more industrialized countries, while perpetuating **poverty** and low levels of education in underdeveloped countries. The issues that will soon need to be addressed are the contradictions embedded in the increasing financial power of TNCs and the distribution of profits that are not being realized by these low-end contributors to globalization.

Physician and tennis player Rene Richards underwent "sex-reassignment" surgery in one of the most publicized cases of the 1970s *(Corbis Corporation [Bellevue]).*

TRANSSEXUALISM

Transsexualism, now more frequently called ''transgenderism,'' is the permanent adoption of a new gender **identity** through changes in costume, mannerisms, and social habits, and within the last fifty years, through hormones and ''sex-reassignment'' surgery. Transsexuals number between .05% and 0.2% of the population of North America and come from every age group, occupational and socioeconomic category, and sexual orientation.

Throughout history, some people have opted to live as members of another sex (female, male, or a third or fourth category); many cultures afford them special roles as shamans, healers, or mystics, while others force them to become beggars or prostitutes. Early sexologists such as Magnus Hirschfeld and R. von Krafft-Ebing frequently discussed people who would today be called transsexuals, but mainstream sociologists usually ignored them, since they did not develop interesting subcultures or **social movements**; only one article about transsexualism appeared in mainstream **sociology** journals before 1980. Today, although transsexuals are still advocating for freedom from discrimination, social **prejudice**, and the increasing threat of hate **crime**, they have become the iconoclasts of contemporary social **theory**, calling into question basic assumptions of gender and sexuality and even of personal identity.

Early writers confused transsexualism with **homosexuality**, presuming that gay and lesbian people were really heterosexuals trapped in the wrong body, or that transsexuals were unable to admit that they were really gay or lesbian. Even today, relationships between the groups are often strained: transsexuals sometimes display intense **homophobia**, and those transsexuals who are gay or lesbian are sometimes denied admission to festivals, banned from organizations, and vilified in the gay press. Nevertheless, a common sense of exclusion from the **ideology** of hegemonic **masculinity** and femininity has created sufficient solidarity to unite gay/lesbian, bisexual, and transsexual people on many social and political

One of the most prominent tranvestites in U.S. culture is television performer RuPaul *(Corbis Corporation [Bellevue]).*

fronts. Refusing the simplistic designations of male-to-female and female-to-male, activist/scholars such as Lesley Feinberg and Kate Boorstein have recently framed transsexuals as the prophets of a new generation, unfettered by inaccurate, outdated, and oppressive gender polarities.

TRANSVESTISM

In current sociological literature, a *transvestite* is loosely defined as an individual who dresses as the opposite gender, often obtaining erotic pleasure from the act. This definition is based on medical diagnostic terminology and has evolved from its original meaning. The term ''transvestism'' was coined by German sexologist Mangus Hirshfeld in 1910 and was used as a way to categorize and separate cross-dressing behavior from sexual orientation. Previously, cross-dressers were thought to be exclusively homosexual, but **case studies** have shown that many (if not most) transvestites are actually heterosexual or bisexual in orientation. Until the 1950s, the category of transvestite included individuals whose cross-

dressing motivations ranged from fetishistic erotic stimulation to convictions of being the opposite gender, despite biological sex assignment. In 1953, sexologist Harry Benjamin categorized these latter individuals as *transsexuals.* Virginia Prince introduced the term *transgenderist* in 1980 to describe individuals who live as the opposite sex, but have not had sex-change surgery.

Transvestites can be both male and female, but most subjects of study have been male. Few empirical studies have been conducted on females who cross-dress, but the fact of their multiplistic existence is evidenced both cross-culturally and historically. Social science literature focuses almost exclusively on the male transvestite, who is likely to be white, middle-class, married, and highly educated. Many of these subjects view their cross-dressing as an expression of their 'feminine side.' In addition, transvestism has come to be associated with fetishism and sexual arousal, which has not been empirically noted in female transvestites.

Sociologists have studied transvestism through the theoretical lenses of **deviance** (D.H. Fienbloom, J.T. Talamini), **ethnomethodology** (S. Hirschauer, S.J. Kessler, W. McKenna), and **symbolic interactionism** (S. Hirschauer, D. King). One of the first sociologists to study transvestism was Harold Garfinkel. In *Gender: An Ethnomethodological Approach* (1967), Garfinkel observed the process of a male transvestite constructing the feminine gender role. In *Male Femaling: A Grounded Theory Approach to Cross-Dressing and Sex-Changing* (1997), social psychologist Richard Ekins identified five phases of what he termed *male femaling,* which ranges from discovery of the desire to cross-dress to obtaining a sex-change operation. He was careful to note that the phases of the male femaler's career path are not necessarily experienced as linear. An individual may move through any or all of them and in no particular order.

TRIANGULATION

Triangulation is a research technique in which multiple methods are used in the same study. Proponents of triangulation claim that no single system of **data** collection or analysis is wholly valid and reliable. As such, a combination of methods can help to reduce the error associated with any mode. Correctly executed, triangulated research has the power to produce and/or refute strong theories in that the hypotheses tested in this manner withstand the challenges of multiple methodologies.

Styles of triangulation vary greatly according to the research question asked, the funds available, the presence and condition of past research, and the accessibility of the target population. Often a triangulated research design examines data collected using different methods such as combining secondary data analysis with field experiments or interviews with participant observation, or a researcher could systematically reproduce a series of investigations in varied settings in which the contextual focus is shifted to explore and control concepts.

An example of a triangulation study is research attempting to measure the effect of a bilingual education program on

its participants by examining their standardized test scores (secondary quantitative data), while administering a probing, open-ended survey to their parents and teachers (qualitative data). Combining these two data sets would help provide more insight into the overall success of students, particularly those who do not fair well on standardized tests yet have shown growth in the classroom and at home. If the research only examined the test scores, it might have overlooked these other areas of achievement and declared the program less than successful.

TRUTH, SOJOURNER (ca. 1797-1883)
American human rights activist and orator

Sojourner Truth (1797–1883) was a black American freedom fighter and orator. She believed herself chosen by God to preach His word and to help with the abolitionist effort to free her people. Sojourner Truth was born Isabella Baumfree in Ulster County, New York, the daughter of an African named Baumfree (after his Dutch owner) and a woman called Elizabeth. About the age of nine she was auctioned off to an Englishman named John Nealy. The Nealys understood very little of her Dutch jargon and, as a result, she was often brutally punished for no reason.

Eventually Nealy sold her to a fisherman who owned a tavern in Kingston, New York. Here she acquired the idiomatic expressions which came to mark her speech. John J. Dumont, a nearby plantation owner, purchased her next. During her tenure with his family she married and had five children. In 1827, after New York had passed an emancipation act freeing its slaves, she prepared to take her family away. But Dumont began to show reluctance to this, so she ran away with only her youngest child.

She finally wound up in New York City. She worked at a menial job and through some friends came under the sway of a religious fanatic named Mathias. Eventually disillusioned by her life in New York and by Mathias, in 1843 she left on what she termed a pilgrimage to spread the truth of God's word. She assumed the name Sojourner Truth, which she believed God had given her as a symbolic representation of her mission in life. Soon her reputation as an orator spread, and large crowds greeted her wherever she spoke.

A controversial figure for most of the rest of her life, Truth engaged the courts in two rather unusual cases, winning them both and establishing precedents. She became the first black to win a slander suit against prominent whites and the first black woman to test the legality of segregation of Washington, D.C., streetcars.

During the Civil War, Truth bought gifts for the soldiers with money raised from her lectures and helped fugitive slaves find work and housing. After the war she continued her tirade for the Lord and against racial injustice, even when old age and ill health restricted her activities to the confines of a Battle Creek, Michigan, sanatorium. She died there on November 26, 1883.

T-TEST

A t-test is a test of significance that computes an inferential statistic using small samples. The test is similar to large significance tests except that the p-value is calculated according to a t-distribution instead of the standard **normal distribution**. The **degrees of freedom** (d_f) are calculated as ($n-1$) and the larger the d_f, the more closely the distribution will resemble a standard normal distribution. As with large tests, the smaller the p-value, the more likely one is to reject the **null hypothesis**. While the t-test was designed for sample sizes fewer than thirty, it can be used with any size sample. It is important to note, however, that the test cannot go beyond the level of **bivariate analysis**.

T-tests can be used a number of ways. For instance, the means of two groups of a categorical or nominal **variable** can be compared against their distributions on a single continuous variable. This method could be used to compare men to women regarding which sex receives more speeding tickets. Generally, the null hypothesis for this type of t-test would be that the means of the two groups are equal. The two-sided alternative hypothesis would be that the means of the two groups are not equal. A one-sided alternative hypothesis could be that either men receive more speeding tickets than women or that women receive more speeding tickets than men. A low p-value for this test (less than 0.05 for example) indicates that there is evidence that the difference in the two means is statistically significant; therefore, one should to reject the null hypothesis in favor of the alternative hypothesis.

A t-test can also be used for research questions involving only one group or **mean**. A single sample t-test compares the mean of a sample to a known number, such as a population mean or zero. For example, one could compare the average SAT scores of girls from Anytown, USA in 1996 against the 1996 national average SAT scores of girls.

The assumptions of a t-test are that the **data** are random samples selected from a normally distributed population. When comparing two means, the groups need to be equal in size, mutually exclusive, and have equal variances. In these cases, a pre-test for equal variances is necessary. When data do not meet the required assumptions, non-parametric tests, such as Mann-Whitney U Test, can be used in some cases.

TURGOT, ANNE ROBERT JACQUES (1727-1781)
French economist

A member of a noble family, Anne Robert Jacques Turgot, Baron de l'Aulne, administrator under Louis XV, comptroller general under Louis XVI, attempted to bring financial reform to France but was defeated by the privileged classes. A rather fat, shy, and awkward bachelor, his serious demeanor was tinged with humor, but he failed to convince the king of necessary reforms and died in public disgrace.

Turgot, the third son in an old and respected Norman family, was born on May 10, 1727, in Paris. His father, Mi-

Anne Robert Jacques Turgot *(The Library of Congress)*

chel-Étienne, held high office in Paris and was head of the city's municipality from 1729 until 1740. There were three careers open to young men of Turgot's status at the time: civil administration, the military, and the church. As the third son, with his two older brothers having taken the civil and military positions, Turgot was destined for the church. Accordingly, he entered the Seminary of Saint-Sulpice in 1743 and the Sorbonne in 1749. However, just before ordination in 1751, he announced his intention of leaving the church, claiming it was impossible for him to live under false pretences and indicating he would instead enter service for the Crown.

Over the next few years, Turgot held various offices and became interested in economics. He met **Adam Smith**, the great English economist, and also frequented the intellectual salons of Paris. He contributed articles to various publications, developing a distrust of government intervention in the economy and becoming a champion of free trade. Turgot served as deputy solicitor general and later a counselor magistrate in the *parlement* (supreme court of law) in Paris in 1752. According to the **custom** of the time, in 1753 he bought the post of examiner of petitions, a position that often led to appointment as intendant, chief administrator of a district.

In 1761, Turgot had made enough of a name for himself to be noticed by the king. Louis XV appointed him intendant of Limoges, a poor and backward region and a less than desirable post. Over the next 13 years, Turgot tried, with little sup-

port from the central government and not much from the local people, to impose widespread reforms. Although historians dispute his success, he did make some accomplishments and demonstrated a flair for administration and economics. He abolished forced labor on the roads by peasants, known as the *corvee*, substituting a tax. He instituted a fairer means of tax collection and brought tax records up to date in the district. He set up workshops for the unemployed, paid for by funds from landowners. Fighting the famine of 1770–1771, he kept up a free commerce in grain and quelled riots against its movement.

Apart from his administrative duties in Limoges, Turgot continued his interest in economics. He published his best-known work in 1766: *Reflections on the Formation and Distribution of Wealth.* His ideas predated Adam Smith's classic study of 1776.

On August 24, 1774, Turgot was appointed comptroller general (akin to prime minister) by the young and inexperienced king, Louis XVI, the last king of France in the line of Bourbon monarchs before the French Revolution of 1789. By this time, Turgot saw the need for major governmental reforms, but sensing the opposition of the priveleged classes, he proceeded cautiously. In 1776, he presented the king with the Six Edicts. The first four, which took away certain dues and offices, had little opposition. The fifth, which suppressed the guilds of Paris, was not seriously opposed, but the sixth, which would abolish the *corvee* and pay for public roads by a tax on landowners, brought the wrath of the privileged upon Turgot's head. The priveleged were not about to lose this privelege. Everyone, even the queen, was against him, and finally, even Louis, who had supported his minister at first, could not resist the pressure. In May 1776, he requested Turgot's resignation.

Turgot's Six Edicts were the last attempt to reform the French monarchy from within. Before his dismissal, he warned the king that his weakness under pressure would bring disaster, citing Charles I of England who lost his head under similar circumstances. Indeed, Louis XVI and Queen Marie Antoinette were guillotined on charges of counterrevolution in 1792. Turgot, who retired in public disgrace, had died in Paris on March 18, 1781.

TYLOR, SIR EDWARD BURNETT (1832-1917)
English anthropologist

Sir Edward Burnett Tylor, the son of Joseph and Harriet (Skipper) Tylor, was born on October 2, 1832, in Camberwell, London, England. His father, a prosperous Quaker industrialist who owned a brass foundry, sent Tylor to Grove House, a private school operated by the **Society** of Friends. Due to his nonconformist religion, Tylor was prohibited from attending Oxford or Cambridge. Thus, at the age of sixteen, he entered the family business. Six years later, diagnosed with consumption and advised to travel, he set sail for the United States. After spending a year in the southern United States, he visited Cuba. While on an omnibus during his trip, he heard the familiar Quaker use of ''thou'' and subsequently struck up a friend-

ship with Henry Christy, an English banker and amateur ethnologist. Christy invited Tylor on a four-month trip to Mexico, an experience from which Tylor published his first book *Anahuac: or, Mexico and the Mexicans. Ancient and Modern* (1861).

Written in part from the perspective of an amateur anthropologist and in part as a travel log, *Anahuac* is Tylor's first attempt to develop his ideas on **culture** and the prehistoric origins of humanity. In his second book *Researches into the Early History of Mankind and the Development of Civilization* (1865), Tylor made a much clearer attempt to develop a scientific approach to the study of human and cultural development. By studying the language, myths, rites, customs, and beliefs, Tylor concluded that the human mind functions in similar ways under similar conditions; therefore, he created a strong case for the unity of human nature. Either by independent invention or cultural diffusion, a universal pattern exists in all human development.

Tylor's landmark, two-volume work *Primitive Culture: Researches into the Development of Mythology, Philosophy, Religion, Art, and Custom,* which did much to earn for him the title as the founder of modern anthropology, was published in 1871. Operating from the perspective of cultural evolution, Tylor outlined three "grades," or stages, of cultural development: "savagery," which describes culture based on hunting and gathering; "barbarism," which describes cultures based on nomadic herding and primitive agriculture; and "civilization," which describes cultures based on writing and the construction of **cities**. Although he ascribed to the basic doctrine of evolution and the implicit "survival of the fittest" paradigm, Tylor was sensitive to the vast complexities involved in the development of societies. Believing that evolution was primarily progressive, he did allow for the possibility that a civilized society may regress to more primitive forms of behavior (for example, loss of virtues such as simplicity and independence).

Appearing four years after Matthew Arnold's elitist account of culture in *Culture and Anarchy,* Tylor's definition of culture in *Primitive Culture* stood in stark contrast. Directly contradicting Arnold, Tylor believed culture to be an all-encompassing experience that was made manifest in the stuff of everyday living, which belonged to all human existence. As he wrote in the opening of *Primitive Culture,* "Culture, or **Civilization**, taken in its wide ethnographic sense, is that complex whole which includes knowledge, belief, art, morals, law, **custom**, and any other capabilities acquired by man as a member of society." Although some of his work is ethnocentric, he rebuked the Victorian tradition of racism by suggesting that **race** should not be considered a factor in determining the development of the grade of a civilization.

Primitive Culture also proposed a strong critique of religion based on Tylor's development of the ideas of survivals and animism. According to Tylor, animism is primitive society's tendency to place supernatural powers on all things. As society progresses, rational thought overcomes these superstitions and they are ultimately shed by the civilization. Survivals are those things that outlast their proper stages and hang on to

Sir Edward Burnett Tylor *(The Library of Congress)*

occur in a more advanced grade. Tylor considered religion to be a survival. In other words, religion was a superstitious belief held by primitive people that should have been sloughed off as civilization progressed, but somehow remains in civilized society. Although unnecessary to society, these survivals are of great interest to the anthropologist because they allow for the study of past cultural changes. In the tradition of the Victorian intellectual debate raging at the time between science and religion, Tylor was adamantly on the side of science. Much of the focus of *Primitive Culture* is the account of the decay of religion.

Although modern anthropologists have discarded Tylor's emphasis on evolution, many of his basic assumptions and categories continue to form the basic field of anthropology. In his groundbreaking use of statistical **data** in his analysis of societies, Tylor has been heralded for the advancement of social arithmetic. Although he never received a college degree, he was highly regarded in academic circles. He was appointed as curator of the University Museum and as a reader in anthropology at Oxford, in 1883 and 1884, respectively. In 1896 he became Oxford's first professor of anthropology, a position he held until his retirement in 1909. In 1912, five years before his death, he was knighted.

TYPE I (ALPHA) ERROR

A Type I error, also called an alpha error, is the probability of rejecting a **null hypothesis** which is in **fact** true. In other words, in committing a Type I error, the researcher says that a relationship exists between variables when in fact no relationship exists. The null hypothesis is the hypothesis of a statistical test which states that no relationship exists between the variables. This is not the conclusion the researcher expects, but it is what she or he tests. For example, a null hypothesis might be that no relationship exists between a country's literacy and infant mortality rates. This is complemented by the **research hypothesis**, which states that the variables do have a relationship, and may also state a direction of the relationship; the research hypothesis is typically a statement of the researcher's expectations regarding the relationship between the variables. Using the same variables, the research hypothesis might state that a country's literacy and infant mortality rates are related, or it may state a direction for the relationship: as a country's literacy rate rises, its infant mortality rate drops.

A Type I error is also called an alpha error because the chance of making this error is equal to the alpha level selected. The chance of making this type of error can be minimized by selecting a smaller alpha level. Alpha levels are typically set at .05, which means there is a one in twenty chance the researcher will incorrectly reject the null hypothesis. Alpha levels can also be expressed as percentages of confidence: an alpha of .05 means the researcher is 95 percent confident of her or his results.

Although any level may be chosen, the alpha level is generally chosen according to the potential consequences of making the error. If the researcher is simply trying to discover which hypotheses are worth investigating further, the alpha level may be set higher, such as .10. If the hypothesis test may have serious consequences, such as health or safety implications, the researcher may choose a lower alpha level, such .01 or even .001. This means the researcher is less likely to make an error but is also less likely to be able to claim a relationship exists (or it is harder to reject the null hypothesis).

The Type I error is the opposite of Type II, or beta, error which is failing to reject a false null hypothesis. The probability of making a Type I error is inversely related to the probability of making a Type II error, so the researcher cannot simultaneously reduce both but must choose; social scientists typically choose to reduce Type I errors by setting relatively low alpha levels.

See also Null Hypothesis

TYPE II (BETA) ERROR

A Type II error occurs during the hypothesis testing phase of statistical analysis when a researcher accepts a false **null hypothesis**. When a Type II error happens, a theorized relationship is judged to be not supported by the evidence, even though the relationship exists in the real world. Also called the false acceptance or beta error, the Type II error is the opposite of a Type I error, when a true null hypothesis is rejected. The **probability** of a Type II error is referred to as beta, and it is inversely related to the probability of a Type I error.

Type II errors are not unique to **sociology** or the social sciences—the concept is used whenever one is dealing with statistical inferences based on drawing a representative sample from a larger universe. The traditional method for hypothesis testing involves developing a hypothesis which states that a relationship exists between two variables (i.e., X is related to Y) and a null hypothesis which states that such a relationship does not exist (i.e., X is not related to Y). Various statistical tests of statistical significance, such as chi-square or **t-test**, are then used in an attempt to reject the null hypothesis, thereby providing support for the original hypothesis. A Type II error occurs when this null hypothesis is not rejected, based on the statistical tests done on the sample, when in fact in the actual universe from which the sample was drawn, the null hypothesis is not true.

Type II errors are often viewed as less a concern for researchers than Type I errors because a Type II error does not entail incorrectly rejecting the original hypothesis. It simply finds no supporting evidence for it. A Type I error, however, falsely supports the original hypothesis. For this reason, samples are usually drawn to minimize the likelihood of Type I error, which also increases the likelihood of a Type II error. Overall, this strategy provides for a more rigorous test of the original hypothesis.

See also Null Hypothesis

TYPES OF COMPLIANCE

Compliance is defined as the intended result of attempts by the source to influence a target. Compliance is achieved when the behavior of the target changes sufficiently so that it meets the requests or demands of the source. Although the compliance may include both a change in the **attitude** and behavior of the individual, the focus is more on the behavior.

Three types of compliance were outlined by sociologist Amatai Etzioni in his 1961 work *A Comparative Analysis of Complex Organizations*. The types of compliance highlighted in this work were essentially types of power by which an **organization** could gain the loyalty of their members. The types are coercive power, remunerative or utilitarian power, and normative or identitive power.

Coercive power is compliance through the real or potential threat of physical force to enforce the demands of the organization. Examples of compliance through physical force range from prisons to hostage situations and include any situation where the threat of violence or physical harm is used to gain a behavior modification from the target. Remunerative or utilitarian power attains compliance from the target through use of rewards which the organization controls. Compliance through rewards occurs often in business settings where the organization will use monetary bonuses or stock benefits to encourage employees to remain with the company and to continue to work in the way desired by the organization. Final-

ly, normative or identitive power uses symbolic and emotional means to assure continued loyalty to the organization. Collegiate organizations such as alumni groups and fraternal organizations will use ideas like belonging to a prestigious organization or fond reminiscence of the past to encourage members to comply to the wishes of the group. The three style of compliance outlined by Etzioni are often cross-identified with the types of involvement exercised by members of organization (alienative, calculative, and moral) to form a nine-box typology of compliance relationships.

See also Compliance and Conformity

TYPIFICATION

Typfication is the process of organizing things in terms of typical features. Social actors and sociologists organize their social world by categorizing events, people or things in terms of typical features. This concept is a cornerstone of the influential work of Alfred Shutz, a social theorist, in *The Phenomenology of the Social World* (1932). Shutz, a social phenomenonist, believed that everyday actors make sense out of their lives by organizing everyday occurrences and actions and creating common sense knowledges. Shutz and ethnomethodologists believe there is no difference between ''conventional academic sociology'' and ''practical sociology.'' ''Practical sociology'' refers to the process undertaken by everyday actors in their day-to-day lives. From this perspective, individuals are seen as active agents who make sense out of their everyday lives and thereby create social reality.

One area of inquiry that has utilized the concept of typification is social problems research. Constructionists argue that **social problems** are in essence social constructions. Claimsmakers, people who speak on behalf on social problems, draw the public's attention to certain aspects of a social problem. In doing so, claimsmakers characterize, or typify, a problem. Claimsmakers often emphasize how a particular problem can be categorized along with other social problems. For example, abortion can be thought of as a moral problem joined by societal concerns such as changes in family **values** or human rights or debates about free speech. Sociologists analyze how claimsmakers construct and define social problems by focusing on the typification process. For example, alcoholism was once considered a moral problem; alcoholics were immoral people who could not control their drinking. Today, **alcoholism** is most often considered a medical problem; alcoholics are suffering from an illness. When claimsmakers typify or characterize a problem, they in part recommend the root cause and possible solution. In the case of alcoholism, a moral typification of the problem locates the cause in the **morality** of the individual. The medical typification locates the problem in the biological or genetic makeup of the individual. The solutions or cures for the social problem also differ by typification. In the first case, a person can only overcome alcoholism by strengthening moral resolve. From the medical typification, an alcoholic would seek medical treatment.

TYPOLOGIES

A typology is a set of categories created and used for classification purposes. Often in **sociology** the term is used to describe a classification system of types of some particular concept, such as levels of development of societies, forms of **leadership**, or types of bureaucracies. Typologies are useful for drawing attention to certain qualities of a given concept, such as different societies' economic systems, religious ideologies, or political organization, and typologies make it possible for social scientists to compare one **society** with another according to specific traits which they believe are important.

Generally, typological categories are mutually exclusive (meaning a particular entity cannot fit into more than one category at the same time). A particular society could not be both capitalist and socialist at the same time, or primarily Christian and primarily Islamic, or both a **democracy** and a monarchy. Likewise a voter could not be registered as both a Democrat and a Republican or as an Independent and a Socialist. In some instances the categories are not mutually exclusive, but this is avoided whenever possible.

A special set of typologies is what **Max Weber** referred to as ideal types. Through his development of ideal types, Weber created a classification system still used by social scientists today. Ideal types all exhibit certain features. First, they are based on logically constructed concepts. Second, they are derived from the real world of social history. Third, while they are derived from the real world, they do not actually exist there but are exaggerations of the real world. Fourth, they are not meant to describe an ideal (i.e., utopian) world, but rather their purpose is to create theoretical models which can be used to compare real phenomena. Fifth, ideal types must change as necessary since Weber believed that science is always evolving. For example, Weber created an **ideal type** of a **bureaucracy** and then compared actual bureaucracies with his ideal type. He was then able to discuss how real-world examples of bureaucracies compared and contrasted with his **model**. To be included as a bureaucracy, the phenomenon did not have to meet every criteria, but it did have to exhibit certain elements.

The ideal type is not necessarily a goal to be achieved nor is it a perfect example of a specific thing to be discovered, but rather an artificial construct, a concept which exists only hypothetically, in the world of ideas. While a real entity will not exactly match the ideal type, such classifications are still useful for the researcher as a tool to compare with the real-world example. The researcher can then decide if the example and the ideal type match closely enough or can try to provide a better description of the example. The ideal type is used as a measure of comparison to see the world more clearly. The criteria of a particular ideal type are determined by a researcher or social scientist as an attempt to distill the essential features or elements of the social phenomenon. Weber believed that, by setting forth these specific criteria which compose the ideal type, sociologists could compare actual real-world examples and discuss how these real-life situations compare with the ideal type and with one another.

A common illustration of ideal types is types of **authority**. Weber developed three ideal types of authority: traditional,

charismatic, and legal (sometimes called rational). Traditional authority is based on the premise that the rulers of the society are accepted as legitimate because history or tradition says it is so. This type of authority exists where there is rule by a monarch, or in patriarchal societies where tradition dictates ruler succession, property inheritance, etc. The second type of authority, charismatic authority, centers on a leader who possesses or is believed to possess some extraordinary gift and/or power. This type of authority is based on the individual leader's characteristics, and respect for this authority is a matter of followers' personal devotion and confidence in these quali-

ties of the leader. Some political leaders (e.g., John F. Kennedy), some **cult** leaders (e.g., Jim Jones), and some religious figures (e.g., Jesus) have charismatic authority. The third type of authority is legal **domination**. Followers believe in and accept leaders' authority because of **rules** or laws. People respect legal codes, so they respect the authority of those set forth to rule by those codes. This is the type of authority of modern bureaucrats. Weber defined and characterized these ideal types, then compared them with real examples of each of these in order to determine how the ideal types reflected the real world.

U

UNANTICIPATED CONSEQUENCES

When we act, we act with the expectation or the ability to anticipate certain consequences from these actions. If we study for exams, we expect to do well. If we speed, we can expect or anticipate the possibility of getting a ticket. While we can anticipate some consequences, there are also consequences that result from our actions that we do not or cannot anticipate. It is useful in sociological observation to distinguish between the intent of actions and the results of action that might even go unrecognized, also termed in the literature unintended consequences. **Robert K. Merton** distinguished between manifest and latent functions. Manifest functions are the overt, recognized effects of social action. Latent functions are the unanticipated consequences. He delineated three types of unanticipated consequences. One set of unanticipated consequences has positive results for social actors or institutions. For example, the Hopi Indians engage in ceremonial dances. The manifest function of these dances is to encourage rainfall. However, regardless of the weather outcomes, these ceremonial dances also bring the tribe together and strengthen tribal unity. This unity is a positive unanticipated consequence of the ritual. A second set of unanticipated consequences has negative results for social actors or institutions. If a teacher is told that a particular student is a troublemaker, the teacher may pay little attention to the student and have little tolerance for the student. Consequently, the student might act out against the teacher's attitudes and become a troublemaker, which has negative implications both for the student and the teacher. Last, Merton expressed that unanticipated consequences could have a neutral impact, neither positive nor negative on social actors or institutions.

A problem with attempting to categorize effects into one of these three categories is that unanticipated consequences can be simultaneously positive for some portion of a social system and negative for another. Evaluation depends on the perspective one takes. For example, Ruth Milkman wrote about women in the auto industry during World War II. Due to assumptions about innate biological competencies, women were largely segregated from men and concentrated in "feminine" jobs before the war. These were jobs that involved manual dexterity. When men went to war, companies brought large numbers of women into the factories to fill the "masculine" jobs, such as working heavy machinery. When men returned from the war and women were being ejected from these new positions, women began to argue over where the boundary of "men's work" and "women's work" should be. The intention of these debates was to expand the repertoire of jobs that women were allowed to fill. However, the attention and effort being made for change were focused at the boundary between men's and women's jobs rather than on dispelling the cultural notions of femininity and **masculinity** that supported the system of job segregation in the first place. This struggle at the margins had the unintended consequence of helping to legitimate the idiom supporting the overall **division of labor** by sex. This unanticipated consequence was negative for women looking to keep their war-time jobs, but it was positive for men and for the employers who, through sex segregation, could pay women less for their labor because of the nature of the jobs considered "feminine."

The concept of unanticipated consequences is prevalent in the research in many areas of **sociology**. It is also useful both at the micro and macro level of research on **society**. At the micro level, the process of the "self-fulfilling prophesy" exemplifies the importance of attention to unanticipated consequences. The example above about the teacher and student is a classic example of this. A series of experiments found that teachers with preconceived notions of students acted on these beliefs and actually produced the very results they were expecting in the first place. The experiment randomly labeled a group children as exceptionally bright. The teacher, with this knowledge, was found to give more attention to these students and challenged them more than the other students. After a period of time, these students who had previously performed similarly to their classmates, were excelling beyond the other students. At the more macro level, **Anthony Giddens** articulat-

ment rate in the United States was 10.8 percent, which occurred in December 1982. U.S. rates have sometimes been challenged by critics who claim the statistics do not project true figures because they ignore so-called discouraged workers who simply stop looking for work because they believe that no suitable positions exist for them.

Unemployment can be divided into three categories: cyclical, structural, and frictional. Cyclical unemployment occurs with depressions in business cycles and when labor supply exceeds labor demand. Structural unemployment is the result of unbalanced labor markets. Demand for labor rises in one region and falls in another, as when a large factory moves its headquarters, but labor supplies do not adjust. Frictional unemployment is often voluntary and short term, the result of people moving from one area to another and/or finding themselves between jobs.

Unemployment insurance (UI) is social insurance that gives financial assistance to workers whose unemployment is involuntary and short term. It is intended to cover a period long enough for them to find other jobs or to be rehired in the original ones. The UI program in the United States does not cover farm and government workers, most self-employed workers, domestic servants, or those with only brief **employment**. Financial benefits from UI are generally related to earnings. In 1998, a presidential directive initiated study of a program to improve UI in such areas as inclusion of farm and parttime workers.

A young woman applies for unemployment compensation *(Corbis Corporation [Bellevue])*.

ed a notion of ''unintended consequences'' in his theory of structuration. He acknowledges in his work that there is the ability for the barriers that face people to be constructed and maintained through their own actions without this being the intention. The example above about women's efforts to overcome sex segregation in the workplace is an illustration of this process.

UNEMPLOYMENT

The term ''unemployment'' applies to anyone who is capable of working and desires to work but cannot find work. Those people who are retired, ill, do not wish to work, or attend school are not classified as part of the **labor force** or counted in the national unemployment rate. This concept of unemployment dates from the late nineteenth century and the rise of industrialized wage economies. The unemployment rate is figured by dividing the number of unemployed by the total number in the labor force. A two percent unemployment rate in the United States is generally cited as the ''base'' rate. In the last half of the twentieth century, the highest unemploy-

UNIT OF ANALYSIS

Conducting sociological research involves gathering information to analyze from someone or something. The component about which information is gathered is called the unit of analysis. It is also often referred to as the unit of observation.

Given the focus of **sociology**, the unit of analysis is often a person or **group** of people, but it can be things as well, such as personal journals or music videos. There are four basic sources that comprise the range of possible units of analysis for sociological research. They are individuals, groups, organizations, and social artifacts.

When the units of analysis are individuals, information is usually gathered via interviews, **surveys**, or by observation. Researchers observe or inquire about individual behaviors, attitudes, orientations, and opinions. A question, such as ''What is your annual income?'', might be asked of individuals in which the individual is the unit of analysis. However, if we were to ask, ''What is your total **household** income?'', the unit of analysis is a group. Although an individual may answer both questions, the information received pertains to individual income in the first question and **family** (a group) income in the second question. Other examples of groups are gangs, sports teams, and ethnic communities.

Information can also be gathered about formal organizations, such as the National Organization of Women (NOW). A sociologist might be interested in investigating the political climate in which NOW originated. The researcher may gather

information about the organization from individual members or archives, but the information gathered pertains to NOW so an organization is the unit of analysis.

A social artifact is a concrete object created by individuals in a society. Any social artifact can be a unit of analysis such as comic books, television shows, books, or photographs. A sociologist may want to identify the level of violence in children's comic books. The researcher may need to view old comic books in a library archive that have been transformed to microfiche; nonetheless, the information gathered pertains to comic books, which are the social artifacts that are the units of analysis.

UNITED STATES CENSUS BUREAU (U.S. CENSUS BUREAU)

The United States Census Bureau, a federal agency under the U.S. Department of Commerce, is responsible for conducting national **surveys** that collect a wide variety of demographic **data** and for compiling and analyzing these data. The most important of these surveys is the decennial census, which attempts to count every person living in the United States. The census is mandated in Article One, Section Two, of the U.S. Constitution in order to determine the population of different states and congressional districts so that representation in Congress can be reapportioned. The present-day census also collects some basic information on individuals, such as **race**, **ethnicity**, and gender so as to determine the demographic makeup of the U.S. population. Other information is also collected from a sample of individuals that can be used in deciding how to allocate funding, such as income, use of public transportation, and the condition of plumbing in the home.

Early censuses were conducted in the early 1600s in Virginia. After independence, the first decennial census in the United States was conducted in 1790 and was overseen by Thomas Jefferson. Approximately 3.9 million people were counted in the 1790 census, although the U.S. president at the time, George Washington, expressed concern to Jefferson about a possible undercount. Undercount is a continuing concern for the Census Bureau, as they result in affected areas not getting proportional representation and can also result in a lack of necessary government funding. In order to decrease the likelihood of an undercount, Congressional representatives debated the costs and benefits of conducting the 2000 Census using a random sampling technique rather than attempting to count the entire population. However, some representatives felt that Article One, Section Two, of the Constitution requires an actual count; therefore, the 2000 Census continued to attempt a complete count of the U.S. population while an experimental random sample was conducted to test whether this method would produce a more accurate count.

The Census Bureau conducts many other surveys that provide vital information for researchers, private industry, and other federal agencies. These surveys cover many topics, including occupations/labor force, **family**, housing, race/ethnicity and nationality, age, wealth/poverty, participation in social programs, education, health/health insurance and technology use. The Bureau also provides access to much of the data while still keeping confidential identifying information of individuals. The raw data can be purchased, and some data files can be downloaded from the Census Bureau website.

UNIVARIATE ANALYSIS

Univariate analysis involves the examination of a single **variable**. Conducting univariate analysis gives the researcher descriptive information about a variable. Information of this kind helps researchers to locate errors in the **data** and to identify trends in the population from which the data was gathered. Descriptive information is analyzed at the univariate level that includes the frequency of the distribution of cases over the attributes of a variable, measures of central tendency, and **measures of dispersion**.

To remember the meaning of a frequency, think of it in terms of the "frequency" of occurrence for each attribute. How many people report that their income falls into category 2 ($10,001-$20,000)? How about category 1 (Up to $10,000)? The count, or frequency, is usually reported as well as the percentage of the total sample that fall into each category or attribute.

Summary information about a variable is also considered univariate analysis. **Measures of central tendency** refer to the **mean**, **median**, and the mode. In a graph of responses to a single variable, each dot on the graph corresponds to the response of each individual surveyed. There are three different ways to locate a "central" area on the graph, the area around which most responses are located. The mean is the numerical average score for responses to a single variable. The median is the middle score. Calculation of the median eliminates cases that extend far below or above the mean and identifies the halfway point. The mode is the attribute into which the largest numbers of responses fall.

Measures of dispersion include the range, standard deviation, variance, and interquartile range. It helps to think of measures of dispersion as measures that estimate how spread out, or "dispersed," the responses are on a given variable. The range simply refers to the number of attributes a variable has. The standard deviation and the variance both estimate the extent to which the responses are clustered around the mean. The interquartile range is the range of scores for the middle 50 percent of cases on a single variable.

UNSTRUCTURED DATA

Unstructured **data** is information that is gathered without consideration given to how it might be coded later for purposes of compilation and examination. Information that is not readily categorized is labeled unstructured, such as **surveys** comprised of open-ended questions, which allow the respondents to answer in their own words rather than choosing from a predetermined list of possible responses. Collection of unstructured

data is used for qualitative social analysis and as a tool for the development of structured questionnaires. Researchers also regard almost all historical data, such as old manuscripts and newspapers, as unstructured. Their goal, then, is to create a structure to superimpose upon the information so that it may be utilized to the fullest possible extent.

Qualitative sociologists use the unstructured and flexible methods of personal interviews and group discussions to elicit information regarding participants' views and behaviors. The interviews and discussions may be completely unstructured, allowing the conversation to be guided primarily by the participants, or it may be semi-structured, whereby participants are asked to discuss matters related to a selected topic list. Methods employed may include sentence completion, where the participant is asked to finish a sentence, indirect questioning, where the participant is asked to assess how they perceive others might feel about a certain topic, and personalization of objects, whereby emotions are attributed to inanimate objects. In each case, the goal of unstructured qualitative data collection is to gain the broadest understanding, allow for the most freedom of thoughts and feelings, and therefore produce the most in-depth assessment of human social behavior and attitudes.

The collection of unstructured data can also be used to assist the proper development of a structured survey. Pilot questionnaires often provide opportunities for unstructured responses. According to Jean Morton-Williams, the primary author of "Unstructured Design Work," which appears in *Survey Research Practice* (Gerlad Hoinville, Roger Jowell, et. al.; 1978), "Data collected from qualitative research differ from large-scale survey data in fitting no rigid structure: each **interview** or discussion covers the same topics, but the ways in which they are covered and the sorts of information obtained may vary considerably. The researcher's task is to educe a structure which he can then apply to the **questionnaire** for the main survey." The main difficulty faced by researchers who deal with unstructured data, either from surveys or historical documents, is the creation of a coding system, or a method of categorization, that not only adequately compartmentalizes information for the purpose of comparison and analysis, but also provides for the uniqueness of different responses.

Urban Sociology

The concerns of urban sociology are in some sense reflected in the works of the founding fathers of the discipline. The transformations in industrial society that interested **Karl Marx, Max Weber**, and Émile Durkheim, are changes associated with **urbanization** and the transformation of societies from rural to urban-based. Important social processes, as the advent of class-consciousness for Marx, or **rationalization** for Weber, take place in city settings. But urban sociology itself—the sociological study of the causes and consequences of urbanization—dates back to the early twentieth century, and is most often associated with North American sociology, and with the Chicago school.

From the 1920s on, sociologists associated with the University of Chicago developed a number of important early the-

ories and studies and developed a distinctive ethnographic style of sociological research of urban problems. Famous early works include close observation of urban cultures and subcultures. **Louis Wirth** developed the approach to urban sociology that studied "urbanism as a way of life." He was concerned with distinctively urban ways of sociability and **interaction**, which included for him a high degree of impersonal contact and a markedly rationalized approach to personal relationships. Robert Park's urban **ecology** approach sought to understand patterns of location and mobility in **cities** as result of competition between groups, as one might find in natural ecosystems. Drake and Cayton's *Black Metropolis* (1945) challenged the urban ecology approach by showing that the distribution of black populations in ghettoes in the city of Chicago was a result of willful acts of exclusion and violence and not natural, competitive forces.

A new urban sociology was developed in the mid-1970s by scholars influenced by critical traditions in social science, most specifically Marxism and Marxist sociology. Conflicts in cities since the 1960s forced sociologists to rethink approaches to urban sociology to include **social movements**, riots, and other conflicts as central to urban settings, and Marxist approaches that emphasized economic exploitation and **domination** proved germane. The Research Committee on Urban and Regional Sociology of the International Sociological Association, is considered a central organization in these developments. Much of this work was published in its journal *The International Journal of Urban and Regional Research*. A hallmark of the new urban sociology was its attention to the economic and political context under which cities developed and the role of cities in capitalist processes. Manuel Castells, whose *Urban Question* (1977) is considered one of the central texts of this body of work, concentrated on the role of cities in capitalist accumulation, consumption, and in guaranteeing the reproduction of labor for production. Christopher Pickvance, William Tabb, Michael Smith, and Jean Lojkine advanced the understanding of the relationship between capitalist modes of production and features of the city. Urban sociologists concerned with questions of **race** relations and exclusion in the city, as Doug Massey and Nancy Denton, and John Logan and Harvey Molotch have also carried out studies in ways influenced by the new urban sociology. Related changes in the field of geography were also influential at the time. David Harvey, a geographer also concerned with capitalist production and accumulation, sought to link the production of space and features of the built environment of cities to capitalist accumulation.

Two important intellectual trends have helped shape the area since the development of the new urban sociology. One is an increasing attention to global process and globalization as linked to processes of urbanization. Largely under the influence of world-systems analysis, scholars have sought to understand the global system of cities. Earlier work, influenced by Dependency Theory, that had sought to isolate the features of urbanization in 'dependent' countries, has given way to analyses of city features linked to the global economy, in the industrialized world or not. Alejandro Portes, John Walton, and

Janet Abu-Lughod have sought to understand the features of the global system of cities. Saskia Sassen (1991) wrote on the Global City, and the common features cities such as Tokyo, London, and New York have by virtue of their occupying structurally similar positions in the world economy. Scholars of race relations like **William Julius Wilson** have also begun to pay attention to global trends as determining urban fates. His book (1996) *When Work Disappears* deals with the impact of the flight of industry from downtown Chicago on the inner city poor and on race relations.

Another important trend in urban sociology is the increased influence of cultural geographers, like Ed Soja, Henri Lefevre, Douglas Entrikin, Tim Cresswell, and others, who focus on the meaning of place as constitutive of social relations. Much of this new work has been associated with the British journal *Progress in Human Geography*. These scholars have emphasized, for instance, the importance of meanings attached to certain parts of town where it is not considered appropriate for certain groups of persons to be. Feminist geographers have also emphasized that certain spaces are considered male preserves. Much work on place and space has been influenced by thinkers associated with **Postmodernism** and Poststructuralism. Michel Foucault, for instance, whose writings on discipline and power have a strong spatial element, has been influential in work that seeks to understand the ways that spatial arrangements reproduce power and hierarchy. The calls to understand the meaning of place could signify a potential return to Chicago school concerns with close observations and emphasis on the lived experience.

URBANIZATION

Urbanization describes the migration of people out of rural areas and into a city. **Cities** are primarily characterized by their size, defined by the United Nations as 20,000 or more people living in close proximity, and by the United States as areas of 2,500 or more residents. Urbanites relate differently to their fellow city-dwellers than individuals residing in small towns or farming communities relate to their neighbors. City residents are interdependent, interacting with a variety of people on a daily basis in order to meet their needs; this relationship makes city life a prime example of Durkheim's concept of organic solidarity. Cities eschew the insularity of small towns in favor of opportunities for dwellers to associate with individuals from every walk of life, but these meetings tend to be fleeting and superficial; while secrets are hard to keep in a small town, an individual can easily disappear in a metropolis.

Until the **Industrial Revolution**, (European) cities were surrounded by walls and occupied at the center by members of the clergy, government officials, and the wealthy; the poor lived on the outskirts, or outside of the walls. As production moved out of the home and into factories, the proletariat moved into the city centers to take advantage of ample opportunities for employment. However, because factory work was not highly remunerative, the workers ended up in slums, living in crowded apartments with vermin and poor sanitation

European immigrants came to the United States in waves, settling in cities, such as New York and Chicago, and

forming enclaves with an ethnic character that continues to define these areas, such as Chinatown, Little Italy, and Hell's Kitchen (Irish) in New York City. Large numbers of African-Americans moved to northern cities at the beginning of the twentieth century, in an attempt to escape the effects of the pervasive racism, such as limited job opportunities and the predomincance of sharecropping, that prevailed in the southern United States. One of the best-known urban settlements formed as a result of this migration is Harlem, in New York City. Harlem became a strong community with its own **culture** and a highly-regarded artistic moment, the Harlem Renaissance, characterized by distinctive music, literature, and visual arts.

Cities, designed to facilitate commerce, expanded to fill the needs of industry and ameliorate overpopulation. Industry, in search of more and cheaper land, moved to the outskirts of urban areas, taking jobs away from the unskilled members of the lower class. European cities followed the precedent set by their pre-industrial predecessors as the working classes moved to their peripheries. American cities took the opposite path; following World War II, the white middle class began to move to the suburbs, where they could escape the dangers and stresses of the city. The suburbs offered fresh air, less crowded conditions, opportunities for home ownership, better schools, and a segregated environment; as middle-class African-Americans made their way into suburban neighborhood, whites moved elsewhere, a **cycle** now known as ''white flight.''

The disappearance of industry and the middle class from core urban areas left inner cities impoverished and host to a number of ailments frequently associated with city life, such as **crime**, dilapidated housing, ineffective schooling, **prostitution**, and **drug abuse**. However, some wealthy persons, able to insulate themselves from unpleasantries, remained in the cities, creating a bifurcated, racialized social **structure** marked by increasing inequality.

The best of any country's culture, dating from the days of ancient Greece and Rome, resides in its cities. Urban areas are fertile ground for cutting-edge artists of all types, and for museums, libraries and other institutions charged with preserving cultural artifacts. Restaurants in cities boast innovative chefs, clubs host new talents, shopping is excellent, and the theater is unparalleled. As a result, cities continue to draw tourists and artistic hopefuls, as well as immigrants.

This enduring urban appeal began to entice members of the upper-middle class to move back to city centers in the mid-1980s. These young, urban professionals bought and refurbished beautiful old houses and apartments in run-down (i.e., less expensive) sectors of America's cities, pushing up property **values** and driving out the less-advantaged residents who had lived in these neighborhoods for many years. This process, known as **gentrification**, continues in cities across the United States, leaving those at the bottom of the socioeconomic ladder with few options for affordable housing, in or outside of the city center.

UTILITARIANISM

Narrowly defined, utilitarianism refers to a moral and social philosophy that, judging actions by their consequences, aims at the greatest happiness of the greatest number. This **philosophy** emerged in late eighteenth-century England and was expounded by **Jeremy Bentham**, **John Stuart Mill**, and Henry Sidgwick. In **sociology**, the term has been more broadly understood to include assumptions about the nature of social action and the basis of **social order**. Talcott Parsons identified four such assumptions. First, utilitarianism tends to conceive of **society** in atomistic terms, as no more than the individuals who make it up. Second, utilitarianism stresses rational action, understood as the individual pursuit of self-interest and the efficient maximization of utility (satisfaction of needs or wants). Third, utilitarianism tends to see concrete action systems as the aggregates of such rational unit acts. Fourth, utilitarianism sees the ends that social actors pursue as arbitrary, unrelated, and therefore random.

While there has always been a utilitarian strand or tradition within sociology—the work of **Herbert Spencer** being an early example—much sociological thinking has been constituted in conscious opposition to it. **Karl Marx**, for example, suggested that the rational actor posited by utilitarianism is the *bourgeois* of modern civil society, the ''historic result'' of the dissolution of **feudalism** and the development of new productive forces, whom the utilitarians have projected into the past as ''history's point of departure.'' Émile Durkheim also rejected utilitarianism's attempt to deduce society from the individual. Indeed, Durkheim argued, contractual exchange between rational actors presupposes social and normative regulation — the celebrated non-contractual basis of the contract. More recently, Talcott Parsons has shown that social order is inexplicable if one begins with the utilitarian assumption that the actor's choice of ends is arbitrary. Nor can the problem be solved by deriving ends from the conditions of action, Parsons insisted, for this would lead to a distorted and reductionistic understanding of action itself. The dilemma can only be resolved, he argued, if we distinguish, ''as the utilitarians did not, between voluntariness and arbitrariness.'' Social norms do not act externally, in the manner of either physical forces or sanctions. Rather, **norms** ''enter directly into the constitution of the actors' ends themselves.'' Adherence to norms is thus at the same time both voluntary and binding, and it is this internalization of norms that ultimately makes social order possible. In place of the rational actor of utilitarianism, Parsonian sociology thus posits a socialized actor oriented toward shared norms and **values**.

Despite these and other criticisms, utilitarianism continues to find expression in contemporary sociology, most notably in the form of rational choice **theory**. James Coleman provides what is perhaps its most sophisticated formulation in *Foundations of Social Theory* (1990). Inverting Durkheim's argument, Coleman argued that social norms themselves can be explained on the basis of strategic and instrumental action. The advantage of **rational choice theory**, in other words, is that it is able to explain what norm-based theories of action merely assume as a given. Coleman argued that for norms to emerge, actors must be (1) rationally motivated to demand them and (2) able to enforce compliance. Demand for norms arises when someone's actions have adverse consequences for us, but we cannot easily gain control over those actions through a process of social exchange. The necessity of applying sanctions to those who violate the norm gives rise to a free-rider problem, but this can be resolved through the introduction of *incremental sanctioning* in which ''the cost incurred by each sanctioner is small, and the effect of each **sanction** is small as well, but the effects are additive, giving a large total effect.'' Coleman was also careful to make room for the internalization of norms in his **model**. Sanctions are not always applied by others; transgressors often apply sanctions to themselves. This is explained by the alignment of ''the agent's interests so fully with those of the principal that the agent's self-interest comes to coincide with the principal's interest.'' However, by introducing what he called the ''expansion of the object self,'' or the identification of an actor with others, Coleman suggested the possibility of a solidaristic rather than an instrumental relation to others. In this way, he seemed to implicitly smuggle in nonutilitarian assumptions.

UTOPIA

A utopia is an ideal **community** whose inhabitants live under perfect conditions. The term was coined in 1516 by Sir Thomas More in his book *Utopia*, the two volumes of which described both the faults that characterized Christian European societies of the period and the contrasting merits of the fictional island of Utopia, a pagan and communist city-state. More derived the term by combing the Greek words for ''not'' (ou) and ''place'' (topos), thus inventing ''utopia,'' which means ''nowhere.'' This meaning suggests More's awareness that utopian thinking was visionary and not possible to be realized.

Utopia themes have been common in literature at least since ancient times, with Plato's *Republic* often cited as the definitive **model**. Writers have used both straightforward argument as well as satire to express utopian visions, which have considered such matters as governance, work, distribution of resources, and social roles. Humanist utopias have been described in such works as Antonio Francesco Doni's *I mondi* (1552), and Francesco Patrizi's *La citt. . .felice* (1553). Tommaso Campanella described a practical utopia in *La citt. . . del sole* (1602). Utopias based on religious principles have included *Antangil* (1616) by''I.D.M.,'' *Christianopolis* (1619) by Johann Valentin Andreae, and *Novae Solymae libri sex* (1648) by Samuel Gott. Among utopian works that focus on economic matters have been James Harrington's *The Common-Wealth of Oceana* (1656) and Edward Bellamy's extraordinarily influential*Looking Backward* (1887), which advocated absolute economic equality. William Morris, attacking Bellamy's emphasis on economics and his support of centralized social controls, imagined in *News From Nowhere* (1890) a utopia of complete individual freedom, in which all work was pleasure. And **B.F. Skinner** envisioned a behaviorist utopia in *Walden Two* (1948).

Among the most widely-known satirical utopian works are Jonathan Swift's *Gulliver's Travels* (1726) and Samuel Butler's *Erewhon* (1872), which is ''nowhere'' spelled backward. A twentieth-century development stemming from the satirical utopian tradition is the bitterly anti-utopian, or dystopian, literature such as Yevgeny Zamyatin's *We* (1925) and George Orwell's *1984* (1949).

Though utopias are generally considered impossible to create in the real world, many groups, particularly religious ones, have attempted to establish working utopian societies. Between 1663 and 1858, about 138 utopian settlements were founded in North America. The first to endure after the death of its founder was the Ehprata Community, founded in 1732 in Pennsylvania. Many religious utopian communities died out, but some still exist, including a small number of Shakers and the flourishing Hutterite communities in several U.S. states and Canada. Among secular utopian communities are the Oneida Community, founded in 1841 and established at Oneida, New York, in 1848, and Brook Farm, established in Massachusetts in the 1840s and one of some 28 colonies established between 1841 and 1859 on the model advocated by French social reformer Charles Fourier.

In the twentieth century, interest in structured utopian communities waned. But some individuals who, during the 1960s and 1970s, rejected what they perceived as militaristic and materialistic societal **norms** formed ''communes,'' or loosely-organized group living arrangements, that offered alternatives to the hegemonic social **structure**. Though these communities did not necessarily identify themselves as utopian, they often structured themselves according to egalitarian ideals, with many producing their own food and practicing open sexual relationships. Other twentieth century utopias have been established by charismatic religious leaders, but in general these have faded after the death of the leader.

Sociologists have critiqued utopian theories for their basis in arbitrary value systems. **Karl Marx** rejected **utopianism** for deflecting attention from real political goals by emphasizing an impossible model. Utopianism, in his view, is based on irrational ideals and cannot lead to practical change. Karl Mannheim, however, in *Ideology and Utopia*, argued that utopian ideas contain the potential to effect at least some degree of change on an existing **social order** and could thus help advance some elements of a particular utopian model.

UTOPIANISM

Utopianism is the search for, the desire for, or the realization of an ideal **society**, as envisioned through literary works, political and religious treatises, and actual social experiments. A pun on the Greek eutopia, ''good place,'' and outopia, ''noplace,'' the term first appeared as the name of the fictional island in Thomas More's **Utopia** (1516). During the next three centuries, many more Utopian novels, satires, allegories, and even epic poems appeared, offering critiques of contemporary social institutions and, in many cases plans (ranging from the workable to the whimsical) for improving them. In the typical

Sir Thomas More coined the term ''utopia'' in 1516 *(The Library of Congress)*.

Utopian novel, a European adventurer stumbles onto an isolated island, valley, or future Earth ruled entirely by inhabitants who live in gigantic dormitories in clockwork cities, work at state-assigned jobs, and engage in sexual relations solely to replenish the supply of workers. If they have a religion at all, they worship at a Temple of Reason instead of in churches or synagogues. The adventurer makes a number of cutting comparisons with the superstition, petty bigotry, oppression, and everyday injustice implemented by **church**, state, and common folk back home.

As a mode of presenting reality rather than a distinct genre, Utopianism continues to influence modern literature, especially magic **realism**, science fiction, and fantasy. Sociologists, however, are more interested in how the desire for social perfection has been transmitted into actual social experiments. During the nineteenth century, the sparsely populated North American continent seemed an ideal locale to start a new, perfect **civilization**, and it was soon riddled with planned communities, communes, cults, autocracies, and theocracies. Some, such as Ephrata in Pennsylvania or the Amana Colonies in Iowa, were designed according to God's precise directions and ruled by God's prophets; some, such as Icaria in Illinois and New Harmony in Indiana, were based upon the socialist ideas of such great utopianists as Étienne Cabet, Robert Owen, and Charles Fourier; and a few, such as John Humphrey Noye's Oneida in upstate New York, were based upon outlandish theories of nutrition and sexuality or simply idiosyncratic rants.

Although a few localized social experiments were attempted later, most notably by the hippies and New Left activ-

ists of the 1960s and 1970s, in the twentieth century most social theorists, politicians, theologians, and philosophers transcended the local, fostering Utopian plans for national and even global transformation. Sometimes the quest for perfection meant eliminating the weak and unfit, and a form of Utopianism lay in the background of the horrors of Nazi Germany, Stalinist purges, and ethnic cleansing elsewhere in the world. Conversely, Israeli *kibbutzim*, family planning in India, and the famous ''Good Society'' debates in the United States evoke Utopia as the potential result of responsible social planning by a liberal, tolerant, and self-aware civilian population.

Nineteenth-century social thinkers tended to disapprove of Utopianism as at best impractical and, more likely, a subtle reinforcement of bourgeois gender and class oppression. However, **Auguste Comte**, Émile Durkheim, and **Karl Marx** all postulated grand Utopian futures, and many first-generation American sociologists spent their childhoods in Utopian communes. Recent generations of sociologists, especially **Karl Mannheim**, Krisnan Kumar, and Zygmunt Bauman, have maintained that Utopianism is central to all social systems, a progressive dynamic that allows us to locate the future within the present, to see things as they could or should be, and to work for **social change**.

V

VALIDITY

Validity refers to the extent to which measurements in social research accurately represent the qualities of the concepts or phenomena they claim to measure. The general concept of validity represents the "truthfulness" of any information. However, the concept of validity as it relates to social research originated in the development of social science in the nineteenth century. As research has become more advanced, the assessment of validity has become more precise. Although validity cannot be "proven" to the extent it is in the physical sciences, several ways exist to assess it. Common areas to evaluate when assessing social measures are **face validity**, construct validity, and criterion validity.

Face validity describes the extent to which a measure makes sense considering one's knowledge of a given concept. A more rigorous examination of face validity would examine a measure for potential biases. An example would be social desirability **bias**. Even though anonymity is usually guaranteed on questionnaires, respondents sometimes give answers that they think a person would want to hear. For example, individuals being asked how many times they take illegal drugs in a typical month might report fewer than they actually do because of social pressure to reject drugs.

Some sociological concepts cannot be adequately measured with one survey item. Socio-economic status, for example, is a combination of measures of education, income, **race**, and other factors. *Construct validity* must be assessed when combining measures into this type of index. This can be done statistically by evaluating the extent to which the individual items in the index are correlated, or how likely it is that an individual who gives a particular response to one item in the index will give a particular response to another item. For example, one would expect a subject's response for a **household** income item to be low if her or his response to an education level item is low.

Another way to assess the validity of a measure is to compare responses from a survey to external criteria that are known to be valid. An example of an evaluation of *criterion validity* would be to compare assessment measures of prospective employees' skills to their performance records after one year on the job. Employees who scored high on management skills before being hired should, after one year, exhibit higher than average performance in management.

Validity of social research measures is relevant in everyday American life. Social measures are often used for evaluation of programs, policymaking, market research, and political polling. The concept of information literacy is related to validity: to gauge the **reliability** of statistical information released by **political organizations**, one must know how the question was asked. It is well known that changing the wording of a question can change the answer. For instance, an individual might answer the two questions differently even though they purport to measure the same thing: "Do you support mandatory gun locks?" and "Would you support legislation to place safety locks on handguns to prevent the accidental deaths of children in the home?"

VALUES

Defined most broadly, values are the criteria individuals or groups use to define and rank practically anything as relatively good or bad, including objects (e.g. fruit, cars, gold, music), styles (of painting, clothing design, writing, etc.), ideas and philosophies (reason vs. intuition, cooperation vs. **competition**), action (praying vs. fighting, lying vs. truth telling), personal characteristics (muscular or lean), and states of being (**war** vs. peace, indifference vs. passion). Values may thus refer to interests, preferences, likes and dislikes, desires, duties and/ or moral obligations. As criteria, values influence human judgement and action. Accordingly, sociologists and other scholars have studied values to help understand and predict human behavior, social change and social continuity.

Sociologists have, perhaps naturally, tended to be more interested in shared or cultural values than strictly individual

values. Individual values are, of course, often also cultural values, although individuals may not be aware of this. Many contemporary Americans, for instance, say they personally value individualized spirituality over organized religion. This is a personally deeply felt value and one also common to millions of Americans who share, consciously or not, in a set of individualistic cultural values. Cultural values may be studied at various levels, from those shared between two individuals or a small gang of youth all the way to the fundamental values which shape the direction of major institutions like national governments and transnational economies.

The **concept** of values gained perhaps its greatest prominence around the middle of the twentieth century, when many sociologists argued the importance of values to societal order and stability. Political sociologists like Seymour Martin Lipset (1922–) argued that widely shared democratic values were crucial to maintaining the stability and vitality of democracies. The prominent twentieth century sociologist **Talcott Parsons** (1902–1979) argued that cultural values are crucial to establishing consensus, to fulfilling societal functions and goals (e.g. education, wealth creation, efficient communication, etc.), and thus to making **society** possible. Parsons theorized that individuals living in a given society tend to internalize the cultural values (and related norms or **rules** guiding behavior) of that society and, consequently, behave in ways which support societal development and maintenance. Critics of Parsons have argued that his **theory** of values does not adequately explain how and why values change, or how the dominant values in a society may, in fact, not only integrate individuals but also serve elite interests.

Beginning in the 1960s, sociologists grew more cautious and skeptical about the importance of cultural values, especially as values may be used to explain or predict human action. Cultural sociologist Ann Swidler, among others, argued that values are often poor indicators of how people actually act. While national surveys may reveal the values which individuals profess, it has been much harder to then explain their actions because action is usually also shaped by so many other factors, including habits, psychological predisposition, material conditions, and institutional costs and benefits. This argument has figured in the 1960s debate about the "culture of poverty" and specifically whether poor people act in self-destructive ways due to having internalized bad values. Some critics of this argument contend that poor people often share the same values as mainstream, middle class Americans, but act differently due to poorer structural circumstances or due to different habits and skills rather than different values.

VARIABLE

The opposite of a constant, a variable is a logical grouping of different attributes that all pertain to the **concept** that the variable is supposed to represent. A variable is best explained by its components and by examples. Variables are composed of attributes (i.e., categories or numbers) that pertain to different aspects of a concept. For instance, sex is a concept that is ex-

pressed by a variable that has two categories, male and female. If the concept under investigation were simply male, then this would not be considered a variable because male has only one attribute. But sex is a variable for which its two logical groupings of attributes vary between the categories of male and female.

Age provides another example of a variable. Age can be measured as a numerical variable or a categorical one. The attributes of age can be represented in the number of years since birth, or they can be represented as the calendar year in which someone is born. The variable age can also be represented in categories. For instance, the question could be asked, In which category is your age represented: (1) 18-25, (2) 26-35, (3) 36-45, (4) 46-55, (5) 56-65, or (6) over 65?

Sociological researchers use what is called a "variable language". They look at how change in one variable relates to change in another variable. For instance, a sociologist might ask how income changes with age. As people age, does their income typically rise or fall? At what age is income typically highest? Does income then generally decline, or does it remain constant, or does it constantly rise as one ages? These are questions set into the variable language that sociologists use to describe and explore relationships among various concepts in the social world.

VEBLEN, THORSTEIN BUNDE (1857-1929)

American political economist

The American political economist, sociologist, and social critic Thorstein Bunde Veblen (1857–1929) wrote about the evolutionary development and mounting internal tensions of modern Western society. Thorstein Veblen was born on July 30, 1857, in Valders, Wisconsin. He was the sixth of twelve children of Norwegian immigrant parents. Veblen graduated in 1880 from Carleton College, Minnesota, and in 1884 he took his doctorate in **philosophy** at Yale. He was a brilliant student, yet failed to get an academic post—apparently because of his "Norski" background and his skepticism of established institutions. For seven years Veblen read books on the farm in Minnesota, tinkered with farm machinery, and took part in village discussions. In 1888 he married Ellen Rolfe.

In 1891 Veblen revived his academic career by enrolling as a graduate student in economics at Cornell. A year later he moved to the University of Chicago, where he stayed for 14 years. Despite numerous papers and book reviews in learned journals, Veblen's academic advancement on the Chicago faculty was slow. His first and best-known book *The Theory of the Leisure Class* (1899) was followed by *The Theory of Business Enterprise* (1904).

Although he produced eight volumes between 1914 and 1923, Veblen's academic fortune did not prosper. In 1906 he had moved from Chicago to Stanford University for three years. His teaching performance was always considered poor: he mumbled inaudibly and consistently flouted the grading system by giving his students "Cs." His domestic difficulties

and associations with other women complicated his situation, according to university administrators. Forced to resign from Stanford, Veblen remained without a post for two years. Then, in 1911, he was appointed lecturer at the University of Missouri, where he remained for seven years. He remarried in 1914.

After a short period of **government** service in World War I, Veblen wrote editorials and essays for magazines and gave occasional lectures at the New School for Social Research. In 1926 he retired to his California shack, ''a defeated man,'' in the words of his biographer Joseph Dorfman. He died in poverty in Menlo Park on August 3, 1929.

Veblen made his readers aware that, in his period, American small-scale competitive capitalism was giving way to large-scale monopoly trusts. Among the implications of this trend were: the monopolistic practice of administered prices—charging what the traffic would bear; the limitation on production in order to raise prices and maximize profits; the subordination of the national state and of universities to the **role** of agents for business; and the emergence of a leisure class devoted to wasteful and **conspicuous consumption** for the sake of **status**.

Veblen also rejected the prevailing late-nineteenth-century social philosophy of the ''survival of the fittest.'' Instead, he adopted a perspective of impersonal institutional change and conflict which owed much to **Charles Darwin** and even more to **Karl Marx**. Another major **influence** on Veblen was the utopian socialism of Edward Bellamy's *Looking Backward* (1888). Yet Veblen was never a social activist or even an open advocate of social reform. He remained for the most part an academic observer and analyst. Implicitly, however, some of his writings were severely critical of the existing social order, with overtones of agrarian populism and utopian socialism. A number of Veblen's basic concepts and insights have become widely accepted in American sociological analysis: these include the ''sense of workmanship,'' ''culture lag,'' ''conspicuous consumption,'' and ''waste.''

In his *Theory of the Leisure Class* (1899) Veblen analyzed the status symbolism of modern bourgeois consumption, with interesting historical and anthropological antecedents. Social prestige, he pointed out, is enhanced by wasteful consumption of time and goods. With few changes, this book remains an excellent source work for many present-day social and liberating movements.

On modern America and its economy, two of Veblen's best books are *The Theory of Business Enterprise* (1904) and *Absentee Ownership* (1923). These works trace the inherent conflict between profit-oriented capitalists and the general welfare—defined by Veblen as maximum productivity of goods and services. *The Higher Learning in America* (1918), a biting analysis of the consequences of business domination of universities, should be read even today by those interested in contemporary issues and conflicts on North American campuses.

Veblen's *Imperial Germany* (1915) and *The Nature of Peace* (1917) are still relevant. His posthumously published *Essays on Our Changing Order* (1934) throws more light on the cold war than do most interpretations.

Though he left no disciples, Veblen influenced economists of varied views, political scientists, public administra-

Thorstein B. Veblen *(Corbis Corporation [Bellevue])*

tors, and policy makers in Franklin Roosevelt's New Deal era, and a minor but significant social movement—technocracy. Originating in the early 1920s, technocracy identified the general welfare with maximum engineering productivity. But Veblen's organizational connection with technocracy was temporary and superficial.

Even his most orthodox contemporaries rated Veblen as one of the few really outstanding American social scientists. After his death his stature grew steadily, for his insights have proved both lasting and prophetic. His vision of America was a dark one. As early as 1904 he wrote of a possible reversion to militarism. The deadpan humor of his literary style only highlighted his conception of America as a system of vested business interests propped up by indispensable canons of waste, artificial scarcity, unproductive salesmanship, war, and conspicuous consumption.

VERSTEHEN

As envisioned by **Auguste Comte**, who first applied the term sociology to the scientific study of **society**, and Émile Durkheim, the first social scientist to use statistical analysis in the study of human behavior, the methods around which the discipline of **sociology** was to be structured were to resemble as closely as possible those of the natural sciences in the late

eighteenth and early nineteenth centuries. Through the use of such scientific methods the objective of early sociologists like Comte and Durkheim was to remove all elements of uncertainly from the study of how society and its members interact and function. Rejecting earlier attempts that had been made to explain and predict social interaction through methods built on philosophical and religious foundations, Comte and Durkheim believed an understanding of society could be attained only through the gathering of **data** using new scientific methods. Their belief was based on the **fact** that data gathered using such methods could be systematically and mathematically analyzed and interpreted. Then hypotheses or theories about the workings of human society could be either proven and accepted or disproven and rejected.

While recognizing the importance and usefulness of the scientific method and process in studying and understanding society, **Max Weber** felt that the ultimate and complete interpretation of such data required an additional element if it was to be properly understood. Weber believed the additional element was a knowledge and understanding of the historical origins and basis of the behavior and acts of individuals and the workings of their society. Weber's "German historicism," as this interpretive process came to be called, when properly applied and incorporated into the analysis of social data, could, he believed, lead to a broader and fuller understanding of man and society than could be attained solely through statistical analysis of data. Grounded in such broad historical knowledge, as well as in current scientifically gathered and analyzed data, the social scientist could understand all the data, both historical and current, with a depth that would be nearly intuitive in nature. Such deeply seated understanding and interpretive knowledge was given the name *verstehen* by Weber. It was Weber's belief that such broadly based understanding and knowledge, or verstehen, would provide a more complete perspective for the social scientist than would mere empirical or statistical analysis of data.

In his comprehensive text, Economy and Society, Max Weber discussed at length the essential issue of attaching correct meaning to any knowledge gained through the use of sociological methods. Referring to social acts performed by actors, Weber makes it clear that the meaning attached to any social act may be of two kinds. One type of meaning is that which the actor may have intended to convey in performing a particular social action. The other type of meaning is that which those surrounding the actor would attach to the act experienced or witnessed. Weber did not envision either type of meaning as being totally true or correct. But he did make it clear that there is a difference between social acts with meaning and those which are mere reactions to other acts, those reactions lacking any subjective meaning. For example, the act of one man striking another may have different meaning to the actors involved, as well as to observers of the act. If the two men have a history of animosity toward each other the act may be interpreted as a provocation for future hostility between the men. If the men are strangers, the act may have been precipitated by something known only to the man delivering the blow, the blow itself having no meaning to the man who was struck beyond his knowledge of the physical attack he has suffered. Those witnessing the act may form their own interpretations of the act depending on their knowledge of the individual actors and their social circumstances. The sociologist, observing the actors and their acts while in possession of knowledge at a level of verstehen would know the history of the actors and their society at a level that would afford a correct interpretation of not only the act committed, but of the intention of the actors, and the effect of the act on the actors and their society. Verstehen, understanding of social action at such a depth, is to be sought by all sociologists ascribing to the **philosophy** of Max Weber as they seek to evaluate and interpret sociological data gathered in the course of research.

VICARIOUS REINFORCEMENT

Vicarious reinforcement is a process that is articulated in social learning theory. People can be reinforced directly or vicariously. When they are reinforced directly, they are experiencing responses to their own behaviors, responses directed specifically at them for behaviors they performed. When individuals are reinforced vicariously, they are observing responses for another's actions. Any response to a behavior that encourages continued behavior is called reinforcement. In every day situations, individuals can repeatedly observe others' behaviors and the reactions to those behaviors that can include either reinforcement or punishment. Through watching others, individuals learn what behaviors are appropriate under particular circumstances and in specific social contexts. This learning has an influential role in the regulation of future behavior. If a child is in a sandbox, sees another child sharing toys, and later sees the child hugged and given a lollipop, the child learns that sharing is what is expected. Vicarious punishment, as an indirect learning process, works in a similar manner to vicarious reinforcement. A punishment is any response that intends to reduce the tendency toward a specific behavior. If the same child is in a sandbox, sees another child fighting over toys, and later sees this child scolded for not sharing toys, the child learns that sharing is expected and socially appropriate.

Vicarious punishment and reinforcement are particularly valuable forms of learning when individuals are presented with situations foreign to them. Behaviors appropriate for one situation cannot always be carried over to other situations. We learn how to act in new situations by observing the behaviors of others and the responses to those behaviors, both those that are reinforcing and those that are punishing. Last, how we have observed others reinforced and punished affects how we perceive reinforcement and punishment directed at ourselves. Going back to the child in the sandbox, if the child starts to share after seeing another child get a lollipop and the child's guardian takes the child out to McDonald's this will be perceived as highly rewarding. This is the case because, in relation to the other child's lollipop, McDonald's is a stronger reinforcer. Should the child only be verbally reinforced, the child may perceive this as less rewarding in relation to the lol-

lipop. This example should illustrate how we interpret direct reinforcements in relation to vicarious reinforcement. In other words, vicarious reinforcement can influence the success of direct reinforcement.

VICO, GIAMBATTISTA (1668-1744)
Italian philosopher and jurist

The Italian philosopher and jurist Giambattista Vico (1668–1744) is considered the founder of the **philosophy** of history. His main work, ''The New Science,'' is an examination of social and political institutions in terms of their connection with phases of human development. Apart from being known by a few German thinkers, such as Johann Georg Hamann and Johann Gottfried von Herder, the work of Giambattista Vico was ignored until modern times. Yet the belated recognition of his genius and contribution is such that some scholars suggest that his mode of historical thinking is capable of modifying the intellectual relations between the pure and social sciences.

Vico was born in Naples on June 23, 1668, the only child of Antonio and Candida Vico. Except for one sustained period he lived his entire life in the city of his birth. During this period of political turmoil Naples was ruled by a succession of foreign powers (Spain, Austria, and France) and domestically controlled by the powerful Jesuit order. Intellectually, the city became the center of Italian Cartesianism. Vico, who was in opposition to all of these forces, was unable to advance his **career**. His lack of recognition and success in his professional work, as well as personal misfortunes, made him a bitter man who was periodically subject to melancholia.

In childhood Vico nearly died as the result of a fractured skull, which prevented him from attending school. Because his father was a bookseller, the child read quite extensively but at random. Although he attended a Jesuit university for a brief time, he went only to those classes that interested him. He spent a great deal of time studying logic and scholastic metaphysics until he found himself attracted to the study of law. Despite his lack of formal legal training, he successfully defended his father in a lawsuit when he was only 16 years old. But he developed a distaste for law as a profession and never practiced again.

From 1685 to 1695 Vico tutored relatives of the bishop of Ischia and lived in Vatolla. These were the happiest years of his life, and he used his free time to pursue his intellectual interests. He read widely in the fields of philosophy, history, ethics, jurisprudence, and poetry. His knowledge of science remained cursory, and he had a positive dislike for mathematics.

Vico returned to Naples in 1697 and became professor of rhetoric at the University of Naples. Part of his duties consisted of offering a lecture at the opening of each academic year from 1699 to 1708. These essays show the development of his thought, and *On the Study Methods of Our Time* ranks as a classic defense of liberal education. Between 1720 and 1722 he published a three-volume study *Universal Law*. In 1725 he wrote his *Autobiography;* the same year he published the first edition of *The New Science,* which he modified and expanded in editions of 1730 and 1744. Despite these activities, Vico was not appointed to the chair of civil law and, because of his large **family**, he was forced to supplement his income by writing commissioned poems and prose encomiums. He died on January 22 or 23, 1744, in Naples after a long and painful illness.

While René Descartes, credited with being the originator of modern classical philosophy, attempted to reform scientific thinking by a strict adherence to mathematical reasoning, Vico, who came to the study of philosophy from law, questioned the criterion of rationalist truth on the basis that real knowledge is by way of causes. He believed that ultimately we can know fully only that which we have caused. The true, or *verum,* is identical with the created *factum*. Despite its obscurities, Vico's intuition about history remains quite suggestive. Only God knows the natural cosmos perfectly, and the rationalist model of perfect demonstrable knowledge is attainable only in the realm of mathematical abstractions. But we can know history because it has been created by man, and its originative principles can be discovered by a reconstructive interpretation of our own mind.

Accordingly Vico's *New Science* anticipates the later thought of G. W. F. Hegel, **Auguste Comte**, and Arnold Toynbee: ''Our philosophical and philological investigations revealed an ideal eternal history which has been traversed in time according to the division of the three ages . . .'' Vico was indebted to Egyptian mythology for his basic metaphor of poetic, heroic, and natural natures. But the scope of his immense and diffuse learning enabled him to systematically associate these three types as reflected in customs, laws, **language**, institutions, and political authority; or, in brief, in the manifestations of nations as well as individual characters.

For example, primitive cultures are notoriously mythological in their thinking. To Vico this fact was a clear reflection of their ignorance of natural causes and the compensating strength of their imaginations. He believed the study of common language in its progression from oracular to expressive to vernacular provides a ''mental dictionary'' of character, nation, and time. Similarly, he believed a close study of laws and the facts of commerce yields more insight about a **civilization** than a study of its science or philosophy.

Vico's **comparative method** issued in a **concept** of political organization. In aristocracies the nobles ''by reason of their native lawless liberty'' will not tolerate checks upon their power. When plebeians increase in number and military training, they force the aristocracy to submit to law, as in democracies. Finally, in order to preserve their privileges, the lords accept a single ruler, and monarchies are established.

VIOLENT CRIME

In the United States, violent crime accounts for around ten percent of reported crimes. Central **cities** have the highest rates, while small towns have the lowest. Both victims and perpetra-

Violent crime rate

Violent crimes (murder, rape, robbery and aggravated assault) per 100,000, 1976-1998

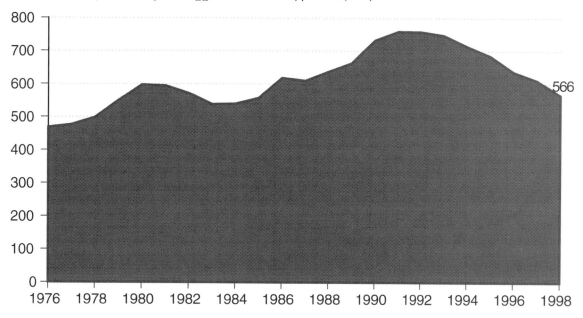

Source: "Uniform Crime Reports, 1998," October 1999, Federal Bureau of Investigation

tors tend to be young and poor, while perpetrators are overwhelmingly male. Although representations of violence in the media focus on violence by strangers, most violent crimes are perpetrated on family members or acquaintances.

For many years, sociologists have debated the reasons why the rate of violent crime in the United States is far higher than in other advanced industrialized nations. Most give some responsibility to the easy availability of firearms. However, in the experience of other countries, the existence of an armed population has not necessarily led to a violent society. As the social psychologist Leonard Berkowitz has shown, aggressive feelings do not translate into violent actions without specific linking mechanisms.

Many sociologists and historians have argued that the history of the United States has produced an inherently violent culture. For nearly three centuries, the social and economic order of the southern states relied on the forced labor of African-Americans, underpinned by the threat of extreme violence. After the emancipation of the slaves, white southerners employed violence to restore and maintain white supremacy in the southern states from the 1890s to the 1950s.

The South is not unique in its history of community-sanctioned violence and murder. During the long years of westward expansion, frontier settlements developed ahead of **law enforcement**. Native Americans were considered fair target for armed intimidation and murder, and between whites the threat of violence often prevailed over the rule of law. One out-

come of the weak law enforcement in frontier America was a long tradition of vigilante movements. Starting with the eighteenth-century Regulators of backwoods South Carolina, the vigilante tradition culminated in the white supremacist, anti-Semitic, and anti-Catholic Ku Klux Klan, which reached a membership of four million in the mid-1920s. At the same time, the great cities suffered from turbulent ethnic rivalries throughout the nineteenth century, expressed in frequent murders and riots. Nineteenth century urban police officers were low ranking hacks within corrupt local political machines, and were both brutal and ineffective in comparison to their northern European counterparts. The **subculture** of violence always present in the large American cities has been stimulated in the late twentieth century by the development of a mass-market in illegal narcotics. While consumers of these drugs come from a wide variety of background and ethnic groups, those working as street-level drug dealers are disproportionately African-American men from poor families, whose opportunities in the legal labor market are extremely limited.

The high rate of violent crime in the United States is matched by its very high rates of imprisonment. At the beginning of 1998, one in every 117 American men was imprisoned, more than in any other country in the world with the exception of Russia. Ironically, many men convicted of violent crimes have been discharged early to make way for prisoners convicted of nonviolent drug offenses which carry non-negotiable mandatory sentence.

The stringent crime policies implemented over the last twenty years are seen by some sociologists as a product of the national enthusiasm for crime as entertainment. During the 1970s American film and **television** moved away from the anti-authoritarian civil rights themes popular in the dramas of the 1960s. Instead of storylines about lawyers fighting corruption and injustice gained popularity. The films and shows of the late 1970s featured overworked police struggling to maintain public order and frequently violating the law in order to do so. Using feature films as an example, the investigation of police corruption dramatized in *Serpico* (1973) was superseded by the kind of vigilante police violence pioneered by the *Dirty Harry* films (1971-1988).

The continuing popularity of police dramas has been complemented by television reality crime programs, tabloid-style collaborations between police departments and television journalists which appeared in the late 1980s. In addition to the usual identification created by filming from the point of view of the police, these kinds of programs create an alliance between the audience and the on-screen police officers by using information and even videotapes provided by the public. Sociologists have found that reality crime programs focus on crimes with African-American perpetrators and white victims, (although such crimes are relatively rare if compared to intra-racial crimes), and that viewers of such programs tend to strongly overestimate the prevalence of violent crime in **American society**.

In *Television and the Drama of Crime*, Richard Sparks argued that fear is much more than a predictable response to danger. Rather fear has become a primary mode of perception in American culture, a language through which people develop identities and practices. The fear of crime explains and justifies the **privatization** of everyday life and the neglect of urban public space. The representation of violent crime in both politics and entertainment has, therefore, become a primary space for the expression of a political discourse which privileges the protection of individual property over the collective needs of those less affluent Americans from whose ranks convicted felons are overwhelmingly drawn.

VOGEL, LISE (? - ?)
American sociologist

Lise Vogel grew up in New York City during the 1950s, the child of well-educated parents. Her father, of German-Jewish descent, was a doctor and her mother, of Russian-Jewish descent, held a college diploma. Nonetheless, her parents continually struggled to remain economically solvent as her father, who was prone to depressive states of melancholy, could never establish a successful medical practice. Also, the time of Vogel's childhood paralleled the McCarthy years. Because her parents had been involved in leftist politics since the 1930s, they worried about repression. Her mother, a member of the Communist Party, insisted that a collectivist society was necessary to institute **peace**, **justice**, and the end to racial oppression. Because of her parents' politics and their inability to

maintain financial stability, Vogel never found a comfortable place within her middle-class existence. Vogel wrote in the introduction to *Woman Questions: Essays for a Materialist Feminism* (1995), ''I can say that my memories of growing up are filled not with a sense of middle-class economic and emotional entitlement, but with feelings of contradiction, **marginality**, and dread.''

After graduating from the Bronx High School of Science, Vogel enrolled at Radcliffe College, and her feelings of marginality intensified in the midst of her predominately white, affluent classmates. Although she was deeply interested in art and art history, Vogel selected mathematics as her major in an attempt to pursue a practical course of study. After growing increasingly frustrated at her inability to be satisfied with mathematics, Vogel dropped out of college and spent the next two years in Paris. Upon her return, she completed her senior year at Radcliffe, changing her major to art history. At that time, attending Radcliffe was the means by which a woman could receive a Harvard education, and so, upon completing her undergraduate degree, Vogel enrolled as a doctoral candidate in art history.

During her graduate studies, Vogel became involved in the 1960s civil rights movement. She began by picketing Woolworth's and ended by spending the summers of 1964 and 1965 in rural Mississippi as part of a Student Nonviolent Coordinating Committee initiative. Arrested twice and jailed for 12 days, Vogel credited her time working with the civil rights movement and the Vietnam War protest as highly influential in the later development of her Marxist feminist ideology. Upon completing her doctorate in art history, Vogel accepted a position as an assistant professor of art history at Brown University in Providence, Rhode Island. While at Brown during the late 1960s, Vogel became involved with women activist groups, later writing in *Woman Questions,* ''A powerful longing for freedom and **community** flooded through these first moments of women's liberation, offering, it seemed to me, a reprise of the vision already conjured in Mississippi. The notion of a **women's liberation movement** struck me with an intensity of feeling I could not resist.''

As she became increasingly involved in the feminist movement, Vogel began to feel disengaged from her **career** as a professor of art history. Eventually she resigned from Brown and, after a period of freelance teaching and writing, enrolled as a graduate student in the sociology program at Brandeis University. Completing her doctorate in sociology, Vogel pursued a new academic career. She became a member of the sociology faculty at Rider University in Lawrenceville, New Jersey, teaching **family**, social deviance, feminist social theory, and the senior seminar. She is the author of four books: *The Column of Antoninus Pius* (1973), *Marxism and the Oppression of Women: Toward a Unitary Theory* (1983), *Mothers on the Job: Maternity Policy in the U.S. Workplace* (1993), and *Woman Questions: Essays for a Materialist Feminism* (1995). She has also contributed numerous articles and essays to journals and books on socialist feminism.

Vogel's feminist perspective is understood in the context of Marxist, or materialist, thought. Whereas the feminists

Recent sociological scholarship has noted the decline of civic and political participation by U.S. citizens *(AP/Wide World Photos, Inc.).*

Talcott Parsons developed a **theory** of voluntary action in his 1937 book *The Structure of Social Action*, in which he synthesized the work of Durkheim, Marshall, Pareto, and Weber to construct an all-encompassing theory of **society**. His theory of voluntary action was greatly dependent upon Weber's concept of rational social action; Parsons used this concept to demonstrate the relationship between objective conditions and adherence to **norms** and values and how they affect people's decisions to act in a particular ways.

Accepting voluntarism as a component of social life significantly complicates the development of predictive social theory, although proponents claim it results in **sociological theory** that more realistically depicts human behavior. Theorists using **symbolic interactionism** and **ethnomethodology** tend to emphasize the voluntarism in human behavior, although theories that depend exclusively on voluntarism are often criticized for neglecting the effects of social structure and, therefore, not being sociological.

VOLUNTARY ASSOCIATIONS

A voluntary association is any formally constituted **group** in which membership is optional. Churches, social-service organizations, parent-teacher associations, even junior sports leagues can serve as voluntary associations. Scholarly attention usually focuses on the ways in which voluntary associations are expressions of democratic citizenship. Numerous social and political theorists have written about the importance of voluntary associations for involving citizens in public life. Voluntary associations are understood to comprise that realm of civil society in which members of a society participate in democratic government. They are the means through which like-minded citizens express their desires.

The right to a "peaceful assembly" guaranteed by the Constitution has been interpreted to imply that voluntary associations can organize around any agenda, even ones that advocate currently illegal behavior, providing that the associations themselves do not break the law. The unlimited right of association in America has prompted the spread of voluntary associations with agendas that some observers find unusual. European visitors were surprised to learn of the temperance unions that dotted the American political landscape in the nineteenth and early twentieth centuries. They were surprised not so much at the sentiment against alcohol but at the idea of an organized group opposing its use. The unrestrained right of association has also meant that even militia groups that deny the legitimacy of American government have the right to assemble and pursue their aims.

Alexis de Tocqueville brought attention to the importance of voluntary associations for democratic vitality. In his classic work *Democracy in America,* published between 1835 and 1840, Tocqueville wrote that he was particularly impressed with the way American citizens organized to make their voices heard. Formed by the private agency of individuals, voluntary associations were the "public assent to which individuals give to certain doctrines and their attempt to pro-

of the women's liberation movement named **patriarchy** as the primary culprit in the oppression of women, socialist feminists looked more to class and **capitalism** as the foundational issues. In "Marxism and Socialist-Feminist Theory: A Decade of Debate," which appeared in *Readings in Contemporary Sociological Theory: From Modernity to Post-Modernity* (1995; edited by Donald McQuarie), Vogel wrote that socialist feminists assert "that the key oppressions of sex, class, and race are interrelated and that the struggles against them must be coordinated—although the precise character of that coordination remains unspecified." She continued by suggesting that "the essence and strength of the socialist-feminist movement lay not in its view of **socialism** but in its particular interpretation of the feminist insights that sisterhood is powerful and that personal is political."

VOLUNTARISM

Voluntarism is a term denoting the capacity of individuals to act upon their desires or needs without the imposition of external forces determining their behavior. Voluntarism is associated with agency and thus is often juxtaposed with **structure** in the agency-structure debate that is common in sociological discourse. It is commonly used to describe changes in contemporary social relations, such as the increased voluntarism in religious participation.

mote the spread of those doctrines.'' Tocqueville noted several strengths of voluntary associations. First, they allow for cooperative effort. An individual acting alone can accomplish very little in terms of influencing policy, but a group of like-minded individuals joined together commands more attention in the public square. Along these same lines, Tocqueville noted that the very act of association required a certain level of articulation of the group's goals. Thus, the potential for mobilized action is more readily directed by the mere act of associating. Sociologists have long recognized that the coming together of like-minded individuals creates propensity for action, thus providing another advantage of voluntary associations over individual actors.

When Tocqueville toured America in the 1830s he was struck by the existence of so many associations and by the number of people that participated in them. More recent scholarship has noted the decline of participation by Americans in political and civic associations. In a series of controversial articles Robert Putnam has argued that participation in voluntary associations has declined over the past two generations. Putnam and others hold that the decline of voluntary associations could threaten the vitality of civil society because it lowers the level of ''social capital'' in America. Although Putnam's assessment is contested by several scholars (as is his indictment of **television** as one of the culprits), he holds that membership in such diverse voluntary associations as parent-teacher groups and bowling leagues has dropped significantly in the last three decades. Regardless of whether the current state of voluntary associational life in America is stronger or weaker than it has been in the past, virtually everyone agrees that voluntary associations are crucial for the involvement of the citizenry and therefore for the maintenance of a democratic society.

VOODOOISM

Voodooism is the practice of traditional beliefs and rituals derived from traditional African religions. The word *voodoo* is African and means ''god,'' ''spirit,'' or ''sacred object.'' Followers believe in the existence of one supreme being and in the existence of strong and weak spirits, with each person having a protector spirit who may reward or punish the person. Voodoo practitioners, called Vodousians, also use spells, incantations, and animal sacrifice.

Voodoo is practiced in Haiti and the Caribbean, Brazil, Benin, and in parts of the United States. Voodoo originated in Benin, and spread with the slave trade into the West Indies. As West African slaves brought their traditions to colonial Haiti, tribes and families shared their individual practices and beliefs. Influences from **Christianity** and Native American religions were also introduced, producing a spiritual practice based on an amalgam of cultural references. Though Voodoo uses no written scriptural text for reference, many practitioners see Voodoo as a way in which African societies have preserved their **culture** and have retained their ties between communities and with the environment.

Voodoo customs are still practiced in Haiti, the Caribbean, Brazil, Benin, as well as parts of the United States *(Archive Photos, Inc.).*

VOTING BEHAVIOR

In democratic societies like the United States, the general public can take part in governmental action in two ways. Voters may vote directly for social action or they can vote for a representative who is trusted to implement social action in the best interest of the public. In the United States, citizens age 18 and over are eligible to vote, but not all Americans do vote. Some groups vote more often than other groups and voting behavior tends to follow set patterns.

On the whole between fifty and sixty percent of eligible Americans vote in presidential elections. Individuals vote even less for state and local elections. Participation in local elections can be as low as ten percent in some communities. One reason cited for low voter turnout in the United States is the sometimes cumbersome registration process. One has to register to vote in the area of residence. Each time individuals move, they have to register again in the new area. Legislation has been enacted to help make voter registration easier. One approach is the ''motor voter'' program which allows an individual to register to vote when they apply for a driver's license. Since most states require individuals to change their addresses on their driver's licenses each time they move, the motor voter program reaches those who have changed residences. Preliminary research suggests that this program has increased voter participation.

Sociologists and other researchers study trends in voting behavior to find out why so few take an active **role** in the election process. The United States has one of the lowest percentages of voter turnouts of all other democratic nations. Austria, Australia, and New Zealand are among other democratic countries with high voter turnouts. These countries show over an eighty percent voter turnout.

Through research, sociologists have created the following profile of voters in America. People who are older are more likely to vote than those who are younger. Males and females are equally as likely to vote, though this has not been true throughout American history (women began to vote in equal numbers to men starting in the early 1980s; prior to this males

Participation in Elections for President and U.S. Representatives: 1932 to 1998

[As of **November**. Estimated resident population 21 years old and over, 1932-70, except as noted, and 18 years old and over thereafter; includes Armed Forces. Prior to 1960, excludes Alaska and Hawaii. District of Columbia is included in votes cast for President beginning 1964 and in votes cast for Representative from 1972 to 1992]

Year	Resident population (incl. aliens) of voting age [1] (1,000)	Votes cast				Year	Resident population (incl. aliens) of voting age [1] (1,000)	Votes cast			
		For President [2] (1,000)	Per-cent of voting-age population	For U.S. Representatives (1,000)	Per-cent of voting-age population			For President [2] (1,000)	Per-cent of voting-age population	For U.S. Representatives (1,000)	Per-cent of voting-age population
1932 . . .	75,768	39,758	52.5	37,657	49.7	1966 . . .	116,638	(X)	(X)	52,908	45.4
1934 . . .	77,997	(X)	(X)	32,256	41.4	1968 . . .	120,285	73,212	60.9	66,288	55.1
1936 . . .	80,174	45,654	56.9	42,886	53.5	1970 . . .	124,498	(X)	(X)	54,173	43.5
1938 . . .	82,354	(X)	(X)	36,236	44.0	1972 . . .	140,777	77,719	55.2	71,430	50.7
1940 . . .	84,728	49,900	58.9	46,951	55.4	1974 . . .	146,338	(X)	(X)	52,495	35.9
1942 . . .	86,465	(X)	(X)	28,074	32.5	1976 . . .	152,308	81,556	53.5	74,422	48.9
1944 . . .	85,654	47,977	56.0	45,103	52.7	1978 . . .	158,369	(X)	(X)	55,332	34.9
1946 . . .	92,659	(X)	(X)	34,398	37.1	1980 . . .	163,945	86,515	52.8	77,995	47.6
1948 . . .	95,573	48,794	51.1	45,933	48.1	1982 . . .	169,643	(X)	(X)	64,514	38.0
1950 . . .	98,134	(X)	(X)	40,342	41.1	1984 . . .	173,995	92,653	53.3	83,231	47.8
1952 . . .	99,929	61,551	61.6	57,571	57.6	1986 . . .	177,922	(X)	(X)	59,619	33.5
1954 . . .	102,075	(X)	(X)	42,580	41.7	1988 . . .	181,956	91,595	50.3	81,786	44.9
1956 . . .	104,515	62,027	59.3	58,426	55.9	1990 . . .	185,812	(X)	(X)	61,513	33.1
1958 . . .	106,447	(X)	(X)	45,818	43.0	1992 . . .	189,524	104,425	55.1	96,239	50.8
1960 . . .	109,672	68,838	62.8	64,133	58.5	1994 . . .	193,650	(X)	(X)	70,781	36.6
1962 . . .	112,952	(X)	(X)	51,267	45.4	1996 . . .	196,507	96,278	49.0	89,863	45.8
1964 . . .	114,090	70,645	61.9	65,895	57.8	1998 . . .	200,929	(X)	(X)	66,033	32.9

X Not applicable.   [1] Population 18 and over in Georgia, 1944-70, and in Kentucky, 1956-70; 19 and over in Alaska and 20 and over in Hawaii, 1960-70.   [2] Source: 1932-58, U.S. Congress, Clerk of the House, *Statistics of the Presidential and Congressional Election*, biennial.

Source: Except as noted, U.S. Census Bureau, *Current Population Reports*, P25-1085; Congressional Quarterly, Inc., Washington, DC *America Votes*, biennial (copyright).

outnumbered women at the polls). Whites are more likely to vote than African Americans. Both are more likely to vote than Hispanics. Whites vote twice as often as Hispanics. People with **higher education** tend to vote more often. College graduates vote twice as often as individuals with a grade school education. Individuals who are employed are more likely to vote than those who are unemployed. Finally, people with a higher income are more likely to vote than those with lower incomes.

Researchers question why the unemployed, lower income, less educated, younger, minority status individuals are less likely to vote. Several ideas have been put forth to explain these trends. One **theory** posits that social integration in **society** plays a role. Those who are less socially integrated in society will see less reason to vote in elections than an individual who is wholly social integrated. A socially integrated individual is one whose culture, **values**, and beliefs are recognized by society and by the political system. For example, inhabitants of the inner city slums generally are not as socially integrated as those who live in the middle and upper class suburbs. The political system does not address the needs of the people in the inner city as it does those in the suburbs. These individuals

begin to recognize this fact and, therefore, a poor, uneducated, Hispanic woman may feel that her needs are not being addressed by politicians, and may choose not to vote.

Alienation and apathy are describe other reasons for poor voter turnout. The Hispanic woman mentioned above feels alienated from the political system. Individuals like her feel that their vote will not affect their situation or their lives. We also see, however, that people who do fit the voter profile, the upper class, educated, white individual, also stay away from the polls. The reason for this in many cases is voter apathy. Like the alienated individuals, they feel that their vote will not matter, but they also have an indifferent or apathetic attitude toward the **government**. They feel there is little difference between the political parties and politicians and feel that their vote will not be effective in creating change. Regardless of the reasons behind not voting it is a persistent problem in the United States. Researchers continue to explore voting behavior in order to make better assumptions about reasons for poor voter turnout and perhaps enact legislation to increase political participation among Americans.

W

WALLERSTEIN, IMMANUEL MAURICE (1930-)

American sociologist

Immanuel Maurice Wallerstein is best known for world-systems theory, outlined in his series of books, beginning with *The Modern World-System: Capitalist Agriculture and the Origins of the European World-Economy in the Sixteenth Century* in 1974. World-systems theory is a comprehensive theoretical framework and **methodology** for the study of **social change** in the context of the global system of nations. World-systems theory has reshaped the **sociology** of development and has made Wallerstein one of the discipline's single most influential scholars.

Less well-known today are Wallerstein's earlier contributions to African studies throughout the 1960s. His Ph.D. thesis at Columbia, later published as *The Road to Independence: Ghana and the Ivory Coast* (1964), dealt with nationalist independence movements in the two countries. Drawing on **modernization theory**, Wallerstein discussed the **role** of voluntary associations as precursors to independence movements. In his two following books *Africa: The Politics of Independence* (1961) and *Africa: The Politics of Unity* (1967), Wallerstein begun to break with modernization approaches and begun to develop the origins of his distinctive approach. Against the optimism of the earlier generation of scholars who had predicted the industrialization of post-independence Africa, Wallerstein posited that Africa had inherited a set of social relationships as result of European colonialism that made certain kinds of social change more difficult and vitiated further economic development. Like dependency theorists like Samir Amin and Andre Gunther Frank, Wallerstein claimed that the involvement of industrialized nations in the continent of Africa was going to only reproduce a kind of distorted development that was unlikely to bring about general social welfare or broad economic development.

In the late 1960s, Wallerstein wrote a book in reaction to student rebellions, *University in Turmoil: The Politics of Change* (1969) that tied events in the United States at the time to global trends and the U.S. position in the world-system. He left Columbia University, which had been his academic home since his Ph.D., and wrote the first book of his *World Systems* series, eventually settling at the State University of New York in Binghamton, where the Fernand Braudel Center has been established for research into world **systems theory**.

World-systems theory was developed in dialogue with dependency theory, though extending the **unit of analysis** from a single country or continent to the whole global system of trade since the sixteenth century. Also, whereas dependency theory generally focused on explaining social change in the developing world, world-systems also dealt with Industrialized nations. Wallerstein's framework pointed to the original expansion of European colonial powers in the sixteenth century as the beginning of the world system of relations between nations. Core nations, in this framework, tend to have advanced economic and military capacity and advance this advantage by exploitative relations with peripheral nations that maintain those nations in a subordinate status.

In the first period of the world system, core nations were the colonial powers and the periphery was made up of their colonial holdings. In the modern period, core nations are the industrialized powers, while peripheral nations are the less developed countries. Semiperipheral nations are those nations that exhibit characteristics of both core and periphery. Core nations, in **competition** with one another, sought out colonial holdings as prizes necessary for their own survival. Inadequate demand for goods at the core and periodic crises of overconsumption led core nations to constantly seek new areas for incorporation. The demand for cheap raw materials in the core also drives this expansion. Wage pressures in core countries, because of the successes of organized labor there, encourage investments in places where workers have less bargaining power. The international capitalist system thrives as result of the uneven development of certain areas. A key element of the framework, however, is that nations may change **status** in this system by possessing certain comparative advantages.

Societies socialize their members, usually males, to engage in war in a culturally specific manner *(Corbis Corporation [Bellevue]).*

Wallerstein has continued to develop his framework as well as to develop a critique of social science, which, he argued, is still based on inadequate national units of analysis. Some of his important critiques are outlined in *Unthinking Social Science: The Limits of Nineteenth Century Paradigms* (1991). He has continued to develop research at his institute, which publishes *Review,* a journal devoted to world systems research. His students and followers, who include Christopher Chase-Dunn, Daniel Chirot, Fred Block, Albert Bergessen, and others, have continued to develop the world systems paradigm through a series of empirical projects and theoretical extensions.

WAR

War is organized political violence in which two or more armed groups engage in ongoing combat. The characteristics of any war are strongly influenced by the motivations of the parties involved. For example, imperialist wars are motivated by economic expansion. The aggressive empire may be seeking to gain **territory**, new markets, trade routes, or raw materials. Modern balance-of-power wars occur between or among nation-states which may be disputing the location of a border or trying to gain economic or military superiority. Revolution-

ary wars and civil wars are internal to a sovereign polity which, in modern times, usually means the war is internal to a **nation-state**. An ideological war is justified by some reasoning, usually religious, as in the Christian *bellum justum* or the Islamic *jihad*. This type of delineation, between a "good war" and a "bad war", has also been made by secular theorists. For instance, according to political scientist Robert Gilpin, a good war transforms a political system, redistributing power and restabilizing the international system, while a bad war is overly destructive and incapacitating. Of course, any given episode of war may contain elements of many ideal types.

Kenneth Waltz and other political theorists have discussed numerous paradigms to explain the causes of war. Some psychological explanations focus on the belligerence and **aggression** of men. Because men are aggressive, any social or political institution men form will also tend towards aggression. This line of reasoning is closely linked to biological theories that propose war is an instinctual part of **human nature**. Others theorists focus on war as a learned behavior or as a social institution. Societies socialize their members, usually male members, to engage in war in a culturally specific manner, including how enemies are defined, how the chain of command is maintained, and what techniques of war-making are considered "fair" and "appropriate."

Still other researchers focus on the structure of war, both on the level of the international system and that within a state. Realists, like Waltz and Bueno de Mesquita, propose that the world is an anarchic system of states. Because of this lack of central authority, conflicts are difficult to mediate. Further, some classic liberalists believe that war is necessary for states to be able to maintain **justice** in their foreign policy. Within the nation-state, researchers note that states are structured to make war because of their orientation toward law and order, and their function in maintaining security. Conflict theorists point out that economic strain within a nation-state is frequently the impetus for revolution. Military sociologists examine the composition and **norms** of the military as a social institution.

WARD, LESTER FRANK (1839-1913)
American paleontologist and professor

Lester Frank Ward is one of American sociology's most colorful characters. The first president of the American Sociological Society (now called the American Sociological Association) Ward came to the discipline after several years of government service in geological science. Born in 1839 to working class parents Ward developed an appreciation for education early in his life. He considered learning to be the chief mechanism for self-improvement and progress. However, his **family** had limited means, and he could not afford a formal education as a young man. Ward taught himself many subjects including five classical languages and mathematics. After being wounded in combat service, during the Civil War, he earned a formal degree. Ward completed a bachelor's degree at Columbian (now George Washington) University through night school while

working in Washington as a government clerk. Using veteran's benefits he went on to earn a law degree, and medical degree from the same institution.

Despite his humble beginnings Ward established himself as an important contributor to science and ideas. While in school, he socialized with a group of government scientists and intellectuals and contributed to a free-thought magazine called *The Iconoclast*. During these years, he also formulated his central philosophy on evolution. Expanding on the popular philosophy of **Utilitarianism**, Ward speculated that the greatest happiness for the greatest number of people comes through mass education. The natural product of education, he reasoned, is knowledge and that leads to progress and happiness. In the mid–1870s, through his social network of scientists and intellectuals, Ward landed a job as a paleobotanist with the United States' Geological Survey which changed the scope of his **career**.

Doing scientific work exposed Ward to the theories of Auguste Comte and Darwin. He began incorporating their concepts into his thesis. Knowledge, he claimed, not only has the capacity to expand happiness but prevent crises as well. Ward concluded that disruptions, such as labor strikes and populist movements, could be prevented if the public were educated. Evolution, controlled through education, would eliminate uncontrolled social revolution. Ward began his first formal work in **sociology** with these ideas in mind.

Dynamic Sociology was published in 1883. Here, Ward depicted a world driven by social forces. Biological evolution was the conceptual fulcrum on which all social forces operate. Organic matter, Ward argued, including the human mind, is shaped by centuries of progressive evolution. But human beings, through their **intelligence**, can understand the laws of nature and statistically use them. As the title of his book attests, society and social forces exist in reciprocal relationship. Ward next turned attention to the functions of society. He accepted economic competition as a progressive social force but worried about the extent to which population density impedes it. His solution proposed that sociocracy, a professional body that would design wise policy based on study of social laws. Science, he proclaimed, will tame the social forces.

Ward continued to build upon the theme of knowledge as the key to evolutionary progress. In 1891 he published *The Psychic Factors in Civilization*, *Pure Sociology* in 1903, and *Applied Sociology* in 1906. All these works were efforts to elaborate on the evolution of humanity. Whereas in the earlier work Ward focused on psychic human development, the later two developed on issues of societal growth and control. All of his work generated considerable controversy. Ward's lack of formal education in philosophy allowed him to escape the intellectual orthodoxy of his peers but also opened his arguments to criticism. The debate over his work opened further publishing and lecturing opportunities for Ward. His prolific writing led Brown University to offer him a chair of sociology in 1906. Ward spent the remainder of his career at this institution. Soon after his appointment at Brown he was elected as the first president of the American Sociological Society. The year before he agreed to edit the new *American Journal of Sociology*. He continued to be an avid correspondent with the most important thinkers of the day and was a popular public lecturer.

Ward's most important contribution to sociology was his insistence that social laws, once identified, can be harnessed and controlled just as wind, water, and electricity. Unlike his contemporary, **William Graham Sumner**, Ward was an optimistic sociology, conceptualized as an instrument to improve the lot of humanity. This tradition continues today in the form of applied sociology where **sociological theory** and methods guide efforts to improve social conditions.

WARNER, WILLIAM LLOYD (1898-1970)
American social anthropologist

William Lloyd Warner was born on October 26, 1898, in Redlands, California. He was the son of William Taylor, a rancher and engineer, and Clara Belle (Carter) Warner. He attended San Bernadino High School until he joined the army in March 1917 and was discharged from his military duties the following year after contracting tuberculosis. Warner's early twenties were a time of unrest. He studied at the University of Southern California for one year before transferring to the University of California at Berkeley. At the University of California, he studied English and became active in the Socialist Party. Briefly married to Billy Overfield, probably from 1918 to 1921, he left California in 1921 to pursue an acting career in New York City. Failing to secure any acting work outside a few small parts, Warner returned to Berkeley to complete his studies.

Upon his re-admittance to the University of California, Warner developed a lifelong friendship with anthropology professor Robert H. Lowie, who encouraged Warner to pursue his bachelor's degree in anthropology. He also established close and lasting relationships with anthropologists Alfred Kroeber and Theodora Kroeber and was deeply influenced by **Bronislaw Malinowski** and A. R. Radcliffe-Brown during their visits to Berkeley. Malinowski and Radcliffe-Brown introduced Warner to the British functionalist approach to social anthropology. Graduating in 1925 with a bachelor's degree in anthropology, Warner traveled to northern Australia in 1927 on a Rockefeller Foundation and Australian National Research Council fellowship to pursue doctoral research among the Murngin people. During his two-year stay, Warner applied social anthropological methodology to the study of the Murngin's social and kinship organization. In 1937, Warner published *A Black Civilization: A Social Study of an Australian Tribe,* basically his doctoral dissertation, but he never defended it and he never received his doctoral degree.

Upon returning to the United States in 1929, Warner turned his attention to the study of contemporary society. While working on his graduate studies at Harvard University, he taught at Harvard, Radcliffe, and the Graduate School of Business Administration. He was also appointed to the Committee on Industrial Psychology. Working with behavioral scientist Elton Mayo, Warner studied the workplace structure and organization of the Western Electric Hawthorne plant in Chicago. His desire to apply his methodology to an entire community led Warner to his next, and most influential, project. Hoping to find a town small enough to handle the data collec-

tion but big enough to embody the major traits of contemporary **American society**, Warner located his new research project in Newburyport, Massachusetts. From 1930 to 1935, Warner and thirty assistants conducted extensive interviews, compiling research on 17,000 members of the small industrial town. Warner, himself, moved to Newburyport in 1932 and married a local resident, Mildred Hall. They had three children: Ann, Caroline, and William Taylor.

The comprehensive study, popularly called the "Yankee City Series," addressed the issues of class, **community**, factory life, **ethnicity**, and religious organization. Ultimately, Warner would be the primary author of the five-volume series: *The Social Life of a Modern Community* (1941; with Paul S. Lunt), *The Status System of a Modern Community* (1942; with Lunt), *The Social Systems of American Ethnic Groups* (1945; with Leo Srole), *The Social System of the Modern Factory* (1947; with J. O. Low), and *The Living and the Dead: A Study of the Symbolic Life of Americans* (1959). The study received significant coverage by the media, adding to the influence of the research results. Well written, the series portrays typical American life as it is influenced by social, ethnic, religious, and work relationships. Working from the assumption that relationships determine personal identity, Warner developed a social scheme, still commonly in use, consisting of six ranks within the class system: upper, middle, and lower, with each being divided again into upper and lower. Although he was criticized as being ahistorical and too prone to generalization, Warner's social anthropological methodology of relating social personality to social structure heavily influenced continuing research in **social stratification** and **social mobility**.

In 1935, Warner became professor of anthropology and **sociology** at the University of Chicago. During his twenty-five year tenure, he conducted numerous other community studies based on his Yankee City Series, focusing in particular on **urbanization**, ethnicity, and education. He served as a member of the Committee on Human Development from 1942 to 1959, and co-founded Social Research, Inc., in 1946, created as a means to apply social anthropologic research in such areas as marketing and human relations to the business world. In 1959 Warner moved from the University of Chicago to accept the position of University Professor of Social Research at Michigan State University in East Lansing, where he remained until his death in 1970. Warner produced numerous works during his career outside the Yankee City Series, including *Structure of American Life* (1952), *Occupational Mobility in American Business and Industry, 1928-1952* (1955; with James C. Abegglen), and *The Corporation in the Emergent American Society* (1961).

WEBB, BEATRICE POTTER (1858-1943)
English social reformer

The English social reformer Beatrice Potter Webb (1858–1943) was a leading Fabian socialist and a partner with her husband, **Sidney Webb**, in their projects for social and educational reform and in their research into the history of politi-

cal and **economic institutions**. Beatrice Potter was born on January 2, 1858, at Standish House near Gloucester. Her father, Richard Potter, was a man with large railroad interests and many contacts among politicians and intellectuals. She was educated at home by governesses and also by extensive travel, wide reading, and direct contact with many of the leading figures of politics, science, and industry. **Herbert Spencer** in particular gave her attention and encouragement.

Potter's involvement with **social problems** began in 1883, when she became a rent collector in London. This work, in turn, led to her participation in Charles Booth's survey published as *Life and Labour of the People in London*. In 1887 the results of her inquiries into dock life in the East End of London were published in *Nineteenth Century,* soon followed by other articles and studies of sweated labor.

Increased confidence and deeper study culminated in Potter's *The Co-operative Movement in Great Britain* (1891). It was in connection with this that she met Sidney Webb. They were married in 1892, and their life together became one of single-minded dedication to research and social reform. Together they produced a veritable torrent of books, pamphlets, essays, and memoranda amounting to over a hundred items.

Until 1906 Potter's role in the partnership was primarily that of researcher, writer, and hostess for gatherings of Cabinet ministers and members of Parliament who came to hear the Webb opinion on social legislation. At the end of 1905 Beatrice was appointed a member of the Royal Commission on the Poor Laws, which sat from 1906 to 1909. The minority report, drafted by the Webbs, played an important role in the dismantling of the old Poor Law and in its replacement by the new systems of social insurance.

In the period after 1910 the Webbs abandoned their nonpartisan stance and became an important force in building the Labour party. Another cornerstone of their earlier **philosophy** was abandoned with the publication of their *Soviet Communism: A New Society?* (1935). They, who had always held that **social change** cannot come about by the violent destruction of existing institutions, endorsed the Russian Revolution in spite of its totalitarianism. Beatrice Webb died at Liphook, Hampshire, on April 30, 1943. In 1947, shortly after Sidney's death, their ashes were buried in Westminster Abbey.

WEBB, SIDNEY JAMES [BARON] (1859-1947)
English social economist

Baron Passfield of Passfield Corner, Sidney James Webb was a social reformer, co-founder of the London School of Economics, Cabinet minister, and historian, who deeply affected social ideas and institutions in England. He was born in London on June 25, 1865, into a lower middle class family, his father a freelance accountant, his mother a shopkeeper. Anxious for her children to do well in life, Elizabeth Webb sent Sidney and his brother Charles to Switzerland for a time to learn French. Upon his return, Sidney was admitted to the civil service and passed the bar examination in 1884. For some time,

he had been the friend of young Bernard Shaw, who introduced him to the newly formed Fabian Society, a socialist organization, in 1885. This group was jokingly named for the Roman consul Fabius Cunctator, who was said to have defeated Hannibal with cautious tactics. Webb became a dominating **influence** in the society, writing the first edition of *The Fabian Tract Facts for Socialists* in 1889. A year later he met Beatrice Potter, daughter of a wealthy businessman. They were married in 1892, much to the delight of caustic friends who thought of them as the odd couple: she was beautiful, tall, graceful, and wealthy; he was ugly, short, rather scruffy, and the son of a hairdresser. But they thought and wrote as one, so much so that it is difficult to distinguish one **career** from the other after their **marriage**, and indeed, most biographies cite the two of them together.

The first joint works of the Webbs were *The History of Trade Unionism* (1894) and *Industrial Democracy* (1897). The former educated economists to a segment of British social life and the later covered areas of historical and social research and reforms. Throughout their married life, the Webbs published numerous tracts, pamphlets, and books, establishing themselves as top historical researchers. This work was secondary, however, to their commitment to establishing institutions to serve the socialist cause.

Webb served on the London County Council from 1892 to 1910, creating a system of secondary state schools and a scholarship system. He provided a blueprint that became the Education Acts of 1902 and 1903, setting a pattern for public school education in England for decades, and he remodeled the University of London into a federation of teaching institutions. Webb and his wife founded the London School of Economics during this time, with R. D. Haldane, a liberal statesman. In 1913, the Webbs founded the *New Statesman* to debate socialist and Fabian causes. But by 1914, the Fabian society had ceased to further their ideals, so the Webbs joined the Labour Party, and Sidney became a member of the executive committee. Elected to parliament in 1920, he was appointed president of the Board of Trade in the first Labour administration of 1924. Two years later, he refused to support the general strike, believing that universal voting rights now made mass action unnecessary. This caused his unpopularity and he retired in 1928. However, he was called back and given the title of baron (which Beatrice refused to share) in 1929 so that he could take a seat in the House of Lords and serve as Colonial Secretary. This was a rather unsuccessful post for him, mostly due to the trouble in Palestine at the time. In 1932, the Webbs, now retired and discouraged with labor's progress in their home country, traveled to Russia and pronounced themselves "in love" with the system there. Their last work was *Soviet Communism: A New Civilization?* (1935). Retired again to their home in Hampshire, Beatrice died in 1943 and Sidney on October 13, 1947.

The Webbs exerted a good deal of influence on British radical thought and in radical circles during the first half of the twentieth century. Never concerned with credit for their ideas, many of which were followed and expanded by others, the Webbs worked as a remarkably effective and complementary

Beatrice Potter Webb *(Corbis Corporation [Bellevue])*

team, sometimes much to the irritation of colleagues who found them impervious to criticism. Said G.B. Shaw in his book on the Webbs, "The collaboration is so perfect...[that] I who have been behind the scenes of it, cannot lay my hand on a single sentence and say this is Sidney or that is Beatrice."

WEBER, MAX (1864-1920)
German scientist

The German social scientist Max Weber initiated modern sociological thought and his historical and comparative studies are a landmark in the history of **sociology**. Weber was interested in charting the varying paths taken by universal cultural history as reflected in the development of the great world civilizations. In this sense, he wished to attempt a historical and analytical study of the themes sounded so strongly in Hegel's philosophy of history, especially the theme, which Weber took as his own, of the "specific and peculiar rationalism of Western culture." Weber's detailed training as a legal and economic historian led him to reject simplistic formulas of economic base and corresponding cultural superstructure that were so often used to account for cultural development and were a strong part of the intellectual environment of Weber's early years as student and professor. He went beyond Hegel and Marx to create a comparative study of sociocultural processes in West and East.

Max Weber *(Archive Photos, Inc.)*

Weber was born on April 21, 1864, in Erfaut, Thuringia, the son of a lawyer. After three terms at Heidelberg University, Weber served a year in the military. Resuming his studies at the Universities of Berlin and Göttingen in 1884, he passed his bar examination in 1886 and later practiced law for a time.

In 1893 Weber married Marianne Schnitger. He taught briefly at Freiburg University and at Heidelberg. In 1903 he joined Werner Sombart in editing the *Archiv für Sozialwissenschaft and Sozialpolitik* (Archives for Social Science and Social Policy), the most prominent German social science journal of the period. Here, Weber began to write perhaps his most renowned essays, published in the *Archiv* in 1904–1905 under the title *The Protestant Ethic and the Spirit of Capitalism*. He linked the rise of a new **capitalism** to the religious ethics of Protestantism, especially Calvinists.

Weber argued that the **asceticism** of the medieval Catholic monastery brought into the conduct of everyday affairs contributed greatly to the systematic rationalization and functional organization of every sphere of existence, especially economic life. He viewed the Reformation as causing a fundamental reorientation of basic cultural frameworks of spiritual direction and human outlook. Within the context of his larger

questions, Weber tended to view Protestant rationalism as one step in the series of stages of increasing rationalization of every area of modern society.

In 1904 Weber went to the United States where he saw evidence for his thesis in *The Protestant Ethic and the Spirit of Capitalism*. He also recognized that contemporary American economic life had been stripped of its original ethical and religious impulse. Intense economic competition assumed the character almost of sport.

Weber attempted to weigh the relative importance of economic, religious, juridical, and other factors in contributing to the different historical outcomes seen in any comparative study of world societies. This larger theme formed one of his central intellectual interests throughout the remainder of his life, and it resulted in the publication of *The Religion of China* (1915), *The Religion of India* (1916–1917), and *Ancient Judaism* (1917–1919).

Weber's break with the Verein für Sozialpolitik (Union for Social Policy), a long-standing German political and social scientific organization, over the question of the relation of social scientific research to social policy led to the establishment in 1910, with the collaboration of other social scientists, of the new Deutsche Soziologische Gesellschaft (German Sociological Society).

Weber and his collaborators argued that social science could not be simply subordinated to political values and policies. Rather, there was a logical distinction between the realms of **fact** and value, one which required a firmly grounded distinction between the analyses of the social scientist and the policies of any political order. Social science must develop "objective" frames of reference, ones "neutral" to any particular political policies and ethical values. This ever-renewed tension between particular ethical stances and "objectivity" in the sciences remained a central part of Weber's concerns.

In 1909 Weber took over the editorship of a projected multivolume encyclopedic work on the social sciences entitled *Outline of Social Economics*, and when he did not get the contributions from other writers he took on much more than originally planned, the one volume *Economy and Society*. The work became a construction of a systematic sociology in world historical and comparative depth and it occupied a large portion of his time and energies during the remainder of his life.

Economy and Society differed in tone and emphasis from Weber's comparative studies of the cultural foundations of Chinese, Indian, and Western civilizations. This massive work was an attempt at a more systematic sociology, not directed toward any single comparative, historical problem but rather toward an organization of the major areas of sociological inquiry into a single whole.

Despite time spent in the medical service during World War I, Weber devoted from 1910 to 1919 to the completion of his studies on China, India, and ancient **Judaism** and to his work on *Economy and Society*. Many younger as well as more established scholars formed part of Weber's wide intellectual circle during these years.

In 1918 Weber resumed his teaching duties. One result was a series of lectures in 1919–1920, "Universal Economic

History,'' which was published posthumously from students' notes as *General Economic History*. Along with this lecture series, Weber delivered two addresses in 1918, ''Science as a Vocation'' and ''Politics as a Vocation,'' in which he voiced ethical themes that had occupied him in his scholarly work.

Weber sounded ethical themes that have become a central part of the ''existentialist'' philosophical orientation of our time. He gave no simple solutions and was willing neither to wait for new prophets nor to abdicate all ethical responsibility for the conduct of life because of its seeming ultimate ''meaninglessness.'' Weber died in Munich on June 14, 1920. His work forms a major part of the historical foundation of sociology.

WELFARE STATE

A welfare state is created when a **government** uses its powers to guarantee a certain **standard of living** for its constituents. The actual level of aid provided depends upon the individual government; Communist states, such as Cuba and China, provide for all of their people, while capitalist states vary widely in type and amount of aid. The welfare state was developed as a remedy for the ills of *laissez-faire* capitalism, which dictated that the government stay out of economic matters and let them run their course. However, the *laissez-faire* approach left some people uncared for, such as the impoverished and unemployed. During the Great Depression, Western governments were forced to expand aid programs for their residents because the majority were living in financial hardships.

Social insurance, known in the United States as Social Security, is the primary feature of welfare state programs. Social insurance is intended to give aid to those who are unable, for whatever reason, to work and earn money, or provide for themselves in other ways. Common recipients of social insurance are people who are injured on the job, are so ill that they cannot work, are elderly, become unemployed, or have suffered the death of a spouse or the absence of another family member that provides income. Participation in these programs is mandatory and often tied to previous work involvement; in the United States, one must have worked a certain number of years to qualify for social security payments upon **retirement**, and people seeking unemployment insurance must have lost their jobs under a particular set of circumstances to receive such aid.

Great Britain and Canada have socialized medicine, so their populations receive medical treatment regardless of income level. Sweden, on the other hand, offers its residents far more than medical benefits; Swedish people also receive subsidized day care, paid medical leave from their occupations, and paid maternity and paternity leave. Great Britain and Sweden are also generous with their unemployment benefits; in Great Britain, receiving these benefits is known as ''being on the dole.''

Welfare programs are funded in a number of ways. Residents of Canada and Sweden pay a high percentage of their income for taxes because of the increased level of benefits offered by their governments. U.S. citizens pay for social security through payroll deductions, and employers pay for unemployment insurance. Other U.S. aid programs, such as **Medicare** and **Medicaid**, are federal programs financed by a variety of federal taxes. The tax systems themselves can be a sort of welfare program; progressive tax systems attempt to redistribute wealth by requiring those in higher tax brackets to pay more than those with lower incomes.

One problem with social insurance is that the payments are rarely adequate to cover living expenses for a given individual. Moreover, many of these programs are being dismantled, particularly in the United States. Conservatives often object to the amount of **money** spent on programs other than Social Security, blaming these ''handouts'' for a variety of the nation's ills. Canada, on the other hand, is experiencing a ''brain drain;'' highly-trained professionals, most of whom have enjoyed state-subsidized educations, are moving to the United States, where they can earn more money and pay a smaller proportion out for taxes.

WELLS-BARNETT, IDA. B. (1862-1931)
American journalist

Ida B. Wells-Barnett (1862–1931), an African American journalist, was an active crusader against lynching and a champion of social and political justice for African Americans. Ida B. Wells was born a slave in Holly Springs, Mississippi, on July 16, 1862, six months before the Emancipation Proclamation freed all of the slaves in the Confederate states. Her father, James, was a carpenter and her mother, Elizabeth, a cook. James Wells was a hardworking, opinionated man who was actively interested in politics and in helping to provide educational opportunities for the liberated slaves and for his own eight children. He was on the board of trustees of Rust College, a freedmen's school, where his daughter Ida received a basic education. Elizabeth Wells supervised her children's religious training by escorting them to **church** services and by insisting that the only book that they could read on Sunday was the Bible. Young Wells was an avid reader and stated that as a result of this rule she had read through the Bible many times.

Tragedy struck the Wells family when she was about 16 years old. Her parents and some of her brothers and sisters died in a yellow fever epidemic while Wells was in another town visiting relatives. With a small legacy left by her parents, she was determined to assume the **role** of mothering her younger brothers and sisters. By arranging her hair in an adult style and donning a long dress, Wells was able to obtain a teaching position by convincing local school officials that she was 18 years old. A few years later, after placing the older children as apprentices, she moved to Memphis with some of the younger children to live with a relative. She was eventually able to earn a teaching position there by obtaining further education at Fisk University.

In 1884, while she was travelling by train from school, Wells was forcibly thrown out of a first-class car by the conductor because she refused to ride in the car set aside for Afri-

can Americans which was nicknamed the "Jim Crow" car. She had purchased a first-class ticket and was determined not to move from her seat, but she was not able to defend herself against the conductor, who literally dragged her from her seat while some of the white passengers applauded. However, Wells, who was determined to fight for **justice**, sued the railroad and won her case. When the decision was later overturned by the Tennessee Supreme Court, Wells just became more determined to fight against racial injustice wherever she found it.

When Wells joined a literary society in Memphis, she discovered that one of their primary activities was to write essays on various subjects and read them before the members. Wells' essays on social conditions for African Americans were so well received that the society members began to encourage her to write for church publications. When she was offered a regular reporting position and part ownership of the *Memphis Free Speech and Headlight* in 1887 she eagerly accepted. The name of the newspaper was later shortened to the *Free Speech,* and Wells eventually became its sole owner. She was not afraid to speak out against what she perceived to be injustices against African Americans, especially in the school system where she worked. She believed that the facilities and supplies available to African American children were always inferior to those offered to whites. As a consequence of her editorials about the schools, Wells lost her teaching position in 1891.

One year later, in 1892, three of Wells' friends, who were successful businessmen in Memphis, were killed and their businesses destroyed by whites who Wells accused of being jealous of their success. The *Free Speech* ran a scathing editorial about the murders in which Wells harshly rebuked the white community. It was probably not coincidental that she was out of town by the time local whites read her paper. An angry mob of whites broke into her newspaper office, broke up her presses, and vowed to kill her if she returned to Tennessee.

Wells became a journalist "in exile," writing under the pen name "Iola" for the *New York Age* and other weekly newspapers serving the African American population. She systematically attacked lynching and other violent crimes perpetrated against African Americans. She went on speaking tours in the northeastern states and England to encourage people to speak out against lynching. She wrote well-documented pamphlets with titles such as *On Lynchings, Southern Horrors, A Red Record*, and *Mob Rule in New Orleans.*

In 1895 Wells moved to Chicago, where she married a widower named Frederick Barnett. She remained active after she was married and carried nursing children with her during her crusades. She and her husband owned a newspaper for a while and she continued to write articles for other journals. She actively participated in efforts to gain the vote for women and simultaneously campaigned against racial bigotry within the women's movement. In 1909 she attended the organizational meeting of the National Association for the Advancement of Colored People (NAACP) and continued to work with the organization's founders during its formative years, although her association with the organization was not always peaceful.

Wells-Barnett did agree with one of the major thrusts of the **organization**, however, and that was their desire to see the enactment of federal anti-lynching legislation. She found a settlement house in Chicago for young African American men and women, regularly taught a Bible class at the house, and also worked as a probation officer there. After her death in 1931 her contributions to the city of Chicago were acknowledged when a public housing project was named after her.

WIDOWHOOD

As a sociological phenomenon, widowhood was not studied in-depth until about thirty years ago, although some research was done in the fields of anthropology and **psychology**. Anthropologists focused on various cultural and tribal practices surrounding widowhood, while psychologists focused mainly on the bereavement process. Several reasons are cited for the initial lack of interest in the subject on the part of sociologists and other researchers. First, the vast majority of those that experience widowhood are women of old age, and both women and older people have historically been ignored or understudied as subjects of research. Additionally, the cultural taboos associated with death and dying contributed to the stigma associated with widowhood and, therefore, to the dearth of researchers willing to study the phenomenon. An increase in life span has resulted in unsurpassed growth in the population of persons age 65 and above. Widows, due to the **feminization of poverty**, are also among the poorest, and outlive their husbands by an average of about twenty years. A steadily growing population brought with it an increased need for societal resources. Together, these factors clearly delineated the need for more research on widowhood.

In *Suicide: A Study in Sociology* (1897), Émile Durkheim incorporated widowhood into his findings. He found a correlation between widowhood and **suicide**, due to the survivor's loss of social connection, which he termed *domestic anomie*. Among sporadic early sociological studies that focused on widowhood were Peter Marris' in-depth interviews of London widows suffering from the recent loss of their mates (1958) and Felix Berardo's 1968 study of the widowed in the state of Washington. Berardo found that widowers, especially those in rural areas, had few social skills and difficulty performing the domestic tasks formerly accomplished by their wives. Effects of widowhood have since been found to be qualitatively different for men and women, but more or less equal in terms of traumatic effect.

Undoubtedly, the most comprehensive sociological contribution to the study of widowhood came from Helena Znaniecka Lopata. Her thirty years of research focused mainly on urban widows in **American society**, although she incorporated cross-cultural, comparative data into her later work. Lopata's early work consisted of in-depth interviews and observation of widows (not widowers) in Chicago. Lopata's work incorporated Florian Znaniecki's concept of the *social role*, which is based on the relations, duties, and rights of a member of a social circle. In *Widowhood in an American City* (1973), Lopata

found that loneliness, followed by financial worries, was most problematic for widows. Nevertheless, levels of social isolation did not change significantly from married life to widowhood, and the stronger a widow's identification with the traditional 'wife' role, the greater her level of social isolation in widowhood. Widows whose marriage integrated egalitarian values were less likely to feel socially isolated. Subjects also cited long-term positive outcomes of the transition into widowhood, including personal growth, greater freedom, less work (emotional and household), and a greater sense of independence and confidence.

Lopata's **concept** of *support systems* has been widely incorporated into the social sciences (*Women as Widows: Support Systems*, 1979). She found that different types of cultural and community support systems produced different initial and long-term adjustments to widowhood. Changes in western culture, such as greater mobility, urbanization, and a tendency toward **egalitarianism**, allowed widows greater access to societal resources. Other factors that affected the widow's transition from wife role to the **status** of widowhood include **race**, class, education level, age, **ethnicity**, geographic location, and length of time in caretaker role prior to husband's death. Lopata argued that widowhood is a transitory role, rather than a permanent one, particularly in modern culture. The role of widow becomes a *pervasive identity*, and, as such, enters into other social roles in varying degrees, in the same manner as gender identity. Lopata's most recent work *Current Widowhood: Myths and Realities* (1996) examines myths and stereotypes associated with widows and widowhood. Current sociological literature can be found in the areas of bereavement (**death and dying**), **marriage** and family, women and **aging**, and population studies (R. Gibson, D. K. van den Hoonard, L. Howie, R. Kalish, and D. Umberson, among others).

WILSON, WILLIAM JULIUS (1935-)
American sociologist and educator

William Julius Wilson, a professor at Harvard University's John F. Kennedy School of Government, is an authority on **race** and **poverty** in the United States. Wilson has built his reputation on three controversial and widely-read books: *The Declining Significance of Race* (1978), *The Truly Disadvantaged* (1987) and *When Work Disappears* (1996). Before 1996, Wilson taught at the University of Chicago for 25 years, where he conducted his research in local poor African American neighborhoods.

Respected beyond academia, Wilson is consulted by U.S. presidents on issues of race and poverty. While his advice has not always been accepted, Wilson's **influence** is undeniable. President Clinton, for example, told *Time* magazine that Wilson's books "made me see race and poverty and the problems of the inner city in a different light."

Wilson was born on December 20, 1935, in Derry Township, Pennsylvania, and raised in Blairsville, Pennsylvania, a working-class community east of Pittsburgh. His father, Esco Wilson, a coal miner, and his mother, Pauline Wilson,

had to struggle to support the family. The Wilson home was so small that all six children shared one bedroom. When Wilson was 12, his father died of lung disease. Then the family was forced to accept public assistance until his mother managed to find a job as a housekeeper. Wilson recalled in an interview with the magazine *Chicago*: "We were desperately poor. But I don't remember being unhappy.... We simply had no idea how bad off we were."

As a child, Wilson spent summers with his aunt, Janice Wardlaw, a psychiatric social worker in New York City. Wardlaw had a profound influence on Wilson's early life, taking him to cultural attractions in New York and encouraging him to read. Later, when Wilson won a church scholarship to attend Wilberforce University, Wardlaw helped to support him financially. Yet Wilson wishes his life would not be used as an argument government assistance for the poor is unnecessary. His work attempts to show that the obstacles those in the inner cities now face are nearly insurmountable.

As a sociology major at Wilberforce, Wilson became interested in urban sociology and the politics of race. He earned a B.A. in 1958, then spent several years in the army. In 1961, he earned an M.A. in sociology from Bowling Green State University in Bowling Green, Ohio. In 1966, Wilson earned a Ph.D. from Washington State University.

From 1965 until 1971, Wilson taught at the University of Massachusetts, Amherst, where in 1970, he was honored with a "Teacher of the Year" distinction. Wilson was offered a position in the sociology department at the University of Chicago in 1971. Hoping to disprove any suspicion that he was hired because of his race, Wilson resolved to work harder and do better than other scholars.

Wilson's achievements at the University of Chicago were remarkable. He won tenure in his first year and was appointed as a full professor in 1975. Three years later, at the age of 42, he became chair of the sociology department. In 1984, he was given the title of distinguished service professor and became a university professor in 1990. The following year, Wilson was elected to the National Academy of Sciences.

Disillusioned by the **urban sociology** produced in the 1960s and 1970s, Wilson developed a fact-based approach, relying heavily on statistical analysis. His first book *Power, Racism, and Privilege: Race Relations in Theoretical and Sociohistorical Perspectives*, a comparative study of race relations in the United States and South Africa (1973), was based on such methods. In his second book, Wilson decided to focus on class distinctions within the African American community. *The Declining Significance of Race: Blacks and Changing American Institutions* (1978) explained that social class was becoming more important than race in determining the prospects of African Americans. For middle-class blacks, Wilson wrote, there were fewer and fewer impediments to success, whereas for very poor black Americans, options were increasingly limited.

In his next book Wilson distanced himself from conservative scholars. *The Truly Disadvantaged: The Inner City, The Underclass, and Public Policy* (1987). Here, Wilson argued that many middle-class and working-class African Americans

had moved out of ghetto neighborhoods, taking with them traditional values. The only solution to this problem, in Wilson's view, would be for the government to implement a major, race-neutral project of social and economic reconstruction for American cities. The book was well-received by many liberals and moderates.

Wilson's project, the Urban Poverty and Family Life Study, became an extensive ethnographic survey of urban poor. Assisted by a large number of graduate students, Wilson organized interviews with 2,500 poor Chicago residents and 190 area employers. On the basis of this extensive study, Wilson secured grant money to establish a permanent **organization** for poverty research at the University of Chicago, The Center for the Study of Urban Inequality (begun 1993).

In 1996, Wilson admitted disappointment when Clinton signed the welfare-reform bill. According to the new **rules**, virtually all welfare recipients, including children, are entitled to receive only five years of welfare assistance throughout their lifetime. After receiving aid for two years, recipients must find work or lose their benefits.

In *When Work Disappears: The World of the New Urban Poor* (1996) Wilson argued that chronic, community-wide unemployment produces deviant behavior. The central reality has come to be not just poverty, but community-destroying joblessness which results in characteristics that trap ghetto residents in poverty. Wilson advocated an extensive, race-neutral program of social reforms, including universal health insurance, and a system of low-wage public jobs to replace welfare.

In 1996, Wilson left the University of Chicago to join Harvard University's prestigious John F. Kennedy School of Government. In 1997, Wilson and a team of researchers began a study to track the impact of welfare reform on 4,500 low-income workers and welfare recipients in Boston, Chicago, and Baltimore. The five-year study will determine whether Wilson's predictions of disaster are fulfilled.

WIRTH, LOUIS (1897-1952)

German sociologist

Louis Wirth was born August 28, 1897, in Gümenden in the Rhineland district of Germany. Wirth's family was a relatively prosperous family of the Jewish community in their small village. The Wirths were cattle merchants and farmers as were most Jews in the rural areas of Rhineland and Westphalia. Gümenden was a small rural community of only about nine hundred people. Wirth immigrated to United States in 1911, when his mother's brother visited the Wirth family in rural Germany. Wirth's uncle offered to take Wirth and an older sister back to America. Wirth's mother had high educational aspirations for her children, and she welcomed the opportunity to send Wirth and his sister to America to pursue educational opportunities. In America, Wirth lived first in Omaha, Nebraska. Wirth left Omaha after winning a regional scholarship to study at the University of Chicago. His intellectual pursuits were deeply influenced by University of Chicago sociology faculty

including Robert Park and Ernest Burgess. After his under-graduate degree, Wirth became the director of the division of delinquent boys for the Bureau of Personal Service of the Jewish Charities of Chicago.

Wirth married Mary Bolton, a University of Chicago trained social worker, in 1923. Soon after his marriage, Wirth returned to University of Chicago to pursue his graduate degree in sociology. His doctoral dissertation *The Ghetto*, a study of the Jewish community, was completed in 1925. A classic in ethnic studies, Wirth traced the segregation of Jewish communities from self-isolation in late antiquity to the Middle Ages when Jews were required under law to live in segregated areas and up to the contemporary Jewish community in Chicago. He first held a temporary teaching position at the University of Chicago and then at a brief appointment at Tulane University after receiving his doctorate. A fellowship from the Social Science Research Council allowed him to travel through Europe with his family during 1931. On his travels, he saw the presence of Nazis in Germany becoming more pronounced. On his return to America, Wirth began the necessary steps to bring his family to America. From 1932 to 1937, the Wirth family resettled in America. When Wirth returned to America in 1931, he also joined the sociology faculty at the University of Chicago under the chairmanship of Park. His intellectual pursuits during his long tenure at Chicago included involvement in community affairs in Chicago, **sociology of knowledge**, **sociological theory**, and urban sociology. He was politically and intellectually interested in the improvement of urban living conditions and minority rights. Wirth was appointed the president of the American Sociological Association in 1946. He also helped to establish the International Sociological Association and became its first president in 1950. He died suddenly on May 10, 1952, in Buffalo, New York, after speaking at a conference on community relations.

Although Wirth spent many of his early years in rural environments in both Germany and Nebraska, Wirth's writings on urban life became classics of in the field of **urban sociology**. In *Urbanism as a Way of Life* (1938), Wirth proclaimed that urbanism is the prevailing way of life in modern society. Wirth defined a city as a relatively large, dense, and permanent settlement of heterogeneous people. Wirth theorized that physical features of the city (size, density, and heterogeneity) have profoundly changed both the urbanite and the nature of interpersonal relationships. Due to city size people cannot possibly know all other urbanites. Out of necessity, there is a shift away from primary relationships to secondary relationships. Urbanites interact with others not as individuals but with others in certain roles. For example, an urban dweller deals with many people in the course of the day such as the deli cashier and the doorman of his or her apartment building. The urbanite does not develop deep personal connections with these people but only interacts with them in terms of their roles. Personal relations become superficial and transitory. Urban life is marked by utilitarianism and efficiency. The density of living and heterogeneity of urban residents leads people to live in homogenous groups resulting in a "mosaic of social worlds" in a city. Transitions across groups are difficult, and numerous social orders result adding to the segmentation of urban life.

WOLLSTONECRAFT, MARY (1759-1797)

English writer

Nearly two centuries after her death in 1797 from complications following the birth of her famous daughter, Mary Shelley, Mary Wollstonecraft occupies an important place in feminist literary studies. During her life, the popular press attacked her "radical" views; after her death, Wollstonecraft served as an example to women of the nineteenth century, either as an "unsex'd female" or, to an important few, as a model author in the male-dominated world of letters. The twentieth century has witnessed Wollstonecraft's emergence as a seminal figure in feminist writing.

Wollstonecraft's early life predisposed her to find the radical politics of the 1780s and 1790s appealing. The second of seven children born to an abusive father, she learned firsthand the limits of her gendered social position. The young Wollstonecraft attempted all the respectable employment options for unmarried middle-class women: she worked as a paid companion, as a governess, and as a school proprietor. She witnessed the failure of contemporary education for girls and young women, as well as the powerless position of women in unhappy marriages. During the mid–1780s, she read authors who helped shape her political and social thinking and she met an important resource for her career change, liberal publisher Joseph Johnson.

Her first publication *Thoughts on the Education of Daughters* (1787) argued against many accepted child-rearing and educational practices of the eighteenth century. With this conduct book—written to satisfy the growing appetite of an emerging middle class—Wollstonecraft worked within an accepted genre for women writers. Here, she applies the lessons of her self-education, drawing on the ideas of Locke, Rousseau, and other liberal writers.

Wollstonecraft again remains very clearly within the female tradition of authorship with her 1788 novel *Mary: A Fiction.* Published by Johnson (like all her books), the novel fuses autobiographical elements with an assessment of the self-defeating effects of morbid sentimentalism. A third-person account of a woman dissatisfied with her arranged marriage and overcome with affection for another man, Mary's story admits of only one outcome—her death from a fever after she accepts the hopelessness of her life. The novel concludes with its heroine "hastening to that world where there is neither marrying, nor giving in marriage."

In London, Wollstonecraft's friendship with Johnson and her success as a professional writer brought her into association with some of the leading radical and dissenting minds of the time at dinners the publisher hosted, for example, William Blake and Thomas Christie, Johnson's partner in launching his new periodical *The New Analytical Review.* Wollstonecraft's self-confidence no doubt benefited from these contacts as she entered the traditionally male domain of authorship.

Johnson, who would later be imprisoned for selling Thomas Paine's *Rights of Man,* encouraged the radicals among his authors, and he supported Wollstonecraft when she responded to an attack on the ideals of the French Revolution by one of England's leading political figures, Edmund Burke. In his *Reflections on the Revolution in France,* published in November 1790, Burke set the tone for reactionary opposition and inspired a series of responses from liberal and radical authors. Her *Vindication of the Rights of Man* was published anonymously by Johnson the following month, a second edition appearing shortly afterwards bearing her name on the title page.

Wollstonecraft reasons from immutable principles. She emphasized reason, individual merit, and moral virtue. She was not the first woman to enter the male-dominated domain of political discourse, but she was clearly the most visible and least diffident. Early in 1792 Wollstonecraft made the connection which few others would make between the rights of men and the situation of women. By far her best known book—and the one on which her reputation as an early feminist rests—Wollstonecraft's *Vindication of the Rights of Woman* stimulated a new debate on sexual injustice and earned her the moral condemnation of conservative men and women alike. Her appeal opens with a dedication to Tallyrand, one of the principle figures behind reform of education in revolutionary France; it then assaults Rousseau's sexist notions of female education in his otherwise enlightened *Émile.*

Although acknowledging certain differences between men and women from the outset, *Vindication of the Rights of Woman* bases its argument on the spiritual equality of all human beings. From this first principle, Wollstonecraft ridiculed the contemporary gender construction of females as weak and modest, attractive and shallow playthings for men, reinforced by an education based in sentiment and focused on luring a suitable mate, however deceptively. Wollstonecraft reasoned that if women are indeed capable of being moral beings, then their education should be designed to help them achieve a moral and intellectual development equal (or very nearly so) to men's. In **marriage**, she maintains, women should be the equal partners of their husbands, not merely attractive and desirable objects of male passion.

After publication of *Vindication of the Rights of Woman,* Wollstonecraft went to Paris to write a history of the revolution. *An Historical and Moral View of the French Revolution, and the Effect it Has Produced in Europe* suffers from her lack of understanding of the nation and its limited scope. Her personal distractions—a relationship with Gilbert Imlay, the first real love of her life, and the birth of their daughter Fanny in 1794—were not conducive to writing something so different from her previous work.

After her relationship with Imlay soured, Wollstonecraft left France with Fanny to tour Scandinavia as his business agent. During these months, she kept up a personal correspondence with Imlay, chronicling the manners of local people. These letters, returned by her estranged lover, formed the bulk of *Letters Written during a Short Residence in Sweden, Norway, and Denmark,* the book Godwin later claimed led him to fall in love with Wollstonecraft. The work is generally regarded as stylistically her best writing. Wollstonecraft's last important work, the unfinished novel *Maria, or the Wrongs of*

The Women's Liberation movement drew momentum from the 1960s Civil Rights movement *(Corbis Corporation [Bellevue]).*

Woman, addresses legal injustices perpetrated against women in regard to **property**, child custody, sexual and reproductive freedom, extra-legal incarceration, and **divorce**.

WOMEN'S LIBERATION MOVEMENT

The Women's Liberation Movement, as such, began in the 1960s as an outgrowth of the Civil Rights Movement. Various women's movements have arisen through history, usually focusing on one particular cause such as abolition of slavery, suffrage, or labor rights; when that cause disappeared the movement would temporarily lose power. When women were granted national suffrage in the United States in 1920, for instance, the question of women's rights seemed, for a time, to be settled.

In the 1960s, however, the movement was reborn with the more radical goal of equality for women in all areas of **society**. The civil rights campaigns of the 1950s and early 1960s had created a framework of activism that these women could use to mobilize members and attract media attention. Ironical-

ly, the sexism *within* the Civil Rights Movement was greatly responsible for the new sense of urgency for women's liberation.

In addition to the civil rights demonstrations, Betty Friedan's 1963 book *The Feminine Mystique* was an important factor in empowering women to expand their roles. Previously, most women worked outside their homes only when it was necessary to support their families, but now careers were seen as important for personal fulfillment; it became more common for middle-class women to seek **employment**, and women surpassed men in college enrollment.

The movement reached its peak in the early 1970s, particularly focusing on abortion rights and the Equal Rights Amendment (ERA), an unsuccessful effort to ensure gender equality constitutionally. The National Organization for Women (NOW), founded by Friedan and others in 1966, had become a major political force, and in 1973 the Supreme Court ruling on *Roe v. Wade* legalized abortion under certain conditions.

In the 1980s a conservative revival caused the Women's Liberation Movement to lose some momentum once more. ERA failed to be ratified by Congress, and anti-abortion groups became more militant, while NOW's leaders often feuded over goals and tactics. Nevertheless, women continued to narrow the gender gap in the workplace, and some became prominent leaders.

The term ''women's liberation'' has mostly fallen into disuse due to the disparaging way in which it was often used, but the struggle for equality is ongoing. The movement has fragmented, with women active on opposing sides of almost every political argument, but they still share goals for equal voice and the right to make their own choices.

WOMEN'S STUDIES

Women's Studies (WST) is a multidisciplinary curriculum that identifies and challenges the androcentric (male-biased) foundation of **society**. It seeks to integrate information about women into society at both the individual and the structural or institutional levels and to illuminate the male biases that permeate society, particularly in academia. A suporter of women's studies generally contends that knowledge is socially created. What has historically been accepted as ''knowledge'' and ''fact'' is actually androcentric, based primarily, if not completely, on the experiences of men. Historically, men have controlled society, they have been able to define whom and what is considered important or appropriate to study as well as how to study it. As a result of this male bias, much academic scholarship has excluded women and other minorities. Women's studies programs are based on the idea that enlightenment comes through education and that education can change or help eliminate gender inequality. Thus, women's studies seeks to re-educate people about the place of women in society and history, highlighting the contributions women have made to social, economic, intellectual, and political life. Through this re-education, scholars intend to make a place for women in the social construction of knowledge.

Emerging from the second wave of **feminism** in the 1960s and 1970s, women's studies became a part of some university curricula in 1969. In the early 1970s, several universities developed separate departments with degree programs. Today, most colleges and universities have a women's studies program or department or offer courses in women's studies. This marginalized discipline, however, has not become an integral part of the academic curriculum in the United States. Unfortunately, the faculty and staff of many departments are subjected to verbal and sometimes physical threats. This violence is usually attributed to the threat women's studies poses to the institution of academia. Some people believe that women's studies is not a valid or necessary area of study and have tried to intimidate schools and individuals into eliminating the programs.

Women's studies is rooted in feminist theory and method. Feminist work challenges the separations between academic fields and encourages inter-disciplinary work. This counters the traditional educational structure that is based on separation of disciplines. Women's studies focuses on the social contributions and the diverse experiences of women in an effort to supplement women's voices and experiences to our cultural knowledge. Women's studies also analyzes the experiences of women living in a patriarchal world, which is, in part, an attempt to raise academic and public awareness of the subordinate position of women in society. Another branch of women's studies developed in the 1980s, focusing on the diverse voices of racial, ethnic, and sexual minorities in conjunction with gender. This area of study has been led by Black feminist scholars who have explored the interconnected effects of these oppressive systems.

Women's studies has also challenged the androcentric nature of academia by developing new research methodologies. Unlike traditional research pedagogy, feminist research pedagogy contends that object and subject should not be separated in research because this leads to a dehumanization of research participants and puts researchers in a falsely superior position. Traditional researchers claim that a personal connection with research topics or participants creates unreliable results. Thus, according to traditional researchers, the separation of object and subject allows them to remain objective.

Objectivity, however, is rejected by many researchers in women's studies. They do not believe that objectivity is attainable because all people are to some extent guided by their subjective experiences. Where the traditional model supports male biases under the guise of objectivity, women's studies pursues unbiased research. This means that researchers should admit to their own personal biases based in areas such as **race, ethnicity**, class, gender, sexual orientation, and religious affiliation and compensate for their subjectivity in how they do research, what they ask, and who and what they choose to study. An open acknowledgment of one's biases allows researchers to be more honest about their findings and contributes to a greater understanding of the life experiences of the people they are studying. It also helps them move away from a male-defined model of research and create one that is more compatible with the lives and experiences of women and other minority groups.

See also Gender Studies; Men's Studies

WORK AND OCCUPATIONS

Economically, work can be thought of as productive effort to produce goods and services for the market with the expectation of compensation. Work, however, does not only occur in economic settings. Work can also be considered the exertion of effort in order to achieve a specific goal. People engage in many types of productive work with no expectation of compensation. People engage in leisure activities, such as working in the garden; community activities, such as volunteer work; and housework, such as doing the dishes. While all types of productive activities have been of interest to sociologists, compensated work within the economy has been of particular concern. Paid work within the economy helps to determine an individual's lifestyle, social status, identity, and overall well-being.

Social scientists distinguish between jobs and occupations. A job is set of work activities that one or more persons perform in a specific work setting. For example, a job is being a cook at a local restaurant. Occupations, on the other hand, are collections of specific jobs that perform a single economic role. Occupations are transferable across employers and business settings. The 1990 U.S. Census identified 503 detailed occupations (e.g., janitor, lawyer, teacher, etc.). Since the **Industrial Revolution**, there has been an increase in the number of occupations in the United States reflecting a more complex **division of labor** within the U.S. economy.

Sociologists have long been interested in what occupations people hold. The occupational structure of **society** is a tabulation of the number of workers in each occupation. Sociologists are interested in the occupational structure partly because it reflects the economic order of a society. For example, in 1870 half of all Americans were employed in agriculture. By 1990, only two-percent of all Americans were employed in agriculture. During this time, the economy of the United States shifted from agriculturally based to industrial and service based.

Sociologists are concerned with not just shifts in the number of persons employed within an occupation; they are also concerned with what groups make up an occupation. Since occupations differ in terms of social prestige and income, the distribution of individuals and groups within the occupational structure can be an indication of **discrimination** and unequal opportunity. Occupational sex segregation refers to the distribution of men and women across occupations. Female-dominated occupations include secretarial work, domestic work, and nursing. Male-dominated occupations include auto mechanic, lawyer, and police officer. Although men and women can work in any occupation, most men and women in the United States still work in sex-segregated occupations. The sex segregation of occupations is seen as a primary cause of the sex gap in pay. Today, and for most of the last century,

women in the work force have earned about sixty percent of men's income. Not only are women under represented in high paying **professions**, such as law or engineering, male-dominated occupations generally pay more than female-dominated occupations. An auto mechanic usually makes more than a practical nurse despite the fact that the occupations may be comparable in terms of training required, **skill**, and responsibility.

In the United States, the occupational structure is also segregated by **race** and **ethnicity**. For example, African Americans are under-represented in the professions, including law, medicine, and teaching, and well-paid technical jobs, such as computer programming. African Americans are over-represented in low paying, low-prestige jobs including many service-industry jobs such as fast-food servers, domestic work and retail sales.

When examining the occupational structure in society, sociologists also consider those who are unemployed. The unemployment rate in the United States varies greatly across groups. In 1997, the unemployment rate for Caucasians was only four percent, but for African Americans it was eleven percent—almost triple the rate for Caucasians. The picture is even bleaker for young African-American males who are far less likely to be employed than their Caucasian counterparts. In 1984, 58.3 percent of African-American men aged twenty to twenty-four were employed. In that same year, seventy-eight percent of Caucasian men aged twenty to twenty-four were employed. William J. Wilson and others have theorized why African Americans have such high rates of unemployment. Reasons include the history of racial discrimination in the United States, lack of informal networks to learn about employment opportunities, and discrimination by employers.

An occupation is more than what an individual does to gain income. Sociologists have long been interested in how what one does for a living affects identity. Karl Marx, a political and economic theorist, found that work under a capital system profoundly altered the souls of workers. Under the economic system of **capitalism**, the product that workers produce, such as a pair of shoes, belongs to the employer. Workers are thus alienated from the fruits of their labor. This **alienation** leads workers to become estranged from fellow workers and ultimately leaves workers spiritually bankrupt. Other sociologists, including Howard Becker, consider work the primary socialization mechanism for adults and see work as the basis of an adult's personality.

Sociologists have also studied how people balance their work and non-work lives. Arlie Hochschild, a sociologist, studied the domestic responsibilities of dual-job marriages. She found that in marriages where both partners work, women do most of the household chores including cleaning and childcare. Although their participation in the workforce has increased over the last century, women still bear the majority of the responsibility for household chores and child rearing.

Throughout most of human history, most people did not distinguish between paid and unpaid work. People consumed what they produced, such as food and clothing. Only with the rise of capitalism and industrialism, did people begin to leave the home and sell their labor to an employer. People then began to distinguish between paid work and unpaid work. Today, most people think of work as some activity they do for an employer for a wage. For sociologists, work in the economy is a fruitful and important area of sociological inquiry. Sociologists have been interested in all aspects of the work process from the structure of occupations within a society to the interpersonal relationships in the work setting.

WORK ORIENTATION

Work orientation is the social psychological quality of mind that people have about the work that they perform. How does someone feel about his or her work? What are the feelings and sentiments that people have about the work that they perform? And how do these feelings shape how an individual approaches their work? Work orientation refers to the symbolic ideas, belief, and emotions that a worker has about their work-related experience. Work orientation creates a person's sense of self.

Work orientation is constantly shifting and is supported by many rationales. Extrinsic motivations (such as **money** or **status**) and intrinsic motivations (such as self-expression or a sense of accomplishment) are both components of work orientation. Individuals have varying ideas about their work. Work itself varies widely in what it provides to the individual worker. Some aspects of work are very enjoyable, others are not.

Work is valued by workers even if the particular tasks performed may be disliked. The status of being a productive member of American society is embedded in the idea of working. Americans uniformly define life without work as a useless or meaningless existence. Therefore, the notion of being a productive and valued member of **American society** as a whole is connected to meeting the requirements of work even if these stipulations are difficult. People alter their behavior to meet the requirements of work rather than changing work to meet their personal and idiosyncratic needs, such as changing one's routine so that they can be punctual. The way that people relate to their work is important for both the individual and the larger society.

Juliet Schor has noted that since World War II, American workers have engaged in a trade off of sorts. Workers working longer in order to accumulate greater amounts of pay rather than working less for the same amount of compensation. The productive capacity of the United States since the 1950s was such that workers could have mobilized to re-organize the workplace to allow for greater flexibility. But because American workers desired more material goods rather than greater **leisure**, work time has increased. This has led to a situation that Schor calls ''the overworked American.'' Work has become the central issue in our lives. People are more focused on the outcome of spending money for the purchase of commodities rather than the emotional benefits of working less and having more vacation and free time with one's **family** and friends.

The consumption of commodities that is possible through one's labor becomes the main focus of work rather than the nature of the work itself. Although work is the means

by which people can get what they want, the work is seen as drudgery. Whether or not workers share this interpretation of the nature of work, workers tend to view work in negative terms.

Therefore, instead of viewing work as an enjoyable task, most workers believe that work is a synonym to suffering. Over time, most work has come to be defined as arduous labor rather than tasks that have intrinsic joy and value. Play and work become defined, for most workers, in an antithetical fashion. Work becomes viewed as action that is hard to complete. Work, thus, becomes something that people flee from during vacations or other restful activity rather than seeking out because of intrinsic rewards. Most corporations are involved in efforts to encourage and increase a worker's commitment to their jobs by adding workplace flexibility.

Researchers in the sociology of work have tried to determine what creates greater appreciation by workers for the kind of work that they do. Before a person learns a particular job, he or she learns how to feel or think about work. Worker satisfaction is closely correlated with the experience of work autonomy. Autonomy is defined as the amount of control that a worker has over their labor power, the level of respect a worker experiences, and the perceived value of the work rather than the amount of pay received for the completion of work tasks.

The relationship between the work and person is not one-sided. Not only does a person's work affect his or her orientation to the work, but also a person's orientation affects the work itself. The connection between individuals and their work settings is reciprocal. And the nature of this reciprocity varies based on the individual worker, their employer, the industry, and the specific workplace. People tend to either find work that matches their perspectives or try to change the content of the work so that it more closely matches their personality. For example, a worker who values autonomy might make changes in their work so that less direct supervision occurs in their workplace.

WORLD RELIGIONS

Although a long-neglected sub-discipline, the sociology of religion has been a growing area of research interest since the 1960s. Researchers focus on how **society** influences the origins, practices, and doctrines of religion and how religion, in turn, influences social activity. Sociologists of religion do not make judgments about whether a **belief system** is true or false. Instead, they see all religions as products of particular cultures and all religions as created in similar manners across all cultures.

This field attempts to define *religion*. Some very small societies do not recognize religion as a separate element, as do Judeo-Christian cultures. Many features that Western cultures associate with religion, such as a belief in a divinity, a set of ethical rules, a separation between the natural and the supernatural, and a link between how life is lived on earth and what happens in the afterlife, do not appear in other religions. Hard-to-label belief systems add to the challenge of defining reli-

gion. In this effort, sociologists have identified six dimensions that all religions share: **ritual**, mythology, doctrine, code of ethics, **influence** on society, and experiences, such as revelations or visions, that directly affect some individuals.

A formal study of the **sociology of religion** was developed in the late nineteenth century. Before that, sociologists dismissed religion as a relic of man's primitive and superstitious past. Religion was seen as harmless myth, but social scientists did not think it was worth serious study until Emile Durkheim reasoned that so universal a phenomenon could not simply be dismissed. Durkheim studied Australian **totemism**, which he determined to be the most primitive religion. He concluded that religious rites embed and transmit values within a society, maintain prohibitions and taboos, and bring people together to confirm community solidarity. Religious forces are moral forces, Durkheim said. In his view, every society needs a religion or a comparable system of secular beliefs.

Max Weber studied the influence of religious ideas, such as the Protestant work ethic, on the economy and examined how religious belief can accelerate or retard capitalist development in particular societies. Weber also distinguished between religion and magic. In religion, he said, societies relate to divinities through supplication, **prayer**, and worship; in magic, supernatural forces are not worshiped but are made to be obedient to human will through the use of charms, formulas, or rites. Weber defined religions as *this-worldly*, meaning aimed at mastering the social environment (such as Protestantism) or *other-worldly*, meaning aimed at withdrawing from materialistic, earthly concerns (such as **Buddhism**).

In recent years, sociologists have been concerned with secularization, or the increasing involvement of religious institutions with the material world. They explore the extent religious ideas and influences are fading from modern society and why this process is taking place. There are no easy answers, but some sociologists believe that the changes are caused by urbanization, the rise of technology, and the increasing tendency to approach life from a rational rather than a spiritual perspective. At the same time, however, we see the rise of evangelicalism and the staying power of organized religion. Plus relatively new, unorganized belief systems, such New Age beliefs—which incorporate elements from various sources, including organized religion, astrology, and the paranormal—are on the rise.

Contemporary sociologists of religion also are interested in how personality and social status correlate to religious beliefs. For example, fundamentalist sects attract many low-income individuals who migrate from rural to urban areas. Research suggests that the upwardly mobile often change not only their political and economic lifestyle but their church affiliation. Sociologists studying the *Jesus Freak* phenomenon of the 1980s learned that it drew its support primarily from disillusioned youth who had a feeling of being disconnected from and alienated by mainstream society; after their religious conversion, they became markedly more conservative and conformist.

Experience shows that no religious institution exists that has not faced criticism and challenges. Outside challenges

often lead to internal clashes which ultimately result in reform. Ultimately, sociologists say, no aspect of any religious tradition escapes being influenced by society, and no society is left unmarked by religion.

WORLD-SYSTEMS THEORY

Immanuel Wallerstein is acknowledged as the ''father'' of world-systems theory, which is associated with his publication in 1974 of the first of three volumes of *The Modern World-System*. The work, which outlines rise and expansion of the modern world-system, was shaped by the work of earlier scholars. First, Wallerstein's work was influenced by the work of Fernand Braudel, renowned French historian who first formulated the concept of the world-system and who proposed an interdisciplinary approach to the study of **social change** on a world scale. Braudel and Wallerstein were both influenced by **Karl Marx** from whose materialist conception of history Wallerstein drew heavily. For instance, Wallerstein's approach to class and class struggle is similar to Marx's. Wallerstein, however, extended those concepts to the global level, proposing that world historical development is the product of class struggles both internal to nation-states and between national and regional entities. Another influence on Wallerstein was the work of Andre Gunder Frank, who with other Latin American scholars had earlier developed **dependency theory**. Frank theorized about the ''development of underdevelopment,'' in which he identified underdevelopment of the periphery as the product of modern capitalist development imposed by core nations upon those that were weaker.

Wallerstein identified two basic types of world-systems: world-empires and world-economies. A third concept, mini-systems, is frequently used to identify smaller, less complex, pre-capitalist formations. A world-empire is a world-system that is politically and militarily unified, like the Roman Empire. A world-economy is an intricate network of economic, social, and political relations that transcends national boundaries. It differs from a world-empire in that it lacks political and military unity although its economic system extends across national boundaries. Only one world-economy, the capitalist world-economy which emerged in western Europe around 1450 and became consolidated around 1650, has lasted for a significant length of time without becoming a world-empire. However, Wallerstein contends that it is the nature for a world-economy to disintegrate into a world-empire as is evidenced by the perpetual competition between core powers. The capitalist world-economy has several characteristics. First, it is autonomous; regardless of its interactions with external systems, it can persist on its own. Second, it is comprised of a single, complex **division of labor** that organizes economic activity along both specialized economic lines and geographical zones. Finally, it is made up of any number of cultural forms.

Wallerstein adopted and expanded the concept of economic zones, which Frank had described as the metropolis and its satellites, and introduced a third type, the semiperiphery. The three zones, the core, periphery, and semiperiphery, are all intricately involved in the capitalist world-economy and are hierarchically related to each other. Core nations are the central political and economic powers; for example, the United States in the West and Japan in the East represent the most technologically and industrially advanced core nations. The periphery is comprised of underdeveloped countries, some that continue to use pre-capitalist forms of exploitation, such as peasant-labor, forced labor, and other non-economic forms of **coercion**, and others that specialize in primary production, such as mining and agricultural commodity production. These peripheral economies are technologically retarded by their relationship to the core, and advanced industries located there result from direct core capitalist investments and are under core control. The semiperiphery is comprised of two economic forms: those that share features with both core and periphery zones and those that are at an intermediate level of economic development. Modern examples of semiperipheral countries are Brazil, South Korea, Taiwan, and Singapore. The semiperiphery is important because it stabilizes and mediates the polarization inherent in the relationship between the core and periphery.

The core, periphery, and semiperiphery interact within the world- economy such that, first, the core exploits the periphery and, to a lesser extent, the semiperiphery, generating large profits and a high rate of return on investments, often through superexploitation (the taking of social surplus and portions of the socially necessary production). This process happens in the absence or near absence of labor laws and unions that protect workers and regulate the externalization of the social costs of production (e.g., pollution, environmental degradation, etc.). To a lesser degree, the semiperiphery also exploits the periphery and frequently acts as a middle man in economic transactions between the core and the periphery. Second, economic rivalry exists among the core countries over the military and political domination of territories, often with political and military implications. Finally, the world-economy changes; for instance, a peripheral country may, with difficulty, enter the semiperiphery; others frequently move from the semiperiphery to the periphery. While a core state rarely falls to peripheral status, several have receded to the semiperiphery. Although it is much more rare, at least one peripheral country has become a core country, the United States.

The world-system would disintegrate into perpetual **war** and instability with the mediating influence of the interstate system, which is the political structure of the world-system. The world-system involves nation-states (some 180 of them at present) competing, for the opportunity to establish hegemony over the world-system or to attain status as a world-empire. This competition within the world-system is mediated by the interstate system, or various formal and informal networks of trade and diplomacy; the World Bank, International Monetary Fund, United Nations, World Trade Organization, and other such organizations attempt to institutionalize and formalize the interstate system. However, although currently the world labors under U.S. **hegemony** (just as it did under the Dutch in the sixteenth century and the British less than a century ago), there is no single world government. As a consequence, inter-

national economic actors quite easily avoid the laws, policies, and practices of sovereign states, leading some world-systems scholars to propose that the world-system is an economic system free from state constraint.

X

XENOPHOBIA

The meaning of the term ''xenophobia'' has roots in Greek, meaning ''fear of what is strange''. It can manifest itself in responses to people of different races, ethnic backgrounds, national origins, or religions. It is based on **prejudice** and can result in **discrimination**. Xenophobia is a backlash to recent immigrants. Legislation such as California's 1994 passage of Proposition 187 which denies **social services**, including schooling, to illegal immigrants may express fear of assimilating newcomers into the social system. Evidence of xenophobia can be found in almost every country. During the 1980s Germans felt hostility toward people of Turkish descent whose families settled in the area to help rebuild Germany after World War II. Rwanda experienced conflict between the Hutus and Tutsis. Serbians fought against Bosnian neighbors in the last years of the twentieth century.

The opposite of xenophobia is xenocentrism which assumes that other cultures are better than one's own. Xenocentric individuals prefer to associate with those of different races, ethnicities, national origins or religions. They prefer to purchase imported rather than domestic products. There are cases of American products adopting product names that sound foreign, for example, Haagen-Dazs ice cream.

Y

YOUTH CULTURE

Youth culture emerged as a sociological concept in the United States around 1940. It was developed to explain youthful **deviance**. Drawing on a life course **model** of human development, youth culture represented an adolescent social system that facilitates the transition from childhood to adulthood. The theory presumed that as children grow older they experience biological, social, and psychic changes that create strain and crisis. The socially structured set of **norms**, **values**, and behaviors legitimated in youth culture allows individuals to work out such tensions in a relatively safe manner. Sociologists argued that despite the appearance of irresponsibility, youth culture actually serves a social function in facilitating development.

This notion of youth culture as a homogenous social structure experienced by most youth in most places in modern societies began to be challenged in the 1960s. Critics argued that there is no singular youth culture. Rather, the more accurate term should be youth culture(s). Adolescents, like all human beings, are diverse; their social groupings and associated structures of norms and values should be viewed accordingly. Studies of youth culture(s) tend to focus on the ways that youth band together in order to re-shape their identity. Typically, youth culture(s) organize themselves around particular cultural objects such as musical styles or fashion (recent examples include hip-hop, grunge, and punk).

Youth culture is becoming a larger area of inquiry among sociologists who study popular and mass culture. In industrialized western nations, like the United States, the adolescent age **cohort** has consistently gained discretionary spending resources each year. Accordingly, much of contemporary popular culture (music, **television**, motion pictures, and fashion) is oriented to the tastes and consumption patterns of youth. Sociologists study youth culture(s) to understand how such trends and trajectories shape life in the broader society.

Much of contemporary popular culture is oriented to the tastes and consumption patterns of youth *(AP/Wide World Photos, Inc.).*

Z

ZEITGEIST

Though eighteenth century philosophers were intrigued by the concept of *zeitgeist,* it was not popular until Friedrich Hegel more fully developed it. Zeitgeist is the characteristic spirit (geist) of a specific historical era (zeit). Hegel argued that artistic and philosophical expression cannot escape the zeitgeist in which they are produced because they are always imperfect and symbolic and do not provide for the progress of the human spirit over time. In popular parlance, it is described as ''the spirit of the age.'' The current definition of the word applies the meaning of the term more loosely and uses it to describe the general cultural quality of any given period; it largely excludes the historicist connotations of Hegelian philosophy.

Sources Consulted

Books

Abercrombie, Nicolas, Stephen Hill, and Bryan S. Turner. *The Penguin Dictionary of Sociology*. 3rd ed. London: Penguin, 1988.

Abrahamson, Mark. *Functionalism*. Englewood Cliffs, NJ: Prentice-Hall, Inc., 1978.

Abrams, Philip. *Historical Sociology*. Ithaca, NY: Cornell University Press, 1982.

Adam, Barry D. *The Rise of a Gay and Lesbian Movement*. Boston: Twayne, 1987.

Adams, Carol J., ed. *Ecofeminism and the Sacred*. New York: Continuum, 1993.

Adler, Emily Stier and Roger Clark. *How It's Done: An Invitation to Social Research*. Belmont, CA: Wadsworth Publishing Company, 1999.

Adler, Freda, Gerhard O. W. Mueller, and William S. Laufer. *Criminology: The Shorter Version* 4th ed. Boston: McGraw-Hill, 1998.

Adorno, Theodor W. et al. *The Authoritarian Personality: Studies in Prejudice*. Edited by Max Horkheimer and Samuel H. Flowerman. New York: Harper & Brothers, 1950.

Agger, Ben. *Critical Social Theories: An Introduction*. Oxford: Westview Press, 1998.

Agresti, Alan and Barbara Finlay. *Statistical Methods for the Social Sciences*. 3rd ed. Upper Saddle River, NJ: Prentice-Hall, 1997.

Ahmed, Akbar. *Postmodernism and Islam: Predicament and Promise*. New York: Routledge, 1992.

Akerd, William Keith. *Wocante Tinza: A History of the American Indian Movement*. Ann Arbor: UMI, 1988.

Akers, Ronald L. *Criminological Theories: Introduction and Evaluation*. Los Angeles: Roxbury Publishing Company, 1997.

Al-Azmeh, Aziz. *Islams and Modernities*. New York: Verso, 1996.

Allen, Dennis. "Lesbian and Gay Studies: A Consumer's Guide." In *The Gay Nineties: Disciplinary and Interdisciplinary Formations in Queer Studies*. Edited by Thomas Foster et al. New York: New York University Press, 1997.

Alley, Robert S. *Without a Prayer: Religious Expression in Public Schools*. Amherst, NY: Prometheus Books, 1996.

American Men and Women of Science: the Social and Behavioral Sciences. Ed. By the Jacques Cattell Press. 12th ed - 13th ed. New York: Bowler, 1973–78.

Amin, Samir. *Accumulation on a World Scale: A Critique of the Theory of Underdevelopment*. Translated by Brian Pearce. New York: Monthly Review Press, 1974.

Ammer, Christine and Dean S. Ammer. *Dictionary of Business and Economics*. Rev. ed. New York: Free Press, 1984.

Andersen, Margaret L. and Howard F. Taylor. *Sociology: Understanding a Diverse Society*. Belmont, CA: Wadsworth Thompson Learning, 2000.

Anderson, B. A. "Regional and Cultural Factors in The Decline of Marital Fertility in Western Europe." In *The Decline of Fertility in Europe*. Edited by A. J. Coale and S. C. Watkins. Princeton: Princeton University Press, 1986.

Anderson, Benedict. *Imagined Communities: Reflections on the Origin and Spread of Nationalism*. Rev. ed. London: Verso, 1991.

Aptheker, Bettina. *Woman's Legacy: Essays on Race, Sex, and Class in American History*. Amherst: University of Massachusetts Press, 1982.

Arendt, Hannah. *The Origins of Totalitarianism.* New York: Harcourt Brace Jovanovich, 1951.

Arestis, Philip and Malcolm Sawyer, eds. *A Biographical Dictionary of Dissenting Economists.* Hants, England: Edward Alger Publishing Limited, 1992.

Ashley, David and David Michael Orenstein. *Sociological Theory: Classical Statements.* 4th ed. Boston: Allyn and Bacon, 1998.

Ashton-Jones, Evelyn, Gary A. Olsen, and Merry G. Perry. *The Gender Reader.* 2nd ed. Boston: Allyn and Bacon, 2000.

Assiter, Alison and Avedon Carol, eds. *Bad Girls and Dirty Pictures: The Challenge to Reclaim Feminism.* London: Pluto Press, 1993.

Atkins, Robert A. *Egalitarian Community: Ethnography and Exegesis.* Tuscaloosa: University of Alabama Press, 1991.

Auerbach, Susan, ed. *Encyclopedia of Multiculturalism.* New York: Marshall Cavendish, 1994.

Avery, John. *Progress, Poverty, and Population: Re-reading Condorcet, Godwin, and Malthus.* London: Frank Cass, 1997.

Avey, Albert. *Handbook in the History of Philosophy: A Chronological Survey of Western Thought, 3500 B. C. to the Present.* New York: Barnes and Noble, Inc., 1954.

Avineri, Shlomo. *The Social and Political Thought of Karl Marx.* New York: Cambridge University Press, 1968.

Babbie, Earl. *The Basics of Social Research.* Belmont, CA: Wadsworth Publishing Company, 1999.

——. *The Practice of Social Research.* 6th ed. Belmont, CA: Wadsworth Publishing Company, 1992.

——. *The Sociological Spirit: Critical Essays in a Critical Society.* 2d ed. Belmont, CA: Wadsworth Publishing Company, 1994.

——. *What is Society? Reflections on Freedom, Order, and Change.* Thousand Oaks, CA: Pine Forge Press, 1994.

Babkin, B. P. *Pavlov: A Biography.* Chicago: University of Chicago Press, 1949.

Bahr, Howard M., Bruce A. Chadwick, and Joseph H. Strauss. *American Ethnicity.* Lexington, Massachusetts: D.C. Heath and Company, 1979.

Bailey, Beth L. *From Front Porch to Back Seat: Courtship in Twentieth Century America.* Baltimore: Johns Hopkins University Press, 1988.

Baker, Keith Michael, ed. *Condorcet: Selected Writings.* Indianapolis: Bobbs-Merrill Company, Inc., 1976.

Bancroft, Anne. *Religions of the East.* New York: St. Martin's Press, 1974.

Banks, James A. "Multicultural Education: Its Effects on Students' Racial and Gender Role Attitudes." In

Handbook of Research on Social Studies Teaching and Learning. Edited by James P. Shraver. New York: Macmillan, 1991.

Bannister, Robert C. *Sociology and Scientism: The American Quest for Objectivity, 1881–1940.* Chapel Hill: University of North Carolina Press, 1987.

Barak, Gregg. *Integrating Criminologies.* Boston: Allyn and Bacon, 1998.

Baran, Paul A. *The Political Economy of Growth.* New York: Monthly Review Press, 1957.

Barfield, Thomas, ed. *The Dictionary of Anthropology.* Cambridge: Blackwell Publishers, 1997.

Barkan, Steven E. *Criminology: A Sociological Understanding.* Upper Saddle River, NJ: Prentice Hall, 1997.

Barnard, F. M., ed. and trans. *J. G. Herder on Social and Political Culture.* Cambridge: University of Cambridge Press, 1969.

Barry, John. *Environment and Social Theory.* New York: Routledge, 1999.

Bartollas, Clemens and Larry D. Hahn. *Policing in America.* Boston: Allyn and Bacon, 1999.

Bartowski, Francis. *Feminist Utopias.* Lincoln: University of Nebraska, 1989.

Baumann, Zygmunt. *Modernity and the Holocaust.* Cambridge: Polity Press, 1989.

——. *Socialism: The Active Utopia.* New York: Holmes & Meier, 1976.

Bayley, David H. *Police for the Future.* New York: Oxford University Press, 1994.

Beck, Lewis White and Robert L. Holmes. *Philosophic Inquiry: An Introduction to Philosophy.* 2nd ed. Englewood Cliffs, NJ: Prentice-Hall, Inc., 1968.

Becker, Howard S. *Outsiders: Studies in the Sociology of Deviance.* New York: Free Press, 1963.

Becker, Mary, Cynthia Grant Bowman, and Morrison Torrey. *Cases and Materials on Feminist Jurisprudence: Taking Women Seriously.* St. Paul: West Publishing Company, 1994.

Bedford, Henry F. and Trevor Colbourn. *The Americans: A Brief History Since 1865.* New York: Harcourt Brace, 1972.

Beecher, Jonathan. *Charles Fourier: The Visionary and His World.* Berkeley: University of California Press, 1986.

Beeghley, Leonard. *The Structure of Social Stratification in the United States.* 3rd ed. Needham Heights, MA: Allyn and Bacon, 2000.

Bell, Daniel. *The Coming of Post-Industrial Society: A Venture*

in Social Forecasting. New York: Basic Books, Inc., Publishers, 1973.

Bell, Roger T. *Sociolinguistics: Goals, Approaches, and Problems*. New York: St. Martin's Press, 1976.

Bellah, Robert N. *Habits of the Heart: Individualism and Commitment in American Life*. Updated ed. Berkeley: University of California Press, 1996.

———. *Tokugawa Religion: The Cultural Roots of Modern Japan*. New York: Free Press, 1957.

Bellah, Robert N., Richard Masden, William M. Sullivan, Ann Swindler, and Steven M. Tipton. *The Good Society*. New York: Vintage Books,1991.

Beirne, Piers and James Messerschmidt. *Criminology*. 3rd ed. Boulder, CO: Westview Press, 2000.

Benford, Robert D, ed. *Social Issues: Selections from Macmillan's Four-Volume Encyclopedia of Sociology*. New York: Macmillan Library Reference, 1992.

Benjamin, Harry. *The Transsexual Phenomenon*. New York: Julian Press, Inc., 1966.

Benjamin, Walter. *Illuminations*. Edited by Hannah Arendt. Translated by Harry Zohn. New York: Schocken Books, 1968.

Benokraitis, Nijole V. *Marriage and Families: Changes, Choices, and Constraints*. 3rd ed. Upper Saddle River, NJ: Prentice Hall, 1999.

Berg, Bruce L. *Qualitative Research Methods for the Social Sciences*. 2nd ed. Boston: Allyn and Bacon, 1995.

Berger, Joseph, B.P. Cohen, and M. Zelditch, Jr., eds. *Sociological Theories in Progress*. Boston: Houghton Mifflin, 1966.

Berger, Monroe, et al. *Freedom and Control in Modern Society*. New York: Octagon Books, 1964.

Berger, Peter L. *The Sacred Canopy: Elements of a Sociological Theory of Religion*. New York: Anchor Books, 1967.

Berger, Peter L. and Thomas Luckemann. *The Social Construct of Reality*. New York: Doubleday, 1966.

Bernard, H. Russell. *Research Methods in Anthropology: Qualitative and Quantitative Approaches*. 2d ed. Walnut Creek: AltaMira Press, 1995.

Bernard, Jessie. *The Future of Marriage*. 2d ed. New Haven: Yale University Press, 1982.

Berryman, Sue E. *Who Serves? The Persistent Myth of the Underclass Army*. Boulder, CO: Westview Press, 1988.

Best, Joel. *Images of Issues: Typifying Contemporary Social Problems*. New York: Aldine De Gruyter, 1995.

Black, Henry Campbell. *Black's Law Dictionary*. 6th ed. St. Paul: West Publishing Company, 1991.

Blake, Lord and C. K. Nicholls, eds. *The Dictionary of*

National Biography: 1971–1980. Oxford: Oxford University Press, 1986.

Blanchard, Dallas. *The Anti-Abortion Movement and the Rise of the Religious Right: From Polite to Fiery Protest*. New York: Twayne Publishers, 1994.

Blau, Peter M. and Otis Dudley Duncan. *The American Occupational Structure*. New York: John Wiley & Sons, 1967.

Blaug, Martin, ed. *Great Economists Since Keynes*. Brighton: Wheatsheaf Books, 1985.

———. *Who's Who in Economics: A Biographical Dictionary of Major Economists 1700–1986*. Cambridge: MIT Press, 1986.

Blume, Stuart S., ed. *Perspectives in the Sociology of Science*. Chichester: John Wiley and Sons, 1977.

Blumer, Herbert. *Symbolic Interactionism: Perspective and Method*. Englewood Cliffs, NJ: Prentice-Hall, Inc., 1969.

Blumstein, Philip and Pepper Schwartz. *American Couples: Money, Work, Sex*. New York: William Morrow and Company. Inc., 1983.

Bognanno, Mario F. and Kathryn J. Ready, eds. *The North American Free Trade Agreement: Labor, Industry, and Government Perspectives*. Westport, CT: Quorum Books, 1993.

Bohannan, Paul and Philip Curtin. *Africa and Africans*. 4th ed. Prospect Heights, IL: Waveland Press, 1995.

Bohrnstedt, George W. and David Knoke. *Statistics for Social Data Analysis*. 3rd ed. Itasca, IL: F. E. Peacock Publishers Inc., 1994.

Borgatta, Edgar F. and Marie L. Borgatta, eds. *Encyclopedia of Sociology*. New York: Macmillan, 1992.

Bornstein, Kate. *Gender Outlaw: On Men, Women, and the Rest of Us*. New York: Routledge, 1994.

Botwinick, Jack. *Aging and Behavior*. 3rd ed. New York: Springer Publishing Company, 1984.

Boucher, Jerry, Dan Landis, and Karen Arnold Clark, eds. *Ethnic Conflict: International Perspectives*. Newbury Park: Sage Publications, 1987.

Boudon, Raymond and Francois Bourricaud. *A Critical Dictionary of Sociology*. Translated by Peter Hamilton. Chicago: University of Chicago Press, 1989.

Bourdieu, Pierre. *Distinction*. Translated by Richard Nice. Cambridge: Harvard University Press, 1984.

Bourdieu, Pierre and Loc J. D. Wacquant. *An Invitation to Reflexive Sociology*. Chicago: University of Chicago Press, 1992.

Bowles, Samuel and Herbert Gintis. *Schooling in Capitalist America: Educational Reform and the Contradictions of Economic Life*. New York: Basic Books, 1976.

Bowling, Ann. *Measuring Health: A Review of Quality of Life Measurement Scales.* Bristol, PA: Open University Press, 1997.

Bowman, John S., ed. *The Cambridge Dictionary of American Biography.* Cambridge: Cambridge University Press, 1995.

Bravmann, Scott. "Postmodernism and Queer Identity." In *Queer Theory/Sociology.* Edited by S. Siedman. London: Blackwell, 1996.

Braverman, Harry. *Labor and Monopoly Capital: The Degradation of Work in the Twentieth Century.* New York: Monthly Review Press, 1974.

Breuilly, John. *Nationalism and the State.* New York: St. Martin's Press, 1982.

Broom, Leonard. "Social Differences in Stratification." In *Sociology Today: Problems and Prospects.* Edited by Robert K. Merton, Leonard Broom, and Leonard S. Cottrell, Jr. New York: Basic Books, 1959.

Brown, A. Lee, Jr. *Rules and Conflict: An Introduction to Political Life and Its Study.* Englewood Cliffs, NJ: Prentice-Hall, Inc., 1981.

Brown, Stephen E., Finn-Aage Esbensen, and Gilbert Geis. *Criminology: Explaining Crime and Its Context.* 2d ed. Cincinnati: Anderson Publishing Company, 1996.

Brubaker, Rogers. *The Limits of Rationality: An Essay on the Social and Moral Thought of Max Weber.* New York: Routledge, 1984.

Brunn, S. D. and K. A. Mingst. "Geopolitics." In *Progress in Political Geography.* Edited by Michael Pacione. London: Croom Helm, 1985.

Bryfronski, Dedria and Robert L. Brubaker, eds. *Contemporary Issues Criticism.* Detroit: Gale Research, 1983.

Bryk, T. and Stephen Raudenbush. *Hierarchal Linear Models: Application and Data Analysis Methods.* Newbury Park, CA: Sage Publications, 1992.

Buhle, Mari Jo, Paul Buhle, and Dan Georgakas, eds. *Encyclopedia of the American Left.* New York: Oxford University Press, 1998.

Bulato, R.A. and R. D. Lee. "A Framework For The Study of Fertility Determinants." In *Determinants of Fertility Decline in Developing Countries.* Edited by R.A. Bulato. New York: Academic Press, 1983.

Bunton, R. S. Needleton, and R. Burrows, eds. *The Sociology of Health Promotion: Critical Analyses of Consumption, Lifestyle, and Risk.* New York: Routledge, 1995.

Burgess, Ernest W., Robert E. Park, and Roderick D. McKenzie. *The City.* Chicago: University of Chicago Press, 1967.

Burn, Shawn Meghan. *Women Across Cultures: A Global Perspective.* London: Mayfield Publishing Company, 2000.

Burston, W. H. *James Mill on Philosophy and Education.* London: Athlone Press, 1973.

Cain, Maureen and Alan Hunt. *Marx and Engels on Law.* New York: Academic Press, 1979.

Califia, Pat. *Public Sex: The Culture of Radical Sex.* San Francisco: Cleis Press, 1994.

———. *Sex Changes: The Politics of Transgenderism.* San Francisco: Cleis Press, 1997.

Campbell, A. *The Sense of Well-Being in America: Recent Patterns and Trends.* New York: McGraw-Hill, 1981.

Cardoso, Fernando Herique and Enzo Faletto. *Dependency and Development in Latin America.* Translated by Marjory Mattingly Urquidi. Berkeley: University of California Press, 1979.

Carmins, Edward G. and Richard A. Zeller. *Reliability and Validity Assessment.* Newbury Park: Sage Publications, 1979.

Cashmore, Ellis and Chris Rojek, eds. *Dictionary of Cultural Theorists.* London: Edward Arnold Publishers, 1999.

Castells, Manuel. *The Urban Question: A Marxist Approach.* Translated by Alan Sheridan. London: Edward Arnold, 1977.

Castells, Manuel, Alejandro Portes, and Lauren A. Benton. "World Underneath: The Origins, Dynamics, and Effects of the Informal Economy." In *The Informalized Economy: Studies in Advanced and Less Developed Countries.* Baltimore: Johns Hopkins University Press, 1989.

Cayton, Horace R. and St. Clair Drake. *Black Metropolis.* London: Jonathan Cape, 1946.

Cayton, Mary Kupiec, Elliot J. Gorn, and Peter W. Williams, eds. *Encyclopedia of American Social History.* New York: Charles Scribner's Sons, 1993.

Chancer, Lynn S. *Reconcilable Differences: Confronting Beauty, Pornography, and the Future of Feminism.* Berkeley: University of California Press, 1998.

Chapkis, Wendy. *Live Sex Acts: Women Performing Erotic Labor.* New York: Routldege, 1997.

Charnon, Joel M. *Symbolic Interactionism: An Introduction, An Interpretation, An Integration,* 5th ed. Englewood Cliffs, NJ: Prentice Hall, 1995.

Chodorow, Nancy J. *The Reproduction of Mothering.* Berkeley: University of California Press, 1978.

Choudhury, Masadul A. *Studies in Islamic Social Sciences.* New York: St, Martin's Press, 1998.

Christian, Charles M. *Black Saga: The African American Experience.* Boston: Houghton Mifflin Company, 1995.

Coates, Charles H. and Roland J. Pellegrin. *Military Sociology: A Study of American Military Institutions and Military Life*. University Park, MD: Social Science Press, 1965.

Cockerham, William C. *This Aging Society*. 2d ed. Upper Saddle River, NJ: Prentice Hall, 1997.

———. *Medical Sociology*. 7th ed. Upper Saddle River, NJ: Prentice Hall, 1998.

Coe, R. *Sociology and Medicine*. 2d ed. New York: McGraw-Hill, 1978.

Cohen, Marcia. *The Sisterhood*. New York: Fawcett Columbine, 1988.

Coleman, James S. *Foundations of Social Theory*. Cambridge: Harvard University Press, 1990.

———. *Longitudinal Data Analysis*. New York: Basic Books, Inc., Publishers, 1981.

Coleman, James William and Donald R. Cressey. *Social Problems*. 7th New York: Longman, 1999.

Colfax, J. David and Jack L. Roach, eds. *Radical Sociology*. London: Basic Books, Inc.,

Collins, Patricia Hill. *Black Feminist Thought: Knowledge, Consciousness, and the Politics of Empowerment*. Rev. ed. New York: Routledge, 2000.

Collins, Randall. *The Credential Society: An Historical Sociology of Education and Stratification*. Orlando: Academic Press, Inc., 1978.

———. *Theoretical Sociology*. San Diego: Harcourt Brace Jovanovich, Publishers, 1988.

———. *Three Sociological Traditions*. New York: Oxford University Press, 1985.

Comstock, Gary. *Violence Against Lesbians and Gay Men*. New York: Columbia University Press, 1991.

Conley, Dalton. *Being Black, Living in the Red*. Berkeley: University of California Press, 1999.

Connell, R.W. *Gender and Power: Society, the Person, and Sexual Politics*. Stanford: Stanford University Press, 1987.

Conrad, Peter and Joseph W. Schneider. *Deviance and Medicalization: From Badness to Sickness*. St. Louis: C.V. Mosby Company, 1980.

Constantine, Larry L. and Joan M. *Group Marriage: A Study of Contemporary Multilateral Marriage*. New York: Macmillan Company, 1973.

Cook, Karen S., ed. *Social Exchange Theory*. Newbury Park: Sage Publications, 1987.

Cook, Karen S., Gary Alan Fine, and James E. House, eds. *Sociological Perspectives on Social Psychology*. Boston: Allyn and Bacon, 1995.

Cook, Richard I. *Bernard Mandeville*. New York: Twayne Publishers, Inc.,

Cooley, Charles Horton. *Human Nature and the Social Order*. Rev. ed. New York: Charles Scribner's Sons, 1922. 1974.

———. *Social Organization: A Study of the Larger Mind*. New York: Schocken Books, 1962.

Contemporary Authors. Detroit: Gale Research, 1994.

Coser, Lewis A. *Masters of Sociological Thought: Ideas in Historical and Social Context*, 2d ed. Fort Worth: Harcourt Brace Jovanovich College Publishers, 1977.

Coupland, Nikolas and Adam Jaworski. *Sociolinguistics: A Reader*. New York: St. Martin's Press, 1997.

Cox, Steven M. *Police: Practices, Perspectives, Problems*. Boston: Allyn and Bacon, 1996.

Craib, Ian. *Modern Social Theory: From Parsons to Habermas*. New York: St. Martin's Press, 1984.

Craig, Edward, ed. *Routledge Encyclopedia of Philosophy*. London: Routledge, 1998.

Crook, Stephen. *Moderist Radicalism and Its Aftermath: Foundationalism and Anti-Foundationalim in Radical Social Theory*. London: Routledge, 1991.

Crooks, Robert and Karla Bauer. *Our Sexuality*. 7th ed. Pacific Grove: Brooks/Cole Publishing, 1999.

Critchlow, Donald T. *Intended Consequences: Birth Control, Abortion, and the Federal Government in Modern American*. New York: Oxford University Press, 1999.

Croteau, David and William Hoynes. *By Invitation Only: How the Media Limit Political Debate*. Monroe, ME: Common Courage Press, 1994.

Crystal, David. *The Cambridge Biographical Encyclopedia*. Cambridge: Cambridge University Press, 1994.

Cullen-DuPont, Kathryn. *The Encyclopedia of Women's History in America*. New York: Facts on File, Inc., 1996.

Curry, Tim, Robert Jiobu, and Kent Schwirian. *Sociology for the Twenty-First Century*. 2d ed. Upper Saddle River, NJ: Prentice Hall, 1999.

Czaja, Ronald and Johnny Blair. *Designing Surveys: A Guide to Decisions and Procedures*. Thousand Oaks, CA: Pine Forge Press, 1996.

Dahbour, Omar and Micheline R. Ishay, eds. *The Nationalism Reader*. New Jersey: Humanities Press, 1995.

Dahl, Robert A. *Who Governs? Democracy and Power in an American City*. New Haven: Yale University Press, 1961.

Dahrendorf, Ralf. *Class and Class Conflict in Industrial Society*. Stanford: Stanford University Press, 1959.

Daleiden. Joseph L. *The Science of Morality*. Amherst, NY: Prometheus Books, 1998.

Dandeker, Christopher, ed. *Nationalism and Violence* New Brunswick: Transaction Publishers, 1998.

Davies, Norman. *Europe: A History.* Oxford: Oxford University Press, 1996.

Davis, Lennard J. *Enforcing Normalcy: Disability, Deafness, and the Body.* New York: Verso, 1995.

Davis, Mike. *Ecology of Fear: Los Angeles and the Imagination of Disaster.* New York: Henry Holt and Company, Inc., 1998.

Deegan, Mary Jo. *Jane Addams and the Men of the Chicago School, 1895–1918.* New Brunswick: Transaction Books, 1988.

Delacoste, Frederique and Priscilla Alexander, eds. *Sex Work: Writings by Women in the Sex Industry.* San Francisco: Cleis Press, 1987.

Delgado, Richard and Jean Stefancic, eds. *Critical White Studies: Looking Behind the Mirror.* Philadelphia: Temple University Press, 1997.

Deloria, Vine. *Custer Died for Our Sins: An Indian Manifesto.* Norman: University of Oklahoma Press, 1988.

D'Emilio, John. *Sexual Politics, Sexual Communities: The Making of a Gay and Lesbian Movement.* Chicago: University of Chicago Press, 1983.

Denzin, Norman and Yvonne Lincoln. *The Landscape of Qualitative Research: Theories and Issues.* Thousand Oaks: Sage Publications, 1998.

Diamond, Irene and Gloria Femand Orenstein, eds. *Reweaving the World: The Emergence of Ecofeminism.* San Francisco: Sierra Club Books, 1990.

DiCanio, Margaret. *The Encyclopedia of Marriage, Divorce, and the Family.* New York: Facts on File, 1989.

Dillman, Don L. *Mail and Telephone Surveys: The Total Design Method.* New York: John Wiley and Sons, 1978.

D'Lange, N. R. M. *Judaism.* Oxford: Oxford University Press, 1986.

Docter, Richard F. *Transvestites and Transsexuals: Toward a Theory of Cross-Gender Behavior.* New York: Plenum Press, 1988.

Donahue, John D. *The Privatization Decision: Public Ends, Private Means.* New York: Basic Books, 1989.

Donaldson, S. *Fertility Transition: The Social Dynamics of Population Change.* Cambridge: Basil Blackwell, 1991.

Donnelly, Dorothy. *Patterns of Order and Utopia.* New York: St. Martin's Press, 1998.

Doob, Christopher Bates. *Sociology: An Introduction.* 6th ed. Fort Worth: The Harcourt Press, 2000.

Dougherty, James E. and Robert L. Pfaltzgraff, Jr. *Contending Theories of International Relations.* Philadelphia: J.B. Lippincott Company, 1971.

Douglas, Jack D. *The Social Meanings of Suicide.* Princeton: Princeton University Press, 1967.

Douglas, Jack D. and John M. Johnson. *Existential Sociology.* Cambridge: Cambridge University Press, 1977.

Downie, R., C. Tannahill, and A. Tannahill. *Health Promotion: Models and Values.* 2d ed. New York: Oxford University Press, 1996.

Drabble, Margaret, ed. *The Oxford Companion to English Literature.* Oxford: Oxford University Press, 1995.

Dryden, Caroline. *Being Married, Doing Gender: A Critical Analysis of Gender Relationships in Marriage.* London: Routledge, 1999.

Duff, Raymond and August B. Hollingshead. *Sickness and Society.* New York: Harper and Row, 1968.

Duncan, Otis Dudley. *Notes on Social Measurement: Historical and Critical.* New York: Russell Sage Foundation, 1984.

Duneier, Mitchell. *Introduction to Sociology.* 3rd ed. New York: W. W. Norton and Company, Inc., 2000.

Dunlap, John, et al. *Industrialism and Industrial Man Reconsidered: Some Perspectives on a Study Over Two Decades of the Problems of Labor and Management in Economic Growth.* Princeton, NJ: The Inter-University Study of Human Resources in National Development, 1975.

Dunlap, Riley E. and Angela G. Mertig. *American Environmentalism.* Philadelphia: Taylor and Francis, 1992.

Dunn, Dana and David V. Waller, eds. *Analyzing Social Problems: Essays and Exercises.* Upper Saddle River, NJ: Prentice Hall, 1997.

Durkheim, Émile. *The Division of Labor in Society.* New York: Free Press, 1984.

——. *The Elementary Forms of Religious Life.* Translated by Joseph Ward Swain. New York: Free Press, 1915.

——. *Essays on Morals and Education.* Edited by W. S. F. Pickering. London: Routledge & Kegan Paul, 1979.

——. *The Rules of Sociological Method.* Edited by Steven Lukes and translated by W.D. Halls. New York: Free Press, 1982.

——. *Suicide: A Study in Sociology.* Edited by George Simpson. Translated by John A. Spaulding and George Simpson. New York: Free Press, 1951.

Dynes, Russell R., et al. *Social Problems: Dissensus and Deviation in An Industrial Society.* New York: Oxford University Press, 1964.

Easton, Susan M. *The Problem of Pornography: Regulation and the Right to Free Speech.* London: Routledge, 1994.

Edwards, Ruth Dudley, ed. *The Best of Bagehot*. London: Hamish Hamilton, 1993.

Einstadter, Werner and Stuart Henry. *Criminological Theory: An Analysis of Its Underlying Assumptions*. Fort Worth: Harcourt Brace College Publishers, 1995.

Eitzen, D. Stanley and Maxine Baca Zinn. *In Conflict and Order: Understanding Society*. 8th ed. Boston: Allyn and Bacon, 1998.

Ekins, Richard. *Male Femaling: A Grounded Theory Approach to Cross-Dressing and Sex-Changing*. London: Routledge, 1997.

Elder, Glen H., Jr. *Children of the Great Depression: Social Changes in Life Experience*. Chicago: University of Chicago Press, 1974.

Elliot, Anthony, ed. *The Blackwell Reader in Contemporary Social Theory*. Oxford: Blackwell Publishers, Ltd., 1999.

Elliot, Robert. *The Shape of Utopia: Studies in a Literary Genre*. Chicago: University of Chicago Press, 1970.

Ellis, Lee and Anthony Walsh. *Criminology: A Global Perspective*. Boston: Allyn and Bacon, 2000.

Elrod, Preston and R. Scott Ryder. *Juvenile Justice: A Social, Historical, and Legal Perspective*. Gaithersburg, MD: Aspen Publishers, Inc., 1999.

Emprey, LaMar T., Mark C. Stafford, and Carter H. Hay. *American Delinquency: Its Meaning and Construction*. Belmont: Wadsworth Publishing Company, 1999.

Encyclopedia of Sociology. Guilford, CN: The Duskin Publishing Group, Inc., 1974.

Epenshade, T.J and G.A. Huber. "Fiscal Impacts of Immigrants and The Shrinking Welfare State." In *The Handbook of International Migration: The American Experience*. Edited by C. Hirschmand, P. Kasinitz, and J. DeWind. New York: Russell Sage Foundation, 1999.

Epstein, Isidore. *Judaism: A Historical Presentation*. Baltimore: Penguin, 1959.

Eshleman, Ross J. *The Family*. 9th ed. Needham Heights, MA: Allyn and Bacon, 2000.

Eshleman, Ross J., Barbara G. Cashion, and Lawrene A. Basirico. *Sociology: An Introduction*. 4th ed. New York: Harper Collins College Publishers, 1993.

Esler, Philip F. *The First Christians in Their Social Worlds: Social-Scientific Approaches to New Testament Interpretation*. London: Routledge, 1994.

Espisito, John. *The Straight Path*. 3rd ed. New York: Oxford University Press, 1998.

Espriritu, Yen Le. *Asian American Women and Men: Labor, Laws, and Love*. Thousand Oaks, CA: Sage Publications, 1997.

Essential Schopenhauer. London: George Allen and Unwin Ltd., 1962.

Etzioni, Amitai. *The Moral Dimension: Toward New Economics*. New York: Free Press, 1988.

———. *The New Golden Rule: Community and Morality in a Democratic Society*. New York: Basic Books, 1996.

———. *The Spirit of Community: The Reinvention of American Society*. New York: Touchstone, 1993.

Etzioni, Amitai and Paul R. Lawrence, eds. *Socio-economics: Toward a New Synthesis*. Armonk, NY: M. E. Sharpe, Inc., 1991.

Eulau, Heinz and James G. March, eds. *Political Science*. Englewood Cliffs, NJ: Prentice-Hall, Inc., 1969.

The Europa World Year Book 1999. London: Europa Publications Limited, 1999.

Evans, Peter. *Embedded Autonomy: States and Industrial Transformation*. Princeton: Princeton University Press, 1995.

Evans, Sara M. *Born for Liberty: A History of American Women in America*. New York: Free Press, 1989.

———. *Personal Politics: The Roots of Women's Liberation in the Civil Rights Movement and the New Left*. New York: Vintage Books, 1979.

Fackenheim, Emil. *What is Judaism: An Interpretation for the Present Age*. New York: Summit Books, 1987.

Faghirzadeh, Saleh. *Sociology of Sociology: In Search of Khaldun's Sociology, Then and Now*. Tehran: Soroush Press, 1982.

Fanon, Frantz. *The Wretched of the Earth*. Translated by Constance Farrington. New York: Grove Press, 1963.

Feagin, Joe R. and Clairece Booher Feagin. *Racial and Ethnic Relations*. 6th ed. Upper Saddle River, NJ: Prentice Hall, 1999.

———. *Social Problem: A Critical Power-Conflict Perspective*. 5th ed. Upper Saddle River, NJ: Prentice Hall, 1997.

Feinberg, Leslie. *Transgender Warriors: Making History from Joan of Arc to RuPaul*. Boston: Beacon Press, 1996.

Feldman, Shelley and Eveline Ferretti, eds. *Informal Work and Social Change: A Bibliographic Survey*. Ithaca, New York: Cornell University Press, 1998.

Fenwick, Lynda Beck. *Should the Children Pray? A Historical, Judicial, and Political Examination of Public School Prayer*. Waco, TX: Markhan Press Fund, 1989.

Ferguson, Susan J. *Mapping the Social Landscape: Readings in Sociology*. Mountain View, CA: Mayfield Publishing Company, 1996.

———. *Shifting the Center: Understanding Contemporary Families*. Mountain View, CA: Mayfield Publishing, 1998.

Fernald, J.L. "Interpersonal Heterosexism." In *The Social Psychology of Interpersonal Discrimination*. Edited by B.

Lott and D.Maluso. New York: Guilford Press, 1995.

Ferrante, Joan. *Sociology: A Global Perspective.* Belmont, CA: Wadsworth Publishing Company, 1992.

Ferree, Myra Marx and Beth B. Hess. *Analyzing Gender: A Handbook of Social Science Research.* Newbury Park: Sage Publications, 1987.

Ferree, Myra Marx and Beth B. Hess, eds. *Controversy and Coalition: The New Feminist Movement Across Three Decades of Change.* New York: Twayne Publishers, 1994.

Fieldhouse, D. K. *Colonialism, 1870–1945: An Introduction.* New York: St. Martin's Press, 1981.

Fine, Gary Alan, ed. *A Second Chicago School?* Chicago: University of Chicago Press, 1995.

Forisha-Kovach, Barbara. *The Experience of Adolescence: Development in Context.* Glenview, IL: Scott, Foresman and Company, 1983.

Fortes, Meyer. *Kinship and Social Order: The Legacy of Lewis Henry Morgan.* Chicago: Aldine Publishing Company, 1970.

Foster, Mary LeCron and Robert A. Rubinstein, eds. *Peace and War: Cross-Cultural Perspectives.* New Brunswick: Transaction Books, 1986.

Fox, Karl A. *Social Indicators and Social Theory.* New York: John Wiley and Sons, 1974.

Fox, R. *The Sociology of Medicine: A Participant Observer's View.* Englewood Cliffs, NJ: Prentice-Hall, 1989.

Frank, Andre Gunder. *Capitalism and Development in Latin America: Historical Studies of Chile and Brazil.* New York: Monthly Review Press, 1967.

Frank, Irene and David Brownstone. *The Women's Desk Reference.* New York: Viking, 1993.

Fraser, James. *Between Church and State.* New York: St. Martin's Press, 1999.

———. "Developing Definitions of an Adoptee-Birthmother Reunion Relationship." In *Families and Adoption.* Edited by Harriet E. Gross and Marvin B. Sussman. New York: The Haworth Press, Inc., 1997.

Freud, Sigmund. *Introductory Lectures on Psycho-Analysis.* New York: W. W. Norton and Co., 1966.

———. *Totem and Taboo.* Translated by J. Strachey. New York: Norton, 1950.

Freudenheim, Ellen. *Healthspeak: A Complete Dictionary of America's Health Care System.* New York: Facts on File, Inc., 1996.

Freund, Peter E. S. and Meredith B. McGuire. *Health, Illness, and the Social Body: A Critical Sociology.* 2d ed. Englewood Cliffs: Prentice-Hall, 1995.

Friedberg, J. W., ed. *Critical Sociology: European Perspectives.* New York: Irvington Publishers, Inc., 1979.

Friedman, Myles I. *Improving the Quality of Life: A Holistic Scientific Strategy.* Westport, CT: Praeger, 1997.

Fritz, Jan M. "The Contributions of Clinical Sociology in Health Care Settings." In *Sociological Practice.* Edited by Elizabeth J. Clark and Jan M. Frtiz. Lansing: Michigan State University Press, 1991.

Frost-Knappman, Elizabeth. *Women's Progress in America.* Santa Barbara, CA: ABC-CLIO, 1994.

Fulton, Robert, et al, eds. *Death and Dying: Challenge and Change.* Reading, MA: Addison-Wesley Publishing Company, 1978.

Gaines, Larry K., Victor E. Kappeler, and Joseph B. Vaughn. *Policing in America.* 3rd ed. Cincinnati: Anderson Publishing Company, 1999.

Galston, William A. *Justice and the Human Good.* Chicago: University of Chicago Press, 1980.

———. *Liberal Purposes: Goods, Virtues, and Diversity in the Liberal State.* Cambridge: Cambridge University Press, 1991.

Galstung, Johan. *Peace By Peaceful Means: Peace and Conflict, Development and Civilization.* London: Sage Publications, 1996.

Galton, Francis. *Inquiries Into Human Faculty.* London: Macmillan and Company, 1883.

Gamson, Joshua. "Must Identity Movements Self-Destruct: A Queer Dilemma." In *Social Perspectives in Lesbian and Gay Studies: A Reader.* Edited by P. Nardi and B. Schnieder. New York: Routledge, 1998.

Gardner, Howard. *Frames of Mind: The Theory of Multiple Intelligences.* New York: Basic Books, Inc., Publishers, 1983.

Garfinkel, Harold. *Studies in Ethnomethodology.* Englewood Cliffs, NJ: Prentice Hall, 1967.

Garfinkel, Irwin et al, eds. *Fathers Under Fire: The Revolution in Child Support Enforcement.* New York: Russell Sage Foundation, 1998.

Garms-Homolova, Erika M. Hoerning, and Doris Schaeffer, eds. *Intergenerational Relationships.* Lewiston, NY: C. J. Hogrefe, Inc., 1984.

Garraty, John A., ed. *Encyclopedia of American Biography.* New York: Harper & Row, Publishers, 1974.

Garreau, Joel. *Edge City: Life on the New Frontier.* New York: Anchor Books, 1991.

Gates, E. Nathaniel. *Critical Race Theory: Essays on the Social Construction and Reproduction of "Race."* New York: Garland Publishing, Inc., 1997.

Gaventa, John. *Power and Powerlessness.* Urbana, IL: University of Illinois Press, 1980.

Gelles, Richard J. and Anne Levine. *Sociology: An Introduction.* 6th ed. Boston: McGraw-Hill, 1999.

Gellner, Ernest. *Nations and Nationalism*. Oxford: Basil Blackwell Publisher, Ltd., 1983.

Gerhardt, Uta, ed. *German Sociology*. New York: Continuum, 1998.

Gerth, H. H. and C. Wright Mills, eds. *From Max Weber: Essays on Sociology*. Translated by Thomas McCarthy. New York: Oxford University Press, 1946.

Geschwender, James A., ed. *The Black Revolt: The Civil Rights Movement, Ghetto Uprisings, and Separatism*. Englewood Cliffs, NJ: Prentice-Hall, 1971.

Gibb, Hamilton A. R. *Mohammedanism: An Historical Survey*. London: Oxford University Press, 1969.

Giddens, Anthony. *Central Problems of Social Theory: Action, Structure, and Contradiction in Social Analysis*. London: Macmillan Press, 1979.

Giddens, Anthony, ed. and trans. *Émile Durkheim: Selected Writings*. Cambridge: Cambridge University Press, 1972.

Giddens, Anthony and Mithchell Duneier. *Introduction to Sociology*. 3rd ed. New York: W. W. Norton and Company, Inc., 2000.

Gilbert, Margaret. *Living Together: Rationality, Sociality, and Obligation*. Lanham, MD: Rowman and Littlefield Publishers, Inc., 1996.

Gilligan, Carol. *In a Different Voice: Psychological Theory and Women's Development*. Cambridge: Harvard University Press, 1982.

Gillispie, Charles Coulston, ed. *Dictionary of Scientific Biography*. New York: Charles Scribner's Sons, 1972.

Gilpin, Robert. *War and Change in World Politics*. Cambridge: Cambridge University Press, 1981.

Glazer, Nathan. *Affirmative Discrimination: Ethnic Inequality and Public Policy*. New York: Basic Books Inc., 1975.

———. "From Socialism to Sociology." In *Authors of Their Own Lives: Intellectual Autobiographies By Twenty American Sociologists*. Edited by Bennett M. Berger. Berkeley: University of California Press, 1990.

Glendon, Mary Ann. *Rights Talk: The Impoverishment of Political Discourse*. New York: The Free Press, 1991.

Goffman, Erving. *Asylums*. Garden City, NY: Anchor Books, 1961.

———. *Interaction Ritual: Essays on Face-to-Face Behavior*. Garden City, NY: Anchor Books, 1967.

———. *The Presentation of Self in Everyday Life*. Edinburgh: University of Edinburgh, 1956.

Golla, Victor, ed. *The Sapir-Kroeber Correspondence: Letter Between Edward Sapir and A. L. Kroeber, 1905–1925*. Berkeley: University of California, 1984.

Goode, William J. *The Family*. Englewood Cliffs, NJ: Prentice-Hall, Inc., 1964.

Goodman, Norman. *Introduction to Sociology*. New York: Harper Collins, 1992.

Gordon, Linda. *Women's Body, Women's Right: A Sociological History of Birth Control in America*. New York: Viking, 1976.

Gordon, Milton M. *Assimilation in American Life: The Role of Race, Religion, and National Origins*. New York: Oxford University Press, 1964.

———. *Social Class in American Sociology*. Durham, NC: Duke University Press, 1958.

Gottwald, Norman K. *The Tribes of Yahweh: A Sociology of the Religion of Liberated Israel, 1250–1050 B.C.* Maryknoll, New York: Orbis Books, 1979.

Gould, Julius and William L. Kolb, eds. *A Dictionary of the Social Sciences*. New York: Free Press, 1964.

Gramsci, Antonio. *Selections from the Prison Notebooks*. Edited and translated by Quintin Hoare and Geoffrey Nowell Smith. New York: International Publishers, 1971.

Grant, Carl A. and Gloria Ladson-Billings, eds. *Dictionary of Multicultural Education*. Phoenix, AZ: Oryx Press, 1997.

Green, Rayna, ed. *That's What She Said: Contemporary Poetry and Fiction by Native North American Women*. Bloomington: Indiana University Press, 1984.

———. *Women in American Indian Society*. New York: Chelsea House Publishers, 1992.

Griffin, Em. *A First Look at Communication Theory*. 4th ed. Boston: McGraw Hill, 2000.

Gross, Leonard, ed. *Sexual Issues in Marriage: A Contemporary Perspective*. New York: Spectrum Publications, Inc., 1971.

Grunsky, David B., ed. *Social Stratification: Class, Race, and Gender in Sociological Perspective*. Boulder, CO: Westview Press, 1994.

Gubrium, Jaber F. and James A. Holstein. *The New Language of Qualitative Method*. New York: Oxford University Press, 1997.

Gujarati, Damodar. *Essentials of Econometrics*. 2d ed. Boston: McGraw-Hill, 1999.

Gusfield, Joseph R. *Community: A Critical Response*. New York: Harper and Row, 1975.

Habermas, Jürgen. *Communication and the Evolution of Society*, Translated by Thomas McCarthy. Boston: Beacon Press, 1979.

———. *Legitimation Crisis*. Boston: Beacon Press, 1975.

———. *The Structural Transformation of the Public Sphere: An Inquiry into a Category of Bourgeois Society*. Translated by Thomas Berger and Frederick Lawrence. Cambridge: Massachusetts Institute of Technology Press, 1989.

————. *The Theory of Communicative Action*. In *Lifeworld and System: A Critique of Functionalist Reason*. Vol. 2. Translated by Thomas McCarthy. Boston: Beacon Press, 1987.

Haddad, Yvonne. *Contemporary Islam and the Challenge of History*. Albany: SUNY Press, 1981.

Haller, Mark. *Eugenics: Hereditarian Attitudes in American Thought*. New Brunswick, NJ: Rutgers University Press, 1963.

Harrington, Michael. *Socialism*. New York: Saturday Review Press, 1970.

Harris, Leonard, ed. *Racism*. Amherst, NY: Humanity Books, 1999.

Hartmann, Betsy. *Reproductive Rights and Wrongs: The Global Politics of Population Control*. Boston: South End Press, 1995.

Harvey, Sir Paul and J. E. Heseltine, eds. *The Oxford Companion to French Literature*. Oxford: Clarendon Press, 1959.

Hauser, P.M. and O.D. Duncan. *The Study of Population: An Inventory and Appraisal*. Chicago: University of Chicago Press, 1959.

Healey, Joseph F. *Statistics: A Tool for Social Research*. 5th ed. Belmont, CA: Wadsworth Publishing Company, 1999.

Health Policy Tracking Service. *Major State Health Care Policies: Fifty State Profiles, 1997*. Washington, D.C.: Health Policy Tracking Service, 1998.

Hedrick, Terry E., Leonard Bickman, and Debra J. Rog. *Applied Research Design: A Practical Guide*. Newbury Park: Sage Publications, 1993.

Hennekens, Charles H. and Julie E. Burning. *Epidemiology in Medicine*. Boston: Little, Brown, and Company. 1987.

Henslin, James M. *Social Problems*. 5th ed. Upper Saddle River, NJ: Prentice Hall, 2000.

————. *Sociology: A Down-to-Earth Approach*. 4th ed. Boston: Allyn and Bacon, 1999.

Herbert, Melissa S. *Camouflage Isn't Only for Combat: Gender, Sexuality, and Women in the Military*. New York: New York University Press, 1998.

Herek, Gregory M. "Beyond Homophobia: A Social Psychological Perspective on Attitudes toward Lesbians and Gay Men." In *Homophobia: An Overview*. Edited by J. DeCecco. New York: Haworth, 1984.

Hewitt, John P. *Self and Society: A Symbolic Interactionist Social Psychology*. 8th ed. Boston: Allyn and Bacon, 2000.

Hickman, Edgar P. and James G. Hilton. *Probability and Statistical Analysis*. Scranton: Intext Educational Publishers, 1971.

Hochschild, Arlie. *The Second Shift*. New York: Avon Books, 1989.

Hoinville, Gerald and Roger Jowell. *Survey Research Practice*. London: Heinemann Educational Books, 1977.

Holland, Dorothy and Margaret Eisenhart. *Educated in Romance: Women, Achievement, and College Culture*. Chicago: University of Chicago Press, 1990.

Hollander, Edwin P. and Raymond G. Hunt, eds. *Current Perspectives in Social Psychology*. New York: Oxford University Press, 1967.

Homans, G. C. *Social Behavior: Its Elementary Forms*. New York: Harcourt Brace and World, 1961.

Honderich, Ted, ed. *The Oxford Companion to Philosophy*. Oxford: Oxford University Press, 1995.

Honneth, Axel. "Critical Theory." In *Social Theory Today*. Edited by Anthony Giddens and Jonathan H. Turner. Stanford: Stanford University Press, 1987.

Hoover, Kenneth and Todd Donovan. *The Elements of Social Scientific Thinking*. 6th ed. New York: St. Martin's Press, 1995.

Horkheimer, Max. *Eclipse of Reason*. New York: Continuum, 1947.

————. *Critical Theory: Selected Essays*. Translated by Matthew J. O'Connell, et al. New York: Herder and Herder, 1972.

————. *Critique of Instrumental Reason*. New York: Continuum, 1974.

Horkheimer, Max and Theodor W. Adorno. *Dialectic of Enlightenment*. Translated by John Cumming. New York: Continuum, 1993.

Horn, Robert V. *Statistical Indicators for the Economic Social Sciences*. Cambridge: Cambridge University Press, 1993.

Horowitz, Irving Louis. *Ideology and Utopia in the United States: 1956–1976*. New York: Oxford University, 1977.

————. *Taking Lives: Genocide and State Power*. 3rd ed. New Bruswick: Transaction Publishers, 1980.

Horowitz, Irving Louis and Mary Symons Strong, eds. *Sociological Realities: A Guide to the Study of Society*. New York: Harper and Row, Publishers, 1971.

Hoselitz, Bert F. *Sociological Aspects of Economic Growth*. New York: Free Press of Glencoe, 1960.

Hughes, John A, Peter J. Martin, and W. W. Sharock. *Understanding Classical Sociology: Marx, Weber, Durkheim*. London: Sage Publications, 1995.

Hughest, Henry Stuart. *Oswald Spengler: A Critical Estimate*. New York: Scribner, 1952.

Hughey, Michael W. *Civil Religion and Moral Order: Theoretical and Historical Dimensions*. Westport, CT: Greenwood Press, 1983.

Hunt, Chester L. and Lewis Walker. *Ethnic Dynamics: Patterns of Intergroup Relations in Various Societies.* 2nd ed. Holmes Beach, FL: Learning Publications, Inc., 1979.

Hunter, Ian, David Saunders, and Dugland Williamson. *On Pornography: Literature, Sexuality, and Obscenity Law.* New York: St. Martin's Press, 1993.

Ingraham, Larry H. *The Boys in the Barracks: Observations on American Military Life.* Philadelphia: Institute for the Study of Human Issues, 1984.

Inkeles, A. *What is Sociology?* Englewood Cliffs, NJ: Prentice Hall, 1964.

Ireland, Patricia. "The State of NOW: A Presidential (and Personal) Report." In *Getting There: The Movement Toward Gender Equality.* Edited by Diana Wells. New York: Carroll and Graf, 1994.

Jacobs, James B. "The Emergence and Implications of American Hate Crime Jurisprudence." In *Hate Crime: The Global Politics of Polarization.* Edited by Robert J. Kelly and Jess Maghan. Carbondale: Southern Illinois University Press, 1998.

Janowitz, Morris. *Military Institutions and Coercion in the Developing Nations.* Chicago: University of Chicago Press, 1977.

———. *The Professional Soldier: A Social and Political Portrait.* London: Collier-Macmillan, 1960.

Janowitz, Morris, ed. *W. I. Thomas on Social Organizations and Social Personality.* Chicago: University of Chicago Press, 1966.

Jary, David and Julia Jary. *The Harper Collins Dictionary of Sociology.* New York: Harper Collins, 1991.

Jencks, Christopher, et al. *Who Gets Ahead? The Determinants of Economic Success in America.* New York: Basic Books, Inc., 1979.

Jenness, Valerie. "Hate Crimes in the United States: The Transformation of Injured Persons Into Victims and the Extension of Victim Status to Multiple Constituencies." In *Images of Issues: Typifying Contemporary Social Problems.* Edited by Joel Best. New York: Aldine de Gruyter, 1995.

Joas, Hans. *Pragmatism and Social Theory.* London: University of Chicago Press, 1993.

Joffe, Carole. *The Regulation of Sexuality: Experiences of Family Planning Workers.* Philadelphia: Temple University, 1986.

Johnson, Allan G. *The Blackwell Dictionary of Sociology: A User's Guide to Sociological Language.* Cambridge: Basil Blackwell Inc., 1995.

Johnstone, Ronald L. *Religion and Society in Interaction: The Sociology of Religion.* Englewood Cliffs, NJ: Prentice Hall, 1975.

Jones, Robert Alun. *Émile Durkheim: An Introduction to Four Major Works.* Beverly Hills: Sage Publications, 1986.

Jones, Robert Alun, ed. *Research in Sociology of Knowledge, Sciences, and Art: An Annual Compilation of Research.* Greenwich, CT: JAI Press, Inc., 1978.

Joreskog, K. G. and D. Sorbom. *LISREL III: Estimation of Linear Structural Equation Systems by Maximum Likelihood Methods.* Chicago: International Educational Services, 1976.

Kane, Robert. *The Significance of Free Will.* New York: Oxford University Press, 1996.

Kanellos, Nicolas, ed. *The Hispanic American Almanac: A Reference Work on Hispanics in the United States.* Detroit: Gale Research, 1993.

Kanter, Rosabeth Moss. *Men and Women of the Corporation.* New York: Basic Books, 1977.

Kappeler, Victor E. *The Police and Society: Touchstone Readings.* 2d ed. Prospect Heights, IL: Waveland Press, Inc., 1999.

Karenga, Maulana. *Introduction to Black Studies.* 2d ed. Los Angeles: University of Sankore Press, 1993.

Katz, Jonathan. *The Invention of Heterosexuality.* New York: Penguin, 1995.

Kelly, Delos H. *Deviant Behavior: A Text-Reader in the Sociology of Deviance.* 3rd ed. New York: St. Martin's Press, 1989.

Kendall, Diana. *Race, Class, and Gender in a Diverse Society.* Boston: Allyn and Bacon, 1997.

———. *Social Problems in a Diverse Society.* Boston: Allyn and Bacon, 1998.

———. *Sociology in Our Times.* 2d ed. Belmont, CA: Wadsworth Publishing Company, 1999.

Kendall, Patricia L., ed. *The Varied Sociology of Paul F. Lazarfeld.* New York: Columbia University Press, 1982.

Kerlinger, Fred N. and Elazar J. Pedhazur. *Multiple Regression in Behavioral Research.* New York: Holt, Reinhart and Winston, Inc., 1973.

Kessler, Suzanne J. and Wendy McKenna. *Gender: An Ethnomethodological Approach.* New York: John Wiley and Sons, 1978.

Kimmel, Michael. *Manhood in America: A Cultural History.* New York: Free Press, 1996.

Kimmel, Michael, ed. *Changing Men: New Directions in*

Research on Men and Masculinity. Newbury Park: Sage Publications, 1987.

Kinnell, Susan K., ed. *People in History: An Index to U.S. and Canadian Biographies in History Journals and Dissertations.* Santa Barbara: ABC-CLIO, 1988.

Knapp, Elise F. "William Godwin." In *British Prose Writers, 1600–1800.* Edited by Donald T. Seibert. Detroit: Gale Research, 1991.

Knox, David and Caroline Schacht. *Choices in Relationships: An Introduction to Marriage and the Family.* 6th ed. Australia: Wadsworth Thomson Learning, 2000.

Kohler, Josef. *On the Prehistory of Marriage: Totemism, Group Marriage, Mother Right.* Translated by R.H. and Ruth Barnes. Chicago: University of Chicago Press, 1975.

Kohn, Hans. *The Idea of Nationalism: A Study in Its Origins and Backgrounds.* New York: Collier Books, 1944.

Kornblem, William. *Sociology in a Changing World.* 5th ed. Fort Worth: Harcourt College Publishers, 2000.

Kornhauser, William. *The Politics of Mass Society.* New York: Free Press, 1959.

Kotarba. Joseph A. and Andrea Fontana, eds. *The Existential Self in Society.* Chicago: University of Chicago Press, 1984.

Kottak, Conrad Phillip. *Anthropology: The Exploration of Human Diversity.* 7th ed. New York: McGraw-Hill, 1996.

Kourvetaris, George A. and Betty A. Dobatz, eds. *World Perspectives in the Sociology of the Military.* New Brunswick: Transaction Books, 1977.

Kranzler, Gerald and Janet Moursund. *Statistics for the Terrified.* 2d ed. Upper Saddle River, NJ: Prentice Hall, 1999.

Kreft, Ita and Jan de Leeuw. *Introducing Multilevel Modeling.* London: Sage Publications, 1998.

Kroeber, A. L. *Style and Civilizations.* Ithaca, NY: Cornell University Press, 1957.

Kronenfield, Jennie Jacobs. *The Changing Federal Role in U.S. Health Care Policy.* Westport, CT: Praeger, 1997.

Kumar, Krisdan. *Utopianism.* Minneapolis: University of Minnesota Press, 1990.

Kuper, Leo. *Genocide: Its Political Use in the Twentieth Century.* New Haven: Yale University Press, 1981.

Kurtz, R. and H. Chalfant. *The Sociology of Medicine and Illness.* 2d ed. Needham Heights, MA: Allyn and Bacon, 1991.

Lachmann, Richard, ed. *The Encyclopedic Dictionary of Sociology.* 4th ed. Guilford, CN: The Duskin Publishing Group, Inc., 1991.

Lamont, Michele. *Money, Morals, and Manners.* Chicago: University of Chicago Press, 1992.

Lang, Kurt. *Military Institutions and the Sociology of War: A Review of the Literature with Annotated Bibliography.* Beverly Hills, CA: Sage Publications, 1972.

Lauer, R. *Social Problems and the Quality of Life.* Madison, WI: Brown and Benchmark, 1995.

Lawrence, Frederick M. *Punishing Hate: Bias Crimes Under American Law.* Cambridge: Harvard University Press, 1999.

Lazerwitz, Bernard. *Jewish Choices: American Jewish Denominationalism.* Albany: SUNY Press, 1998.

Lederer, Laura, ed. *Take Back the Night: Women on Pornography.* New York: William Morrow and Company, Inc., 1980.

Lefrancois, Guy R. *Of Children: An Introduction to Child Development.* Belmont, CA: Wadsworth Publishing, 1973.

Leichter, Howard M. *Health Policy Reform in America: Innovations from the States.* 6th ed. Armonk, NY: M. E. Sharpe, 1997.

Lemert, Charles, ed. *Social Theory: The Multicultural and Classic Readings* Boulder: Westview Press, 1993.

Lemert, Edwin M. *Social Pathology: A Systematic Approach to the Theory of Sociopathic Behavior.* New York: McGraw-Hill Book Company, Inc., 1951.

Lemkin, Raphael. *Axis Rule in Occupied Europe: Laws of Occupation, Analysis of Government, Proposals for Redress.* Washington: Carnegie Endowment for International Peace, 1944.

Lenin, V. I. *The State and Revolution: The Marxist Theory of the State and the Tasks of the Proletariat in the Revolution.* Moscow: Progress Publishers, 1975.

Lenski, Gerhard. *Power and Privilege: A Theory of Social Stratification.* New York: McGraw-Hill Book Company, 1966.

———. *The Religious Factor: A Sociological Study of Religion's Impact on Politics, Economics, and Family Life.* Garden City, NY: Doubleday and Company, Inc., 1961.

Lenski, Gerhard and Jean Lenski. *Human Societies: An Introduction to Macrosociology.* New York: McGraw-Hill Book Company, 1970.

Leslie, Gerald R. and Sheila K. Korman. *The Family in Social Context.* 7th ed. New York: Oxford University Press, 1989.

Levin, Jack, et al. *Social Problems: Causes, Consequences, Interventions.* 2d ed. Los Angeles: Roxbury Publishing, 1983.

Levine, Donald L. *Visions of the Sociological Tradition.* Chicago: University of Chicago Press, 1995.

Levinson, David, ed. *Encyclopedia of Marriage and the Family.* New York: Macmillan Reference, 1995.

Levinson, David and Melvin Ember, eds. *Encyclopedia of Cultural Anthropology*. New York: Henry Holt and Company, 1996.

Levitas, R. *The Concept of Utopia*. Syracuse, NY: Syracuse University Press, 1990.

Lewis, Oscar. *The Children of Sanchez: Autobiography of a Mexican Family*. New York: Vintage Books, 1963.

Lieberman, Jethro K. *The Enduring Constitution*. New York: Harper and Row, 1987.

Likert, Rensis and Jane Gibson Likert. *New Ways of Managing Conflict*. New York: McGraw-Hill Book Company, 1976.

Lin, Nan. *Foundations of Social Research*. New York: McGraw-Hill, 1976.

Lindsey, Linda and Stephen Beach. *Sociology: Social Life and Social Issues*. New Jersey: Prentice Hall, 2000.

Linton, Ralph. *The Study of Man: An Introduction*. New York: Appleton-Century-Crofts, Inc., 1936.

Lipset, Seymour Martin. *Political Man: The Social Bases of Politics*. Baltimore: Johns Hopkins University Press, 1981.

Lombard, Charles M. *Joseph de Maistre*. Boston: Twayne, 1976.

Lopata, Helena Znaniecka. *Current Widowhood: Myths and Realities*. In *Understanding Families*. Vol. 3. Edited by Bert M. Adams and David M. Klein. Thousand Oaks: Sage Publications, 1996.

———. *Widowhood in an American City*. Cambridge: Schenkman Publishing Company, Inc., 1973.

———. *Women as Widows: Support Systems*. New York: Elsevier, 1979.

Lorber, Judith. *Paradoxes of Gender*. New Haven: Yale University Press, 1994.

Loustaunau, M. and E. Sobo. *The Cultural Context of Health, Illness, and Medicine*. Westport, CT: Bergin and Garvey, 1997.

Lowman, Rodney L. "What Is Clinical Method?" In *Exploring Clinical Methods for Social Research*. Beverly Hills, Sage Publications, 1985.

Lyon, Larry. *The Community in Urban Society*. Lexington, MS: Lexington Books, 1987. 1999.

Macionis, John. *Society the Basics*. 5th ed. Englewood Cliffs, NJ: Prentice-Hall, 2000.

———. *Sociology: An Annotated Instructor's Edition*. 7th ed. Upper Saddle River: Prentice Hall, 1999.

Mackenzie, Gordene. *Transgender Nation*. Bowling Green: Bowling Green State University Press, 1994.

MacKinnon, Catherine A. *Toward a Feminist Theory of the State*. Cambridge: Harvard University Press, 1989.

Mackintosh, N. J. *Conditioning and Associative Learning*. New York: Oxford University Press, 1983.

Magill, Frank N., ed. *International Encyclopedia of Sociology*. London: Fitzroy Dearborn Publishers, 1995.

Malim, Tony and Ann Birch. *Introductory Psychology*. London: Macmillan Press Ltd., 1996.

Malina, Bruce J. *The Social World of Jesus and the Gospels*. London: Routledge, 1996.

Mandelker, Ira. *Religion, Society, and Utopia in Nineteenth-Century America*. Amherst: University of Massachusetts Press, 1984.

Mankiller, Wilma et al. *The Reader's Companion to U. S. Women's History*. Boston: Houghton Mifflin Company, 1998.

Mann, Michael. *A History of Power from the Beginning to A.D. 1760*. In *The Sources of Social Power*. Vol 1. Cambridge: Cambridge University Press, 1986.

Mann, Michael, ed. *The International Encyclopedia of Sociology*. New York: The Continuum Publishing Company, 1984.

Mannheim, Karl. *Ideology and Utopia*. Translated by Louis Wirth. New York: Harcourt Brace and World, 1936.

Manstead, Anthony R. and Miles Hewstone, eds. *The Blackwell Encyclopedia of Social Psychology*. Oxford: Basil Blackwell, Ltd., 1995.

Margolis, Maxine. *Mothers and Such: Views of American Women and Why They Changed*. Berkeley: University of California Press, 1984.

Marris, Peter. *Widows and Their Families*. London: Routledge and Kegan Paul, 1958.

Matcha, D. *Medical Sociology*. Needham Heights, MA: Allyn and Bacon, 2000.

Maquet, Jacques. *The Sociology of Knowledge: Its Structure and Its Relation to the Philosophy of Knowledge*. Westport, CT: Greenwood Press, 1951.

Marcuse, Herbert. *One-Dimensional Man: Studies in the Ideology of the Advanced Industrial Society*. Boston: Bacon Press, 1964.

Marger, Martin N. *Race and Ethnic Relations: American and Global Perspectives*. 4th ed. Belmont: Wadsworth Publishing Company, 1997.

Marshall, Gordon, ed. *The Concise Oxford Dictionary of Sociology*. Oxford: Oxford University Press, 1994.

Marshall, T. H. *Citizenship and Social Class*. Concord, MA: Pluto Press, 1992.

———. *Class, Citizenship, and Social Development*. Garden City, NY: Doubleday and Company, 1964.

Martineau, Harriet. *Society in America*. New Brunswick: Transaction Publishers, 1994.

Marx, Karl and Frederick Engels. *On Colonialism: Articles from the "New York Tribune" and Other Writings*. New York: International Publishers, 1972.

Maslow, A. H. *Motivation and Personality*. New York, Harper and Row, 1970.

———. *Toward a Psychology of Being*. New York: Van Nostrand, 1962.

Massey, Douglas S. "Why Does Immigration Occur? A Theoretical Synthesis." In *The Handbook of International Migration: The American Experience*. Edited by C. Hirschmand, P. Kasinitz, and J. DeWind. New York: Russell Sage Foundation, 1999.

Massey, Douglas S. and Nancy A. Denton. *American Apartheid: Segregation and the Making of the Underclass*. Cambridge: Harvard University Press, 1993.

Mastrofski, Stephen D. "The Police." In *Criminology*. Edited by Joseph F. Sholey. 2d ed. Belmont: Wadsworth Publishing Company, 1995.

McCalister-Smith, Peter. *International Humanitarian Assistance: Disaster Relief Actions in International Law and Organization*. Dordrecht: Marinus Nijhoff Publishers, 1985.

McElroy, Wendy. *A Woman's Right to Pornography*. New York: St. Martin's Press, 1995.

The McGraw-Hill Encyclopedia of World Biography. New York: McGraw-Hill, 1973.

McGovern, William Montgomery. *From Luther to Hitler: The History of Fascist-Nazi Political Philosophy*. Cambridge: The Riverside Press, 1941.

The McGraw-Hill Dictionary of Modern Economics: A Handbook of Terms and Organizations. 3rd ed. New York: McGraw-Hill Book Company, 1983.

McGreal, Ian P., ed. *Great Thinkers of the Western World*. New York: Harper Collins, 1992.

McIntyre, Lisa J. *Law in the Sociological Enterprise*. Boulder: Westview Press, 1994.

———. *The Practical Skeptic: Core Concepts in Sociology*. London: Mayfield Publishing Company, 1999.

McLemore, S., Dale and Harriet D. Romo. *Racial and Ethnic Relations in America*. 5th ed. Boston: Allyn and Bacon, 1998.

McNaron, Toni A. H. *Poisoned Ivy: Lesbian and Gay Academics Confront Homophobia*. Temple University Press, 1997.

McNeil, William Hardy. *Arnold J. Toynbee, A Life*. New York: Oxford University Press, 1976.

Mead, George H. *Mind, Self, and Society: From the Standpoint of a Social Behaviorist*. Chicago: University of Chicago Press, 1934.

———. *On Social Theory: Selected Papers*. Edited by Anselm Strauss. Chicago: University of Chicago Press, 1977.

Meek, Ronald L., ed. and trans. *Turgot on Progress, Sociology and Economics: A Philosophical View of the Successive Advances in the Human Mind on University History, Reflections on the Formation and the Distribution of Wealth*. Cambridge: Cambridge University Press, 1973.

Mendenhall, William and Terry Sinich. *A Second Course in Statistics: Regression Analysis*. 5th ed. Upper Saddle River, NJ: Prentice Hall, 1996.

Merton, Robert. *Social Theory and Social Structure*. Glencoe, IL: Free Press, 1949.

Mesquita, Bruce Bueno de and David Lalman. *War and Reason: Domestic and International Imperatives*. New Haven: Yale University Press, 1992.

Michel, Sonya and Robyn Muncy. *Engendering America: A Documentary History, 1865 to the Present*. Boston: McGraw-Hill, 1999.

Michels, Robert. *Political Parties*. New York: Free Press, 1962.

Michener, H. Andrew and John D. DeLemater. *Social Psychology*. 3rd ed. Fort Worth: Harcourt Brace College Publishers, 1994.

Mies, Maria and Vandana Shiva. *Ecofeminism*. London: Zed Books, 1993.

Midlarsky, Manus I. *On War: Political Violence in the International System*. New York: Free Press, 1975.

Mills, C. Wright. *The Power Elite*. New York: Oxford University Press, 1956.

———. *The Sociological Imagination*. London: Oxford University Press, 1959.

Min, Pyong Gap, ed. *Asian Americans: Contemporary Trends and Issues*. Thousand Oaks: Sage Publications, 1995.

Misztal, Bronislaw and Anson Shupe, eds. *Religion and Politics in Comparative Perspective: Revival of Religious Fundamentalism in East and West*. Westport, CT: Praeger, 1992.

Mitchell, G. Duncan, ed. *A New Dictionary of Sociology*. London: Routledge and Kegan Paul, 1979.

Mittlberg, David. *Strangers in Paradise: The Israeli Kibbutz Experience*. New Brunswick: Transaction Books, 1988.

Moody, Harry R. *Aging: Concepts and Controversies*. 2d ed. Thousand Oaks, CA: Pine Forge Press, 1998.

Mooney, Linda A., David Knox, and Caroline Schacht. *Understanding Social Problems*. Minneapolis-St. Paul: West Publishing Company, 1997.

Moore, Barrington. *Social Origins of Dictatorship and Democracy: Lord and Peasant in the Making of the Modern World*. Boston: Beacon Press, 1966.

Moore, David S. *The Basic Practice of Statistics*. New York: W. H. Freeman and Company, 1995.

Moore, Wilbert E. *World Modernizations: The Limits of Convergence*. New York: Elsevier, 1979.

More, Thomas. *Utopia*. New York: Penguin, 1965.

Moreno, J. L. *Who Shall Survive? Foundations of Sociometry, Group Psychotherapy, and SocioDrama*. Beacon, NY: Beacon House Inc., 1953.

Morgan, David L. *Focus Groups as Qualitative Research*. In *Qualitative Research Methods Series*. Vol. 16. 2d ed. Thousand Oaks: Sage Publications, 1997.

Morgan, Gareth. *Images of Organization*. 2d ed. Thousand Oaks: Sage Publications, 1997.

Morgan, Lewis H. *Houses and House-Life of the American Aborigines*. Chicago: University of Chicago Press, 1965.

Morris, Charles G. *Psychology: An Introduction*. 5th ed. Englewood Cliffs, NJ: Prentice-Hall, Inc., 1985.

Morris-Suzuki, Tessa. *Beyond Computopia: Information, Automation, and Democracy in Japan*. London: Kegan Paul International, 1988.

Morton, A. L. *The Life and Ideas of Robert Owen*. New York: International Publishers, 1969.

Munch, R. *Sociological Theory from the 1850s to Present*. Glencoe, IL: Free Press, 1957.

Muraskin, Rosyln and Ted Alleman. *It's a Crime: Women and Justice*. Englewood Cliffs, NJ: Regents/Prentice Hall, 1993.

Murnstein, Bernard L., ed. *Exploring Intimate Life Styles*. New York: Springer Publishing Company, 1978.

Murry, William O. *American Gay*. Chicago: University of Chicago Press, 1998.

Myers, Dowell. *Analysis With Local Census Data: Portraits of Change*. Boston: Academic Press, Inc., 1992.

Nachmias-Frankfort, Chava. *Social Statistics for a Diverse Society*. Thousand Oaks, CA: Pine Forge Press, 1999.

Nagel, Joane. *American Indian Ethnic Renewal: Red Power and the Resurgence of Identity and Culture*. New York: Oxford University Press, 1997.

Nagle, Jill. *Whores and Other Feminists*. New York: Routledge, 1997.

Naisbitt, John. *Megatrends Asia: Eight Asian Megatrends That Are Reshaping Our World*. New York: Simon and Schuster, 1996.

Nam, C. B. *Understanding Population Change*. New York: F. E. Peacock, 1994.

NesSmith, William C. *Thinking Sociologically: An Introduction to the Discipline*. Fort Worth: Harcourt Brace College Publishers, 1995.

Neubeck, Kenneth J. and Davita Silfen Galsberg. *Sociology: A Critical Approach*. New York: McGraw-Hill, Inc., 1996.

Neuman, W. Lawrence. *Social Research Methods: Quantitative and Qualitative Approaches*. 4th ed. Boston: Allyn and Bacon, 2000.

Newell, Colin. *Methods and Models in Demography*. New York: Guilford Press, 1988.

Newman, David M. *Sociology: Exploring the Architecture of Everyday Life*. 3rd ed. Thousand Oaks, CA: Pine Forge Press, 2000.

———. *Sociology of Families*. Thousand Oaks, CA: Pine Forge Press, 1999.

Newman, Oscar. *Defensible Space: Crime Prevention Through Urban Design*. New York: The MacMillan Company, 1972.

Newton, Esther. *Cherry Grove, Fire Island: Sixty Years in America's First Gay and Lesbian Town*. Boston: Beacon, 1993.

Nisbet, Robert A. *The Quest for Community: A Study in the Ethics of Order and Freedom*. San Francisco: Institute for Contemporary Studies Press, 1990.

———. *Tradition and Revolt: Historical and Sociological Essays*. New York: Random House, 1968.

———. *Twilight of Authority*. New York: Oxford University Press, 1975.

Norton, Mary Beth, et al. *A People and a Nation: A History of the United States*. 3rd ed. Boston: Houghton Mifflin Company, 1990.

Notestein, F. W. "Population—the Long View." In *Food for the World*. Edited by T. W. Schultz. Chicago: University of Chicago Press, 1945.

Nye, Ivan F. and Felix M. Berardo. *The Family: Its Structure and Interaction*. New York: The Macmillan Company, 1973.

O'Brian, Robert M. "Crime and Victimization Data." In *Criminology: A Contemporary Handbook*. Edited by Joseph F. Sheley. 2nd ed. Belmont: Wadsworth Publishing Company, 1995.

Ogburn, William F. *On Culture and Social Change: Selected Papers*. Chicago: University of Chicago Press, 1964.

Oliver, Willard M. *Community Policing: Classical Readings*. Upper Saddle River, NJ: Prentice Hall, 2000.

Olson, Mancur. *The Logic of Collective Action: Public Goods and the Theory of Groups*. New York: Basic Books, 1965.

Omi, Micheal and Howard Winant. *Racial Formation in the United States: From the 1960s to the 1990s*. New York: Routledge Press, 1994.

Oppenhaimer, Martin, Martin J. Murray, and Rhonda F. Levine, eds. *Radical Sociologist and the Movement:*

Experiences, Lessons, and Legacies. Philadelphia: Temple University Press, 1991.

Outhwaite, William and Tom Bottomore, eds. *The Blackwell Dictionary of Twentieth Century Social Thought.* Cambridge: Blackwell, 1994.

Page, James A. and Jae Min Roh. *Selected Balck American, African, and Caribbean Authors: A Bio-Bibliography.* Littleton, CO: Libraries Unlimited, Inc., 1985.

Paine, Thomas. *Collected Writings.* Compiled by Eric Foner. New York: The Library of America, 1995.

———. *The Rights of Man.* London: J. M. Dent and Sons Ltd., 1958.

Paludi, Doyle. *Sex and Gender: The Human Experience.* Boston: McGraw-Hill, 1998.

Parrillo, Vincent N. *Strangers to These Shores: Race and Ethnic Relations in the United States.* 5th ed. Boston: Allyn and Bacon, 1997.

Parrillo, Vincent N., John Stimson, and Ardyth Stimson. *Contemporary Social Problems.* 4th ed. Boston: Allyn and Bacon, 1999.

Parrinder, Geoffrey, ed. *World Religions: From Ancient History to the Present.* New York: Facts on File Publications, 1971.

Parry, Melanie, ed. *Chambers Biographical Dictionary.* 6th ed. New York: Chambers Harrap Publishers, 1997.

Parsons, Talcott. *Action Theory and the Human Condition.* New York: Free Press, 1978.

———. *Essays in Sociological Theory.* Glencoe, IL: The Free Press, 1954.

———. *The Evolution of Societies.* Edited by Jackson Toby. Englewood Cliffs, NJ: Prentice-Hall, 1977.

———. *On Institutions and Social Evolution.* Edited by Leon H. Mayhew. Chicago: University of Chicago Press, 1982.

———. *The Social System.* Glencoe, IL: Free Press, 1951.

———. *The Structure of Social Action.* New York: Free Press, 1968.

Parsons, Talcott, R. Bales, and E. Shils. *Working Papers in the Theory of Action.* Glencoe, IL: Free Press, 1953.

Payne, Michael. *A Dictionary of Cultural and Critical Theory.* Oxford: Blackwell Publishers, Ltd., 1996.

Payne, Richard J. *Getting Beyond Race: The Changing American Culture.* Boulder, CO: Westview Press, 1998.

Pearce, Joseph R. *Analytical Sociology: Its Logical Foundations and Relavance to theory and Empirical Research.* Lanham: University Press of America, Inc., 1994.

Peoples, James and Garrick Bailey. *Humanity: An Introduction to Cultural Anthropology.* 5th ed. Belmont, CA: Wadsworth Thompson Press, 2000.

Perry, John and Erna Perry. *The Social Web: An Introduction to Sociology.* San Francisco: Canfield Press, 1974.

Persell, Caroline Hodges. *Understanding Society: An Introduction to Sociology.* 2d ed. New York: Harper and Row Publishers, 1987.

Persons, Stow. *Ethnic Studies at Chicago: 1905–45.* Urbana and Chicago: University of Illinois Press, 1987.

Peterson, Marvin. *Organization and Governance in Higher Education: An Ashe Reader.* 4th ed. Needham Heights, MA: Simon and Schuster, 1991.

Peterson, R. Dean, Delores F. Wunder, and Harlan L. Meuller. *Social Problems: Globalization in the Twenty-First Century.* Upper Saddle River, NJ: Prentice-Hall, 1999.

Phelps, Edmund S. *Political Economy: An Introductory Text.* New York: W. W. Norton and Company, 1985.

Plant, Judith. *Healing the Wounds: The Promise of Ecofeminism.* Philadelphia: New Society Publishers, 1989.

Poloma, Margaret M. *Contemporary Sociological Theory.* New York: Macmillan Publishing Co., 1979.

Popenoe, David. *Sociology.* 11th ed. New Jersey: Prentice-Hall, 2000.

Porter, Ray, ed. *The Bibliographic Dictionary of Scientists.* 2d edition. New York: Oxford University Press, 1994.

Portes, Alejandro, Manuel Castells, and Lauren A. Benton, eds. *The Informal Economy: Studies in Advanced and Less Developed Countries.* Baltimore: Johns Hopkins University Press, 1989.

Pressler, Charles A. and Fabio B. Dasilva. *Sociology and Interpretation: From Weber to Habermas.* Albany: State University of New York Press, 1996.

Putnam, Robert D. *Making Democracy Work: Civic Traditions in Modern Italy.* Princeton: Princeton University Press, 1993.

Queen, Carol and Lawrence Schimel, eds. *PoMoSexuals: Challenging Assumptions About Gender and Sexuality.* San Francisco: Cleis Press, Inc., 1997.

Quinney, Richard. *Class, State, and Crime: On the Theory and Practice of Criminal Justice.* New York: David McKay Company, Inc., 1977.

Radford, John and Ernest Govier, eds. *A Textbook of Psychology.* London: Routledge, 1980.

Radice, Lisanne. *Beatrice and Sydney Webb: Fabian Socialists.* New York: St. Martin's Press, 1984.

Rafter, Nicole. *White Trash: The Eugenic Family Studies, 1877–1919.* Boston: Northeastern University Press, 1988.

Ragan, Pauline K., ed. *Aging Parents.* Los Angeles: University of Southern California Press, 1979.

Ragin, Charles C. *Constructing Social Research.* Thousand Oaks: Pine Forge Press, 1994.

Rebach, Howard M. and John G. Bruhn, eds. *Handbook of Clinical Sociology.* New York: Plenum Press, 1991.

Reed, Michael I. *The Sociology of Organizations.* New York: Harvester Wheatsheaf, 1992.

Renzetti, Claire M. and Daniel J. Curran. *Living Sociology.* 2d ed. Boston: Allyn and Bacon, 1999.

———. *Women, Men, and Society.* 4th ed. Needham Heights, MA: Allyn and Bacon, 1999.

Reskin, Barbara and Irene Padavic. *Women and Men at Work.* Thousand Oaks, California: Pine Forge Press, 1994.

Rich, Adrienne. *Of Women Born: Motherhood as Experience and Institution.* New York: W. W. Norton and Company, 1976.

Richardon, Laurel, Verta Taylor, and Nancy Whittier. *Feminist Frontiers IV.* New York: The McGraw-Hill Companies, Inc., 1997.

Ridgeway, Cecilia L. "Gender, Status, and Social Psychology of Expectations." In *Theory on Gender/Feminism on Theory.* Edited by Paula England. New York: Aldine De Gruyter, 1993.

Riley, Matilda White. *Sociological Lives.* Newbury Park: Sage Publications, 1988.

Ritchey, Ferris J. *The Statistical Imagination: Elementary Statistics for the Social Sciences.* Boston: McGraw-Hill, 2000.

Ritzer, George. *Contemporary Sociological Theory.* New York: McGraw-Hill, Inc., 1992.

———. *Modern Sociological Theory.* New York: McGraw-Hill, Inc., 1996.

Ritzer, George, ed. *Frontiers of Social Theory: The New Synthesis.* New York: Columbia University Press, 1990.

Robbers, Monica Leone Pia. "An Interdisciplinary Examination of Juvenile Delinquency." Ph.D. diss., American University, 1999.

Robbins, Richard H. *Global Problems and the Culture of Capitalism.* Boston: Allyn and Bacon, 1999.

Robinson, Neal. *Islam: A Concise Introduction.* Washington: Georgetown University Press, 1999.

Robinson, Paul A. *The Freudian Left: Wilhelm Reich, Geza Roheim, Herbert Marcuse.* New York: Harper and Row, 1969.

Roemer, John E. *Egalitarian Perspectives: Essays on Philosophical Economics.* Cambridge: Cambridge University Press, 1994.

Roemer, M. I. *Comparative National Policies on Health Care.* New York: Marcel Dekker, Inc., 1980.

Root, Maria P. P., ed. *Racially Mixed People in America.* Newbury Park: Sage Publications, 1992.

Ropers, Richard H. *Persistent Poverty: The American Dream Turned Nightmare.* New York: Plenum, 1991.

Rosenberg, Morris and Ralph H. Turner, eds. *Social Psychology: Sociological Perspectives.* New Brunswick: Transaction Publishers, 1992.

Rosenblaum, Dennis P., ed. *The Challenge of Community Policing: Testing the Promises.* Thousand Oaks: Sage Publications, 1994.

Ross, Edward Alsworth. *Foundations of Society.* 5th ed. New York: Macmillan Company, 1919.

Rossi, Alice S., ed. *Sexuality Across the Life Course.* Chicago: University of Chicago Press, 1994.

Rossi, Alice and Peter H. Rossi. *Of Human Bonding: Parent-Child Relations Across the Life Course.* New York: Aldine de Gruyter, 1990.

Rossi, Peter H. *Down and Out in America: The Origins of Homelessness.* Chicago: University of Chicago Press, 1989.

Rostow, W. W. *The Stages of Economic Growth: A Non-Communist Manifesto.* Cambridge: Cambridge University Press, 1960.

Rothman, Robert A. *Inequality, and Stratification: Class, Color, and Gender.* 2d ed. Englewood Cliffs, NJ: Prentice Hall, 1993.

Rovner, Julie. *Health Care Policy and Politics A to Z.* Washington. D. C.: CQ Press, 2000.

Rummel, R.J. *The Just Peace.* In *Understanding Conflict and War.* Vol. 5. Beverly Hills: Sage Publications, 1981.

Ryan, Alan, ed. *Mill: Texts, Commentaries.* New York: W. W. Norton and Company, 1997.

Ryan, Barbara. *Feminism and the Women's Movement.* New York: Routledge, 1992.

Sader, Marion, series ed. *The Reader's Advisor: The Best in Social Sciences, History, and the Arts.* New Providence, NJ: R. R. Bowker, 1994.

Sainsbury, Peter. *Suicide in London: An Ecological Study.* London: Chapman and Hall, 1955.

Salant, Pricilla and Don A. Dillman. *How to Conduct Your Own Survey.* New York: John Wiley and Sons, Inc., 1994.

Salvaggio, Jerry L., ed. *The Information Society: Economic, Social, and Structural Issues.* Hilldale, NJ: Lawrence Erlbaum Associates, Publishers, 1989.

Sapiro, Virginia. *Women in American Society: An Introduction to Women's Studies.* 4th ed. Mountain View, CA: Mayfield Publishing Company, 1999.

Scarbrough, Elinor. *Political Ideology and Voting: An Exploratory Study.* Oxford: Clarendon Press, 1984.

Schaefer, Richard T. *Racial and Ethnic Groups.* 8th ed. New Jersey: Prentice Hall, 2000.

———. *Sociology: A Brief Introduction.* 3rd ed. Boston: McGraw-Hill, 2000.

Scheff, Thomas J. *Being Mentally Ill: A Sociological Theory.* 3rd ed. Hawthorne, NY: Aldine De Gruyter, 1999.

Scheff, Thomas J. and Robert P. Lamm. *Sociology.* 6th ed. New York: McGraw-Hill Companies, Inc., 1998.

Schmalleger, Frank. *Criminology Today: An Integrative Introduction.* 2nd ed. Upper Saddle River, NJ: Prentice Hall, 1999.

Schneider, Dorothy and Carl J. *American Women in the Progressive Era, 1900-1920: Change, Challenge, and the Struggle for Women's Rights.* New York: Anchor Books, 1993.

Schroyer, Trent. *The Critique of Domination: The Origins and Development of Critical Theory.* New York: G. Braziller, 1973.

Schultz, Alfred. *Collected Papers.* The Hague, Netherlands: Martinus Nijhoff, 1962.

Schultz, Quentin J., et al. *Dancing in the Dark: Youth, Popular Culture, and the Electronic Media.* Grand Rapids, MI: William B. Eerdmans Publishing Company, 1991.

Schuman, Howard and Stanley Presser. *Questions and Answers in Attitude Surveys: Experiments in Question Form, Wording, and Context.* Thousand Oaks: Sage Publications, 1996.

Schur, Edwin M. *Radical Nonintervention: Rethinking the Delinquency Problem.* Englewood Cliffs, NJ: Prentice-Hall, Inc., 1973.

Schutt, Russell K. *Investigation the Social World: The Process and Practice of Research.* Thousand Oaks, CA: Pine Forge Press, 1996.

Scott, Barbara Marliene and Mary Ann Schwartz. *Sociology: Making Sense of the Social World.* Boston: Allyn and Bacon, 2000.

Scott, W. Richard. *Organizations: Rational, Natural, Open Systems.* 4th ed. Upper Saddle River, NJ: Prentice Hall, 1998.

Scruton, Roger. *A Dictionary of Political Thought.* New York: Harper and Row, Publishers, 1982.

Segal, David R. *Recruiting for Uncle Sam: Citizenship and Military Manpower Policy.* Lawrence: University of Kansas Press, 1989.

Segal, David R. and H. Wallace Sinaiko. *Life in the Rank and File: Enlisted Men and Women in the Armed Forces of the United States, Australia, Canada, and the United Kingdom.* Washington: Pergamon-Brassy's, 1986.

Seidman, Steven. *Contested Knowledge: Social Theory in the Postmodern Era.* Cambridge: Blackwell Publishers, 1996.

———. "Identity and Politics in a 'Postmodern' Gay Culture: Some Historical and Conceptual Notes." In *Fear of a Queer Planet: Queer Politics and Social Theory.* Edited by M. Warner. Minneapolis: University of Minnesota Press, 1993.

Seligman, Edwin R. A., ed. *Encyclopedia of the Social Sciences.* New York: Macmillan Company, 1933.

Sidel, Ruth. *America's War on the Poor.* Rev. ed. New York: Penguin Books, 1998.

Siegel, Larry J. *Criminology.* 7th ed. Australia: Wadsworth Thomson Learning, 2000.

Sills, David, ed. *International Encyclopedia of the Social Sciences.* New York: Macmillan Company and Free Press, 1968.

Silvey, Jonathan. *Deciphering Data: The Analysis of Social Surveys.* London: Longman Group, Ltd., 1975.

Sim, Stuart, ed. *The Rutledge Critical Dictionary of Postmodern Thought.* New York: Routledge, 1998.

Simmel, Georg. *The Philosophy of Money.* Translated by Tom Bottomore and David Frisby Boston: Routledge and Kegan Paul, 1978.

———. *The Sociology of Georg Simmel.* Edited and translated by Kurt H. Wolff. Glencoe, IL: Free Press, 1950.

Singleton, Royce A., Jr. and Bruce C. Straits. *Approaches to Social Research.* 3rd ed. New York: Oxford University Press, 1999.

Sils, David L. *International Encyclopedia of the Social Sciences.* New York: Macmillan Company, 1968.

Silverman, David. *The Theory of Organisations: A Sociological Framework.* London: Heinemann, 1970.

Sinn, Maxine Baca and Stanley D. Eitzen. *Diversity in Families.* 5th ed. New York: Longman, 1999.

Sklare, Marshall. *Observing America's Jews.* Boston: Brandeis University Press, 1993.

Skelton, R. *Population Mobility In Developing Countries: A Reinterpretation.* London: Belhaven Press, 1990.

Skocpol, Theda. *States and Social Revolutions: A Comparative Analysis of France, Russia, and China.* Cambridge: Cambridge University Press, 1999.

Skocpol, Theda, ed. *Vision and Method in Historical Sociology.* Cambridge: Cambridge University Press, 1984.

Smelser, Neil J. *Handbook of Sociology.* Newbury Park: Sage Publications, 1988.

———. *Social Change in the Industrial Revolution: An Application of Theory to the British Cotton Industry.* Chicago: University of Chicago Press, 1959.

———. *The Sociology of Economic Life*. 2d ed. Englewood Cliffs, NJ: Prentice-Hall, Inc., 1976.

Smith, Anna Marie. "The Good Homosexual and the Dangerous Queer." In *New Sexual Agendas*. Edited by L. Segal New York: New York University Press,1997.

Smith, Anthony D. *Nations and Nationalism in a Global Era*. Cambridge: Polity Press, 1995.

Smith, Christian. *American Evangelism: Embattled and Thriving*. Chicago: University of Chicago Press, 1998.

Smith, D. *The Geography of Social Well-Being in the United States*. New York: McGraw-Hill, 1973.

Smith, Huston. *The World's Religions*. San Francisco: Harper San Francisco, 1991.

Smith, Jane. *Islam in America*. New York: Columbia University Press, 1999.

Snipp, Matthew. *American Indians: The First of This Land*. New York: Russell Sage Foundation, 1989.

Snyder, Louis L. *Varieties of Nationalism: A Comparative Study*. Hinsdale, IL: Dryden Press, 1976.

Social Indicators: Problems of Definition and of Selection. Paris: Unesco Press, 1974.

Spector, Malcom and John I. Kitsuse. *Constructing Social Problems*. New York: Aldine De Guyter, 1987.

Spengler, Oswald. *The Decline of the West*. New York: Knopf, 1926.

Spretnak, Charlene and Frijof Capra. *Green Politics: The Global Promise*. Sante Fe: Bear and Company, 1986.

St. John-Stevas, Norman. *Walter Bagehot*. London: Longmans, Green and Co., 1963.

Starr, Paul. *The Social Transformation of American Medicine*. New York: Basic Books, 1982.

Stearns, Peter N., ed. *Encyclopedia of Social History*. New York: Garland, 1994.

Steele, James, ed. *The Sociology of Sport*. 3rd ed. Washington, DC: American Sociological Association, 1999.

Steinmetz, Suzanne K., Sylvia Clavan, and Karen F. Stein. *Marriage and Family Realities: Historical and Contemporary Perspectives*. New York: Harper and Row, 1990.

Stewert, Elbert W. and James A. Glynn. *Introduction to Sociology*. 4th ed. New York: McGraw-Hill Book Company, 1985.

Stinnett, Nick and Craig Wayne Birdsong. *The Family and Alternate Life Styles*. Chicago: Nelson-Hall, 1978.

Strenski, Ivan. *Durkheim and the Jews of France*. Chicago: Univeristy of Chicago Press, 1997.

Stroll, Avrum and Richard H. Popkin. *Introduction to Philosophy*. 3rd ed. New York: Holt, Rinehart, and Winston, 1979.

Strong, Bryan, Christine DeVault, and Barbara Werner Sayad. *Core Concepts in Human Sexuality*. Mountain View, CA: Mayfield Publishing Company, 1996.

Stuhr, John. *Pragmatism and Classical American Philosophy*. New York: Oxford University Press, 2000.

Sudman, Seymour. *Applied Sampling*. New York: Academic Press, 1976.

Sullivan, Thomas J. *Introduction to Social Problems*. 4th ed. Boston: Allyn and Bacon, 1997.

Sutherland, Edwin H., Donald R. Cressey, and David F. Luckenbill. *Principles of Criminology*. 11th ed. Dix Hills, NY: General Hall, Inc., 1992.

Takaki, Ronald. *A Different Mirror: A History of Multicultural America*. Boston: Little Brown and Company, 1993.

Tannenbaum, Frank. *Crime and the Community*. Boston: Ginn and Company, 1938.

Tarrow, Sidney. *Power in Movement: Social Movements and Contentious Politics*. Cambridge: Cambridge University Press, 1998.

Tausig, Mark, Janet Michello, and Sree Subedi. *A Sociology of Mental Illness*. Upper Saddle River, NJ: Prentice Hall, 1999.

Taylor, John G. *From Modernization to Modes of Production: A Critique of the Sociologies of Development and Underdevelopment*. London: Macmillan Press Ltd., 1979.

Thomas, W. I. *The Unadjusted Girl: With Cases and Standpoint for Behavior Analysis*. Edited by Benjamin Nelson. New York: Harper Torchbooks, 1967.

Theories of Sociology: Foundations of Modern Sociological Theory. New York: Free Press, 1961.

Thio, Alex. *Sociology: A Brief Introduction,* 4th ed. Boston: Allyn and Bacon, 2000.

Thompson, Kenneth, ed. *Readings from Émile Durkheim*. Translated by Margaret Thompson. London: Routledge, 1985.

Thompson. William E. and Joseph V. Hickey. *Society in Focus: Introduction to Sociology*. 3rd ed. New York: Addison Wesley Longman, Inc., 1999.

Thornberry, Terence P., ed. *Developmental Theories of Crime and Delinquency*. In *Advances in Criminological Theory*. Vol. 7. New Brunswick: Transaction Publishers, 1997.

Tilly, Charles. *The Vende*. Cambridge: Harvard University Press, 1964.

Tischler, Henry L. *Introduction to Sociology*. 6th ed. Fort Worth: Harcourt Brace College Publishers, 1999.

●

Tocqueville, Alexis de. *Democracy in America.* Rev. ed. New York: Vintage Books, 1945.

Todaro, M. P. "Internal Migration In Developing Countries: A Survey." In *Population and Economic Change In Developing Countries.* Edited by R.A. Easterlin. Chicago: University of Chicago Press, 1980.

Tönnies, Ferdinand. *Gemeinschaft und Gesellschaft.* Translated and edited by Charles P. Loomis. East Lansing, MI: Michigan State University Press, 1964.

Toynbee, Arnold Joseph. *Mankind and Mother Earth: A Narrative History of the World.* New York: Oxford University Press, 1989.

Treiman, Donald J. *Occupational Prestige in Comparative Perspective.* New York: Academic Press, 1977.

Trotten, Samuel, William S. Parsons, and Israel W. Charny, eds. *Century of Genocide: Eyewitness Accounts and Critical Views.* New York: Garland Publshing, Inc., 1997.

Trudgill, Peter. *Applied Sociolinguistics.* London: Academic Press, 1984.

Tucker, Robert. *The Marx-Engels Reader.* 2d ed. New York: W. W. Norton and Company, 1978.

Turk, Austin T. *Criminology and Legal Order.* Chicago: Rand McNally and Company, 1969.

Turkle, Sherry. *The Second Self: Computers and the Human Spirit.* New York: Simon and Schuster, 1984.

Turner, Bryan S. *Religion and Social Theory.* 2d ed. London: Sage Publications, 1991.

Turner, Jeffrey S. *Encyclopedia of Relationships Across the Lifespan.* Westport, CT: Greenwood Press, 1996.

Turner, Jeffrey S. and Donald B. Helms. *Marriage and Family: Traditions and Transitions.* San Diego: Harcourt Brace Jovanovich, Publishers, 1988.

Turner, Jonathan H. *Classical Sociological Theory: A Positivist's Perspective.* Chicago: Nelson-Hall Publishers, 1993.

Turner, Jonathan H., Leonard Beeghley, and Charles H. Powers. *The Emergence of Sociological Theory.* 3rd ed. Belmont, CA: Wadsworth Publishing Company, 1995.

Turner, Ralph H. and Lewis M. Killian. *Collective Behavior.* 3rd ed. Englewood Cliffs, NJ: Prentice-Hall, Inc., 1972.

Turner, Stephen P. and Regis A. Factor. *Max Weber: The Lawyer as Social Thinker.* London: Routledge, 1994.

Urmson, J. O. and Jonathan Ree. *The Concise Encyclopedia of Western Philosophy and Philosophers.* London: Unwin Hyman, 1989.

Uttal, William R. *The War Between Mentalism and Behaviorism: On the Accessability of Mental Processes.* Mahwah, NJ: Lawrence Erlbaum Associates, Publishers, 2000.

Van Gennep, Arnold. *The Rites of Passage.* Translated by Monica B. Vizedom and Gabrielle L. Caffee. Chicago: University of Chicago Press, 1960.

Velody, Irving and Robin Williams, eds. *The Politics of Constructionism.* London: Sage Publications, 1998.

Vogel, Lise. "Marxism and Socialist-Feminist Theory: A Decade of Debate." In *Readings in Contemporary Sociological Theory: From Modernity to Post-Modernity.* Edited by Donald McQuarie. Englewood Cliffs, NJ: Prentice Hall, 1995.

———. *Woman Questions: Essays for Materialist Feminism.* London: Pluto Press, 1995.

Vold, George B, Thomas J. Bernard, and Jeffrey B. Snipes. *Theoretical Criminology.* 4th ed. New York: Oxford University Press, 1998.

Volkart, Edmund, ed. *Social Behavior and Personality: Contributions of W. I. Thomas to Theory and Social Research.* Westport, CT: Greenwood Press, 1951.

Wald, Alan M. *The New York Intellectuals: The Rise and Decline of the Anti-Stalinist Left From the 1930s to the 1980s.* Chapell Hill: University of North Carolina Press, 1987.

Walker, James T. *The Psychology of Learning.* Upper Saddle River, NJ: Prentice-Hall, 1996.

Wallace, Ruth A. and Allison Wolf. *Contemporary Sociological Theory: Continuing the Classical Tradition.* 4th ed. Englewood Cliffs, NJ: Prentice Hall, 1995.

Wallerstein, Immanuel. *The Capitalist World Economy.* Cambridge: Cambridge University Press, 1979.

———. *The Modern World System I: Capitalist Agriculture and the Origins of the European World-Economy in the Sixteenth Century.* San Diego: Academic Press, Inc., 1974.

Wallimann, Isisdor and Michael N. Dobkowski, eds. *Genocide and the Modern Age: Etiology and Case Studies of Mass Death.* New York: Greenwood Press, 1987.

Walzer, Lee. *Between Sodom and Eden: A Gay Journey Through Today's Changing Israel.* New York: Columbia University Press, 2000.

Waters, Malcolm. *Modern Sociological Theory.* London: Sage Publications, 1994.

Watson, John B. *Behaviorism.* Rev. ed. Chicago: University of Chicago Press, 1930.

Watson, Tony J. *Sociology, Work, and Industry.* 3rd ed. London: Routledge, 1995.

Weber, Max. *Ancient Judaism.* Glencoe, IL: Free Press, 1952.

———. *Economy and Society.* 2 vols. Edited by G. Roth and C. Wittich. Berkeley: University of California Press, 1978.

———. *From Max Weber: Essays in Sociology.* Edited by H. H.

Gerth and C. Wright Mills. New York: Oxford University Press, 1946.

——. *The Protestant Ethic and the Spirit of Capitalism.* Translated by Talcott Parsons. New York: Charles Scribner's Sons, 1958.

Weeks, J. R. *Population: An Introduction to Concepts and Issues.* 7th ed. New York: Wadsworth, 1999.

Wellman, Barry and S. D. Berkowitz, eds. *Social Structures: A Network Approach.* Cambridge: Cambridge University Press, 1997.

Welsh, Brian W. W. and Pavel Butorin, eds. *Dictionary of Development: Third World Economy, Environment, Society.* New York: Garland Publishing, Inc., 1990.

Wei, William. *The Asian American Movement.* Philadelphia: Temple University Press, 1993.

Weiss, G. and L. Lonnquist. *The Sociology of Health, Healing, and Illness.* Englewood Cliffs, NJ: Prentice Hall, 1994.

Weyler, Rex. *Blood of the Land: The Government and the Corporate War Against the American Indian Movement.* New York: Everest House Publishers, 1982.

Whitehead, John T. and Steven P. Lab. *Juvenile Justice: An Introduction.* 3rd ed. Cincinnati: Anderson Publishing Company, 1999.

Wiggins, James A., Beverly B. Wiggins, and James Vander Zanden. *Social Psychology.* 5th ed. New York: McGraw-Hill, Inc., 1994.

Williams, Frank P. III and Marilyn D. McShane. *Criminology Theory: Selected Classic Readings.* Cincinnati: Anderson Publishing Company, 1993.

Wilson, James and Richard J. Herrnstein. *Crime and Human Nature.* New York: Simon and Schuster, 1985.

Wilson, John. *Religion in American Society: The Effective Presence.* Englewood Cliffs, NJ: Prentice-Hall Inc., 1978.

Wilson, William J. *The Truly Disadvantaged: The Inner City, the Underclass, and Public Policy.* Chicago: University of Chicago Press, 1987.

——. *When Work Disappears: The World of the New Urban Poor.* New York: Alfred A. Knopf, 1996.

Wirth, Louis. *On Cities and Social Life: Selected Papers.* Edited by Albert J. Reiss, Jr. Chicago: University of Chicago Press, 1964.

Wolf, Deborah. *The Lesbian Community.* Berkeley: University of California Press, 1979.

Wolff, Janet. *Hermeneutic Philosophy and the Sociology of Art.* London: Routledge and Kegan Paul, 1975.

Wolff, Kurt H., ed. and trans. *The Sociology of Georg Simmel.* New York: Free Press, 1950.

Wright, Eric Olin. *Classes.* London: Verso, 1985.

Wright, Harrison M. *Problems in European Civilization.* Lexington: D. C. Heath and Company, 1961.

Wright, W. *The Social Logic of Health.* Hanover, NH: Wesleyan University Press, 1994.

The Writer's Directory. 10th ed. Chicago: St. James Press, 1991.

Yetman, Norman R., ed. *Majority and Minority: The Dynamics of Race and Ethnicity in American Life.* 6th ed. Boston: Allyn and Bacon, 1999.

Yolten, John W., et al. *The Blackwell Companion to the Enlightenment.* Oxford: Basil Blackwell, Ltd., 1991.

Yorburg, Betty. *Family Relationships.* New York: St. Martin's Press, 1993.

Zack, Naomi. *Thinking About Race.* Belmont, CA: Wadsworth Publishing Company, 1998.

Zeitlin, Irving M. *The Social Condition of Humanity: An Introduction to Sociology.* 2d ed. New York: Oxford University Press, 1984.

Zelizer, Viviana A. *The Social Meaning of Money.* New York: Basic Books, 1994.

Zellner, William W. *Countercultures, A Sociological Analysis.* New York: St. Martin's Press, 1995.

Zimmerman, Carle C. and Merle E. Frampton. *Family and Society: A Study of the Sociology of Reconstruction.* New York: D. Van Norstrand Company, Inc., 1935.

Zinn, Maxine Baca, Pierrette Hondagneu-Sotelo, and Michael A. Messner. *Through the Prism of Difference: Readings on Sex and Gender.* Boston: Allyn and Bacon, 1997.

Zuriff, G. E. *Behaviorism: A Conceptual Reconstruction.* New York: Columbia University Press, 1985.

Journal Articles

Acker, Joan. "Between Feminism and Labor: The Significance of the Comparable Worth Movement." *American Journal of Sociology* 97 (January 1992): 1154–56.

Adam, Barry D. "Theorizing Homophobia." *Sexualities* 1 (1998): 387–404.

Alba, Richard D. and Reid M. Golden. "Patterns of Ethnic Marriage in the United States." *Social Forces* 65 (September 1986): 202–23.

Aneshensel, Carol S. "Social Stress: Theory and Research." *Annual Review of Sociology* 18 (1992): 15–38.

Archer, Margaret S. "The Myth of Cultural Integration." *British Journal of Sociology* 36 (1985): 333–53.

Arnett, Jefrey Jensen. "High Hopes in a Grim World." *Youth and Society* 31 (March 2000): 267–86.

Atkinson, Dorothy. "Soviet and East European Studies in the United States." *Slavic Review* 47 (Fall 1988): 397–413.

●

Awe, Susan C. Review of *Financing the American Dream: Debt, Credit, and the Making of American Consumer Culture,* by Lendol Calder. *Library Journal* 124 (March 15, 1999): 88.

Badran, Margot. "Feminisms and Islamisms." *Journal of Women's History* 10 (1999): 196–204.

Bailey, Ronald. "Thwarting the Grim Reaper: Agricultural Production in Developing Countries." *Forbes* 152 (November 8, 1993): 122–25.

Becker, Howard S. "The Career of the Chicago Public Schoolteacher." *American Journal of Sociology* 57 (March 1952): 470–77.

Becker, Howard S. and Anselm L. Strauss. "Careers, Personality and Adult Socialization." *American Journal of Sociology* 62 (1956): 253–263.

Bello, Walden. "U.S. Imperialism in the Asia-Pacific." *Peace Review* 10 (1998):367–73.

Berbrier, Mitch. "Half the Battle: Cultural Resonance, Framing Processes, and Ethnic Affections in Contemporary White Separatist Rhetoric." *Social Problems* 45 (1998): 431–50.

Berger, Joseph and M. Hamit Fisek. "Consistent and Inconsistent Status Characteristics and the Determination of Power and Prestige Orders." *Sociometry* 33 (September 1970): 287–304.

Berk, Richard. "Thinking About Hate-Motivated Crimes." *Journal of Interpersonal Violence* 5 (September 1995): 334– 49.

Blumstein, Philip, Judith A. Howard, and Pepper Schwartz. "Social or Evolutionary Theories? Some Observations on Preferences in Human Mate Selection." *Journal of Personality and Social Psychology* 53 (July 1987): 194–200.

Blumstein, Philip, Peter Kollock, and Pepper Schwartz. "The Judgement of Equality in Intimate Relationships." *Social Psychology Quarterly* 57 (December 1994): 340–51.

Bobo, Lawrence. "Race, Interests, and Beliefs about Affirmative Action." *The American Behavioral Scientist* 41 (April 1998): 985–1003.

Bongaarts, J. W. "A Framework for Analyzing The Proximate Determinants of Fertility." *Population and Development Review* 4 (1978): 105–132.

Bower, Bruce. "A World that Never Existed: Researchers Debate the Pervasive View of Modern Hunter-Gatherers as a Window to Humanity's Past." *Science News* 135 (April 29, 1989): 264–66.

Boyd, Richard. "The Unsteady and Precarious Contribution of Individuals: Edmund Burke's Defense of Civil Society." *Review of Politics* 61 (Summer 1999): 465–91.

Breazeale, Daniel. "Fichte on Skepticism." *Journal of the History of Philosophy* 29 (July 1991): 427–33.

———. "The Theory of Practice and the Practice of Theory: Fichte and the 'Primacy of Practical Reason.'" *International Philosophical Quarterly* 36 (March 1996): 47–64.

Britton, Dana M. "Homophobia and Homosociality: An Analysis of Boundary Maintenance." *Sociological Quarterly* 31.3 (1990): 423–39.

Brown, Doug. "Thorstein Veblen Meets Eduard Berstein: Toward a Institutionalist Theory of Mobilization Politics." *Journal of Economic Issues* 25 (September 1991): 689–209.

Brulle, Robert J. "Environmental Discourse and Social Movement Organizations: A Historical and Rhetorical Perspective on the Development of U.S. Environmental Organizations." *Sociological Inquiry* 66 (Winter 1996): 58–83.

Buell, John. "Slow-tracking NAFTA." *Humanist* 59 (May 1999): 38–9.

Caldwell, J. C. "Demography and Social Science." *Population Studies* 50 (1996): 305–33.

Camic, Charles. "Three Departments in Search of a Discipline: Localism and Interdisciplinary Interaction in American Sociology." *Social Research* 62 (Winter 1995): 1003–33.

Caspi, Avshalom. "The Child is Father of the Man: Personality Continuities from Childhood to Adulthood." *Journal of Personality and Social Psychology* 78 (January 2000): 158–72.

Catton, William R. and Riley E. Dunlap. "Environmental Sociology: A New Paradigm." In *The American Sociologist* 13 (February 1978): 41–49.

Cervone, Daniel. "Evolutionary Psychology and Explanation in Personality." In *American Behavioral Scientist* 43 (March 2000): 1001–14.

Chand, Ganeshwar. "Capitalism, Democracy, and Discrimination—The Rise and Decline of Racism in Cox's Caste, Class, and Race." *The Review of Black Political Economy* 23 (Fall 1994): 71– 92.

Cleland, J. and C. Wilson. "Demand Theories of Fertility Transition: An Iconoclastic View." In *Population Studies* 41 (1987): 5–30.

Clow, Frederick R. "Cooley's Doctrine of Primary Groups." *American Journal of Sociology* 25 (November 1919): 326– 47.

Coale, A. J. "The Demographic Transition" *International Union for the Scientific Study of Population* 1 (1973): 53–72.

Cole, W. E. and R. D. Sanders "Internal Migration and Urban Employment in the Third World." In *American Economic Review* 75 (1985): 481–94.

Colson, Charles and Nancy Pearcey. "How Evil Became

Cool." In *Christianity Today* 43 (August 9, 1999): 80.

Cook, Bernard. "Winds of Change Bring a 'Paradigm Shift': Now the Faithful Must Speak Up." In *National Catholic Reporter* 32 (August 8, 1996): 9–11.

Cook, K. S. and J. M. Whitmeyer. "Two Approaches to Social Structure: Exchange Theory and Network Theory." In *Annual Review of Sociology* 18 (1992): 109–27.

Cornfield, Daniel B. "The U.S. Labor Movement: Its Development and Impact on Social Inequality and Politics." In *Annual Review of Sociology* 17 (1991): 27–49.

Costelloe, Timothy M. "Shultz, Music, and Temporality: A Wittgensteinian Assessment." In *Philosophy of the Social Sciences* 24 (December 1994): 439–.

Cottrell, Ann Baker. "Cross-National Marriages: A Review of the Literature." In *Journal of Comparative Family Studies* 21 (Summer 1990): 151–69.

Cowley, Geoffrey. "First Born, Later Born: Personality Differences between First and Later Born Siblings." *Newsweek,* October 7, 1996, 65–71.

Cramer, Elizabeth P. "Hate Crime Laws and Sexual Orientation." In *Journal of Sociology and Social Welfare* 26 (1997): 5–25.

Crimmins, E. M. "Demography: The Past 30 Years, The Present, and The Future." *Demography* 30 (1993): 579–91.

Crow, James F. "Francis Galton: Count and Measure, Measure and Count." In *Genetics* 135 (September 1993): 1–4.

Dancer, L. Suzanne. "Louis Guttman." *American Psychologist* 45 (June 1990): 773–74.

Davies, Christie. "Goffman's Concept of the Total Institution: Criticism and Revisions." In *Human Studies* 12 no. 1–2 (1989): 77–95.

Davis, K. "The World In Demographic Transition." *Annals of the American Academy of Political and Social Science* 237 (1945): 1–11.

Davis, K. and J. Blake. "Social Structure and Fertility: An Analytic Framework." In *Economic Development and Cultural Change* 4 (1956) 211–235.

Demeny, P. "Early Fertility Decline in Austria-Hungary: A Lesson in Demographic Transition." In *Daedalus* 97 (1968): 502–22.

DeMont, John. "Is 'Sorry' Good Enough?" *World Press Review* 45 (March 1998): 14.

DeVoe, Deborah. "Communication Skills: Learn to Resolve or Avoid Work Conflicts." In *InfoWorld* 21 (August 23, 1999): 84.

Didsbury, Howard F. "Hedonists vs. the Future." *The Futurist* 33 (December 1999): 60.

Doherty, Brian. "Blame Society First." In *Reason* 30 (June 1998): 8.

Draper, Roger. "Blacks in the White Establishment?" *The New Leader* 74 (April 8, 1991): 15.

Droel, William. "Social Justice is a Full-Time Job." *U.S. Catholic* 64 (December 1999): 40.

Drucker, Peter F. "In Defense of Japanese Bureaucracy." *Foreign Affairs* 77 (September-October 1998): 68– 81.

Dugger, William M. "Markets and Democracy: Participation, Accountability, and Efficiency." In *Journal of Economic Issues* 28 (September 1994): 946–49.

Dunn, Samuel L. "Christianity's Future: The First World-Church Takes a Back Seat." In *The Futurist* 23 (March-April 1989): 34–38.

Easterlin, R. A. "An Economic Framework for Fertility Analysis." In *Studies in Family Planning* 6 (1975): 53– 63.

Edwards, Cynthia A. "Leadership in Groups of School-Age Girls." In *Developmental Psychology* 30 (November 1994): 920–27.

Ehrenreich, John H. "A Case of Intellectual and Social Isolation?" In *Journal of Psychology* 131 (January 1997): 33–44.

Eide, Asbjorn. "The Human Rights Movement and the Transformation of the International Order." In *Alternatives* 11 (1986): 367–402.

Elder, Glen H. Jr., et al. "Symposium: The American Occupational Structure." In *Contemporary Sociology* 21 (September 1992): 632–61.

Elkin, Frederick and William A. Westley. "The Myth of Adolescent Culture." In *American Sociological Review* 20 (1955): 680–84.

Emerson, Richard M. "Power-Dependence Relations." *American Sociological Review* 27 (February 1962): 31–40.

England, Paula and Dana Dunn. "Evaluating Work and Comparable Worth." In *Annual Review of Sociology* 14 (1988): 227–28.

Epstein, Jeffrey H. "Reducing Government Bureaucracy." *The Futurist* 32 (January-February 1998): 10– 12.

Falcone, Lauren Beckham. "Winging It: 20–Somethings Take a Step Back Now to Avoid Mid-Life Crisis Later." In *Boston Herald* March 28, 2000.

Fallows, James. "The Screw-You Spirit: Tribalism and Group Antipathy." In *Washington Monthly* 21 (March 1989): 42– 44.

Faris, Ellsworth. "The Primary Group: Essence and Accident." In *American Journal of Sociology* 38 (July 1932): 41– 50.

Farrington, Keith. "The Modern Prison as Total Institution?" *Crime and Delinquency* 38 (1992): 6–26.

Ferman, Patricia R. and Louis A. Ferman. "The Structural Underpinnings of the Irregular Economy." In *Poverty and Human Resources Abstracts* 8 (1973): 3–17.

Ficarrotto, Thomas J. "Racism, Sexism, and Erotophobia: Attitudes of Heterosexuals Toward Homosexuals." In *Journal of Homosexuality* 19.1 (1990): 111–16.

Field, M. G. "The Health System and the Polity: A Contemporary American Dialectic." In *Social Science and Medicine* 14 (1980): 397–413.

Fitzgerald, Tina Katherine. "Who Marries Whom? Attitudes and Behavior in Marital Partner Selection." Ph.D. diss., 1999. Abstract in *Dissertation Abstracts International* 60 (1999): 1346–47.

Fletcher, Arthur A. "Business and Race: Only Halfway There." In *Fortune* 141 (March 6, 2000): 76–78.

Foley, Donald L. "The Sociology of Housing." *Annual Review of Sociology* 6 (1980): 457–78.

Foner, Eric. "Hiring Quotas for White Males Only." In *Nation* 260 (June 26, 1995): 924–26.

Foss, Nicolai Juul. "Spontaneous Social Order: Economics and Schwartzian Sociology." In *American Journal of Economics and Sociology* 55 (January 1996): 73–87.

Foster, John Bellamy. "A Classic in Our Time: 'Labor and Monopoly Capital' After a Quarter-Century." In *Monthly Review* 8 (January 1999): 12–18.

———. "Remarks on Paul Sweezy on the Occasion of His Receipt of the Veblen-Commons Award." In *Monthly Review* 51 (September 1999): 39–44.

Franke, Volker C. "Duty, Honor, and Country: The Social Identity of West Point Cadets." In *Armed Forces and Society* 26 (2000): 175–90.

Fuller, Richard K. and Susanne Hiller-Sturmhofel. "Alcoholism Treatment in the United Sates: An Overview." In *Alcohol Research and Health* 23 (1999): 69–77.

Galbraith, John Kenneth. "The Affluent Society 40 Years On." In *Dollars and Sense* 226 (November/December 1999): 49.

Galton, David J. and Clare J. Galton. "Francis Galton: An Eugenics Today." In *Journal of Medical Ethics* 24 (April 1998): 99–105.

Garrety, Karin and Richard Badham. "The Politics of Socio-Technical Intervention: An Interactionist View." In *Technology Analysis and Strategic Management* 12 (March 2000): 103–118.

Garvery, Michael O., et al. "Vox Pouli: Four Perspectives on Catholicism and Popular Culture." In *Commonwealth* 22 (September 22, 1995): 16–20.

Gibson, Rose C. "Blacks at Middle and Late Life: Resources and Coping." In *The Annals of The American Academy of Political and Social Science* 464 (November 1982): 79–90.

Gideonse, Ted. "Baby by Proxy." *The Advocate,* June 22, 1999, 83.

Giobbe, Dorothy. "'Political Correctness': Journalists Attempt to Define What it Means Today." In *Editor and Publisher* 127 (October 22, 1994): 13–14.

Goldberg, Barry. "Let Them Eat Multiculturalism." *New Politics* 6 (1997): 3–26.

Goldstein, Herman. "Toward Community-Oriented Policing" Potential, Basic Requirements, and Threshold Questions." In *Crime and Delinquency* 33 (January 1987): 6–30.

Gould, Stephen Jay. "The Smoking Gun of Eugenics." In *Natural History* 12 (December 1991): 8–17.

Grahn, Lance. "Integrating Latin America and the Caribbean Into Global History." In *Journal of General Education* 46 (1997): 107–24.

Grecas, Viktor. "The Self-Concept." *Annual Review of Sociology* 8 (1982): 1–35.

Greider, William. "Shopping Till We Drop." *The Nation* 270 (April 10, 2000): 11.

Guttman, Louis. "Social Problem Indicators." *The Annals of the American Academy of Political and Social Science* 393 (January 1971): 40–46.

Hacken, Richard. "The Current State of European Studies in North American and of Scholarly Publishing in Western Europe." In *The Journal of Academic Librarianship* 24 (May 1998): 201–207.

Hansen, Drew D. "The American Invention of Child Support: Dependency and Punishment in Early American Child Support Laws." *Yale Law Journal* 108 (March 1999): 1123–53.

Haque, Akhlaque U. and Micheal W. Spicer. "Reason, Discretion, and Tradition: A Reflection on the Burkean Worldview and Its Implications for Public Administration." In *Administration and Society* 29 (March 1997): 78–96.

Hart, Keith. "Informal Income Opportunities and Urban Employment in Ghana." In *The Journal of Modern African Studies* 11: 61–89.

Hartman, Ann. "Ideological Themes in Family Policy." In *Families in Society: The Journal of Contemporary Human Services* (March 1995): 182–92.

Harvey, Van A. "Feuerbach on Luther's Doctrine of Revelation: An Essay in Honor of Brian Gerrish." In *The Journal of Religion* 78 (January 1998): 3–17.

———. "The Re-discovery of Ludwig Feuerbach." In *Free Inquiry* 17 (Winter 1996/1997): 45–6.

Harwood, Henrick J. "Cost Estimates for Alcohol and Drug Abuse" In *Addiction* 94 (May 1999); 621–47.

Heckathorn, Douglas D. "The Dynamics and Dilemmas of Collective Action." In *American Sociological Review* 61 (April 1996): 250–77.

Heilbroner, Robert. "Rereading the Affluent Society." *Journal of Economic Issues* 23 (June 1989): 367–77.

Henkin, Louis. "The United Nations and Human Rights." *International Organization* 19 (Summer 1965): 504–17.

Hexter, Maurice B. "Implications of a Standard of Living." In *American Journal of Sociology* 22 (September 1916): 212–25.

Hogan, J. Michael. "George Gallup and the Rhetoric of Scientific Democracy." In *Communication Monographs* 64 (June 1997): 161–79.

Hoover, Judith D. and Leigh Anne Howard. "The Political Correctness Controversy Revisited." In *American Behavioral Scientist* 38 (June-July 1995): 963–76.

Horner, Jim. "Henry George on Thomas Robert Malthus: Abundance Vs. Scarcity." In *American Journal of Economics and Sociology* 56 (October 1997): 595–607.

Hout, Micheal and Andrew M. Greeley. "The Center Doesn't Hold: Church Attendance in the United States, 1940–1984." In *American Sociological Review* 52 (June 1987): 325–45.

Howie, Linsey. "Old Women and Widowhood: A Dying Status Passage." In *Omega* 26 (1992): 223–33.

Hruby, Olga S. "Keeping the Faith." *National Review* 42 (January, 22 1990): 27–29.

Huber, Peter. "Junk Credit Cards: Backruptcy Law Needs Reform." In *159 (March 24, 1997): 172.*

Hu-DeHart, Evelyn. "The History, Development, and Future of Ethnic Studies." In *Phi Delta Kappan* 75 (September 1993): 50–5.

Hunt, Alan. "Perspectives in the Sociology of Law." In *Sociological Review Monograph: The Sociology of Law* December 1976, 22–43.

Jacobs, James B. and Kimberly A. Potter. "Hate Crimes: A Critical Perspective." In *Crime and Justice* 22 (1997): 1–50.

Jacobs, Jerry A. "Comparable Worth: Theories and Evidence." In *Contemporary Sociology* 22 (September 1993): 728–30.

Janush, Rosa Taikon. "The Sharing Caring Family." *UNESCO Courier* (October 1984): 18–21.

Johnson, Trebbe. "The Second Creation Story." *Sierra* 83 (November 1998): 50.

Johnston, Hank and David A. Snow. "Subcultures and the Emergence of the Estonian Nationalist Opposition 1945–1990." *Sociological Perspectives* 41(1998): 473–97.

Kalish, Richard A. "Death and Survivorship: The Final Transition." In *The Annals of the American Academy of Political and Social Science* 464 (November 1982): 163–73.

Kalmijn, Matthijs. "Intermarriage and Homogamy: Causes, Patterns, and Trends." In *Annual Review of Sociology* 24 (1998): 395–421.

Kane, Pat. "There's Method in the Magic." *New Statesman* 125 (August 23, 1996): 24–8.

Kaplan, Robert D. "Technology as a Magnifier of Good and Evil." In *Forbes* 158 (December 2, 1996): S51.

Kapp, Clare. "WHO Examines the Health of Indigenous Peoples." In *The Lancet* 354 (December 4, 1999): 1982.

Katz, I., J. Goldston, and L. Benjamin. "Behavior and Productivity in Bi-Racial Work Groups." In *Human Relations* 11 (1958): 123–41.

Kelley, R. Lynn. "An Area Studies Approach: Globalizing the Curriculum." In *Liberal Education* 77 (November-December 1991): 14–.

Kennedy, Eugene and Sara C. Charles. Excerpt from "Authority: The Most Misunderstood Idea in America." In *National Catholic Reporter* 34 (February 13, 1998): 13–16.

Keyfitz, N. "Thirty Years of Demography." *Demography* 30 (1993): 533–49.

Khazanov, Anatoly. "The Collapse of the Soviet Union: Nationalism During Perestroika and Afterwards." In *Nationalities Papers* 22 (1994): 157–73.

Kirk, D. "Demographic Transition Theory." *Population Studies* 50 (1945): 361–87.

Kizer, Edgar and Michale Hechter. "The Role of General Theory in Comparative-Historical Sociology." In *American Journal of Sociology* 97 (July 1991): 1–30.

Koeppel, Barbara. "Paul Sweezy." *The Progressive* 56 (May 1992): 34–6.

Kohn, Melvin L. "Social Structure and Personality: A Quintessentially Sociological Approach to Social Psychology." *Social Forces* 68 (September 1989): 26–33.

Kraly, E. P. and R. Warren. "Estimates of Long-Term Immigration to the United States: Moving to the U.S. Statistics Toward United Nations Concepts." In *Demography* 29 (1992): 613–26.

Krippner, Stanley. "New Myths for the New Millenium." In *The Futurist* 32 (March 1998): 30–35.

Laczko, Leslie. "Attitudes Towards Aboriginal Issues in Canada: The Changing Role of Language Cleavage." In *Quebec Studies* 23 (Spring/Summer 1997): 3–12.

●

Lee, E. S. and A. S. Lee. "Internal Migration Statistics for the United States." In *Journal of the Maerican Statistical Association* 55 (1960): 644–97.

Lee, Gary R.. Marion C. Willetts, and Karen Seccombe. "Widowhood and Depression: Gender Differences." In *Research on Aging* 20 (September 1998): 611–31.

Lenski, G.E. "Social Participation and Status Crystallization." In *American Sociological Review* 21 (August 1956): 458–64.

Lerner, Michael. "Spirituality in America." *Tikkun* 13 (November-December 1998): 33.

Levin, Irene. "Family as Mapped Realities." *Journal of Family Issues* 14 (March 1993): 82–91.

Levy, Daniel S. "Your Family." *Time,* August 2, 1999, 100.

Lieberman, Devorah A. and Candice L. Goucher. "Multicultural Education and University Studies." In *Journal of General Education* 48 (1999): 118–.

Lieblich, Julia. "Beliefs Drive Racial Hatred, Violence Against the 'Damned.'" In *National Catholic Reporter* 31 (September 8, 1995): 5.

Linden, Eugene. "Borneo: The Penans Stand By Their Land." In *Time,* September 23, 1991, 54.

———. "Megacities." In *Time,* January 11, 1993, 30–38.

Livingstone, David N. "The Gift of Science: Examining the Relationship Between Christianity and Science." In *Christianity Today* 43 (December 1999): 52.

Long, L. and D. DeAre. "U.S. Population Redistribution: A Perspective on the Nonmetropolitan Turnaround." In *Population and Development Review* 14 (1988): 433–50.

Long, Norton E. "Politics, Political Science, and Public Interest." In *Political Science and Politics* 24 (December 1991): 671–75.

Macklin, Eleanor D. "Nontraditional Family Forms: A Decade of Research." In *Journal of Marriage and the Family* (November 1980): 175–85.

Malos, Stanley B. "The New Affirmative Action." *Journal of Applied Behavioral Science* 36 (March 2000): 5–22.

Mandt, A. J. "Fichte, Kant's Legacy, and the Meaning of Modern Philosophy." In *The Review of Metaphysics* 50 (March 1997): 591–633.

Mann, Thomas. "The Downfall of Idealism." *UNESCO Courier* (June 1994): 46–48.

Maoz, Zeev and Bruce Russett. "Normative Structural Causes of Democratic Peace, 1946–1986." In *The American Political Science Review* 87 (September 1993): 624–38.

Marcus, David L. "After the Buses Stop Virtual Resegregation?" In *US News and World Report* December 13, 1999, 38.

Martin, P. and J. Widgren. "International Migration: A Global Challenge." In *Population Bulletin* 51 (1996): 1–48.

Marty, Martin E. "Circulation of Elites." *The Christian Century* 113 (March 20, 1996): 369.

Massey, D. S. "The Social and Economic Origins of Immigration." In *Annals of the American Academy of Political and Social Sciences* 510 (1990): 60–72.

Massey, D. S., J. Arango, G. Hugo, A. Kouaouci, A. Pelligrino, and J. E. Taylor. "Theories of International Migration: A Review and Appraisal." *Population and Development Review* 19 (1993): 431–6.

Massey, D. S., M. D. Maudlin, and J. F. Phillips. "The Demographic Impact of Family Planning Programs." In *Studies in Family Planning* 21 (1990): 299–310.

Maxwell, Joe and Andres Taplia. "Guns and Bibles: Militia Extremists Blend God and Country Into a Potent Mixture." In *Christianity Today* 39 (June 19, 1995): 34–9.

McClenahen, John S. "NAFTA Works." *Industry Week* 249 (January 10, 2000): 5–6.

McCorkel, Jill. "Going to the Crackhouse: Critical Space as a Form of Resistance in Total Institutions and Everyday Life." *Symbolic Interaction* 21.3 (1998): 227–52.

McNicoll, G. "Institutional Determinants of Fertility Change." In *Population Review* 6 (1980): 441–62.

Mechanic, D. "The Role of Sociology in Health Affairs." In *Health Affairs* 9: (1990): 85–97.

———. "Sociological Dimensions of Illness Behavior." In *Social Science and Medicine* 41 (1995): 1207–16.

Miele, Frank. "Darwin's Dangerous Disciple." *Skeptic* 3 (1995): 80–85.

Milke, Melissa A., Robin W. Simon, and Brian Powell. "Through the Eyes of Children: Youth's Perceptions and Evaluations of Maternal and Paternal Roles." In *Social Psychology Quarterly* 60 (1997): 218–37.

Milke, Melissa A. and Pia Petola. "Playing All the Roles: Gender and the Work-Family Balancing Act." In *Journal of Marriage and the Family* 61 (May 1999): 476–90.

Mitchell, Barbara. "Transitions to Adulthood in a Changing Economy: No Work, No Family, No Future?" In *Journal of Marriage and the Family* 62 (February 2000): 274–75.

Moberg, Dennis J. "The Big Five and Organizational Virtue." In *Business Ethics Quarterly* 9 (April 1999): 245–72.

Moore, J. C., Jr. "Status and Influence in Small Group Interactions." In *Sociometry* 31 (March 1968): 47–63.

Monaghan, Peter. "A New Momentum in Asian-American Studies." In *Chronicle of Higher Education* 45 (April 2, 1999): A16–A18.

Morales, Isidoro. "NAFTA: The Governance of Economic Openness." In *Annals of the American Academy of*

Political and Social Science 565 (September 1999): 35–65.

Morrow, Lance. "Guerillas in Our Midst: Passive Aggression is Spreading Like a Drug-Resistant Strain of Civic Anger." *Time,* March 18, 1996, 102.

Morse, Claire K. "Age and Variability in Francis Galton's Data." In *Journal of Genetic Psychology* 160 (March 1999): 99–104.

Motavalli, Jim. "Enough! (Dissatisfaction with the Consumer Culture)." In *E* 7 (March-April 1996): 28–36.

Muthen, Bengt O. and Patrick J. Curran. "General Longitudinal Modeling of Individual Differences in Experimental Design: A Latent Variable Framework for Analysis and Power Estimation." In *Psychological Methods* 2 (1997): 371–402.

Nakansishi, Don T. "Linkages and Boundaries: Twenty-Five Years of Asian American Studies." In *Amerasia Journal* 21 (Winter 1995/1996): xvii–xxv.

Newcomb, T. "An Approach to the Study of Communicative Acts." In *Psychological Review* 60 (1953): 393–404.

Ogburn, William Fielding. "Technology and the Standard of Living in the United States." In *American Journal of Sociology* 60 (January 1955): 380–86.

Olsen, Ted. "Missions Leaders Seek to 'De-Westernize' the Gospel." In *Christianity Today* 41 (February 3, 1997): 86.

Oser, Fritz K. "Kohlberg's Dormant Ghosts: The Case of Education." In *Journal of Moral Education* 25 (September 1996): 253+.

Palmer, Bryan. "Before Braverman: Harry Frankel and the American Worker's Movement." In *Monthly Review* 8 (January 1999): 33–46.

Paterson, Eva. "Equal Opportunity for a Post-Proposition 209 World." In *Human Rights* 26 (Summer 1999): 9–12.

Pearlin, Leonard I. "The Sociological Study of Stress." In *Journal of Health and Social Behavior* 30 (September 1989): 241–56.

Pearlin, Leaonrard I., et al. "The Stress Process." *Journal of Health and Social Behavior* 22 (December 1981): 337–56.

Pebley, A. R. "Demography and Environment." *Demography* 35 (1998): 377–89.

Perry, Constance M. "How Do We Teach What is Right? Research and Issues in Ethical and Moral Development." In *Journal for a Just and Caring Education* 2 (October 1996): 400–10.

Pescosolido, B. and J. Kronenfeld. "Health, Illness, and Healing in an Uncertain Era: Challenges From and For Medical Sociology." *Journal of Health and Social Behavior* extra issue (1995): 5–35.

Peskind, Steve. "Buddha's Way." *The Advocate,* July 22, 1997, 11.

Petersen, William. "A New Look at Malthus." *Society* 36 (November 1998): 60–65.

Peterson, Trond. "On the Promise of Game Theory in Sociology." In *Contemporary Sociology* 23 (July 1994): 498–502.

Phelps, Christopher and Andros Skotnes. "An Interview with Paul Sweezy." *Monthly Review* 51 (May 1999): 31–53.

Piroth, Scott. "Social Issues and Voting Behavior." In *Social Education* 60 (October 1996): 368–73.

Polachek, Solomon William. "Conflict and Trade." In *Journal of Conflict Resolution* 24 (March 1980): 55–78.

Population Council. "Research on the Determinants of Fertility." In *Population and Development Review* 7 (1981): 11–24.

Powers, Charles H. "Clarification and Extension of Emerson and Cook's Exchange." In *Sociological Theory* 3 (Spring 1985): 58–65.

Press, Julie and Eleanor Townsley. "Wives' and Husbands' Housework Reporting: Gender, Class, and Social Desirablility." In *Gender and Society* 12 (April 1998): 88–218.

Prier, Phillipe. "Le Play and His Followers: Over a Century of Achievement." In *International Social Science Journal* 157 (September 1998): 343–48.

Putnam, Robert D. "Bowling Alone: America's Declining Social Capital." In *Journal of Democracy* 6.1 (1995): 65–78.

———. "The Strange Disappearance of Civic America." In *The American Prospect* (Winter 1996): 34.

Ramey, James W. "Emerging Patterns of Innovative Behavior in Marriage." In *The Family Coordinator* (October 1972): 435–57.

Revelle, William. "Personality Process." *Annual Review of Pscyhology* 46 (1995): 295–328.

Ridgeway, Cecilia L. "Expectations, Legitimation, and Dominance Behavior in Task Groups." In *American Sociological Review* 51 (October 1986): 603–17.

Robey, John S. "Civil Society and NAFTA: Initial Results." *Annals of American Academy of Political and Social Science* 565 (September 1999): 113–25.

Rothman, Kenneth J. "Lessons from John Graunt." *The Lancet* 347 (January 6, 1996): 37–40.

Rothman, Stanley and Amy Black. "Elites Revisited: American Social and Political Leadership of the 1990's." *International Journal of Public Opinion Research* 11 (1999): 169–95.

Rubin, Alfred P. "Are Human Rights Legal?" *Israel Yearbook on Human Rights* 20 (1991): 45– 70.

Rushton, J. Philippe. "Sir Francis Galton, Epigenetic Rules, Genetic Similarity Theory, and Human Life History Analysis." *Journal of Personality* 58 (March 1990): 117–140.

Sampson, E. E. "Status Congruence and Cognitive Consistency." *Sociometry* 26 (1963): 146–62.

Seiple, Robert A. "Ministry in the Real World Order." *Christianity Today* 40 (July 15, 1996): 14–16.

Shapiro, Svi. "Killing Kids: The New Culture of Destruction." *Tikkun* 13 (July-August 1998): 23–26.

Sharpe, T., M. Browne, and K. Crider. "The Effects of A Sportsmanship Curriculum Intervention on Generalized Positive Social Behavior of Urban Elementary School Students."*Journal of Applied Behavior Analysis* 28, (1995): 401–16.

Shea, Christopher. "Multiculturalism Gains an Unlikely Supporter." *Chronicle of Higher Education* 43 (April 11, 1997): A16–A18.

Simon, Rita J. and James P. Lynch. "The Sociology of Law: Where We Have Been and Where We Might Be Going." *Law and Society Review* 23 (1989): 825–45.

Simpson, Michael D. "Affirmative Action Under Attack." *NEA Today* 18 (November 1999): 20.

Skvoretz, John and Thomas J. Fararo. "Generating Symbolic Interaction." *Sociological Methods of Research* 25 (August, 1996): 60.

Smith, George W. and Dorothy E. Smith. "The Ideology of 'Fag': The School Experience of Gay Students." *Sociological Quarterly* 39.2 (1998): 309–35.

South, S. J. and K. D. Crowder. "Residential Mobility Between Cities and Suburbs: Race, Suburbanization, and Back-to-the-City Moves." *Demography* 4 (1997): 525–38.

Sowell, Thomas. "Drive a Stake Through It: Affirmative Action." *Forbes* 158 (August 26, 1996): 53.

———. "Surrendering to the Multiculturalists." *Forbes* 159 (June 16, 1997): 72–78.

Spohn, William C. "Conscience and Moral Development." *Theological Studies* 61 (March 2000): 122–38.

Spratt, Margaret. "Beyond Hull House: New Interpretations of the Settlement Movement in America." *Journal of Urban History* 23 (September 1997): 770–76.

Stanford, Peter. "Would You Believe It? Unrevealed Truths About the Christian Church." *New Statesman* 127 (December 18, 1998): 45–47.

Strauss, R. "The Nature and Status of Medical Sociology." *American Sociological Review* 22 (1957): 200–204.

Strickland, Debra Higgs. "Monsters and Christian Enemies." *History Today* 50 (February 2000): 45.

Stycos, J. M. "Demography As An Interdiscipline." *Sociological Forum* 2 (1987): 616–18.

Sutton, John R. "Crime and Punishment in American History." *Contemporary Sociology* 23 (July 1994): 573–75.

Swinder, Ann. "Culture in Action: Symbols and Strategies." *American Sociological Review* 51 (1986): 273–86.

Szreter, S. "The Idea of Demographic Transition and the Study of Fertility Changes: A Critical Intellectual History."*Population and Development Review* 19 (1993): 659–701.

Tarde, Gabriel. "Criminality and Social Health." Translated by Andrew Scull. *Revue philosophique* 39 (1895): 148–62.

Taylor, Marylee C. "Improved Conditions, Rising Expectations, and Dissatisfaction: A Test of the Past/Present Relative Deprivation Hypothesis." *Social Psychology Quarterly* 45 (March 1982): 24–33.

Thoits, Peggy A. "Stress, Coping, and Social Support Processes: Where are We? What Next?" *Journal of Health and Social Behavior* Extra Issue (1995): 53–79.

Thompson, W. "Population." *American Journal of Sociology* 34 (1929) 959–75.

Thomson, Keith Stewart. "1798: Darwin and Malthus." *American Scientist* 86 (May 1998): 226–29.

Thornton, Stephen P. "Facing Up to Feuerbach." *Philosophy of Religion* 39 (April 1996): 103–20.

Thurman, Robert. "The Dalai Lama on China, Hatred, and Optimism." *Mother Jones* 22 (November-December 1997): 28–34.

Tickamyer, Ann R. "Sex, Lies, and Statistics: Can Rural Sociology Survive Restructuring? (or) What is Right with Rural Sociology and How Can We Fix It?" *Rural Sociology* 61 (Spring 1996): 5–24.

Timson, Judith. "Our So-Called Social Lives." *Chatelaine* 69 (December 1996): 30.

Tiryakian, Edward A. "Existential Phenomenology and the Sociological Tradition." *American Sociological Review* 30 (October 1965): 674–88.

Tobin, James. "Macroeconomics in the Conservative Era." *Challenge* 40 (July-August 1997): 27–36.

Todaro, M. P. "A Model of Labor Migration and Urban Unemployment in Less Developed Countries." *American Economic Review* 59 (1969): 138–48.

Torrance, E. P. "Some Consequences of Power Differences on Decision-Making in Permanent and Temporary Three-Man Groups." *Research Studies* 22 (1954): 130–40.

Turner, Ralph H. "Collective Behavior and Resource Mobilization as Approaches to Social Movements: Issues

and Continuities." *Research in Social Movements, Conflict, and Change* 4 (1981): 1–24.

———. "Personality in Society: Social Psychology's Contribution to Sociology." *Social Psychology Quarterly* 51 (1988): 1–10.

Twohey, Megan. "Desegregation is Dead." *National Journal* 31 (September 18, 1999): 2614–20.

Umberson, Debra, Camille B. Wortman, and Ronald C. Kessler. "Widowhood and Depression: Explaining Long-Term Gender Differences in Vulnerability." *Journal of Health and Social Behavior* 33 (March 1992): 10–24.

Van Bierma, David and Nadya Labi. "Pop Goes the Kabbalah: Jewish Mysticism Makes a Comeback with Younger People Yearning for a More Individual Spirituality." *Time,* November 24, 1997, 92–5.

Van Den Berghe, Pierre. Review of *The Scope of Sociology* by Milton M. Gordon. *Social Forces* 69 (September 1990): 644–45.

Vaughn, Lewis and Theordore Schick, Jr. "Do We Have Free Will?" *Free Inquiry* 18 (Spring 1998): 43–47.

Volokh, Alexander. "Faithful Incentives." *Reason* 29 (November 1997): 21–2.

Wagner, David G. Review of *A Measure for Measures: A Manifesto for Empirical Sociology,* by Ray Pawson. *American Journal of Sociology* 96 (March 1991): 1314–17.

Wallace, Paul. "The Rebirth of Malthusian Gloom." *New Statesman and Society* 11 (January 9, 1998): 21–2.

Wallach, Frances. "A Partnership That's Saving Kids." *Parks and Recreation* 26 (October 1991): 52–5.

Walsh, Catherine. "The Life and Legacy of Lawrence Kohlberg." *Society* 37 (January 2000): 36.

Walters, Andrew S. and David M. Hayes. "Homophobia Within Schools: Challenging the Culturally Sanctioned Dismissal of Gay Students and Collegues." *Journal of Homosexuality* 35 (1998): 1–23.

Walton, Paul. "Max Weber's Sociology of Law: A Critique." *Sociological Review Monograph: The Sociology of Law* December 1976, 7–21.

Waltz, Kenneth N. *Man, the State, and War: A Theoretical Analysis.* New York: Columbia University Press, 1959.

Webster, Murry and John B. Kervin. "Artificiality in Experimental Sociology." *Canadian Review of Sociology and Anthropology* 8 (1971): 263–72.

Weis, Lois. "Seeing Education Rationally: The Botton and the Top." *International Journal of Sociology and Social Policy* 5 (1985): 61–73.

Wellman, Barry. "The Community Question: The Intimate Networks of East Yorkers." In *American Journal of Sociology* 84 (1979):1201–.

Whitham, Larry. "Apocalypse Eventually." *Insight on the News* 11 (May 29, 1995): 33.

Wiley, Mary Glenn. "How Expectation States Organize Theory Construction." In *Contemporary Sociology* 15 (May 1986): 338–41.

Williams, J. Allen, Jr. and Suzanne T. Ortega. "Dimensions of Ethnic Assimilation: An Empirical Appraisal of Gordon's Typology." *Social Science Quarterly* 71 (December 1990): 697–703.

Willoughby, Robert E. "The Creative Role of Controversy within the Church." *The Humanist* 59 (September 1999): 46.

Yates, Micheal D. "Braverman and the Class Struggle." *Monthly Review* 50 (January 1999): 2–11.

Youngman, Nicole. "Interview With Patricia Ireland, President of National Organization for Women." *The Harbinger* 17 (May 4, 1999).

Zelinsky, W. "The Hypothesis of the Mobility Transition." *Geographical Review* 61 (1971): 219–49.

Zweigenhaft, Richard L. and G. William Domhoff. "The New ower Elite." *Mother Jones* 23 (1998) 44–47.

Zukier, Henri. "The Essential 'Other' and the Jew: From Antisemitism to Genocide." In *Social Research* 63.4 (1996): 1110–1154.

Internet Sites

About.com. http://www.about.com.

Alcoweb: The World Wide Web about Alcohol and Alcoholism. http://www.alcoweb.com.

American Anthropological Association. http://www.aaanet.org.

American Health Care Association. http://www.ahca.org/.

American Humanist Association. http://humanist.net.

American National Biography Online. http://www.anb.org.

American Sociological Association. http://www.asanet.org.

The Anarchist Theory FAQ Homepage. http://www.geocities.com/CapitolHill/1931.

The Anti-Defamation League. http://www.adl.org.

Assembly of First Nations. http://www.afn.ca/.

Atlantic Unbound. http://www.theatlantic.com.

Athabasca University. Online Dictionary of the Social Sciences. http://datadump.icaap.org/cgi-bin/glossary/SocialDict.

Best.com. "Hermeneutics." http://www.best.com/~szabo/hermeneutics.html.

Bookreporter.com. http://www.bookreporter.com.

Boston University. School of Theology. "Peter L. Berger, University Professor." http://www.bu.edu.

Bowling Green State University. Department of Popular Culture. http://www.bgsu.edu/departments/popc.

Bureau of Indian Affairs Homepage. http://www.doi.gov/bureau-indian-affairs.html.

Center for World Indigenous Studies. http://www.cwis.org/who.html.

Centers for Disease Control and Prevention. http://www.cdc.gov.

The Chronicle of Higher Education. http://chronicle.com.

CNN. "U.S. Hate Groups Hard to Track." http://www.cnn.ru/US/9907/07/hategroups.

The Daily News. "Hermeneutics." http://www.tdn.com/ntm/questions/hermeneutics.htm.

Disaster Relief: Worldwide Disaster Aid and Information. http://www.disasterrelief.org.

Electronic Library. http://www.elibrary.com.

Facts on File. http://www.facts.com.

Federal Bureau of Investigation. "Counterterrorism." http://www.fbi.gov/contact/fo.jackson/cntrterr.htm.

Federal Emergency Management Agency. http://www.fema.org.

Fordham University. Modern History Sourcebook. "Thorstein Veblen: The Theory of the Leisure Class" by Paul Halstall. http://www.fordham.edu/halstall/mod/1899veblen.html.

Hate Watch. http://www.HateWatch.org.

Indiana University. "Cultural Materialism" by Soo Kyung Lim. http://www.indiana.edu/~wanthro/mater.htm.

Infotrac. http://www.infotrac.com.

Inlink Communications. "Social Norms: William Graham Sumner." Http://www.inlink.com/-tfc/norms.html.

Journal Storage. http://www.jstor.org/.

London School of Economics and Political Science. http://www.lsc.ise.ac.uk.

Marxists Internet Archive. http://www.marxists.org.

National Adult Literacy Database. http://www.nald.ca/.

National Center for Education Statistics. http://www.nces.ed.gov/.

National Institute for Literacy. http://www.nigl.gov/.

National Organization for Women. http://now.org.

Nobel E-Museum. http://www.nobel.se/index.html.

Office of Juvenile Justice and Delinquency Prevention. http://ojjdp.ncjrs.org.

Ohio State University. "Michel Foucault." http://cohums.ohio-state.edu/philo/foucault.html.

Princeton University Press. http://www.pupress.princeton.edu.

The Proceedings of the Friesian School. Electronic Journal of Philosophy. http://www.friesian.com.

The Public Interest. "The End of Courtship" by Leon R. Kass. http://www.thepublicinterest.com/notable/article7.html.

Radford University. "Dead Sociologists Index" by Larry Ridener. http://www.runet.edu/~lridener/DSS/INDEX/HTML.

Ron's Home Page. "Michel Foucault." http://www.connect.net/ron/foucault.html.

San Francisco State University. "Michel Foucault." http://userwww.sfsu.edu/-rsauzier/Foucault.html.

Sinclair Community College. "Health and Illness Behavior." http://www.sinclair.edu/classenhancements/aih103e/MulticulturalConecpts/sld008.htm.

Social Security History Home Page. http://www.ssa.gov/history/history.html.

Society of Applied Sociology. http://www.appliedsoc.org.

Sociocite: Sociological Information System Based at the University of Amsterdam. http://www.pscw.uva.nl/sociocite.

Sociological Practice Association. http://www.socpractice.org.

The Southern Poverty Law Center. http://www.splcenter.org.

Time. http://www.time.com

United States Bureau of the Census. International Database. http://www.census.gov/ipc/www/idbnew.html.

United States Committee for Refugees. "Worldwide Refugee Information." http: www.refugees.org/world/world-main.html.

United States Department of Education. http://www.ed.gov/.

University of Alabama. Department of Anthropology. "Cultural Materialism" by Jon Marcoux. http://www.as.ua.edu/ant/Faculty/murphy/cultmat.htm.

University of California. "A Brief Biography of G. William Domhoff." http://psych.ucsc.edu/dreams/About/bill.html.

University of California, Berkeley. Department of Demography. "Intergenerational Transfers and the Economic Life Cycle: A Cross Cultural Perspective" by Ronald Lee. http://www.demog.bekeley.edu/~rlee/papers/ccig.

———. Department of Sociology. http://sociology.berkeley.edu.

———. "Alfred Kroeber as Museum Anthropologist" by Ira Jacknis. http://www.qal.berkeley.edu/~kroeber/kromus.htm.

————. Free Speech Movement Archives. http://www.fsm-a.org.

University of California Press Online. http://www.ucpress.edu.

University of California Riverside. "Edna Bonacich." http://web.ucr.edu/web/schools/CHSS/soc/ebobacic/ebonacic.html.

University of Chicago. Department of Sociology. http://socialsciences.uchicago.edu/sociology/hist.html.

University of Chicago Press Online. http://www.press.uchicago.edu.

University of Massachusettes. "Game Theory Evolving." http://www-unix.oit.umass.edu/~gintis/.

University of Missouri. "Sociology Timeline" by Edward Brent. http://www.web.missouri.edu/~socbrent/timeline.htm.

University of Nebraska at Kearnley. Department of Sociology. http://www.unk.edu/departments/soc.

University of New Mexico. Department of Sociology. Sociology 371. "Weber and Conflict Theory." http://soc.unm.edu/soc371/wbconflict.htm.

University of Notre Dame. "Hermeneutics." http://www.nd.edu/~theo/glossary/hermeneutics.html.

University of Tennessee. "The Internet Encyclopedia of Philosophy." Edited by James Feiser. http://www.utm.edu/research/iep.

University of Texas. "Phl 347, Lecture 14: Obscentity." http://www.utexas.edu/course/phl247/lectures/lec14.html.

University of Turku, Finland. Department of Sociology. http://www.utu.fi/yht/sosiolgia.

University of Virginia. American Studies. http://xroads.virginia.edu.

University of Washington. School of Public Health and Community. "Health Policy Analysis Program." http://depts.washington.edu/hpap/index.html.

The White House. "Lyndon B. Johnson." http://www.whitehouse.gov/WH/glimpse/presidents/html/lj36.html.

The World of Richard Dawkins. "Revolutionary Evolutionist."

In *Wired Magazine*. July 1995. http://www.world-of-dawkins.com/bio.htm.

1640 Thomas Hobbes, an English philosopher, mathematician, and linguist, publishes *Elements of Law and Natural Politics*. Treatises concerning politics and government date back to Greek and Roman philosophers and are two of the oldest topics of concern for scholarly writing.

1651 Thomas Hobbes publishes *Leviathan*. The *Leviathan* was written during the English Civil War. In it, Hobbes argues that without states, there is inevitable war, and inhabitants will live in constant fear of death. His work influences many later writers and theorists.

1670 Benedict de Spinoza publishes *A Theologico-Political Treatise*. This work is often cited as Spinoza's most influential. In it, he argues that civil and religious thought should be kept separate, and distinctly different theories about them should be articulated. This argument is relatively new to philosophy at this time.

1677 Benedict de Spinoza publishes *Ethics*. In it, he discusses the nature of the human mind, how ideas are formulated, types of knowledge, and emotion. Ethics and morals are topics common to ancient philosophers. Concern for these topics later leads scholars to inquire about values and norms—two main topics for sociologists.

1677 Benedict de Spinoza publishes *On the Improvement of Understanding*. In it, he discusses multiple causation and the finiteness of causation. It serves as a methodological foundation for the social sciences on which future sociologists and statisticians expand. This is one of the first epistemological essays to spawn the question of how we know what we know.

1690 John Locke publishes his *Essay Concerning Human Understanding*. In it, he investigates the boundaries between opinions, or faith, and knowledge from the origin of ideas through the manner in which they are expressed through behavior.

1690 John Locke publishes the *Second Treatise on Government*. In the two volumes of this document, Locke develops his theory of natural laws and natural human rights—what is now known as inalienable rights—and this work forms the foundation of American freedom. Locke's work also influenced the creators of the American Constitution legitimizing revolts against tyrannical governments. This idea is the basis for checks and balances in U.S. government.

1721 Charles de Montesquieu publishes his *Persian Letters*. This famous compilation of letters is a social criticism of gender, politics, the self, history, religion, and culture. Montesquieu believed that humans are guided by greed and self-interest, and that these things drive all human interaction. This philosophy is called utilitarianism and remains a prominent philosophy in social, political, and criminological theory.

1733 The Industrial Revolution is estimated to have begun with the advent of the prototype for the cotton gin by John Kay in Britain (although most scholars estimate 1760 as the true beginning of the Industrial Revolution). The Industrial Revolution is a period of transition in which manual tools were replaced by machines in the manufacturing of goods. These changes revolutionized manufacturing, economics, politics, culture, and society in general. Social theory, during this time period, begins to focus on relations among social classes, and the role of government and business in the lives of individuals.

1739   David Hume writes his *Treatise on Human Nature.* He states that the purpose of this Treatise was to "introduce the experimental method of reasoning into moral subjects." In this work, Hume questions what human nature is and contrasts existing views of human nature.

1748   David Hume publishes his *Metaphysical Essays.* Hume sought to discover the true nature of things, and he believed that these things were discoverable outside of individual situations. Metaphysics led to, and made possible, scientific investigation of social phenomena.

1748   David Hume publishes *An Enquiry Concerning Human Understanding.* In this work, Hume agrees with John Locke in asserting that people are born as blank slates, and they come to develop a sense of self through interaction with others. This is a fundamental assertion for many modern sociologists.

1748   Charles de Montesquieu publishes the *Spirit of Laws.* This is considered Montesquieu's most influential work. In it, he describes three types of government: republic, monarchy, and despotism. Montesquieu was heavily influenced by John Locke, and both philosophers' work strongly influenced the writers of the U.S. Constitution.

1751   David Hume publishes the *Inquiry Concerning the Principles of Morality,* in which he questions the substance and definition of human nature. This work is criticized for its utilitarianism, but it was, nonetheless, a significant contribution to literature of its time.

1755   Jean Jacques Rousseau publishes *A Discourse upon the Origin and Foundation of the Inequality Among Mankind.* Here, he attempts to distinguish between what is human nature and what aspects of the human condition are brought about through interaction.

1760–1830

The Industrial Revolution spanned these years. It was Frederick Engels who much later coined the term "Industrial Revolution." The term refers to a transition period in which the market economy was transformed into an industrial economy where massive production was aided by the advent and usage of machine labor.

1762   Jean Jacques Rousseau publishes *The Social Contract.* In this work, Rousseau regards the social contract of states as protection of social rights, not as the states' obligation to award rights to individuals.

1775   Thomas Paine publishes an article in the *Pennsylvania Journal and the Weekly Advertiser* called "African Slavery in America." Some historians argue that Paine's article was instrumental in the formulation of the first anti-slavery society in America that was established in Philadelphia on April 14, 1775, just a few weeks following the article's publication.

1775–1781

The American Revolution.

1776   Thomas Paine publishes *Common Sense.* It is a pamphlet regarding the abuses of power in government, particularly, American government. Thomas Paine's discussions of power in politics and government inform later theorists in political economy.

1776   Jeremy Bentham publishes *Fragment on Government.* In it, Bentham proclaims that because it is human nature to act upon one's self-interest, that this type of action will always produce the "right" outcome. This idea is heavily criticized, but sparks a resurgent debate about human nature.

1776   Adam Smith publishes *An Inquiry into the Nature and Causes of the Wealth of Nations.* In it, he investigates the laws of supply and demand that later contribute to shaping the American economic system and purpose.

1777   John Howard publishes *The State of Prisons.* He was a sheriff in Europe whose primary job was to guard the judge. In fulfilling his duties, he witnessed grave injustice and maltreatment of prisoners. His book brought much attention to prison reform and resulted in at least three major prison reform policies enacted in Europe.

1781   Immanuel Kant publishes his *Critique of Pure Reason.* In this book, Kant denounces the existence of a God. His work epitomizes typical debates in the late eighteenth century over the connections between scientific inquiry and the production of reason. Questions of truth and human reason arise in these debates that often pit religion against science.

1782–1789

Jean Jacques Rousseau writes about the corrupt social customs and institutions of his time in *Confessions.*

1785   Watt's steam engine is invented. This invention expands exports and imports of goods during the industrial revolution, and aides in the manufacturing of goods.

1787   The United States Constitution is signed into law. The influence of many philosophers and philosophical debates on government, law, politics, and even human nature can be seen in the U.S. Constitution.

1787   Jeremy Bentham writes a series of letters to a friend that is later called the *Defense of Usury.* In the letters, he critiques legal restraints on bargaining.

1788   Immanuel Kant publishes *Critique of Practical Reason.* In this work, Kant continues with his denunciation of the existence of a God, and a soul, but says that in practice, people must accept these things as real. Otherwise, there is no moral basis for behavior.

1789–1799

The French Revolution. Many European philosophers, political analysts, and economists are strongly influenced by the French Revolution, including Karl Marx and Frederick Engels.

1789   Jeremy Bentham publishes the *Introduction to the Principles of Morals and Legislation,* wherein he describes his view of human nature that depicts humans as pleasure seeking and pain avoiding. This utilitarian view of human nature guides Bentham's view of legislation and the enforcement of laws. Many criminological and sociological theories of human behavior begin with Bentham's theory of human nature, although many of Bentham's critics call him the "great compiler" due to his ability to compile other people's theories into his own.

1790   On March 1, the first United States census begins. Today, the US census is extensively used in social research.

1790   Edmund Burke writes a series of unpublished letters called *Reflections on the Revolution in France.* The French revolution provides many political theorists of this time a practical case study for analyzing political crises.

1790   Mary Wollstonecraft writes *A Vindication Of The Rights Of Men* in response to Edmund Burke's Reflections on the Revolution in France. Harriet Martineau, in *Illustrations of Political Economy* (1832), describes Wollstonecraft as the first English public advocate of women's rights.

1791   The Corresponding Society is established. This organization is the first English revolutionary labor organization. Karl Marx and Frederick Engels later became active supporters of this movement.

1795   Thomas Paine publishes *The Age of Reason.* In this work, Paine examines the Bible objectively and critically. At the time this was written, such examinations of the Bible were uncommon. This work later influences Weber's extensive work on world religions.

1798   Thomas Malthus publishes his *Essay on the Principle of Population.* In it, he suggests that society can only be improved by keeping the size of the population at a minimum. Malthus' theories help to inform later demographers. Charles Darwin attributes much of his own thinking to the theories of Malthus.

1798   Mary Wollstonecraft publishes *Maria: Or, The Wrongs of Woman.* This is a novel in which Wollstonecraft describes the oppression of women through the various laws and customs of her time.

1807   Georg Wilhelm Freidrich Hegel publishes *The Phenomenology of Mind.* Hegel believed that only through interaction with other—through experience—could humans evolve to perfection. His dialectical theories of the mind, logic, and realism influenced Marx, Engels, and many modern theorists. There remain, even today, Hegalian societies worldwide, although his philosophy was much more popular in his own time. Hegel continued to publish though 1837, but *The Phenomenology of Mind* proves to be his most influential work.

1813   Weaving machines are invented. These machines aid and expanded the Industrial Revolution.

1813   Harriet Taylor and John Stuart Mill publish "A New View of Society" in the *Unitarian.* The focus of her work centered on the degrading realities of marriage and the economic dependence of women on men in her time. Many believe that Harriet wrote much of what is now credited solely to John Stuart Mill. Mill is quoted as saying, "when two persons have their thoughts and speculations completely in common it is of little consequence in respect of the question of originality, which of them holds the pen."

1814   Joseph de Maistre publishes his *Essay on the Generative Principle of Political Constitutions.* Maistre's work focused on the irrational aspects of politics and, specifically, on violence.

1814   Saint-Simon, who advocated a society based on a scientific division of labor, publishes *The Reorganization of European Society.* His main contribution to sociology is his tutelage of Auguste Comte.

1822   Auguste Comte publishes *Plan of the Scientific Operations Necessary for Reorganizing Society.* In this text, Comte coins the term "sociology," and so today is considered the "father of sociology." His work concentrates on social change and social stability. Comte is also known as the "father of French positivist thought." He emphasized that society should be studied in the same manner as nature.

1830   Auguste Comte publishes *The Positive Philosophy* (6 volumes; 1830, 1835, 1838, 1839, 1841, 1842). *The Positive Philosophy* had a huge impact on Harriet Martineau, and in 1896, she translated and condensed all six volumes.

1833   Harriet Martineau publishes *Poor Laws and Paupers*. Jeremy Bentham, John Stuart Mill, and Harriet Taylor heavily influenced Martineau's work.

1833–1843

The Young Hegelians flourish in Germany. This time period marks their heyday.

1834   Harrriet Martineau publishes *Illustrations of Political Economy*. She later settled in London and was consulted by cabinet ministers. Martineau's work influenced the feminist movement of the 1960s, and continues to inform social feminist theory.

1834–1836

Harriet Martineau visits America and offends many with her abolitionist views.

1835   Lambert Adolphe Jacques Quetelet publishes *Sur l'homme et le développement de ses facultés* (translated into English in 1842 as *A Treatise on Man and the Development of His Faculties*). Quetelet is credited with developing the application of the normal curve, a statistical phenomena, to social research. His social research concentrated on the numerical consistency of crimes.

1835–1840

Alexis de Tocqueville writes *Democracy in America*. In 1831, Tocqueville traveled to America from France to study the U.S. prison system. His main objective, though, was to study democracy. This book results from his travels. In it, he says that he intends to discover what there is to fear, and what there is to hope for, in modern democracy.

1837   Harriet Martineau publishes *Society in America*. This work is the result of her two-year stay in America (1934–1936) in which she studies American morals and their effects on American institutions. Martineau is one of the earliest feminists whose work also includes discussions on the political non-existence of women, inadequacies in the American educational system, and slavery.

1841   It is estimated that Frederick Engels and Karl Marx meet around this time, both as members of the German intellectual group called "The Young Hegelians." Their work, which was strongly influenced by Hegel, Montesquieu, and political and industrial changes occurring around them in Europe at the time, focused on the structural aspects of economic relations. Ironically, both Engels and Marx disagreed with Hegel's theories and eventually separated from the Young Hegelians.

1842   Karl Marx writes his first article for *Rheinische Zeitung*, a German revolutionary newspaper. Shortly

following publication, Marx became the editor for the paper and, due to its radical content, publication ended within one year.

1842   The Webster-Ashburton Treaty is signed to abolish the African slave trade.

1843   Karl Marx and Frederick Engels begin publishing the first of their radical philosophical theories in the journal *Deutsch-Franzîsischen JahrbÅcher* (Translated as "*Franco-German Year Books*").

1843   John Stuart Mill publishes his *System of Logic*. In it, Mill establishes an inductive method for finding proof.

1844   Frederick Engels publishes *Outlines of a Critique of Political Economy*. It is one of many articles that compile the *Deutsch Franzosische Jahbucher*, a series of Marx and Engels' personal journals.

1844   Karl Marx writes his *Thesis on Feuerbach*. Marx and Engels were heavily influenced by Feuerbah's humanitarian philosophy.

1844–1845

Karl Marx writes *The Economic and Philosophic Manuscripts of 1844*, in which he develops the thesis for *Das Kapital*. These early manuscripts were never intended for publication.

1846   Karl Marx publishes *The German Ideology.*

1847   Frederick Engels writes *The Principles of Communism,* the predecessor to Marx and Engels' *Communist Manifesto* published one year later.

1847   Karl Marx publishes *The Poverty of Philosophy,* which was a direct response to, and critique of, J. P. Proudhon's *The Philosophy of Poverty.*

1848   Karl Marx and Frederick Engels publish the *Communist Manifesto.* The two theorists had been commissioned to write the book by the Communist League to which they both belonged.

1848   John Stuart Mill publishes *Principles of Political Economy*. This work expands the political theories of Adam Smith.

1849   Harriet Martineau publishes the *History of England During the Thirty Years' Peace 1816–1846.*

1849   Karl Marx delivered a series of lectures entitled the "Wage-Labor and Capital" that are transformed into articles published the same year in the *Neue Rheinische Zeitung.*

1850   Frederick Engels publishes "The Peasants' War in Germany" in the *Neue Rheinische Zeitung*. In this article, Engels parallels the events leading to both the German Revolution of 1525 and that of 1848–1849. He attributes the cause of both revolutions to class

conflict. Prior to this article, the revolutions had been blamed on religious conflict.

1850 Karl Marx and Engels publish "England's 17th c. Revolution" in the *Politisch-Okonomische Revu*. It is a review of Francios Guizot's 1850 pamphlet *Pourquoi la revolution d'Angleterr a-t-elle reussi?* Critics of the earlier publication argue that the historical facts of the French Revolution were distorted and confused even as they were occurring. These criticisms become a case study in the sociology of knowledge.

1850 Karl Marx's *The Class Struggle in France, 1848 to 1850* is published.

1850 Herbert Spencer publishes *Social Statics*. In this work, Spencer traces evolutionary changes in social structures and institutions.

1851 John Stuart Mill and Harriet Taylor publish "The Emancipation of Women" in the *Westminster Review*. Mill published with Taylor until her death in 1858. For fifteen years following her death, he published with her daughter Helen Taylor.

1851 Harriet Martineau publishes *Letters on the Laws of Man's Nature and Development*. In it, Martineau articulates agnostic views that alienated her friends.

1851–1854

Comte writes his four-volume manifesto titled *System of Positive Polity*.

1852 Karl Marx publishes *The Eighteenth Brumaire of Louis Bonaparte*. In this book, Marx makes his most radical and controversial conclusion that the bourgeois must be completely eliminated for a revolution to succeed.

1853 Lambert Adolphe Jacques Quetelet organizes the first international statistics conference.

1854 Harriet Martineau publishes a letter in the London *Daily News* regarding wife-beating and the state of women's rights in divorce. The letter helped to shape parliamentary acts regarding women's rights in these matters.

1857 Karl Marx's *Pre-Capitalist Economic Formations* is published. It originated as part of *A Contribution to the Critique of Political Economy* published two years later.

1857 Karl Marx publishes *Grundrisse: Foundations of the Critique of Political Economy*. In this huge body of work compiled as personal notebooks, Marx begins to develop the theoretical foundations for his next two books on political economy.

1859 Charles Darwin publishes *The Origin of Species*. This famous work influenced sociology in many

ways and continues to center the debate between influences of biology and sociology on human behavior. In fact, it was sociologist Herbert Spencer who later coined the term "survival of the fittest" when referencing Darwin's theory.

1859 John Stuart Mill publishes *On Liberty*. This work is widely cited within political economy. It describes how legitimacy is established and exercised by society over the individual.

1861–1865

The U.S. Civil War occurs.

1861 Henry Sumner Maine writes *Ancient Law*. This work is widely cited in the study of the sociology of law. It traces the evolution of law and legal thought through history.

1864 Herbert Spencer publishes his controversial book titled *Reason for Dissenting from the Positivist Philosophy of M. Comte*. Spencer's work is thought by many as a continuation of Comte's work, but Spencer vehemently disagreed. Nonetheless, Spencer and Comte share an emphasis on evolution and organist explanations of social phenomena.

1867 Herbert Spencer publishes *Principles of Biology* (two volumes). In it, he develops his theory of social evolution, which draws heavily on Darwin's theory of biological evolution.

1868 Karl Marx's first volume of *Das Kapital* is published. In it, he articulates his famous and influential theory of materialist alienation.

1868 The U.S. Congress ratifies the Fourteenth Amendment to the Constitution allowing equal rights to all natural born citizens. It took several subsequent constitutional laws to interpret this amendment.

1870 The U.S. Congress ratifies the Fifteenth Amendment to the Constitution allowing African American men the right to vote in elections. The 1965 Voter Rights Act was enacted to enforce this law.

1871 Charles Darwin publishes *The Descent of Man*. Darwin's work significantly influenced biological theories in the study of criminal behavior, which were popular from 1800 through 1915.

1876 Cesare Lombroso publishes *Criminal Man*. Lombroso developed the most often cited biological theory of criminal personality, although research discounts the theory. He believed that one could predict the propensity for criminal behavior by mapping the bumps and crevices on peoples' heads.

1881 Ferdinand Tönnies publishes *Gemeinschaft und Gesellschaft*, which was translated into English in

1957 (*Communities and Society: Gemeinschaft und Gesellschaft*). In it, he describes two basic social groups, Gemeinshaft (community), and Gesellschaft (society). These basic concepts still form the foundation of lectures on the structure of society in general sociology courses.

1882   Karl Marx and Frederick Engels publish *Socialism, Utopian and Scientific*. In Engels' preface to the book, he traces German socialist theories to the influence of Saint Simon, Fourier, Own, Kant, Fichte and Hegel.

1889   Sir Francis Galton produced probability theory in mathematics. This is the statistical theory upon which social scientific research is based.

1892   The Chicago School of Sociology opens. Housed at the University of Chicago, this is the first school of sociology in the United States. Prominent early faculty members include Albion Small, Robert Park, Earnest Burgess, and William Ogburn. William Ogburn is the first sociologist in the United States to incorporate the use of statistics into the analysis of social data.

1893   Émile Durkheim publishes the first of four of his most famous works *The Division of Labor in Society*. In it, he describes his functionalist perspective on economic stratification. Durkheim is considered as a structural theorist whose primary focus centered on the development and function of norms within a society.

1895   Jane Addams publishes *Hull-House Maps and Papers, by Residents of Hull-House, A Social Settlement, A Presentation of Nationalities and Wages in a Congested District of Chicago, Together With Comments and Essays on Problems Growing Out of the Social Conditions*. Addams wrote about elitism, patriarchy, and intellectualism. She was shunned by most sociologists because of her radical ideas, feminist perspective, and because she was a woman. Nonetheless, Addams' work strongly influenced the work of others in the Chicago School, such as Park and Burgess, although her work is rarely cited. During this time, women who earned academic degrees in sociology were channeled into social work, while men were channeled into the field of sociology.

1895   Émile Durkheim publishes *The Rules of Sociological Method*. In each of Durkheim's publications, he emphasized the importance of using the scientific method to study social phenomenon. In this work, he describes the sociological method in detail and identifies and defines social facts.

1897   Émile Durkheim publishes *Suicide*. This is perhaps his most famous and most often cited work. In it, he identified three forms of suicide brought about by societal changes: egoistic, altruistic, and anomic. His theory of anomie continues to inform sociological theory.

1897   Max Weber publishes *The Methodological Foundations of Sociology*. Weber is possibly the most influential theorist in the history of sociology. His influence on social research methods includes his creation of the analytical and conceptual tool, the "ideal type", and his view of objectivity in social research.

1897   William Edward Burghardt Du Bois publishes *The Suppression of the African Slave Trade to the United States of America, 1638–1870*. In Du Bois' lifetime, he founded and/or edited at least six major newspapers including *The Moon* in Tennessee, *The Horizon*, in Washington, D.C., *The Crisis, The New Review, The Brownies' Book,* and *Phylon*. Du Bois was extremely instrumental in informing the public about the harsh realities of being African American.

1898   Émile Durkheim establishes the first social science journal in France called the *Annee Sociologique*. It was published annually and provided an outlet for philosophical writings on society and the scientific method as it applied to the study of society.

1899   T. B. Veblen publishes *The Theory of the Leisure Class: An Economic Study of Institutions*. In it, he discusses the economic role that the leisure class plays in modern life. He also coins the term "conspicuous consumption." The term is often used today in writings on the American middle-class's tendency to overspend.

1900   Georg Simmel publishes *Philosophy of Money*. Simmel's work constitutes a reaction to the organicist emphasis in social theory as written by Comte and Spencer. Instead, Simmel thought that human interaction was subject to different interpretation depending upon the historical period and cultural setting in which people were being studied. Simmel's theories mark the beginning of social interactionist theories.

1902   Vilfredo Pareto publishes *Les Systemes Socialistes*. The entirety of this work has yet to be published in English. This work directly opposes the theories of Karl Marx and Frederick Engels. Pareto warns against the "suicidal dangers of humanitarianism."

1902   Charles Horton Cooley publishes *Human Nature and Social Order*. In this work, Cooley lays the foundation for his theory of "the looking glass self."

1903   Émile Durkheim publishes *Moral Education: A Study in the Theory and Application of The Sociology of Education*. Durkheim's theory of education remains a prominent theory in the sociology of education.

1903 Lester Ward publishes *Pure Sociology*. Ward developed a theory of planned progress called telesis. His theory suggests that, through education and intellect, man can direct social evolution. He was one of the first American sociologists.

1904 Robert Ezra Park publishes *The Crowd and the Public*. Park's work stemmed from the work of previous social and ecological theorists. He develops a theory of social place that influences current theories of deviance and criminology.

1904 T. B. Veblen publishes *The Theory of Business Enterprise*. Veblen writes extensively on what is now referred to as the sociology of knowledge as well as business. He believes that man's position in the occupational and social order informs his way of knowing the world around him. He further theorizes that preference for different scientific approaches also stems from occupational and social order. His theories later influenced Robert Merton's theory of latent and manifest functions.

1904 Max Weber publishes *Objectivity in Social Science and Social Policy*. Weber argued that the method of social inquiry should be "value free," meaning that society should be studied objectively. He argued that objectivity is paramount to understanding the subjective meaning that humans attach to their actions.

1904 Max Weber visits the United States (St. Louis Exposition). Two years later, he publishes *The Protestant Ethic and the Spirit of Capitalism*. In this work, he traces the form of capitalism found in the United States to the Protestant ethic that developed in early America.

1905 The American Sociological Association (ASA) is founded. Its mission is to serve sociologists in their work, advance sociology as a science and profession, and to promote the contributions and use of sociology to society. Today, the ASA is the leading sociological association in the United States.

1906 William Graham Sumner publishes *Folkways: A Study of the Sociological Importance of Usages, Manners, Customs, Mores, and Morals*. Sumner was a Social Darwinist. He believed that the power and nature of social customs, mores, and folkways would direct human evolution, and that no political or legal intervention, such as socialism, was necessary.

1908 Georg Simmel publishes *Sociology: Investigations on the Forms of Sociation*. Most of what appears in this book comes from previous journal articles. His impact on sociology comes through his protégée Robert Park.

1909 William Edward Burghardt Du Bois establishes the National Association for the Advancement of Colored People (NAACP).

1909 Charles Horton Cooley publishes *Social Organization: A Study of the Larger Mind*. At about the same time as W. I. Thomas and George H. Mead, Cooley begins to emphasize the important roles that individuals play in the interpretation of their individual situations.

1910 William Edward Burghardt Du Bois establishes the magazine titled *The Crisis*. This magazine operates between 1910 and 1934. Included in one of the early editions of the magazine is Du Bois' famous treatise on race, *The Souls of Black Folk*.

1912 Émile Durkheim publishes *Elementary Forms of Religious Life*. In it, he identifies and describes the most basic forms of religion.

1913 Rosa Luxemburg writes *The Accumulation of Capital*. This work explains the capitalist movement towards imperialism. Luxemburg was a Marxist.

1913 Edmund Hussel, the founder of the field known as "phenomenology", publishes *Ideas: A General Introduction to Pure Reason,* which is not translated into English until 1931. Phenomenology—the study of the phenomena of consciousness—leads to the development of "the sociology of knowledge."

1914–1918

World War I spans these years. All major wars, skirmishes, and conflicts affect sociology and social theory.

1914 Émile Durkheim publishes *Pragmatism and the Question of Truth*. His philosophy on what is now known as the sociology of knowledge is that religious commitments can be traced to social commitments and not the other way around, as was most commonly thought at the time.

1915 Vilfredo Pareto publishes a *General Treatise on Sociology*. This is argued to be his most famous work. In it, Pareto emphasizes the importance of using scientific methods to study human structure and action.

1916 Vladimir Lenin publishes *Imperialism, The Highest Stage of Capitalism*. Lenin is accredited with bringing together advocates of Karl Marx' theories and initiating the "Marxist" school of thought.

1918 Rosa Luxemburg writes *The Russian Revolution,* which is published in 1922. In it, she describes the dictatorial powers of the Bolshevik party as dangerous. She was imprisoned for her political activities.

1918–1921

William I. Thomas and Florian Znaniecki publish *The Polish Peasant in Europe and America* (five volumes). This famous work traces the experiences

of Polish immigrants into America. It continues to inform social thought, theories about immigration, social change, and adaptation.

1919 Pitirim A. Sorokin publishes *System of Sociology* (two volumes). This work stemmed from Sorokin's Ph.D. dissertation and would never have been published had the censorship permission from the Russian government that appeared on the title page not been forged. Sorokin lived a tumultuous life, primarily because of his radical involvement in the Russian Revolution.

1920 The U.S. Congress ratifies the Nineteenth Amendment to the Constitution allowing women to vote in public elections.

1921 Ernest Burgess and Robert Ezra Park publish *An Introduction to the Science of Sociology.* In it, they emphasize the importance of establishing a practical focus for social research. This concise history of U.S. sociology is considered to be Park's most famous work.

1921 The Tulsa race riot of 1921 occurs on May 31st in Tulsa, Oklahoma. This is the most gruesome riot to have ever occurred in the United States. Some refer to the incident as the "Black Holocaust." Fifteen thousand African Americans were literally run out of town and white authorities murdered thousands of black men, women, and children. Riots are of particular significance to sociologists who study race relations, criminology, and political economy.

1922 John Dewey publishes *Human Nature and Conduct.* This social psychological work focuses on the role and definition of habit.

1922 Max Weber's *Economy and Society* (two volumes) is published postpartum. This work includes his famous analysis of bureaucracy and power.

1923 W. I. Thomas publishes *The Unadjusted Girl.* In it, he describes his theory on the formation of perspectives about life. He suggests that life perspectives develop through a series of individual definitions of each situation that is encountered.

1923 George Herbert Mead writes "Scientific Method and the Moral Sciences." Most of Mead's work was not published until after his demise. Many of his manuscripts are compiled in a book titled *Selected Writings on George Herbert Mead.*

1924 Edwin H. Sutherland publishes *Criminology.* This book marks the beginning of the branching off of the study of crime into its own subfield of sociology. In 1960, the American Society of Criminology establishes an award honoring Sutherland for his major contributions to the field of criminology.

1924 The U.S. Congress ratifies the National Origins Act, which limits immigration into the United States. Patterns of immigration and the effects that they were having on communities were being studied in human ecology and sociology at the Chicago School during this time.

1925 George Herbert Mead publishes "The Genesis of the Self and Social Control" in the *International Journal of Ethics.* Mead was a social psychologist whose work concentrated on defining the interaction between the mind and society.

1925 Ernest Burgess and Robert Ezra Park publish *The City.* In this work, the authors describe their "concentric zone theory" that was later transformed into the theory of social disorganization. This theory emphasizes the influence that neighborhoods have over the individuals who reside within them.

1925 Karl Mannheim publishes *The Problem of Sociology of Knowledge.* Mannheim is attributed to developing Husserl's phenomenology into the sociology of knowledge.

1927 The world's first television broadcast is transmitted from Washington D. C. to New York. The impact of television on society is profound.

1928 Louis Wirth publishes *The Ghetto.* Wirth was from the Chicago School of Ecology, but his work focused more extensively on urbanism and urban lifestyles than on the ecology of the city.

1929 Karl Mannheim further develops the phenomenology of Edmund Husserl into the "sociology of knowledge" in his *Ideology and Utopia.* He coined the term "sociology of knowledge", which today is a subfield of interest for sociologists.

1929 The New York Stock Exchange crashes, marking the beginning of the Great Depression. October 29 is forever known as "Black Thursday."

1932 Franklin Delano Roosevelt is elected president of the United States. This marks "The New Deal Era" in which many social and economic programs helped to put millions of people back to work during the Great Depression.

1932 George Herbert Mead writes "The Philosophy of the Present." Mead is described as a pragmatist philosopher whose work is primarily symbolic interactionist.

1932–1972

The Tuskegee Syphilis Study is conducted. The federal government's experiment lasted over forty years in which six hundred African American males were purposely injected with syphilis. The effects of which were monitored during the experiment, and at

least one hundred men lost their lives as a result. This experiment has prompted drastic changes in the ethical restraints placed upon social and medical researchers. The American Sociological Association updates its code of ethics annually.

1933 W. I. Thompson and P. K. Whelpton publish *Population Trends in the United States.* This work is an early example of demography—the statistical study of human populations—a subfield of sociology.

1934 William Edward Burghardt Du Bois begins to reject the conservative views of the NAACP and withdraws his support for the organization.

1934 George Herbert Mead publishes *Mind, Self, and Society.* In this work, Mead describes the development of the self as it occurs through socialization.

1935 Houston Stuart Chapin publishes *Contemporary American Institutions.* This work marks the beginning of the sociology of institutions.

1937 Talcott Parsons publishes the *Structure of Social Action.* Parsons believed that social structure is an entity in and of itself and, therefore, should be treated in social theory is if it is capable of acting.

1937 Herbert Blumer coins the term "symbolic interaction" in *Man and Society.* The concept of symbolic interaction stems from the logic of John Locke, David Hume, and Adam Smith, and from the theoretical contributions of George Herbert Mead. Symbolic interaction is a micro-sociological perspective that continues to influence both theory and method. It emphasizes the importance of meaning to the individual in theory and direct empirical observation as a methodology.

1937 Edwin H. Sutherland publishes *The Professional Thief: By a Professional Thief.* It is one of the very first ethnographic studies in criminology.

1937–1941

Pitirim A. Sorokin publishes *Social and Cultural Dynamics* (four volumes). His distinct theories on the sociology of knowledge contrasted with earlier thinkers. Instead of focusing on social structures, he emphases the influences of culture on individuals and on social change.

1938 On June 25th, the Wages and Hours (Fair Labor Standards) Act is passed. After several failed attempts, this act is the final ban on child labor in the United States. The act also limits the workweek to forty hours. The act goes into effect in October 1940. Another subfield of sociology is the sociology of occupations.

1939–1945

World War II spans these years.

1939 Edwin H. Sutherland publishes *Principles of Criminology.* In it, Sutherland defines his theory of differential association in which he explains criminal behavior as the result of learned behavior. This theory is still widely used today.

1948 Kingsley Davis publishes *Human Society.* In this and other works, he defines his functionalist approach to social class and social stratification.

1949 Talcott Parsons publishes *Essays in Sociological Theory, Pure and Applied.* Parsons' sociological theories take a functionalist perspective and his views are very conservative within sociology.

1949 Edwin H. Sutherland publishes *White Collar Crime.* In this work, Sutherland coins the term "white collar" and, in so doing, distinguishes differences in crime types associated with social class. Today, the terms white collar crime and white collar criminals are widely used, not only in criminology, but among the general public as well.

1949 Robert K. Merton, considered as one of the most influential twentieth century theorists, publishes *Social Theory and Social Structure.* In it, he describes his theory of manifest and latent functions, which he describes as the intended and unintended consequences of motivation. This theory helps to shape sociological research in many areas including deviance, criminology, criminal justice, race, political economy, aging, and education. In this book, Merton also describes bureaucratic structure and personality, as well as his theories of anomie and goal disjunction.

1950 Karl Mannheim publishes another treatise on what is now known as the sociology of knowledge, *Freedom, Power, and Democratic Planning.*

1950 Amos Hawley publishes *Human Ecology; A Theory of Community Structure.* Hawley wrote about population issues through human ecology and urban sociology. He is also credited with introducing family planning concepts to Thailand.

1950 Sheldon and Eleanor Glueck publish *Unraveling Juvenile Delinquency.* The data from their study of juveniles is the best-known and most often analyzed data in criminology.

1951 C. Wright Mills publishes *White Collar: The American Middle Classes.* In this book, Mills describes the transformation of the old middle class to the new middle class, emphasizing power structures and lifestyles.

1951 Talcott Parsons publishes *Toward a General Theory*

of Action. This work was published during the heyday of conservative political theory.

1952   Robert Ezra Park publishes *Human Communities.* This work extends his previous work with Burgess in human ecology published in *The City* (1925).

1954   Following the decision in *Brown v. Board of Education of Topeka, Kansas* the United States declares that school segregation is unconstitutional. This legal decision is of particular significance to political economists, racial analysts, and education sociologists.

1955   Talcott Parsons publishes *Family, Socialization and Interaction Process.* Parson's work on the family is politically conservative. His work and the conservative leanings of social theory that were widely accepted during the late 1940s and 1950s begin to fade into the background in the late 1950s and the 1960s.

1956   C. Wright Mills publishes *The Power Elite.* This work concentrates on people who have attained power in U.S. society including politicians, military personnel, celebrities, and executives. He explains that powerful people in our society make most of the decisions for which common people suffer the consequences. The book remains an important essay in political economy.

1956   Lewis Coser publishes *The Functions of Social Conflict.* In it, Coser addresses the varied conditions under which social conflict contributes to the maintenance, adjustment, or adaptation of social relationships and social structures.

1959   Karl Raimund Popper's *The Logic of Scientific Discovery,* originally published in 1934, is published for the first time in English. Popper's most significant and lasting contribution to sociology is his analysis of refutation in scientific research. He stated that hypotheses can only be refuted and never proven. This idea is particularly important to probabilistic sciences such as sociology. Popper is also remembered for his stark criticisms of Marxism and linguistic philosophy.

1959   C. Wright Mills publishes *The Sociological Imagination.* In it, he describes the role of the individual in society and the process and ethic of social scientific research. He also provides excellent illustrations of the different focuses of macro- and microsociological research. Today, most undergraduate students of sociology are required to read at least excerpts from this work.

1959   Lord Ralf Gustav Dahrendorf publishes *Class and Class Conflict in Industrial Society.* This helps to shape a functional definition of social class for the purpose of research in social stratification. His focus primarily concentrates on the construction of group conflict.

1959   Erving Goffman publishes *The Presentation of Self in Everyday Life.* In this book, he describes his theory of dramaturgy in which he parallels social interaction with acting on a stage.

1959   Pitirim Sorokin publishes *Social and Cultural Mobility,* in which he describes routes of social mobility as being both horizontal and vertical. This work is a major contribution to the sociological subfield of stratification.

1960   Eleanor Roosevelt writes her autobiography *You Learn By Living.* In it, she describes her life and achievements. She is considered as the most influential woman of the twentieth century because of her social activism.

1961–1970 (1974)

The Vietnam War significantly affects social, political, and military theory. The academic field of sociology was also affected. Many young men who opposed the War entered college as a way of escaping the draft. For many of them, their political views paralleled Marxist ideology. As a result, during the 1960s the emphasis in popular social theory took a radical turn from conservative to extremely liberal.

1961   Michel Foucault, a French philosopher whose work questions cultural assumptions in historical texts, publishes *Madness and Civilization.* Among his topics of inquiry are insanity, politics, sexuality, and power.

1961   Erving Goffman publishes *Asylums: Essays in the Social Situations of Mental Patients and Other Inmates.* In this famous work, Goffman emphasizes the significance of social structure in producing conforming behavior. He coins the term "total institutions."

1962   Max Weber's *Basic Concepts in Sociology by Max Weber* is published postpartum. This work combines many of his papers and lectures on several of his theories. Weber's legacy to sociology includes a host of topics including bureaucracy, research methods, social action, religion, social class, social status, and power.

1962   Thomas Kuhn publishes *The Structure of Scientific Revolutions.* In it, he defines a scientific paradigm. This concept is used in sociology to illustrate movements and emphasis on various methods in social research.

1963   The March on Washington convenes to protest racial injustice, at which Martin Luther King, Jr. gives his famous speech on race relations, "I Have a Dream."

1963   Erving Goffman publishes *Stigma: Notes on the management of Spoiled Identity*. This book inspires research in deviance and investigates the effectiveness of sanctions for deviant behavior.

1963   Betty Friedan publishes *The Feminine Mystique*. This book served as the modern-day catalyst for advances in the feminist movement of the 1960s. Friedan is the founder of the National Organization for Women (NOW) and is the convener of the National Women's Political Caucus.

1964   The U.S. Congress ratifies the Civil Rights Act of 1964. The passage of this act and significant social changes and events that lead to it mark a reemphasis in the field of sociology on social justice and Marxist thought. These events inform theories of the family, politics, economics, law, crime, education, and institutions. It marks a major shift in sociological thought.

1964   The U.S. Congress ratifies the Twenty-fourth Amendment to the Constitution outlawing the poll tax, which had been used to prevent African Americans from voting in public elections.

1964   Peter M. Blau publishes *Exchange and Power in Social Life*. Blau's theory is known as exchange theory and is based on the utilitarian principle.

1965   The U.S. Congress ratifies the Voter Rights Act to enforce the Fifteenth Amendment to the Constitution that allows African American citizens to vote in public elections.

1965   The Watts Riot occurs during the month of August in Los Angeles County, California. This riot was fueled by the racial harassment of a black motorist by an L.A. County Highway Patrol officer, but quickly escalated into violent protest against over all racial oppression and abuse. It sparked the occurrence of several other riots within the following two years, including the well-known Chicago Riots.

1966   Peter Berger and Thomas Luckmann publish *The Social Construction of Reality: A Treatise in the Sociology of Knowledge*. In this work, the authors describe society, not as an entity in its own right, but as the result of individual construction.

1966   Michel Foucault publishes *The Order of Things*. Here he traces the pre-Darwinian history of evolutionary theory. It is an example of work in the sociology of knowledge.

1967   Marvin Wolfgang and Franco Ferracuti publish *Subculture of Violence*. The theory articulated in this work is widely used today in studies of gangs and youth violence.

1967   Lewis Coser publishes *Continuities in the Study of*

Social Conflict. Coser's work investigates the consequences of group conflict.

1967   George Casper Homans publishes *The Nature of Social Science*. Homans, like Blau, is a social exchange theorist. The exchange model describes human interaction as a process of give-and-take.

1967   Alfred Schutz's *The Phenomenology of the Social World* (1932) is published in English. Schutz was primarily concerned with how people understand the consciousness of others while simultaneously struggling with their own consciousness. The popularity experienced by phenomenology during the 1960s has not been paralleled before or since in U.S. history.

1967   Harold Garfinkel publishes *Studies in Ethnomethodology*. It includes a series of studies in the rules of unspoken communication. Garfinkel sent several of his students out to test the moral order of society by having them conduct breaching experiments in which the students were assigned to brake traditional rules of conversation and communication. Garfinkel's experiments are often discussed in introductory sociology courses today.

1967   Barney G. Glaser and Anselm L. Strauss publish *Discovery of Grounded Theory: Strategies for Qualitative Research*. This book provides a detailed description of how to conduct inductive research. It is considered the essential handbook for conducting this type of research.

1968   Critical theorist Jürgen Habermas publishes *The Idea of the Theory of Knowledge as Social Theory*. In this work, he defines three types of knowledge: work, practical, and emancipatory.

1968   Lord Ralf Gustav Dahrendorf publishes *Essays in the Theory of Society*. Dahrendorf believes that theory should be divided into two sets, one composed of conflict, the other consensus. Each group of theories should explain phenomena specific to each set of theories.

1968   Robert K. Merton publishes *Social Theory and Social Structure*. Merton is a student of Talcott Parsons, but his form of functionalism is very different from Parsons's theories. Merton is called a "middle-range" theorist because his theories are not intended to explain groups of phenomena, but focus instead on more limited phenomena.

1969   Travis Hirschi publishes *Causes of Delinquency*. In it, he describes his now famous control theory. Briefly, this theory purports that four things are necessary to inhibit deviant behavior: attachment, commitment, involvement, and belief.

1969   Michel Foucault publishes *The Archeology of Knowledge*. Foucault is considered a poststructural-

ist whose work exemplifies a variety of philosophical influences. He combines aspects of theory from Marx, Weber, and Nietzsche. Consequently, his impact on social theory is widespread.

1969 Herbert Blumer publishes *Symbolic Interactionism: Perspectives and Methods.* Blumer is considered as the leading figure in symbolic interactionism. This book summarizes interactionist thought with respect to theory and social research methods. Symbolic interactionism is considered a perspective as well as a theory of social interaction.

1971 The first microcomputer is invented, enabling citizens to own home computers.

1972 Marvin E. Wolfgang, Robert M. Figlio, and Thorsten Sellin publish *Delinquency in a Birth Cohort.* The study depicted in this book remains one of the only comprehensive studies of the behavior for a single birth cohort over time.

1974 Glen Elder publishes *Children of the Great Depression: Social Change in Life Experience.* In it, Elder begins to develop his theory that has now come to be known as life-course theory. It has quickly become a new perspective with which to explain individual behavior as it results from life's processes and experiences.

1974 George Homans publishes *Elementary Forms of Social Behavior.* In this work, Homans articulates a system of propositions as a composite theory of social behavior that have previously existed separately in psychological behaviorist theories.

1975 Freda Adler publishes *Sisters in Crime.* This is one of the first comprehensive studies of female involvement in criminal behavior.

1976 Immanuel Wallerstein publishes *The Modern World-System: Capitalist Agriculture and the Origins of the European World-Economy in the Sixteenth Century.* In it, he describes his theory of world systems that has now become a perspective in its own right within political economy.

1976–1984

Michel Foucault writes *The History of Sexuality.* The work is never finished due to his death in 1984.

1977 On September 8th, Margaret Mead appeared as a witness in a hearing before the Committee on Aging of the U.S. House of Representatives. Although she is an anthropologist, not a sociologist, her statements center on stereotyping, television and age discrimination, and her claims lead to much research by sociologists.

1981 Erving Goffman publishes *Frame Analysis.* In this essay on the organization of experience, Goffman explains how experiences are shaped and categorized.

1981 Stephen Jay Gould publishes *The Mismeasure of Man* as a reaction to a controversial book titled *The Bell Curve* in which all human behaviors are considered innate. Gould confronts racism, biological determinism, and faulty research methods during the politically conservative climate of the 1980s.

1982 Anthony Giddens publishes "Class Structuation and Class Consciousness." This work significantly contributes to theories of social stratification by explaining how it comes to be that economic classes become social classes. His theory of structuration focuses on the reproduction of social systems.

1985 Anthony Giddens helps to establish the academic publishing house, Polity Press. He has published 34 books that have been translated into 29 languages and more than 200 articles. He is a significant figure in modern social theorizing. Giddens' most famous work includes his theory of structuration and globalization.

1987 Jürgen Habermas publishes *The Theory of Communicative Action.* Habermas describes a "metabiological" model of situational communication. Communicative action is a circular process in which the actor is described as both an "initiator" and a "product" of his/her process of socialization.

1989 The fall of the Berlin Wall marks the reunification of East and West Germany and symbolizes the fall of communism in Eastern Europe.

1990 Elijah Anderson publishes *Streetwise: Race, Class, and Change in an Urban Community.* This ethnographic study of two communities is already considered a classic study of social class, race, and urban social change.

1993 Robert J. Sampson and John H. Laub publish *Crime in the Making: Pathways and Turning Points Through Life.* The authors reanalyze the Glueck and Glueck studies from a life-course perspective on criminal behavior.

1996 The U.S. Congress ratifies the Personal Responsibility and Work Opportunity Reconciliation Act of 1996. This act changes the manner in which financial and social assistance is awarded to families in need. Many sociologists predict that this act will have devastating affects on families and children in the future.

1997 Jürgen Habermas publishes *A Berlin Republic: Writings on Germany.* In this book, he discusses German history and its consequences, the challenges facing German society in the post-Berlin wall era, and Germany's place in contemporary world society.

2000   Anthony Giddens publishes *Runaway World: How Globalization is Reshaping Our Lives.* Based upon his 1999 lecture series, the book presents Giddens's views on the ways globalization is re-ordering society. He takes a philosophical, rather than an economic perspective, examining the affects of globalization on gender, family, tradition, and democracy.

Nationality Index

Indian

Gandhi, Mohandas Karamchand, **I:** 259

Irish

Berkeley, George, **I:** 52

Italian

Vico, Giambattista, **II:** 699

Northern Irish

Burke, Edmund, **I:** 71

Polish

Gumplowicz, Ludwig, **I:** 287

Russian

Pavlov, Ivan Petrovich, **II:** 497

Scottish

Carlyle, Thomas, **I:** 78
Ferguson, Adam, **I:** 233
Hume, David, **I:** 323
Mill, James, **I:** 446
Smith, Adam, **II:** 595

Swiss

Jung, Carl Gustav, **I:** 365
Piaget, Jean, **II:** 504

Welsh

Owen, Robert, **II:** 486

GENERAL INDEX

A

AA (Alcoholics Anonymous), **II**: 546–547

AARP (American Association of Retired Persons), **I**: 18

ABC of Anarchism (Berkman), **I**: 31

Abnormal, **I: 1**

Abolition, **I: 1–2**
 See also Slavery and involuntary servitude

Abrams, Philip, **I**: 110

ABS (Association of Black Sociologists), **I: 40**

Absolute mobility, **II**: 479

Absolute poverty, **II**: 518–519

Absolutism, **I: 2–3**

Abuse prevention, **I**: 228–229

Academic authority, **I**: 43

Accountability, **I: 3**

Accounts, **I**: 261

Acculturation. *See* Cultural integration

The Accumulation of Capital (Luxemburg), **II**: 767

Achieved status, **I: 3**

Acquired Immune Deficiency Syndrome (AIDS), **I: 3–5, I**: 202

Action research, **I**: 35

Active euthanasia, **I**: 209

ADA (Americans with Disabilities Act), **I**: 168–169

Adaptation, **I: 5**

Adarand Constructors v. Pena, **I**: 12

Addams, Jane, **I: 5–6, I**: *6,* **I**: 319–320, **II**: 626

Adler, Freda, **II**: 772

Adolescence, **I: 6–8**

Adoption, **I: 8**

Adoption of innovation, **I**: 19

Adorno, Theodor W., **I: 8–10**

Adult Basic Education Program, **I**: 10

Adult education, **I: 10**

Adulthood, **I: 10–11**
 See also Fatherhood; Motherhood

Advance directives (death), **I**: 210

AFDC (Aid to Families with Dependent Children), **I: 19**

Affect control theory, **I: 11–12**

Affective involvement, **II**: 496

Affective neutrality, **II**: 496

Affirmative Action, **I: 12–13, II**: 558–559
 See also Discrimination

Affluent society, **I: 13–14**

The Affluent Society (Galbraith), **I**: 255

African-American studies, **I: 14**

African studies, **I: 15**

Afrocentricity (Assante), **I**: 14

Against Our Will: Men, Women, and Rape (Brownmiller), **II**: 588

Age cohorts, **I**: 99

Age of Enlightenment, **I: 15–16**

The Age of Reason (Paine), **II**: 763

Age-sex pyramid. *See* Population pyramid

Aggregate data. *See* Group data

Aggregation, **II**: 610

Aggression, **I: 16–17**

Aging, **I: 17–18**

Aging Parents (Bengtson), **I**: 348

Agrarian society, **I: 18–19**

Agricultural innovations, **I**: 19

Aid to Families with Dependent Children (AFDC), **I: 19**

AIDS (Acquired Immune Deficiency Syndrome), **I: 3–5, I**: 202

AIDS cases, **I**: *4*

AIM (American Indian Movement), **I: 27–28**

Alcoholics Anonymous (AA), **II**: 546–547

Alcoholism, **I: 19–22**

Alcoholism and medicalization, **I**: 438

Alcoholism and Native Americans, **II**: 557

Alexander, Jeffrey Charles, **I**: 22

Alienation, **I: 22**

All-volunteer military force, **I**: 446

Allport, Gordon W., **II**: 501

Almoners, **II**: 618

Alpha error. *See* Type I error

Althusser, Louis, **I: 23–24, I**: *24*

Altruism, **I: 24–25**

Altruistic suicide, **I**: 25

Amalgamation, **I: 25**

American Apartheid (Denton, Massey), **I**: 272

American Association of Retired Persons (AARP), **I**: 18

American Capitalism: The Concept of Countervailing Power (Galbraith), **I**: 255

American colonies (map), **I:** *103*

American Couples: Money, Work, Sex (Blumstein, Schwartz), **I:** 62, **II:** 576

American Crisis (Paine), **II:** 489

American embassy hostages (1979), **II:** *671*

American families, **I: 25–27**

American Indian Movement (AIM), **I: 27–28**

 See also Native American identity

American Indian Studies Center, **I:** 85

The American Occupational Structure (Blau, Duncan), **I:** 60, **I:** 179, **II:** 496, **II: 648–649**

American Political Science Association (APSA), **II:** 510

American Revolution, **II:** 529, **II:** 762

American society, **I: 28–29**

American Sociological Association (ASA), **I: 29–30, II:** 767

The American Soldier (Stouffer), **II:** 652

The American Way of Death (Mitford), **I:** 155

Americans and work, **II:** 718

Americans with Disabilities Act (ADA), **I:** 168–169

Analysis of covariance (ANCOVA), **I: 30, I:** 132

Analysis of the Phenomenon of the Human Mind (Mill), **I:** 446

Analysis of variance (ANOVA), **I:** 30

Analytical Marxism, **I:** 423

Anarchy, **I: 30–31**

Ancestor worship, **I: 31**

Ancient Law (Maine), **II:** 765

Ancient Society, or Researches in the Lines of Human Progress (Morgan), **I:** 457

ANCOVA (Analysis of covariance), **I: 30, I:** 132

Anderson, Benedict, **II:** 466

Anderson, Elijah, **II:** 772

Androcentrism, **I: 31–32**

 See also Patriarchy

Animism, **I:** 462

Année Sociologique, **II:** 766

Anomic health care systems, **I:** 298

Anomie, **I: 32**

Anomie theory, **I:** 32

ANOVA (Analysis of variance), **I:** 30

Anthony, Susan B., **I: 32–33, I:** *33,* **II:** 643–644

Anthropocentrism, **I:** 200

Anti-colonial nationalism, **II:** 465–466

Anti-feminist backlash, **I:** 232, **II:** 464

Anticipatory socialization, **I: 33–34**

Anxiety, **II:** 530

Apartheid, **I: 34–35**

 See also Discrimination; Segregation and desegregation

Apellate courts, **I:** 131

Apparel industry workers, **I:** 64

Applied research, **I: 35–36**

Applied sociology, **I: 36**

APSA (American Political Science Association), **II:** 510

The Archeology of Knowledge (Foucault), **II:** 771–772

Archer, Margaret, **II:** 655

Archetypes, **I: 36–37**

Arendt, Hannah, **I:** 424, **I:** *425*

Arnett, Jefrey Jensen, **I:** 11

Arranged marriage, **I:** 418

Art and society, **I: 37–38**

ASA (American Sociological Association), **I: 29–30, II:** 767

Asceticism, **I:** 38

Asch, Soloman, **I:** 285

Ascribed status, **I:** 3, **I: 38–39**

 See also Caste and class; Social stratification

Asian-American studies, **I: 39–40**

Asimov, Isaac, **I:** 105

Assante, Molefi, **I:** 14

Assertiveness, **I:** 16

Assimilation, **I:** 145, **I:** 206, **I:** 279, **I:** 458

Assimilation in American Life (Gordon), **I:** 279

Assisted suicide, **I:** 209

Association of Black Sociologists (ABS), **I:** 40

Associationism, **II:** 531

Asylees, **I:** 351

Asylums: Essays in the Social Situations of Mental Patients and Other Inmates (Goffman), **I:** 440, **I:** 441, **II:** 770

Attitude receptional assimilation, **I:** 279

Attitudes, **I: 40**

Attribution theory, **I: 40–41**

Audience studies, **I:** 424

Authoritarian personality, **I:** 41

Authoritarianism, **I:** 2–3, **I:** 280

Authority, **I: 41–43**

Autonomous man, **I:** 43

Autonomy, **I: 43**

Aversion therapy, **I:** 48

Avery, Dennis, **I:** 19

Axiomatic theory. *See* Metatheory

B

Baby Boomer Generation, **I:** 269

Bacterial vaginosis, **II:** 589

Bagehot, Walter, **I: 45–46**

Bakke, University of California Regents v., **I:** 12, **II:** 559

Balance, **II:** 608

Balance theory, **I:** 98–99

Bandura, Albert, **I:** 392, **I:** 454

Banishing Bureaucracy (Osborne, Plastrik), **I:** 70

Bankruptcy and credit, **I: 46–47**

Bankruptcy cases, **I:** *46*

Banyard, John, **I:** 119

Bar charts, **I: 47**

Baran, Paul, **I:** 139

Barnett, Samuel A., **II:** 618

Base-superstructure model, **I:** 184

Basic Concepts in Sociology by Max Weber (Weber), **II:** 770

Basic social needs, **I:** 410

Baudrillard, Jean, **II:** 518

Bauer, Raymond, **II:** 604

Beauvoir, Simone de, **I:** 3, **II:** 496

Beccaria, Cesare, **II:** 499

Beck, Lewis White, **II:** 503

''Begging the question.'' *See* Tautology

Behavior, **I:** 241–242

Behavior personality theory, **II:** 500–501

Behavior receptional assimilation, **I:** 279

Behaviorism, **I: 47–48, II:** 531

Being and Time (Heidegger), **I:** 302–303

Being Mentally Ill (Scheff), **I:** 441

Belief systems, **I: 48**

Bell, Alexander Graham, **I:** *358*

Bell, Buck v., **I:** 208

Bell, Daniel, **I: 48–50, I:** *49,* **II:** 517

Bell curve, **II:** 646

E

H

Hegel, Georg, **I: 300–301, II:** 763

Hegemony, **I: 301–302**

Heidegger, Martin, **I:** 216, **I: 302–304,** I: *303,* **I:** 305

Heider, Fritz, **I:** 40

Heise, David, **I:** 11–12

Hendry, L., **I:** 8

Henotheism, **I:** 451–452

Henry, William, **II:** 603–604

Hepatitis, **II:** 589

Herder, Johann Gottfried von, **I: 304,** I: *305*

Hermeneutics, **I: 304–305**

Heroin use, **I:** *176*

Herrnstein, Richard, **I:** 345

Heterogamy, **I: 305**

Heteronomy, **I:** 43

Heterosexism, **I:** 306, **I:** 317

Heterosexuality, **I: 305–307**

> *See also* Bisexuality; Homosexuality

Hierarchical linear models, **I: 307**

Hierarchy of needs, **I: 307–308**

High mass-consumption stage of economic growth, **II:** 642

Higher education, **I: 308–309**

The Highest Stage of Capitalism (Lenin), **II:** 767

Hightower, James, **I:** 19

Hinduism, **I:** 80, **I: 309–310**

Hirschi, Travis, **I:** 369, **II:** 771

Hirshfeld, Magnus, **II:** 680

Hispanic, **I:** 310

Hispanic-American income statistics, **I:** *333*

Hispanic-American studies, **I: 310–311**

Histograms, **I: 311**

Historical-comparative research, **I: 311–312**

Historical materialism, **I:** 428

Historical sociology, **I: 311**

Historical Sociology (Abrams), **I:** 110

History of England During the Thirty Years' Peace 1816-1846 (Martineau), **II:** 764

The History of Sexuality (Foucault), **II:** 772

Hitler, Adolf, **I:** *42*

HIV (Human immunodeficiency virus). *See* AIDS

HMO (Health maintenance organizations), **I:** 437

Hobbes, Thomas, **I:** 67, **I: 312–313,** I: *313,* **II:** 761

Hochschild, Arlie, **II:** 628

HOLC (Home Owners' Loan Corporation), **II:** 547

Hollingshead, August, **I: 313–314**

Holmes, Robert L., **II:** 503

Holocaust, **I:** *269*

Homans, George, **I:** 155, **I:** 215, **I: 314–315**

Home Owners' Loan Corporation (HOLC), **II:** 547

Homelessness, **I: 315–316, II:** 563

Homogamy, **I: 316,** I: 427

Homophily, **I:** 354

Homophobia, **I: 317**

Homosexuality, **I: 317–318**

> *See also* Bisexuality; Heterosexuality

Homosexuality in Perspective (Johnson, Masters), **I:** 364

Hopwood v. Texas, **I:** 12

Horkeheimer, Max, **I:** 140, **I: 318**

Horowitz, Irving Louis, **I: 318–319**

House, James, **II:** 612

Households, **I:** 319

Housing, sociology of, **II: 629**

Housing and the Urban Poor: A Critical Analysis of Federal Housing Policy (Solomon), **II:** 629

Housing projects, **I:** *157*

Howard, John, **II:** 763

Hoynes, William, **I:** 122

Hoyt, Henry, **II:** 581

Hughes, Everett, **I:** 425

Hula hoops, **I:** *223*

Hull House, **I:** 6, **I: 319–321,** I: *320,* **II:** 618, **II:** 766

Human capital, **I:** 178, **I: 321**

Human-centered technology, **I: 322–323**

Human Communities (Park), **II:** 770

Human Ecology: A Theory of Community Structure (Hawley), **II:** 769

Human ecology theory, **I:** 108

The Human Group (Homans), **I:** 314–315

Human immunodeficiency virus (HIV). *See* AIDS

Human nature, **I: 321**

Human Nature and Conduct (Dewey), **II:** 768

Human Nature and Social Order (Cooley), **II:** 766

Human papiloma virus, **II:** 589

Human Problems in Technological Change (Spicer), **I:** 19

Human Relations School, **I: 322**

Human rights, **I: 322, II:** 484

Human Sexual Response (Johnson, Masters), **I:** 363, **I:** 364, **I:** 426

Human Societies (Lenski), **I:** 396

Human Society (Davis), **II:** 769

Human subjects in social research, **I:** 205

Humanistic personality theory, **II:** 500

Hume, David, **I:** *323,* **I: 323–324, II:** 762

Hunter-gatherers, **I: 324–325**

Huss, Magnus, **I:** 20

Hussel, Edmund, **II:** 767

Hyman, Herbert, **II:** 548

Hymes, Dell, **II:** 623–624

I

Ibd-Khaldun, Abdel Rahman, **I: 327**

Id, **I: 327–328**

The Idea of a Social Science (Winch), **II:** 566

The Idea of the Theory of Knowledge as Social Theory (Habermas), **II:** 771

Ideal type, **I: 328, II:** 685

Idealism, **I: 328**

Ideas: A General Introduction to Pure Reason (Hussel), **II:** 767

Identification assimilation, **I:** 279

Identity, **I: 328–329**

Identity crisis, **I: 329**

Identity theory, **I:** 329, **II:** 584

Ideographic explanation, **I:** 218

Ideology, **I: 329–330**

Ideology and Utopia (Mannheim), **I:** 330, **II:** 630, **II:** 768

Illegal immigrants, **I:** 351

Illegitimate births, **I:** 330

Illegitmacy, **I: 330**

Illiteracy, **I: 331**

Illuminism, **I:** 461

Illustrations of Political Economy (Martineau), **II:** 764

Imagined Communities (Benedict), **II:** 466

Immigrant Entrepreneurs: Koreans in Los Angeles (Bonacich, Light), **I:** 64

Immigrants, **I:** 351

Immigration. *See* International migration

J

K

N

Q

R

Symbolic Interactionism: Perspectives and Methods (Blumer), **II:** 772

Symbolic interactionist paradigm, **II:** 491

Symbols, **I:** 430, **II: 664**

Syphilis, **II:** 588–589, **II:** *589*

A System of Logic (Mill), **I:** 109, **II:** 764

System of Positive Polity (Comte), **II:** 765

System of Sociology (Sorokin), **II:** 768

Systems of Consanguinity and Affinity of the Human Family (Morgan), **I:** 457

Les Systems Socialistes (Pareto), **II:** 766

Systems theory, **II: 664–665**

T

T-test, **II: 681**

Taboo, **II: 667**

Tabula rasa, **II: 667–668**

Tachyon, Catarhine, **I:** 95

Tacit knowlege, **I:** 346

Take-off stage of economic growth, **II:** 641–642

Taking the role of the other, **II: 668**

Tannenbaum, Frank, **I:** 381

Tarde, Jean Gabriel, **II: 668–669**

Tautology, **II: 669**

Taylor, Edward Burnett, **II:** *683*

Taylor, Frederick William, **II:** 578

Taylor, Harriet, **I:** 448, **II:** 763

Taylorism. *See* Scientific management

Technical design philosophy, **I:** 322–323

Teleology, **II: 669**

Telephone surveys, **II:** 663

Telesis, **II:** 767

Television, **II:** *669,* **II: 669–670**, **II:** 768

Television and crime, **II:** 701

Television and popular culture, **II:** 513

Television and the Drama of Crime (Sparks), **II:** 701

Temporary Assistance for Needy Families (TANF) recipients, **I:** *20*

Territory, **II: 670**

Terrorism, **II: 670–671**

Test-retest methods, **II: 671–672**

    See also Reliability

Test-retest reliability, **II:** 551

Texas, Hopwood v., **I:** 12

Theocracy/caesaropapism model, **II:** 551

A Theologico-Political Treatise (Spinoza), **II:** 761

Theoretical Sociology (Collins), **II:** 560

Theory, **II: 672**

The Theory of Business Enterprise (Veblen), **II:** 767

Theory of cognitive dissonance, **I:** 98–99

A Theory of Cognitive Dissonance (Festinger), **I:** 234

The Theory of Communicative Action (Habermas), **I:** 292, **II:** 772

Theory of Moral Sentiments (Smith), **II:** 595–596

The Theory of Organizations (Silverman), **I:** 111–112

The Theory of Social and Economic Organization (Weber), **I:** 386

Theory of stratification, **I:** 315

The Theory of the Leisure Class (Veblen), **I:** 394, **II:** 633, **II:** 697, **II:** 766

Theosophy, **I:** 461

Thesis on Feuerbach (Marx), **II:** 764

Thirteenth Amendment, **I:** 2, **II:** 594

Thomas, William Isaac, **I:** 159, **II: 672–673**

Thomas theorem. *See* Definition of the situation

Thompson, Robert, **I:** 11

Thompson, Warren, **I:** 161, **II:** 769

Thoughts on Death and Immortality (Feuerbach), **I:** 235–236

Thoughts on the Education of Daughters (Wollstonecraft), **II:** 715

Three Dialogues between Hylas and Philonous (Berkeley), **I:** 52

Tilly, Charles, **I:** 108

Time series analysis, **II: 673–674**

Tit-for-tat strategy, **I:** 259

Title IX, **II:** 634

Tocqueville, Alexis de, **I:** 336, **I:** 424, **II: 674, II:** *674,* **II:** 702–703

Tolman, E. C., **I:** 47

Tönnies, Ferdinand, **I:** 107–108, **I:** 263, **II: 674–675**

Total institution, **II: 675–676**

Totalitarianism, **I:** 2, **II: 676**

Totem and Taboo (Freud), **II:** 667

Totemism, **II:** 542, **II: 676–677**

Totemism (Lévi-Strauss), **II:** 677

Tourism and built environment, **II:** 634

Toward a General Theory of America (Parsons), **II:** 769–770

Toynbee, Arnold, **II:** *677,* **II: 677–678**

Toynbee Hall, **II:** 618

Traditional authority, **II:** 484, **II:** 565, **II: 685–686**

Traditional legitimacy, **I:** 393

Traditional societies, **II: 678**

Traditional society stage of economic growth, **II:** 641

"Trail of Broken Treaties," **I:** 28, **I:** 69

Training of social workers, **II:** 618

Trait theories of personality, **II:** 501

Trajectories, **I:** 399

Trancendental idealism, **I:** 328

Transitions, **I:** 399

Transnational corporations, **II: 678–679**

Transsexualism, **II: 679–680**

Transvestism, **II: 680**

A Treatise Concerning the Principles of Human Knowledge (Berkeley), **I:** 52

Treatise on Human Nature (Hume), **II:** 762

A Treatise on Man and the Development of His Faculties (Quetelet), **II:** 538–539, **II:** 764

The Treatise on Sociology (Pareto). *See The Mind and Society* (Pareto)

Trend components, **II:** 673

Triads, **I:** 97

Trial courts, **I:** 131

Triangulation, **II: 680–681**

Trichmoniasis, **II:** 589

The Truly Disadvantaged: The Inner City, the Underclass, and Public Policy (Wilson), **II:** 713–714

Truth, Sojourner, **II: 681**

Truzzi, Marcello, **I:** 37–38

Tulsa (OK) Race Riot of 1921, **II:** 768

Turgot, Anne Robert Jacques, **II: 681–682**, **II:** *682*

Turner, Barry S., **II:** 551

Turner, Ralph, **II:** 562

Tuskegee Syphilis Study, **II:** 768–769

Twenty-Fourth Amendment, **II:** 771

Twenty Statements Test, **I:** 377

Two-powers model, **II:** 551

Two Treatises of Government (Locke), **II:** 599

Tylor, Sir Edward Burnett, **II: 682–683**

Type I error, **II: 684**

    See also Null hypothesis

Type II error, **II: 684**

    See also Null hypothesis

religion, **II:** 719

social closure and credentialism, **I:** 133

society, **II:** 621

status, **II:** 648

status group, **II: 650**

verstehen, **II: 697–698**

Webster-Ashburton Treaty, **II:** 764

Wedding ceremonies and rituals, **I:** 418–419

Weighted cross sectional research, **I:** 141

Weil, Felix, **I:** 343

Weiner, Bernard, **I:** 41

Weiner, Norbert, **I:** 148–149

Welfare services. *See* Social services

Welfare state, **II: 711**

Wells-Barnett, Ida B., **II: 711–712**

Whelpton, P. K., **II:** 769

When Work Disappears: The World of the New Urban Poor (Wilson),
I: 272, **II:** 714

White, Harrison, **II:** 608

White, Leslie A., **I:** 5

White Collar: The American Middle Class (Mills), **II:** 769

White Collar Crime (Sutherland), **II:** 769

White flight, **I:** 188

Who Rules America? (Domhoff), **I:** 174

Who Shall Survive (Moreno), **II:** 562

Whorf, Benjamin Lee, **I:** 145, **II:** 572

Widowhood, **II:** 554, **II: 712–713**

Widowhood in an American City (Lopata), **II:** 712–713

Wiener, Norbert, **I:** *149*

Wilcoxon matched-pairs signed-ranks test, **II:** 474

The Will to Believe (James), **I:** 361

Willoughby, Robert E., **I:** 92

Wilson, Pete, **I:** *13*

Wilson, William Julius, **I:** *95,* **I:** 96, **I:** 272, **II: 713–714**

Winch, Peter, **II:** 566

Wirth, Louis, **II: 714,** **II:** 768

Wolfgang, Marvin E., **II:** 771, **II:** 772

Wollstonecraft, Mary, **I:** 231, **II: 715–716**

Women and role conflict, **II:** 561

Women and status conflict, **II:** 649–650

Women as Widows: Support Systems (Lopata), **II:** 713

Women's Liberation Movement, **II: 716**

Women's studies, **II:** 562–563, **II: 716–717**

See also Gender studies; Men's studies

Women's suffrage. *See* Anthony, Susan B.; National American Woman
Suffrage Association (NAWSA)

Woodstock, **I:** 131

Work, sociology of, **II: 636–637**

Work and occupations, **II: 717–718**

Work orientation, **II: 718–719**

Workforce Investment Act, **I:** 10

World-economies, **II:** 720

World-empires, **II:** 720

World Modernization: The Limits of Convergence (Moore), **I:** 125

World religions, **II: 719–720**

World-systems theory, **I:** 118–119, **I:** 164–165, **I:** 410, **II:** 626–627, **II:**
705, **II: 720–721**

World Trade Center bombing, **II:** 670–671

World War I, **II:** 767

World War II, **II:** 769

Wounded Knee conflict, **I:** 28

The Wretched of the Earth (Fanon), **I:** 229

Wundt, Wilhelm, **II:** 530–531

X

Xenocentrism, **II:** 723

Xenophobia, **II: 723**

Y

Yankee City Series, **II:** 707–708

Yorburg, Betty, **I:** 428

You Learn By Living (Roosevelt), **II:** 770

Young, Michael, **I:** 441–442

Young Hegelians, **II:** 764

See also Engels, Friedrich; Marx, Karl

Youth culture, **II: 725–726**

Z

Zald, Mayer, **II:** 607

Zeitgeist, **II: 727**

Zelizer, Viviana, **I:** 451

Znaniecki, Florian, **II:** 672

Zopf, Paul E., Jr., **II:** 567

For Reference

Not to be taken from this room